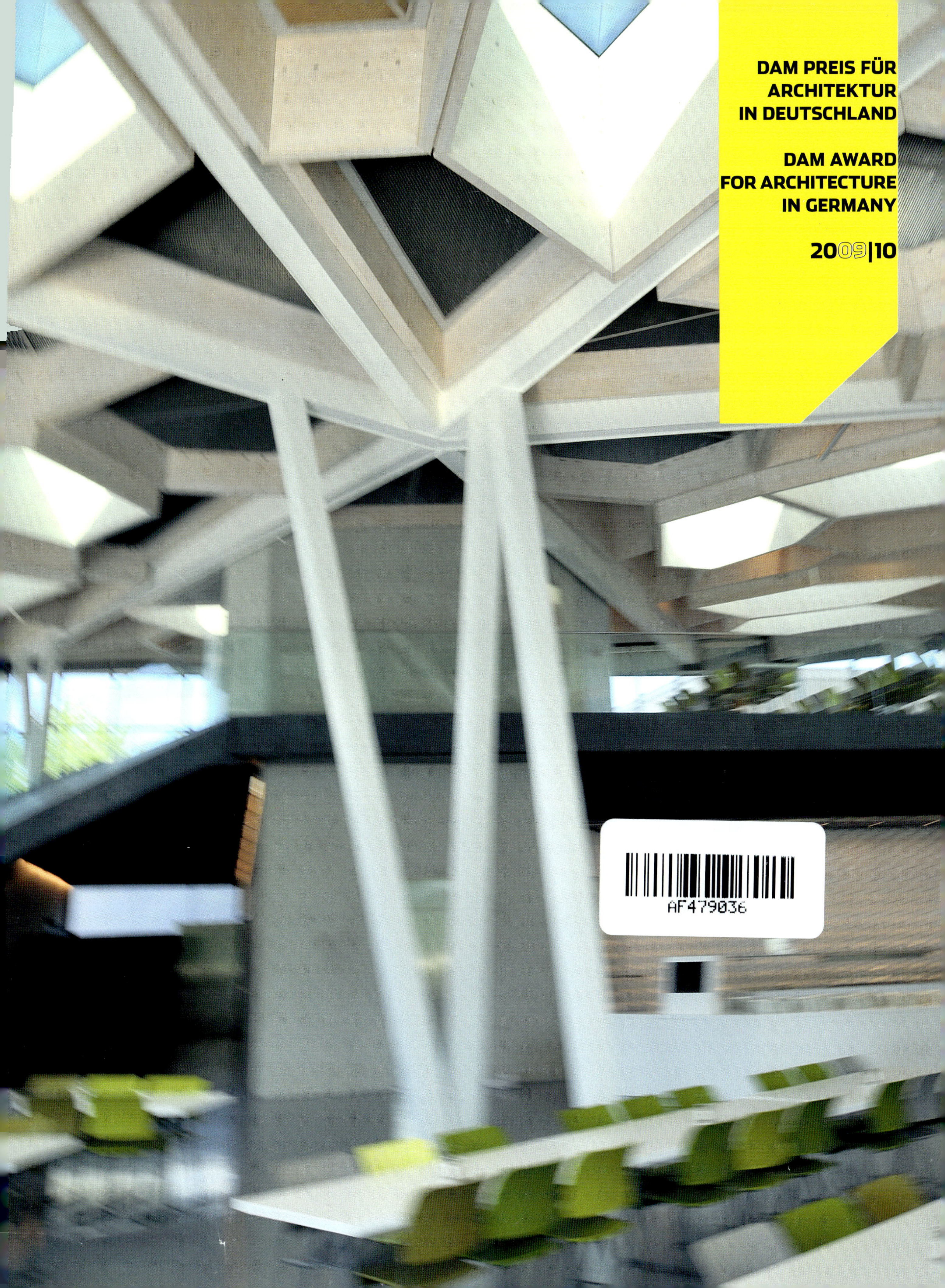
DAM PREIS FÜR
ARCHITEKTUR
IN DEUTSCHLAND

DAM AWARD
FOR ARCHITECTURE
IN GERMANY

2009|10

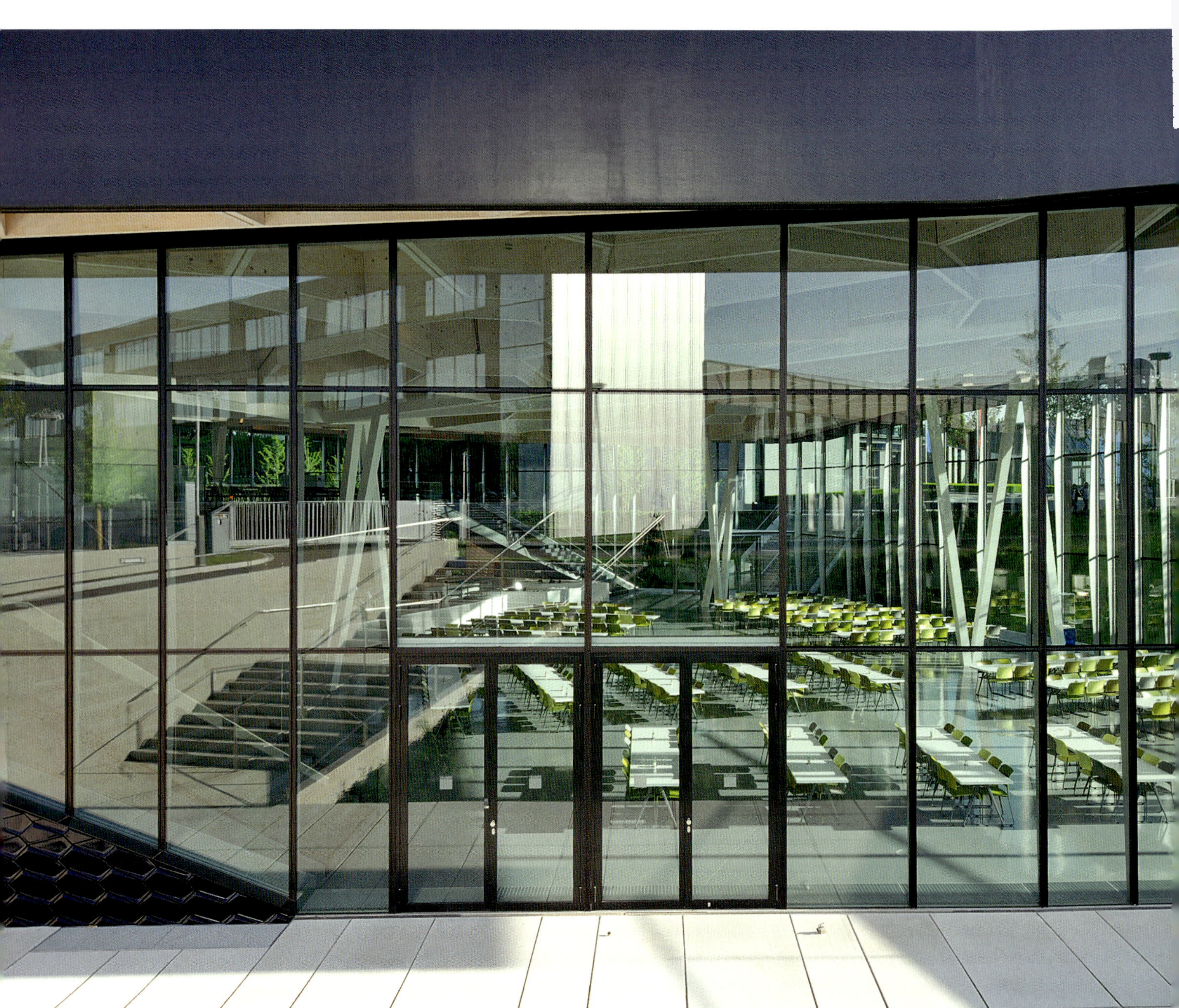

Schräg stehende Baumstützen im lichten Einraum | Tilted tree-like supports in the bright, soaring interior

HANS IBELINGS

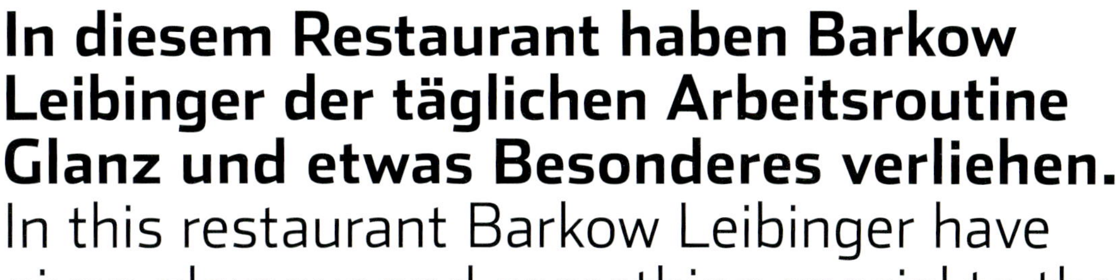

In diesem Restaurant haben Barkow Leibinger der täglichen Arbeitsroutine Glanz und etwas Besonderes verliehen.

In this restaurant Barkow Leibinger have given glamour and something special to the daily routine of working.

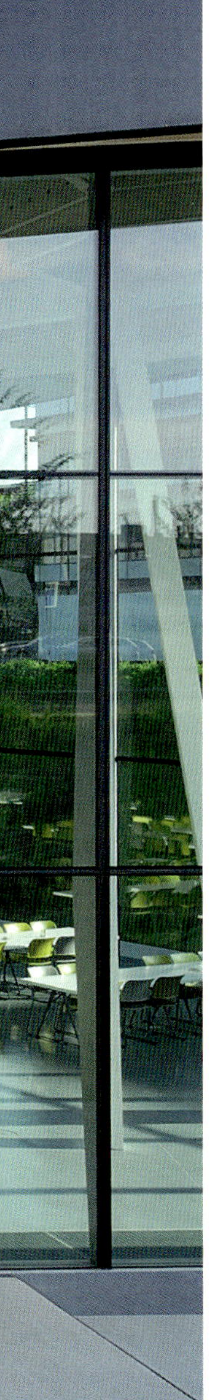

LAYLA DAWSON

Eine elegante bauliche und architektonische Lösung für einen Schirm, der eine Vielzahl gemeinschaftlicher Aktivitäten überspannt und den Sozialpakt zwischen Arbeitgeber und Arbeitnehmer symbolisiert.

An elegant structural and architectural solution for an umbrella over a multitude of community events, symbolising the social pact between employer and employee.

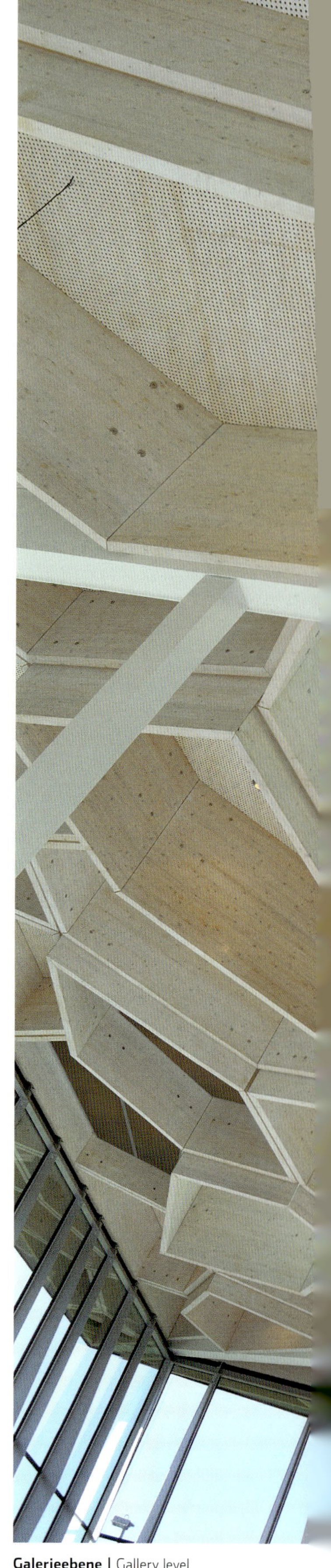

Galerieebene | Gallery level

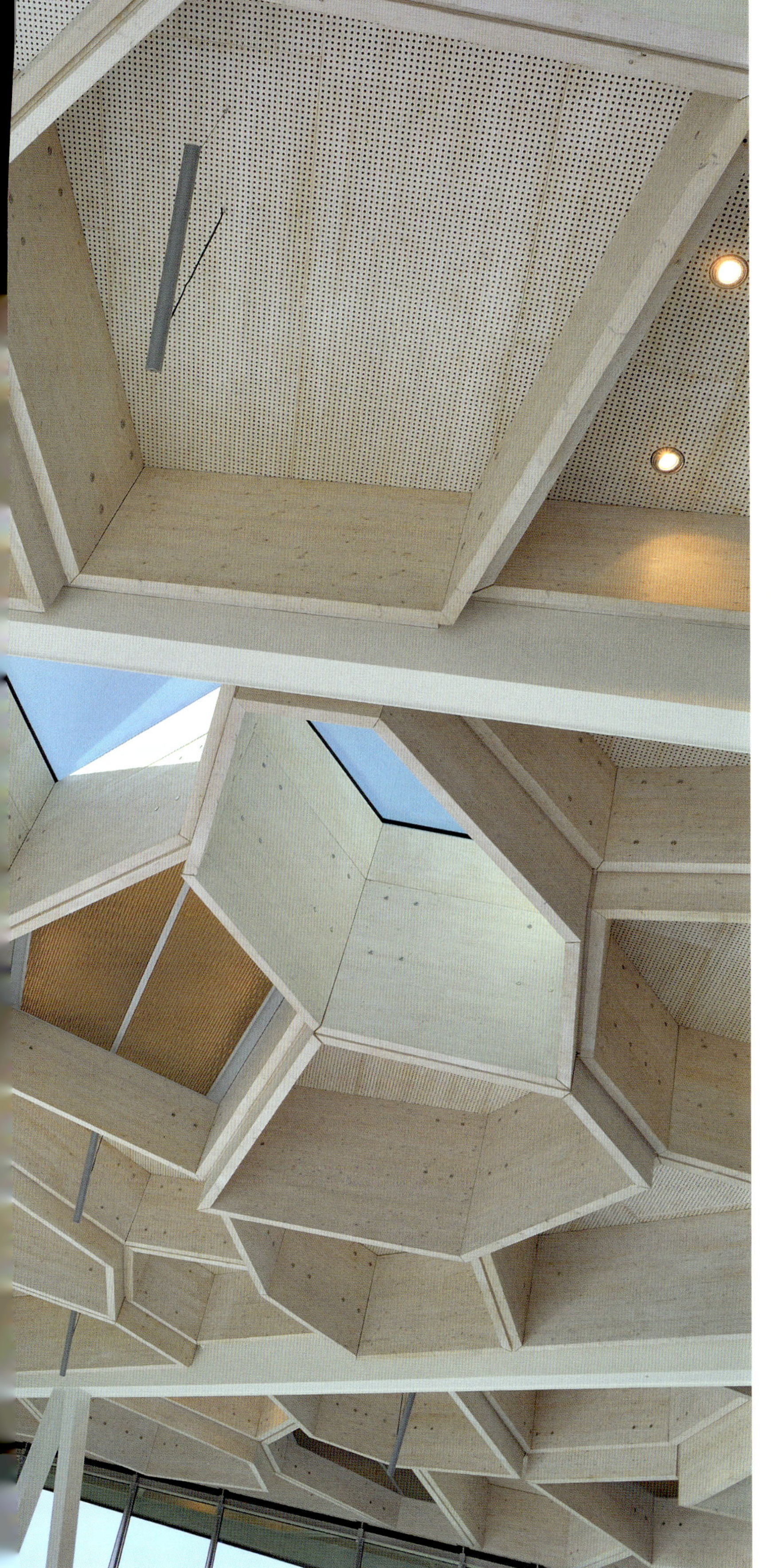

CHRISTIAN SCHITTICH

Mit einer faszinierenden Konstruktion schaffen die Architekten ein räumliches Erlebnis und eine für die Bauaufgabe durchaus nicht selbstverständliche besondere Atmosphäre. With a fascinating construction, the architects have created a spatial experience and an atmosphere that is anything but a matter of course for a building project of this kind.

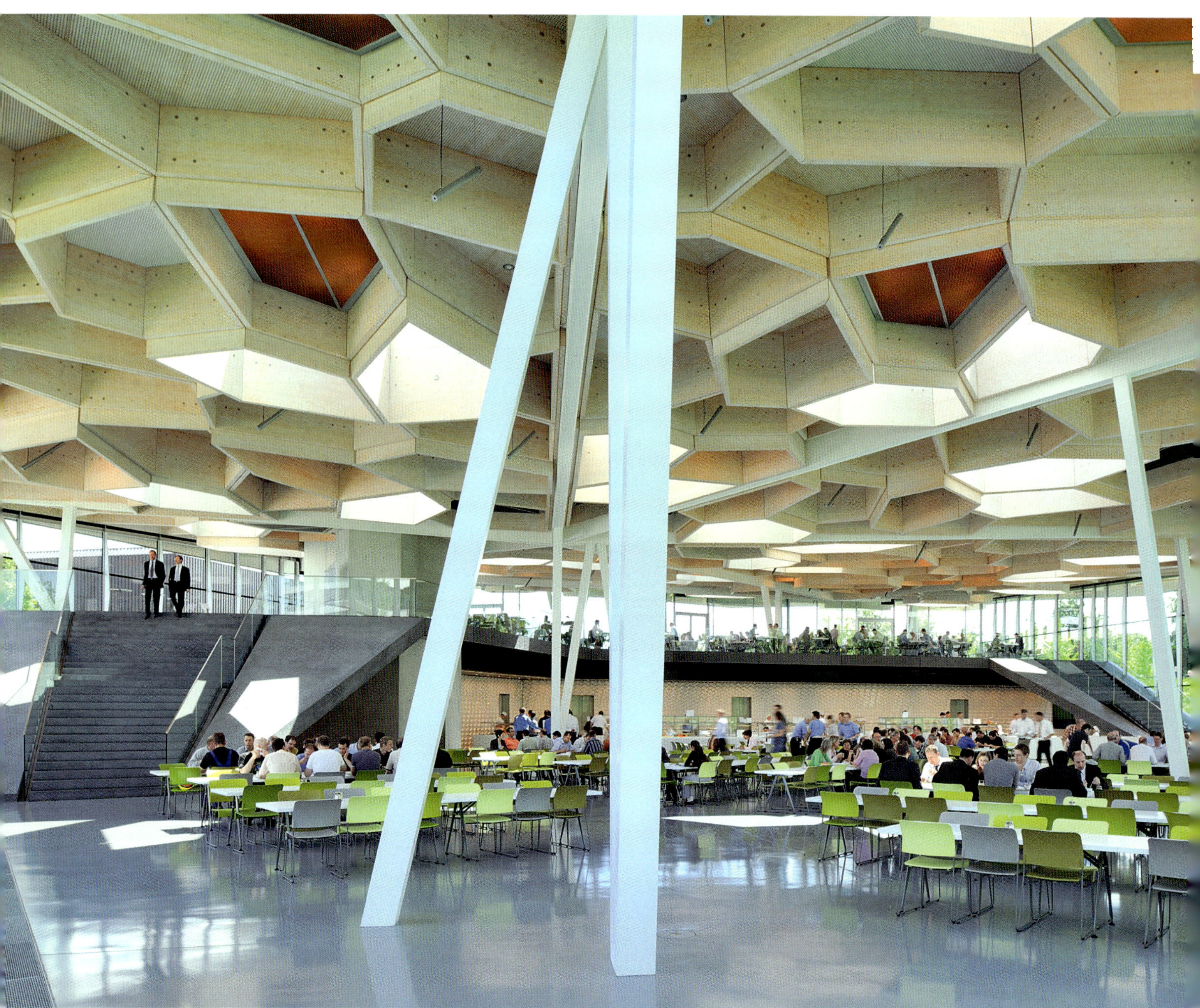

Die Hauptebene des Betriebsrestaurants ist von der Geländeoberkante um vier Meter abgesenkt.
The main level of the company restaurant is sunk four metres into the ground.

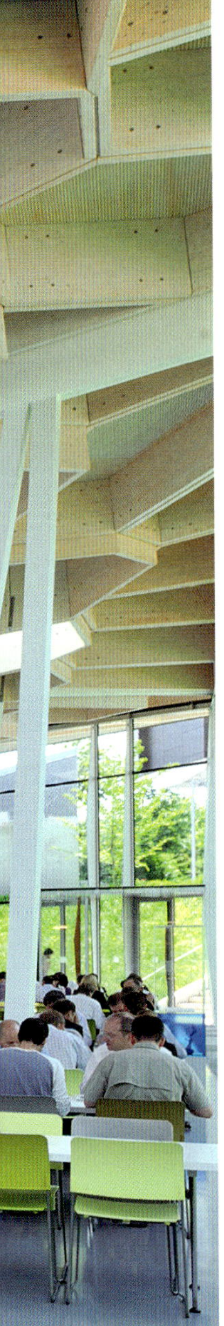

PETER CACHOLA SCHMAL

Barkow Leibinger schaffen es, für eine banale Allerweltsaufgabe wie eine Kantine einen Ort zu kreieren, der angenehm ist, und bauen das Bild eines ‚beschützenden Blattes über einer Kuhle'.

Barkow Leibinger manage to create for an ordinary everyday project like a company cafeteria a place that is pleasant to be in, evoking the image of a 'sheltering leaf over a hollow'.

FALK JAEGER

Der Raum hat etwas von Musik, eine souveräne, schwebende Leichtigkeit, die befreiend wirkt. ‚Schöner Essen' gehört ebenso wie die Gestaltung hochwertiger, optimaler Arbeitsplätze zur Philosophie einer High-End-Firma von Weltrang.

This room has something musical about it – a self-assured, floating lightness that has a liberating effect. Just like the provision of high-quality, optimised workplaces, 'beautiful dining' is part of the philosophy of a high-end company with international standing.

In die fünfeckigen Zellenstruktur des Daches sind Oberlichter, Leuchtfelder oder Akustikpaneele integriert.
Skylights, light fields and acoustic panels are integrated into the five-sided cell structure of the roof.

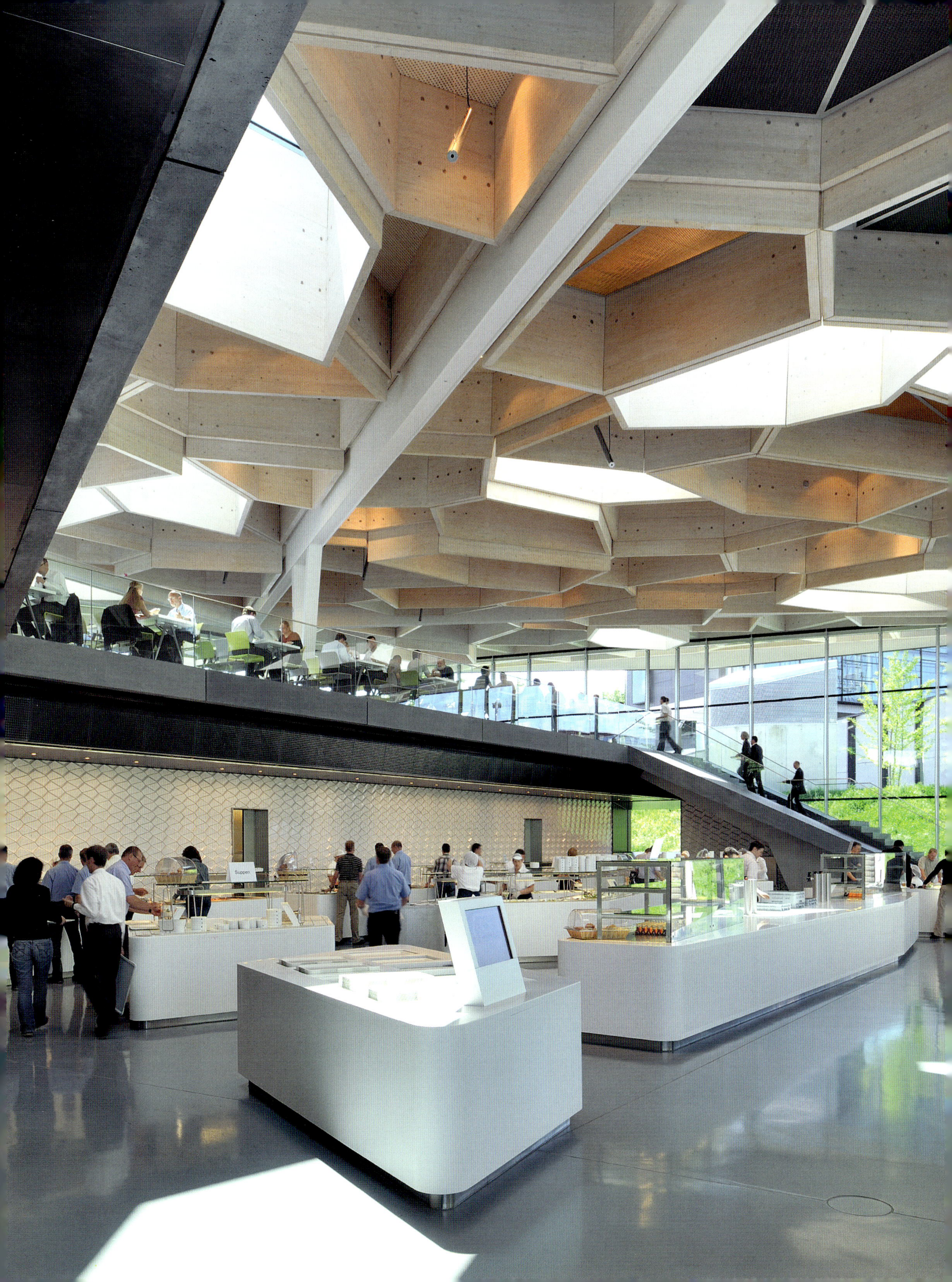

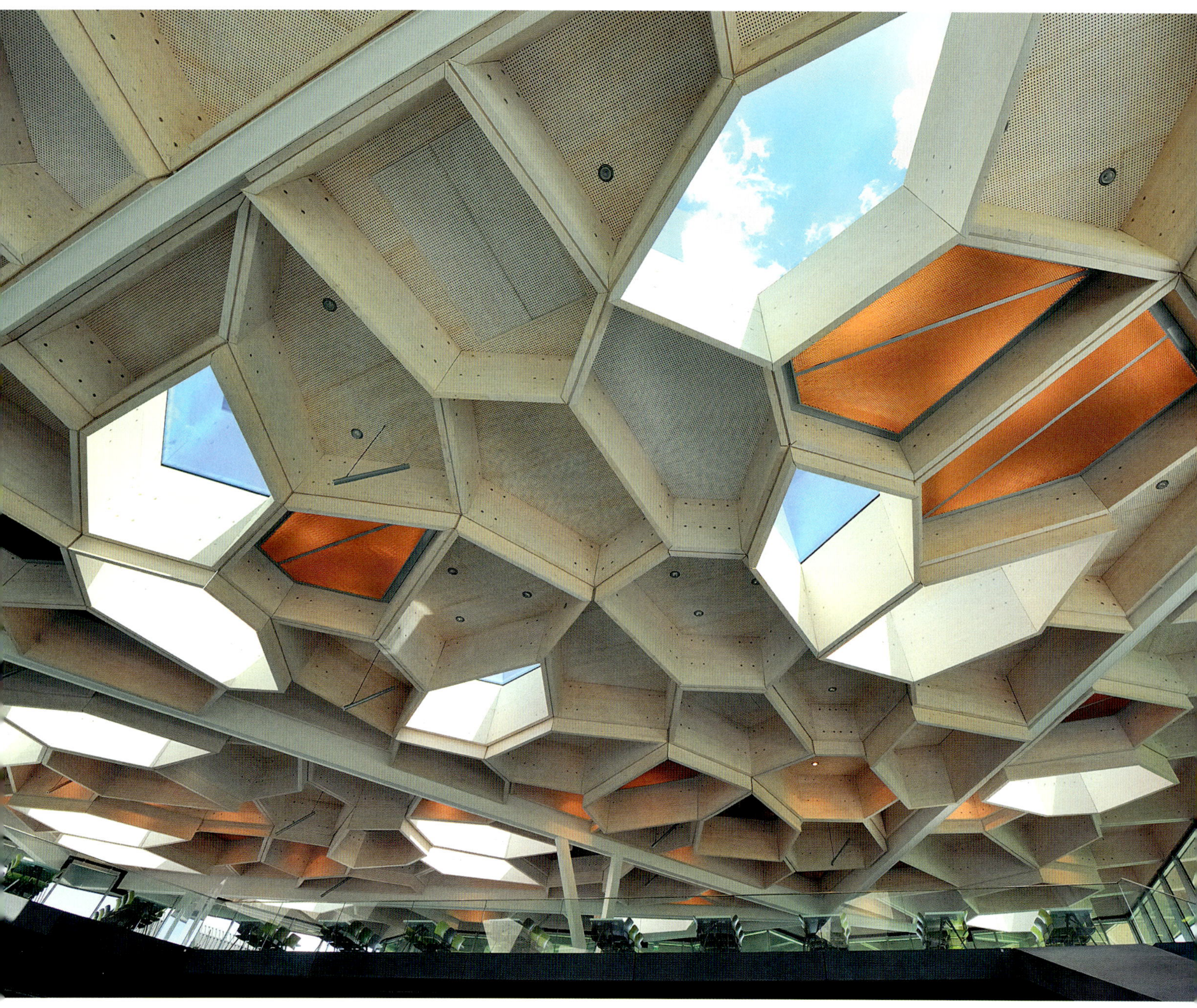

Die Tiefe der Dachwaben variiert von 90 bis 150 Zentimetern, so dass die Untersicht plastisch ausgeformt wirkt.
The depth of the roof cells varies between 90 and 150 centimetres, making the lower surface seem to be moulded sculpturally.

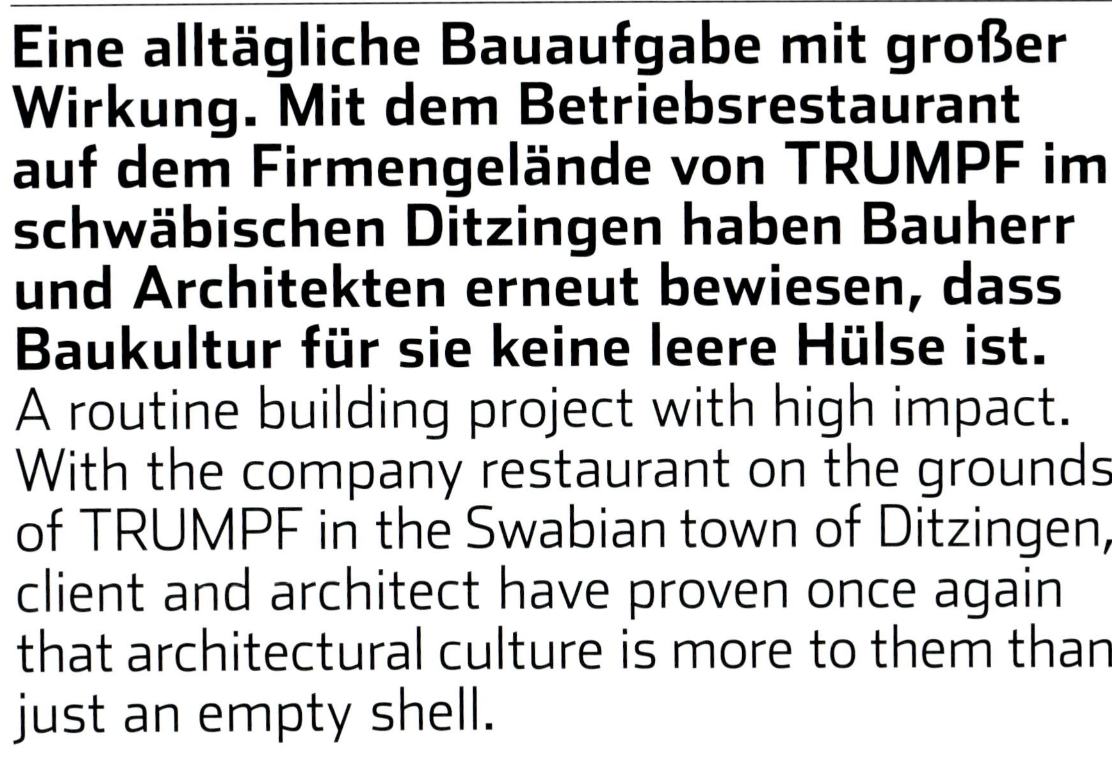

URSULA KLEEFISCH-JOBST

Eine alltägliche Bauaufgabe mit großer Wirkung. Mit dem Betriebsrestaurant auf dem Firmengelände von TRUMPF im schwäbischen Ditzingen haben Bauherr und Architekten erneut bewiesen, dass Baukultur für sie keine leere Hülse ist.

A routine building project with high impact. With the company restaurant on the grounds of TRUMPF in the Swabian town of Ditzingen, client and architect have proven once again that architectural culture is more to them than just an empty shell.

BARKOW LEIBINGER ARCHITEKTEN

GEBÄUDE | BUILDING

BETRIEBSRESTAURANT TRUMPF

TEXT PETER CACHOLA SCHMAL

01

ARCHITEKTEN | ARCHITECTS

Barkow Leibinger Architekten
Schillerstraße 94
10625 Berlin
www.barkowleibinger.com

MITARBEITER | TEAM

Entwurf | design:
Jason Sandy, Johanna Doherty,
Christina Eickmeier, Klaus Reintjes
Ausführung | execution:
Lukas Weder (Projekt-
leitung | project architect**),**
Philipp Heydel (Projektmana-
gement | project management**)**
Philipp Heidemann,
Caspar Hoesch, Mathias Oliva,
Christina Möller, Dagmar Pelger,
Jason Sandy

BAUHERR | CLIENT

TRUMPF GmbH & Co. KG

TRAGWERK | STRUCTURE

Werner Sobek, Stuttgart

AUSFÜHRUNG DACHTRAGWERK
CONSTRUCTION OF ROOF
SUPPORT STRUCTURE

Holzbau Amann,
Weilheim-Bannholz

LANDSCHAFTSARCHITEKTEN
LANDSCAPE ARCHITECTS

Büro Kiefer, Berlin

FARBGESTALTUNG
COLOUR CONCEPT

Friederike Tebbe, Berlin

FERTIGSTELLUNG | COMPLETION

2008

STANDORT | LOCATION

Johann-Maus-Straße 2
71254 Ditzingen

FOTOS | PHOTOS

Stephan Sahm

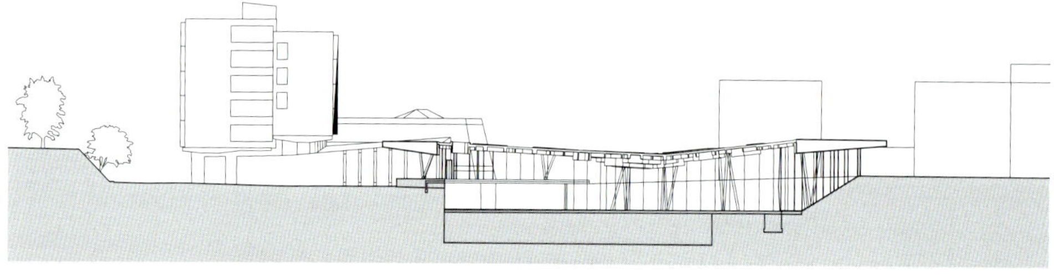

Geländeschnitt | Section of grounds

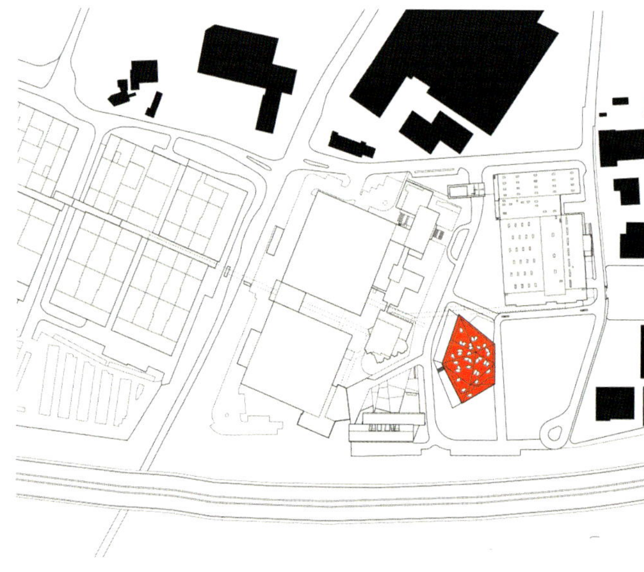

Lageplan | Site plan

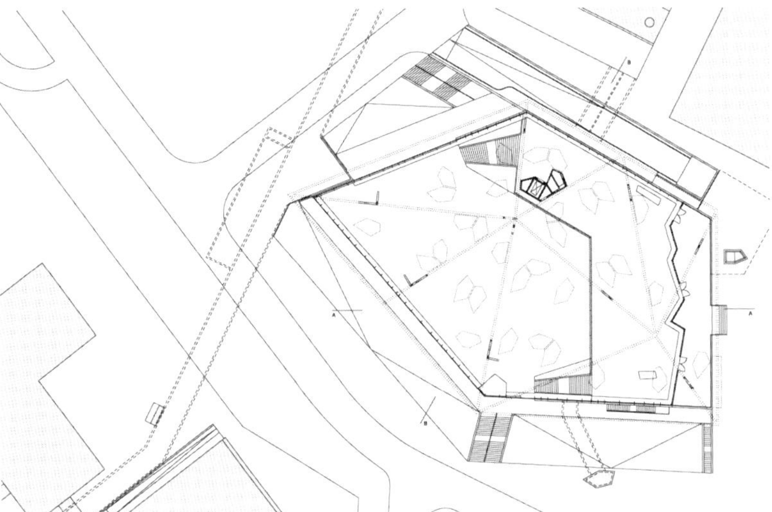

Grundriss Erdgeschoss | Floor plan of ground floor

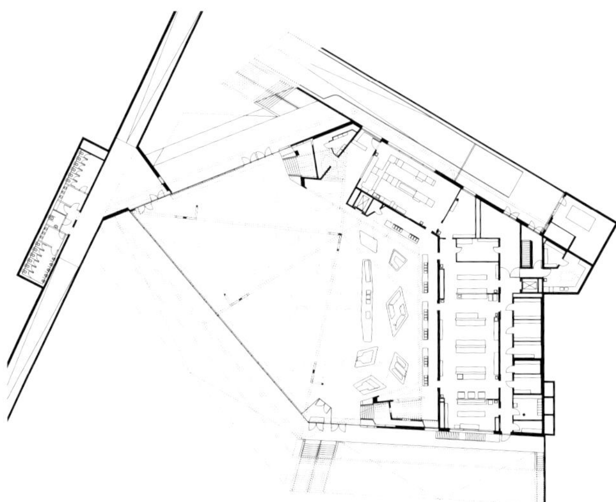

Grundriss Untergeschoss | Floor plan of basement

„Wir sind wirklich daran interessiert, diese alltäglichen Raumprogramme oder Typologien zu erhöhen und zu etwas ganz Besonderem zu machen." Frank Barkow

An alltäglichen gewerblichen Bauaufgaben mangelt es nicht bei der Firma TRUMPF, einer Spezialfirma der Hochtechnologie für Werkzeugmaschinen und Lasertechnik im schwäbischen Ditzingen, einer kleinen Stadt im Umland von Stuttgart und in verkehrsgünstiger Lage direkt an der A81 zwischen Zuffenhausen und Leonberg. Seit zwölf Jahren realisieren die Architekten Barkow Leibinger Stück für Stück ihren Masterplan der Trumpf Corporate Architecture, der das Werksgelände gründlich verändert hat – zu etwas Besonderem. Es ist das Verdienst der Berliner Architekten, dass sie dabei die notwendige Funktionalität im Industriebau mit innovativen Herstellungsmethoden und Gestaltungsvorschlägen gepaart und ein stimmiges Gesamtbild von höchster Qualität erzeugt haben.
Eine Laserfabrik mit speziellem Faltdach sowie ein Logistikzentrum waren 1998 und 2000 die ersten Bauabschnitte, gefolgt 2003 von einem vielfach ausgezeichneten Vertriebszentrum; und vier Jahre später von einem neuen Schulungszentrum und einer kleinen, kühn überdachten Pforte zum Betriebsgelände. Im Herbst 2009 geht diese langjährige Transformation zu Ende, wenn als vorerst letzter Schritt ein großes Entwicklungszentrum mit Produktionshallen eingeweiht wird. Alle Bauten entwickeln sich entlang einer unterirdischen Versorgungsachse, die Fabriken sind dabei quer zu dieser Achse angeordnet. Barkow spricht von einer typischen Struktur, wie sie auch die umliegende Landwirtschaft mit ihren streifenförmigen Anbauflächen quer zu den Haupterschließungswegen kennzeichnet. Das einzige Bauwerk, das nicht nur geometrisch aus dem Rahmen fällt, ist das etwa 60 x 40 Meter große Pentagon des Betriebsrestaurants. Dies entspricht auch seiner herausragenden Bedeutung, denn es dient nicht nur der Nahrungsaufnahme, sondern stellt auch den zentralen Veranstaltungs- und Versammlungsort des Unternehmens dar. Die Firma hat sich diesen, auch von den Kosten her herausragenden Bau geleistet. Und es hat sich gelohnt.
Entstanden ist ein lichter hoher Einraum, der zur Hälfte in der Erde eingegraben ist, so dass das vorhandene unterirdische Tunnelsystem aus den Fabriken, den Verwaltungen und den

"We're really interested in elevating these everyday building programmes or types into something that can be very special." Frank Barkow

There is no lack of everyday commercial building projects these days at the TRUMPF company, a specialist in high-tech machine tools and laser technology based in Ditzingen, a small Swabian town near Stuttgart conveniently situated directly on the A81 motorway between Zuffenhausen and Leonberg. For the past twelve years, the architects Barkow Leibinger have been realising bit by bit their master plan for Trumpf's corporate architecture, transforming the company site from the ground up – into something unique. It is to the credit of the Berlin architects that they have been able to unite the necessary functionality of industrial construction with innovative production methods and design suggestions, resulting in a coherent overall picture at the highest level of quality.
A laser plant with a special folded roof as well as a logistics centre were the first construction projects in 1998 and 2000, followed in 2003 by a multi-award-winning distribution centre, and four years later by a new training centre and a small, daringly roofed main gate to the company grounds. In autumn 2009 the years of transformation will be over for the time being when, as the last step in the current plans, a large-scale development centre with production halls will open its doors. All of the buildings have been developed along an underground supply channel, with the factories arranged perpendicular to its axis. Barkow speaks here of a typical structure, echoing the way the ploughed strips of the surrounding agricultural fields are set perpendicular to the main access routes. The only building that stands out from the orderly whole – and not only due to its geometry – is the 60 x 40 metre pentagon holding the company restaurant. This distinctive look is fitting in view of the cafeteria's exceptional importance, because it

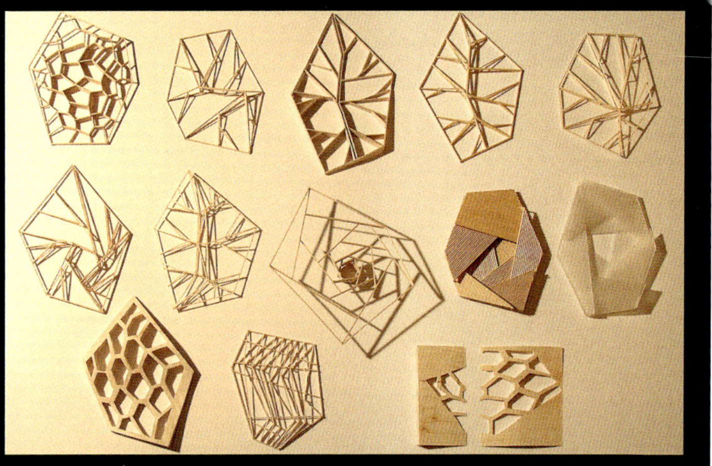

Modellstudien/Skizzen | Model studies / sketches

anderen Bereichen angeschlossen und die notwendigen Räume wie Küche, Lager, Technik und Andienung unsichtbar untergebracht werden konnten. Von außen in seiner halben Höhe noch relativ harmlos wirkend, entfaltet der Raum erst im Innern seine ungewöhnliche Präsenz. Wie ein großes Blatt schwebt das markanteste architektonische Element des Baues, ein ungewöhnlich konstruiertes Dach, über einer Mulde. Die Architekten haben sich, nicht nur statisch, von Blattstrukturen mit ihren Haupt- und Nebenadern inspirieren lassen. Das Dach erinnert auch an den Mies'schen Trägerrost der Neuen Nationalgalerie, allerdings in zeitgemäßer Umdeutung und ohne dabei den dunklen und lastenden Raumeindruck zu erzeugen. Die wenigen, teils schräg stehenden Stahlstützen werden zu sieben Bündeln zusammengefasst und wirken wie schlanke Baumstämme unter einem gemeinsamen Blätterdach, das von einer Vielzahl von Lichteinfällen durchbrochen wird. Die Stahlstützen sind durch schlank wirkende, hochkant stehende Stahlträger miteinander verbunden und bilden so unregelmäßige Fünfeckfelder von beträchtlicher Spannweite. Diese neun Felder werden wiederum in eine Vielzahl von fünfeckigen Zellen aus hellen Fichtenholz-Leimbindern unterteilt, die nicht nur tragende Funktionen übernehmen, sondern auch solche der Belichtung und Akustik – durch unterschiedliche Ausfüllungen mit Oberlichtern, Leuchtfeldern oder Akustikpaneelen. Die Tiefe dieser Zellen variiert sehr stark, von 90 bis 150 Zentimetern, so dass die Untersicht des Daches nicht ‚so irgendwie geraten' ist, sondern skulptural ausgeformt wurde. Der unter diesem Dach entstandene Raum der Kantine ist beeindruckend großzügig, die Atmosphäre dennoch angenehm und geschützt, unterstützt durch die eingesetzten Materialien: das helle Grau des Epoxydharz-Estrichs, die in vielen Grüntönen gehaltene Bestuhlung, die eleganten abgerundeten Ausgabetheken aus acrylgebundenem Mineralwerkstoff (einem Corian-ähnlichen Material) sowie die experimentell geformten weißen Kacheln an den Wänden. Dazu kommen die perfekt ausgeführten, anthrazit eingefärbten Betontreppen und die in der Wirkung zurückgenommenen, aus dünnen Stahlschwertern geformten Fassadenprofile. Eine Galerie geht auf halber Höhe in eine Außenterrasse über. Insgesamt

serves not only as a dining facility, but also forms a central place for the firm's events and assemblies. The company decided to invest in a building that is really outstanding – in terms of cost, too. And it was worth it.

The result is a single soaring, light and airy space, half embedded in the ground so that the existing underground tunnel system leading from the plants, offices and other areas could be connected and used to invisibly accommodate the necessary rooms such as kitchen, storage, technical equipment and delivery services. Seen from outside at half its actual height, the structure looks quite harmless, but once inside the room develops extraordinary presence. Like a giant leaf, the building's most striking feature – its unusually constructed ceiling – floats atop the hollow that is the dining area. The architects drew inspiration from both the structure and aesthetic of leaves with their main and subsidiary arteries. The roof recalls Mies van der Rohe's support grid for the Neue Nationalgalerie in Berlin, but translated into present-day style, having cast off all the darkness and heaviness. The sparsely placed, sometimes slanting steel stanchions are gathered together into seven bundles and look like slim tree trunks under their leafy canopy, which is pierced by a number of skylights. The steel pillars are linked by slender steel girders, thus forming irregular five-sided fields spanning sizeable open spaces. These nine fields are subdivided into a number of five-sided cells made of light-coloured spruce gluelam that not only have a load-bearing function but also serve lighting and acoustic purposes – filled variously with skylights, lighting or acoustic panels. The depth of these cells varies considerably, from 90 to 150 centimetres, so that the ceiling has not 'just turned out like that', but rather constitutes a sculptural form in its own right. The dining room beneath this ceiling is impressively spacious, the atmosphere nonetheless pleasant and sheltered, a feeling that is enhanced by the materials used: the light grey of the epoxy resin flooring, the many green tones of the chairs, the food counters with their elegantly rounded corners, which are made of an acrylic composite (similar to Corian), as well as the experimentally shaped white tiles on the walls. Added to this are perfectly executed anthracite-coloured concrete steps and the restrained façade profiles made of thin steel swords. A gallery halfway up leads out onto a terrace. Overall, the impression is that of a stage, which one can imagine would lend itself well to company parties and the concerts planned for the space. It is more important,

Schnitte | Sections

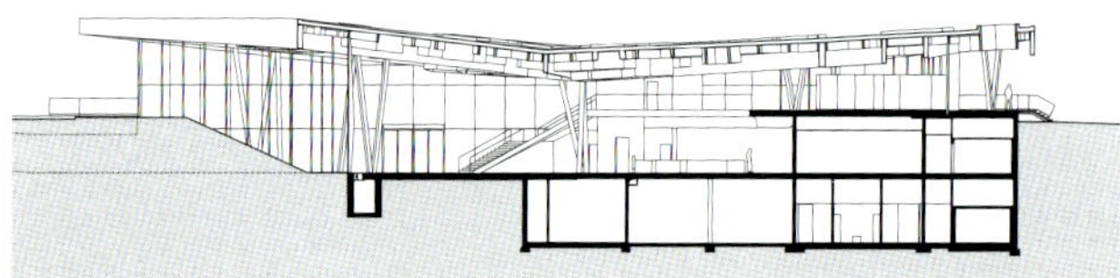

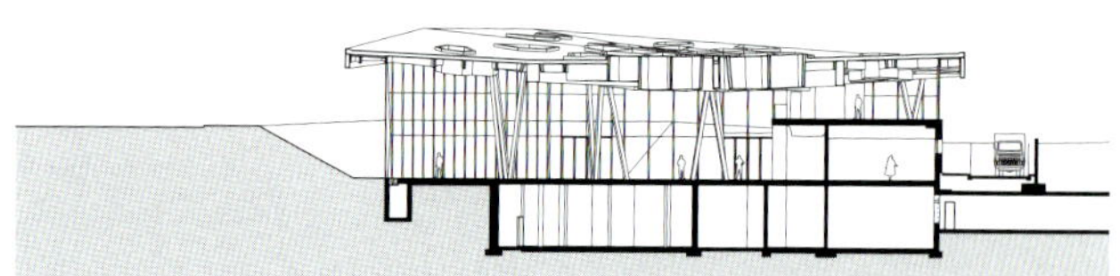

wird ein bühnenartiger Raumeindruck erzeugt, den man sich gut für Betriebsfeste und die geplanten Musikveranstaltungen vorstellen kann. Wichtiger allerdings ist, dass dieser Raum von den Mitarbeitern der Firma TRUMPF in ihrem alltäglichen Leben genossen werden kann. Da er gut 700 Sitzplätze anbietet, essen die heute etwa 2000 Mitarbeiter in Schichten.

Die individualisierte Massenfertigung (Mass-Customization), in der industriellen Produktion von Kleidung, Schuhen, Uhren oder Lebensmitteln bereits üblich, wurde nun auch für größere Bauprojekte eingeführt. Entworfen als digitales 3D-Modell in enger Abstimmung mit den Ingenieuren von Werner Sobek, und gefertigt mithilfe von CNC-Verfahren von der außergewöhnlichen Holzbaufirma Amann aus dem badischen zwischen Freiburg und Zürich gelegenen Weilheim-Bannholz, ist mit diesem Dach ein Meilenstein nicht nur der Baukonstruktion entstanden. Denn die Entwicklung nichtorthogonaler Architektur zeigt ihr volles Potenzial nicht bei den freigeformten Blobs, wie vor einiger Zeit noch angenommen, sondern in solchen geometrisch komplexen Sonderbauten.

Das Deutsche Architekturmuseum ist stolz, den „DAM Preis für Architektur in Deutschland 2009/10" dem Betriebsrestaurant von TRUMPF verleihen zu können, und damit seinen Architekten Barkow Leibinger Architekten aus Berlin, seinen Fassaden- und Tragwerksplanern Werner Sobek aus Stuttgart und seinem Bauherrn, der TRUMPF Werkzeugmaschinen GmbH + Co. KG aus Ditzingen.

however, that this fine building can be enjoyed every day by TRUMPF staff. Since it has some 700 seats, the 2,000 company employees eat in shifts. Mass customisation, common today in the industrial production of clothing, shoes, watches and food products, has now been discovered for large-scale construction projects. Designed as a digital 3D model in close collaboration with the engineers at Werner Sobek, and fabricated with the help of CNC processes by a specialist in unusual wooden structures, Amann from Weilheim-Bannholz between Freiburg and Zurich, this roof is a milestone – and not only in terms of its construction. The fact is that the evolution of non-orthogonal architecture really shows its full potential not in free-form blobs, as once assumed, but rather in geometrically complex, special buildings like this one.

The Deutsches Architekturmuseum is proud to present the DAM Award for Architecture in Germany 2009/10 to the TRUMPF company restaurant, and thus to its architects, Barkow Leibinger Architekten from Berlin; its façade and structural planners, Werner Sobek from Stuttgart; and its client, TRUMPF Werkzeugmaschinen GmbH + Co. KG, Ditzingen.

DIE SUCHE NACH OPTIMALEN ARBEITSBEDINGUNGEN

Für ein Unternehmen wie TRUMPF, weltweit führender Werkzeugmaschinenhersteller und Laserspezialist, ist gute und hochwertige Architektur nicht so sehr eine Frage der Selbstdarstellung nach außen. Sie ist vielmehr Ausdruck einer Suche nach optimalen Arbeitsbedingungen und somit ein Zeichen der Wertschätzung gegenüber den eigenen Mitarbeitern: Gute Arbeit, das ist die Grundüberzeugung der Bauherren des Unternehmens, kann nur unter guten Bedingungen entstehen. Dazu zählt auch die Architektur unserer Bauten. Hier zu investieren ist eine bewusste Entscheidung – nicht aus Übermut, sondern weil sich diese Investition im Laufe der Jahre durch geringere Kosten im Unterhalt und auch die flexiblere Anpassbarkeit an neue Rahmenbedingungen mehr als bezahlt macht.

Was für Gebäude in den Bereichen Produktion und Verwaltung gilt, nämlich dass sie durch eine hohe Qualität und Präzision in der Ausführung einen idealen Rahmen für gute Arbeit bieten sollen, das gilt im übertragenen Sinne umso mehr für ein Betriebsrestaurant. Hier verbringt man die knappe Zeit der Mittagspause, hier stehen Entspannung und informelle Kommunikation im Vordergrund, hier tankt man neue Kräfte auf.

Mit dem neuen Betriebsrestaurant ist ein heller und offener Raum entstanden, der auch für Preisverleihungen oder Betriebsversammlungen genutzt wird. Die Innovation der Konstruktion passt zum Selbstverständnis des Unternehmens, die Wärme des Holzes und die hervorragende Akustik zur gewünscht erholsamen Atmosphäre. Unter dem markanten, fast schwebenden Dach hat das Firmengelände nun eine ‚soziale Mitte' bekommen.

Jürgen Schäfer
Leiter der Bauabteilung / TRUMPF Immobilien GmbH & Co. KG

THE SEARCH FOR OPTIMAL WORKING CONDITIONS

For a company like TRUMPF, a world-leader at producing machine tools and in laser technology, good, high-class architecture is not so much a question of the image we project to the outside world. Rather, it is an expression of our search for optimal working conditions and hence a sign of appreciation for our own employees. We are convinced that good work can only be done in the right environment. This includes the architecture of our buildings. Investing in good buildings is a conscious decision – not out of pride, but because this investment more than pays off over the years in the form of lower maintenance costs and greater flexibility to adapt to changing conditions.

The demands placed on buildings used for production and as offices, namely that they should form an ideal framework for good work through a high level of quality and precision workmanship, apply even more in a figurative sense to a company restaurant. This is where our employees spend their brief lunch breaks, where the priorities are relaxation and informal communication, where people can recharge their batteries.

The new company restaurant provides us with a bright, open space that can also be used for awards ceremonies or company assemblies. The innovative building fits in well with the company's aspirations, with the warm wood and excellent acoustics creating the desired restorative atmosphere. Under the striking, almost floating roof, the company site has now acquired a new social focal point.

Jürgen Schäfer
Director of the Buildings Department /
TRUMPF Immobilien GmbH & Co. KG

INHALT

DEUTSCHES ARCHITEKTUR JAHRBUCH

GERMAN ARCHITECTURE ANNUAL

2009|10

DEUTSCHES ARCHITEKTURMUSEUM FRANKFURT AM MAIN

PRESTEL VERLAG MÜNCHEN | BERLIN | LONDON | NEW YORK

VORWORT | FOREWORD

PETER CACHOLA SCHMAL
MICHAELA BUSENKELL

Das Deutsche Architektur Jahrbuch, herausgegeben vom Deutschen Architekturmuseum (DAM), hat sich mit der letzten Ausgabe 2008/09 in seiner neuen Form etabliert, ebenso der „DAM Preis für Architektur in Deutschland". Zur Ausstellungseröffnung und Preisverleihung am 16. Januar 2009 kamen fast alle ausgewählten Architekten ins DAM, ein reges Presseecho folgte. Das lag natürlich auch am Gewinner Peter Zumthor. Er erhielt den DAM Preis für sein Diözesanmuseum Kolumba in Köln. Sein Vortrag war eine Sternstunde für das DAM. Auch die Pritzkerpreis-Jury nahm die Fertigstellung dieses Museums wie auch der kleinen Bruder Klaus Kapelle (ebenfalls in unserer Auswahl von 2008) zum Anlass, das Werk von Zumthor mit dem Pritzkerpreis 2009 zu adeln.

Die diesjährigen DAM-Preisträger, das Berliner Büro Barkow Leibinger von Frank Barkow und Regine Leibinger, sind auch keine Unbekannten – ihre kühn auskragende Pforte (Jahrbuch 2008/09) und das Betriebsrestaurant der Firma TRUMPF in Ditzingen begeistern die Kritik. Inzwischen haben sie sogar einem großen Hamburger Architekturbüro dessen traditionellen 1. Platz der Baunetz-Rankingliste streitig gemacht, was die Häufigkeit der publizistischen Nennungen angeht. Wir freuen uns sehr, dass sich unsere Jahrbuch-Jury für das Betriebrestaurant als Preisträger entschieden hat und sind stolz, zusammen mit Barkow Leibinger und ihren Fachplanern von Werner Sobek eine kleine Ausstellung im Ungerschen Haus-im-Haus im 3. OG, dem Herzstück des DAM, pünktlich zur Eröffnung der Ausstellung „DAM Preis 2009. Die 26 besten Bauten in/aus Deutschland" am 13. November 2009 präsentieren zu können.

ESSAYS

Im ersten Essay untersucht der Berliner Kunsthistoriker Christian Welzbacher den anhaltenden Bauboom von Museen und Ausstellungshäusern in Deutschland. Dabei hat sich das Verhältnis von Gebäude und Inhalt verschoben. Heute kennt mancher ein Ausstellungshaus von flamboyanter Gestalt, ohne etwas über dessen Inhalt zu wissen; mal wertet die Architektur nachrangige Ausstellungsstücke auf (oder die

In its last edition in 2008/09, the German Architecture Annual, published by the German Architecture Museum (DAM), established its new format as well as its "DAM Award for Architecture in Germany". Almost all of the featured architects came to the DAM for the awards ceremony on 16 January 2009, and wide coverage in the press followed, thanks in part of course to an appearance by the winner Peter Zumthor. Zumthor received the award for his Kolumba Art Museum for the archdiocese of Cologne. The talk he gave at the ceremony was a great moment for the DAM. The Pritzker Prize jury took the completion of this museum, as well as the small Bruder Klaus Kapelle (also in our last selection of 2008), as an occasion to award him the 2009 Pritzker Prize.

This year's DAM Award winners, Frank Barkow and Regine Leibinger of the Berlin architecture office Barkow Leibinger, are likewise no unknowns on the German architecture scene. Their boldly cantilevered main gate (2008/09 annual) and restaurant for the TRUMPF corporation in Ditzingen have met with widespread acclaim. In the meantime they are even vying for first place in the Baunetz press ranking with a major Hamburg architecture firm that traditionally occupied that position. We are delighted that the jury for our German Architecture Annual chose the TRUMPF corporation restaurant as winner, and are proud to present in conjunction with Barkow Leibinger and their structural engineers from Werner Sobek, a small exhibition of this project in Ungers' house-in-a-house on the third floor, the heart of the DAM, to coincide with the opening of the show "DAM Award 2009. The 26 Best Buildings in/from Germany" on 13 November 2009.

ESSAYS

In the first essay , Berlin-based art historian Christian Welzbacher looks at the ongoing boom in museums and exhibition spaces in Germany. Over the years, the relationship between building and content has shifted. Today some museums are famous for their flamboyant design while nobody has any idea what's inside; in other cases, the architecture has the effect of upgrading mediocre exhibits (or the institution behind the construction project); or the museum functions as a kind of moral money-laundering machine – because whoever funds a museum certainly can't be a bad person. The author

dahinter stehende Institution); oder das Museum fungiert als moralische Geldwaschanlage – denn wer Museen stiftet, kann kein schlechter Mensch sein. Der Autor erörtert, wie weit die Transformation vom bürgerlichen Ausstellungswesen zum spätkapitalistischen Kulturmarketing gediehen ist und erörtert unterschiedliche Aspekte des zeitgenössischen Ausstellungswesens und seiner Architekturen, auch im Zeichen der Krise. Mit den internationalen Autohäusern von Audi – als einer kommerziellen Form des Ausstellungsbaus – setzt sich die Mitherausgeberin Michaela Busenkell auseinander. Audi beauftragte die Architekten Allmann Sattler Wappner aus München, ein neues Autohaus in Serie zu entwickeln – samt Manual mit differenzierten Vorgaben und detaillierter Einweisung für eine internationale Realisierung. Zukunftsweisend ist, dass die Planung nicht auf singuläre Eventarchitektur (wie bei den Automuseen der Konkurrenz), sondern auf die adäquate Einbindung in die jeweilige urbane Stadtkultur setzt. Mit dem Schwerpunkt auf innen- wie stadträumliche Qualitäten könnte der neue ‚terminal' ein Zeichen für eine Weiterentwicklung von Markenarchitektur setzen, bei der nicht nur der überstrapazierte Aufmerksamkeitskoeffizient entwurfsbestimmend wirkt.

DIE JURY DES JAHRBUCHS

Bei der Auswahl der Projekte für dieses Jahrbuch nominierte eine Jury aus Kuratoren und wissenschaftlichen Mitarbeitern des DAM und fünf auswärtigen Experten insgesamt über 100 aktuelle Bauten. Im Februar 2009 bestimmte diese Jury den Gewinner des „DAM Preises für Architektur in Deutschland 2009" und legte fest, welche weiteren 25 Bauwerke im Jahrbuch gewürdigt werden sollen. Mit Marc Frohn von „FAR Frohn Rojas" aus Köln/Santiago de Chile nahm ein Architekt des letzten Jahrbuchs teil. Mit ihm gemeinsam entschieden Hans Ibelings, Chefredakteur des Magazins „A10" aus Amsterdam, Christian Schittich, Chefredakteur der Zeitschrift „Detail", Ursula Kleefisch-Jobst, die neue Leiterin von „M:AI Museum für Architektur und Ingenieurkunst NRW", die freien

explores the progress that has been made from bourgeois exhibition scheme to late-capitalist cultural marketing tool and discusses different aspects of the contemporary exhibition scene and its architecture within the context of the credit crunch.

In the second essay, co-editor Michaela Busenkell analyses Audi's international automobile showrooms – as a commercial form of exhibition buildings. Audi has commissioned the Munich-based architects Allmann Sattler Wappner to develop a new kind of automobile showroom as a series – complete with a manual with varying specifications and detailed instructions geared for execution worldwide. What's forward-looking about this project is that the planning does not aim at one-of-a-kind event architecture (as do the auto museums of the competitors), but rather at suitable integration into each city's own urban culture. Placing the emphasis on interior qualities and urban planning aspects, the new 'terminal' could be a sign of the further development of brand architecture in which more goes into the design than merely the already overtaxed attention-grabbing coefficient.

THE JURY OF THE GERMAN ARCHITECTURE ANNUAL

To choose the projects for this year's annual, a jury of curators and research associates of the DAM, along with five external experts, nominated more than 100 recent buildings. At a session in February 2009 the jury selected the winner of the "DAM Award for Architecture in Germany 2009" and established which other 25 buildings would be included in the annual. One member of the jury, Marc Frohn of FAR Frohn Rojas from Cologne/Santiago de Chile, had his project featured in last year's annual. Joining him on the jury were Hans Ibelings, editor-in-chief of "A10" magazine from Amsterdam, Christian Schittich, editor-in-chief of "Detail" magazine, Ursula Kleefisch-Jobst, new director of the "M:AI Museum für Architektur und Ingenieurkunst NRW", freelance architecture critics Falk Jaeger and Christian Brensing from Berlin, as well as Layla Dawson from Hamburg and the team from DAM, which included, in addition to director Peter Cachola Schmal, curator Oliver Elser and archive director Inge Wolf, the freelance staff members Michaela Busenkell, Karen Jung, Christina Gräwe, Yorck

Architekturkritiker Falk Jaeger und Christian Brensing aus
Berlin sowie Layla Dawson aus Hamburg und das Team des
DAM: neben dem Direktor Peter Cachola Schmal, dem Kurator
Oliver Elser und der Archivleiterin Inge Wolf die freien Mitar-
beiter Michaela Busenkell, Karen Jung, Christina Gräwe, Yorck
Förster, Hester Robinson, Anna Hesse, Sebastian Tokarz, und
Dorothea Deschermeier.
Bei der Bestimmung des Preisträgers gab es intensive Diskus-
sionen. In einer Stichwahlentscheidung obsiegte das Ditzinger
Betriebsrestaurant gegenüber dem sehr beeindruckenden
Kunstmuseum Moritzburg in Halle der Madrider Architekten
Nieto Sobejano. Wie in den vergangenen Jahren wurde das
Gewinnerprojekt exklusiv für das Jahrbuch neu fotografiert.
Dank der gemeinsamen Auslobung des diesjährigen Europäi-
schen Architekturfotografiepreises, zusammen mit „architek-
turbild e. V." aus Stuttgart, haben wir den Preisträger, den
jungen Fotografen Stefan Sahm aus München, gewinnen und
beauftragen können.

KULTURBAUTEN UND
ALLTAGSKULTUR

Das Spektrum der Bauten in diesem Jahrbuch reicht vom
Parlamentsgebäude bis zum Kuhstall, von der Kunsthalle
zum Einfamilienhaus, vom Shopping Center zum umgebauten
Bauernhof. Während im Jahrbuch 2008/09 überwiegend
Umbauten vorgestellt wurden, liegt in diesem Jahr der Schwerpunkt auf Neubauten. Fast ein Drittel aller Gebäude sind
Museen und Ausstellungshäuser. Mit welchen Mitteln reagieren
die jeweiligen Architekturen auf Aspekte des historischen und
gegenwärtigen Kontextes und weisen dennoch über diese
hinaus? Bei der Erweiterung des Museums Schloss Moritzburg
bilden Alt und Neu eine kontrastierende Ganzheit, die zeitgenössischen Elemente wurden mit Fugen auf Abstand zum
Bestand gesetzt (Nieto Sobejano). Landschaftlich sorgfältig
implantiert wurde das künftige Architekturmuseum Hombroich
(Álvaro Siza mit Rudolf Finsterwalder), während der Erweiterungsbau des Franz Marc Museums in Kochel am See auf

Förster, Hester Robinson, Anna Hesse, Sebastian Tokarz, and Dorothea
Deschermeier. Intensive discussions were involved in selecting this
year's award winner. In a run-off vote, the Ditzingen TRUMPF corporation restaurant prevailed over the very impressive Kunstmuseum
Moritzburg in Halle by Madrid architects Nieto Sobejano. As in previous
years, new photographs were taken of the winning project, exclusively
for this publication. As DAM joined "architekturbild e.V." of Stuttgart in
awarding this year's European Architectural Photography Prize, we
were able to retain the services of the prize winner, young photographer
Stefan Sahm from Munich, to take these pictures.

CULTURAL EDIFICES AND
EVERYDAY CULTURE

The spectrum of structures featured in this year's annual ranges from
parliament buildings to a cowshed, from an art exhibition space to a
single-family home, from shopping centre to restored farmhouse.
While in the 2008/09 annual most of the buildings presented were
refurbishment projects, the emphasis this year is on new construction.
Almost one third of the buildings are museums or exhibition spaces.
How does the architecture respond to aspects of its historic and
present-day context and yet point beyond these toward the future?
In the extension of the Schloss Moritzburg Museum, old and new
come together to form a contrast-rich whole, with the contemporary
elements set off from the existing by means joints (Nieto Sobejano).
The upcoming architecture museum Hombroich by contrast was
carefully implanted in its riverside landscape (Álvaro Siza with Rudolf
Finsterwalder). The extension of the Franz Marc Museum in Kochel am
See was designed to harmonise with the paintings on exhibit (Diethelm & Spillmann). A contrast to the historic city backdrop is formed
by both the Ozeanum maritime museum in Stralsund (Behnisch) and
the ensemble of Kunstschule and municipal Galerie Stihl in Waiblingen
(Hartwig N. Schneider). The temporary Kunsthalle on Berlin's Schlossplatz (Adolf Krischanitz) on the other hand is a low-budget pavilion
with its stapled-together façades adorned with a pixel cloud. With the
Sammlung Brandhorst a colourful building block has been set down
in Munich to frame its urban museum quarter (Sauerbruch Hutton).
And while the Information and Exhibition Pavilion at Hamburg's

das Werk des Künstlers abgestimmt wurde (Diethelm & Spillmann). Einen Kontrast zur historischen Stadtkulisse setzen
sowohl das Meeresmuseum „Ozeanum" in Stralsund (Behnisch)
als auch das Ensemble für die Kunstschule und kommunale
Galerie Stihl in Waiblingen (Hartwig N. Schneider). Die temporäre Kunsthalle auf dem Berliner Schlossplatz (Adolf Krischanitz) hingegen ist ein low-budget-Pavillon mit billigster Fassade
und dem abstrakten Fassendenbild einer Pixelwolke. Mit der
Sammlung Brandhorst wiederum wurde ein farbiger Baustein
gesetzt, um das Museumsareal in München städtebaulich zu
rahmen (Sauerbruch Hutton). Während der Informations- und
Ausstellungspavillons dem Hamburger Überseequartier in
einem komplexen Bezugssystem verbunden ist (Bolles+Wilson),
erschafft die waghalsige Inszenierung des Porsche Museums
bei Stuttgart (Delugan Meissl) ihr eigenes Ordnungsprinzip.
Doch nicht weniger wichtig als die Ausstellungs- und Kultur-
bauten sind die unspektakulären, ja profanen Bauaufgaben:
der dreischiffige Selbstbau-Kuhstall auf einer Wiese bei Thankirchen (Florian Nagler); ein markanter Aussichtsturm in
der Lausitz (Stefan Giers und Susanne Gabriel), und nicht
zuletzt die Betriebskantine von TRUMPF in Ditzingen, deren
prägnantes Dachtragwerk aus einem fünfeckigen Zellengefüge
von Blattstrukturen inspiriert ist.
Neubauten können mit Materialien, durch städtebauliche Vorgaben oder den Dialog mit bestehenden Bauten in Beziehung
zum Umfeld treten. So prägt die ungewöhnliche Anwendungs-
form des traditionellen Ziegels die Mittelpunktbibiliothek in
Berlin-Köpenick (Bruno Fioretti Marquez mit Nele Dechmann),
das Stadthaus in Neu-Ulm (Fink+Jocher) oder das Münchner
Dominikuszentrum (Meck) auf jeweils unterschiedliche Weise.
Das IG Farben-Hochhaus von Hans Poelzig aus dem Jahr
1929 bestimmte den weiteren Ausbau des neuen Campus der
Goethe-Universität in Frankfurt am Main (Ferdinand Heide),
und die Idealplanung Karlsruhes setzt den Rahmen, in den
sich die L-Bank harmonisch einfügt (Weinmiller). Neue Inter-
pretationen bekannter Bautypen sind das Hanse Carré in
Münster als Fortführung des giebelständigen Kaufmannshauses
(R. M. Kresing mit A. Deilmann) oder die spektakuläre Shopping-

evolving Überseequartier is tied into a complex system of references
(Bolles+Wilson), the audaciously dramatic Porsche Museum outside
of Stuttgart creates its own ordering principle (Delugan Meissl). No
less important than the exhibition and cultural buildings, however,
are the less spectacular construction projects: the three-aisled DIY
cowshed on a meadow near Thankirchen, (Florian Nagler); or the
striking observation tower in the Lausitz region (Stefan Giers and
Susanne Gabriel); and, last but not least, the restaurant for TRUMPF
in Ditzingen, whose striking roof system with its five-sided cells was
inspired by the structure of leaves.
New buildings can relate to their surroundings through the use of
materials, by responding to urban planning conditions, or by making
reference to existing structures; An unusual use of traditional brick
characterises the Mittelpunktbibiliothek in Berlin-Köpenick for
example (Bruno Fioretti Marquez with Nele Dechmann), as well as the
Stadthaus in Neu-Ulm (Fink+Jocher) and the Munich Dominikuszentrum (Meck Architekten), although each time in a different manner.
The IG Farben highrise Hans Poelzig built in 1929 informed the further
extension of the new campus of the University of Frankfurt am Main
(Ferdinand Heide). Karlsruhe's planning as an ideal city in turn set the
framework into which the L-Bank was harmoniously integrated (Weinmiller Architekten). Reinterpretations of time-honoured architectural
types can be found in the Hanse Carré in Münster as a take on the
gabled commercial building (R. M. Kresing with A. Deilmann) or the
spectacular MAB MyZeil shopping mall in Frankfurt am Main (Massimiliano Fuksas). The extravagant shape of the residence Dupli.Casa
in Marbach is based on the contours of the footprint of the previous
home (J. Mayer H.). Further contributions to residential issues are
made by Haus_L in Augsburg (hiendl_schineis) the Kithier residential
complex in Diessen am Ammersse (Bembé Dellinger) and the semi-
detached homes in Weiden in the Upper Palatinate (WEBERWÜR-
SCHINGER). In a renovation project called "Birg mich, Cilli!" a dilapidated farmhouse in the Bavarian Forest was implanted with concrete
cells – a radical approach to landmark preservation and restoration
(Peter Haimerl, Jutta Görlich).

mall „MyZeil" in Frankfurt am Main (Massimiliano Fuksas).
Die extravagante Form des Wohnhauses Dupli.Casa in Marbach
basiert auf der Umrisslinie des Vorgängerbaus (J. Mayer H.).
Weitere Beiträge zum Thema Wohnen leisten das Haus_L in
Augsburg (hiendl_schineis), die Wohnanlage Kithier in Dießen
am Ammersee (Bembé Dellinger) und die Doppelhäuser in
Weiden in der Oberpfalz (WEBERWÜRSCHINGER). Beim Umbau
„Birg mich, Cilli!" wurden in ein marodes Anwesen im Bayeri-
schen Wald Betonzellen implantiert – als radikaler Ansatz zum
Thema Denkmalpflege und Umbau (Peter Haimerl, Jutta
Görlich).

EXPORT

Das Jahrbuch dokumentiert nicht nur herausragende Bauten
in, sondern auch aus Deutschland. So unterstreicht Hansjörg
Göritz die Bedeutung des Forums und Landesparlaments des
Fürstentums Liechtenstein in Vaduz mit seiner präzisen,
modularen Architektursprache. Um das deutsche Exportgut
‚Know-How' geht es dagegen bei dem Projekt von Roswag &
Jankowski. Aufgrund seiner einschlägigen Erfahrung mit
Lehmbauten wurde er mit der Aufgabe der Sanierung einer
historischen Festungsanlage in der arabischen Wüste betraut.
Das Jahr 2009 wird als das große Wirtschaftskrisenjahr in
unsere Geschichtsbücher eingehen. Eines der aufregendsten
Projekte des DAM, der Bau des DAM Pavillons im Park des
Museums für Angewandte Kunst konnte wegen der Krise
nicht mehr finanziert werden, stattdessen wurde die Planung
von Barkow Leibinger und Werner Sobek zum Thema einer
Ausstellung gemacht, mit einem 1:1 Mock-Up eines Teils des
Pavillons im DAM als hoffentlich gelungenem Ersatz.

Dem Prestel Verlag sei an dieser Stelle für sein großes Engagement gedankt. Ebenso dem gesamten Team des Deutschen
Architekturmuseums und allen Architekten und Fotografen
für die große Unterstützung bei Nominierung und Auswahl,
Publikation und Ausstellung.

EXPORT

The annual documents not only outstanding buildings located in
Germany, but also others outside the country authored by German
architects. Hansjörg Göritz underscores the significance of the Forum
and State Parliament of the Principality of Liechtenstein in Vaduz with
a precise, modular architectural vocabulary. Roswag & Jankowski's
project is all about exporting German expertise. Thanks to his wealth
of experience in mud structures, he was entrusted with the task of
restoring a historic fortification complex in the Arabian Desert.
2009 will go down in history as the year of great economic crisis.
One of the most exciting DAM projects, the construction of the DAM
pavilion on the grounds of Museum of Applied Arts, could no longer
be financed due to the crisis. Instead, the plans conceived by Barkow
Leibinger and Werner Sobek will form the theme of an exhibition,
with a 1:1 mock-up of a part of the pavilion inside the DAM.

We would like to take this opportunity to thank Prestel Verlag for its
hard work and dedication to this project. Many thanks as well to the
team at the Deutsches Architekturmuseum and all architects and
photographers involved for their generous support with the nomina-
tion and selection process, publication and exhibition.

Das DAM zeigt seit 2008 alle Projekte des Deutschen Architektur Jahrbuchs auch in einer Ausstellung. Der Preisträger des DAM Preises für Architektur in Deutschland 2008/2009, das Kolumba Kunstmuseum des Erzbistums Köln, wurde im „Haus im Haus" präsentiert.

Since 2008 the DAM has shown all projects featured in the German Architecture Annual in an exhibition. The winner of the DAM Award for Architecture in Germany 2008/2009, the Kolumba art museum of the archdiocese of Cologne, was presented in the 'House within a House'.

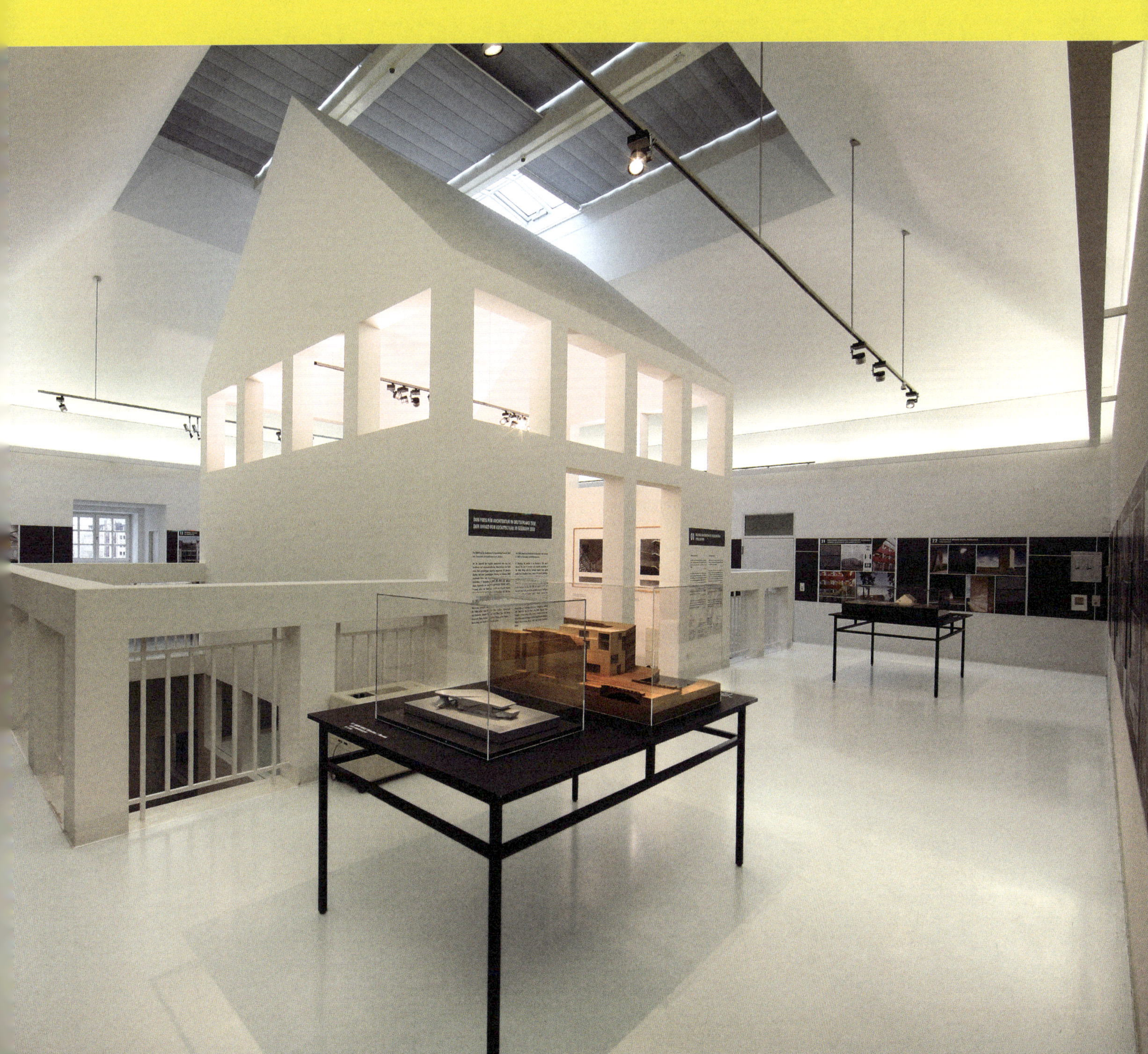

DIE LÜGE IM GEWAND DER WAHRHEIT
A LIE CLOAKED IN TRUTH

DER NEUE DEUTSCHE MUSEUMSBAUBOOM UND DIE KRISE DES MUSEUMS

THE NEW BOOM IN GERMAN MUSEUM CONSRUCTION AND THE CRISIS OF THE MUSEUM

CHRISTIAN WELZBACHER

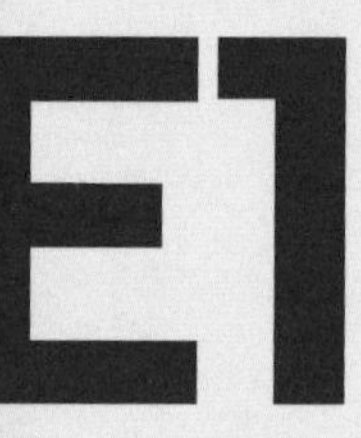

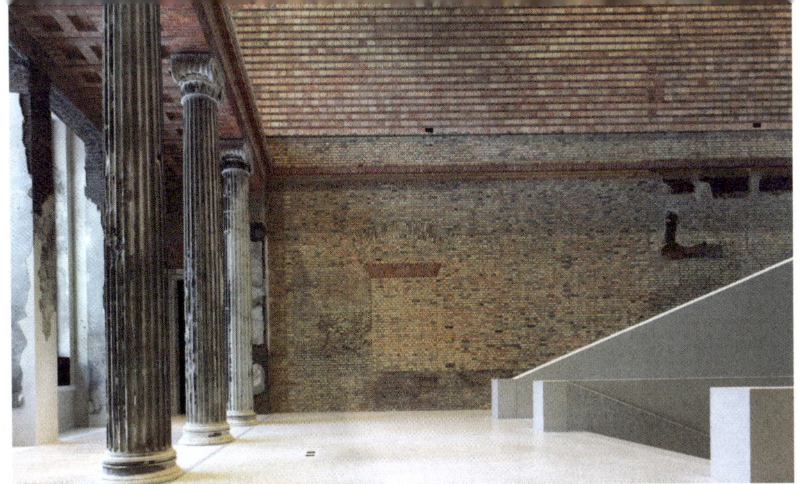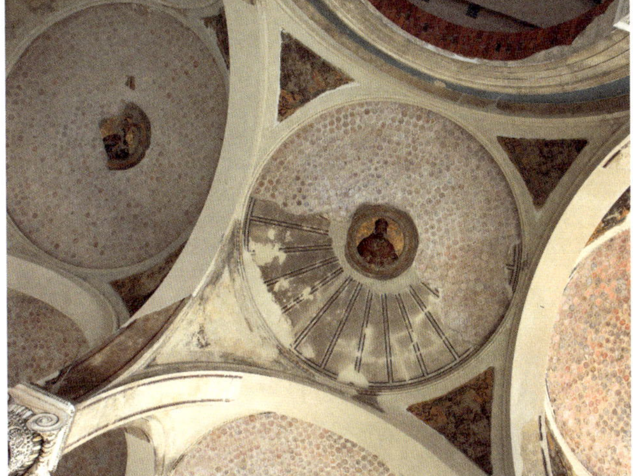

Neues Museum, Berlin; Architekt: David Chipperfield; Treppenhaus (links) / Gewölbe im Mittelalterlichen Saal (rechts)
Neues Museum, Berlin; architect: David Chipperfield; staircase (left) / vault in Medieval Hall (right)

„Der Wunsch nach Authentischem scheint in Zeiten virtueller Überpräsenz immer größer zu werden. Das Museum, das ich als Institution der Aufklärung verstehe, befriedigt sowohl die Altgier als auch die Neugier, es ist ein Ort der Zeitenvermengung. Es hat das, was wir vergessen haben, das, was wir begehren und vor allem vieles, was wir noch nicht kennen. Das Museum ist ein Ort der Streifzüge, des Auges und vor allem ein Ort des Entdeckens."
HG Merz

Es ist schon eine Weile her, da ging man zu Zwecken der Selbstvergewisserung in die Kirche. Heute, da das Vertrauen in jenseitige Versprechungen erschöpft ist, geht man ins Museum. Das Museum wirkt als letzter Ort unserer Kultur, an dem die Dinge ihre Ordnung haben. Hier erscheint die Welt noch logisch. Räume und Bedeutungen sind umgrenzt, Objekte werden tückenlos eingepfercht in Vitrinen, eindeutig katalogisiert und erläutert. Die These drängt sich auf: je undurchdringlicher die Realität, desto größer die Konjunktur des Museums. Tatsächlich etablierte sich dieses Paradoxon im 19. Jahrhundert, der Gründerzeit der Moderne, die gleichzeitig rasenden Fortschritt und manische Rückbesinnung auf die Geschichte zelebrierte. Offenbar haben wir diesen Denk- und Handlungshorizont auch heute nicht wirklich verlassen, denn das Paradoxon wirkt weiter fort. Immer mehr Museen jeglicher Form und Art entstehen, zumal in Deutschland, das mit der Selbstvergewisserung von jeher haderte und deshalb die Bauaufgabe besonders intensiv pflegt. Allein bei vorsichtiger Schätzung kommt man für 2007 und 2008 auf jeweils gut 20 bis 30 Institutionen, die sich einen Neu-, Erweiterungs- oder Umbau leisteten. Solche Quantitäten haben die Kirchen zuletzt zwischen 1945 und 1960 umgesetzt. Doch nach der verlustig gegangenen baukulturellen Mitte – der Sakralarchitektur – avancierte das Museum schnell zur letzten großen gesamtgesellschaftlichen Bauaufgabe.

Die unerhörte Karriere dieses Bautyps ist oft beschrieben worden. Nicht nur die Museumsbauten selbst, auch die Reflexionen über sie sind mittlerweile Legion – wobei sich schnell zeigt, dass die heutige Entwicklung nahtlos an die jüngste Vergangenheit anschließt. Konzeptuell, strukturell und finanziell lässt sich der aktuelle Museumsboom als

"In these days when the virtual is exerting an overpowering presence, there seems to be a growing desire for authenticity. The museum, which I see as an institution of enlightenment, satisfies our curiosity about both the old and the new; it is a place where time converges. It harbours things we have forgotten, things we covet and above all much that we do not yet know. The museum is a place of forays, of the eye and above all a place of discovery."
HG Merz

It's been some time since people went to church to obtain a feeling of self-affirmation. Today, now that our trust in the promise of a hereafter has been exhausted, people go to the museum instead. The museum seems to be the last place in our culture where things have a reliable order. Here, the world still seems to make logical sense. Rooms and meanings are defined, objects are crowded into display cases with no ulterior motives, catalogued and explained clearly. The thesis suggests itself that the more impenetrable reality becomes, the greater the popularity of the museum. In fact this paradox, which celebrated rapid progress while demonstrating a manic appreciation of history, took hold in the 19th century, when the foundations of Modernism were laid. Apparently we have yet to depart from this intellectual horizon today, because the paradox continues to apply. More and more museums are being built in every conceivable form – at least in Germany, which has always had its difficulties with self-affirmation and therefore takes this building task particularly seriously. A cautious estimate shows that a good 20 to 30 institutions undertook a new building, extension or remodelling in each of 2007 and 2008. These numbers were last seen in churches between 1945 and 1960. But after the loss of our architectural focal point – ecclesiastical building – the museum quickly advanced to become the last major building task involving all of society.

The unprecedented career experienced by museum architecture has frequently been described. Not only are the museum buildings themselves by now legion, but also reflections on them – whereby it is soon evident that today's developments pick up seamlessly on the most recent past. Conceptually, structurally and financially, the current explosion of museums can be understood as a continuation of the 'postmodern' museum boom, which in the 1970s and 80s brought (western) Germany a series of notable projects of international standing. Most of the museums of that era – art museums for example – were publicly funded or sponsored by donors and patrons. However, the first larger

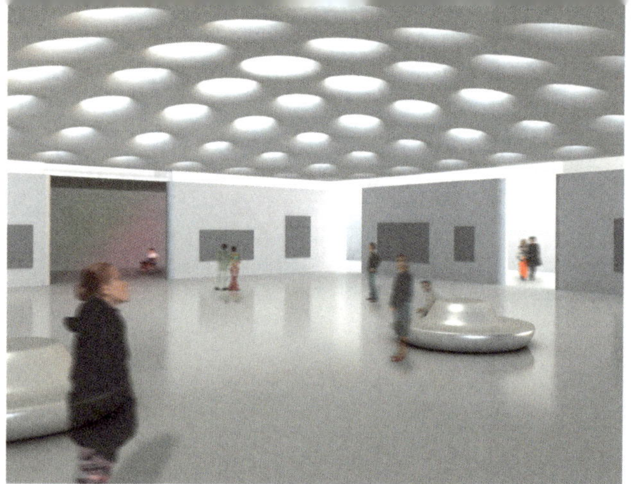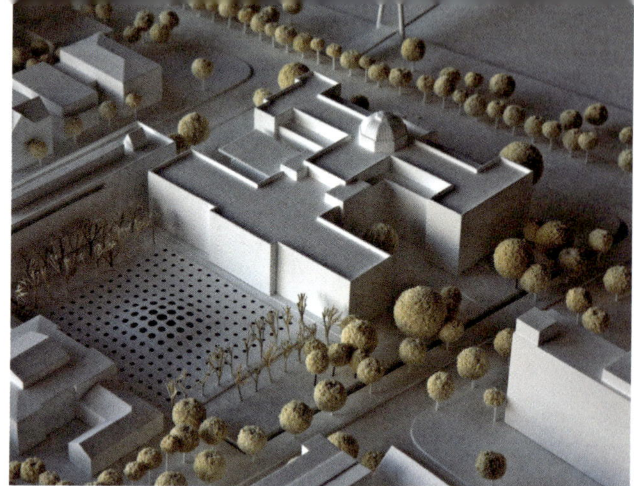

Städel-Erweiterung in Frankfurt am Main; Architekten: schneider+schumacher; Rendering des neuen unterirdischen Ausstellungsflügels (links), Modell (rechts) | Städel-extension in Frankfurt am Main; architects: schneider+schumacher; Rendering of new underground exhibition wing (left), model (right)

Weiterführung des „postmodernen" Museumsbooms begreifen, der (dem westlichen) Deutschland der 1970er- und 1980er-Jahre markante Projekte von internationaler Ausstrahlung bescherte. Die Museen dieser Ära waren – beispielsweise im Kunstbereich – in erster Linie Bauten der öffentlichen Hand, von Mäzenen und Stiftern unterstützt. Aber auch erste größere Privat- und Firmenmuseen entstanden, die neben die Präsentation von Inhalten die Repräsentation der Auftraggeber stellten (wie schon bei den Vorläufern des Museums üblich, den fürstlichen Kunstkammern und Galerien). Gleichzeitig wurden damals die ersten Objekte der Industrie- und Alltagskultur musealisiert, wie es zuvor nur Lebensstätten von Dichtern und Denkern zuteil geworden war.

Es ist nicht unwichtig, das Verhältnis der postmodernen Museumsrenaissance zur Protestbewegung um 1968 zu sehen, als Künstler und Intellektuelle die vermeintlich leeren Pathosformeln bourgeoiser Selbstbeweihräucherung entlarven wollten. Opernhäuser sollten geschlossen werden und es etablierte sich eine Kunst außerhalb der engen Ausstellungskontexte, jenseits der Akademien und staatlichen Fördertöpfe. Analog dazu verkündeten Provokateure, auch Architektur müsse endlich brennen. Zu den Ironien der Geschichte gehört es sicher, dass die großen Clowns dieser Revolutionszeit später zu erfolgreichen Museumsmanagern und Museumsarchitekten aufstiegen. Ihr Weg durch die Instanzen hat dem antibürgerlichen Stachel die Spitze genommen, die Relativierung der Kritik durch die Kritiker selbst formierte eine positive Neubewertung, eine regelrechte Stählung einstiger bürgerlicher Hohlformeln. Im Zuge dieser Restauration rückte das Museum zur entscheidenden Bauaufgabe auf: Es bekam die Schlüsselstellung im neubürgerlichen Kulturbetrieb, die es bis heute einnimmt.

Diese gesellschaftliche Relevanz spiegelt sich seither in der gestalterischen Ambition. Wer ein Museum entwirft, bewegt sich in der Königsdisziplin der Baukunst. Architektonische Kreativität, gediegene Bauausführung, formschöne Ausstellungsinszenierung – das zeigen die Bauten der letzten Jahre – setzen weiterhin Maßstäbe. Dass Museen dabei als frivole Eyecatcher erdacht werden, ihre Konzeption marken- und verkaufsorientiertes Branding einschließt, Shops immer größere Flächen verschlingen – all das irritiert in seiner Penetranz zwar

private and corporate museums also rose up during this period, designed not only to present content but also to represent their clients (as was already common in the museum's precursor, the royal art display chamber or gallery). At the same time, the 1970s and 80s witnessed objects from industrial and everyday culture being turned into museum exhibits, something done previously only for the places where great writers and thinkers lived and worked.

It is not unimportant to place the postmodern museum renaissance in the context of the protest movement of 1968, when artists and intellectuals endeavoured to expose the allegedly empty emotional formulas of bourgeois self-adulation. There were demands that opera houses be closed down, and an art scene established itself outside the narrow exhibition context, beyond the academies and state-funded projects. Agitators proclaimed that architecture, too, should finally go up in flames. One of the ironies of history is surely that the great clowns of those revolutionary times later went on to become successful museum managers and museum architects. Their path through the various levels of authority gradually wore down the sharp point of the anti-bourgeois thorn; as the critique was relativised by the critics themselves, a positive revaluation took shape, a veritable steeling of erstwhile empty bourgeois formulas. In the course of this restoration the museum was elevated to a vital building task: it took on a key standing on the new middle-class cultural scene, one it still occupies today.

This societal relevance has been reflected ever since in the ambitions of those shaping these institutions. He who designs a museum has the privilege of representing the supreme architectural discipline. Architectural creativity, sound construction and beautiful exhibition staging are still setting high standards – as evinced by the museums of recent years. The way that museums are often devised as frivolous eye-catchers, their concepts featuring sales-oriented branding and their shops taking up more and more space, can still prove irritating at times, but at least these trends document undisguisedly the extent to which their transformation from bourgeois exhibition system to late-capitalist cultural marketing platform has in fact flourished. Current admission fees likewise tell the education-hungry visitor of this change – with high prices that some exhibitions apparently try to compensate for by taking on the character of events. "The unquenchable thirst for new stimulation and attractions does not stop at the institution of the museum, however. We have been observing for some time that the opening of works in storage for public viewing* and special exhibitions are outstripping the permanent exhibitions in

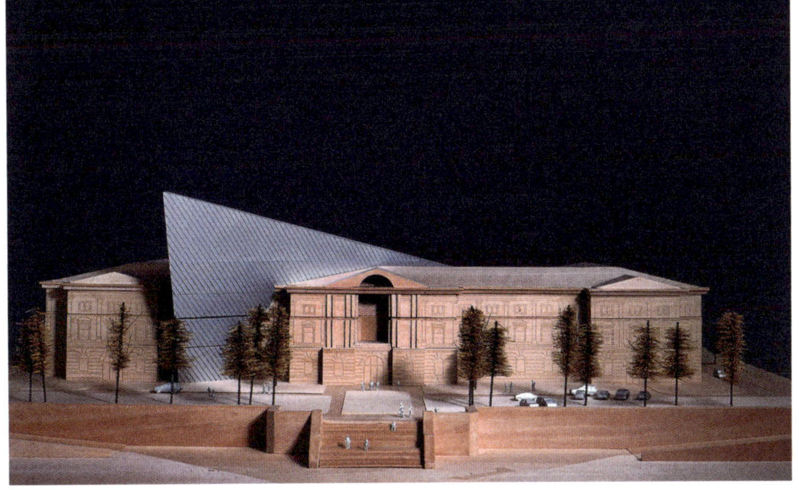 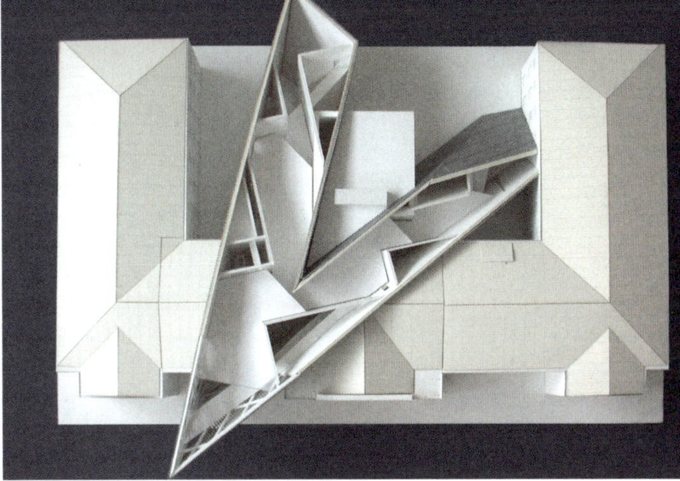

Erweiterung des Militärhistorischen Museums in Dresden; Architekt: Daniel Libeskind; Modelle | Extension of the Museum of Military History in Dresden; architect: Daniel Libeskind; models

bisweilen, aber es dokumentiert zumindest unverhohlen, wie weit die Transformation vom bürgerlichen Ausstellungswesen zum spätkapitalistischen Kulturmarketing tatsächlich gediehen ist. Von dieser Wandlung erzählen dem bildungshungrigen Besucher auch die aktuellen Eintrittspreise, die den Eventcharakter mancher Ausstellungen anscheinend kompensieren soll. „Das unstillbare Bedürfnis nach neuen Reizen und Attraktionen macht allerdings vor der Institution Museum nicht halt: Wir beobachten seit einiger Zeit, dass die Öffnung der Depots zu Schausammlungen* und Sonderausstellungen der klassischen Dauerausstellung den Rang ablaufen", konstatiert HG Merz. (*Nicht ausstellen, abstellen! Joseph Beuys) Dennoch zeigt sich wieder ein Paradoxon: Trotz elementarer Veränderung im Selbstverständnis, was ein Museum sei und welchen Auftrag es habe, sind in den letzten 30 Jahren konkrete Folgen für die Architektur ausgeblieben. Keiner der vielen neuen Bauten stellt Typologien grundlegend in Frage oder prahlt mit umstürzenden didaktischen Innovationen (von deren Versprechungen etwa die multimedialen 1990er-Jahre geprägt waren). Die aktuellen Museumsbauten sind Affirmationen des postmodernen Status quo. Damals war es die Architektur, die das Museum zur gebauten Ikone erhob, ihm eine neue Aura verschaffte. Dieses hohe Gut sichern die neu entstandenen Häuser auf eindringliche Weise. Natürlich fordert die skizzierte Entwicklung ihre Konsequenzen. Seit der Postmoderne hat sich das Verhältnis von Bau und Inhalt relativiert. Mal weiß man nicht, was bestimmte Museen präsentieren (der Bilbao-Effekt: jeder kennt das Haus, kaum jemand den Inhalt), mal wertet die architektonische Hülle nachrangige Ausstellungsstücke aller Art und Provenienz erst auf – Automobile, Fische, bemalte Leinwände, stillgelegte Hochöfen (oder die dahinter stehende Institution). Museen sind Vehikel zur Veredlung von Banalitäten und fungieren als moralische Geldwaschanlage: Durch Ausstellungshäuser suggerieren Firmen, Privatleute und der Staat, sie gäben den Bürgern einen kulturellen Mehrwert zurück, statt Gewinne oder Steuern einfach einzustreichen. Überspitzt könnte man zusammenfassen: das Museum als Bautyp wird so inflationär bemüht, weil es als Chiffre solider Bürgerlichkeit inmitten der chaotischen Weltordnung gilt. Wer Museen stiftet, kann kein schlechter Mensch sein. Noch der windigste Geschäftemacher, noch die

popularity," HG Merz confirms. (*Don't show, stow! Joseph Beuys) Nonetheless, a paradox can be found here as well: despite the elementary change that has taken place in museums' idea of what they are and what their mission is, during the last 30 years there have been no concrete consequences for their architecture. None of the many new buildings fundamentally calls into question the conventional typologies or shows off groundbreaking didactic innovations (of the sort that were promised by the development of multimedia in the 1990s). The current museum buildings are affirmations of the postmodern status quo. Back then it was the architecture that elevated the museum to a built icon, that lent it a new aura. The newly built edifices forcefully underscore the high value placed on this institution. Of course, the development we have sketched above does entail some consequences. Since the days of postmodernism, the relationship of building to content has been relativised. Sometimes people don't even know what certain museums exhibit (the Bilbao effect: everyone knows the building, no one knows what's inside it), and sometimes the architectural shell upgrades the perceived value of objects of all kinds and provenance exhibited therein – automobiles, fish, painted screens, disused blast furnaces (or the institution behind them). Museums are a vehicle for ennobling banalities, functioning as a moral money-laundering machine. By erecting exhibition buildings, companies, private individuals and the State suggest that they are giving back to the citizens a kind of cultural added value, rather than simply pocketing profits and taxes. To exaggerate slightly, one might conclude that the museum as building type is experiencing such an inflation because it is seen as a code for solid middle-class values in the midst of a chaotic world order. Anyone founding a museum can't be a bad person. Even the dodgiest wheeler-dealer, the most moribund community suddenly seems respectable and forward-looking with a shiny new exhibition palace to show off. Notabene (another paradox): it is not despite, but due to this very fact that outstanding museum architecture comes about. The building as bluff – the lie cloaked in truth: the stronger the crisis and decline, the more important the museum becomes. This is admittedly a bitter stocktaking as a foil against which to present the fulsome architectural praise that necessarily follows. In the past year alone, a number of exemplary museum building projects have been completed, taking their place as part of the canon as soon as they opened. This kind of living architectural legend was indulged in for example by Porsche in Stuttgart (design: Delugan Meissl), a huge, enigmatic,

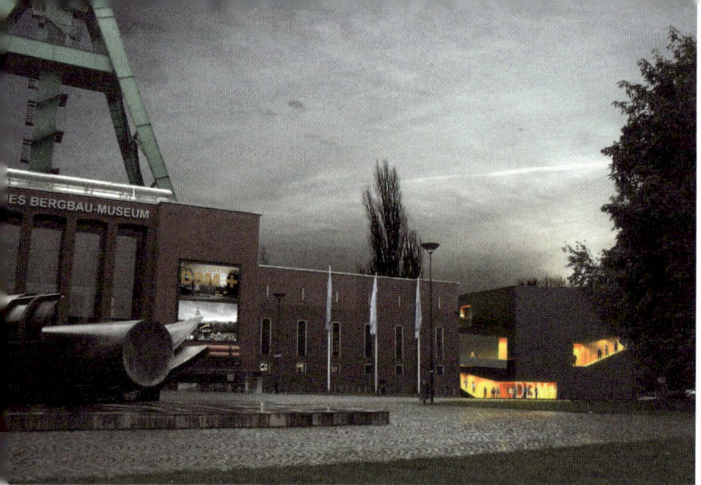

Erweiterung des Deutschen Bergbau-Museums Bochum;
Architekten: Benthem Crouwel | Extension of the German
Mining Museum in Bochum; architects: Benthem Crouwel

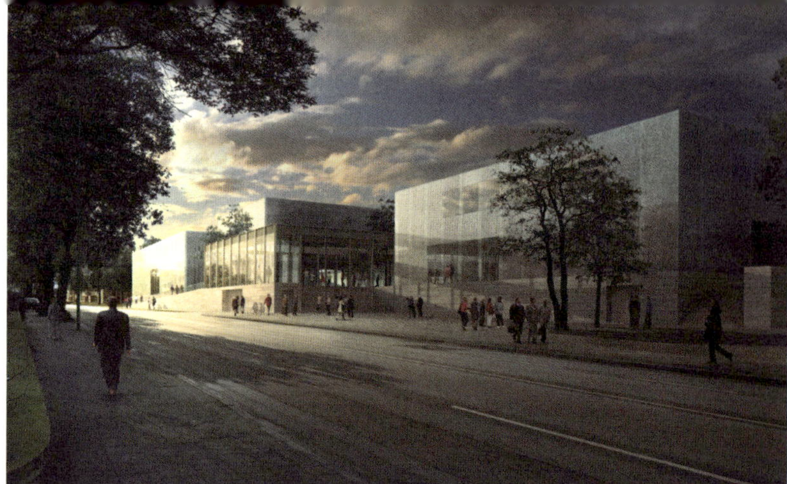

Neubau Museum Folkwang, Essen; Architekt: David Chipperfield
New Museum Folkwang building, Essen; architect: David Chipperfield

marodeste Kommune wirkt dank eines Ausstellungshauses plötzlich seriös und zukunftsfroh. Notabene (ein weiteres Paradoxon): Nicht trotzdem, sondern gerade zu diesem Zweck entsteht herausragende Museumsarchitektur.

Der Bau als Bluff – die Lüge im Gewand der Wahrheit: Je stärker Krise und Verfall, umso wichtiger wird das Museum. Dies ist nun freilich eine bittere Bilanz als Folie für die architekturkritische Lobhudelei, die sich an dieser Stelle zwangsläufig anschließt. Denn allein im letzten Jahr entstanden etliche Musterprojekte des Museumsbaus, die schon bei der Eröffnung zum Kanon gezählt werden müssen. Eine solch lebende Legende der Baukultur gönnte sich etwa das Autohaus Porsche in Stuttgart (Entwurf: Delugan Meissl): eine rätselhaft-abstrakte Großskulptur, von der Kritik gefeiert, von zahlreichen Besuchern interessiert angenommen. Die Selbstdarstellung der Konzerne färbte sogar auf die Zulieferer ab. Das Büro Heinisch.Lembach.Huber errichtete dem Motorenbauer Mahle (Stuttgart) den Rahmen für eine Ausstellung, die polierte Getriebeteile präsentiert wie frisch ergrabene Schätze aus Troja. „Inside Mahle" zelebriert technische Kühle (vielleicht ist coolness gemeint?), in einem Dreiklang aus getöntem Glas, Metallverkleidung und Sichtbeton, der sämtliche neuen Automuseen (auch BMW und Mercedes) kennzeichnet.

Unter den neuen Kunstmuseen seien zwei Bauten benannt. Das Franz Marc Museum im bayerischen Kochel dient nicht nur als süddeutsches Schauhaus des Expressionismus (ergänzend etwa zum privaten Buchheim Museum am Starnberger See). Durch Panoramafenster machten die Architekten Diethelm & Spillmann (Zürich) die Umgebung selbst zum Teil der Ausstellung. Grandiose Öffnungen ermöglichen den Kontakt zur Landschaft, rahmen Blicke, die Marc und seine Künstlerfreunde des „Blauen Reiter" gehabt haben könnten, als sie sich im (nunmehr renovierten) Altbau nebenan versammelten, um im Voralpenland zu malen. Im Idealfall verschmelzen in diesem Haus Bäume und Bilder, Vorbild und Abbild, Inspirationsquelle und Resultate lassen sich direkt miteinander vergleichen. Dieser Effekt hat bei der Präsentation von Werken der klassischen Moderne Tradition. Schon Werner Düttmanns wundersam intimes Berliner „Brücke-Museum" (1964–67) ist in den Grunewald hineinkomponiert, um die Interaktion zwischen Bildtableaus und Natur hervorzurufen.

abstract sculpture, acclaimed by the critics and welcomed with interest by numerous visitors. The corporate image embodied therein has even rubbed off on Porsche's suppliers. The architectural office of Heinisch.Lembach.Huber created an exhibition setting for the Mahle engine-making company (Stuttgart) that presents polished gearbox parts as if they were the freshly excavated treasures of Troy. "Inside Mahle" celebrates cold technical values (perhaps aiming at coolness?) in the three-part harmony of tinted glass, metal cladding and exposed concrete that is the hallmark of every new automobile museum today (including BMW and Mercedes).

Amongst the new art museums, we would like to highlight two buildings in particular. The Franz Marc Museum in the Bavarian town of Kochel not only serves as a southern German showcase for Expressionism (supplementing for example the private Museum Buchheim on Lake Starnberg); by installing panoramic windows, the architects Diethelm & Spillmann (Zurich) made the surroundings themselves part of the exhibition. Magnificent openings allow visitors to make contact with the landscape, framing views that Marc and his artist friends in the "Blaue Reiter" group might have enjoyed when they gathered in the (now renovated) building next door to paint in this beautiful Alpine foothill setting. Ideally, trees and pictures should meld in this building, the model and its depiction, the source of inspiration and the results available for a direct comparison. This effect is already part of the traditional presentation of works of classical Modernism. Werner Düttmann's wonderfully intimate Brücke Museum in Berlin (1964–67) was embedded in the Grunewald forest in order to evoke the interaction between the pictorial tableaux presented within and the nature outside the door.

The architecture of the extension of the Moritzburg Art Museum in Halle relies more strongly on contrasts. Here, the idea is not mediation but rather the collision between the art and its setting. The approach taken by the Madrid architecture office Nieto Sobejano demonstrates a completely altered level of self-assurance in handling monuments (which not infrequently leads to the kind of reserve that reveals weakness of character). This powerful rethinking can be found in Germany in recent years in the work of Anderhalten architects, who shines in the metier of museum building (most recently with the Art Museum in the Diesel Power Plant in Cottbus, opened in May 2008, see German Architecture Annual 2008/09). Not far from the Moritzburg in Halle, Anderhalten architects experimented with a confrontational approach in the Burg Giebichenstein University of Art and Design (2007),

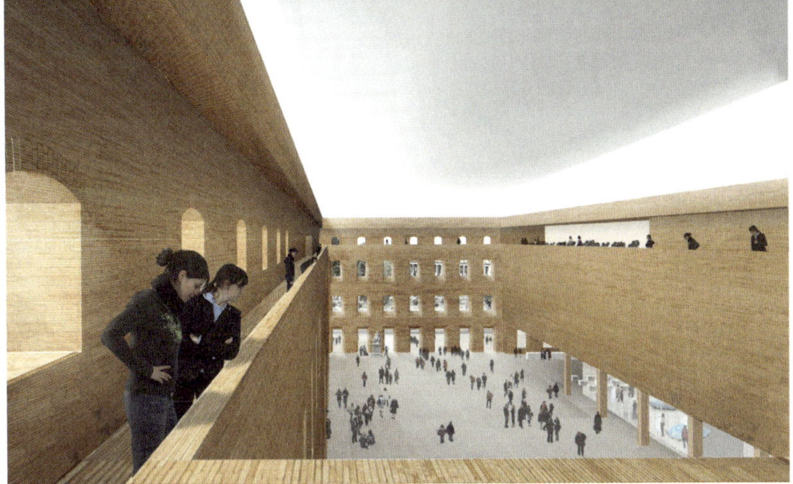

Sonderpreis des internationalen Wettbewerbs für die Wiedererrichtung des Berliner Stadt-schlosses / Humboldt-Forum; Architekten: Kuehn Malvezzi | Special prize in the international competition for the rebuilding of the Berlin City Palace / Humboldt Forum; architects: Kuehn Malvezzi

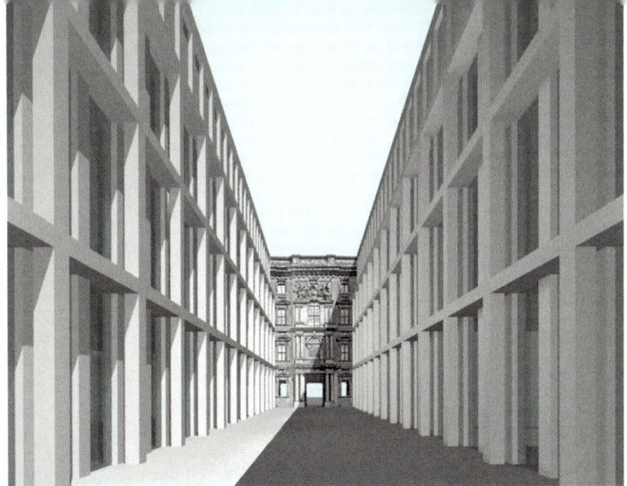

Siegerprojekt des internationalen Wettbewerbs für die Wiedererrichtung des Berliner Stadtschlosses / Humboldt-Forum; Architekt: Franco Stella
Winning project in the international competition for the rebuilding of the Berlin City Palace / Humboldt Forum; architect: Franco Stella

Kontrastiver geriert sich die Architektur der Erweiterung des Kunstmuseums Moritzburg in Halle. Hier geht es nicht um Vermittlung, sondern um den Zusammenprall mit dem Vorhandenen. Der Ansatz des Madrider Büros Nieto Sobejano zeigt ein vollkommen verändertes Selbstbewusstsein im Umgang mit Denkmalen (der nicht selten zu charakterschwacher Zurückhaltung führt). Dieses kraftvolle Umdenken zeichnet sich in Deutschland seit einigen Jahren beispielhaft in den Arbeiten von Anderhalten Architekten ab, die auch im Museumsbau brillierten (zuletzt das Museum Dieselkraftwerk Cottbus, eröffnet im Mai 2008). Unweit der Hallenser Moritzburg, beim Umbau der Kunst- und Designhochschule Burg Giebichenstein (2007), hatten Anderhalten Architekten den konfrontativen Zugang erprobt, ließen bunte, schuppige Blechpaneele auf Putz- und Fachwerkfronten prallen. Vielleicht werden die Lösungen von Nieto Sobejano, Anderhalten oder auch AFF (Umbau des Freiberger Schlosses Freudenstein zum Sächsischen Bergbaumuseum, 2008) nach einigen Jahren zeitgeistig erscheinen. In jedem Fall repräsentieren sie das Zeitalter ihrer Entstehung als markante Statements einer Architektur mit Rückgrat. Radikal war auch der Umgang mit einem Altbau, den der Unternehmer Christian Boros für seine Privatsammlung erwarb: einen Berliner Bunker, aus dessen Innerem mühevoll ein Raumkontinuum herausschält wurde (siehe Jahrbuch 2008/09). Nicht nur die Idee, sich eines dermaßen eigenartigen Altbaus zu bemächtigen und ihn mit einem Penthouse zu bekrönen (der effektsichere Boros kommt aus der Werbebranche), auch die intelligente architektonische Komposition machen das Haus zu einem der originellsten Orte kultureller Selbstdarstellung in Deutschland. Obwohl das Projekt den ganzen Wahnwitz finanzieller Omnipotenz ausstrahlt – nicht zufällig sind auch Werke Damien Hirsts Teil der Sammlung – verhindern der herbe Altbau und das Feingefühl der Architekten aufdringlichen Protz (der Dachaufbau als zeitgemäßes „case-study-house"). Boros' Kunstbunker stellt spielend andere Privatsammler in den Schatten, die sich 2008 ebenfalls imposante Bauten gönnten, etwa das Duisburger DKM-Museum (Egli, Rohr und Partner) oder die Sammlung Gunzenhauser in Chemnitz (Volker Staab).
Kann diese atemberaubende Entwicklung so weitergehen? Scheinbar wohl. Ende 2008 begann das Bochumer Bergbau-

letting brightly coloured, scale-covered sheet-metal panels clash with plaster and half-timbered façades. Perhaps these solutions devised by Nieto Sobejano, Anderhalten or AFF (conversion of Schloss Freudenstein in Freiberg into the Saxon Mining Museum, 2008) will in a few years seem too much stamped with today's own particular zeitgeist. They do however in any case represent the era in which they came about as striking statements of an architecture with backbone. Similarly radical is the way an old building was dealt with that entrepreneur Christian Boros purchased to house his private collection, a Berlin bunker out of whose interior the architects arduously carved out a spatial continuum (see German Architecture Annual 2008/09). Not only the very idea of taking over such an unusual building and crowning it with a penthouse (Boros' deft handling of special effects has been honed in the field of advertising), but also the intelligent architectural composition make the house one of the most original locations of cultural self-expression in Germany. Although the project trumpets the absolute lunacy of financial omnipotence – it's no coincidence that works by Damien Hirst are part of the collection – the austerity of the old building fabric and the sensitivity displayed by the architects prevent any impression of flashy showmanship (the appended penthouse is conceived as a contemporary "case study

Siegerprojekt Wiedererrichtung Berliner Stadtschloss / Humboldt-Forum: Grundriss Erdgeschoss | Winning project fort he rebuilding of the Berlin City Palace / Humboldt-Forum: floor plan of the ground floor

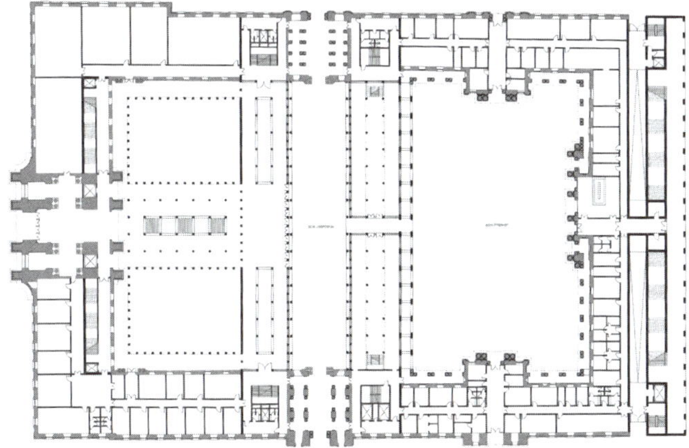

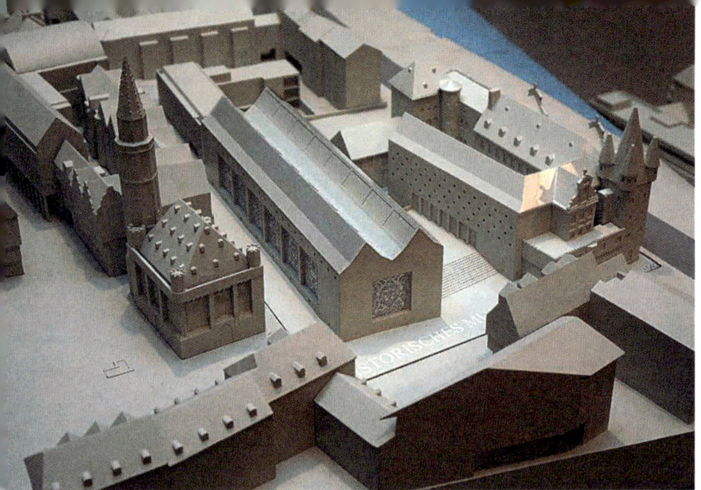

Neubau des Historischen Museums in Frankfurt am Main; Architekten: Lederer Ragnarsdóttir Oei | New History Museum building in Frankfurt/Main; architects: Lederer Ragnarsdóttir Oei

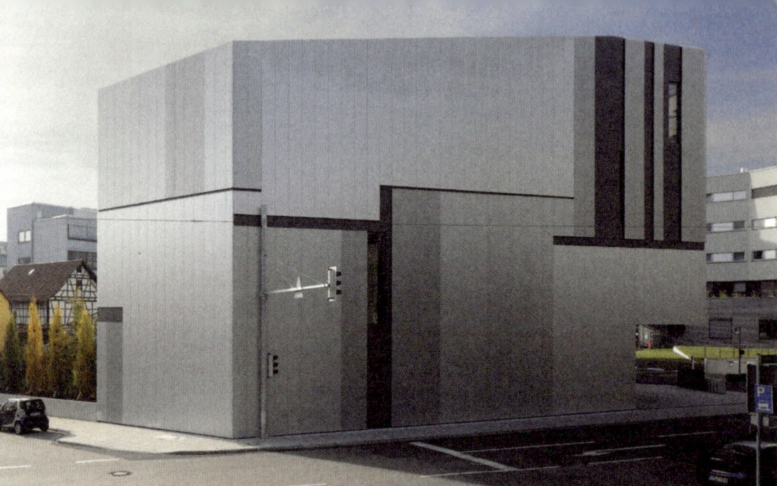

MAHLE Inside, Firmenmuseum des Motorenbauers Mahle in Stuttgart; Architekten: Heinisch.Lembach.Huber | MAHLE Inside, the company museum of engine-makers Mahle in Stuttgart; architects: Heinisch.Lembach.Huber

Museum mit dem schwarzen Kubus seiner Erweiterung (Benthem Crouwel). Daniel Libeskinds Militärhistorisches Museum der Bundeswehr in Dresden wird im Verlauf der nächsten Jahre fertig. Nach dem sanierten und erweiterten „Neuen Museum" auf der Museumsinsel Berlin (David Chipperfield, Eröffnung der Ausstellung: Herbst 2009), folgt die Sanierung des Pergamonmuseums. Frankfurt am Main, seit der Gründung des Museumsufers eine der wichtigsten Museumsstädte des Landes, treibt den Ausbau des Kulturstandorts mehrfach voran: Am Römer entsteht das neue „Historische Museum" (Sieger des Wettbewerbs vom Januar 2008: Lederer, Ragnarsdóttir, Oei), das „Städel" wird durch einen unterirdischen Flügel ergänzt (Sieger des Wettbewerbs vom Februar 2008: schneider+schumacher).

Selbst das größte zukünftige Bauvorhaben der Republik, der Neubau des Hohenzollernschlosses, wird nichts anderes als ein Museum. Am Rande des Bauplatzes, der nach Abriss des „Palast der Republik" als gähnende Leerstelle im Zentrum der Hauptstadt klafft, hat der wacklige Container einer „Temporären Kunsthalle" (Entwurf: Adolf Krischanitz) bereits die Weichenstellung für die Neucodierung des Terrains vorgegeben. Und was auf das letzte öffentliche Filetgrundstück im Herzen unseres Landes zutrifft, gilt auch für die subventionierte Umnutzung vieler Industriebrachen in Ost und West: Wo nichts mehr geht, kommt die Kultur.

Aber wird das wirklich so weitergehen? Zwei Entwicklungen verdeutlichen, dass sich der Umgang mit dem Museums- und Ausstellungswesen weiter verändert. Einerseits wankt die Bestandssicherung vieler Häuser durch die derzeitige Restitutionspraxis. Öffentliche Sammlungen, bis vor Kurzem unantastbar, wandeln durch vorgeblich moralischen Druck rapide ihr Profil, wenn Highlights mit juristischer Gewalt dem Kunstmarkt zugeführt werden. Demnächst wird beispielsweise die Stiftung Preußischer Kulturbesitz um den „Welfenschatz" kämpfen müssen, 42 Artefakte aus dem Vorbesitz der Braunschweiger Herzöge, die das Kunstgewerbemuseum seit 1928 als Kern der Mittelaltersammlung führt. Der Verlust dieser Reliquiare, Büsten, Elfenbeine, profanen und kirchlichen Objekte – die öffentliche Hand könnte sie unmöglich zum heutigen Handelswert zurückkaufen – wäre ein substanzieller Schaden für die Kulturnation.

house"). Boros' art bunker effortlessly upstages other private collectors who treated themselves to similarly imposing structures in 2008, for example the DKM Museum in Duisburg (Egli, Rohr und Partner) or the Gunzenhauser Collection in Chemnitz (Volker Staab).

Can this breathtaking development continue at the same breakneck pace? Apparently, it can. In late 2008 the Mining Museum in Bochum began work on its extension in the form of a black cube (Benthem Crouwel). Daniel Libeskind's German Armed Forces Museum of Military History in Dresden will be completed over the next few years. After the renovation and extension of the Neues Museum (New Museum) on Berlin's Museumsinsel (David Chipperfield, opening of the exhibition: autumn 2009), the redevelopment of the Pergamon Museum is due to follow. Frankfurt am Main, one of the nation's premier museum cities since the establishment of its riverside Museumsufer, is undertaking multiple projects to expand its standing as cultural mecca. The new historical museum, the Historisches Museum, is being built on the Römer (winner of the January 2008 competition: Lederer, Ragnarsdóttir, Oei), the Städel Museum is being given a new underground wing (winner of the February 2008 competition: schneider+schumacher) and the competitions for the extensions to the Museum of World Cultures and the Jewish Museum are in preparation.

Even Germany's biggest future building project, the new Hohenzollern Palace in Berlin, is nothing other than a museum. At the edge of the construction site, where the demolition of the Palace of the Republic opened up a gaping hole in the centre of the capital city, the wobbly container holding the temporary Kunsthalle (art exhibition space, design: Adolf Krischanitz) has already set the tone for recoding this historic terrain. And what applies here to the last prime public plot in the heart of Germany also goes for the subsidised conversion of many industrial wastelands in both East and West: where nothing else is possible, culture comes in to fill the breach.

But will this really continue to be the case? Two trends make it clear that the way we deal with museums and exhibitions is continuing to undergo changes. On the one hand, the once-secure holdings of many museums are now threatened by the current practice of restitution. Public collections, sacrosanct just a short while ago, are rapidly modifying their profiles under ostensible moral pressure, as they are being legally compelled to offer up their highlights on the open art market. The Stiftung Preussischer Kulturbesitz (Prussian Cultural Heritage Foundation), for example, will soon have to go to battle to

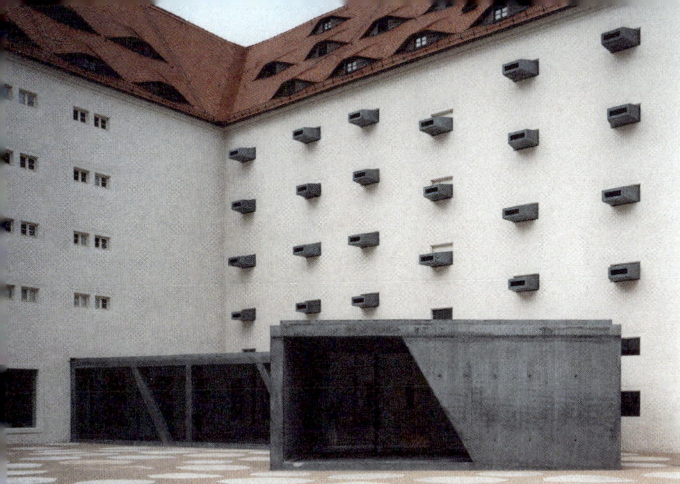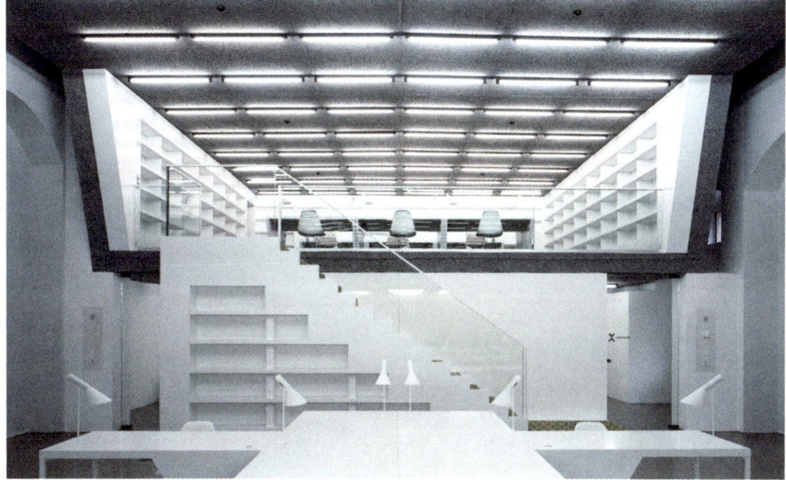

Umbau und Sanierung von Schloss Freudenstein in Freiberg; Architekten: AFF; Eingangsgebäude (links) / Lesesaal (rechts) | Conversion and restoration of Schloss Freudenstein in Freiberg; architects: AFF; entrance building (left) / reading room (right)

Daneben fordert die wirtschaftliche Entwicklung ihren Tribut. „Die globale Finanzkrise hat sicher auch Auswirkungen auf die Museen", bestätigt Barbara Honrath vom Goethe-Institut. „Einerseits führt sie möglicherweise dazu, dass die ohnehin schon knappen Etats gekürzt werden, andererseits birgt sie aber vielleicht auch die Chance, dass die Museen ihre Kernaufgaben und Qualitätsmaßstäbe überdenken und neu definieren." Der Fiskus muss (oder müsste) von nun an strenger über Verteilung von Steuermitteln wachen. Einige Unternehmen haben bereits Schritte eingeleitet und den Ankaufstopp für ihre Kunstsammlungen verhängt. Auch Stiftungen überprüfen ihre Engagements. Im April 2009 sagte die Krupp-Stiftung ein groß angelegtes Ausstellungsprojekt ab, dessen Planungskosten unverhältnismäßig gestiegen waren. Gleichzeitig bestätigte sie ihre Verantwortung für den Neubau des Essener Museum Folkwang (Entwurf: David Chipperfield), die es als Allein-sponsor mit kolossalen 50 Millionen Euro einzulösen gedenkt. Fraglos wird die Eröffnung des Hauses im Kulturstadtjahr 2010 das nächste Großereignis der Museumsgeschichte – es wird bei Weitem nicht das einzige. Und selbst wenn sich bis dahin herumspricht, dass Museen längst keine Orte der Selbstverge-wisserung mehr sind, gilt das alte Paradoxon weiter: Das Museum ist der Krise Kind – es ist selbst eine Krisenerschei-nung. Der Museumsbauboom wird sich daher unweigerlich noch weiter verstärken.

save its 'Guelph Treasure', 42 artifacts previously owned by the Dukes of Braunschweig that have formed the core of the medieval collection of the Museum of Applied Arts since 1928. Forfeiting these reliquaries, busts, ivories, secular and sacred objects – which could never be bought back with public funds at today's market prices – would be a substantial loss for the nation's cultural heritage.

The latest economic developments are also taking their toll. "The global financial crisis will surely affect museums as well," confirms Barbara Honrath, head of the Visual Arts Division in the Goethe Institute. "On the one hand, it will possibly lead to cuts in what are already tight budgets, but on the other hand it perhaps offers an opportunity for the museums to rethink their core tasks and quality standards and redefine them." From now on, the government will have to (or should) monitor the distribution of tax monies more closely. Some enterprises have already taken corresponding steps and imposed a moratorium on acquisitions for their art collections. Foun-dations are also reviewing their cultural commitments. In April 2009 the Krupp Foundation cancelled a large-scale exhibition project whose planning costs had gone up disproportionately. At the same time, it confirmed its responsibility for the new building for the Museum Folkwang in Essen (design: David Chipperfield), which it is planning to fund as sole sponsor for the colossal sum of 50 million euros. The opening of the new museum in 2010, when the Ruhr Valley will take its turn as European Capital of Culture, will no doubt be the next major event in museum history – but by far not the only one. And even if by then word has got around that museums are long since no longer places for self-affirmation, the paradox will continue to apply that the museum is a child of crisis – that it is in fact a manifestation of crisis. The boom in museum building will therefore only grow even stronger.

ARCHITEKTUR IN DEUTSCHLAND
ARCHITECTURE IN GERMANY

02–24

DEUTSCHLAND
GERMANY

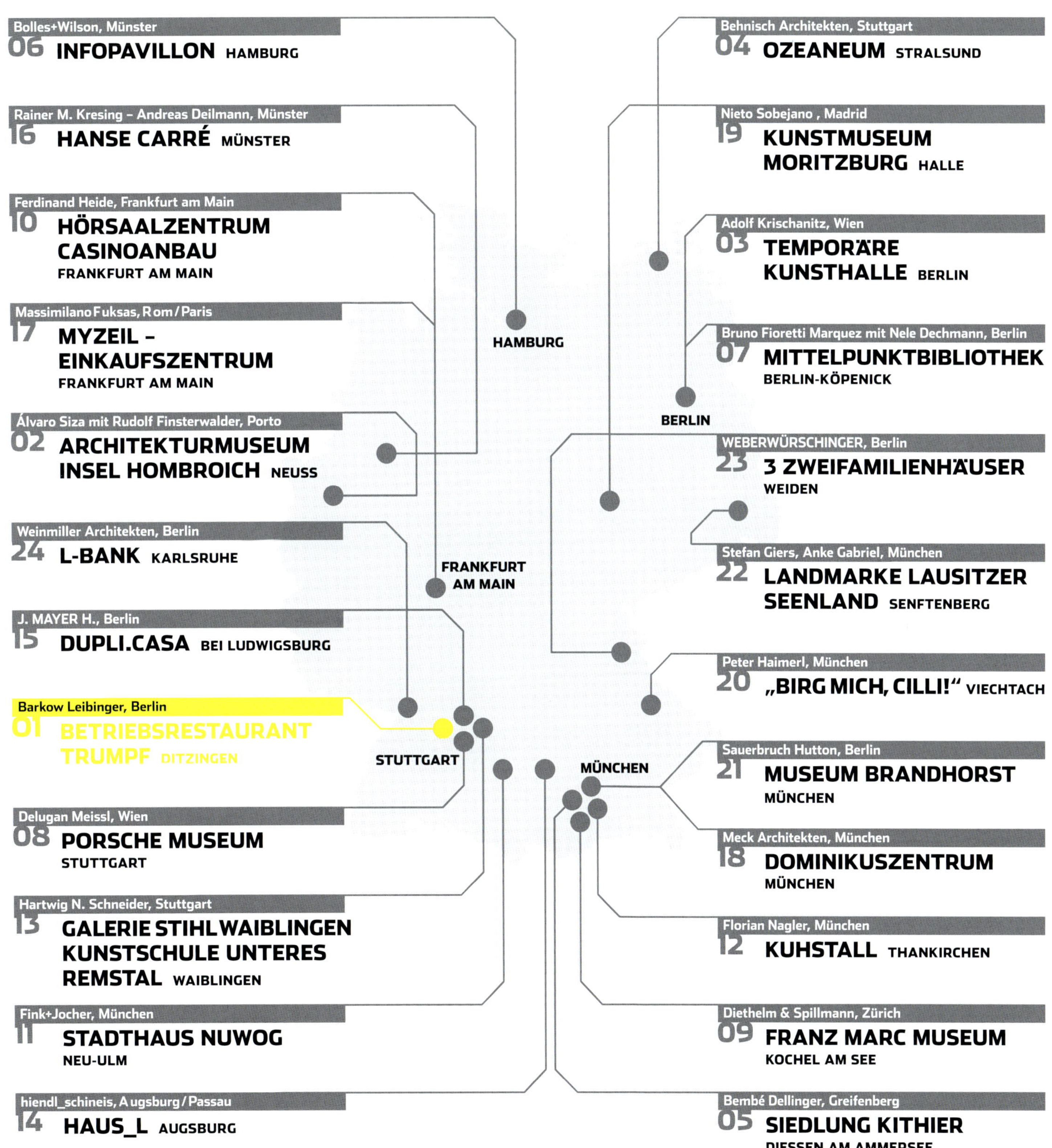

ÁLVARO SIZA MIT RUDOLF FINSTERWALDER

ARCHITEKTURMUSEUM INSEL HOMBROICH

TEXT URSULA KLEEFISCH-JOBST

02

ARCHITEKTEN | ARCHITECTS

Álvaro Siza Vieira
Rua do Alexio 53 – 2°
4150 – 043 Porto
Portugal

Finsterwalder Architekten
Finsterwalderstraße 5
83071 Stephanskirchen
www.finsterwalderarchitekten.com

MITARBEITER | TEAM

Burkhard Damm, José Diniz Santos,
Matthias Heskamp,
Heinz Kirschner, Steffi Zucker

BAUHERR | CLIENT

Stiftung Insel Hombroich

TRAGWERK | STRUCTURE

Horst Kappauf

FERTIGSTELLUNG
COMPLETION
2008

STANDORT | LOCATION

Stiftung Insel Hombroich
Raketenstation
41472 Neuss-Holzheim

FOTOS | PHOTOS

Tomas Riehle / arturimages

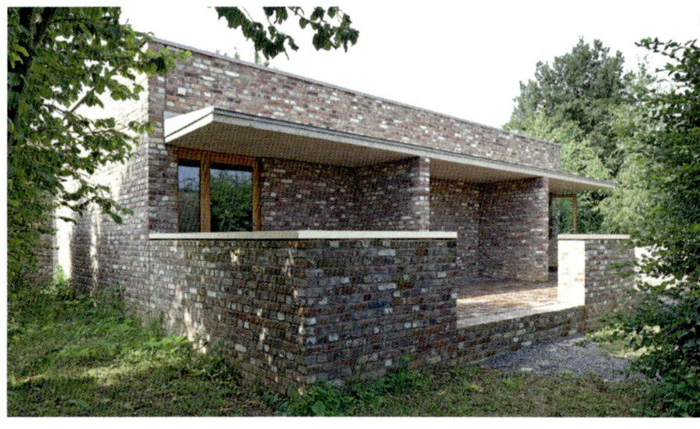

Nordterrasse des Fotoarchivs | North terrace of the photo archive

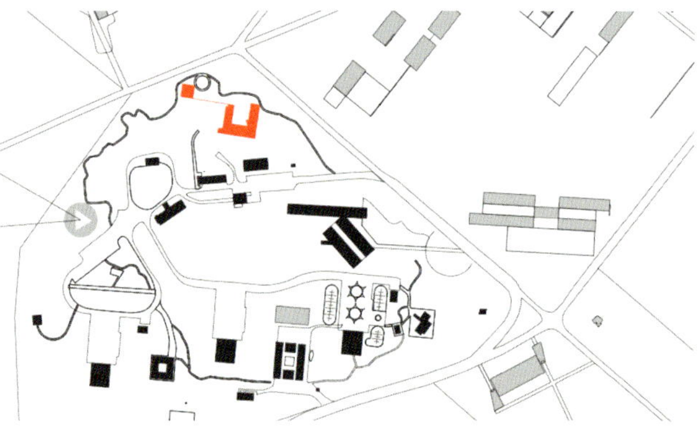

Lageplan | Site plan

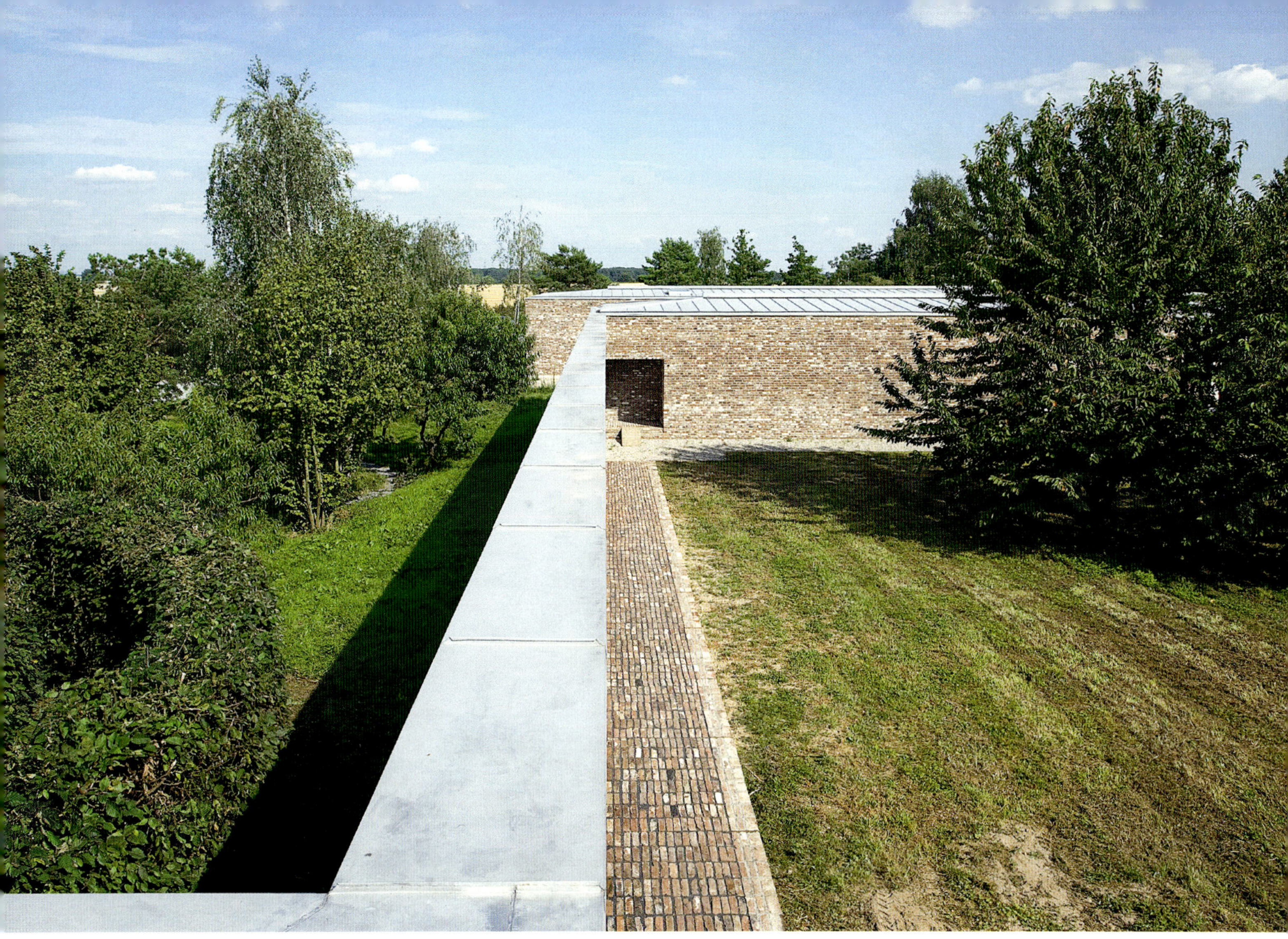

Eine Mauerscheibe verbindet das Museum mit dem Fotoarchiv. | A slice of wall connects the museum to the photo archive.

Ob Architektur Kunst sei, da sie ja immer zweckgebunden bleibt, ist eine alte Streitfrage zahlreicher architekurtheoretischer Erörterungen. Auf der Raketenstation der Insel Hombroich bei Neuss hat Álvaro Siza gemeinsam mit Rudolf Finsterwalder den sichtbaren Beweis geliefert, dass Architektur Kunst sein kann, nämlich Raumkunst.

Nun bedeutete Planen und Bauen auf der Insel Hombroich und seit 1996 auch auf dem angrenzenden Gebiet der ehemaligen US-Raketenstation immer schon Gestalten, befreit von alltäglichen Zwängen. Die Auenlandschaft der Museumsinsel und das überformte Areal der Raketenbasis sind nach dem Willen des vor zwei Jahren verstorbenen Mäzens Karl-Heinz Müller Refugium und Laboratorium für Architektur und Kunst. Landschaft, Kunst und Architektur sollen hier anschaulich und meisterhaft zu einer Symbiose verschmelzen. Dabei hat Karl-Heinz Müller, bei all seinen Eigenheiten als Bauherr, den Architekten, die er ausgewählt hatte, stets große Spielräume gewährt, ihre individuelle Architektursprache bis ins kleinste Detail auszuleben. Entstehen sollten auf der Raketenstation in erster Linie nicht funktionale Bauten, sondern zu Stein gewordene architektonische Haltungen.

So konnte auch ein zunächst als Institut für Biophysik geplantes Gebäude mit geringfügigen Änderungen in ein Architekturmuseum verwandelt werden. Die größte Veränderung gegenüber

Whether architecture, despite the demands of functionality, can still be art, is an old conundrum that is often addressed in discussions of architectural theory. At the old missile base on Hombroich Island near Neuss, Álvaro Siza and Rudolf Finsterwalder have now delivered tangible proof that architecture can indeed be art: namely, spatial art.

Of course, planning and building on Hombroich Island and, since 1996, on the adjacent grounds of the former US missile station has always allowed for creativity free of everyday constraints. In accordance with the wishes of patron Karl-Heinz Müller, who died two years ago, the river bank landscape of the museum island and the restored grounds of the missile base were set aside as a refuge and laboratory for architecture and art. The idea is to create a vivid and masterful symbiosis of landscape, art and architecture. For this reason, Karl-Heinz Müller, despite all his idiosyncrasies as client, always gave his chosen architects free rein to live out their individual architectural vocabulary down to the last detail. Functional buildings were not what was called for on the missile base, but rather architectural attitudes cast in stone.

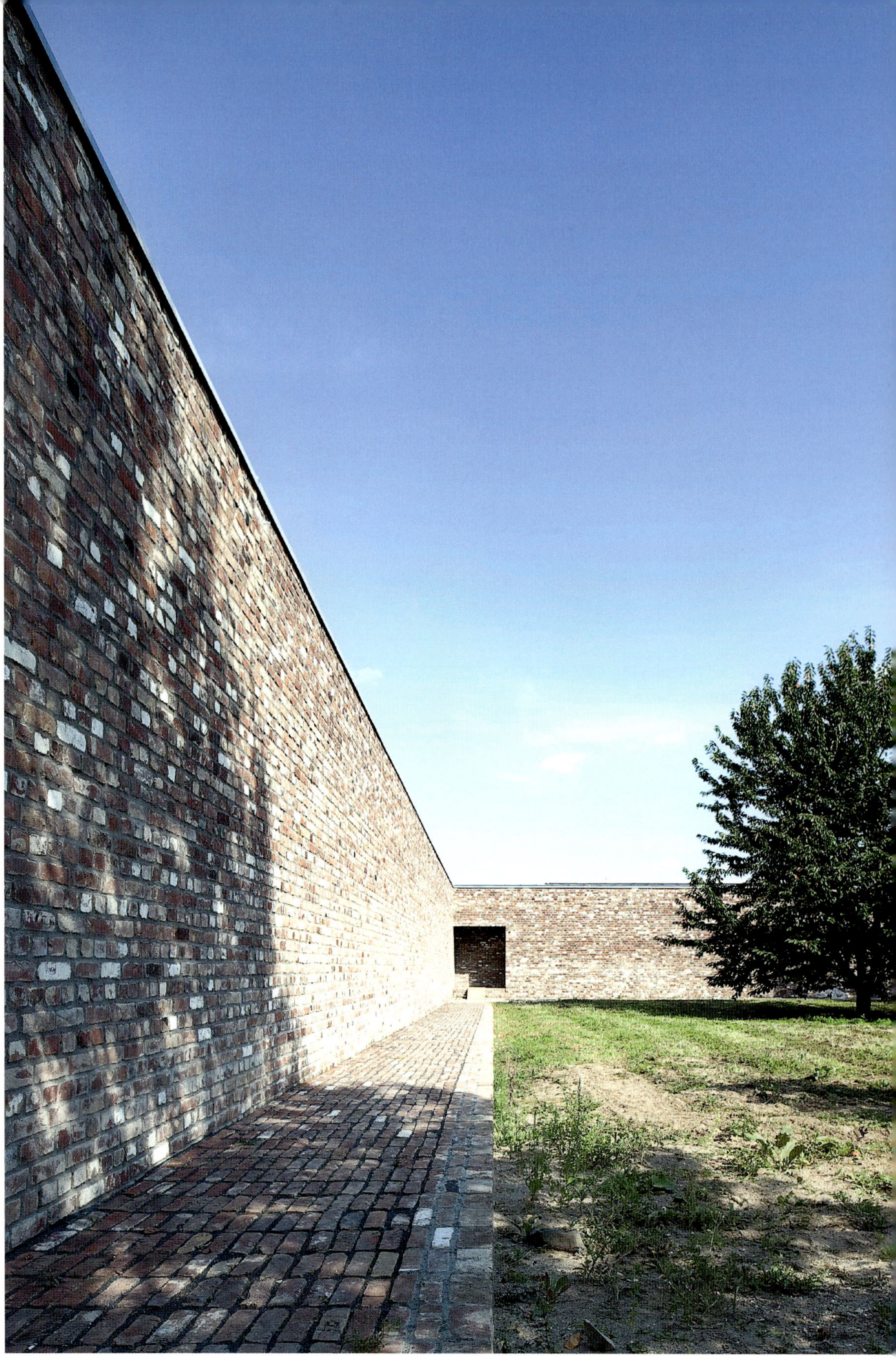

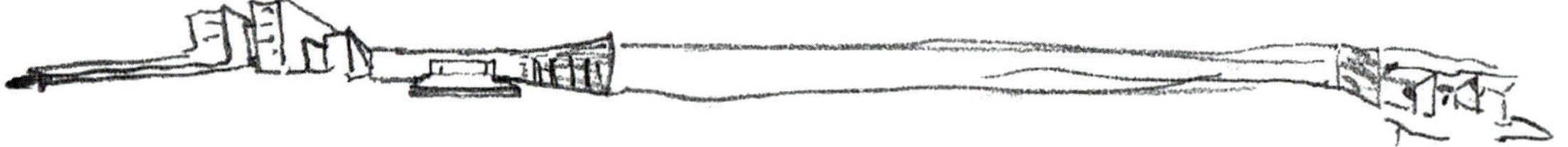

Skizze Gesamtanlage | Sketch of entire complex

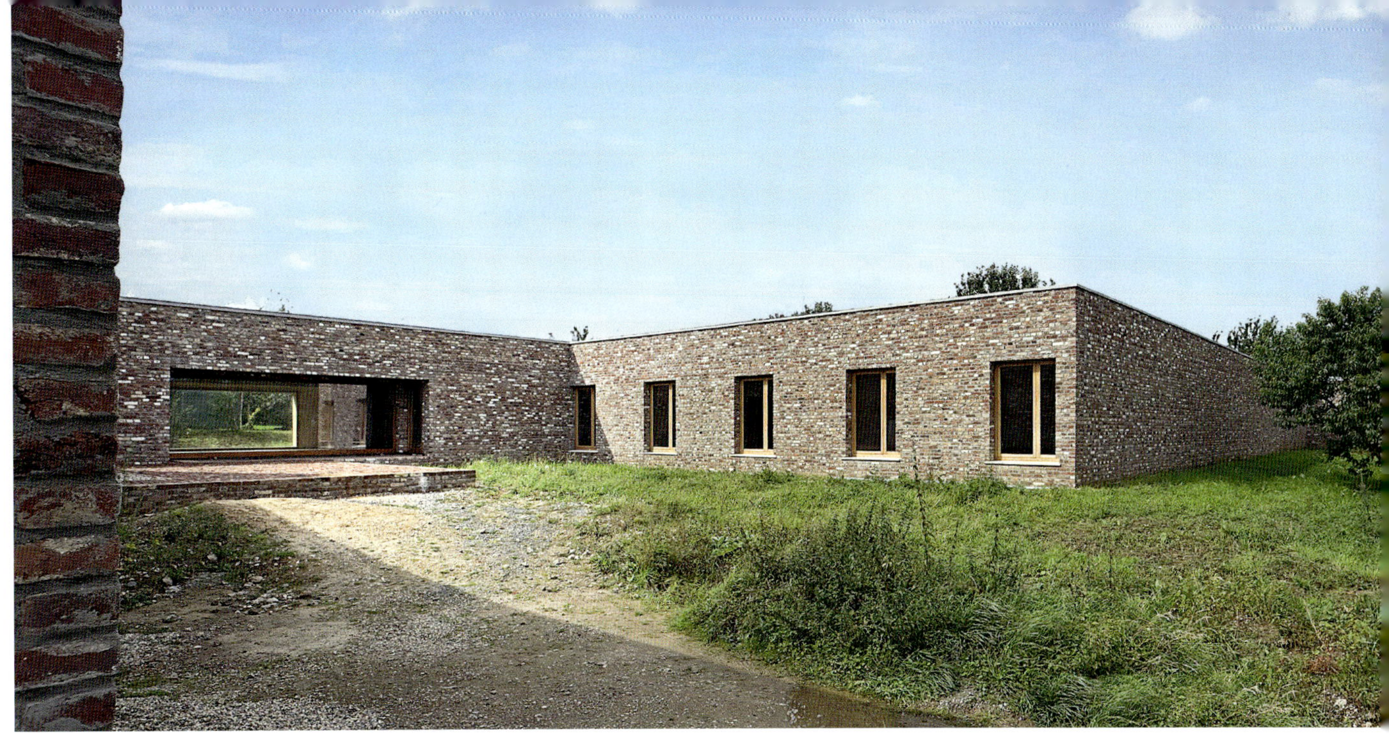

Hofsituation | Courtyard site

der ursprünglichen Planung lag in der Drehung des Gebäudes, so dass der U-förmige Hof, um den sich die Räume gruppieren, nach Norden ausgerichtet ist.

Nähert sich der Besucher der ehemaligen Raketenstation, so rückt der eingeschossige, flach gedeckte Baukörper nur für einen kurzen Moment in sein Blickfeld, um dann sogleich wieder hinter einem kleinen Wall – einem Relikt aus den Zeiten der Militärbasis – zu verschwinden. Álvaro Siza hat wie selbstverständlich, was für ihn so überaus charakteristisch ist, sein Gebäude in die Landschaft eingebettet. Durch einen Einschnitt im Wall betritt der Besucher ein an zwei Seiten von einer sorgfältig gemauerten Ziegelwand umfriedetes Gartenareal. Wer sich auf dem Gelände etwas auskennt, wird sofort an die Ziegelbauten von Erwin Heerich erinnert, auch wenn der hier verwendete unregelmäßige Abbruchziegel dunkler ist als bei den Bauten Heerichs. Die Ziegelmauer gegenüber dem Wall verbindet den Museumsbau im Südosten mit einem kleineren Gebäude im Nordwesten. Dieses war ursprünglich als Gästewohnung für das Biophysikalische Institut gedacht, wird aber künftig das Fotoarchiv von Volker Kahmen und Ursula Schulz-Dornburg beherbergen.

Den Eingang des Museums markiert ein schlichter Portikus aus portugiesischem Kalkstein, das einzige Element, das plastisch aus der Fläche der Mauern heraustritt. Im eher unscheinbar wirkenden Eingangsbereich wird der Blick des Besuchers zunächst nach Norden gelenkt, entlang einer Enfilade von drei Räumen für Wechselausstellungen. Das Ende der Enfilade markiert eine Glastür, die den Blick auf einen Ausschnitt der Backsteinmauer freigibt. Wendet sich der Besucher jedoch nach Süden, so erblickt er einen langen Flur, dessen Ende wiederum von einem Ausblick, nämlich auf einen Laubbaum, abgeschlossen wird. Der Flur weitet sich in der Mitte zu einem großen Raum mit einem zum Hof und in die weite Auenlandschaft weisenden Panoramafenster. Die Mittelachse des Gebäudes wird durch große Fenster zu einer Sichtachse, die Innen- und Außenraum

This enabled what had originally been planned as an institute for biophysics to be transformed into an architecture museum with just a few slight alterations. The biggest change compared with the original plans was to turn the building so that the U-shaped courtyard around which the rooms are grouped now faces north.

When approaching the former missile base, the visitor catches only a brief glimpse of the single-storey, flat-roofed structure, which immediately disappears again behind a small embankment – a relic of the site's military days. As if it were a matter of course, Álvaro Siza has embedded his building in the landscape, as is his habit. Through a break in the embankment, the visitor enters a garden area enclosed on two sides by a wall of carefully executed brickwork. Those who have been to the island before will immediately be reminded of the brick buildings by Erwin Heerich, even though the irregular demolition bricks used here are darker than those in Heerich's structures. The brick wall across from the rampart connects the museum building in the southeast with a smaller building in the northwest. This was originally designated as a guest apartment for the biophysics institute, but in future will instead house the photography archive of Volker Kahmen and Ursula Schulz-Dornburg.

The museum entrance is marked by a simple portico made of Portuguese limestone, the only element that protrudes plastically from the flat surface of the walls. In the low-key entrance area, the visitor's gaze is first directed northward, along an enfilade of three rooms designed for changing exhibitions. The end of this series of rooms is marked by a glass door, through which part of the brick wall can be

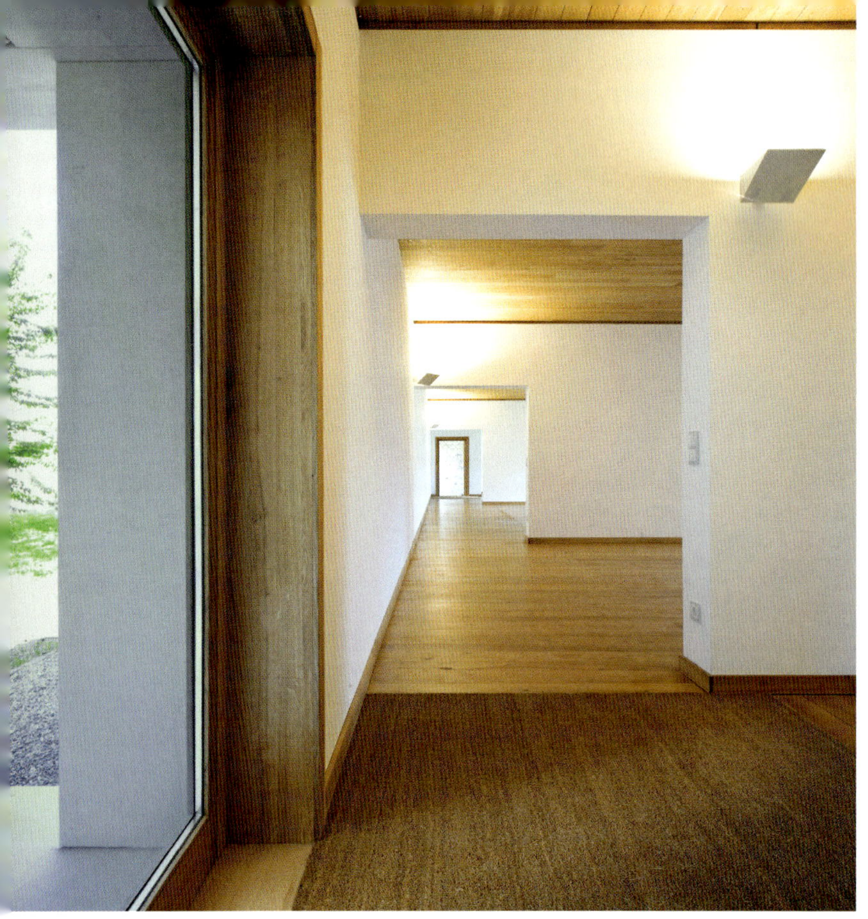

Nach Osten gerichteter Flügel | East wing

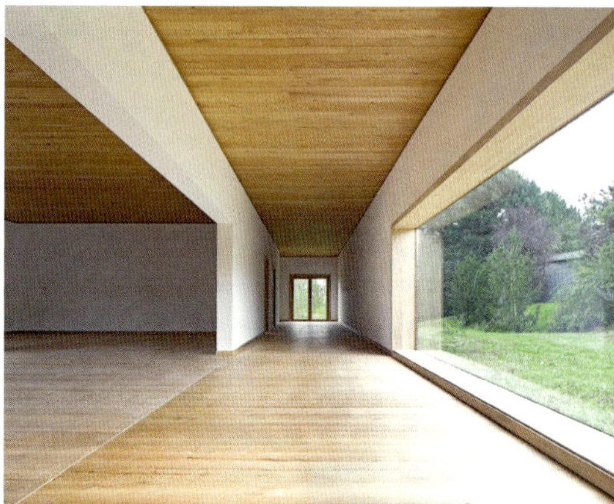

Dauerausstellung | Permanent exhibition

miteinander verbindet. Der Ostflügel des Museums beherbergt neben einem fast intimen Vortragssaal unterschiedliche Räume, die das Erwin Heerich Archiv aufnehmen werden.

Was sich schon am Außenbau ankündigt – nämlich dass das Material den Baukörper moduliert, die Ziegelmauer eine richtige Wand ist, deren Köpfe wiederum echte Binder sind –, setzt sich im Inneren fort: Ein Dreiklang von Materialien vollendet die subtile Raumkomposition. Boden und Decke sind aus Eichenholz, ebenso sind die Türblätter mit einem seltenen Eichenschälfurnier versehen. Die durchlaufende Decke aus massiven Eichenholzbalken betont die Längsausrichtung des Bauwerks. Mit einer schmalen Schattenfuge setzt sich die Decke von den weiß geputzten Wänden ab. Wie der Eingangsportikus bestehen auch die Fensterbänke aus hellem Kalkstein.

Dass hier künftig Skizzen, Pläne, Fotos und Architekturmodelle nur in eigens von Álvaro Siza entworfenem Mobiliar präsentiert werden können, ist naheliegend. Ob man in dieser eleganten, eher wohnlichen Atmosphäre überhaupt etwas ausstellen sollte, ist jedoch die Frage. Das Gebäude ist ein architektonisches Ausstellungsobjekt per se, ein herrliches Stück Architektur!

seen. But if visitors then turn toward the south, they see a long corridor at the end of which there is also a view outside, here of a leafy tree. This corridor widens in the middle to form a large room with a panoramic window giving onto the courtyard and the broad riverside meadows. Large windows turn the building's middle axis into a line of sight that links indoors and outdoors. The east wing of the museum houses, apart from an almost intimate lecture hall, various rooms that will accommodate the Erwin Heerich Archive.

What is already announced by the exterior – namely, that the material modulates the body of the building, that the brick wall is a real wall, whose header bricks are genuine headers – continues in the interior. Here, a triad of materials complements the subtle spatial composition. Floors and ceilings are made of oak, and the door leafs furnished with a rare oaken veneer. The continuous ceiling of solid oak beams emphasises the longitudinal orientation of the structure. The ceiling is set off from the white plaster walls by a narrow shadow joint. Like the entrance portico, the window sills are also made of light-coloured limestone.

It seems clear that sketches, plans, photos and architectural models can in future be presented here only in exhibition furniture designed by Álvaro Siza expressly for this site. The real question is whether it is possible at all to exhibit something in this elegant, domestic-seeming atmosphere. The building itself is an exhibit – a superb piece of architecture!

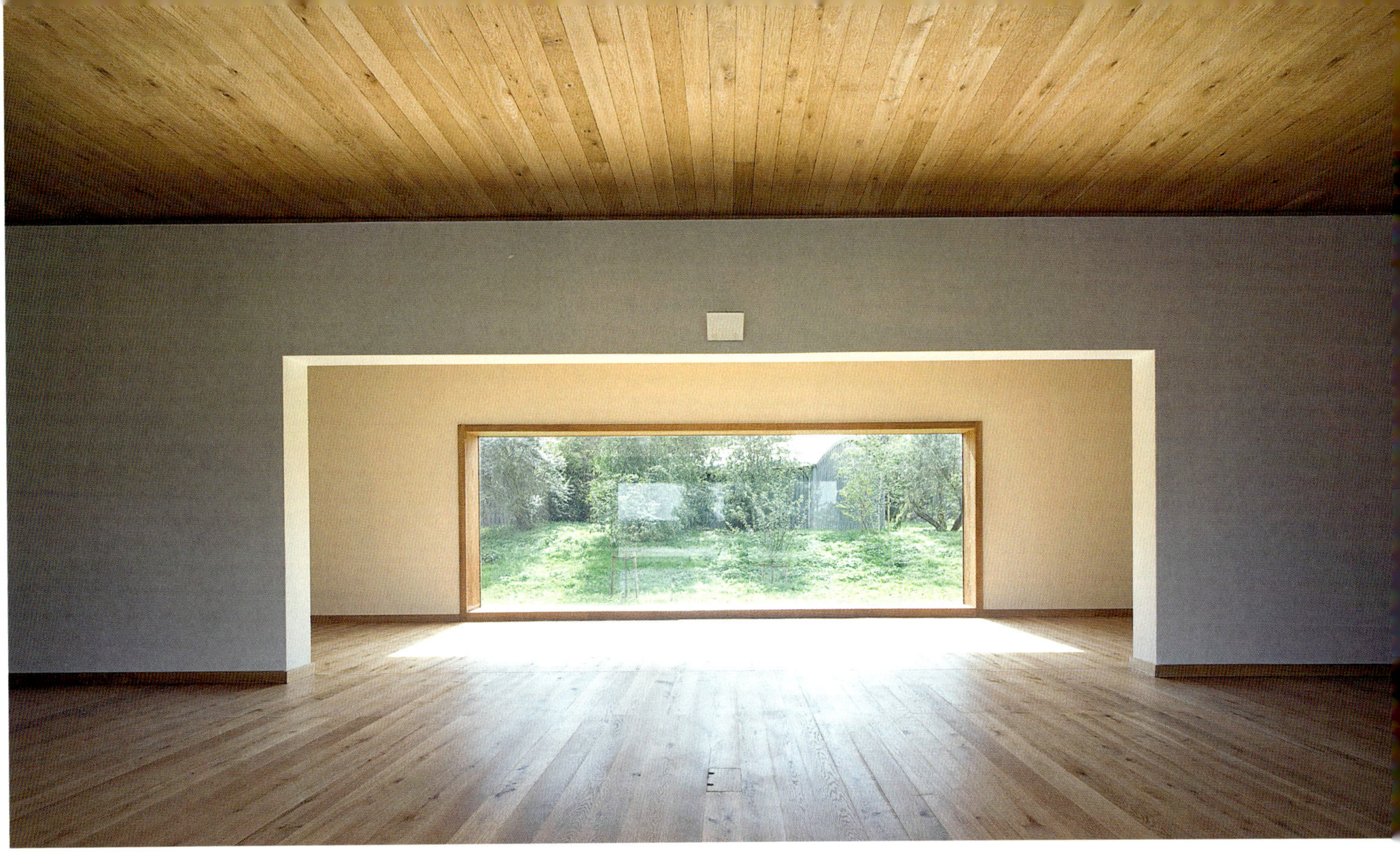

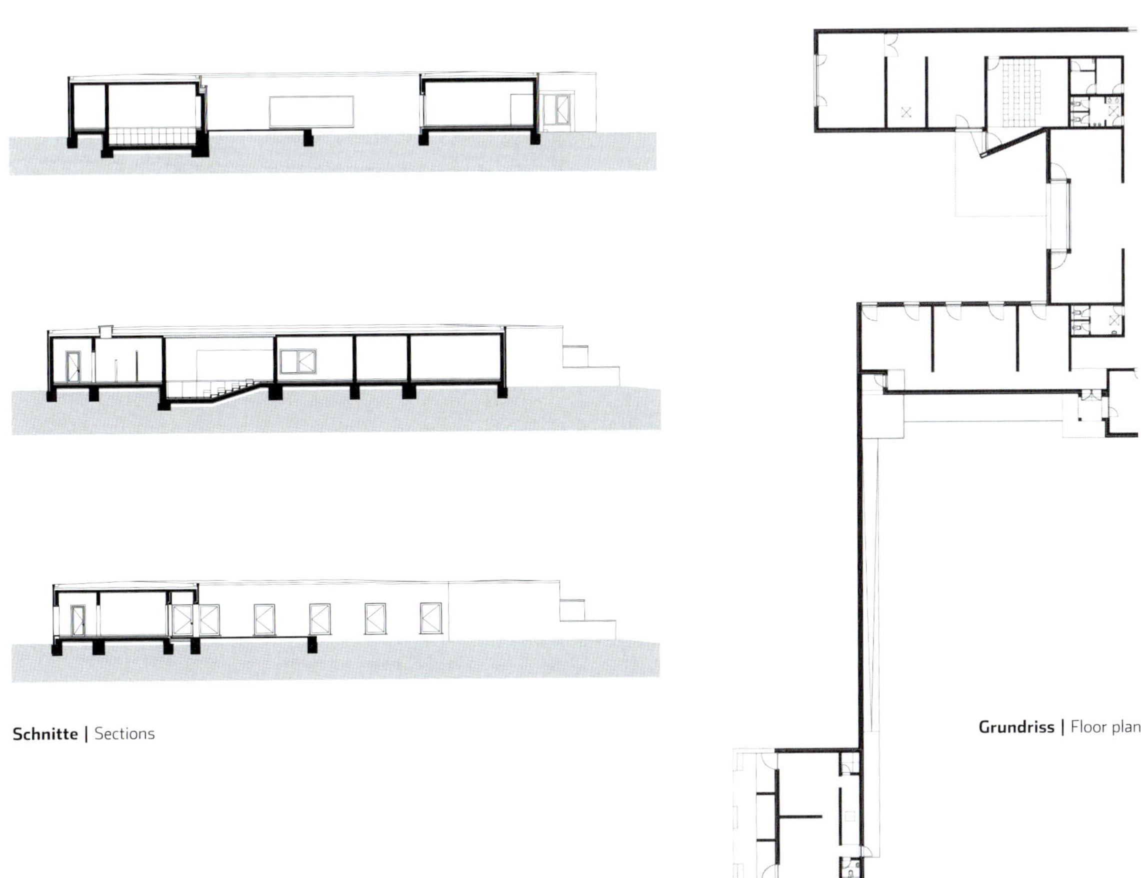

Zentraler Saal für Wechselausstellungen | Central gallery for changing exhibitions

Schnitte | Sections

Grundriss | Floor plan

ARCHITEKT | ARCHITECT

ADOLF KRISCHANITZ

GEBÄUDE | BUILDING

TEMPORÄRE KUNSTHALLE BERLIN

TEXT CHRISTIAN BRENSING

03

ARCHITEKTEN | ARCHITECTS

**Architekt Krischanitz
ZT GmbH
Getreidemarkt 1/11
1060 Wien** | Vienna
Österreich | Austria
www.krischanitz.at

BAULEITUNG
SITE MANAGEMENT

**Groth Development
GmbH & Co. KG,
Berlin**

TRAGWERKSPLANUNG
PLANNING OF THE STRUCTURE

a.k.a. ingenieure.Berlin

ENEV NACHWEIS | CALCULATION
FOR THE GERMAN ENERGY-SAVING
ORDINANCE (ENEV) CERTIFICATE

**Lehrstuhl für
Versorgungsplanung und
Versorgungstechnik
an der UdK-Berlin**

FERTIGSTELLUNG | COMPLETION
2008

STANDORT | LOCATION
**Schlossplatz
10178 Berlin-Mitte**

FOTOS | PHOTOS
Lukas Roth

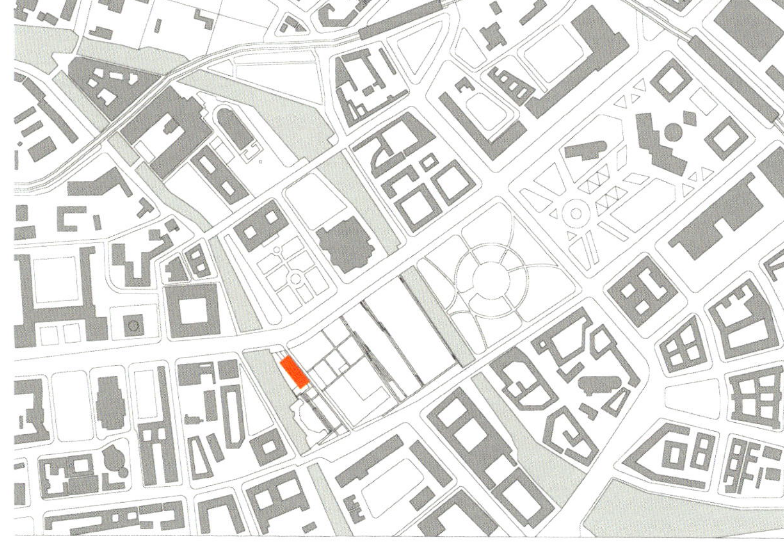

Lageplan | Site plan

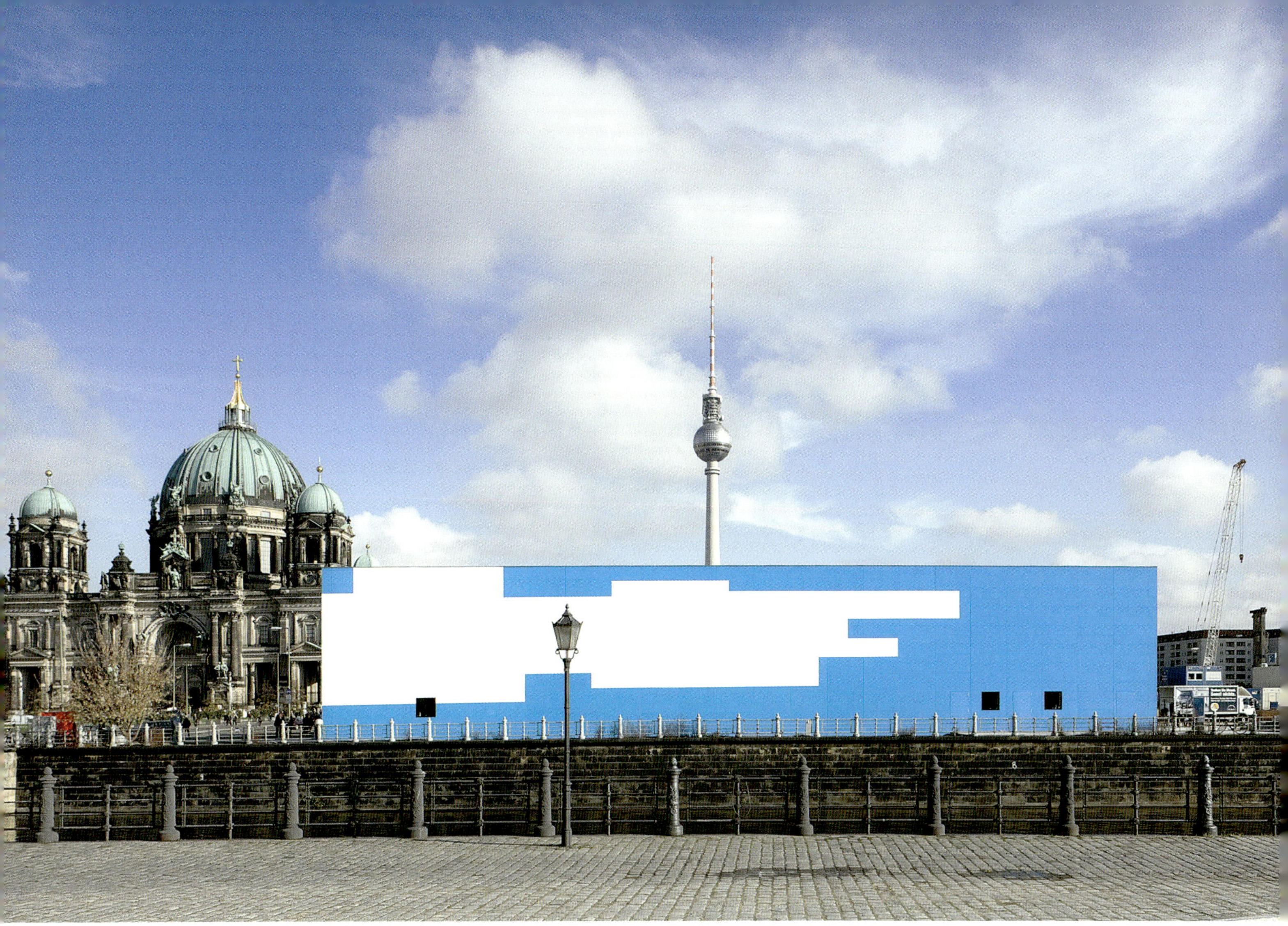

Die Temporäre Kunsthalle auf dem Schlossplatz in Berlin
The Temporäre Kunsthalle on Schlossplatz in Berlin

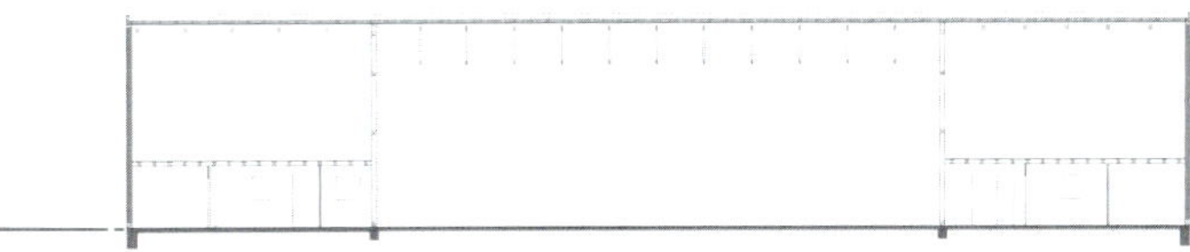

Längsschnitt | Longitudinal section

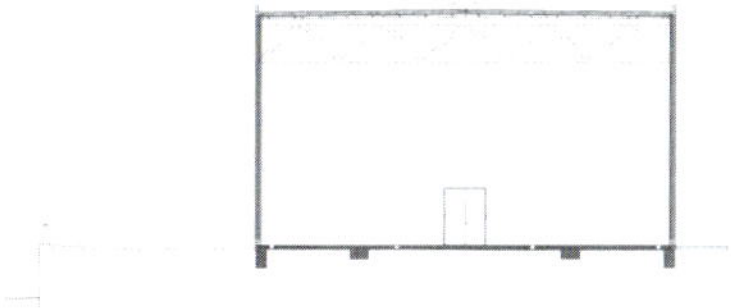

Querschnitt | Cross-section

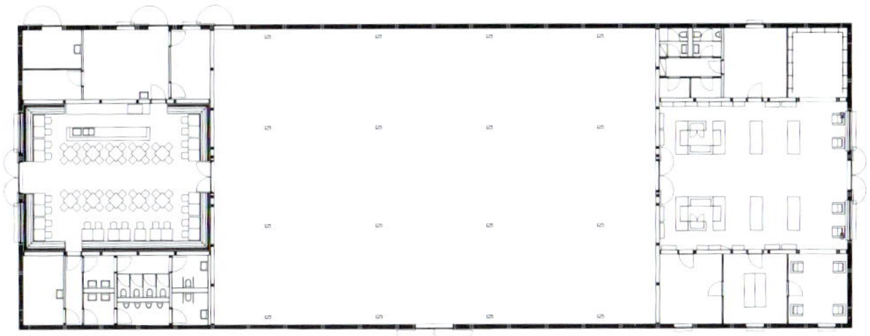

Grundriss | Floor plan

Auf Deutschlands prominentestem und heiß diskutiertem Bauplatz steht seit Oktober 2008 eine temporäre Kunsthalle. Der Berliner Schlossplatz hat ein Jahrhundert kontinuierlicher baulicher Transformation hinter sich. Vom königlichen Stadtschloss der Hohenzollern-Dynastie zum Aufmarschplatz von Deutschlands selbst ernanntem Arbeiter- und Bauernstaat – einschließlich nachfolgendem Palastbau – hat der Schlossplatz ein Maximum an architektonischem Gestaltungswillen über sich ergehen lassen müssen. Auch die Existenz des gegenwärtig temporären Bauwerks ist indirekt einem höheren Ziel geschuldet, nämlich dem Wiederaufbau des Berliner Stadtschlosses als Humboldt-Forum, der offiziell 2010 beginnen soll.

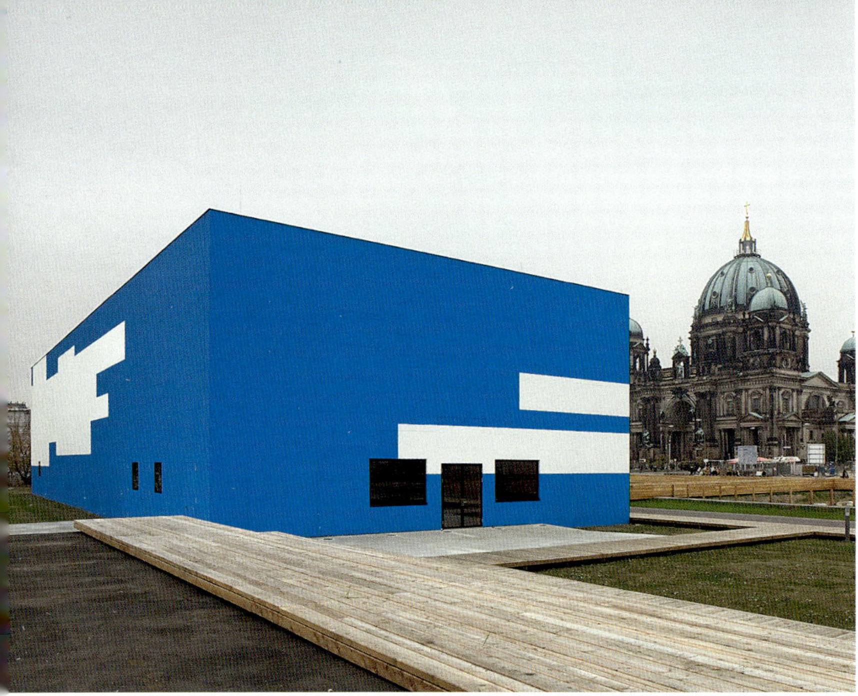

Die „Wolke" im Spannungsfeld des historischen
Ensembles | The "cloud" in the midst of the contrasting
historic ensemble

**Der gegenwärtigen kolossalen Leere zwischen Berliner Dom,
ehemaligem Marstall und DDR-Staatsratsgebäude sowie Schin-
kels Altem Museum und der an einer Ecke wiedererrichteten
Bauakademie zollt der Wiener Architekt Adolf Krischanitz
Referenz mit einem Zitat von Ludwig Wittgenstein: „Eine Wolke
kann man nicht bauen."**
**Die Verkörperung dieses Nichts in Form einer bunten Holzkiste
in Berlins Mitte ist eine provokante Zurschaustellung von
Berlins augenblicklichen Defiziten, aber auch Potenzialen. Unter
der Schirmherrschaft des Berliner Senats entstand, gänzlich
aus privater Initiative und Mitteln des Materialsponsorings, ein
architektonisches enfant terrible auf dem Schlossplatz, das die
Augen und das Aufsehen vieler auf sich zieht. Das gelingt mit
erstaunlich wenigen Mitteln: Eine rechteckige 56 x 20 x 11 Meter
große, fast fensterlose Box aus 100 in Holzrahmenbauweise
vorgefertigten Wandelementen, gegründet auf Streifenfunda-
menten und einer abschließenden Flachdachkonstruktion.
Die Auslegung des 600 Quadratmeter großen Innenraums ist
symmetrisch: vorn zur Schlossbrücke gelegen ein Buchladen,
mittig die Galerie und hinten ein Café mit einer nach Süden
vorgelagerten Terrasse. Die gleiche Bauaufgabe hätte man
kaum mit größerer Effizienz und Wirtschaftlichkeit ausführen
können.**
**Der Erfolg und der Charme der Unternehmung liegen jedoch
im Detail. Das Büro Krischanitz hat durch entsprechend vergleich-
bare Projekte, wie beispielsweise auf dem Wiener Karlsplatz
im Jahr 1992, eine beträchtliche Erfahrung in der Planung, Be-
rechnung und Erstellung vergleichbarer low-budget Kunst-
kuben. Darauf griffen die Bauherrinnen von der White Cube
GmbH gezielt zurück. Vielleicht durch den Erfolg der „Roten
Box" während der Bauzeit des Potsdamer Platzes beflügelt,
spielt Krischanitz bewusst mit der Fernwirkung des Kunst-
pavillons. Nur auf die Distanz ist die abstrakte und grob**

On Germany's most prominent and hotly debated
construction site, the Temporäre Kunsthalle
(temporary art exhibition space) opened in October
2008. Berlin's Schlossplatz has seen centuries of
constant architectural change. From the royal Stadtschloss (City Palace) of the Hohenzollern dynasty to
the parade grounds of the self-proclaimed Socialist
Workers' and Farmers' State – and the subsequent
erection of the Palast der Republik – the Schlossplatz has been subjected to the maximum dose of
political architecture. The temporary structure now
set up there also indirectly owes its existence to a
higher goal, namely the reconstruction of the Stadtschloss as the Humboldt Forum, which is to begin
officially in 2010. Viennese architect Adolf Krischanitz pays tribute to the current colossal void bordered by the Berliner Dom (central Protestant church),
the former Marstall and Staatsratsgebäude (office
of the GDR State Council), by Schinkel's Altes
Museum and the rebuilt Bauakademie on the corner,
with a quote from Ludwig Wittgenstein: "You cannot build a cloud".
The embodiment of this nothingness in the form of
a colourful wooden box in the centre of Berlin is a
provocative display of Berlin's present short-
comings, but also of the city's great potential. Under
the auspices of the Berlin Senate, financed wholly
through private initiatives and with sponsored
materials, an architectural enfant terrible has risen
up on Schlossplatz with an eye-catching exterior
that has attracted much attention. The architects
have achieved this sensation with amazingly modest
means: a rectangular, nearly windowless box meas-
uring 56 x 20 x 11 metres, made of 100 prefabricated
wall panels inserted in a wooden frame, with a
surrounding strip foundation and topped by a flat
roof. The 600-square-metre interior is symmetrical,
with a bookstore at the front on the Schlossbrücke
side, the gallery in the middle and a café at the back
with a terrace extending toward the south. This task
could hardly have been solved with greater efficiency
and economy.
However, the real success and charm of the enter-
prise can be found in the details. The Krischanitz
architectural office has been able to gain considerable
experience in the planning, calculation and execution
of low-budget art spaces through similar projects,
for example on Vienna's Karlsplatz in 1992. The
clients at White Cube GmbH systematically drew
on these prior models. Inspired perhaps by the

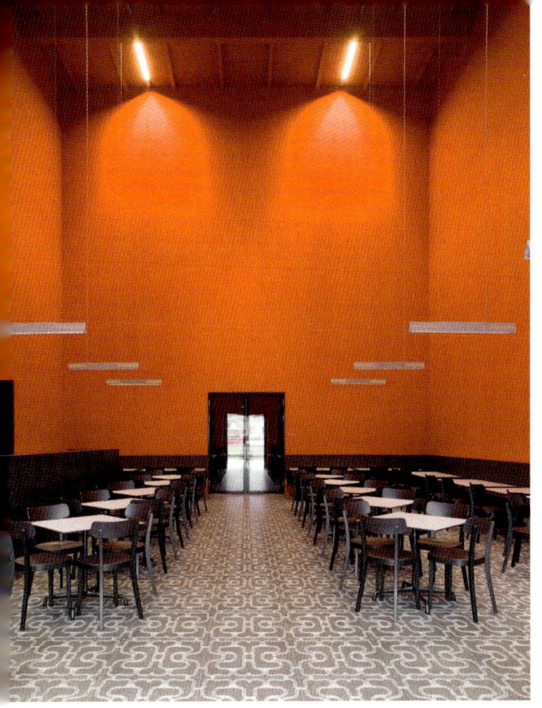

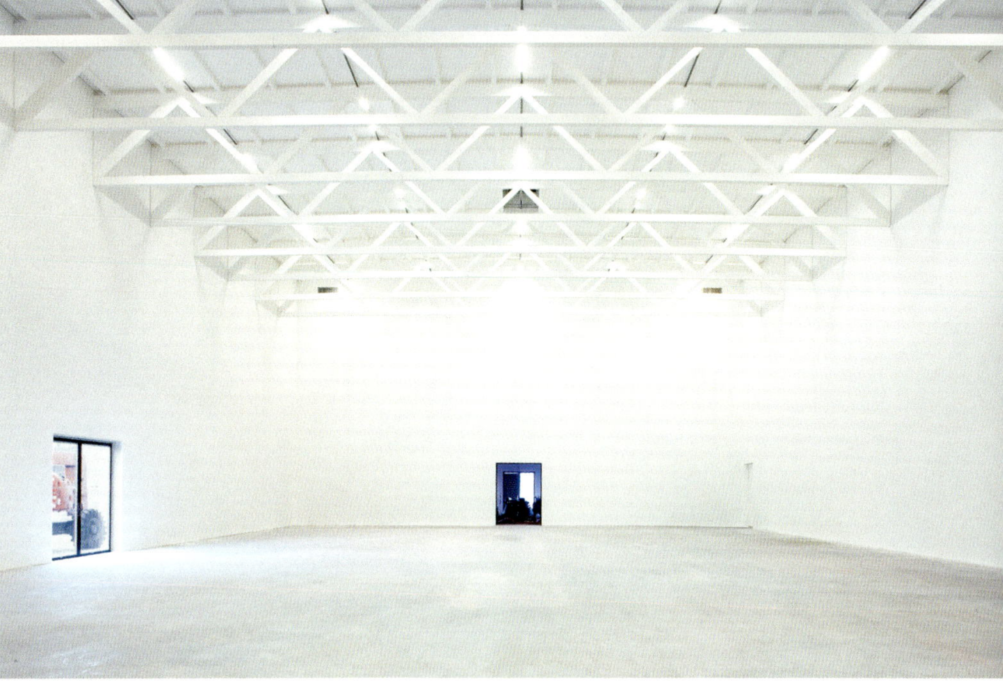

Das Café | The café   **Der Ausstellungsraum** | The exhibition space

gepixelte Wolke (weiß auf cyanblau) des Künstlers Gerwald
Rockenschaub überhaupt erkennbar. Das Bild der Wolke löst
sich zunehmend auf, je näher man kommt. Im Gegensatz dazu
materialisiert sich die Oberfläche. Die 2000 Quadratmeter
große Fassadenfläche entpuppt sich als eine unverputzte, glatte
und fugenlos verlegte Eternit-Faserzementplattenwand, in der
man in kurzen Abständen die Vertiefungen der Befestigungs-
klammern erkennt. Der spröde Charme des Temporären nimmt
einen hier zum ersten Mal gefangen. Der spartanisch-reduktive
Eindruck setzt sich im Inneren fort. Der Trockenbau ist ebenfalls
mit Faserzementplatten verkleidet, diesmal allerdings verspach-
telt und entweder in dunkelgrau (Buchladen), weiß (Galerie)
oder dunkelrot (Café) gehalten. Die größte Überraschung ist
die durchgängige enorme Raumhöhe von 9,78 Metern, welche
schloss-ähnliche Dimensionen aufweist. Da der Eingang zur
Galerie über die hermetischeren und farblich dunkleren Räume
von Café und Buchladen führt, wirkt die Weite der Galerie in
Verbindung mit der Höhe, Helligkeit und dem Lichteinfall von
oben umso effektvoller. Beim Verlassen der Temporären Kunsthalle offenbart sich das Prinzip von Krischanitz' ‚fliegendem
Bau': So unvermutet radikal und direkt das Bauwerk in seiner
Materialität daherkommt, so subtil ist es in seiner metaphori-
schen Bedeutung. Mit der Temporären Kunsthalle festigt Berlin
auf der einen Seite seinen Ruf als Ort populärer Massenattrak-
tionen und andererseits seine prestigeträchtige Position in der
internationalen Kunstszene.

success of the 'Red Boxes' during the construction
of Potsdamer Platz, Krischanitz deliberately
experimented with the effect the art pavilion has
when seen from far off. Only at a distance can the
abstract and roughly pixellated cloud (white on cyan
blue) by artist Gerwald Rockenschaub be recognised
at all. The picture of the cloud increasingly dissolves
the closer one approaches it. The surface, conversely,
then materialises. The 2,000 square metres of
façade reveal themselves to be smooth, unplastered
fibre-cement panels laid without joints, in which the
indentations made by the attachment clamps are
visible at short intervals. The dry charm of the
temporary captivates the visitor the first time here,
on the outside. And then the spartan, reductionist
impression continues in the interior. The walls inside
are also clad in fibre-cement panels, but here they
are plastered and painted either dark grey (bookstore), white (gallery) or dark red (café). The big
surprise is the incredibly high ceiling throughout –
at 9.78 metres it takes on palatial dimensions.
Since the entrance to the gallery leads through the
hermetic and darker-coloured spaces of the café and
bookstore, the broad expanse with its height,
brightness and flood of light has an even more
dramatic effect. Upon leaving the Temporäre Kunsthalle, Krischanitz's principle of the 'flying building'
is revealed: unexpectedly radical and direct in its
use of materials, this structure is equally subtle in
its metaphorical significance. With the Temporäre
Kunsthalle, Berlin consolidates both its reputation
as a city of mass attractions and its prestigious
standing on the international art scene.

BEHNISCH ARCHITEKTEN

OZEANEUM

TEXT YORCK FÖRSTER

04

ARCHITEKTEN | ARCHITECTS

Behnisch Architekten
Rotebühlstraße 163A
70197 Stuttgart
www.behnisch.com

WETTBEWERB UND ENTWURF
COMPETITION AND SCHEMATIC
DESIGN

Behnisch & Partner, Stuttgart

MITARBEITER | TEAM

Peter Schlaier,
Elke Reichel
(Projektleitung | project
management)

BAUHERR | CLIENT

Deutsches Meeresmuseum,
Stralsund

TRAGWERK | STRUCTURE

Schweitzer GmbH
Beratende Ingenieure,
Saarbrücken

AUSSTELLUNGSPLANUNG
EXHIBITION DESIGN

Atelier Lohrer, Stuttgart

LANDSCHAFTSARCHITEKTEN
LANDSCAPE ARCHITECTS

Prof. Nagel,
Schonhoff & Partner,
Hannover

ENERGIEKONZEPT
ENERGY CONCEPT

Transsolar Energietechnik GmbH,
Stuttgart

FERTIGSTELLUNG
COMPLETION

2008

STANDORT | LOCATION

Hafenstraße 11
18439 Stralsund
www.ozeaneum.de

FOTOS | PHOTOS

Roland Halbe,
Johannes-Maria Schlorke,
Ralf Lehm, Frank Ockert

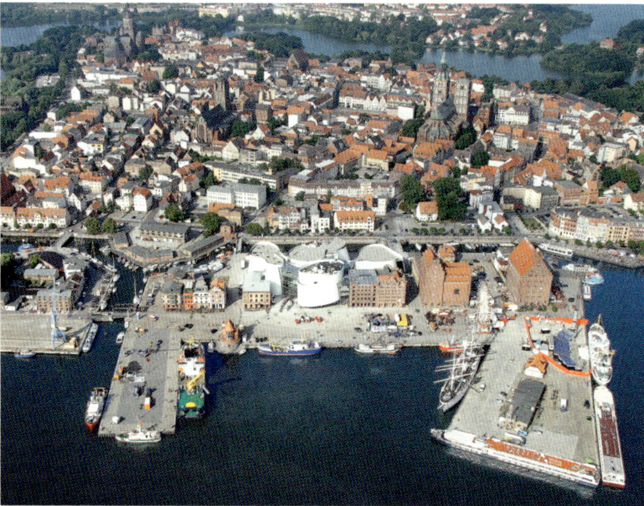

Luftbild Hafeninsel Stralsund mit Ozeaneum | Aerial view of Stralsund's harbour island with Ozeaneum

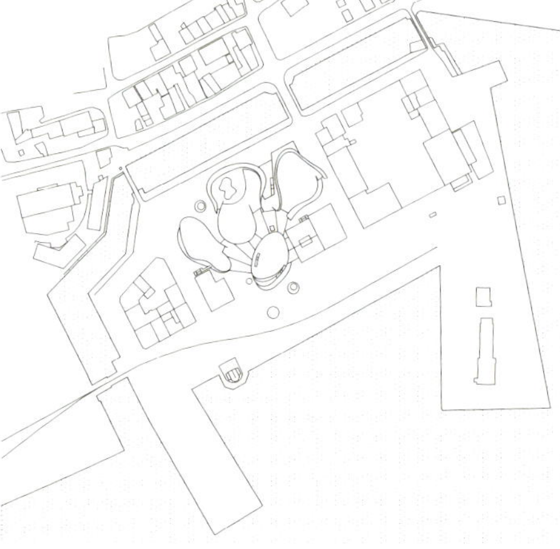

Lageplan | Site plan

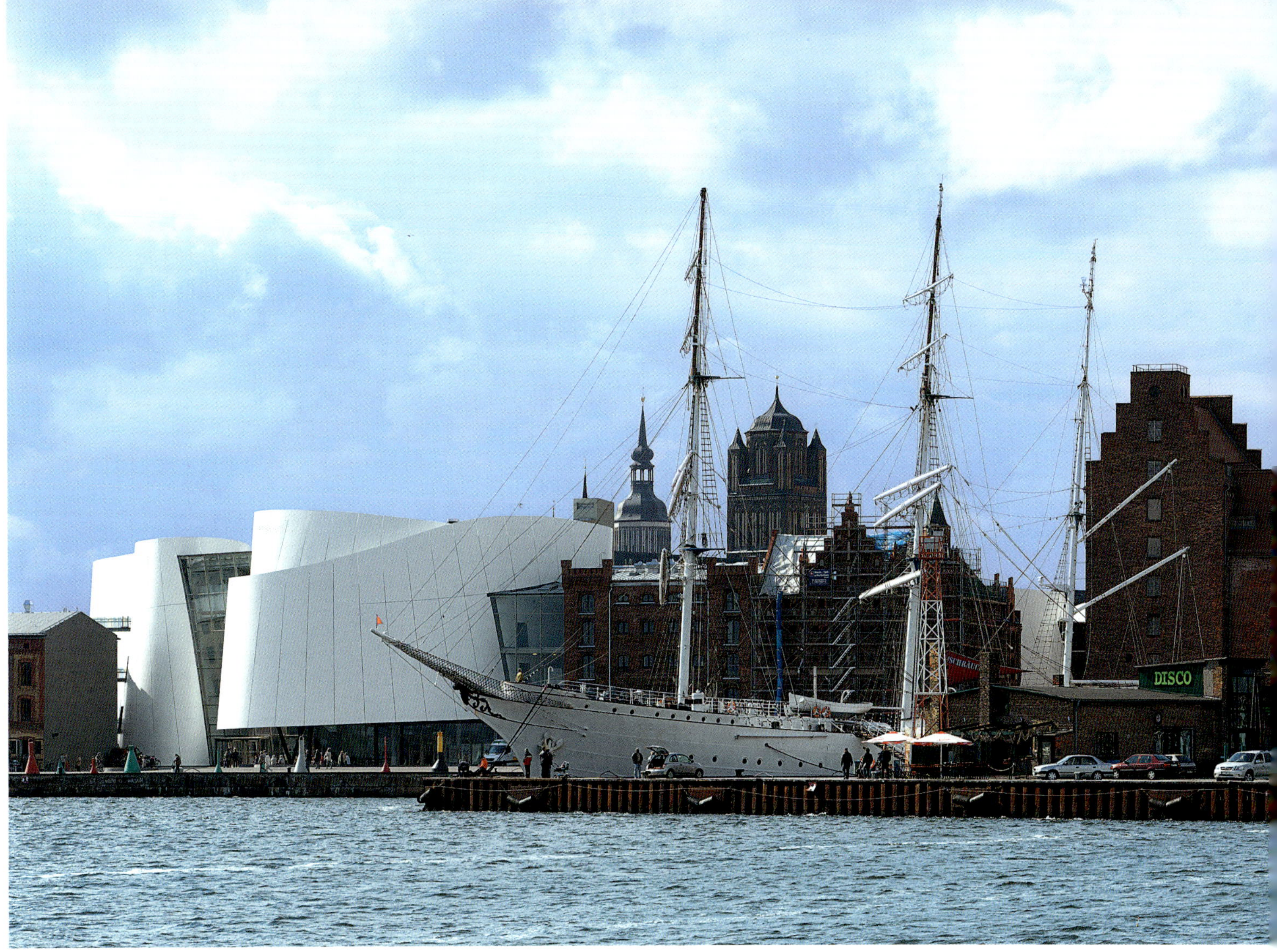

Hafenansicht | Harbour view

Das Deutsche Meeresmuseum in Stralsund ist eines der meist-
besuchten Museen in Deutschland. Am Standort Katharinenberg
in der Altstadt, die als Flächendenkmal Teil der UNESCO-Liste
des Weltkulturerbes ist, bestand keine Erweiterungsmöglich-
keit. Für einen neuen Ausstellungsbau mit Schauaquarien zum
Lebensraum der nördlichen Kaltwassermeere bot sich eine
Brache zwischen denkmalgeschützten Speicherbauten auf der
Hafeninsel an. Den 2001 ausgelobten Wettbewerb konnte
Behnisch & Partner für sich entscheiden, die Ausführung von
2005 bis 2008 oblag dann Behnisch Architekten.
Die Hafeninsel gehört nicht zum Weltkulturerbe und der herbe
Charme eines ehemals gewerblich genutzten Gebiets haftet ihr
bis heute an. Gleichwohl sind die Kais sowie die lang gezogene
Mole für die Besucher Stralsunds eine unbedingte Attraktion.
Der Entwurf sucht die Balance zwischen dem handfesten Charakter eines Umschlagplatzes und der vergnüglichen Leichtigkeit
des Lebens der Sommerfrischler.
Eine vorgehängte Fassade aus weiß lackiertem Stahlblech ist das
prägnante Motiv des Ozeaneums. Die Tafeln sind in Bogenseg-
menten, die sich mal berühren, mal aneinander vorbeilaufen, um
die Baukörper geschlungen. Die sich daraus ergebenden Wellun-
gen und Schwellungen lassen an das Spiel windgefüllter Segel
denken. Beim Wettbewerbsentwurf wurde noch die Idee einer
hölzernen Umkleidung verfolgt, doch aufgrund der Witterung
fiel die Entscheidung für eine Stahlhülle. Das Material steht auch
in Bezug zur Werft- und Hafentradition. Ein lokales Unternehmen

The Deutsches Meeresmuseum (German Oceanographic Museum) in Stralsund is one of the most-
visited museums in Germany. But it had no room to
expand at its former location on Katharinenberg hill
in Stralsund's Old Town, a UNESCO World Heritage
site. Some unused land on Stralsund's port island
between warehouses that are protected monuments
offered a good alternative site for constructing a new
exhibition building with aquarium tanks displaying
the natural habitats of the northern cold-water seas.
Behnisch & Partner submitted the winning proposal
in 2001, and the firm of Behnisch Architekten began
building in 2005, finishing the project in 2008.
The port island is not part of the World Heritage site,
and it still exudes the rough charm of its former
function. At the same time, the quays and the long
jetty are a major attraction for visitors to Stralsund.
The architects' design seeks to balance the stalwart
character of a busy port with the recreational ease
sought by summer visitors. A curtain wall of white-
painted steel sheeting is the signature motif of
Ozeaneum. The sheets are cut into ribbons that
wind their way around the body of the buildings,
sometimes touching, sometimes passing each other
without contact. The resulting waves and swells
call to mind the wind playing across a ship's sails. In

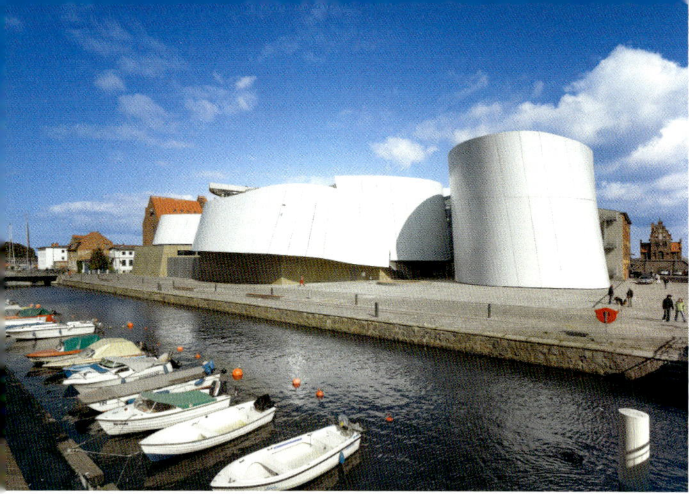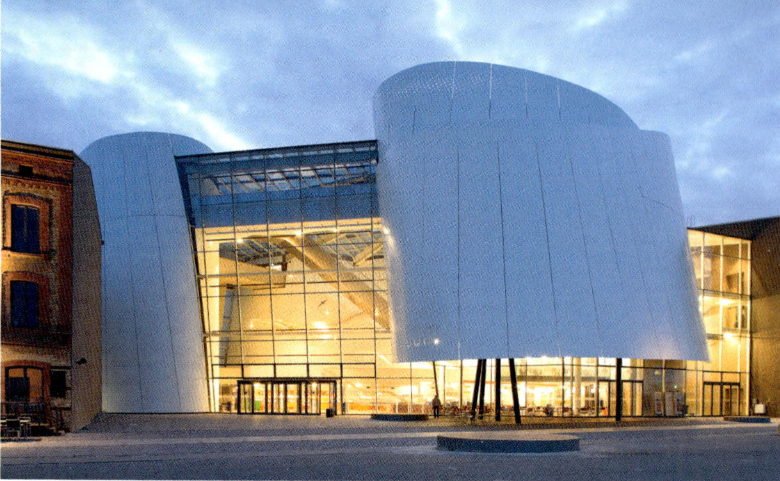

Ozeaneum zur Stadtseite | Ozeaneum on the city side

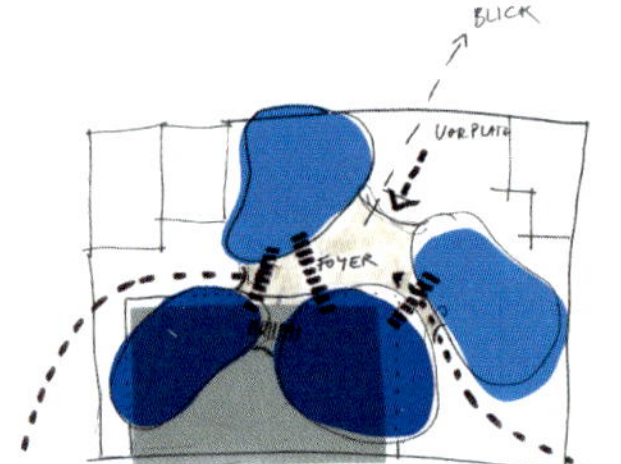

Konzeptskizze | Concept sketch

hat die bis zu 3 x 16 Meter großen Tafeln vorgeformt. Schließlich fand im Jahr 2003 auch noch als Museumsschiff der stählerne Großsegler „Gorch Fock I" vis-à-vis des Ozeaneums seinen Liegeplatz.

Im Grundkonzept ist das Museum ein Ensemble aus vier geschlossen wirkenden unregelmäßig geformten Baukörpern, die wie Findlinge auf dem Grundstück verteilt sind. Die beiden zum Hafen hin orientierten Elemente sind das Gebäude für die ‚Trocken-Ausstellungen' über die Ostsee sowie die Meeresforschung und die Halle mit den spektakulären lebensgroßen Wal-Modellen. Der Stadt zugewandt befinden sich die Aquarienbauten auf einem Techniksockel, dessen Gestalt der durchgängigen subtilen Nobilitierung des Industriellen folgt. Der Sichtbeton zeigt die feine Struktur der Schalungsbretter, die Farbigkeit ist ein warmes Gelbbeige, das Nuancen der Farbe des Backsteins der angrenzenden Speicher aufnimmt.

Zwischen die Baukörper ist ein gläsernes Foyer gespannt, das auch eine Cafeteria und den Museums-Shop aufnimmt. Vom Außenraum durch die Halle ist eine kontinuierliche Fläche aus Granit-Kleinpflaster gezogen. Daraus ergibt sich eine gedeckte Piazza, in der sich sowohl die vom Hafen kommenden Besucher als auch Passanten von den stadtseitigen Zugängen hätten treffen können. Faktisch wurde diese Möglichkeit allerdings aufgegeben. Oberhand hat die Bewältigung des Ansturms von 700 000 Besuchern im ersten dreiviertel Jahr seit der Eröffnung im Juli 2008 gewonnen. So kanalisieren nun Tensa-Barrieren vor dem Hafeneingang den Andrang. Die Innengestaltung der Halle ist nicht übertrieben artifiziell. Auch hier haben die Materialien einen industriellen Charakter; Estrichböden, verzinkte Gitterroste als Brüstungen und mit Heraklith-Platten verkleidete Deckenuntersichten bilden einen robusten Rahmen für die freundliche, lichtdurchflutete Atmosphäre.

Von einer höher gelegenen Galerie gelangen die Besucher über eine Rolltreppe zur Panoramabrücke zwischen den seeseitigen Baukörpern. Dort bietet sich ein Fernblick über den Strelasund, bevor der Rundgang unter die Wasseroberfläche und damit in eine Erlebniswelt im Dunkeln beginnt. Die Architektur beschränkt sich hier darauf, Raum zur Verfügung zu stellen. Die Ausstellungsplanung stammt von Atelier Lohrer und argea fassbender heppert. Im Grundriss dreieckige, je nach Ausstellungsbereich verschieden dimensionierte Vitrinen nehmen die Schauobjekte auf und sind zugleich die Beleuchtungselemente. In den belebten Wunderkammern des Ozeaneums, den 14 Großaquarien, wird die Lebenswelt Meer detailliert vom Hafenkai mit Fahrradschrott, wellenüberspülten Brandungszonen bis

the competition proposal, this outer skin was to be made of wood, but weather conditions made steel the better choice. This material also relates to the shipbuilding and harbour tradition. A local company specialising in steel for shipbuilding fabricated the large panels, which measure up to 3 x 16 metres. Finally, in 2003 the steel-hulled tall sailing ship Gorch Fock I was moored vis-à-vis Ozeaneum as a museum ship.

The basic concept behind the museum entails an ensemble of four closed-looking, irregularly shaped buildings, distributed across the plot like boulders. The two structures facing the harbour house the 'dry exhibitions' about the Baltic Sea and oceanography as well as a hall filled with spectacular life-size whale models. Facing the city two aquaria are set on a plinth holding the technical and maintenance equipment, whose design echoes the subtle ennobling of industrial style that is applied throughout. The exposed concrete retains traces of the fine texture of the boards used for the formwork and has a warm yellowish-beige hue that picks up nuances of the colour of the brick in the neighbouring warehouse.

A glass foyer that also accommodates a cafeteria and museum shop stretches between these structures. As flooring, a continuous surface of small granite paving stones runs from outdoors through the hall. This creates a covered piazza in which visitors streaming in from the harbour might have met passers-by from the city-side entrances. However, in practice this option had to be forfeited in favour of keeping under control the swarms of visitors – 700,000 in just the first nine months since Ozeaneum's opening in July 2008. Now Tensabarriers set up before the harbour entrance keep the crowds at bay. The interior design of the hall is not excessively artificial. The materials used here have the same industrial feel found on the exterior: screed floors, galvanised grates as parapets, and ceilings covered in Heraklith panels form a robust framework for the friendly, light-flooded atmosphere.

From an upstairs gallery, visitors can take an escalator up to a panoramic bridge slung between the

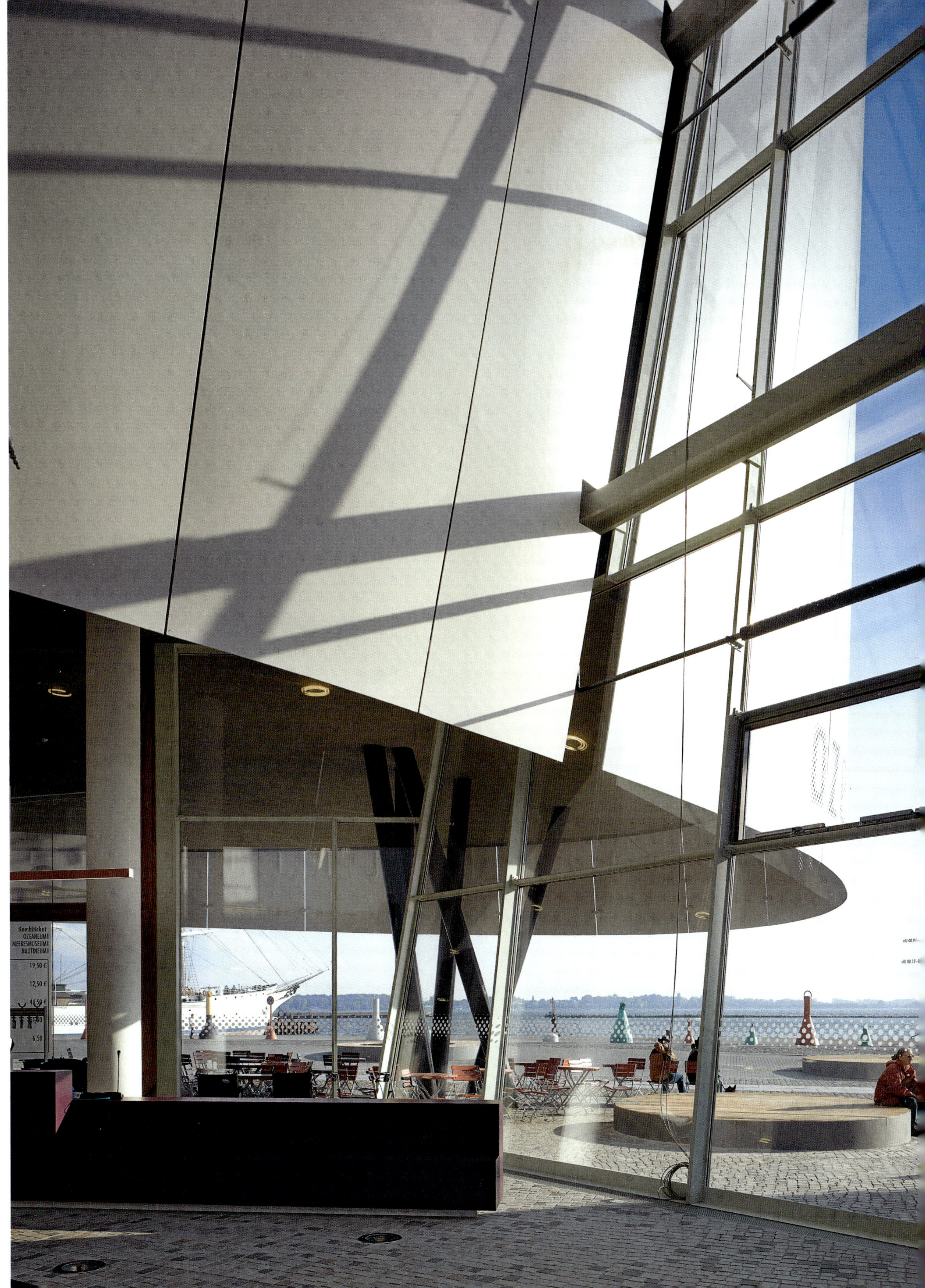

Kombiticket
OZEANEUM
MEERESMUSEUM
NAUTINEUM
19,50 €
12,50 €
44,50 €
6,50

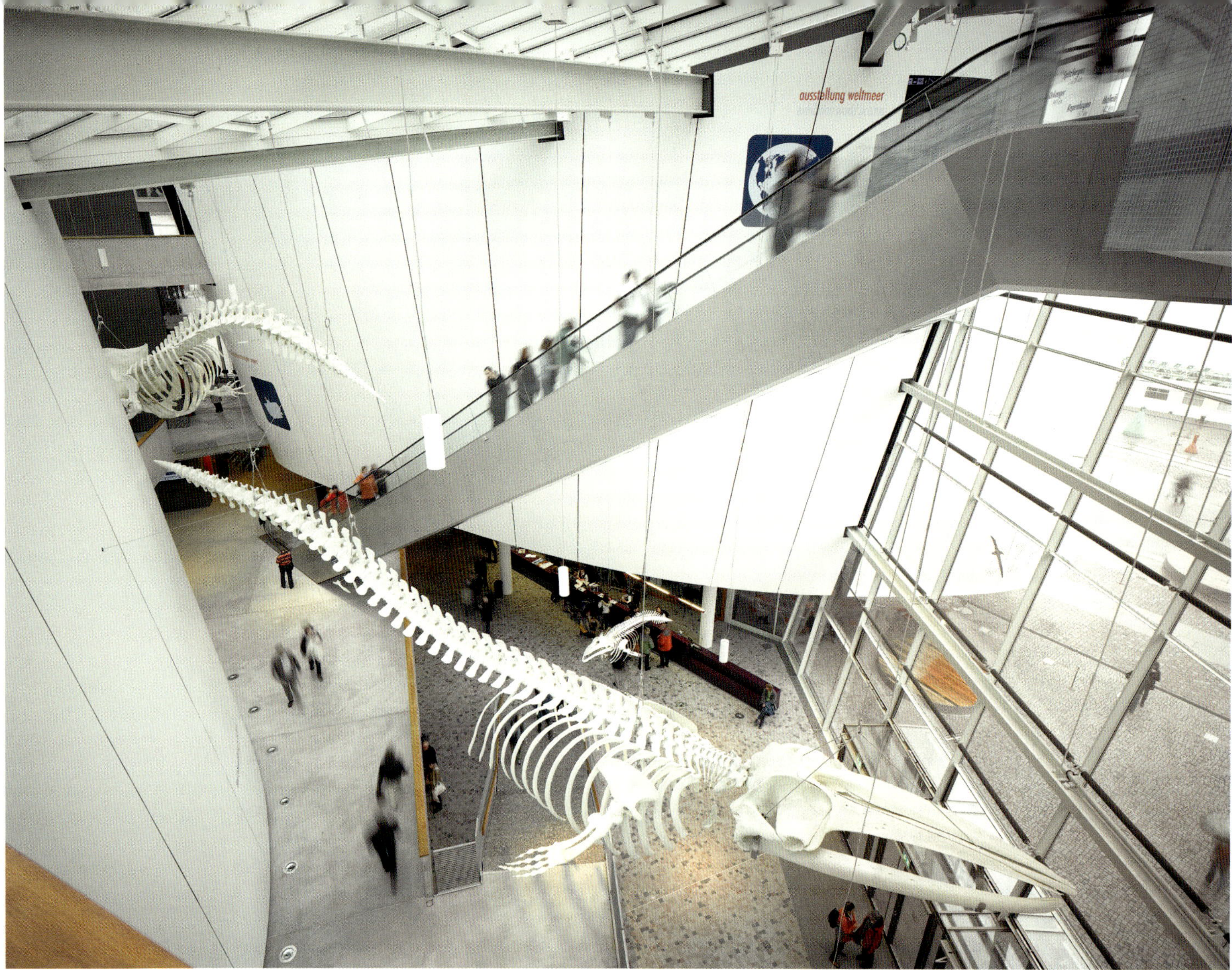

Foyer | Foyer

zum scheinbar unendlichen Becken für Schwarmfische inszeniert.
Letzteres allein hat eine Grundfläche von 300 Quadratmetern
und ist neun Meter hoch, die Füllung umfasst 2,6 Millionen Liter.
Die Aquarien sind ringförmig um das verborgene Herz, die
Technikzone zur Anpassung von Wassertemperatur und Salz-
gehalt sowie die Filter- und Reinigungsanlagen, angeordnet.
Die Verwaltung ist in einem der angrenzenden Speicher unter-
gebracht.
Das Ozeaneum ist ein noch wachsendes Museum. Sobald die
Finanzierung gesichert ist, sollen eine erweiterte Ausstellung
zur Meeresforschung und eine Pinguinanlage auf der Dachterrasse entstehen.

buildings on the sea side. There they can look far off
into the distance over Strela Sound before they set
off on their circuit through the dark underwater
world. Here, the architecture restricts itself to providing the necessary space. The exhibition layout was
planned by Atelier Lohrer and argea fassbender
heppert. Glass cases, triangular in plan and in various
sizes depending on the exhibition area, serve for
both display and lighting. In Ozeaneum's chambers
of wonders, its 14 large-scale life-filled aquaria, marine habitats are recreated in detail – from the harbour
quay littered with discarded bicycle parts and wave-
washed shorelines all the way to the seemingly
infinite tank providing a backdrop for schooling fishes.
This tank alone has an area of 300 square metres
and is nine metres high, holding 2.6 million litres of
water. The aquaria are arranged in a ring around a
hidden core holding the engineering equipment for
adjusting water temperatures and salt content as
well as for filter and cleaning systems. The administrative offices are housed in one of the adjacent
restored warehouses.
Ozeaneum is a still-growing museum. As soon as
financing is secured, an extended oceanographic
exhibition area is to be built, along with a penguin
habitat on the rooftop terrace.

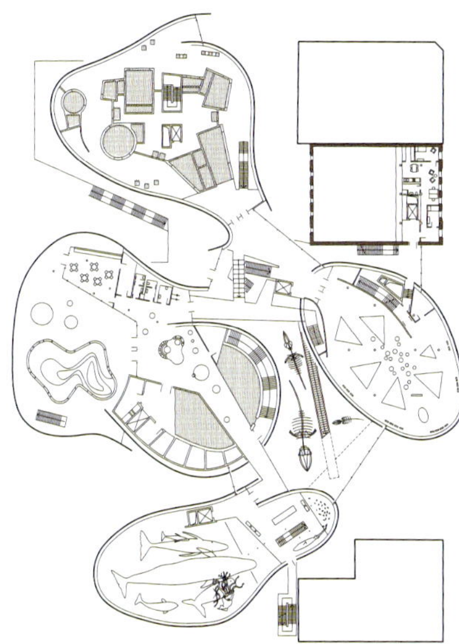

Grundriss Ebene 3 | Floor plan of Level 3

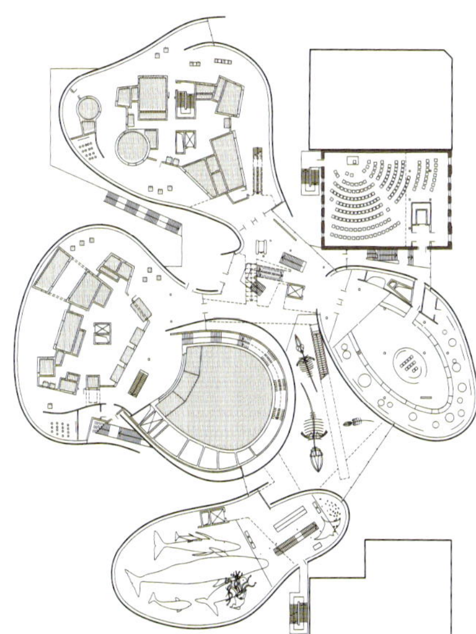

Grundriss Ebene 2 | Floor plan of Level 2

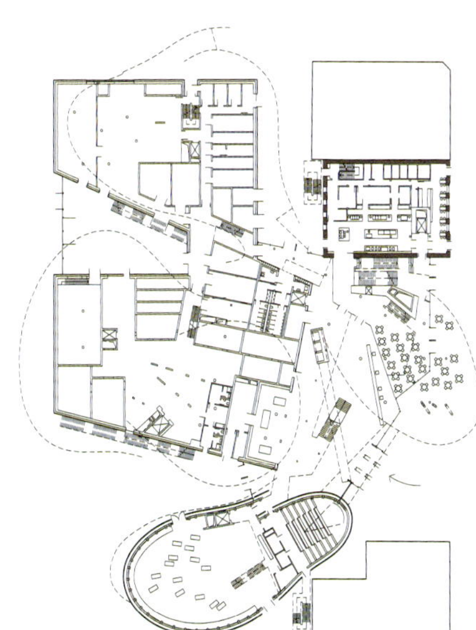

Grundriss Ebene 0 | Floor plan of Level 0

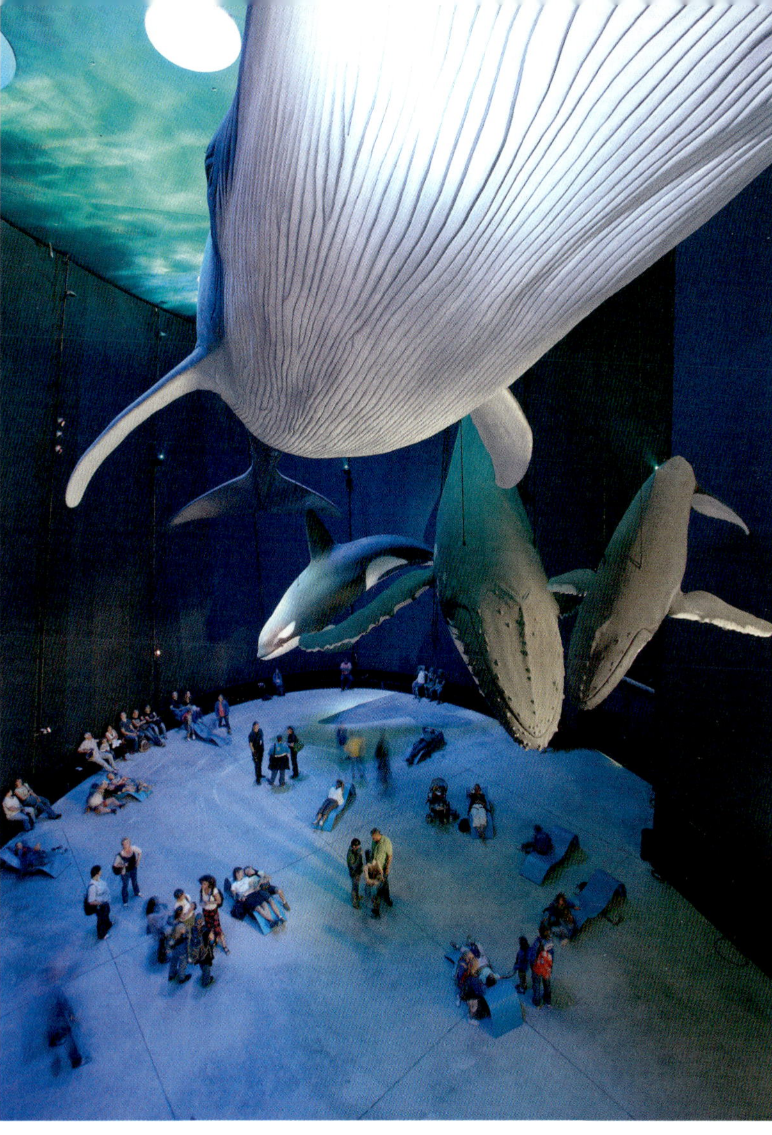

Ausstellung „Riesen der Meere" | "Giants of the Seas" exhibition

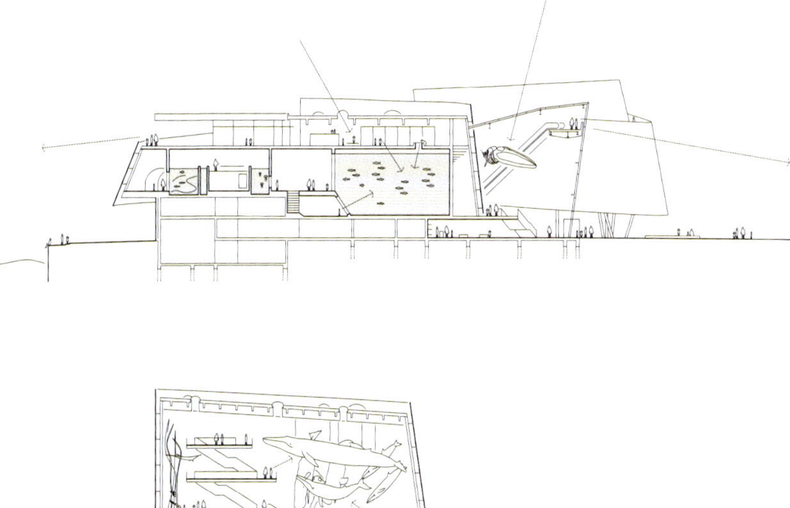

Schnitte | Sections

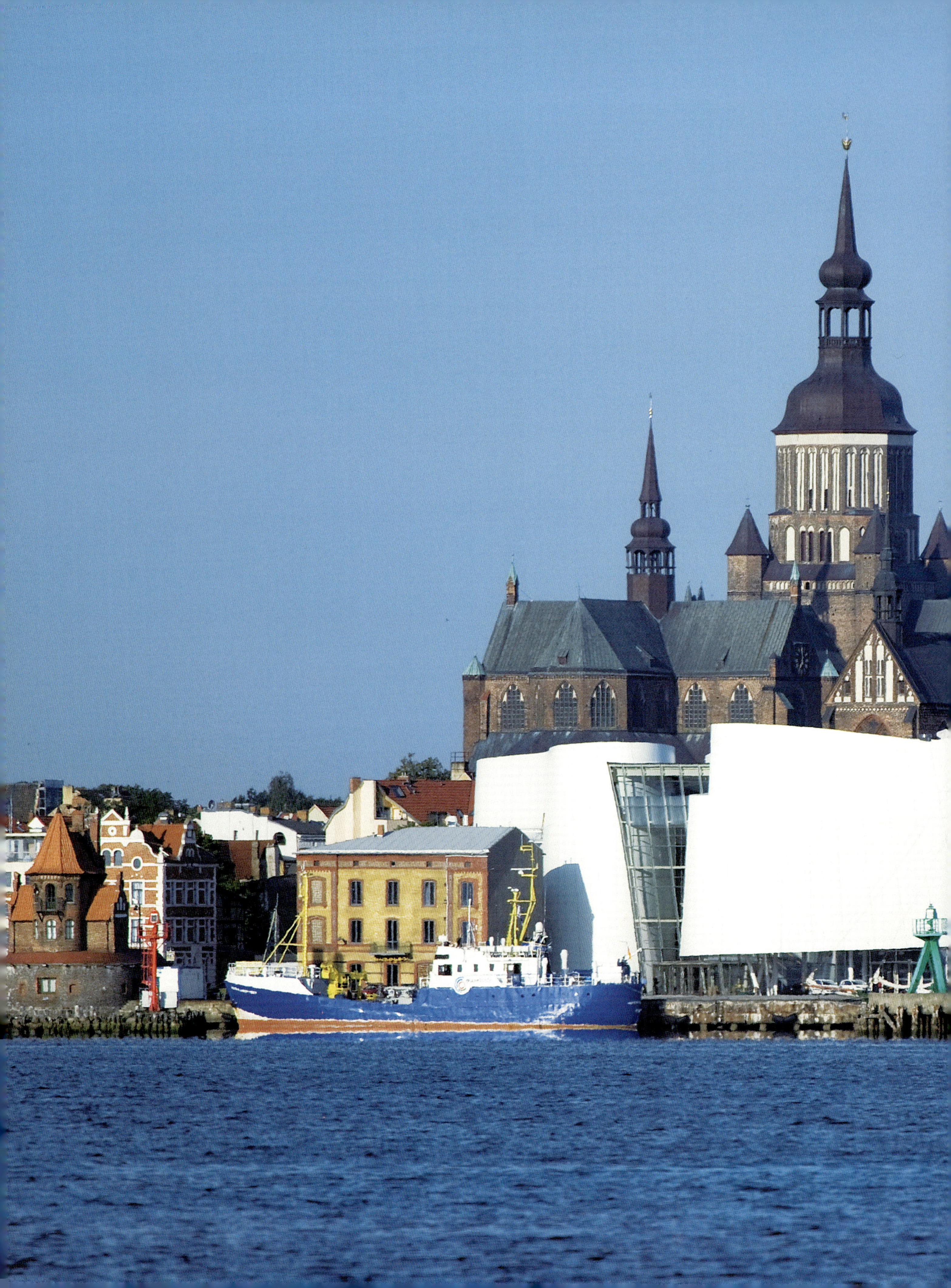

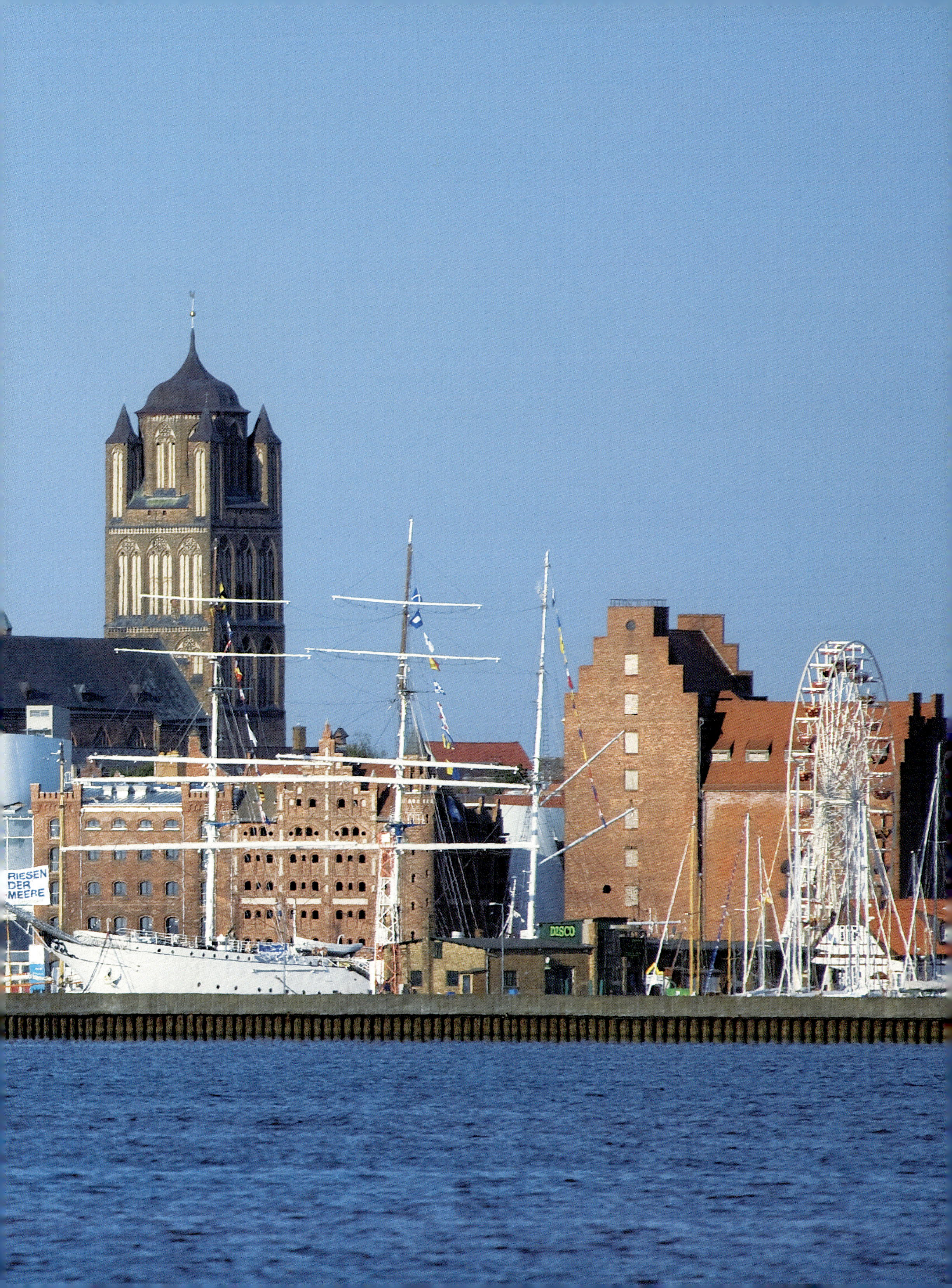

RIESEN
DER
MEERE
DISCO

BEMBÉ DELLINGER

SIEDLUNG KITHIER

TEXT HESTER ROBINSON

05

ARCHITEKTEN | ARCHITECTS

Felix Bembé Sebastian Dellinger
Architekten BDA
Im Schloss
86926 Greifenberg
www.bembe-dellinger.de

MITARBEITER | TEAM

Torben Tjarks (Projektleitung
project management),
Marion Bruns

BAUHERR | CLIENT

Bauherrengemeinschaft Kithier

TRAGWERK | STRUCTURE

Ingenieurbüro Rausch

LANDSCHAFTSARCHITEKTEN
LANDSCAPE ARCHITECTS

Bembé Dellinger

FERTIGSTELLUNG | COMPLETION

Oktober 2007 | October 2007

STANDORT | LOCATION

Lachen-Birkenallee 9–13
86911 Dießen am Ammersee

FOTOS | PHOTOS

Quirin Leppert

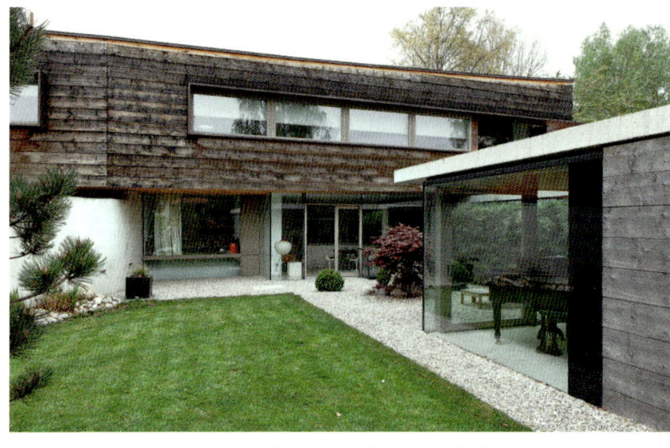

Gartenpavillon mit separatem Zugang für Gäste, Großeltern oder Teenager
Garden pavilion with separate entrance for guests, grandparents or teenagers

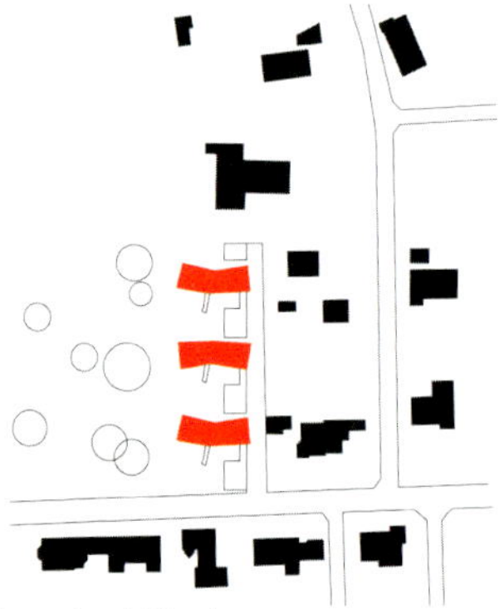

Lageplan | Site plan

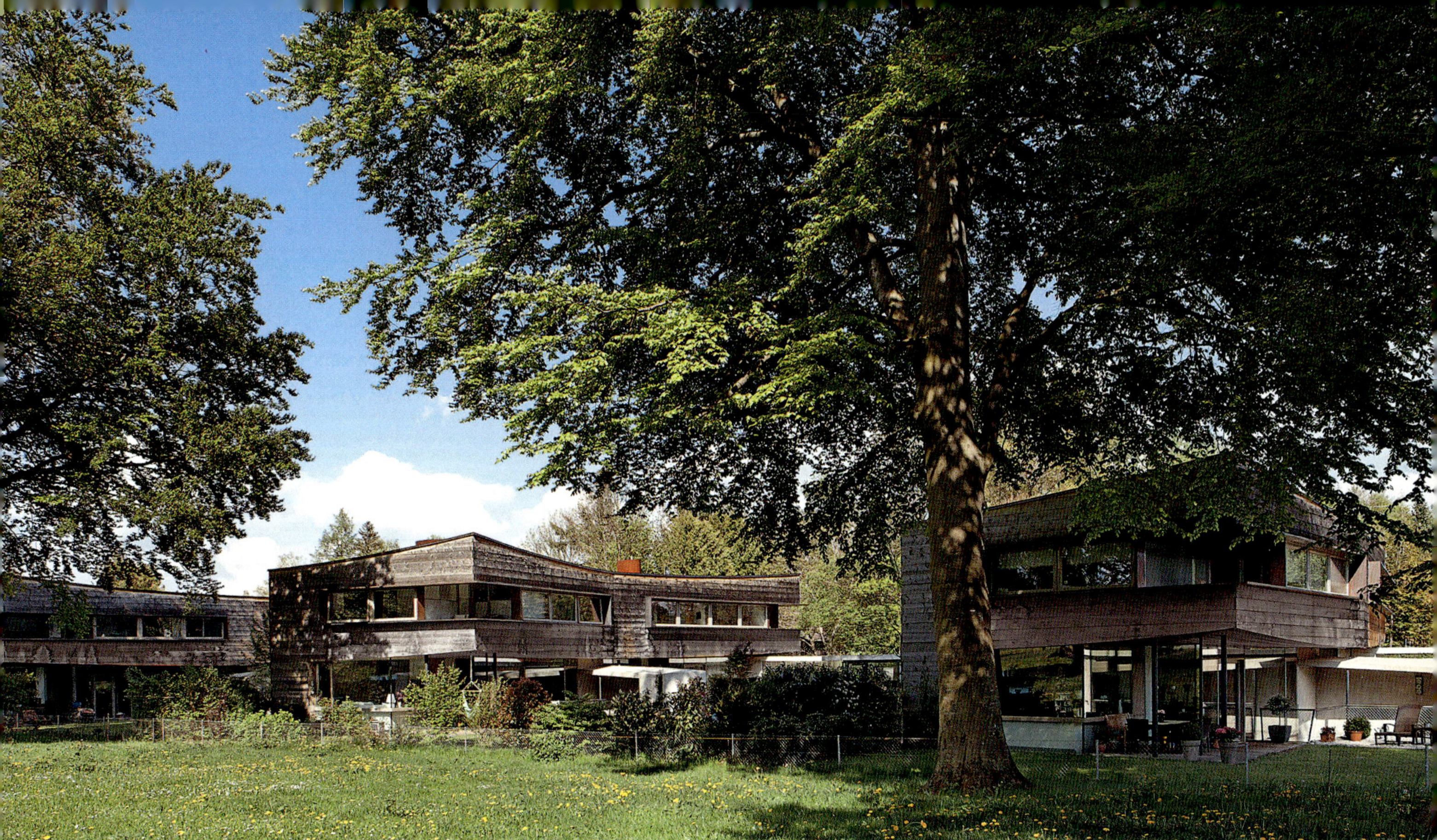

Drei Doppelhäuser im Samba-Rhythmus in die Landschaft gefügt | Three semi-detached houses embedded in the landscape in a samba rhythm

Wer sich drei Doppelhäuser in einer Sackgasse am Rand einer Kleinstadt 60 km südlich von München vorzustellen versucht, dürfte schwerlich auf ein Ensemble kommen, das auch nur im Entferntesten Ähnlichkeit mit diesem kürzlich fertiggestellten Projekt in Dießen am Ammersee hat. Obwohl diese Einfamilienhäuser keinerlei Zugeständnisse an die ortstypische Bauweise ihrer bayerischen Nachbarn machen, fügen sie sich geschickt in ihre Umgebung am Rand dieser idyllischen Stadt am Seeufer ein. Einfallsreicher Materialeinsatz und durchdachte Details gehen Hand in Hand mit einem instinktiven Verständnis dafür, was junge Akademikerfamilien heutzutage suchen, wenn sie sich ein Heim schaffen. Bembé Dellingers Anlage bietet einen hohen Lebensstandard und flexible Nutzungsmöglichkeiten sowie eine findige Lösung des uralten Problems, Wohnraum wechselnden Familienbedürfnissen anzupassen.

Vor gut fünf Jahren beauftragte der Eigentümer dieses 3000 Quadratmeter großen, leicht abfallenden Grundstücks neben einem Bauernhof die ortsansässigen Architekten, Vorschläge für Einfamilienhäuser mit Garten zu entwickeln. Aus dem nur allzu bekannten Dilemma, ein Stück Land in kleine, für Einfamilienhäuser geeignete Parzellen aufzuteilen, fanden Bembé Dellinger einen ebenso originellen wie raffinierten Ausweg, der die Nutzfläche maximierte, aber keinerlei Abstriche bei der Privatsphäre machte. Sie nutzten die gesamte Grundstückstiefe für drei Doppelhäuser, die leicht schräg zueinander versetzt sind und sich sanft in die Landschaft fügen. Da das Grundstück keine verlockenden Ausblicke auf den See bot, konnten die Architekten die Doppelhäuser von Ost nach West anlegen und jedes Haus nach Süden zum Garten hin ausrichten. Was auf den ersten Blick als ungewöhnlich dichte Anordnung für diesen halb ländlichen Standort erscheint, wird durch den zwanglosen Samba Rhythmus der Grundstücksgestaltung abgemildert, die sich vom rechteckigen Zuschnitt des Baugeländes durch die Straßenfront löst. Dass diese Anordnung auch die von der Straße und der angrenzenden Wiese sichtbaren Neubaufronten auf ein Minimum reduziert, könnte man als höfliche Geste gegenüber der Nachbarschaft werten.

Der Auftraggeber verkaufte vier der jeweils 500 Quadratmeter großen Parzellen mit Baugenehmigung und konnte so seine eigenen beiden Häuser der Anlage

If one were to try and picture six semi-detached houses on a cul-de-sac in a small town some 60 kilometres south of Munich, it would be hard to come up with anything even remotely resembling this recently completed project in Diessen am Ammersee. In spite of the fact that these family houses pay no heed to the local typology of their Bavarian neighbours, they nonetheless slot elegantly into the outskirts of this idyllic lakeside town. With an imaginative use of materials and sensitive detailing, combined with an instinctive grasp of what today's young professional families are looking for when they set up home, Bembé Dellinger's scheme offers both a high standard of living and flexibility of use, providing an ingenious solution to the age-old problem of adapting space to meet changing family needs.

Some five years ago, the owner of this 3000-square-metre gently sloping site next to a farm commissioned the local architects to produce a proposal for family homes with gardens. Bembé Dellinger's response to the all-too-familiar conundrum of how to carve up a plot of land into bite-size portions suitable for single houses is both original and sophisticated, maximising the usable area while steadfastly refusing to compromise on privacy. Making full use of the depth of the site, three groups of two back-to-back houses are casually skewed relative to one another and gently weave themselves into the landscape. The fact that there were no tempting lake views from the site allowed the architects to orientate the pairs east-west, so each house faces south towards a garden. What at first glance appears to be an atypically dense arrangement for this semi-rural location is alleviated by the informal rhythmic samba-like site plan that breaks free of the orthogonal geometry set up by the street frontage. And in what might be regarded as a polite gesture towards the neighbourhood, this layout also minimises the bulk of new building facing both the street and the meadow behind.

By selling off the other four 500-square-metre land parcels with building rights, the client was able to pre-finance his own two houses

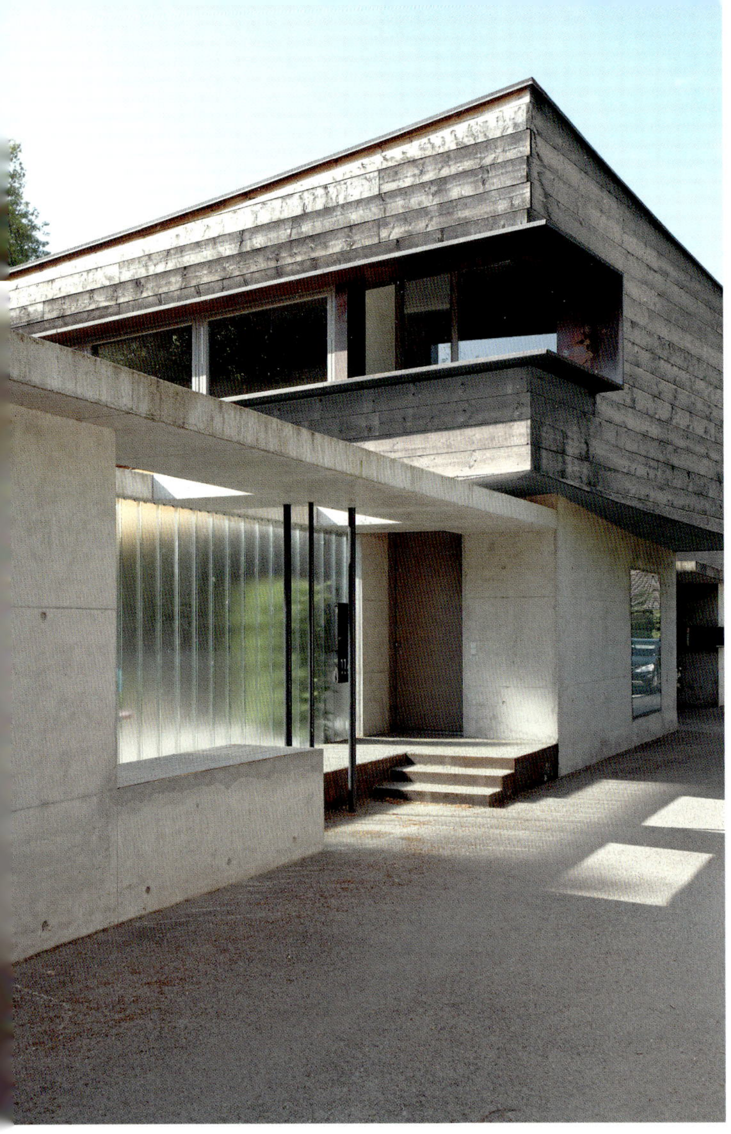

Eingangsbereich | Entrance area

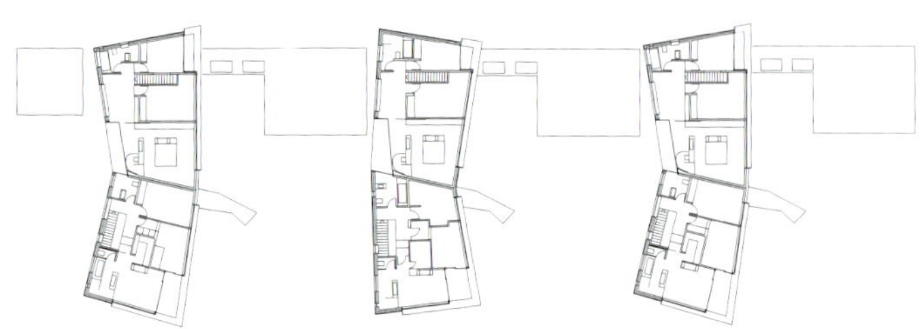

Grundriss Obergeschoss
Floor plan of upper level

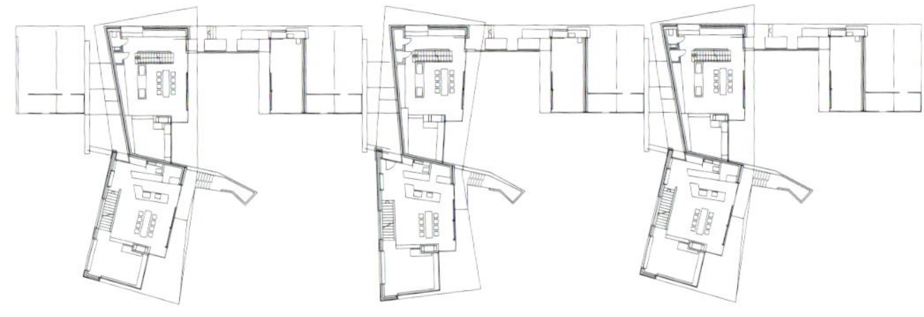

Grundriss Erdgeschoss
Floor plan of ground floor

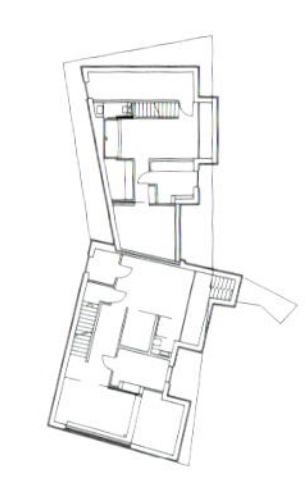
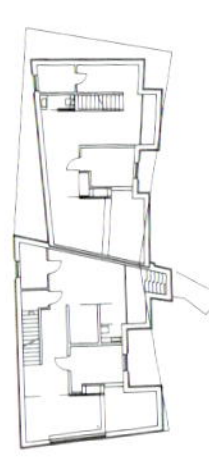
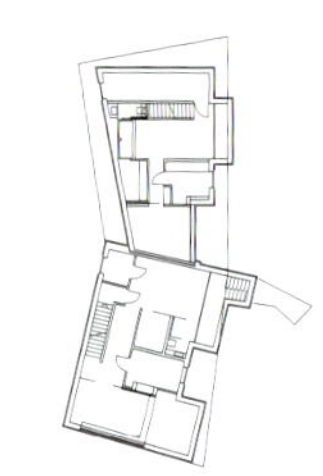

Grundriss Untergeschoss
Floor plan of basement

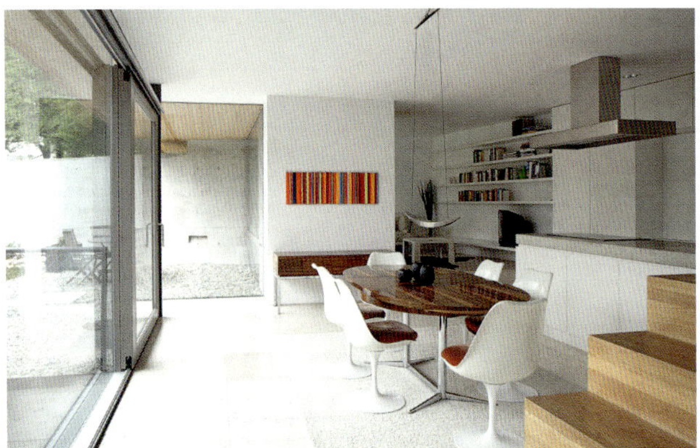

Essbereich mit wandhohen Glasschiebetüren zum Garten
Dining area with floor-to-ceiling sliding glass doors to the garden

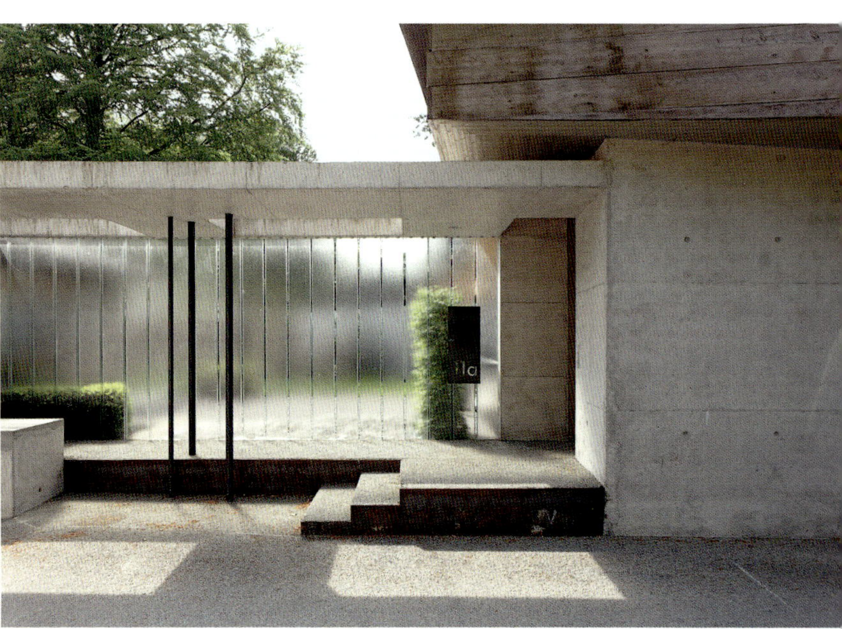

Erschließungsweg | Access route

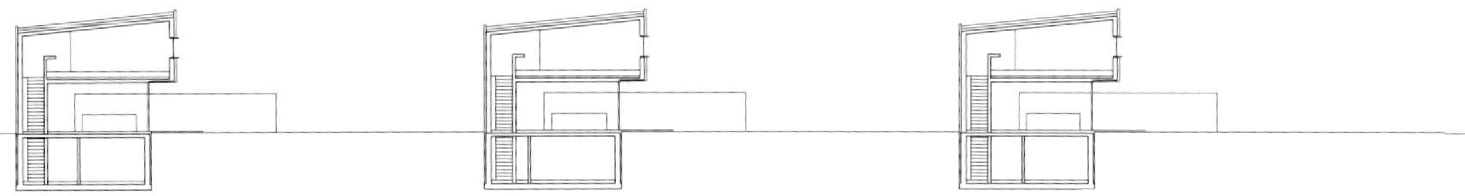

Schnitt | Section

vorfinanzieren. Die Käufer waren vertraglich verpflichtet, sich im äußeren Erscheinungsbild an den Gesamtplan zu halten, konnten aber Raumaufteilung und Detailgestaltung im Inneren eigenen Vorstellungen anpassen. In ihrem selbstbewussten visuellen Vokabular setzen die Architekten eine begrenzte Materialpalette – Glas, Beton, Stahl und Holz – wirkungsvoll ein und erzeugen ein spannendes Spiel der Gegensätze.
Es beginnt gleich mit einem Balanceakt: Die holzverkleideten Obergeschosse ragen schräg über die glatten, rechteckigen Betonfronten im Erdgeschoss hinaus. Im Obergeschoss dient ein langes, tief angesetztes Fensterband mit Stahlrahmen in den Kinderzimmern an den Ecken zugleich als Ausguck auf die Spielstraße. Der Eingangsbereich springt mit einem Sockel vom Erschließungsweg zurück, schafft so einen Übergang von öffentlichem zu privatem Raum und bildet einen minimalen, aber effektiven ‚Schutzbereich'; eine halb transparente Verglasung lässt verlockende, beinahe heimliche Durchblicke in den Garten zu.
Im Inneren öffnen sich großzügige, wandhohe Glasschiebetüren zum Garten mit Rasen- und Kiesflächen. Die vordere Häuserreihe tritt in einem geschickten Spiel mit positiven und negativen Volumen in Beziehung zu den angrenzenden Doppelcarports, denen jeweils ein eingeschossiger Gartenpavillon mit separatem Zugang zur Straße vorgelagert ist. Er bietet einen akustisch getrennten Raum, um zu arbeiten, zu musizieren oder Gäste, Teenager, Oma oder Opa unterzubringen. Badezimmer und Flure im Obergeschoss liegen an der Nordseite und garantieren die Privatsphäre, da sie ihr Licht durch eine lichtdurchlässige Wand oder schmale Fensterbänder mit Dekorglasscheiben erhalten. Tiefe Fensterlaibungen aus Holz dienen bei manchen Bewohnern als Ablagen, auf denen sich alltägliche Gebrauchsgegenstände in dekorative Skulpturen verwandeln, da sie sich als Silhouetten gegen das Licht abheben. Ganz eindeutig besitzen die Architekten beträchtliche Erfahrungen sowohl in der Planung von Wohnhäusern als auch im Familienleben. Doppelwände bieten reichlich Stauraum für Krimskrams aller Art und schaffen äußerst praktische und zugleich durchdachte, handwerklich schön gestaltete Räume. Bembé Dellinger haben sich regional bereits einen Namen mit Entwürfen einmaliger, spektakulär gelegener Häuser gemacht. Mit diesem Projekt setzen sie nun neue Maßstäbe für einen weniger extravaganten Wohnhaustyp. Wenn man ihren Ansatz weiterentwickelt – etwa durch ein zusätzliches Geschoss und einige Kosteneinsparungen in der Innenausstattung –, eignet er sich vielleicht nicht nur für zeitgenössische Einfamilienhäuser im ländlichen Dießen am Ammersee, sondern bietet erhebliches Potenzial als tragfähiges Modell für Wohnbauten in dichter besiedelten Vororten.

on the site. The deal contractually obliged the new buyers to conform to the overall scheme's external appearance, while the interior layout and detailed design was left to the individual clients to negotiate in separate contracts with the architects. Their confident visual vocabulary makes use of a limited palette of materials – glass, concrete, steel and timber – to great effect, producing an intriguing play of opposites.
It starts with a balancing act; the rough timber-clad upper storeys cantilever at an angle over the smooth, rectilinear concrete volumes below. A long steel-lined window set deep into the upper façade also serves as a lookout from the children's corner bedrooms, framing views down the lane. Approaching the front door, the visitor gets a tantalising glimpse of garden, half-spied through a semi-transparent glass screen set back from the street on a plinth that mediates between the public and private realm: a minimal but effective 'defensible space'.
Once inside, generous full-height sliding glass doors open onto the pebbled courtyard and the lawn. In a clever play of positive/negative volumes with the adjacent double carport, the front row of houses have the added bonus of a remote single-storey garden room with separate access to the street, providing an acoustically discreet space in which to work, play music, accommodate guests, teenagers or a grandparent. The north-facing bathrooms and circulation spaces upstairs are ensured complete privacy, as they are lit either by a translucent wall or narrow horizontal slots of etched glass, some with deep timber reveals that serve as shelves, turning everyday objects placed there into decorative sculptures silhouetted against the light. The architects clearly have considerable experience of both house design and of family life; double walls incorporating ample storage hide clutter and paraphernalia, creating highly practical, yet beautifully detailed and crafted spaces.
Bembé Dellinger have already established something of a regional reputation designing one-off, spectacularly located houses. With the completion of this project, they have begun to set new standards for a rather less extravagant type of home. Given further development, perhaps with an additional storey and some cost-paring in the interior fitting-out, their approach may not only prove suitable for contemporary family housing in bucolic Diessen am Ammersee, but offers much potential as a tenable model for residential development in more densely populated suburban areas.

BOLLES+WILSON

INFOPAVILLON

TEXT ULRICH HÖHNS

06

ARCHITEKTEN | ARCHITECTS

BOLLES + WILSON
Julia B. Bolles-Wilson,
Peter L. Wilson
www.bolles-wilson.com

MITARBEITER | TEAM

Christoph Lammers,
Andreas Polzer (Projektleitung
project management),
Cornelia Kober,
Cäcilia Reppenhorst,
Bernd Schnoklake

BAUHERR | CLIENT

Übersee Beteiligungsgesellschaft mbH,
Hamburg

TRAGWERK | STRUCTURE

Dipl.-Ing. Gerhard Abel,
Hamburg

LANDSCHAFTSARCHITEKTEN
LANDSCAPE ARCHITECTS

BB+GG, Barcelona

FERTIGSTELLUNG | COMPLETION

2008

STANDORT | LOCATION

Osakaallee 10
Überseequatier
20457 Hamburg

FOTOS | PHOTOS

Rainer Mader

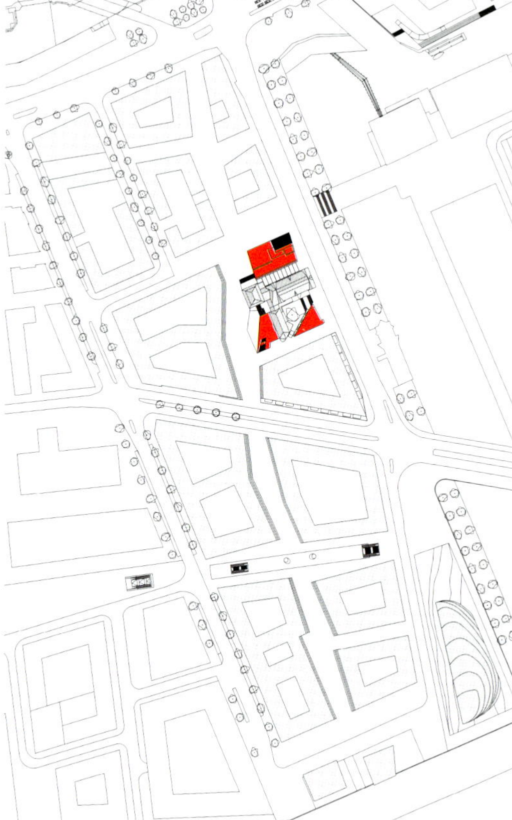

Lageplan | Site plan

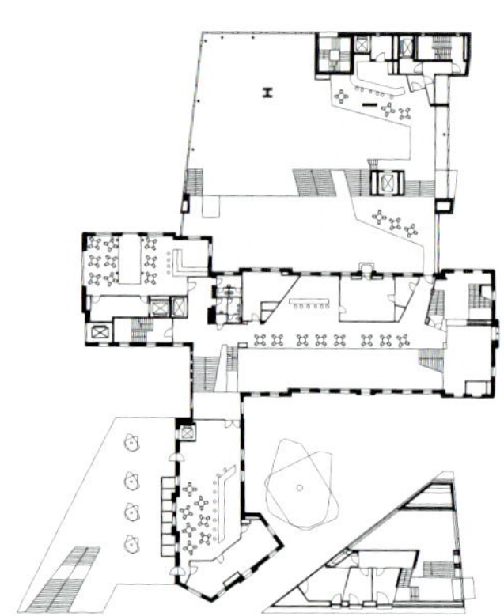

Grundriss 1. Obergeschoss | Floor plan of 1st floor

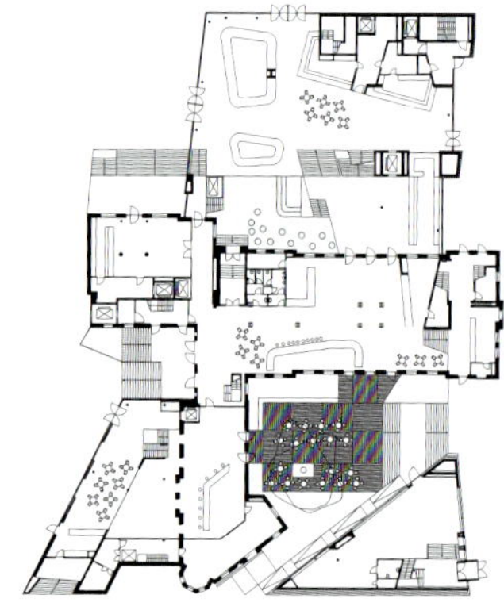

Grundriss Erdgeschoss | Floor plan of ground floor

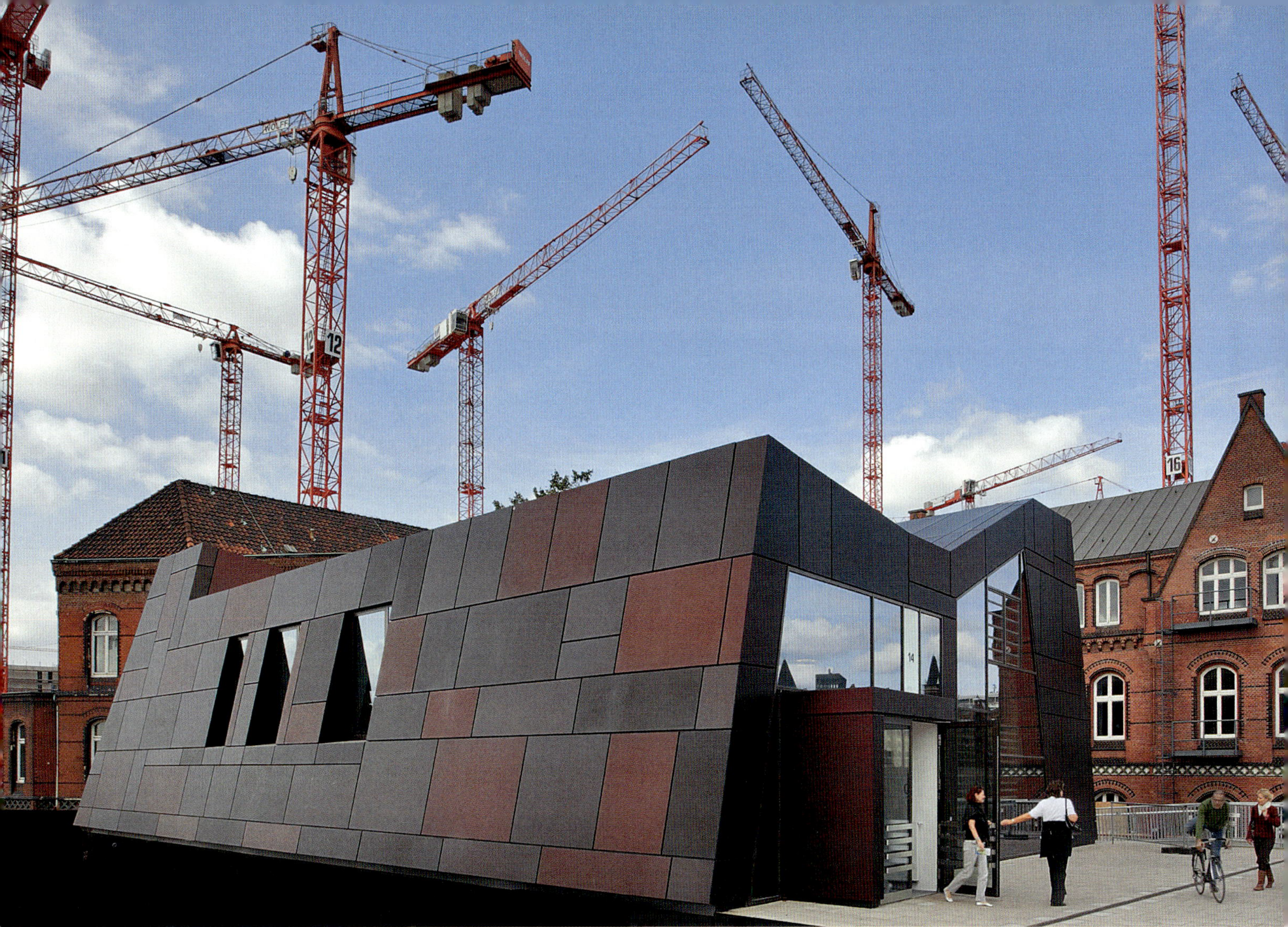

Der Pavillon vor dem Alten Hafenamt, dem einzigen erhaltenen Altbau des Überseequartiers
The pavilion in front of the Altes Hafenamt, the only surviving older building in the Überseequartier

Das geografische Herzstück der entstehenden Hamburger HafenCity ist das Überseequartier. Hier werden einmal 1000 Menschen wohnen, 7000 arbeiten und noch weit mehr das Science Center von Rem Koolhaas und das Kreuzfahrtterminal von Massimiliano Fuksas besuchen. Dieses Gebiet ist ungefähr acht Hektar groß, und entsprechend hoch ist seine Dichte. Deshalb ist es bemerkenswert, dass sich an seiner östlichen Flanke am Magdeburger Hafen ein Freiraum öffnet, in dem sich drei ganz unterschiedliche Kleinformen zu einem Stadtmodul gruppieren, das offenbar nicht dem Primat der Maximalausnutzung des Grundstücks gehorchen musste.

In seinem Zentrum steht das Alte Hafenamt, ein Zeugnis der Architektur der „Hannoverschen Schule", jener bautechnisch zwar grundsoliden, formal aber überdekorierten Neogotik der 1880er-Jahre. Auf weitem, leer geräumtem Gelände war dies leider der einzige Altbau, der bleiben durfte: geschützt als Baudenkmal, in seiner architektonischen Qualität aber überbewertet. Selbst filigrane gläserne Anbauten waren daran nicht diskutabel. Dieser Rest an historischer Bausubstanz gewann so eine vielleicht zu große Bedeutung, damit er nun wenigstens einen Teil der Retortenstadt „durchdringt wie der Sauerteig das Brot" (so Wolfgang Pehnt im Zusammenhang mit der Rekonstruktion des Berliner Schlosses) und dem Ort geschichtlichen Rückhalt gibt.

The geographic heart of Hamburg's emerging HafenCity is the Überseequartier. Some day, 1,000 people will live here, 7,000 will have their workplaces and many more will flock here to visit the Science Center by Rem Koolhaas and the Cruise Terminal by Massimiliano Fuksas. The area spans some eight hectares, and accordingly its density is high. It is therefore all the more remarkable that an open space is emerging on its eastern flank toward the harbour known as Magdeburger Hafen in which three entirely disparate small forms are grouped together into an urban module that evidently need not obey the dictates of maximum utilisation of the available space.

At the centre of the newly developed Überseequartier is the Altes Hafenamt (Old Port Authority Building), a testament to the architecture of the 'Hanoverian School' of the 1880s, characterised by rock solid structures embellished with overexuberant neo-Gothic features. On the vast cleared site this was unfortunately the only old building that was allowed to remain standing: protected as a landmark, but with its architectural quality overestimated. Even filigree glass extensions were out

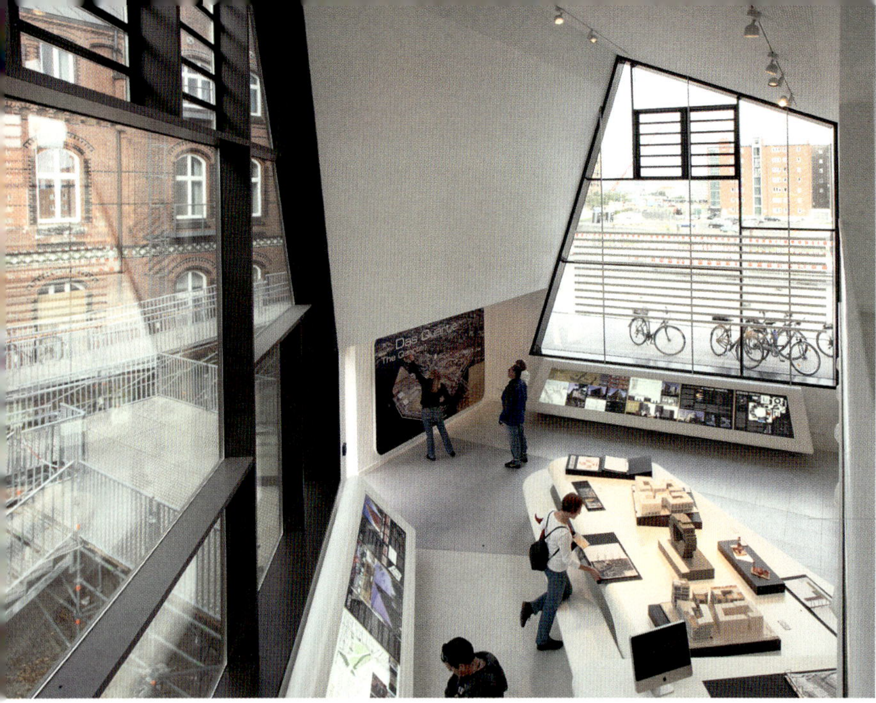

Der Ausstellungsraum mit übergroßen Fensteröffnungen zum Altbau
The exhibition space with oversized windows looking toward the old building

Bolles+Wilson gestalten diesen kleinen Stadtbaustein, der sich inmitten größerer, höher und dichter bebauter, blockartig eingefasster Strukturen angenehm bescheiden ausnimmt, mit Augenmaß. Dem Alten Hafenamt implantieren sie eine Markthalle, die noch nicht fertig ist. Nördlich davon werden sie einen schlanken Turm mit sechs Maisonettewohnungen sowie einer aufgefächerten Nutzung der Sockelzone errichten, und südlich wurde unlängst ein Informationspavillon eröffnet, dessen Ausstellung die baulichen Aktivitäten im Überseequartier erläutert.

Dieses kleinste der Gebäude ist ein unregelmäßig gefaltetes und geknicktes Objekt auf dreieckigem Grundriss mit drei Ebenen, was nicht zuletzt seiner schwierigen Lage in einer Mulde geschuldet ist: drei Meter tiefer als die neue Hochwasserschutzlinie der Warften und Straßen, die auf acht Meter über NN gebracht wurden. Die Camouflage-Ästhetik des Hauses wird wesentlich durch die Schrägstellung einiger Außenwände, einen markanten Knick im Dach sowie die Brechungen seines virtuos geschnittenen und gefügten Metallkleids hervorgerufen. Ziegel- und braunrot eloxierte Bleche unterschiedlicher Formate, durch tiefe Schattenfugen voneinander getrennt, liegend, stehend oder zu grafischen Bändern vereint, umreißen den Bau einerseits mit scharfkantiger Präzision und geben ihm andererseits eine spielerische, zur Auflösung der Form tendierende Anmutung. Natürlich greifen die vielfältig kombinierten Farbfelder der Bleche die Farben der roten, braunen, rauen oder glasierten Steine des Gründerzeitbaus in der Nachbarschaft auf ihre spezifische Weise auf, was ihnen unter wechselndem Lichteinfall auch gut und unaufdringlich gelingt.

Der Wohnturm wird später dasselbe Fassadenbild zeigen, so dass sich dann die gestalterische und städtebauliche Verbindungslinie zwischen beiden Neubauten erklärt. Die ‚hofseitige' Fassade des Pavillons bezieht sich ebenfalls auf den Altbau. Durch ein übergroßes, raumhohes Fenster fällt der Blick frei auf dessen Schauseite, und ihre Ausrichtung folgt der Schrägstellung eines

of the question here. This remainder of the historic building fabric thus took on perhaps too much significance, rooting the area in history and permeating at least part of the test-tube city "like sour dough permeates bread" (in the words of Wolfgang Pehnt, referring to the reconstruction of Berlin's City Palace).

Bolles+Wilson have now shaped this small urban building block, which presents a pleasantly modest contrast to the much larger, higher, densely packed structures in the blocks surrounding it, with a fine sense of proportion. They are implanting a market hall, not yet completed, in the Altes Hafenamt. North of that building they will erect a slim tower containing six maisonette apartments and a base with diversified usage, and to the south the Pavillon, an information pavilion, recently opened with exhibits explaining the building activities in the Überseequartier.

This, the smallest of the planned structures, is an irregularly folded and bent object on a triangular floor plan. It extends over three levels, not least owing to its difficult setting in a depression three metres deeper than the new flood protection line for the wharves and streets, which have been brought up to eight metres above sea level. The building's camouflage aesthetic is attributable mostly to the slant of some of its outer walls, along with a pronounced bend in the roof and the angles of its masterfully cut and jointed metal cladding. Brick-coloured and brownish-red anodised metal plates of various shapes, separated by deep shadow joints, horizontal, vertical or connected to form graphic bands, at once silhouette the building with sharp-edged precision and lend it a playful look tending toward the dissolution of form. The variously combined colour fields of the metal panels naturally pick up the red and brown tones of the rough or glazed stones of the 19th-century neighbouring buildings, doing so beautifully and unobtrusively in the changing light.

The residential tower will later exhibit the same façade aesthetic, building a bridge in terms of design and urban planning between the two new structures. The 'courtyard' façade of the pavilion also relates to the Altes Hafenamt. There is a view through an oversize, full-height window onto the old building's façade, and the new structure is aligned with the angle of one of its wings – doing much honour to the simple edifice. Reference to the

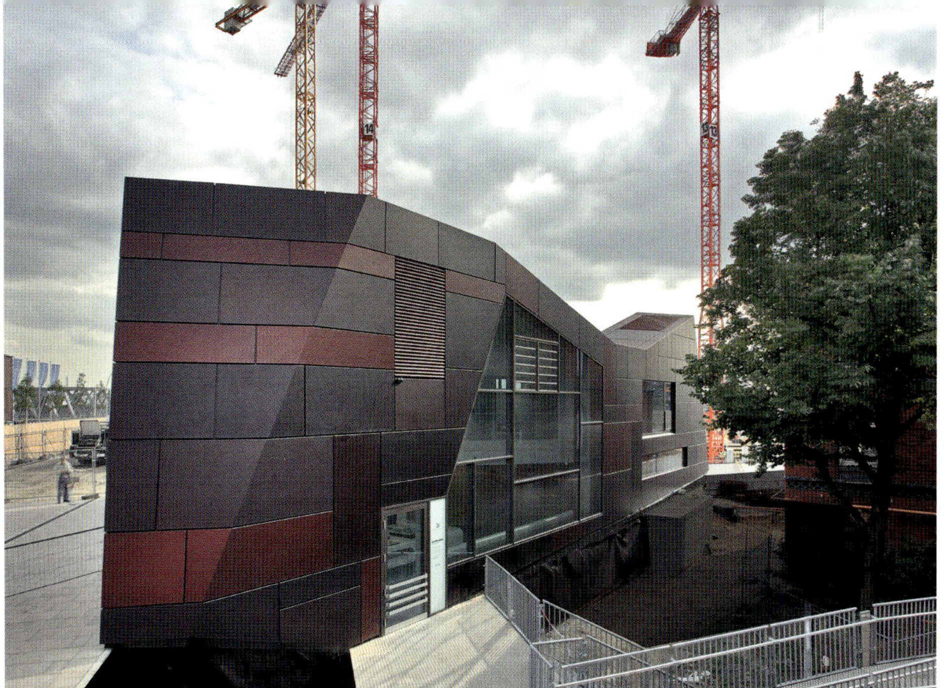

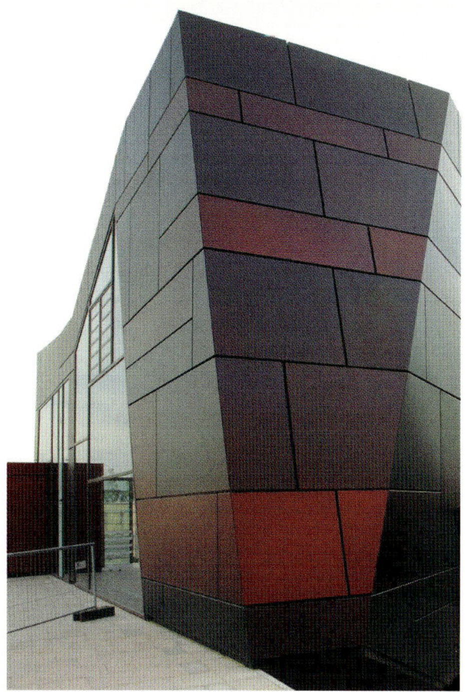

Das ziegel- und braunrot eloxierte Metallkleid des Pavillons nimmt Bezug auf die roten und braunen Steine des Gründerzeitbaus nebenan. | The brick and brownish red anodised metal surface of the pavilion take up the red and brown hues of the turn-of-the-century stone building next door.

Schrägstellung | Tilting

seiner Nebenflügel – viel Ehre für einen schlichten Bau. Die Referenz an die vorgefundene Fluchtlinie bestimmt auch die spitzwinklig auslaufende Dreiecksform des Hauses. So entsteht eine Passage durch den gemeinsamen Hof, die sich zu einem kleinen Platz mit einem Baum darauf weitet. Die für die Zeit nach der Fertigstellung der HafenCity vorgesehene gastronomische Nutzung des Pavillons wird von diesem Wechselspiel zwischen Innen und Außen profitieren.

Innere Größe gewinnt der kleine Bau, weil er als weißer, haushoher Einraum und eingestellter Galerie mit drei kleinen Räumen in seiner ganzen Ausdehnung zu erfassen ist. Das Ausstellungsmobiliar allerdings, nicht von den Architekten entworfen, konterkariert mit den organisch ausschwingenden Formen seiner Tische, Vitrinen und mächtigen Schautafeln, die weder vor einem Fensterband noch vor der markanten spitzen Südwestecke Halt machen, die kristalline Struktur des Gehäuses und ignoriert sein komplexes inneres und äußeres Bezugssystem.

existing building line also dictates the acute angle at the corner of the triangular plan. This creates a passageway through the buildings' shared courtyard, which widens into a small square with a tree. The restaurant planned for the pavilion once HafenCity is completed will benefit from this interplay between indoors and outdoors.

The small building acquires inner grandeur thanks to its conception as a one-room, single-storey white space with an installed gallery containing three small rooms. However, the exhibition furniture (which was not designed by the architects), consisting of organically curving tables, display cases and massive panels, pays no heed to the band of windows or the striking pointed southwest corner, counteracting the crystalline structure of the architecture and ignoring its complex system of interior and exterior references.

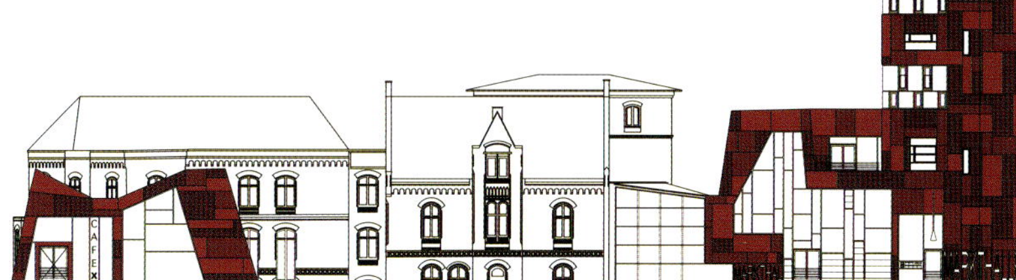

Infopavillon mit Bezug zum noch nicht fertig gestellten Wohnturm
Information pavilion with view of still-unfinished residential tower

BRUNO FIORETTI MARQUEZ MIT NELE DECHMANN

MITTELPUNKTBIBLIOTHEK

TEXT FALK JAEGER

07

ARCHITEKTEN | ARCHITECTS
Bruno Fioretti Marquez
Architekten
Erkelenzdamm 59–61
10999 Berlin
www.bfm-architekten.de

MITARBEITER | TEAM
Anna Saeger, Giovanni Gabai

BAUHERR | CLIENT
Senat Berlin, vertreten durch
das Bauamt Treptow-Köpenick

BAULEITUNG
SITE MANAGEMENT
Häffner + Zenk
Planungsgesellschaft,
Anton Zenk

TRAGWERK | STRUCTURE
Studio C, Rüdiger Ihle

LANDSCHAFTSARCHITEKTEN
LANDSCAPE ARCHITECTS
Bruno Fioretti Marquez
Architekten
mit | with **Nele Dechmann;**
Fugmann Janotta
(Platzgestaltung | design of plaza)

FERTIGSTELLUNG | COMPLETION
2008

STANDORT | LOCATION
Alter Markt 2
12555 Berlin-Köpenick
www.sb-tk.de

FOTOS | PHOTOS
ORCH Chemollo

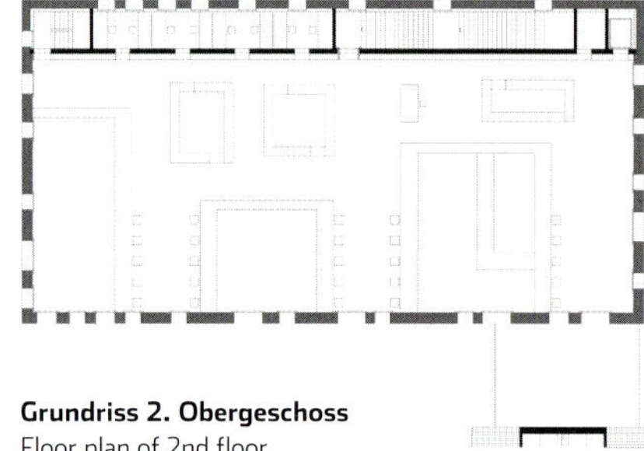

Grundriss 2. Obergeschoss
Floor plan of 2nd floor

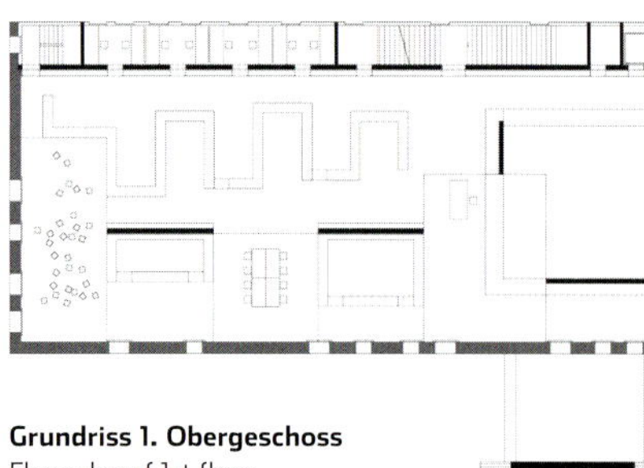

Grundriss 1. Obergeschoss
Floor plan of 1st floor

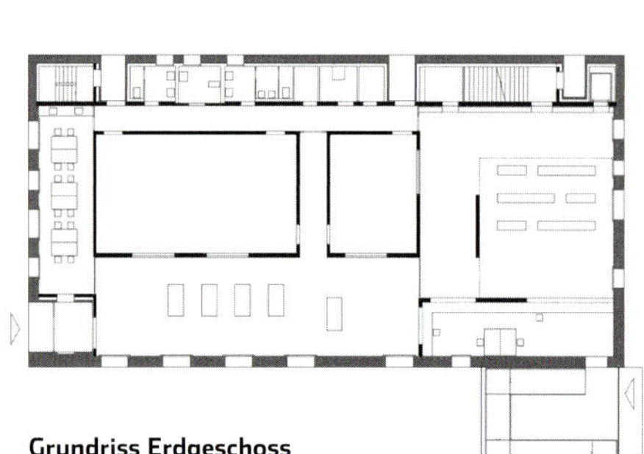

Grundriss Erdgeschoss
Floor plan of ground floor

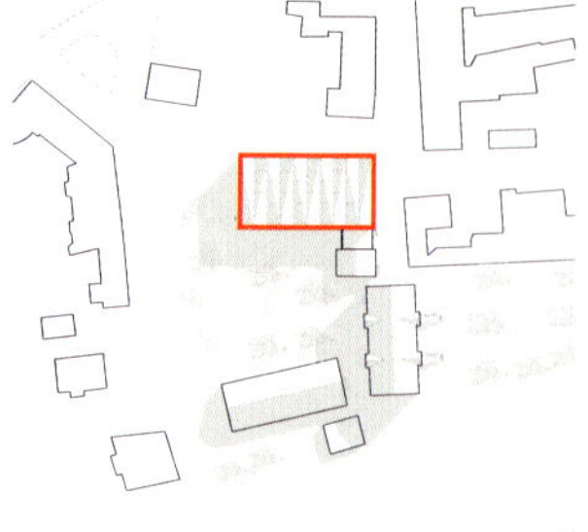

Lageplan | Site plan

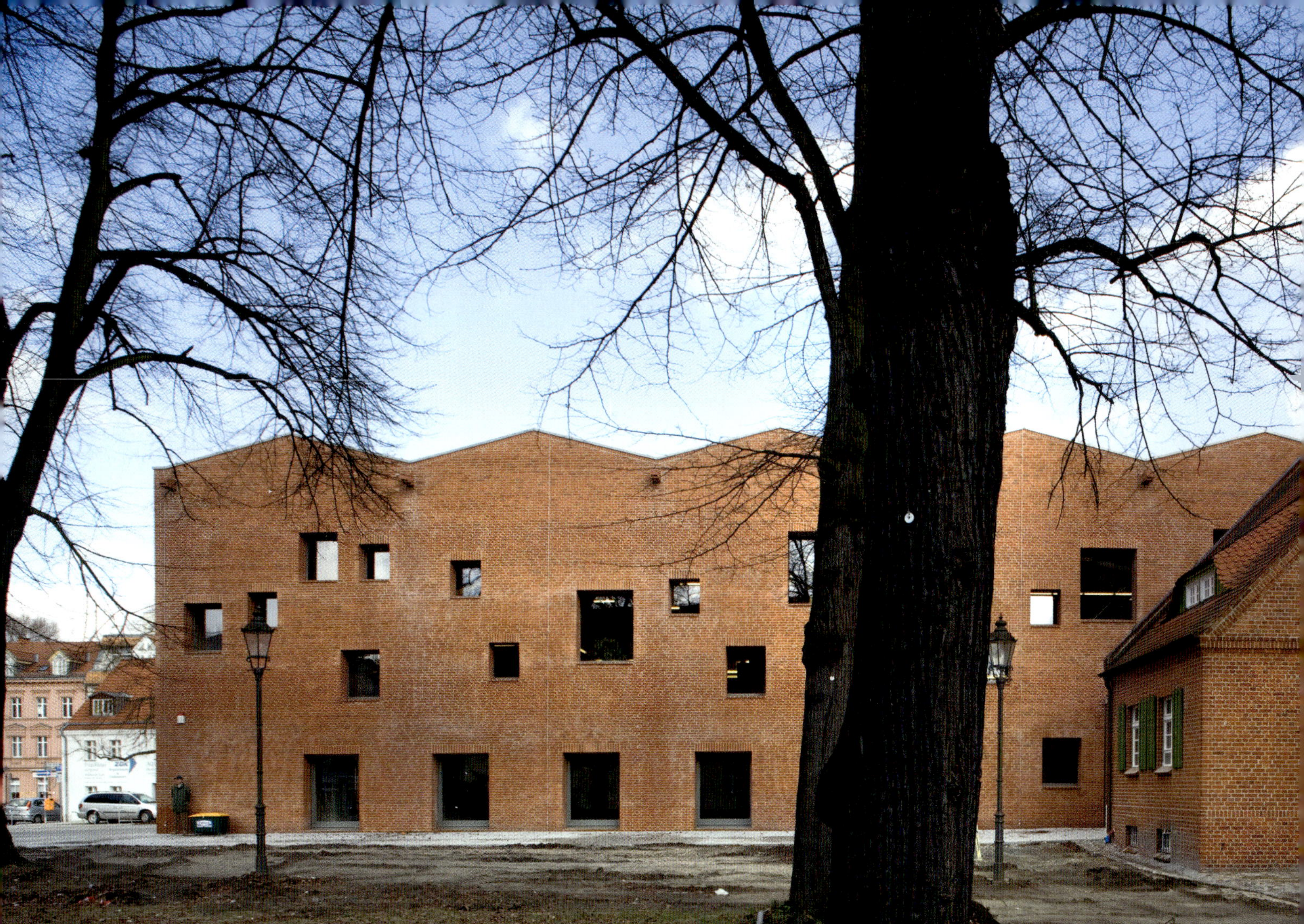

Massives Ziegelmauerwerk für die Bibliothek im mittelalterlich geprägten Stadtkern von Köpenick
Solid brick masonry for the library in the medieval town centre of Köpenick

Die Ausschreibung des beschränkten Wettbewerbs konfrontierte die sieben beteiligten Büros mit einer unlösbaren Aufgabe. Das Gebäude sollte sich mit seiner Maßstäblichkeit als Stadtbaustein in die Situation einfügen. Dies konnte nur ein mindestens dreigeschossiger Baukörper leisten. Die Funktionsbeschreibung der Bibliothek ließ jedoch nur zwei Geschosse zu, um den Personalaufwand beim Betrieb in Grenzen zu halten. Die Architekten setzten sich über die Forderung hinweg, entwarfen einen dreigeschossigen, dazu noch recht voluminösen Neubau und überzeugten das Preisgericht.

Ziegelmauerwerk, etwas anderes kam hier im mittelalterlich geprägten Stadtkern von Köpenick, der wie Berlin mit Ziegeln ,aus dem Kahn gebaut' ist, nicht in Frage. „Geht nicht", war die spontane Reaktion des Statikers auf den Wunsch der Architekten, die Außenwände massiv zu mauern. Doch durch einen etwas erhöhten Wärmedämmaufwand bei Grundplatte und Dach sowie eine zusätzliche Innendämmung der gemauerten Nordwand konnte der vorgeschriebene durchschnittliche Dämmwert erreicht werden. Die übrigen Außenwände haben eine Mauerstärke von 64 Zentimetern entsprechend fünf Köpfen der Ziegel im Reichsformat und bieten die bekannten Vorzüge einschaligen

The brief given the seven architecture offices invited to participate in this competition presented them with an insoluble task. The building was to display proportions that would allow it to fit seamlessly into the surrounding townscape. This called for a structure of at least three storeys. But the functional specifications for the library allowed for only two storeys in order to keep staffing at a manageable level. The architects simply flouted this demand, convincing the jury with a three-storey new building that was also quite voluminous.

Brick masonry – any other material was out of the question in the medieval town centre of Köpenick, which, like Berlin, was built with bricks 'straight off the barge'. "Not possible" was the spontaneous reaction of the structural engineer to the architects' wish to build the library's outer walls of solid masonry. However, it proved possible to achieve the prescribed average insulation value by including some extra heat insulation in the foundation plate and roof as well as additional interior insulation

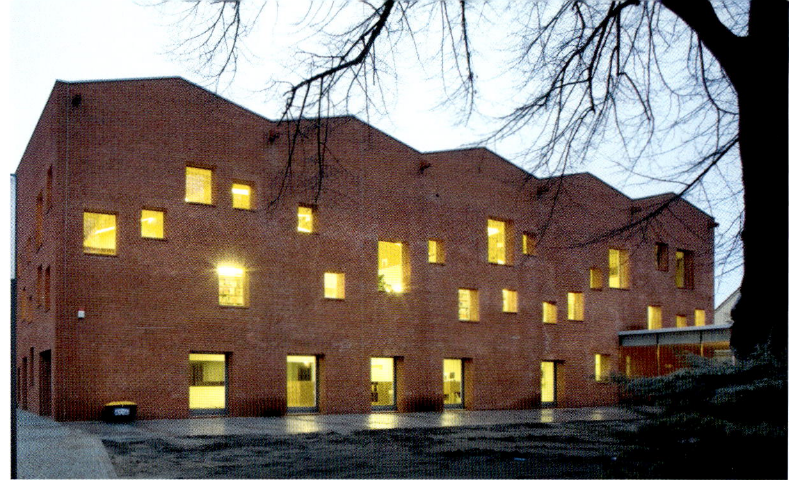

**Die Fenster sind wie Gemälde in einer Art „Petersburger Hängung"
über die Wände verteilt. |** The windows are distributed across the walls in
a kind of "Petersburg hanging".

Mauerwerks: Klima- und Feuchtigkeitsausgleich, Dehnungsfugen
nicht notwendig, dauerhafter, monolithischer Aufbau, wenig
Pflegeaufwand.

Zwei Altbauten waren in den Entwurf funktional einzubinden,
eine Mädchenmittelschule aus dem Jahr 1877 – aus Backstein
natürlich – und das Hausmeisterhaus von 1925, das nun als
Bindeglied zwischen Schulhaus und Neubau fungiert. In den
beiden von den Architekten unauffällig renovierten Altbauten
ist die zentrale Verwaltung aller Bibliotheken Köpenicks untergebracht.

Das massive Mauerwerk ist nicht nur ein von Architekten
geliebtes Prinzip, sondern es gelang den Architekten, die Wände
mit einer ungeheuren skulpturalen Präsenz, fast wie mittel-
alterliches Gemäuer, erlebbar zu machen. Die Fenster sind
innenbündig eingesetzt, wodurch die eindrucksvolle Wandstärke
und die Kraft des Mauerwerks voll zur Wirkung kommen. Der
Haupteingang, eine der tiefen Wandöffnungen, ist nicht besonders hervorgehoben, aber er sitzt genau an jener Stelle, wo
der Besucher ihn erwartet.

Im Inneren ist die bei solchen Objekten übliche standardmäßige
Einheitsästhetik aus dunkelgrauem Gussestrich, weiß getünchten
Wänden, Sichtbetondecken und braunen Holzfenstern nicht
anzutreffen. Stattdessen findet man eine gedeckte, fast erdige
Atmosphäre, die gut mit dem archaischen Mauerwerk harmo-
niert. Wände und Decken sind warmgrau lasiert, Fenster
graubeige lackiert. Wesentlich mitbestimmt wird der Raumeindruck durch die Einrichtung. Die Architekten entwarfen die
Garderoben, Schränke und Regale selbst und ließen sie mit
rotbraunen MDF-Platten mit geölter Oberfläche handwerklich,
aber extrem preisgünstig bauen. So konnten sie mit mäandrie-
renden Regalen Räume gestalten, wo anderswo die Ödnis
serieller Regalreihen herrscht.

Die oberste Ebene wird von dem bewegten hölzernen Dachtragwerk dominiert. Da die Giebel an den beiden Längsseiten
gegeneinander versetzt sind, spannen die weiß gestrichenen
Brettschichtbinder vom Firstpunkt einerseits zum Traufpunkt
andererseits. Als Dachflächen entstehen hyperbolische Para-
boloide. Einzelne Felder sind für Oberlichte offen gehalten. Sie

for the northern brick wall. The other outside walls
are 64 centimetres thick, corresponding to five
header bricks in the German imperial format, and
offer the familiar advantages of single-wall masonry:
heat and moisture exchange, no expansion joints
necessary, long-lived monolithic construction and
low maintenance.

Two older buildings had to be incorporated into the
design for the library: a girls' middle school built in
1877 – naturally of brick – and the custodian's
house from 1925, which now serves as a link between
the schoolhouse and the new structure. These two
older buildings, inconspicuously restored by the
architects, house the central administrative offices
for all of Köpenick's public libraries.

Not only were the architects able to use their
preferred solid masonry for the library – they also
managed to lend the brick walls a singularly sculptural presence, almost like that of medieval stonework. The windows are set in flush with the inside
surface, highlighting effectively the impressive
thickness of the walls and the stalwart masonry.
The main entrance, one of the deep openings in the
façade, is not set off from the rest in any way,
but is located exactly at the spot where visitors
expect it.

Inside, we find nothing like the standard, uniform
aesthetic common to buildings such as this one –
with dark grey cast plaster floors, whitewashed
walls, exposed concrete ceilings and brown wooden
window frames. Instead, the interiors have a subdued, almost earthy atmosphere which harmonises
well with the archaic brickwork outside. Walls and
ceilings are coloured in warm grey, window frames
painted grey-beige. The furnishings play a major
role in the aesthetic of the space. The architects
designed the wardrobes, cupboards and shelves
themselves and had them made in chestnut-col-
oured MDF with oiled surfaces – in carpentry quality,
but done extremely inexpensively. Whereas in other
libraries boring serial rows of shelves set the scene,
here the architects were able to create spaces by
letting the shelves meander.

The top level is dominated by the lively wooden roof
support system. Since the gables on the two longitudinal sides are offset rather than straight across
from each other, the white-painted gluelam beams
span the length from the ridge point on one side to
the eave on the other. The resulting ceiling surfaces
are hyperbolic paraboloids. Some of these fields are

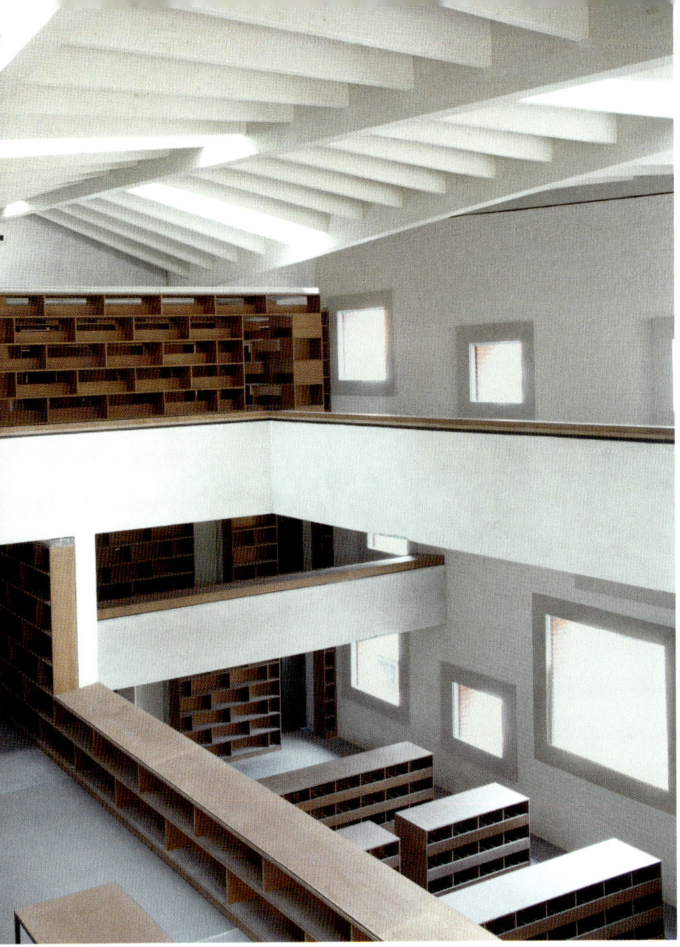

Innenraum | Interior

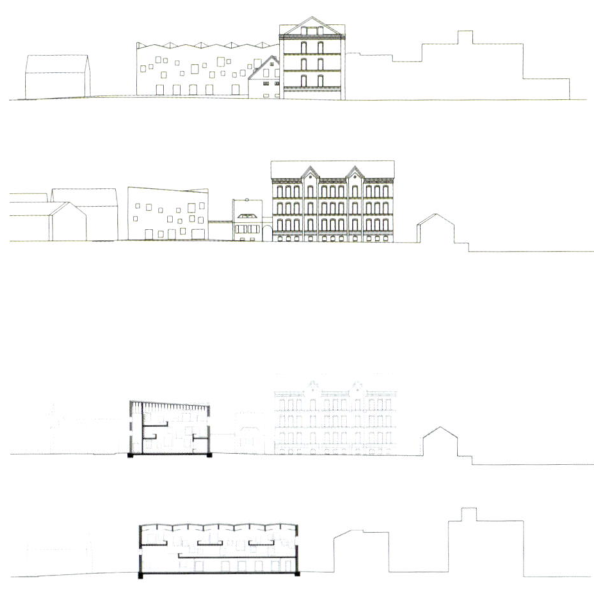

Schnitte | Sections

fügen sich nahtlos in das Beleuchtungskonzept ein, das Einzel-
leuchten vermeidet und mit in die Architektur integrierten
Lichtleisten arbeitet.

In diesem Raumkontinuum wird auch das Prinzip der ohne
Höhen- und Achsbezüge frei verteilten Fensteröffnungen plau-
sibel. Die fest verglasten Fenster sind wie Gemälde in einer Art
‚Petersburger Hängung' über die Wände verteilt: Öffnungen in
drei verschiedenen Größen ‚gehen über die Wände spazieren'.
Dadurch kann auf einzelne Situationen individuell reagiert
werden. So sind zum Beispiel die Fenster in der Kinderbücherei
so tief angebracht, dass auch die kleinen Bilderbuchfreunde
Ausblick haben. Dem Problem der Kältebrücken bei den
innenbündigen Fenstern begegnete man durch breite Fensterrahmen mit rückseitiger Dämmung, die wie breite Bilder-
rahmen wirken.

Lediglich an der Rückseite fügen sich die Fenster in eine
horizontale Ordnung, denn die Ostseite des Grundrisses nimmt
eine schmale Servicezone ein, in der alle Nebenräume, Nass-
räume, die eindrucksvolle einläufige Haupttreppe und ein
Nottreppenhaus untergebracht sind, dazu kleine Kammern als
abgeschirmte Leseplätze. Im Erdgeschoss stehen zwei gefangene
Räume für Vorträge und Seminare zur Verfügung, das kleine
Lesecafé mit Außenbezug wartet noch auf einen Pächter.

kept open for skylights. These fit in seamlessly with
the lighting scheme, which avoids individual lights
and instead works with lighting strips integrated
into the architecture.

In this particular spatial continuum the principle of
freely distributed window openings without any
height or axial references also becomes plausible.
The windows with their fixed panes are scattered
across the walls at various heights like paintings in
a kind of 'Petersburg hanging': openings in
three different sizes 'march across the walls'. This
allows them to react to individual situations. The
windows in the children's library, for example, are
low enough to give the little bookworms a view
outside. The problem of thermal bridges that can
result from set-in windows is countered by broad
window frames with insulation on the back, looking
much like wide picture frames.

Only at the back of the building do the windows
submit to horizontal ordering, because the eastern
side of the floor plan accommodates a narrow service zone in which all ancillary rooms, sanitary facilities, the imposing single-flight main staircase and
an emergency staircase are incorporated, along with
small chambers for use as secluded reading rooms.
On the ground floor two closed rooms are available
for lectures and seminars, and a small reading café
facing outwards still awaits a tenant.

DELUGAN MEISSL

GEBÄUDE | BUILDING

PORSCHE MUSEUM

TEXT CHRISTIAN HOLL

08

ARCHITEKTEN | ARCHITECTS

Delugan Meissl Associated
Architects
ZT Gesellschaft mbH
Mittersteig 13/4
1040 Wien | Vienna
Österreich | Austria
www.deluganmeissl.at

MITARBEITER | TEAM

Martin Josst
(Projektleiter | project manager),
Jörg Rasmussen, Torsten Sauer,
Tapio Lassmann, Zoltan Adorjani,
Philip Beckmann, Hendrik
Steinigeweg, Gerhard Gölles,
Sebastian Brunke, Tom Hindelang

BAUHERR | CLIENT

Dr. Ing. h.c. F. Porsche
Aktiengesellschaft

AUSSTELLUNGSARCHITEKTUR
EXHIBITION ARCHITECTURE

HG Merz Architekten, Stuttgart

TRAGWERK | STRUCTURE

Leonhardt, Andrä und Partner
Beratende Ingenieure VBI, GmbH

AUSFÜHRUNGSPLANUNG
EXECUTION PLANNING

Wenzel + Wenzel Architekten

BAULEITUNG /
PROJEKT-STEUERUNG
SITE MANAGEMENT /
PROJECT MANAGEMENT

Gassmann und Grossmann
Baumanagement GmbH /
Drees & Sommer

FERTIGSTELLUNG | COMPLETION
2008

STANDORT | LOCATION

Porscheplatz 1
70435 Stuttgart-Zuffenhausen
www.porsche.com/germany/
aboutporsche/porschemuseum

FOTOS | PHOTOS

Roland Halbe,
Hertha Hurnaus

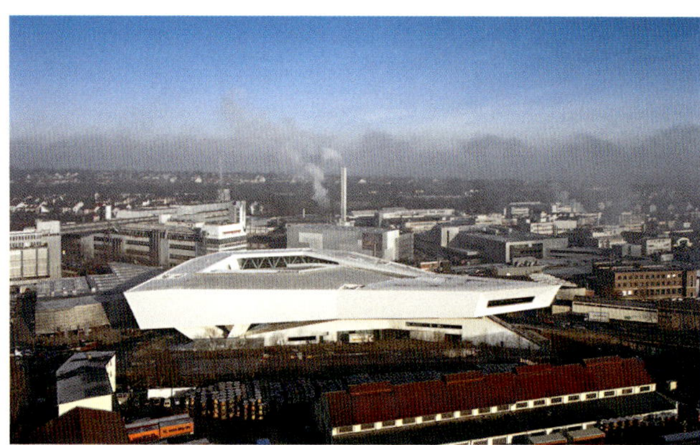

Es ehrt den Bauherrn, dass er das absehbare Risiko nicht gescheut hat, den Siegerentwurf zu verwirklichen. | It is to the clients' credit that they did not balk at the risk involved in realising the winning design.

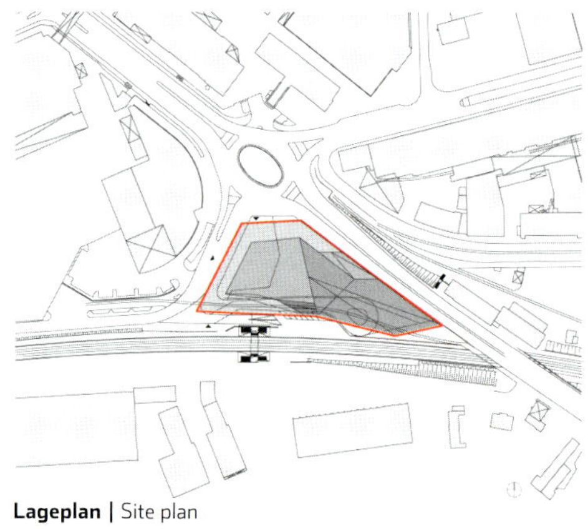

Lageplan | Site plan

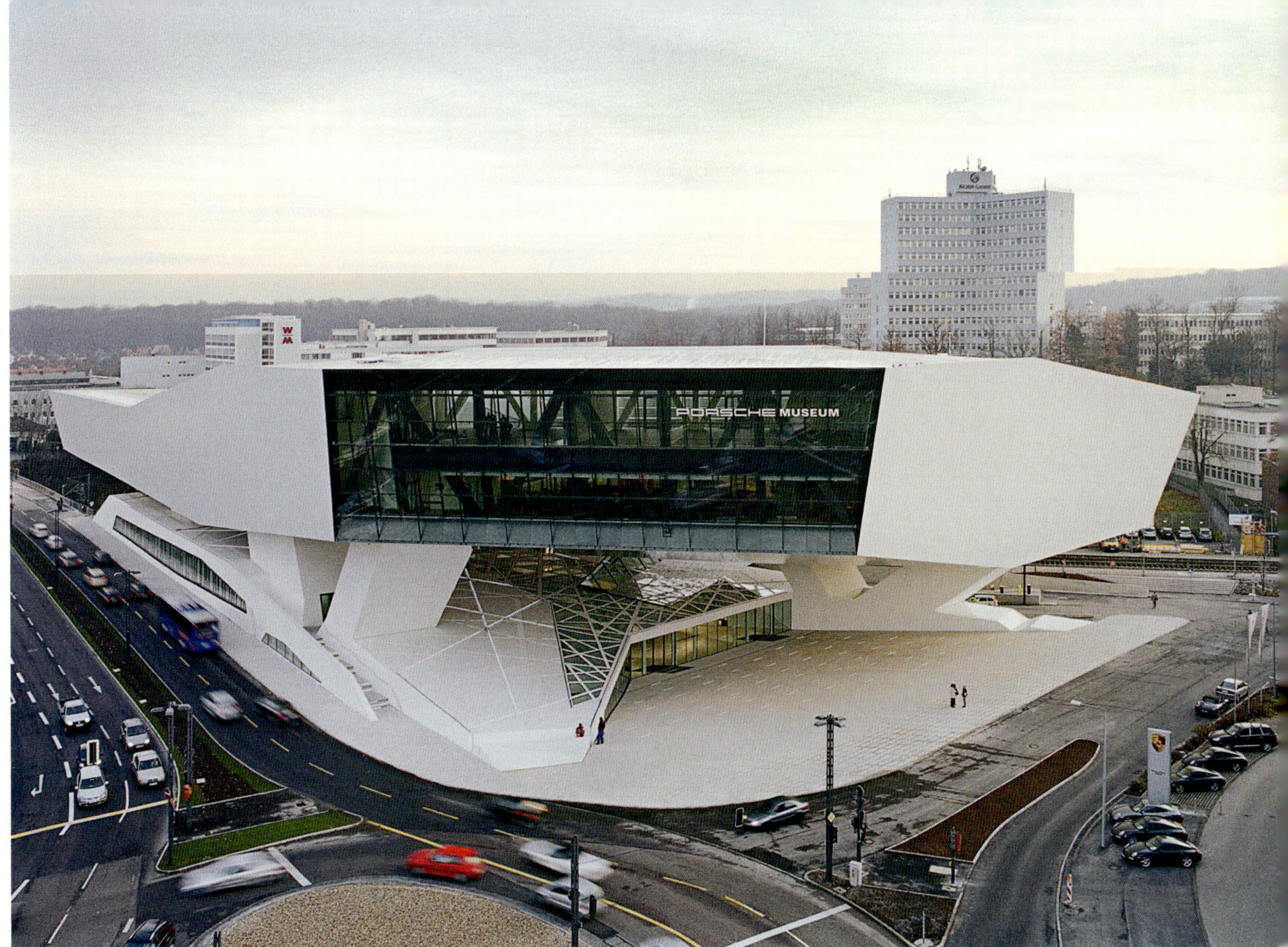

Beeindruckendes Zeichen zwischen Bahntrasse und Autobahnzubringer
An impressive emblem rising up between railway tracks and a feeder road

Im Februar 2005 erhielt der Entwurf der Wiener Architekten Delugan Meissl den ersten Preis im Wettbewerb für den Neubau eines Porsche Museums in Stuttgart. Es ehrt den Bauherrn, dass er das absehbare Risiko nicht gescheut hat, den Siegerentwurf zu verwirklichen. Zwar war man sich sicher darüber im Klaren, dass man mit ihm ein beeindruckendes Zeichen würde setzen können. Doch der Bau hat den Bauherrn, die Architekten sowie die Ausstellungsgestalter vom Büro HG Merz viel Schweiß gekostet und den Tragwerksplanern Leonhardt, Andrä und Partner alles abverlangt. Eigens ein neues Computerprogramm zur Lastenberechnung musste entwickelt werden. Aus 12 000 unterschiedlich geformten Stahlträgern besteht die Konstruktion, dank derer etwa 80 Porsche-Modelle in einem bis zu 60 Meter spannenden, stützenfreien, hohen Saal auf mehreren Ebenen gezeigt werden können. Der Kraftakt ist dem Gebäude anzusehen.

Das Museum ist aber nicht nur ein tragwerksplanerisches Experiment, sondern in erster Linie ein architektonisches. Der Ort und die Aufgabe konnten dafür kaum geeigneter sein. Errichtet wurde das Museum in einem Industriegebiet, an einem viel befahrenen Autobahnzubringer, zwischen einer Bahntrasse, Industriehallen, Verwaltungsgebäuden und einem Kundenzentrum. Hier war keine Stadtbaukunst gefragt.

In February 2005, the design proposal by Viennese architects Delugan Meissl won first prize in the competition for a new Porsche Museum in Stuttgart. It is to the credit of the clients that they did not shy away from the foreseeable risk involved in actually executing the winning proposal. Of course they could be certain of sending a resounding signal with such an imposing structure. But the building would demand plenty of blood, sweat and tears from the clients and the exhibition designers from HG Merz, and made the structural planners Leonhardt, Andrä and Partner give their all. A new computer program had to be developed specially to calculate the loads. Thanks to the 12,000 variously shaped steel girders that make up the structure, some 80 Porsche models can be displayed on several levels in a soaring space reaching across several storeys and spanning as much as 60 metres. The building betrays the effort that went into achieving this tour de force.

But the museum is more than just an experiment in structural planning; it is first and foremost an architectural feat. Its location and task could hardly

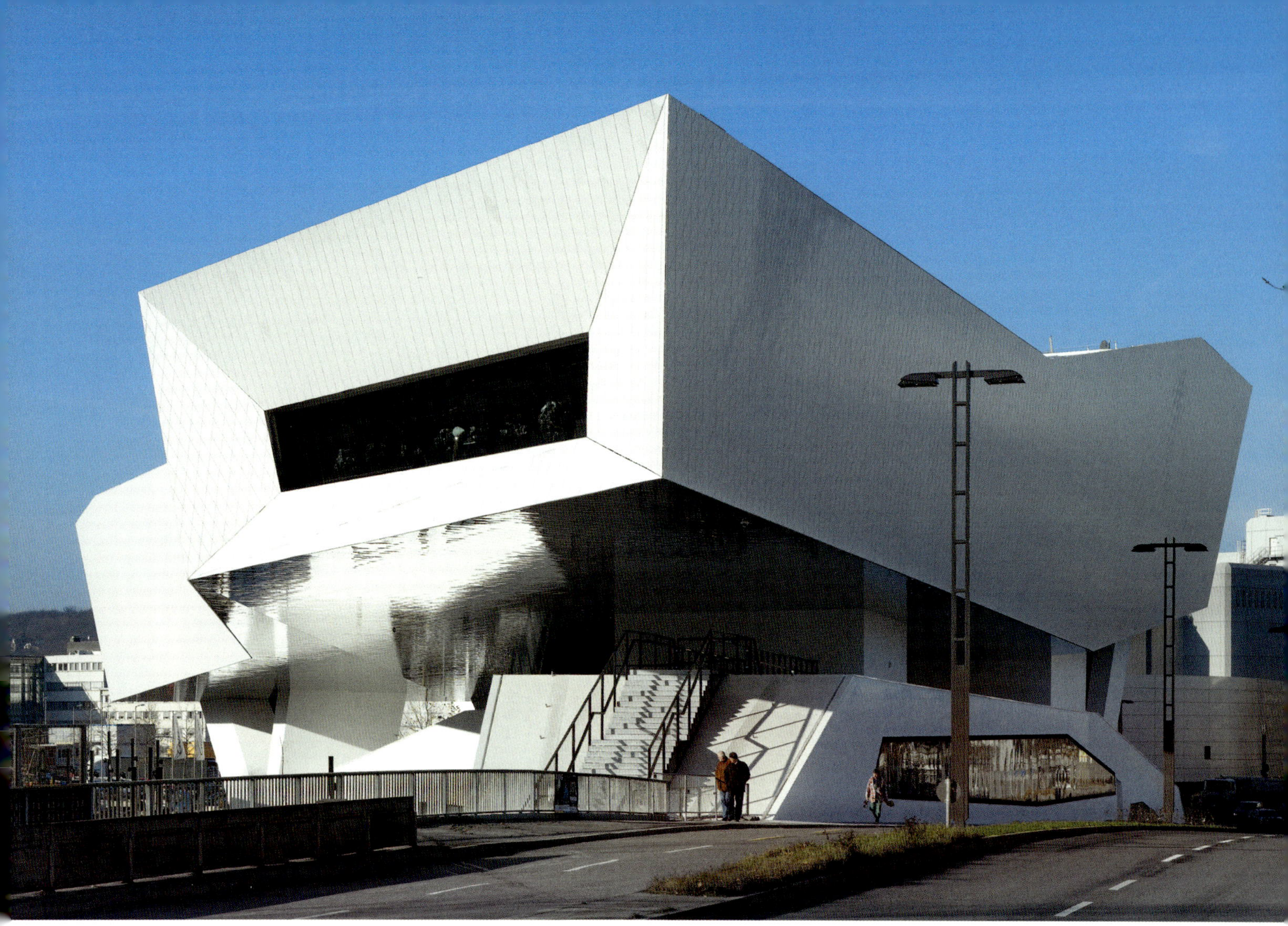

Fassadenansicht Südost | View of southeast façade

Nun wird dieser Ort von dem kraftvollen Neubau geprägt. Das Museum ist in einen Sockel und einen Ausstellungskörper zweigeteilt. Der Sockel nimmt das Foyer, einen Museumsshop, eine Cafeteria, eine Museumswerkstatt, das Archiv und Büroräume auf. Aus diesem Sockel ragen drei mächtige Betonkerne, die den aufgeständerten Ausstellungskörper mit Nobelrestaurant und Konferenzsaal tragen. Die unregelmäßige Gebäudeform ist in weiß beschichtete Metalltafeln gehüllt und an der Unterseite mit glänzenden Metalltafeln verspiegelt. Die polygonale Geometrie, mit der sich der Bau dem etwa dreieckförmigen Grundstück anpasst, lässt sich nicht leicht über einen Vergleich bestimmen, so dass man weiß, wovon die Rede ist. Dieses Haus soll auch nicht einfach mit anderen verglichen werden können, es soll für sich stehen. In dieser Hinsicht trifft es die Erwartungen des Besuchers.

Wer dieses Museum besucht, erwartet Außergewöhnliches. Das Foyer ist vergleichsweise klein, über eine lange Treppe oder eine Rolltreppe kommt der Besucher in eine eigene Welt, einer abgehobenen im wörtlichen Sinne. Der Ausstellungsraum ist bis auf

be better suited for this venture. The museum was built in an industrial area bordered by a busy motorway feeder and set between railway tracks, production facilities, office buildings and a customer centre. Urban architecture was not what was called for here.

Now this location has been given a powerful new landmark. The museum is divided into a plinth and an exhibition area above. The plinth holds the foyer, a museum shop, cafeteria, museum workshop, the archive and offices. Three massive concrete cores rise from this base, supporting the exhibition block with its exclusive restaurant and conference facilities. The irregular outer form of this block is clad in white-coated metal plates and on the underside with shiny, reflective metal panels. The polygonal geometry with which the building conforms to its more or less triangular plot is hard to describe by comparison in a way that makes clear what is

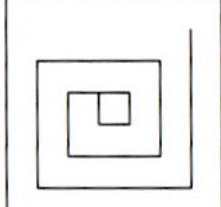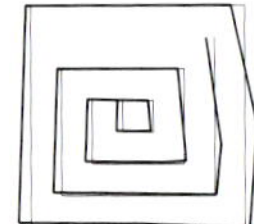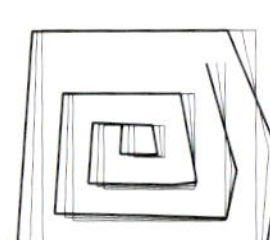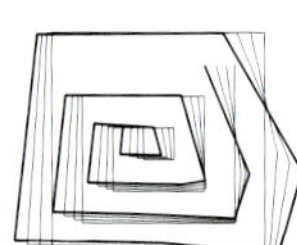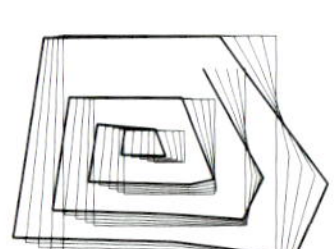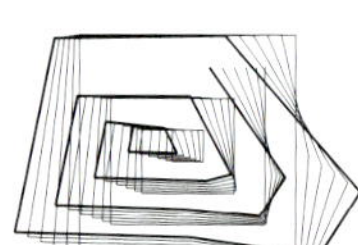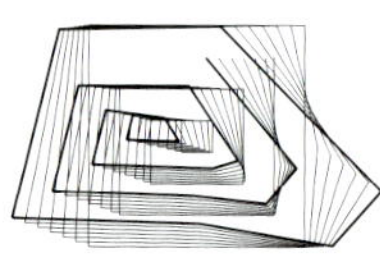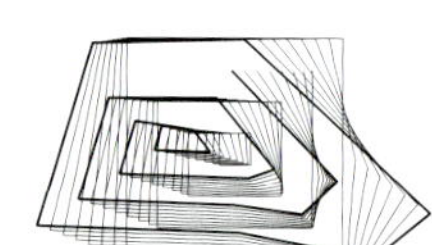

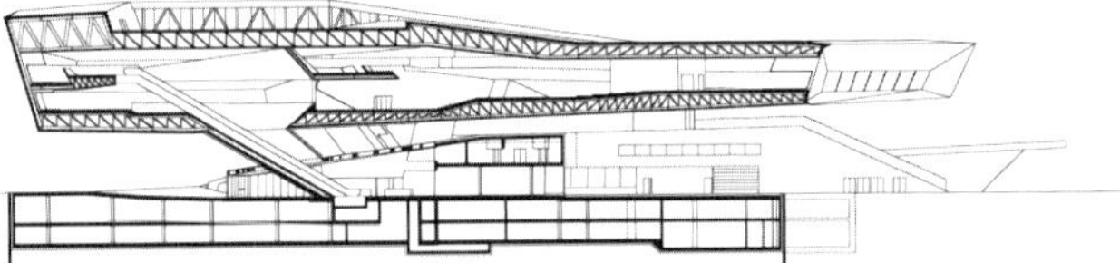

Schnitt | Section

eine Ausnahme fensterlos. Die Ausstellungsgestalter von HG Merz inszenieren geschickt zurückhaltend die Konzentration auf das Exponat. Der 5600 Quadratmeter große Ausstellungsraum besteht aus einer komplexen Struktur aus Flächen, Treppen und Rampen, die sich zu einem die Form des Raumes in der Art einer Spirale nachzeichnenden Parcours verbinden. Trotzdem dominiert der Raumeindruck nicht über die Exponate; die Raumkonzeption lässt dem Besucher viele Wege, auf denen er sich den Exponaten nähern kann. Lediglich entlang der Außenwände stehen die Fahrzeuge in einer schwarzen Fuge, sonst ist der Raum fast durchgehend in Weiß gehalten, so konsequent, dass sich die räumlichen Qualitäten des komplexen Innenraums nicht einfach erschließen.

Mit dieser Inszenierung im Museum wird die Marke als Statussymbol überhöht und ein weiterer Schritt vollzogen, der das Fahrzeug in Distanz zu seiner Funktion setzt: Man kauft sich einen Porsche nicht, weil man mit ihm am besten von A nach B kommt. Es gilt schon lange als Statussymbol, einen Porsche zu haben, der nicht erst zu einem wird, wenn man ihn fährt. Das ist nicht neu, aber die zeitlichen Bezügen enthobene Musealisierung ist ein weiterer Schritt zur Stilisierung der Marke. Dass die Marke damit demonstrativ vom Alltag getrennt wird, heißt aber auch, dass das im Museum Aufbewahrte für die zukünftige Mobilität nicht mehr beispielgebend sein muss. Das Zeichen, das die Architektur setzt, ist insofern Teil dieser Inszenierung, als sie das Einzigartige und Außergewöhnliche zum Ausdruck bringt, das mit der Marke assoziiert werden soll. Delugan Meissl nutzen diese Aufgabe für eine unter anderen Umständen nur schwer zu rechtfertigende Architektur und schufen ein Gebäude, das sich der Bewertung durch ein gängiges System verbindlicher Wertmaßstäbe entzieht – und darin ist es mehr als ein Zeichen. Dies ist aus heutiger Sicht die herausragende Qualität des Museums: Seine Räume und seine Präsenz, die Schwierigkeit, es einzuordnen, zwingt dazu, zu fragen, ob gängige Wertmaßstäbe noch richtig sind, ob nicht Potenziale der Architektur blockiert werden, wenn sie sich einordnen lassen soll. Noch gibt es daher auch keine Antwort auf die Frage, ob der Aufwand und das Ergebnis im richtigen Verhältnis zueinander stehen. Das wird erst in der Zukunft bewertet werden können.

meant. This is a building that is not meant to be simply compared with others – it is meant to stand in a class of its own. In this respect it certainly fulfils visitors' expectations.

Those who come to see this museum want to experience something extraordinary. The foyer is relatively small, but when visitors ascend via a long stairway or escalator, they enter a whole new world, one that is lofty in every sense of the word. The exhibition area is closed off from outside, except for one window. The low-key exhibition concept designed by HG Merz skilfully keeps the focus on the exhibits themselves. The 5,600-square-metre exhibition space consists of a complex structure of planes, stairs and ramps, with visitors following a spiral course through the exhibits that echoes the shape of the space. Nevertheless, the spatial impression is never allowed to dominate the exhibits, but leaves the visitor several options for approaching the pieces on view. Except for a black seam on which the cars along the outer walls are lined up, the room is almost completely white – so consistently in fact that the spatial qualities of the complex interior are not readily discernible.

This stage-setting in a museum has the effect of elevating the brand to even more of a status symbol – a further step in distancing the automobile from its actual function. After all, no one buys a Porsche to get from A to B. Owning a Porsche has long since become a sign of prestige – without even having to take it out on the road. This is nothing new, but removing the brand from a temporal context by placing it in a museum goes even further toward stylising it. Demonstratively separating cars from everyday life like this also means that the items stored in the museum no longer have to set a pioneering example for the mobility of the future. The mark made by the architecture is part of this whole dramatisation, lending expression to the unique and exceptional qualities that are to be associated with the brand. Delugan Meissl seized the opportunity to present an architecture that under other circumstances would be hard to justify, creating a building that defies judgement by any customary system of binding values – and in these terms it is more than just a symbol. This, from today's standpoint, is the outstanding quality of the museum: its spaces and its presence, the difficulty of categorising it, force us to ask if the conventional standards are still appropriate, or if the potential of architecture is not stifled when we try to pin it down. There is still no answer to the question of whether the effort and expense that went into this building are proportionate to the results. Only time will tell.

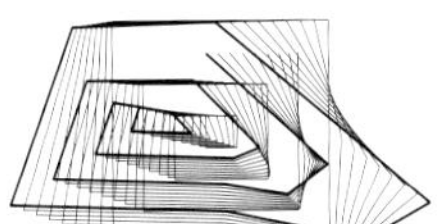
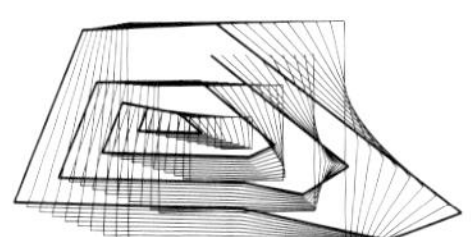
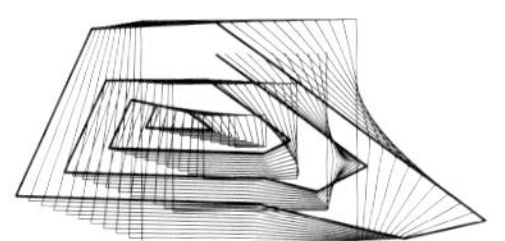
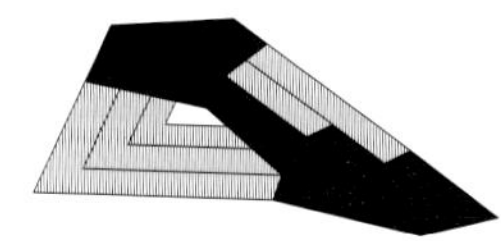

Die Spirale als Ordnungsparameter für das Raumvolumen | The spiral as ordering parameter for the room volume

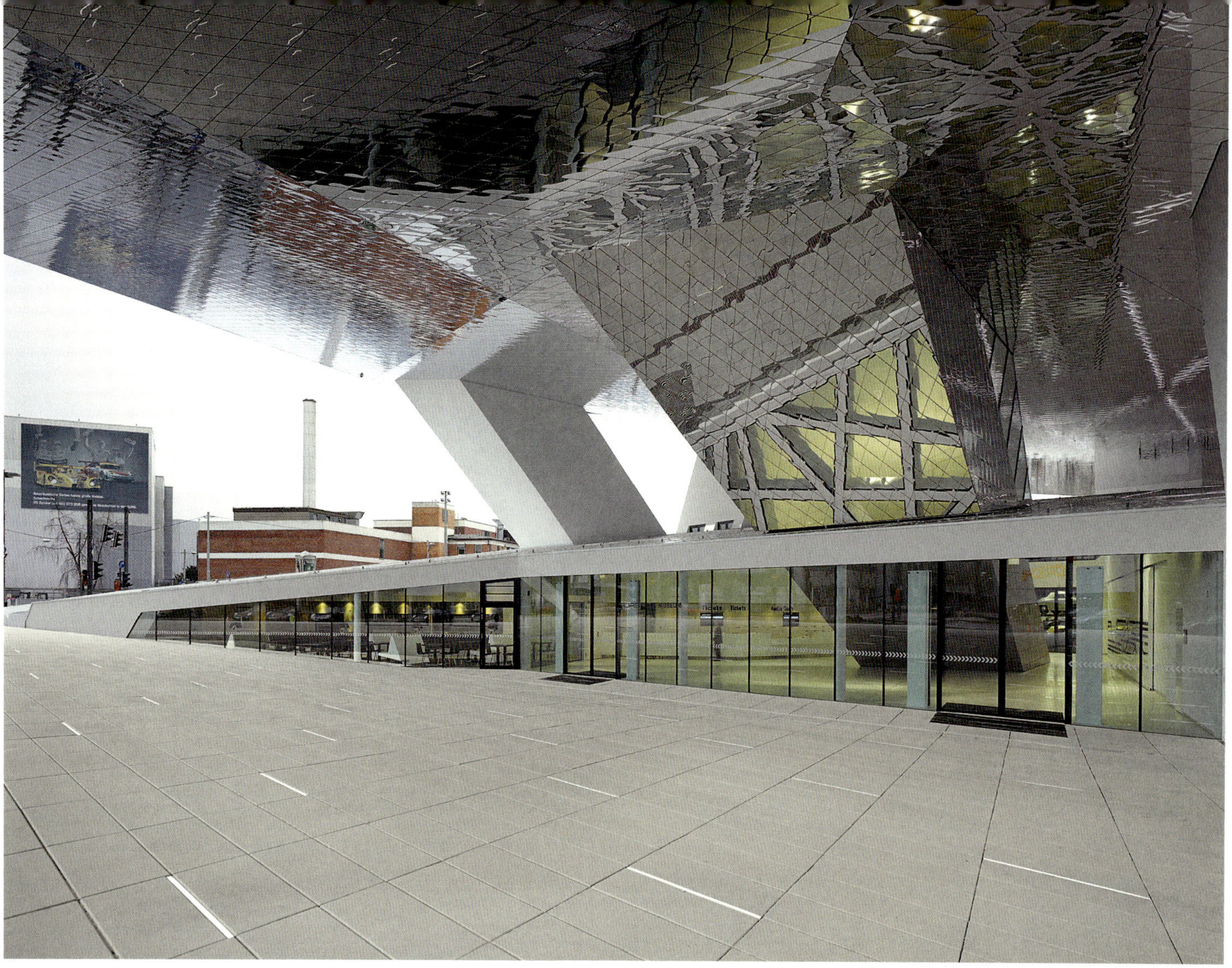

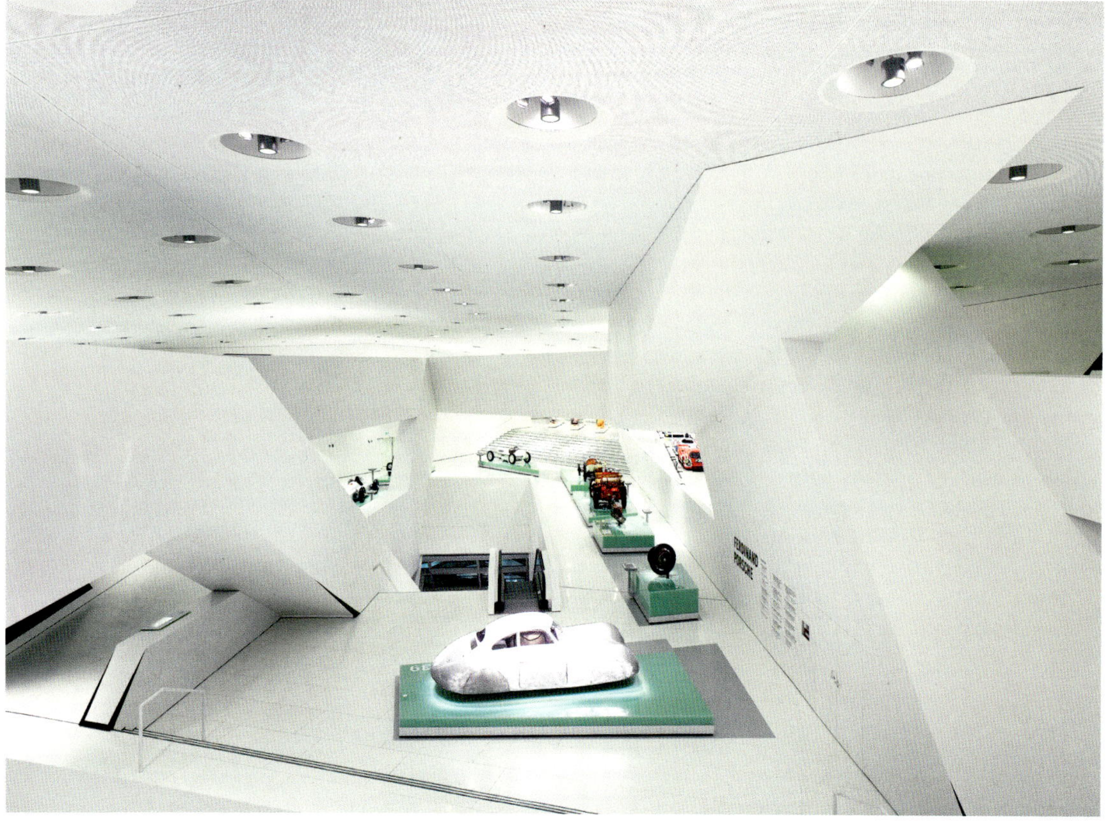

Eingangsbereich | Entrance area

Ausstellung | Exhibition

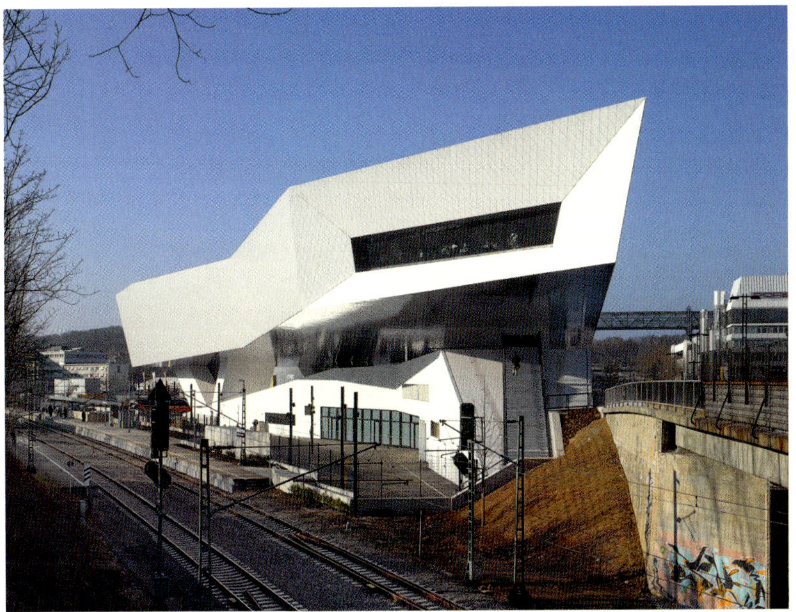

Fassadenansicht von den Gleisen | View of façade from the tracks

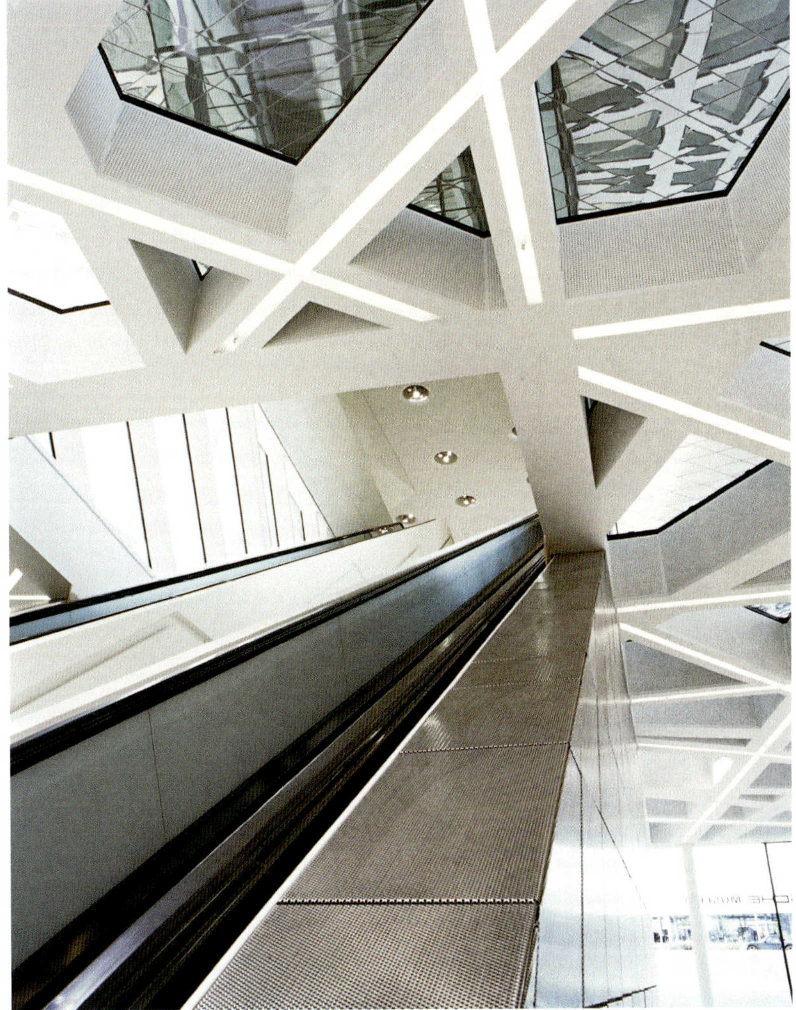

Foyer | Foyer

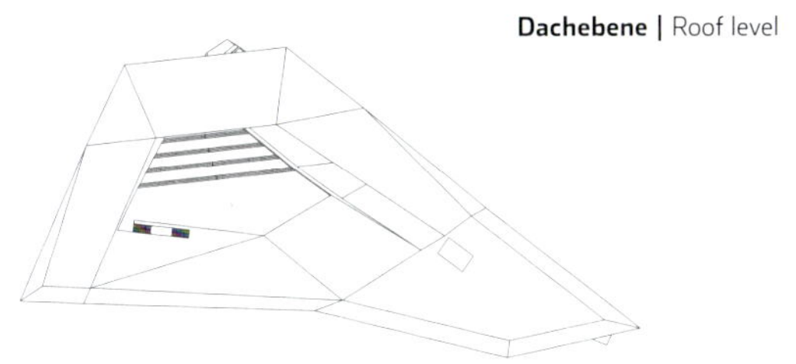

Dachebene | Roof level

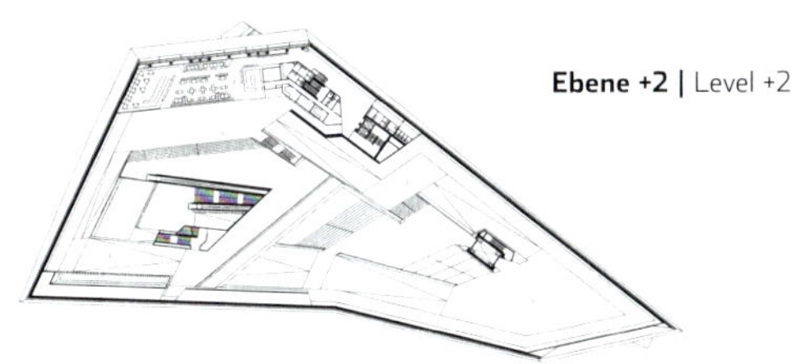

Ebene +3 | Level +3

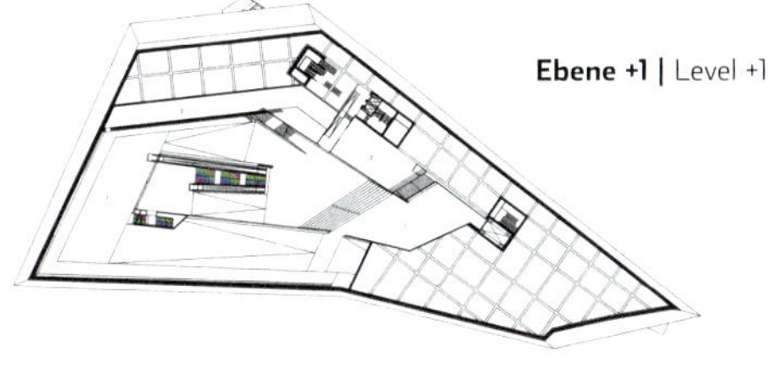

Ebene +2 | Level +2

Ebene +1 | Level +1

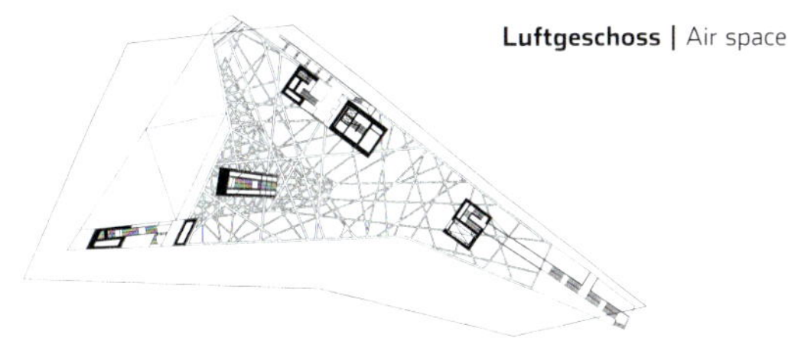

Luftgeschoss | Air space

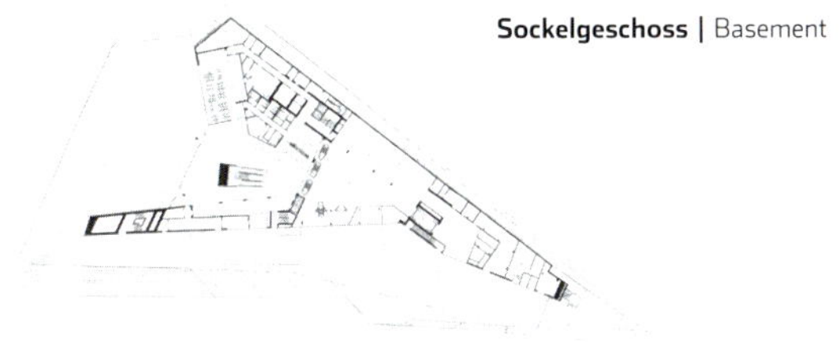

Sockelgeschoss | Basement

ARCHITEKT | ARCHITECT

DIETHELM & SPILLMANN

GEBÄUDE | BUILDING

FRANZ MARC MUSEUM ERWEITERUNG

TEXT SEBASTIAN TOKARZ

09

ARCHITEKTEN | ARCHITECTS

Diethelm & Spillmann
Räffelstrasse 11
8045 Zürich | Zurich
Schweiz | Switzerland
www.dsarch.ch

MITARBEITER | TEAM

Carsten Liewald, Katrin Pohl

BAUHERR | CLIENT

Stiftung Etta und Otto Stangl,
Freiburg im Breisgau

TRAGWERK | STRUCTURE

Ingenieurbüro Klaus Pache,
Dachau

LANDSCHAFTSARCHITEKTEN
LANDSCAPE ARCHITECTS

Mühlbacher und Hilse,
Traunstein

FERTIGSTELLUNG | COMPLETION

2008

STANDORT | LOCATION

Franz Marc Park 8–10
82431 Kochel am See
www.franz-marc-museum.de

FOTOS | PHOTOS

Roger Frei

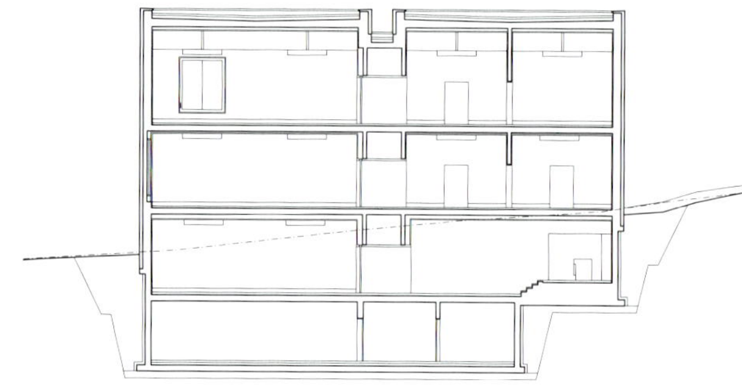

Schnitt | Section

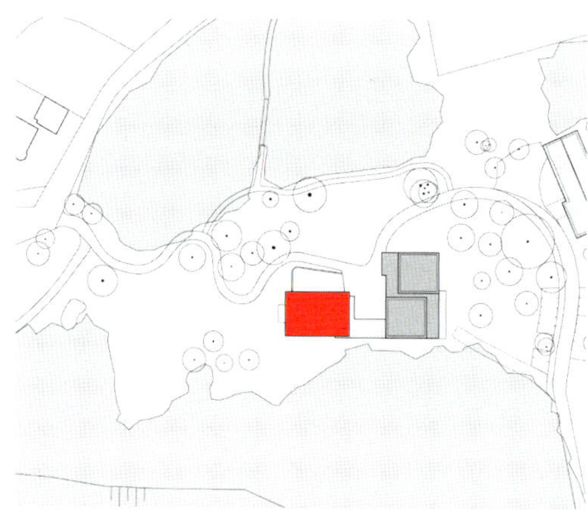

Lageplan | Site plan

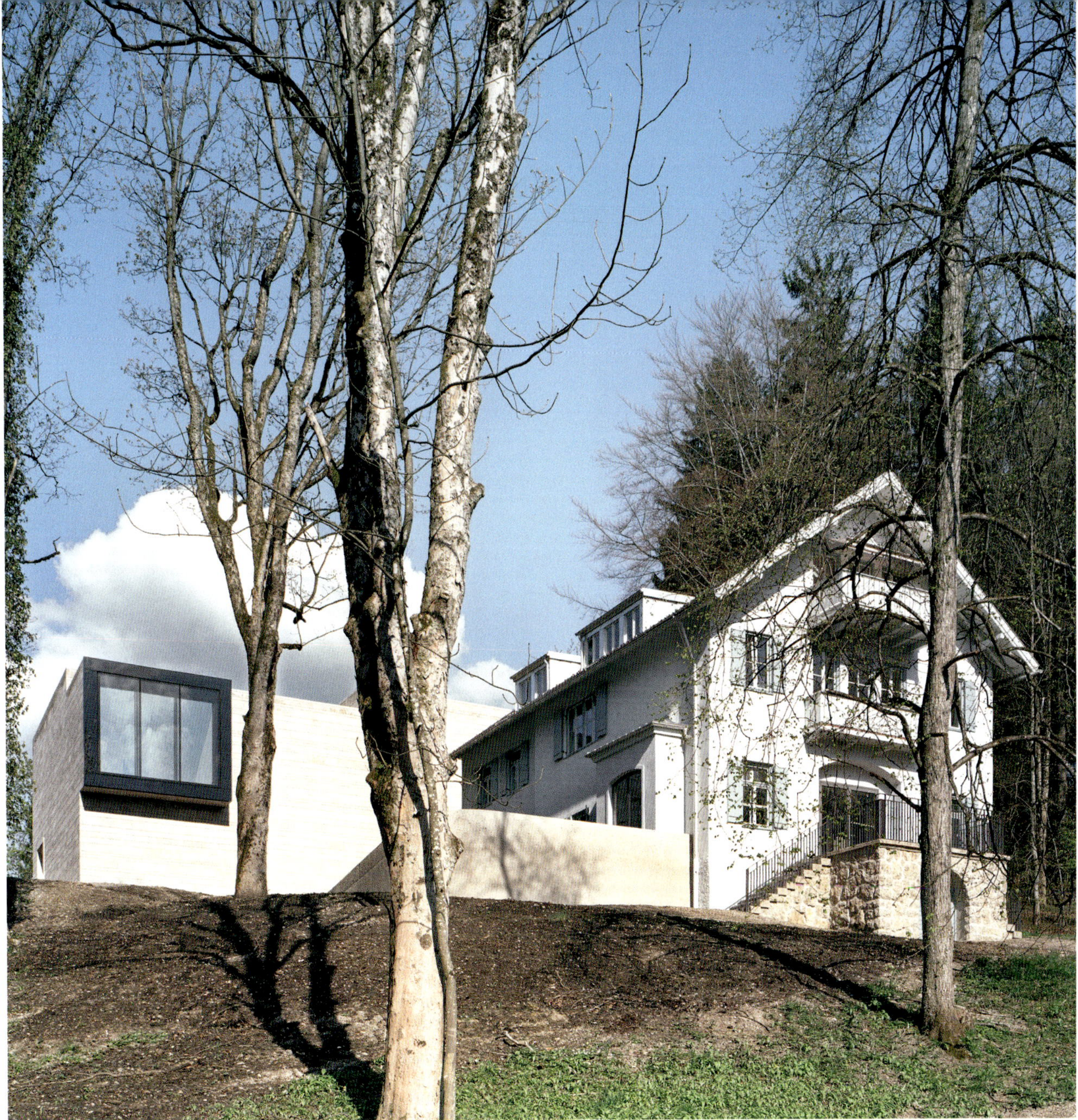

Harmonischer Kontrast von Alt und Neu | Harmonious contrast between old and new

Der Landschaft um Kochel war Franz Marc zeitlebens besonders verbunden. Dieses „Blaue Land" zwischen Kochel, Murnau und Sindeldorf war Ausgangspunkt und Inspirationsquelle seiner Kunst.

Das Franz Marc Museum wurde 1986 in einer Fabrikantenvilla oberhalb des Kochelsees gegründet. 20 Jahre nach seiner Eröffnung sollte es durch einen Neubau erweitert werden, der es erlaubt, neben den Arbeiten von Franz Marc zukünftig auch dessen Einfluss auf die Weiterentwicklung der modernen Kunst in der Nachfolge des „Blauen Reiters" zu präsentieren. Aus einem mehrstufigen Wettbewerb im Jahr 2005 ging das junge Züricher Büro Diethelm & Spillmann als Sieger hervor. Die Architekten stellten der bestehenden Villa einen schlichten, dreigeschossigen Kubus zur Seite, der sämtliche Ausstellungs-

Throughout his brief life, Franz Marc felt a special connection to the landscape surrounding Kochel. This "Blue Land" between Kochel, Murnau and Sindeldorf was the wellspring and source of inspiration for his art.

In 1986, the Franz Marc Museum was established in an industrialist's villa overlooking Lake Kochel (Kochelsee). Twenty years after its foundation, a new building was planned as an extension, allowing not only the presentation of Marc's works, but also the exploration of his influence on subsequent generations of modern artists in the wake of the Blauer Reiter (Blue Rider) group. The young Zurich architectural office Diethelm & Spillmann emerged

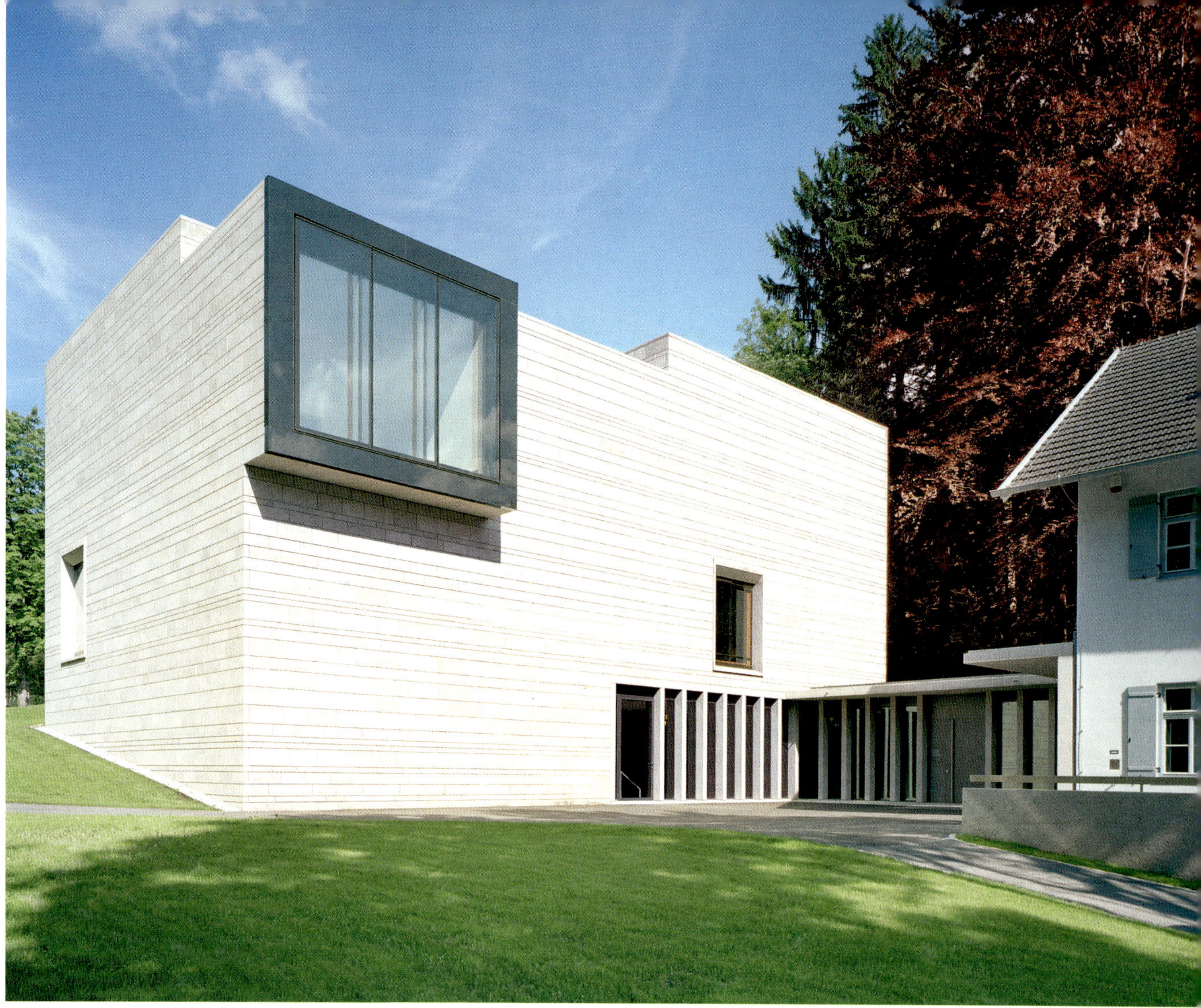

Der Museumsbau verzichtet auf alpenländische Klischees.
The museum building foregoes any Alpine clichés.

und Archivräume aufnimmt. Geschickt nutzten sie die Hanglage des parkähnlichen Grundstücks aus: Das neue Ausstellungsgebäude fängt das abschüssige Gelände ab und schafft zur alten Villa hin einen ebenen Eingangshof, von dem aus das Museum über einen eingeschossigen Verbindungstrakt zugänglich ist. Restaurant, Verwaltung, museumspädagogische Räume sowie die Dienstwohnung des geschäftsführenden Direktors sind nun im behutsam sanierten Altbau untergebracht. Die innere Raumstruktur des neuen Museumsbaus mit 700 Quadratmetern Ausstellungsfläche ist klar und einfach: Treppenaufgang und Aufzug teilen den rechteckigen Grundriss in zwei gegeneinander verschobene quadratische Ausstellungssäle. An diese gliedern sich jeweils kleinere, farblich akzentuierte Kabinette an. Dieses Grundrissschema wird auf den jeweiligen Ebenen geschickt variiert. Die unterschiedlich proportionierten Räume sind in ihrer Größe und Höhe auf die ausgestellten Arbeiten abgestimmt. Die Raumabfolge endet im zweiten Obergeschoss in einem kleinen Raum ohne Exponate, der durch ein auskragendes, raumhohes Panoramafenster einen grandiosen Blick

victorious from a multi-stage competition held in 2005. Next to the existing villa, the architects placed a three-storey cube which holds all exhibition galleries and archives. They skilfully exploit the hillside setting of the park-like site, with the new exhibition building interrupting the sloping ground to create a flat entrance courtyard between itself and the old villa from which the museum can be accessed via a single-storey connecting tract. A restaurant, offices and museum education rooms as well as an apartment for the managing director are now accommodated in the carefully restored villa. The interior layout of the new museum building with its 700 square metres of exhibition space is clear and simple: the staircase and elevator divide the rectangular floor plan into two axially displaced square galleries. From these, smaller chambers lead off, highlighted in different colours. This floor plan is varied cleverly on the different levels, and the size

über den See auf die eindrucksvolle Bergsilhouette eröffnet. Vier großformatige Fenster in den Ausstellungsebenen bieten ebenfalls einen Ausblick in die Landschaft des Voralpenlandes und inszenieren somit den für die Kunst Franz Marcs wesentlichen Dialog zwischen Kunst und Natur.

Der strenge Museumsbau verzichtet mit seiner weitgehend geschlossenen, horizontal gegliederten Natursteinfassade aus Crailsheimer Muschelkalk auf jegliche Anbiederung an alpenländische Klischees. Der bis zu 13 Meter hohe schlichte Kubus behauptet sich mit seiner Formensprache neben dem ehemaligen Haupthaus, welches mit seinem weit auskragenden Satteldach, den Fensterläden und den hell verputzten Fassadenflächen noch ganz dem Bild einer Jahrhundertwende-Villa entspricht.

In Analogie zur künstlerischen Entwicklung Franz Marcs von einer naturalistischen hin zu einer abstrakten Formensprache schufen die Architekten zur traditionell-ländlichen Villa hoch über dem Kochelsee ein modernes Gegenüber als adäquaten Ort, um das künstlerische Schaffen des Wegbereiters der Moderne zu zeigen.

and height of the variously proportioned rooms are adapted to fit the works on display. The sequence of rooms ends on the second floor in a small room without exhibits featuring a protruding, floor-to-ceiling panoramic window opening up a magnificent vista over the lake toward a majestic Alpine silhouette. Four large windows on the exhibition levels likewise offer views of the Alpine foothills, thus staging the dialogue between art and nature that is so important to Marc's work.

The rigorous museum building with its largely closed, horizontally articulated façade of natural shell limestone does not pander to typical Alpine clichés. The sleek 13-metre-high rectilinear structure relies instead on its own formal vocabulary to stand its ground next to the former museum, which with its projecting saddle roof, window shutters and light-coloured stucco façade is the very picture of a turn-of-the-century villa.

In analogy to Franz Marc's artistic development from a naturalistic to a more abstract formal language, the architects have created a modern counterpart to the traditional country villa set high over Lake Kochel – and an ideal place to exhibit the artistic oeuvre of this pioneer of Modernism.

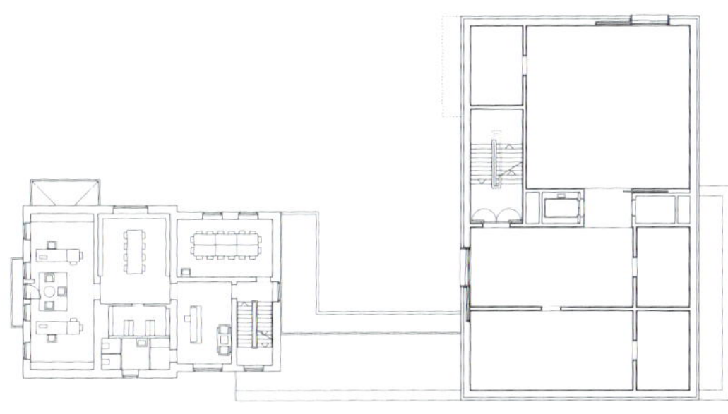

Grundriss Obergeschoss | Floor plan of upper level

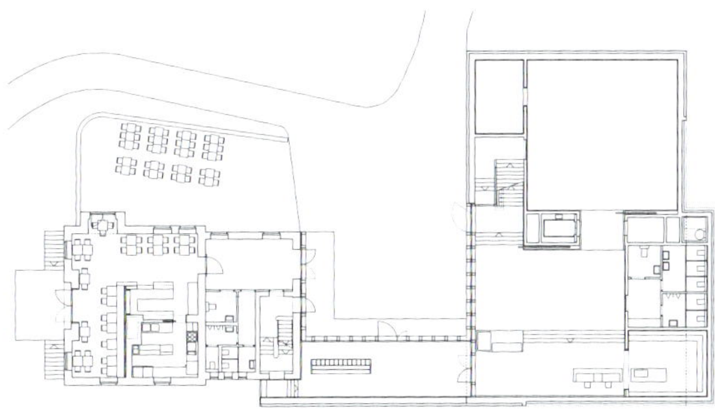

Grundriss Erdgeschoss | Floor plan of ground floor

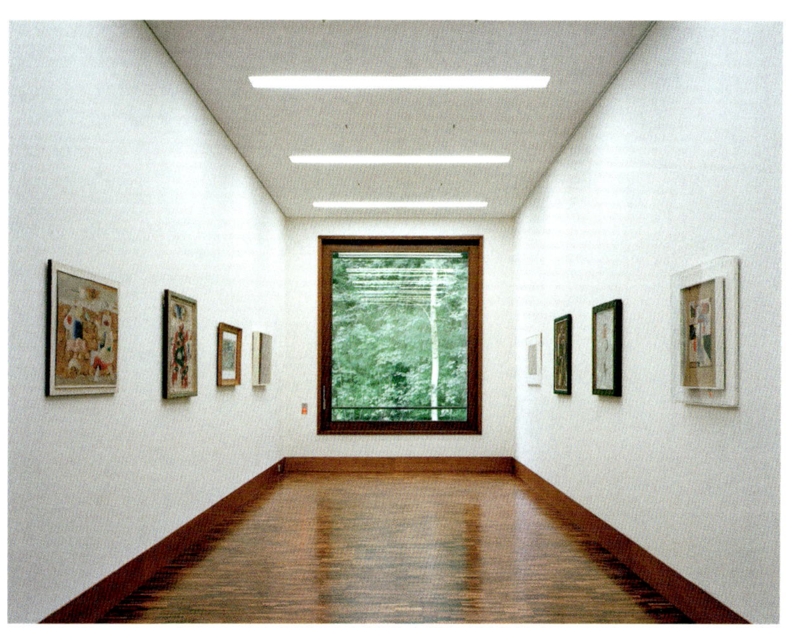

Ausstellungsraum im Dialog mit der Landschaft
Exhibition space in dialogue with the landscape

FERDINAND HEIDE

HÖRSAALZENTRUM CASINOANBAU

TEXT ANNA SCHEUERMANN

10

ARCHITEKTEN | ARCHITECTS

Ferdinand Heide Architekt BDA
Leinwebergasse 4
60386 Frankfurt am Main
www.ferdinand-heide.de

IN ARGE MIT
JOINT VENTURE WITH

Ebert-Ingenieure GmbH & Co. KG,
Niederlassung Nürnberg
(Haustechnik | M&E Engineers)

MITARBEITER | TEAM

Heinrich Großenbach, Christian
Schmitt, Holger Kostmann,
Jessica Gerlach, Frank Heinen,
Heike Kimmig, Tino Koch,
Stefan Kolb, Kaja Kröger,
Dominica Sander, Natalia
Sevillano, Thomas Voss,
Isabell Walter

BAUHERR | CLIENT

Goethe-Universität
Frankfurt am Main
vertreten durch
Hessisches Baumanagement
Regionalniederlassung Rhein-Main
Campus Westend

TRAGWERK | STRUCTURE

Sailer Stepan und Partner GmbH,
Beratende Ingenieure für
Bauwesen VBI, München
(Tragwerksplanung | structural
design, Hörsaalzentrum)

B + G Ingenieure
Bollinger und Grohmann GmbH,
Frankfurt (Tragwerksplanung
structural design, Anbau Casino)

LANDSCHAFTSARCHITEKTEN
LANDSCAPE ARCHITECTS

Topos Berlin / Ferdinand Heide

FERTIGSTELLUNG | COMPLETION

2008

AUSSENANLAGEN | GROUNDS

2014

STANDORT | LOCATION

Campus Westend
Grüneburgplatz 1
60323 Frankfurt am Main

FOTOS | PHOTOS

Barbara Staubach, Frank Heinen

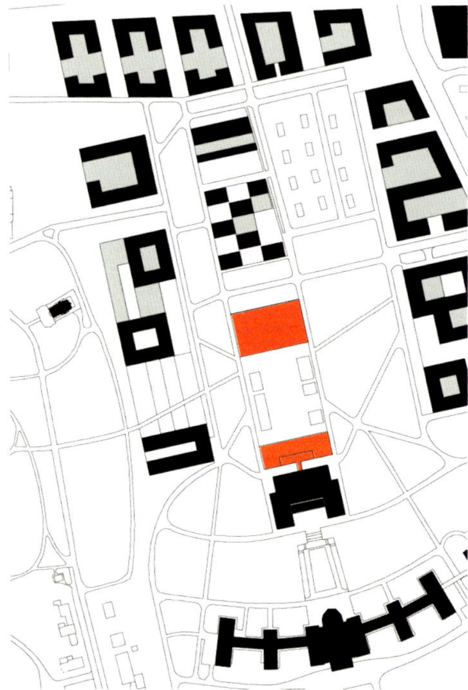

Lageplan | Site plan

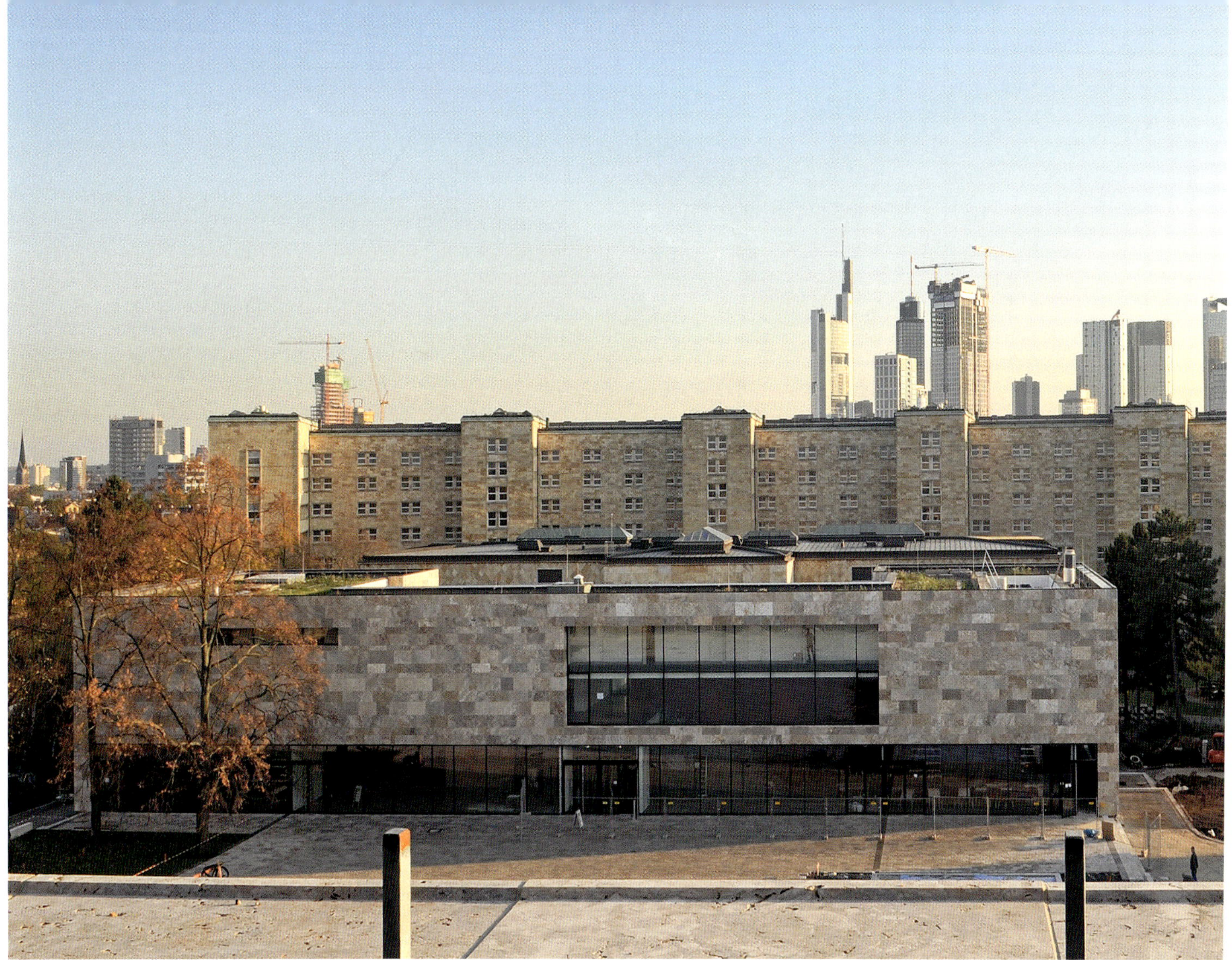

Auf einer Achse: Poelzigs ehemaliges IG Farben-Hochhaus und der Anbau des Casinos
Lined up on an axis: Poelzig's former IG Farben high rise and the dining hall extension

Die noch junge Geschichte des „Campus Westend" begann im Jahr 2001 mit dem Umzug der geisteswissenschaftlichen Fakultäten der Goethe-Universität von dem Stammsitz an der Senckenberganlage im Stadtteil Bockenheim in das IG Farben-Hochhaus im Frankfurter Westend, welches 1929 von Hans Poelzig als Verwaltungssitz für den IG Farben-Konzern errichtet wurde. Im darauf folgenden Jahr wurde ein offener städtebaulicher Wettbewerb für die Gestaltung eines modernen Campus für die Geistes-, Kultur- und Sozialwissenschaften mit insgesamt 25 000 Studenten auf dem 39 Hektar großen, leicht ansteigenden Areal ausgelobt, welches sich im Rücken des Hochhauses erstreckt. Als Sieger ging der Frankfurter Architekt Ferdinand Heide aus dem Rennen, dessen Master-plan bis 2014, dem 100. Geburtstag der Universität, in mehreren Abschnitten umgesetzt werden soll.

Der Poelzig-Bau als markanter Ausgangspunkt war für den weiteren Ausbau bestimmend: seine achsiale Anlage wurde in einem zentralen Band in der Breite des Casinos mit den öffentlichen Einrichtungen (im ersten Bauabschnitt: Anbau des Casinos, Hörsaalzentrum und Studentenwohnheim) fortgeführt. Zwei Grün-spangen mit Fakultätsgebäuden im Westen und Osten fassen das Gelände zum angrenzenden Grüneburgpark und der viel befahrenen Hansaallee ein. Als Gestalt prägend gab der Plan vor, dass die Fassaden der Gebäude passend zu dem Travertin des IG Farben-Hauses ausgeführt werden sollten, um einen dichten und urbanen Campus inmitten eines freizügigen parkähnlichen Areals zu bilden.

The still-young history of the Campus Westend began in 2001 with the relocation of the humanities departments of the University of Frankfurt am Main from their former premises at Senckenberganlage in the Bockenheim district to the old IG Farben high-rise, built as the company's headquarters in 1929 by Hans Poelzig in Frankfurt's Westend. The following year, a public urban planning competition was held for the design of a modern campus for 25,000 students of the humanities and cultural and social sciences on a 39-hectare, slightly sloping plot extending behind the highrise. The winner was Frankfurt architect Ferdinand Heide, whose master plan is to be realised in several stages by 2014, the university's 100th anniversary year.

Poelzig's building is a striking point of departure for new construction on the site: its axial layout was continued as a central band with the width of the campus restaurant to contain a number of public facilities (in the first building phase: a campus restaurant extension, lecture hall centre and student housing). Two swaths of green to the west and east

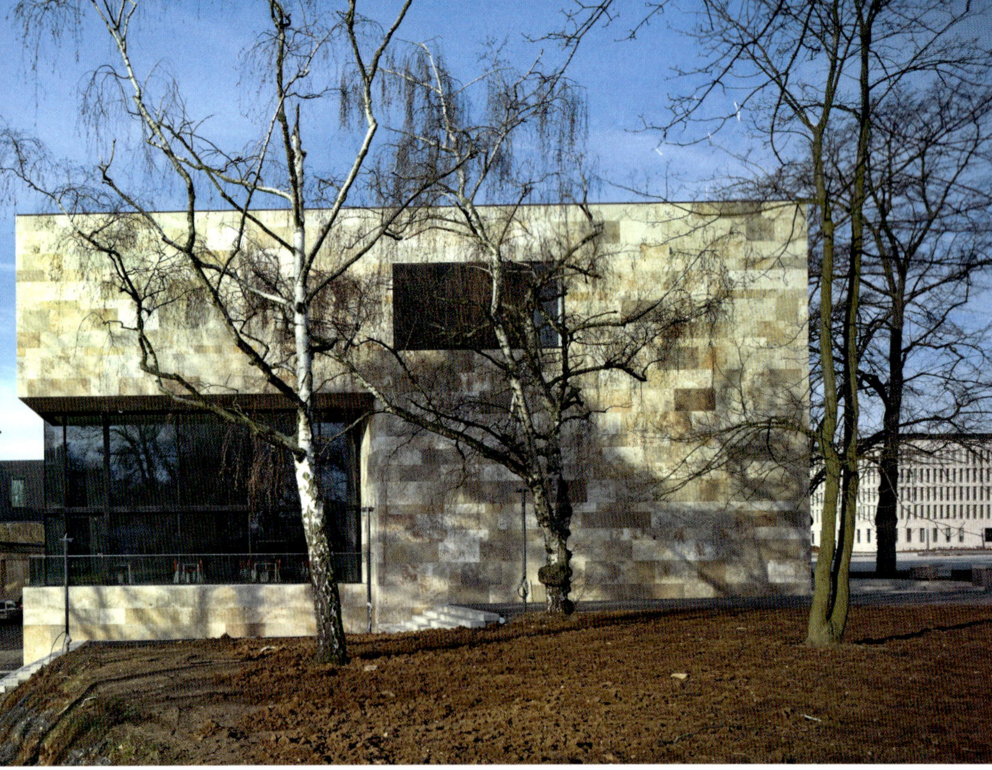

Casino-Anbau | Campus restaurant extension

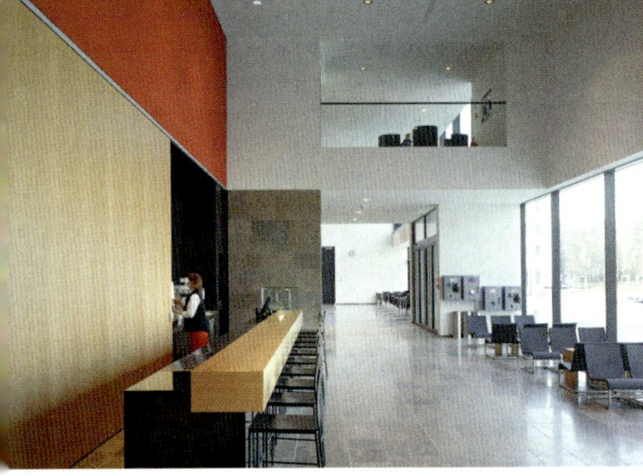

Mensa | Cafeteria

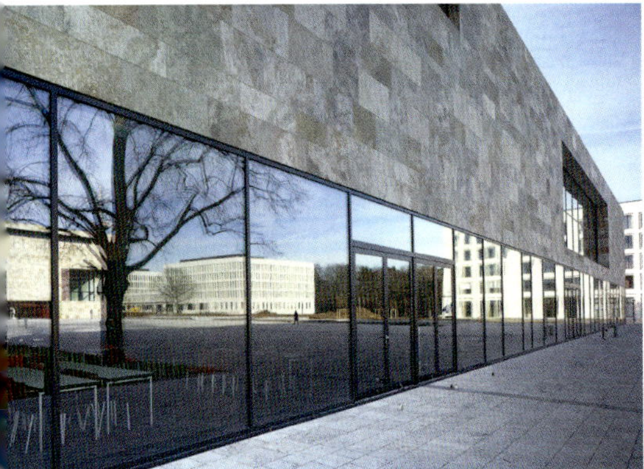

Spiegelungen | Reflections

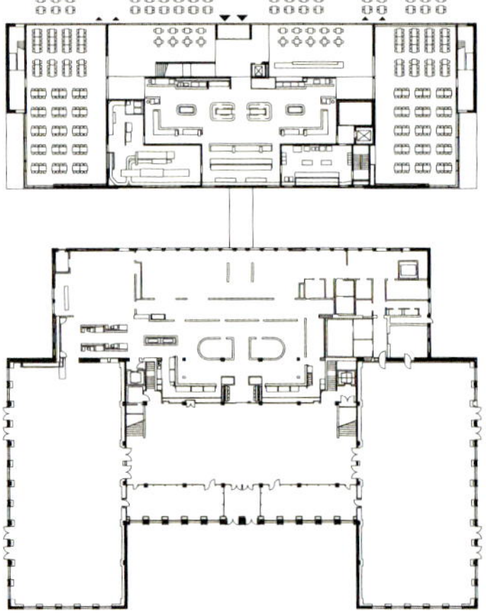

Erdgeschoss Anbau Casino
Ground floor of the dining hall extension

with buildings housing various university departments separate the grounds from adjacent Grüneburg Park and busy Hansaallee. The plan for the new structures specified that their façades must harmonise with the travertine of the IG Farben building in order to form a consolidated urban campus in the middle of wide-ranging, park-like grounds.

Ferdinand Heide also carried the day in the subsequent competitions for two buildings in the first construction phase: the lecture hall centre and the extension of the campus restaurant, with a campus square lying between. The architect was thus able to leave his signature on 'his' campus. The two new buildings front the large square, which has been conceived as a modern counterpart to an existing fountain located further down the slope. In addition to the fountain and various art objects, there is enough space here for outdoor dining, including a sophisticated theft prevention system for the weatherproof seating, as well as for various university events.

The lecture hall centre, which stands out due to its generous window openings and the large wedges cut out of the façade, will in future house large lecture halls that all departments can use for activities which they cannot accommodate in their own buildings. The idea is to create a communicative hub conducive to exchange between the different disciplines. The extremely attractive rooms with skyline views are also to be rented out for external events. Through the compact stacking of twelve different lecture halls – here the ascending parabolic form of the Audimax with its 1,200 seats is very impressive – and seminar rooms on five levels, a great deal of space has been freed up for a generous ground-floor foyer and an open staircase above it. The campus square seems to continue into the interior of the building on all levels, an impression enhanced by the uniform stone flooring outside and in. Unlike the ponderous, stiff new department buildings surrounding it, the lecture hall centre with its openness and daring use of strong colours on the interior, which in some cases shine through to the outside, has a personality of its own and a certain lightness, despite its enormous volume and heavy natural stone façade, a curtain wall of travertine panels.

The much smaller extension to the campus restaurant holds surprises in its contemporary pared-down form and individual choice of materials and colours for its surfaces, as well as its effective use

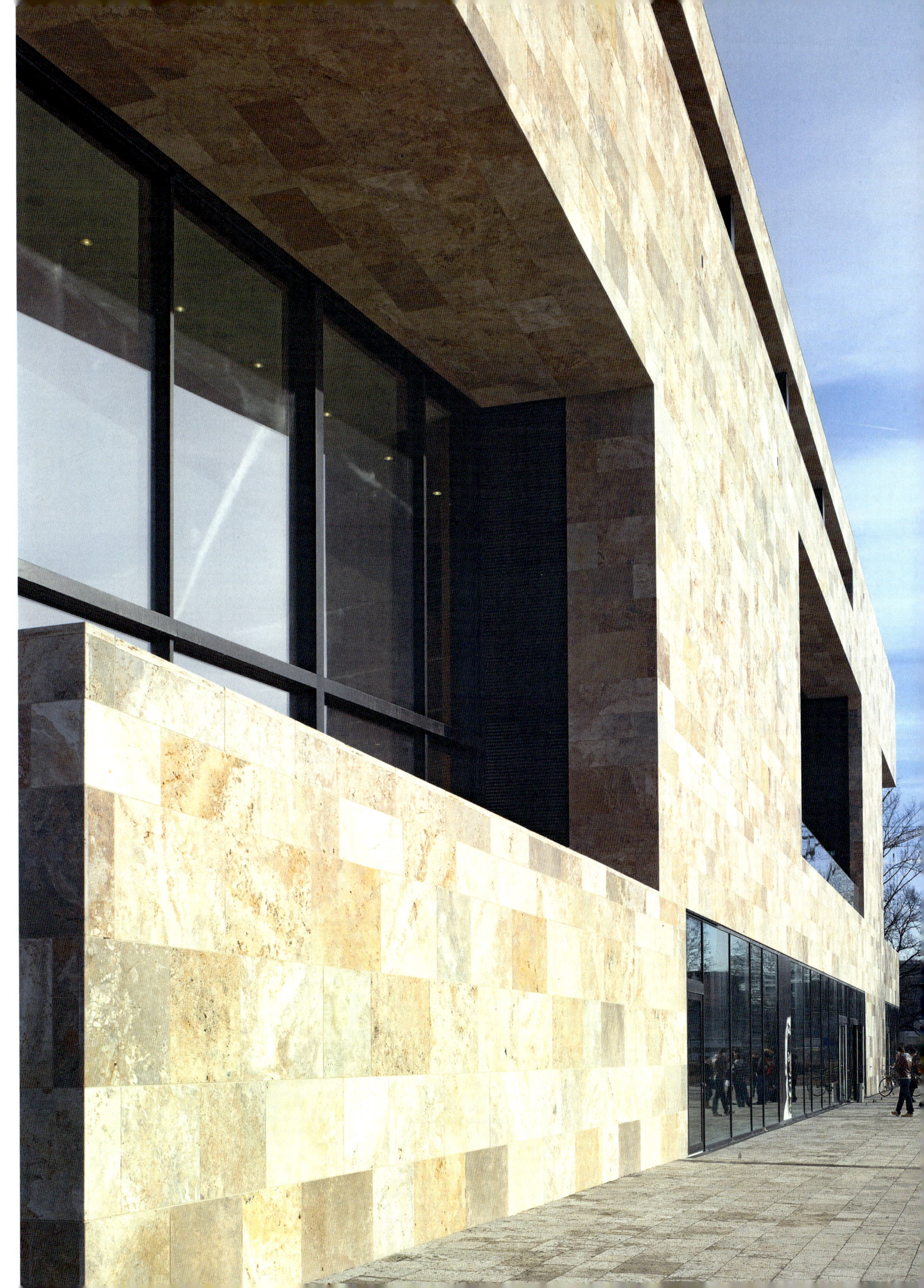

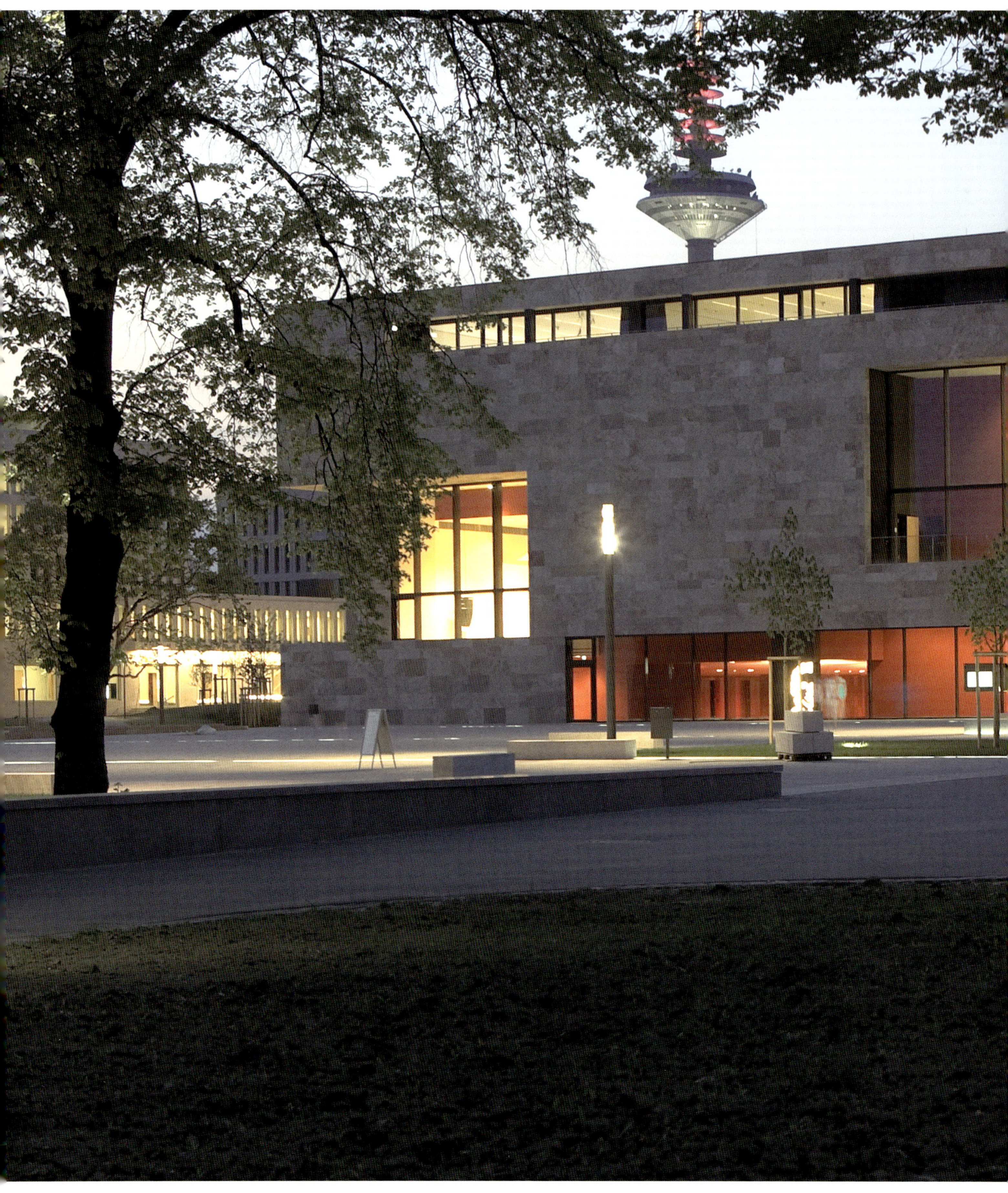

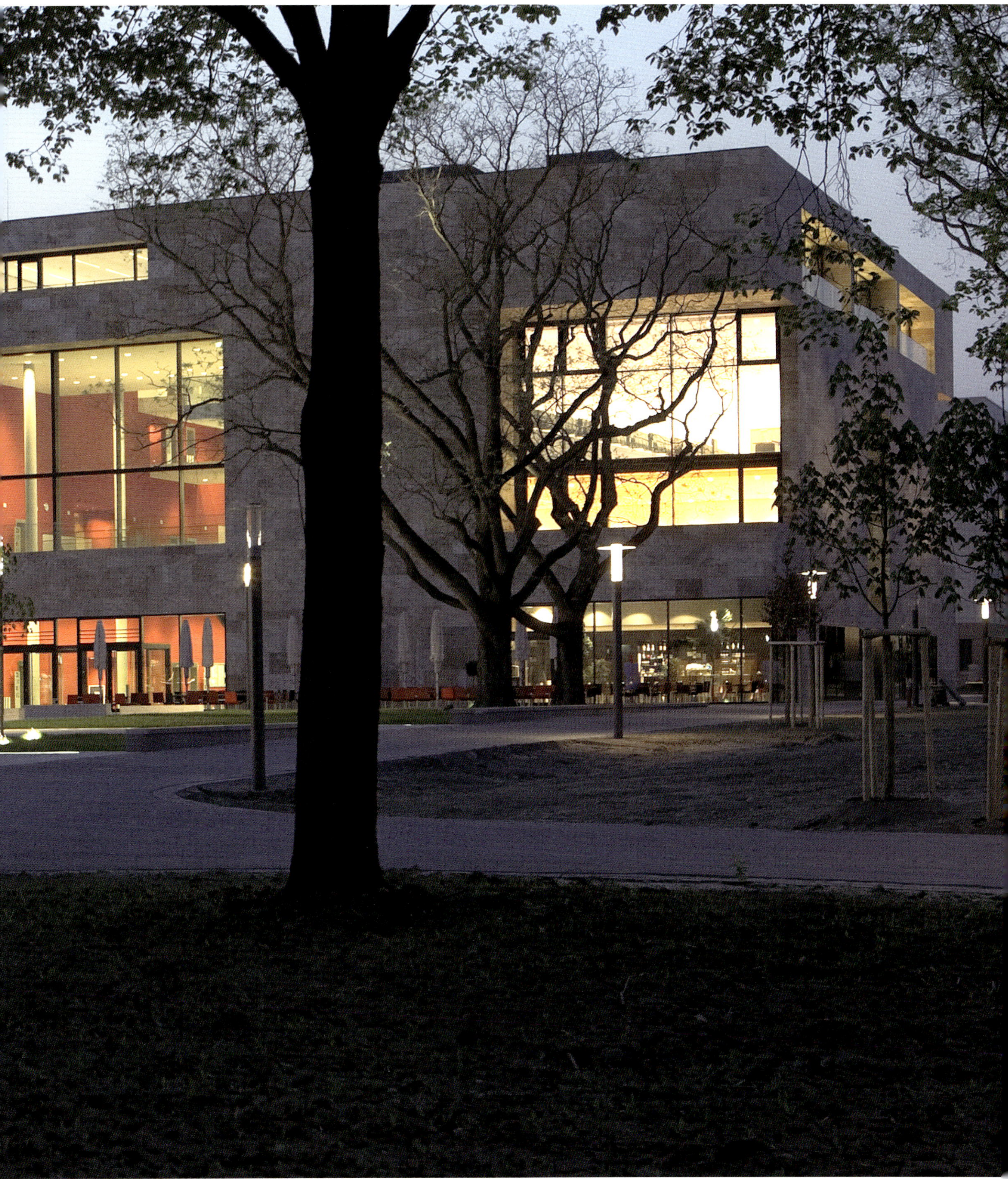

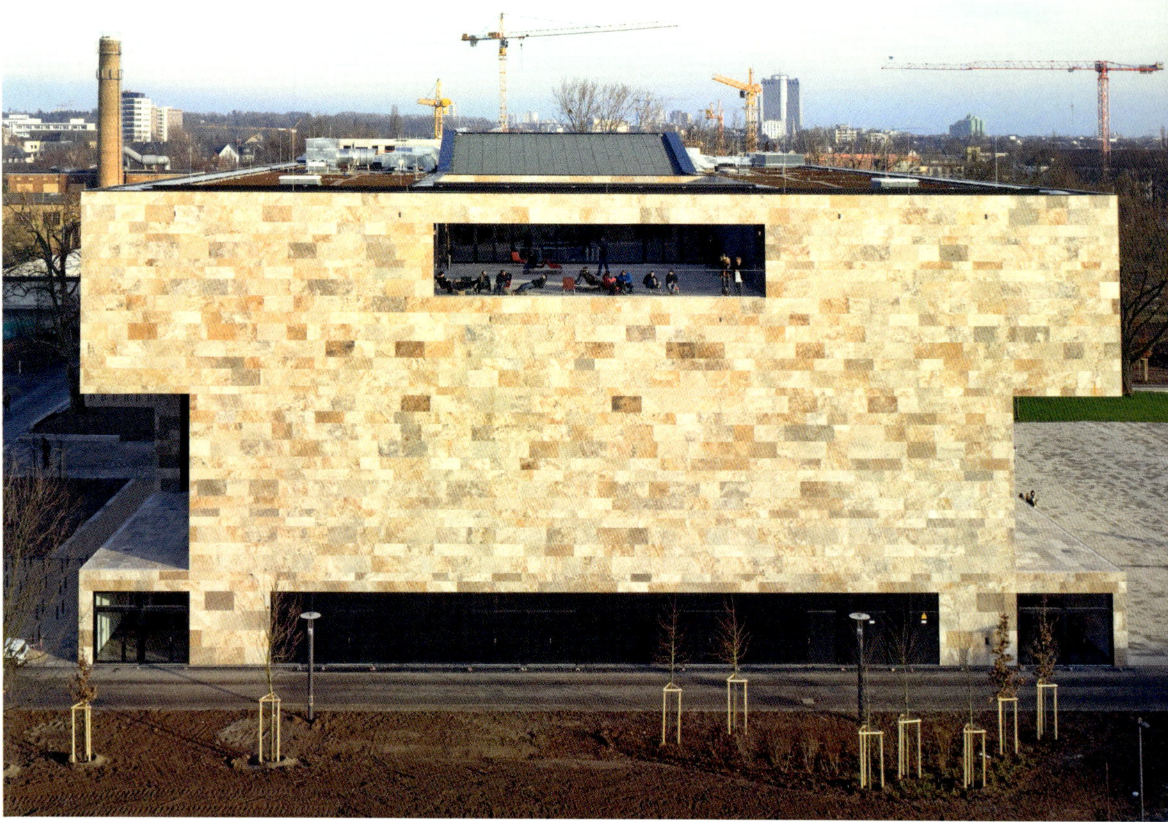

Travertinverkleidung für die Neubauten entsprechend dem Polezig-Bau | Travertine cladding for the new buildings to correspond with Poelzig's structure

Ferdinand Heide konnte auch die anschließenden Realisierungswettbewerbe für zwei Bauten im ersten Bauabschnitt für sich entscheiden: das Hörsaalzentrum und den Anbau des Casinos mit dazwischen liegendem Campusplatz. So konnte der Architekt ‚seinem' Campus tatsächlich die von ihm gewünschte Handschrift geben. Die beiden Neubauten haben ihre Schauseite zum weitläufigen Platz, der als modernes Pendant zum bereits vorhandenen weiter unten liegenden Wasserbecken geschaffen wurde. Hier findet sich neben dem Wasserspiel und verschiedenen Kunstobjekten genügend Freiraum sowohl für die Außengastronomie, mit einer ausgefeilten Anti-Diebstahl-Sicherung für die wetterfeste Bestuhlung, als auch für diverse universitäre Veranstaltungen.

Das Hörsaalzentrum, welches durch seine großzügigen Fensteröffnungen und Einschnitte sehr prägnant ist, bietet in Zukunft allen Fakultäten Raum für größere Veranstaltungen, die nicht mehr in ihren eigenen Gebäuden stattfinden. So soll eine kommunikative Mitte geschaffen werden, die den Austausch der verschiedenen Disziplinen ermöglicht. Außerdem werden die höchst attraktiven Räumlichkeiten mit Skyline-Blick auch für externe Veranstaltungen vermietet. Durch die kompakte Stapelung der zwölf verschiedenen Hörsäle – sehr eindrücklich ist das parabelförmig ansteigende Audimax für 1200 Personen – und Seminarräume auf fünf Etagen, konnte eine große Freizügigkeit im ebenerdigen Foyer und dem darüber liegenden offenen Treppenhaus geschaffen werden. Der Campusplatz scheint sich innerhalb des Gebäudes auf allen Ebenen fortzusetzen, was durch den einheitlichen Bodenbelag im Außen- und Innen-

of the existing dining hall kitchens. The old and new sections are connected via a tunnel and a bridge in order to transport food and people quickly back and forth. Here the old and new architecture of Campus Westend meet directly, and harmonise beautifully with one another. On the ground floor a capacious two-storey café bar opens onto the square, the two dining rooms enclosing the food counter on both sides.

The individual rooms can be closed off or divided at any time using large sliding partitions, thus adapting to changing needs depending on the time of day or semester, while offering additional rental income for the university.

The two buildings and the square designed by Ferdinand Heide demonstrate impressively how the deft deployment of form, material and colour can come together to create a meaningful and dynamic modern urban university campus.

Schnitt durch das Hörsaalzentrum
Section through the lecture hall centre

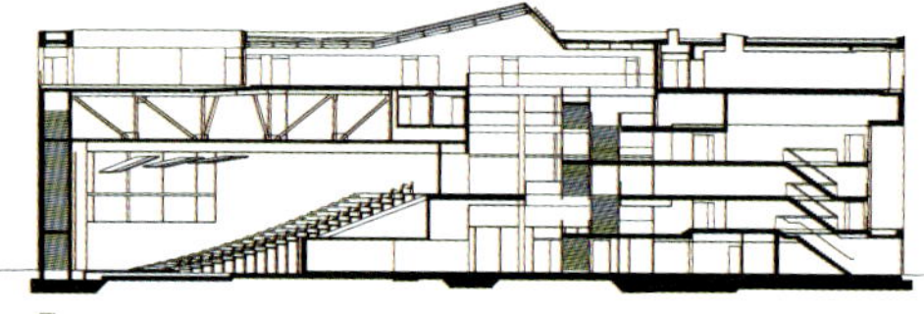

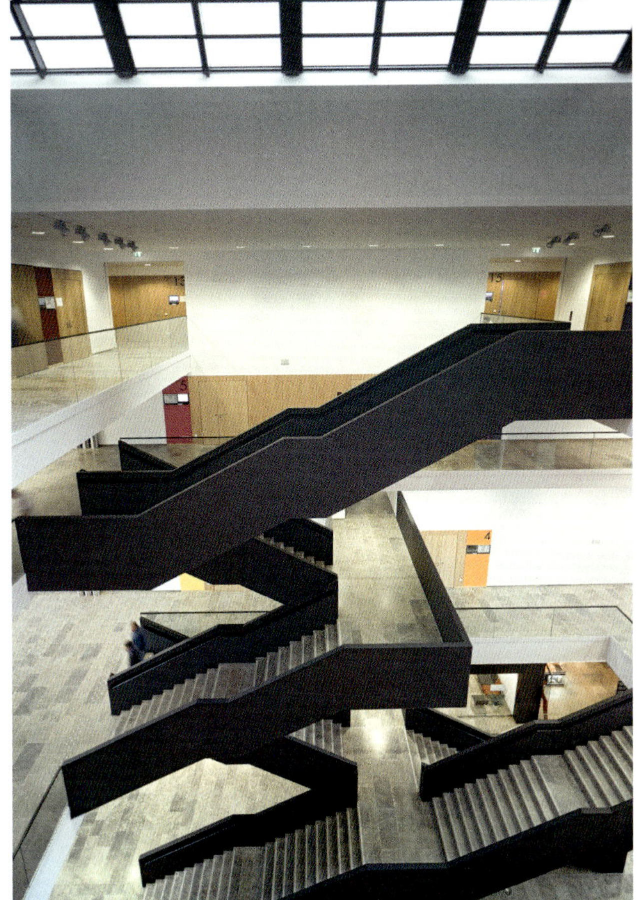

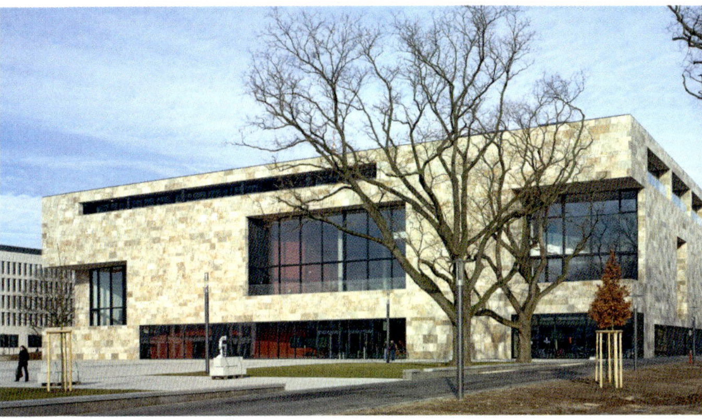

Hörsaalzentrum | Lecture hall centre

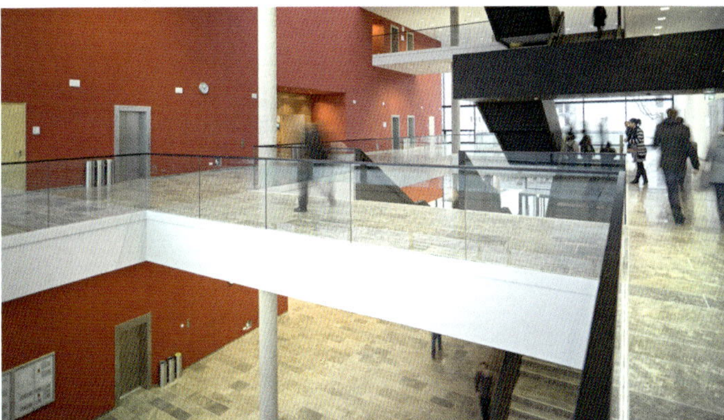

Das offene Treppenhaus des Hörsaalzentrums
The open staircase of the lecture hall centre

Das Wegesystem des Hörsaalzentrums
The hallway system of the lecture hall centre

bereich verstärkt wird. Im Gegensatz zu den schwerfälligen
und steifen neuen Fakultätsgebäuden in der Umgebung verfügt
das Hörsaalzentrum aufgrund seiner Offenheit und dem
mutigen Einsatz von starken Farben, die teilweise bis nach
außen leuchten, über eine eigenständige Note und eine
gewisse Leichtigkeit trotz der schweren Natursteinfassade mit
den vorgehängten Travertinplatten und des enormen Volumens.
Der wesentlich kleinere Anbau des Casinos überrascht durch
eine zeitgemäße Schlichtheit in der Form und eine besondere
Materialität und Farbigkeit der Flächen sowie durch die
effektive Nutzung der bestehenden Großküche der Bestands-
mensa. Über einen Tunnel und eine Brücke sind die beiden
Bauten miteinander verknüpft, um Essen bzw. Menschen
schnell von einem Ort zum anderen zu bringen. Hier treffen die
alte und neue Architektur des Campus Westend direkt aufeinander und harmonieren hervorragend. Im Erdgeschoss öffnet sich
eine weiträumige zweigeschossige Cafébar zum Platz, die
beiden Speisesäle umfassen die Essensausgabe zu beiden Seiten.
Die einzelnen Räume können jederzeit durch große Schiebe-
wände abgeschlossen oder geteilt werden und passen sich so an
die wechselnden Bedürfnisse, abhängig von Uhrzeit und
Semesterzeit, an und bieten weitere Mieteinnahmen für die
Universität.
Die beiden Bauten und der Platz von Ferdinand Heide zeigen
auf eindrückliche Art und Weise, wie bedeutungsvoll und
lebendig ein moderner urbaner Universitäts-Campus durch den
geschickten Einsatz von Form, Material und Farbe gestaltet
werden kann.

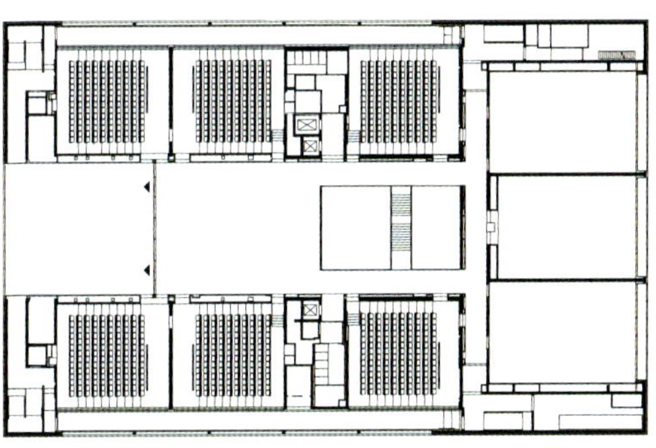

Grundriss 2. Obergeschoss Hörsaalzentrum
Floor plan of the 2nd floor of the lecture hall centre

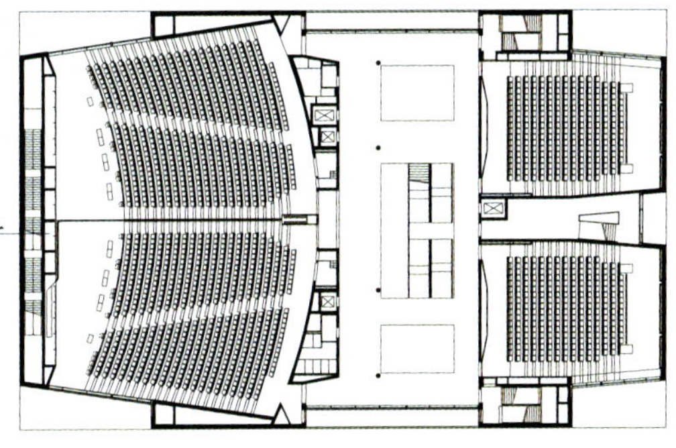

Grundriss 1. Obergeschoss Hörsaalzentrum
Floor plan of the 1st floor of the lecture hall centre

FINK+JOCHER

STADTHAUS NUWOG

TEXT WOLFGANG BACHMANN

ARCHITEKTEN | ARCHITECTS

Architekten Fink+Jocher
Barer Straße 44
80799 München | Munich
www.fink-jocher.de

MITARBEITER | TEAM

Stephan Riedel, Ivan Grafl, Martin
Vaché, Elmar Schaugg

BAUHERR | CLIENT

NUWOG
Wohnungsgesellschaft
der Stadt Neu-Ulm GmbH
Schützenstraße 32
89231 Neu-Ulm

TRAGWERK | STRUCTURE

Ingenieurbüro
Holzmann + Ostertag,
Neu-Ulm

LANDSCHAFTSARCHITEKTEN
LANDSCAPE ARCHITECTS

Burger Landschaftsarchitekten,
Susanne Burger und Peter Kühn
Partnerschaft, München | Munich

FERTIGSTELLUNG | COMPLETION

Ende 2007 | End of 2007

STANDORT | LOCATION

Schützenstraße 32
89231 Neu-Ulm
www.nuwog.de

FOTOS | PHOTOS

Michael Heinrich

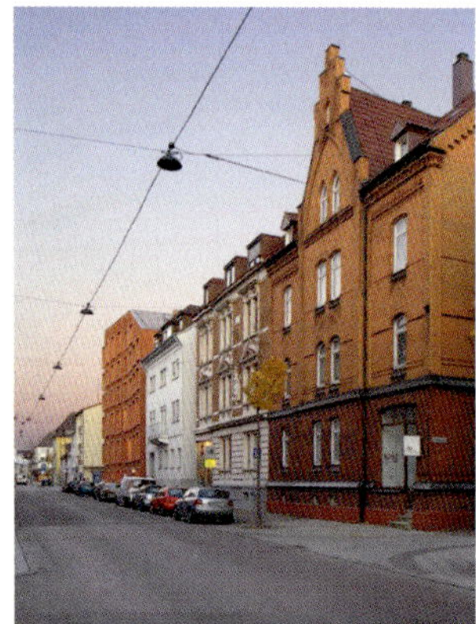

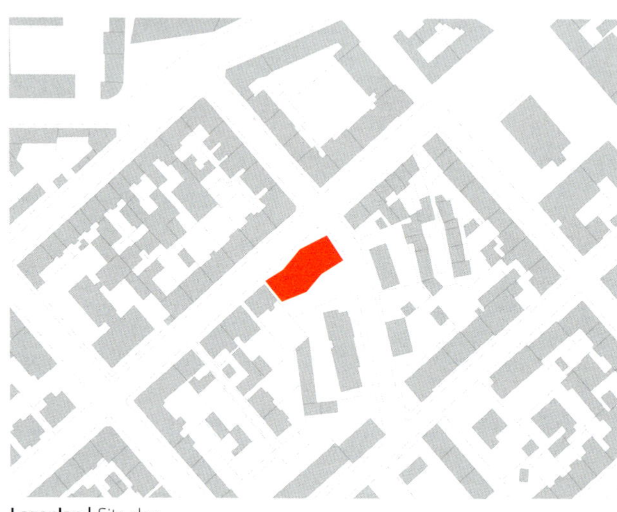

Lageplan | Site plan

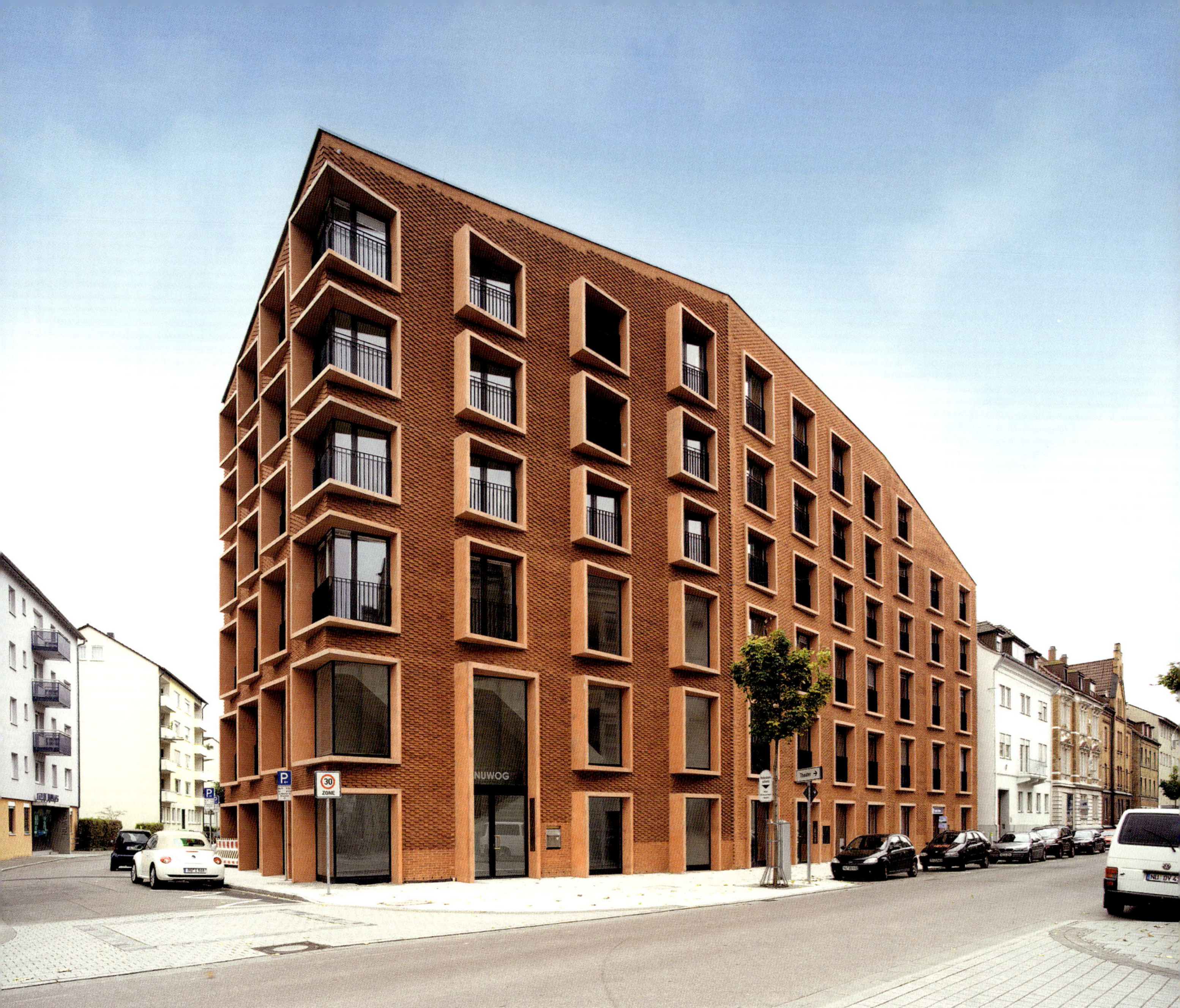

Der Neubau übernimmt die Koordinaten der bestehenden Gründerzeitbebauung und die Störung der Ordnung durch eine Straßendiagonale. | The new building adopts the coordinates of the existing turn-of-the-century structures and the disruption of their order by a diagonal street.

Wohnbau, sofern es sich nicht um Einfamilienhäuser handelt, ist immer mit Bedingungen und Attributen verbunden: Entweder muss er förderfähigen DIN-Normen entsprechen, also ,sozial' sein, oder wenigstens frauen- oder kinderfreundliche Grundrisse aufweisen, vielleicht auch für Alleinerziehende oder Patchworkfamilien taugen. Dass seine Architektur für sich genommen eine Bedeutung hat, wurde erstmals bei der Berliner IBA erprobt – und als Postmoderne gegeißelt.

Nähert man sich jedoch diesem auffallenden roten Haus, liest man als Allererstes ,Architektur'. Über seine Funktion stellt man erst in zweiter Linie Vermutungen an. Der charakteristische Knick des Baukörpers, seine Loggienhöhlen und die zur Rückseite weit auskragenden Balkonkästen samt den rigoros verteilten Öffnungen in der ornamental vermauerten Ziegelfassade lassen Zeitgenossenschaft erkennen. So ein Haus kann nicht in den 1950er- oder 1980er-Jahren entstanden sein.

Residential construction, unless for single-family homes, is always tied to certain requirements and attributes. It either has to comply with the relevant DIN norms in order to be eligible for subsidies as 'social housing', or it at least has to offer floor plans geared to the needs of women and children, perhaps even tailored especially for single-parent or patchwork families. That domestic architecture can be significant in its own right is a thesis that was first tested at the International Building Exhibition in Berlin – where it was hastily chastised as postmodern.

Coming upon this conspicuously red house, however, one reads it first as 'architecture'. It is only on second thoughts that we begin to surmise something about its function. The characteristic angular bend in the

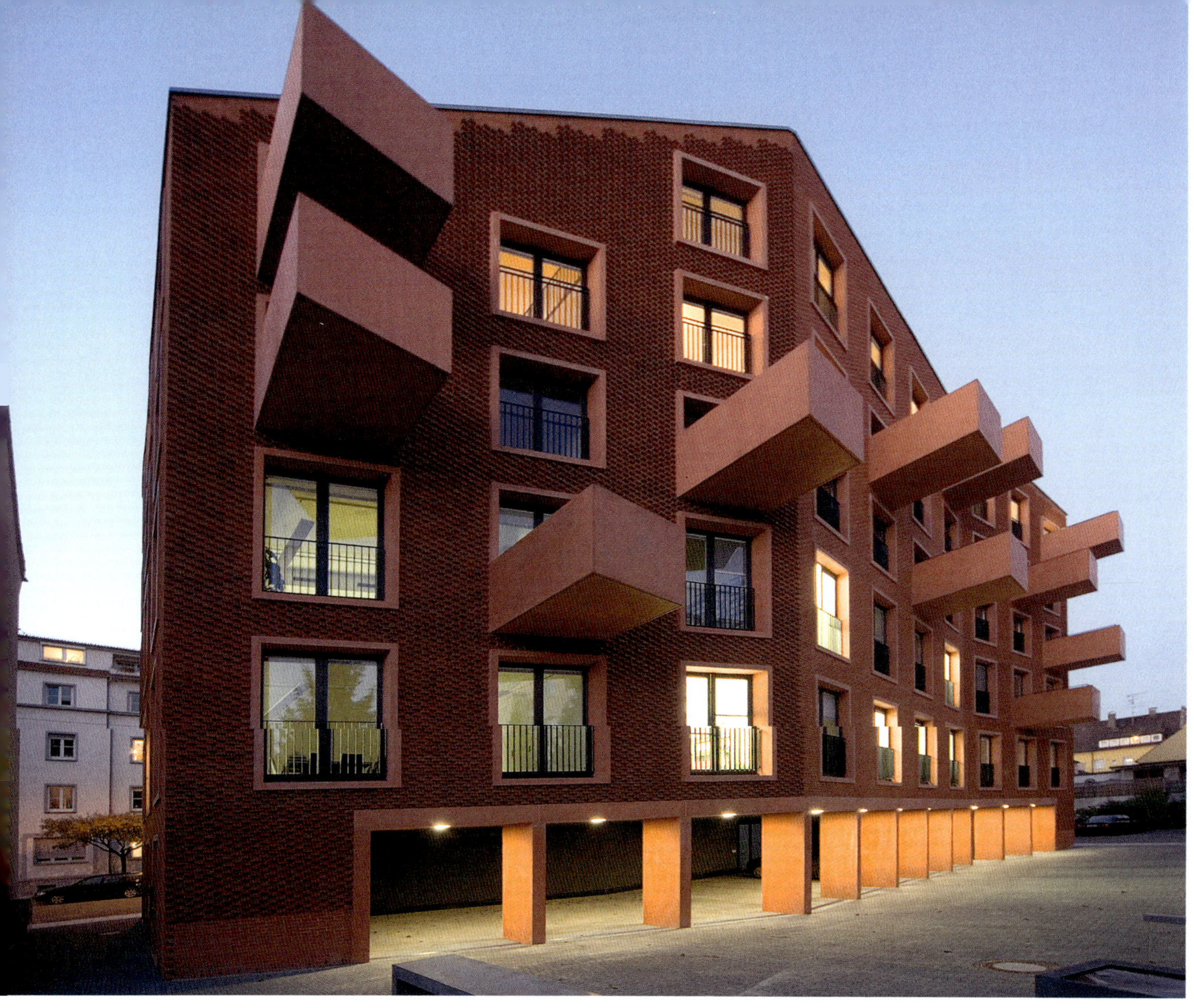

Die Wohnungen sind erkennbar an den wie Schubladen herausgezogenen
Balkones. | The apartments are distinguished by balconies pulled out like drawers.

Dennoch sind die Voraussetzungen für die städtebauliche
Lösung historisch gewachsen. Neu-Ulm (und Ulm) wurden in
den 1840er-Jahren als Bundesfestung ausgebaut. Neben
Ludwigshafen ist Neu-Ulm die bedeutendste schematisch
konzipierte Stadtgründung dieser Zeit. Zur Hauptachse wurde
die Schützenstraße, die der Richtung einer alten (längst abge-
holzten) Lindenallee folgt. Auf diese Situation reagiert der
Neubau. Als ‚verdichtendes Wachstum von innen' – stillschwei-
gende Arbeitshypothese der Architekten – schließt das Haus
eine Blockecke. Dabei nimmt es sowohl die Koordinaten des
Rasters auf, erinnert mit seinem flach geknickten Grundriss
aber auch an die Störung der Ordnung durch die vorhandene
Straßendiagonale. Betont durch die rote, aber quartiertypische
Backsteinfassade fügt es sich in seinen Ort und behauptet sich
gleichzeitig als Adresse.

Dass es überwiegend Wohnungen enthält, verraten die wie
Schubladen herausgeschobenen Balkone. Darunter ist der
Bauherr zu Hause, die NUWOG, eine Wohnungsbaugesellschaft,
die sich regelmäßig auf ambitionierte Architektur einlässt.
Ohne herrschaftliche Repräsentation empfängt der Geschäfts-
eingang allein mit seiner Architekturgeste – einer dreigeschos-

body of the building, its cave-like loggias and the
balcony boxes jutting far out in the back, together
with the rigorously placed openings in the
ornamental masonry of its brick façade, mark it
unmistakably as contemporary. It's impossible that
a house like this could have been built in the 1950s
or 1980s. Nevertheless, the prerequisites for this
particular urban planning solution have historic
roots. Neu-Ulm (and Ulm) was built up in the 1840s
as a confederate fortress. Along with Ludwigshafen,
Neu-Ulm is the most important schematically
conceived city founded during this period. Schützenstrasse was made into the main axis, following
the path of an old (long since deforested) avenue of
limewood trees. The new building responds to this
historical situation. As 'condensed growth from
within' – the tacit working hypothesis adopted by
the architects – the house closes the corner of a
block. In doing so it takes up the coordinates of the
street matrix, but at the same time recalls with the
shallow bend made by its floor plan the disruption

sigen, weiß schimmernden Halle, aus der eine sich nach oben
verjüngende Treppe zu den Geschäftsräumen einlädt. In Gegen-
richtung, nun deutlich schmaler, führt die skulpturale Stiege zu
den Büros der Mitarbeiter, die sich mit ihren breit verglasten
Türfronten wie Geschäfte an einer Straße aufreihen, ein Bild,
das durch den dunklen Epoxydharzestrich noch verstärkt wird.
Die tragenden Wände dieses leicht gewinkelten innen liegenden
Flures setzen sich in den darüber liegenden Wohnungen fort.
Für sie gibt es ein eigenes Treppenhaus, das in einen dunklen,
weniger attraktiven Gang führt. Die Wohnungsgrößen reichen
vom Zweizimmer-Single-Apartement bis zur großen Galerie-
Maisonette unterm Dach, alle barrierefrei. Durch den geknickten
Baukörper und den tragenden Kern haben viele Räume trapez-
förmige oder leicht schiefe Grundrisse. Das kann spannend
sein, falls die Bewohner ein wenig Fantasie und kein
altdeutsches Mobiliar anschleppen, aber würde man beim
Entwerfen mit den Grundrissen beginnen, sähen diese nicht wie
bei sanierten Altbauten aus. Auffallend ist zum Beispiel, dass
gerade die großen Wohnungen bis zu vier verschiedene Innen-
flure brauchen. Das lässt andererseits ein abwechslungsreiches
Familienleben zu. Eine weitere Konsequenz aus der äußeren
Gestaltung sind die niedrigen Fensterstürze, unter denen wie
ein Portal die breiten Rahmen der bodentiefen Öffnungen
anschließen. In den nach Nordosten orientierten Zimmern wird
der Ausblick einseitig durch tiefe Betonleibungen reguliert.
Kein Zweifel, es ist ein städtisches, von außen nach innen
entwickeltes Haus.
Bleiben wir also bei der von der Öffentlichkeit erlebbaren Architektur. Sie übersetzt die Stadtbaugeschichte und die umliegen-
den historischen Fassaden eines Paul Frank in die Gegenwart.
Ziegel, Fugen und die massiven Betonleibungen leuchten im
gleichen Rot. Leben bringt erst die dritte Dimension. Hier ist ein
geradezu philosophisches Konstrukt entstanden, das mit der
Ordnung spielt: Die Ziegel spreizen sich widerborstig wie
Schuppen gegen den Verlauf der Fassaden, sie folgen der Flucht
der Schützenstraße. Mit ihnen verbünden sich die kastenartigen
Betonrahmen, die auf der Rückseite brav in den gewinkelten
Flächen liegen, während die Balkone ihre Stirn gemeinsam
ausrichten. Man könnte eine Metapher darin sehen, wie das
Kleine zum Großen, das Teil sich zum Ganzen verhält. Und
während wir uns von den Dimensionen narren lassen, tritt eine
Frau aus dem Haus und fragt, ob wir wegen der ausblühenden
Fugen neben dem Eingang kommen. Schwaben! Architektur
hält das aus.

Balkon | Balcony

of this order by the existing diagonally running
streets. With its distinctive red brick façade, actually
typical for this district, the house both integrates
itself into its environs and announces itself as an
address.
The fact that it contains mostly apartments is
betrayed by the balconies protruding from the back
wall like drawers. Beneath them are the offices of
the client for the project, the NUWOG building
society, which regularly undertakes ambitious
architectural projects like this one. Without putting
on any ceremonious airs, the company entrance
receives guests in style through an architectural
gesture alone – a three-storey hall shimmering in
white, from which a tapering staircase entices visitors upward to the company premises. In the opposite direction a much narrower, sculptural, staircase
leads up to the offices of the administrative staff
with their broad glass doors reminiscent of shop
windows along a street – an image that is further
underscored by the dark epoxy resin floors. The
supporting walls of this slightly angled interior
corridor are echoed in the apartments above.
The apartments have their own staircase, which
leads up to a dark, not-very-inviting hallway. They
range in size from a two-room studio for singles to
a spacious gallery maisonette under the roof, and all
are barrier-free. Due to the angled body of the
building and the supporting core, the floor plans of
many of the rooms are trapezoid or slightly aslant.

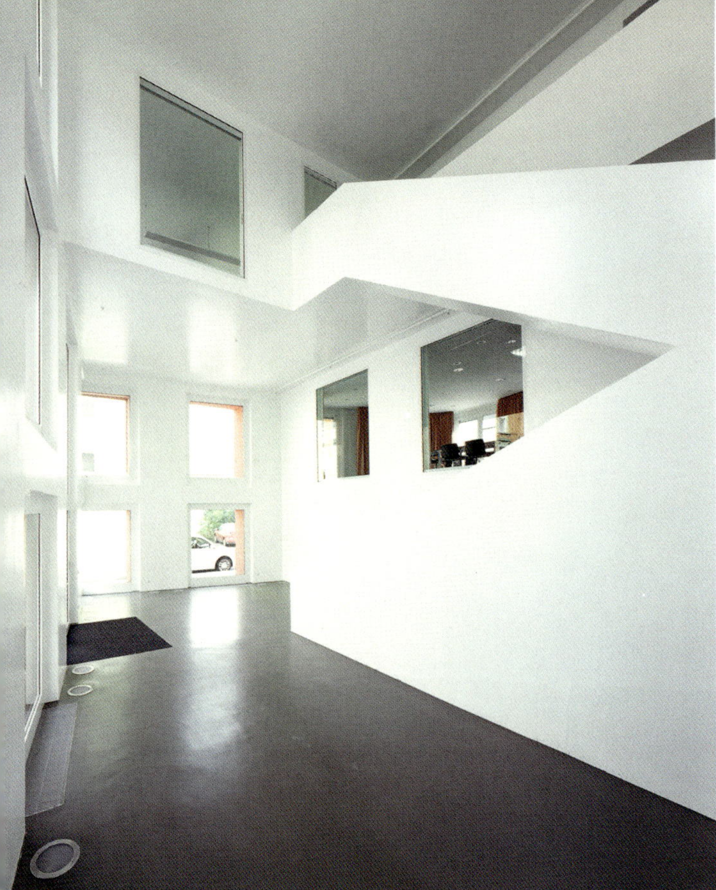

Aufgang | Stairway

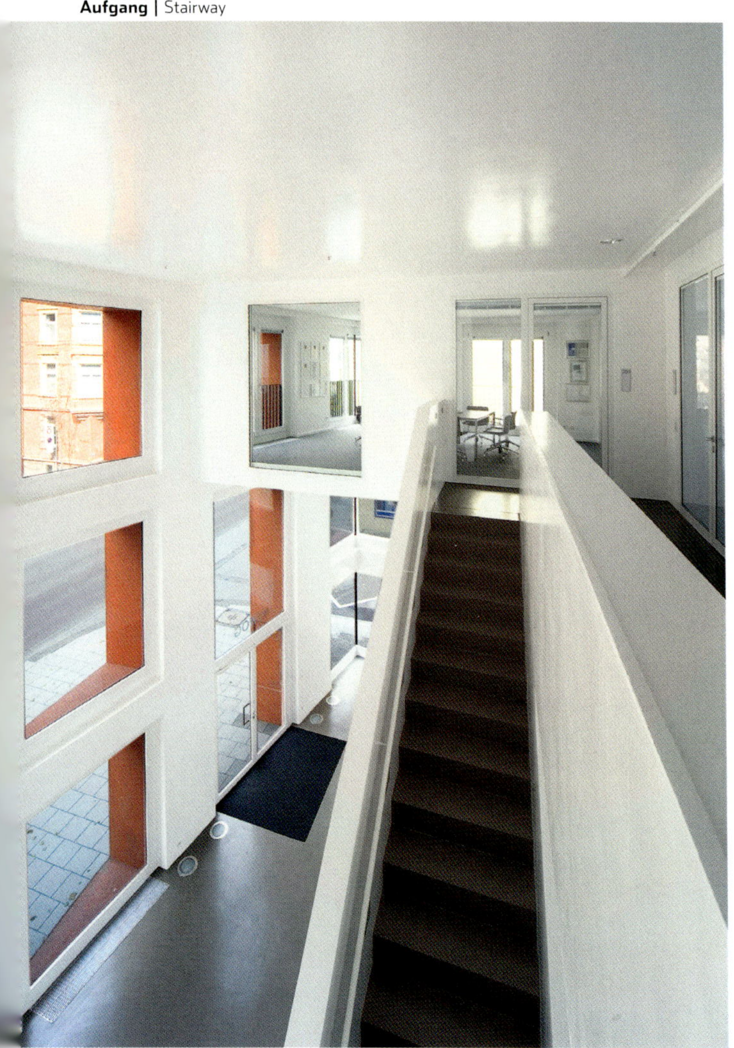

This can be exciting as long as the residents have a bit of imagination and don't move in with their traditional old German furniture. If one began by designing the floor plans, however, they would still not look like the ones in renovated old buildings. Of note for example is that the larger apartments here need up to four different interior hallways. On the other hand, this does leave room for a versatile family life. Another consequence of the exterior design are the low window lintels, bordered underneath like a portal by the wide frames of the floor-level openings. In the rooms facing northeast the view through the windows is regulated on one side by deep concrete reveals. There can be no doubt that this is an urban building, developed from the outside in.

Let us return then to the architecture that can be experienced here by the general public. This architecture translates the city's urban planning history and the surrounding historical façades by architects such as Paul Frank into present-day terms. Bricks, joints and the massive concrete reveals all glow in the same red tone. Life is brought into the composition only in the third dimension. Here a veritably philosophical construct has been created, one that toys with the idea of order. The bricks splay out like fish scales against the surface of the façades, following the line of Schützenstrasse. Joining them are the boxlike concrete window frames, which on the back of the building lie obediently in the angled surfaces, while the balconies align their fronts in unison. One could read into this a metaphor for how smaller elements relate to larger ones, the parts to the whole. And while we're letting these dimensions make a fool of us, a woman comes out of the building and asks if we've come to see about the efflorescence at the joints. Swabians! Architecture can easily withstand a trivial detail like that.

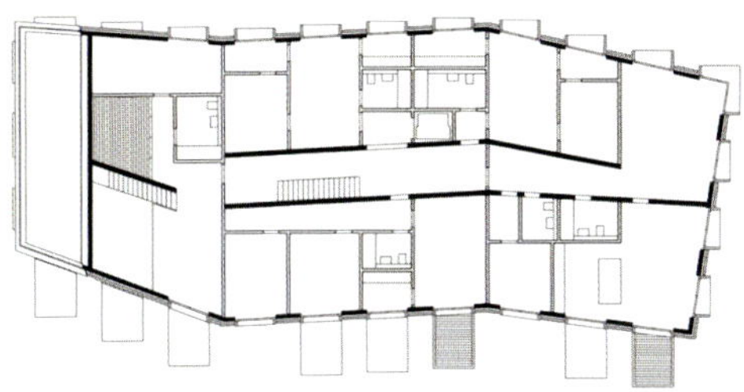

Grundriss 5. Obergeschoss | Floor plan of 5th floor

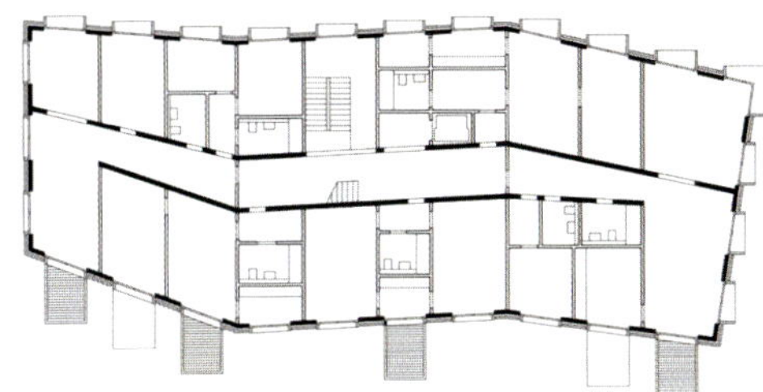

Grundriss 3. Obergeschoss | Floor plan of 3rd floor

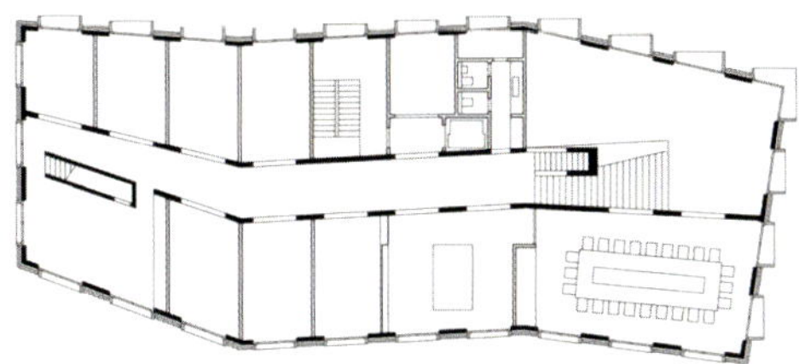

Grundriss 1. Obergeschoss | Floor plan of 1st floor

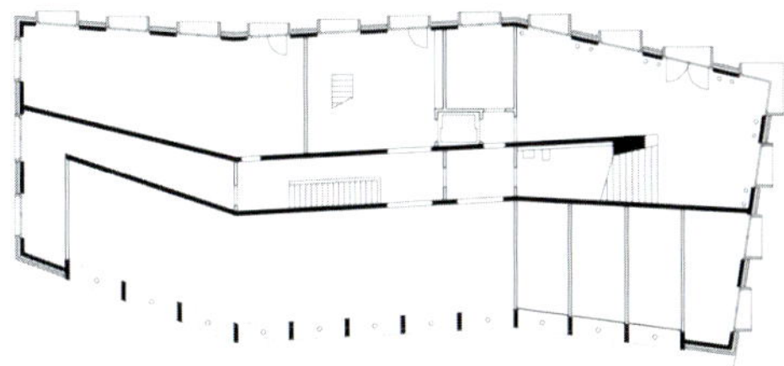

Grundriss Erdgeschoss | Floor plan of ground floor

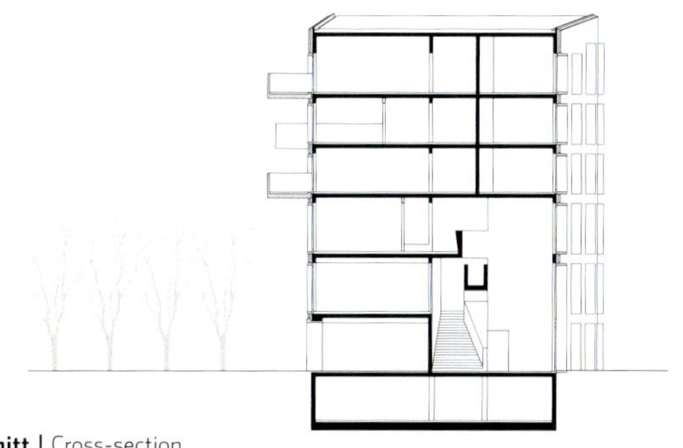
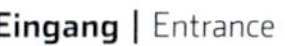

Querschnitt | Cross-section

Eingang | Entrance

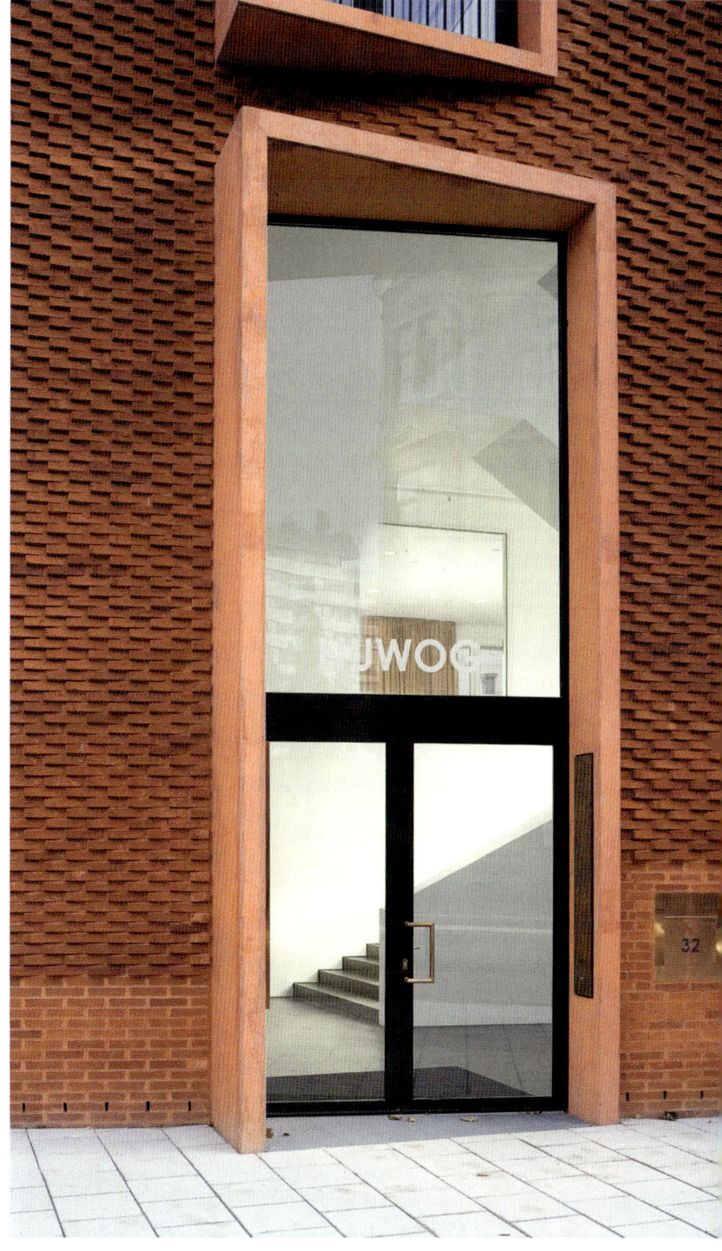

FLORIAN NAGLER

KUHSTALL

TEXT STEFANIE LAMPE

12

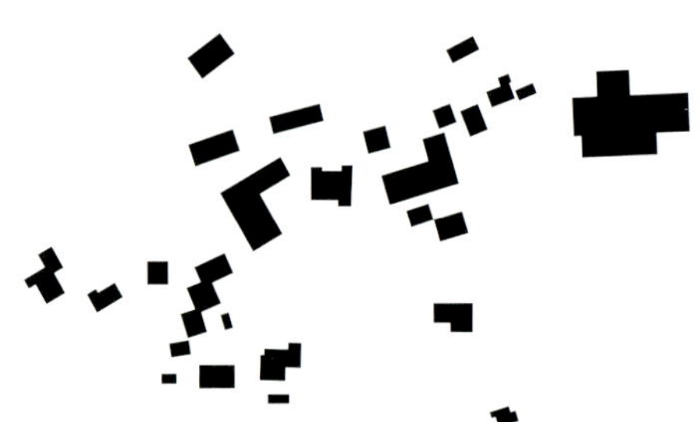

Lageplan | Site plan

ARCHITEKTEN | ARCHITECTS

**Florian Nagler
Architekten GmbH
Theodor-Storm-Straße 16
81245 München** | Munich
www.nagler-architekten.de

MITARBEITER | TEAM

**Almut Schwabe,
Matthias Müller**

BAUHERR | CLIENT

Regina & Kaspar Raßhofer

TRAGWERK | STRUCTURE

merz kley partner GmbH, Dornbirn

FERTIGSTELLUNG | COMPLETION

Oktober 2007 | October 2007

STANDORT | LOCATION

**83623 Dietramszell
Ortsteil Thankirchen**

FOTOS | PHOTOS

Florian Holzherr, Florian Nagler

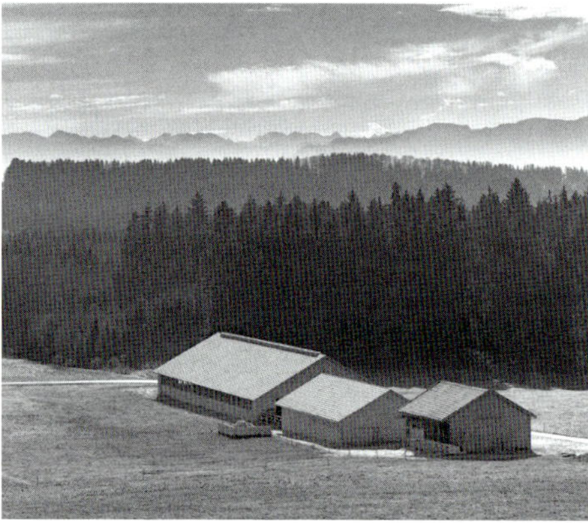

Fortführung ländlich-regionaler Bauweise
Carrying on rural, regional building methods

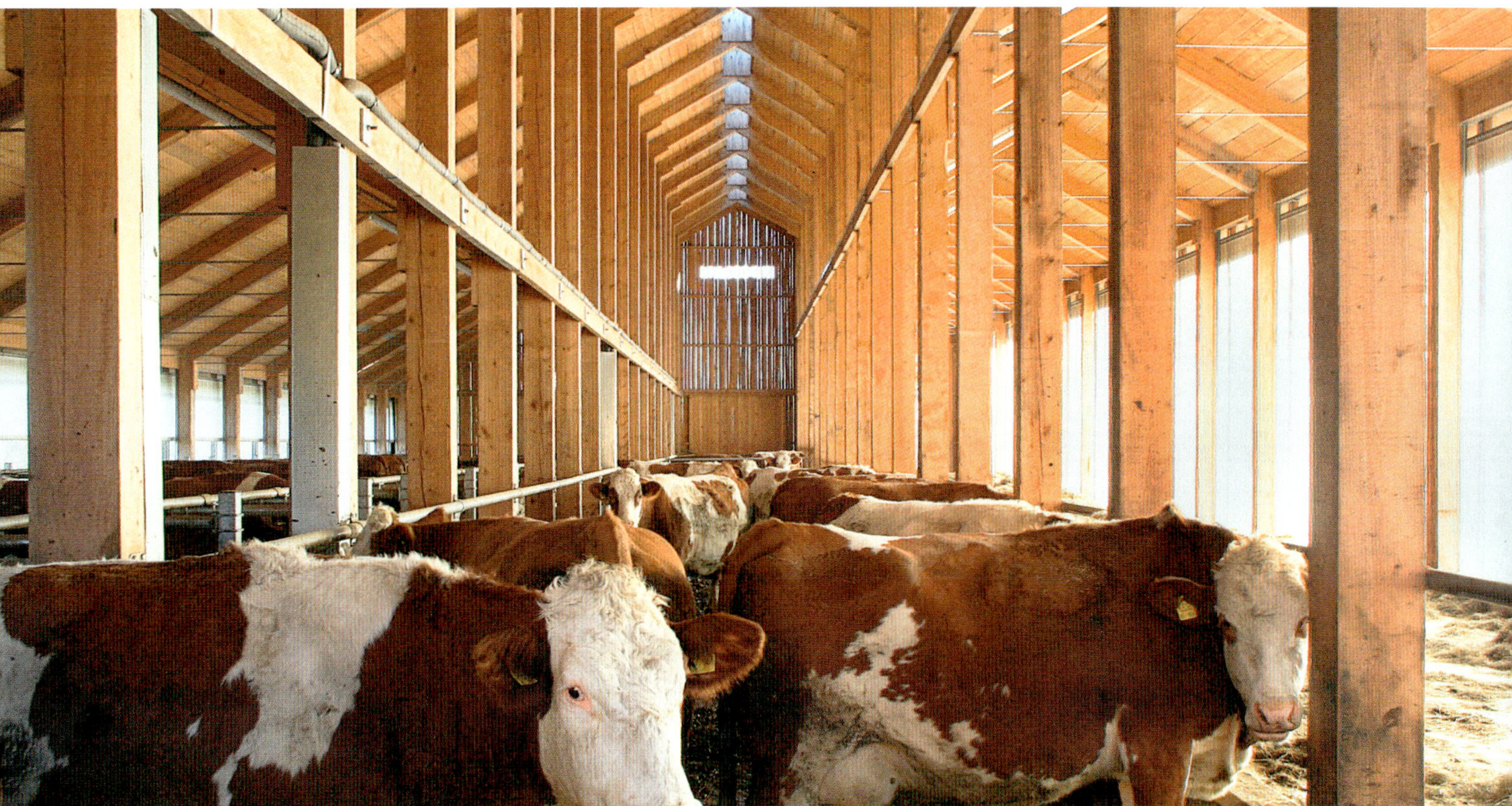

**Traditionelle Dreiteilung des Stalls in Liegebereich,
Fressgang und Futtertisch** | Traditional tripartite division of
the stall into resting area, walking area and feeding alley

**Kuhställe zählen nicht unbedingt zu den Bauaufgaben renommierter Architek-
ten. Da jedoch in diesem Fall die Bauherrin die Schwester des Architekten ist,
plante Florian Nagler im idyllischen bayerischen Alpenvorland bei der Ortschaft
Thankirchen einen Kuhstall und ein Melkhaus. Die neuen landwirtschaftlichen
Nutzgebäude sollten den Standards der Biomilchwirtschaft genügen und der
alte Stall, direkt an das Bauernhaus angegliedert, war für einen solchen Umbau
nicht geeignet – direkt am Hof gab es keine Fläche für eine Erweiterung.
Daher plante Nagler einen neuen Außenklimastall und das Melkhaus außerhalb
der Ortschaft, in linearer Reihung zu einer bestehenden kleinen Scheune am
Rande einer Wiese. Ein für die Kühe frei zugänglicher Freibereich verbindet
Melkhaus und Stall. Die Gebäude sind so in die Landschaft eingebettet, dass sie
weder den Blick von der Wiese zu der höher gelegenen Ortschaft noch den Blick
von Thankirchen auf das entfernte Alpenpanorama stören.
Der Stall wurde aus Tannenholz errichtet, das aus dem eigenen Wald der
Bauherren stammt und im wenige Kilometer entfernten Sägewerk geschnitten
wurde. Das sägerau verarbeitete Vollholz bedingte auch die Konstruktion.**

Cowsheds are not necessarily building projects one
expects prominent architects to devote their attention
to. But since in this case the client happens to be
the architect's sister, so Florian Nagler found
himself planning a cowshed and a milking shed near
the village of Thankirchen, nestled in the idyllic foothills of the Bavarian Alps. The new agricultural
buildings had to comply with the standards for orga-
nic milk production, but the old shed, attached to the
farmhouse, was not suitable for this kind of reconstruction as there was no room in the farmyard to
expand.
Nagler therefore planned a new naturally ventilated
stall and milking house outside Thankirchen, in line
with a small existing barn at the edge of a meadow.
An open-air compound freely accessible to the cows

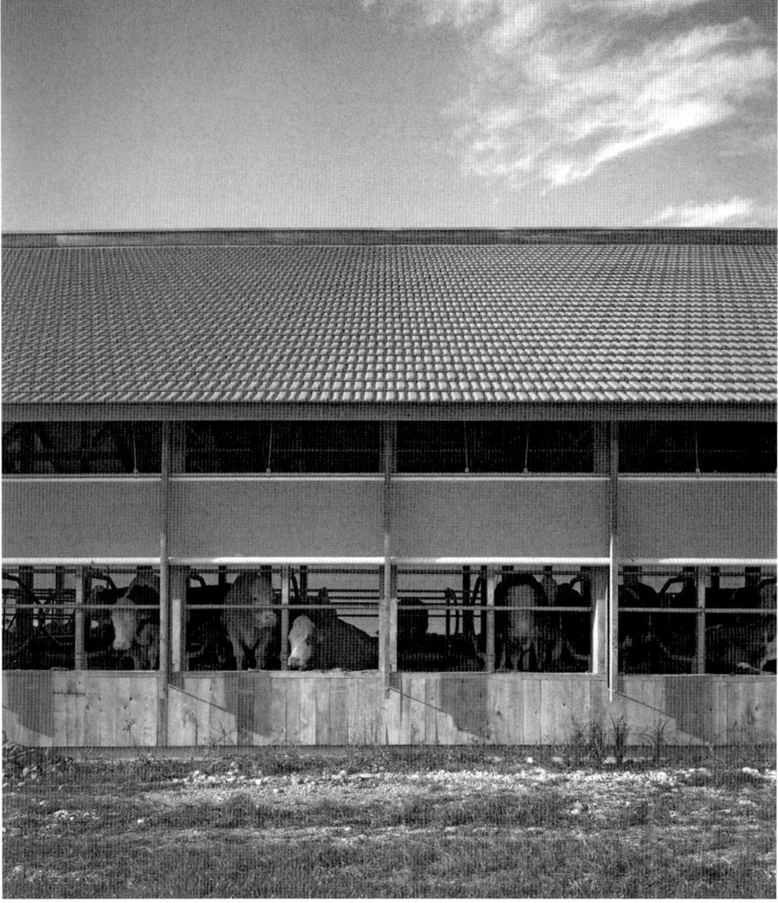

Die Längsseiten des Außenklimestalles sind offen.
The longitudinal sides of the naturally ventilated stall are open.

Nagler, selbst gelernter Zimmermann, betonte die traditionelle Dreiteilung eines Stalles in Liegebereich, Fressgang und Futtertisch mit eng gestaffelten Stützenreihen im Inneren. Jeder der drei funktionalen Bereiche wird nach oben von einer giebelartigen Holzkonstruktion umfasst. Die innere Dreischiffigkeit ist von außen nicht ablesbar. Der Stall erscheint in der Außenansicht als typisches Stallgebäude mit einem tief herabgezogenen Giebeldach, das sich in die Landschaft einfügt.

Die Längsseiten des Außenklimastalls sind nicht verkleidet. Zwischen den Holzstützen, die 2,5 Meter weit auseinander stehen, können nur lichtdurchlässige weiße ‚curtains', ähnlich einem Rollo, herabgelassen werden und die Tiere so vor dem stärksten Wind schützen. Durch eine durchgehende Aussparung im Dachfirst entsteht ein Kamineffekt, der für frische Luft für die Kühe sorgt. An den Giebelseiten schaffen die unterschiedlich breiten Latten der Verkleidung, die sich durch den Zuschnitt ergeben haben, eine lebendige Oberfläche. Wie bei der alten Scheune werden sich auch hier die unbehandelten Latten im Laufe der Zeit verfärben und dann farblich zwischen dunkelbraun und silbergrau changieren. Die Konstruktion war so geplant, dass der Bau komplett in Eigenleistung der Bauherren, ähnlich einem Bausatz, errichtet werden konnte.

Mit einfachen Mitteln plante Nagler ein Gebäude, das gerade dadurch seine Wirkung, vor allem im Inneren, entfaltet. Der Stall will nicht mehr sein als ein Stall und zeigt doch, wie mit traditionellen Mitteln, einer durchdachten Konstruktion und der achtsamen Einbettung in die Landschaft aus einer scheinbar banalen Bauaufgabe ein Stück Architektur erwachsen kann.

connects milking house and shed. The buildings are embedded in the landscape in such a way that they block neither the view from the meadow to the village on higher ground nor the view from Thankirchen to the Alpine panorama in the distance. The stall was constructed of fir from the client's own woodland, which was cut into timber at a sawmill just a few kilometres away. The rough-cut solid timber then also dictated the construction. Nagler, a trained carpenter, emphasised the traditional division of the shed into three parts – resting area, walking area and feeding alley – with closely spaced rows of supports in the interior. Each of the three functional areas is enclosed above by a gable-like wooden structure. The three aisles of the interior cannot be read from outside, however. The shed's exterior looks like a typical stall with a low-pitched gable roof that harmonises with the landscape.

The longitudinal sides of the naturally ventilated stall are not closed. Instead, between the wooden supports, which are 2.5 metres apart, translucent white 'curtains' can be let down like blinds, sheltering the animals when the wind is strong. An opening running along the roof ridge creates a chimney effect, drawing in fresh air for the cows. On the gable ends, the slats of the cladding, sawn into varying widths that the timber yielded, make for a lively surface pattern. Like in the old barn, the untreated slats will change colour over time through weathering, shimmering between dark brown and silver grey. The building was designed in such a way that the clients could construct it themselves, like a building kit.

Using simple means, Nagler planned a building whose very straightforwardness makes a special impact, particularly inside. The shed aspires to be nothing more than a shed, and yet it demonstrates how the use of traditional materials, a carefully thought-out design and mindful embedding in the landscape can turn a seemingly banal building project into a piece of architecture.

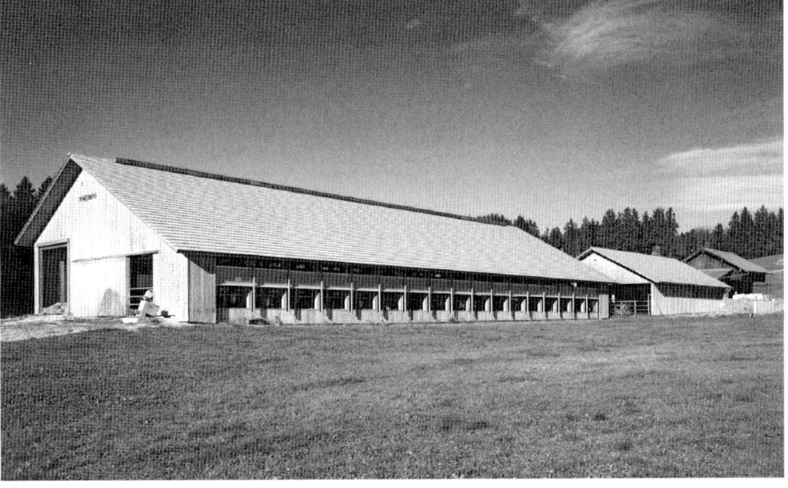

Außenklimastall und Melkhaus in linearer Addition zu einer bestehenden Scheune am Rande einer Wiese | Naturally ventilated stall and milking house as linear addition to existing barn at the edge of a meadow

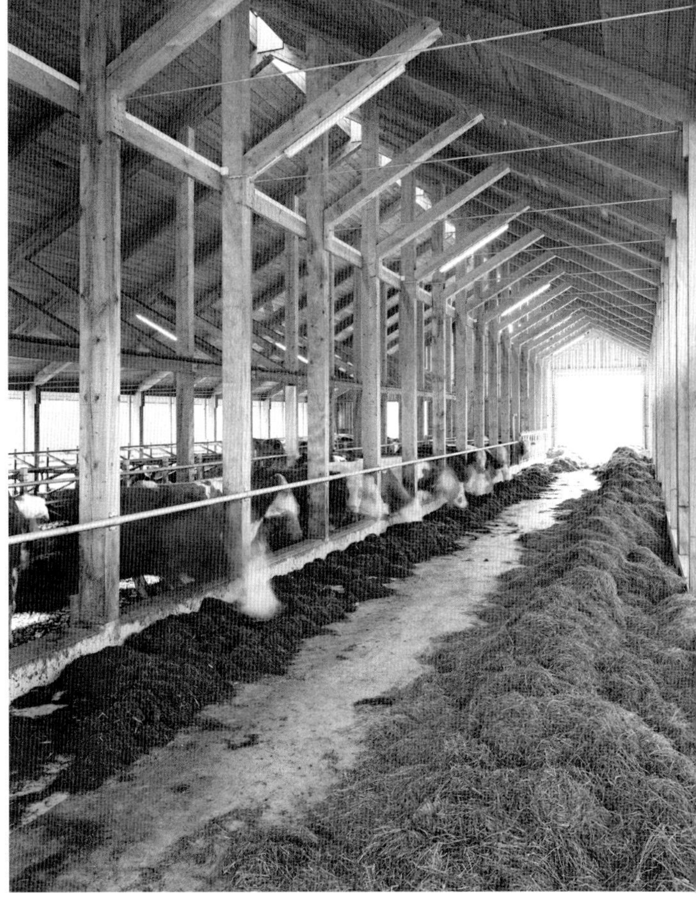

Der Bau ist so geplant, dass er in Eigenleistung vom Bauherrn errichtet werden konnte. | The building was planned for construction by the client.

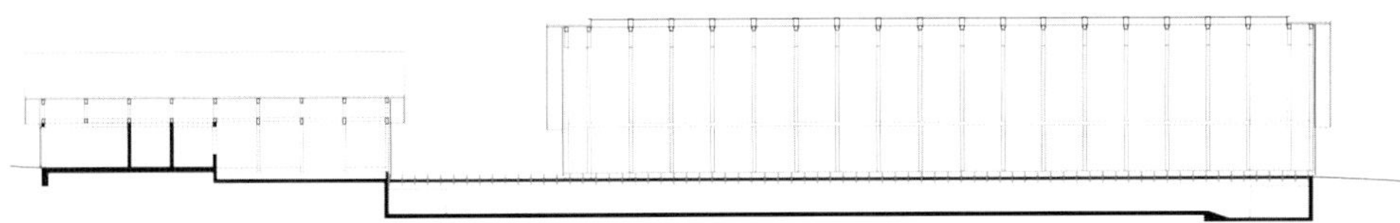

Längsschnitt | Longitudinal section

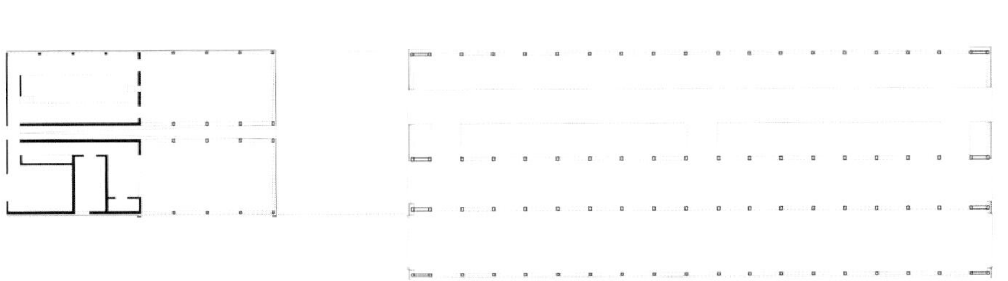

Grundriss | Floor plan

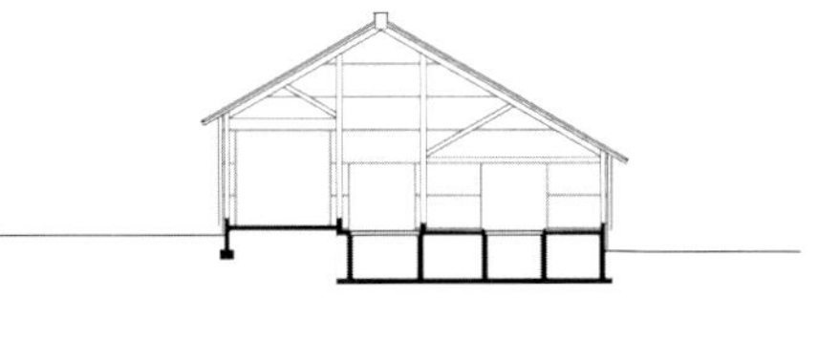

Querschnitt | Cross-section

HARTWIG N. SCHNEIDER

GEBÄUDE | BUILDING

GALERIE STIHL WAIBLINGEN UND KUNSTSCHULE UNTERES REMSTAL

TEXT PAUL ANDREAS

13

ARCHITEKTEN | ARCHITECTS

Hartwig N. Schneider
Architekten BDA
Birkenwaldstrasse 54
D-70191 Stuttgart
www.hartwigschneider.de

MITARBEITER | TEAM

Dennis Mueller,
Ingo Pelchen (Projektleitung
| project management),
Daniel Knieß,
David Mathyl, Alex Pfeiffer
(Wettbewerb | competition),
Marcus Schied, Daniel Seiberts

BAUHERR | CLIENT

Stadt Waiblingen

TRAGWERK | STRUCTURE

Fischer + Friedrich,
Waiblingen

FERTIGSTELLUNG
COMPLETION

2008

STANDORT | LOCATION

Weingärtner Vorstadt 12
71332 Waiblingen
www.galerie-stihl-waiblingen.de
www.kunstschule-rems.de

FOTOS | PHOTOS

Christian Richters

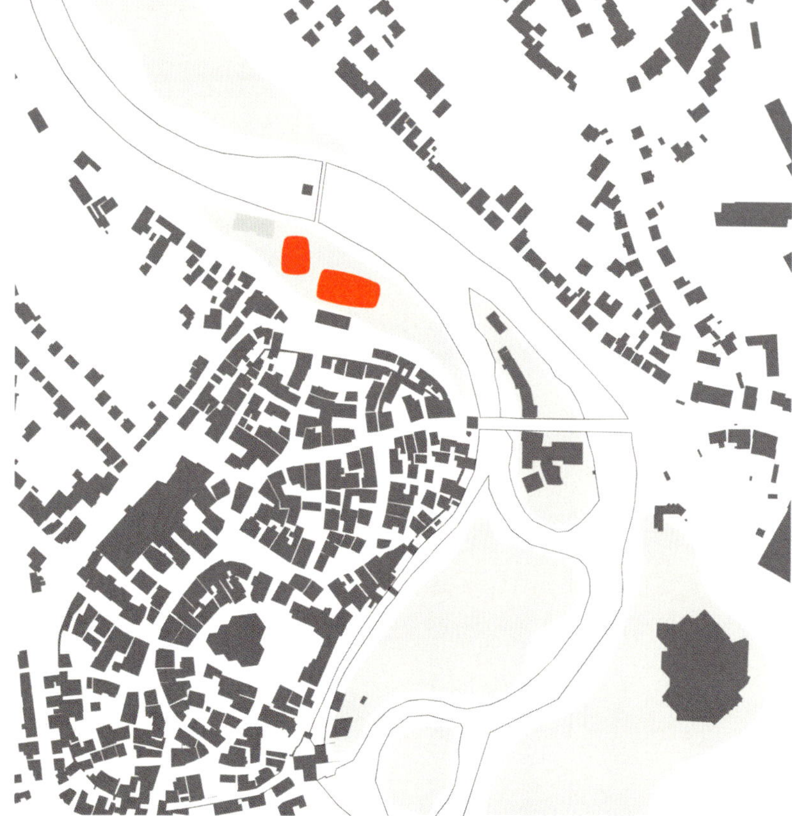

Lageplan | Site plan

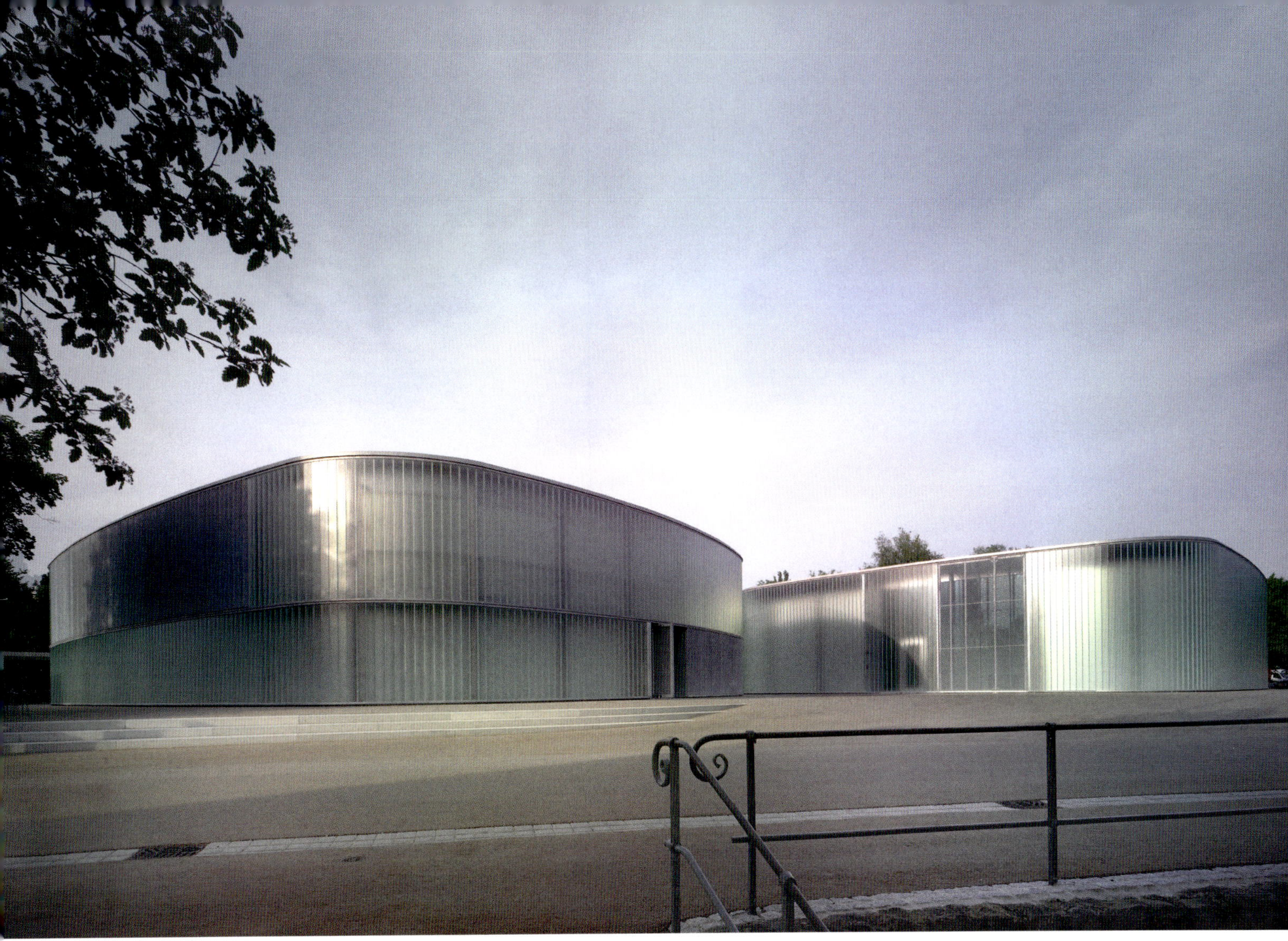

Das Ensemble aus Kunstschule und städtischer Galerie | The ensemble of art school and municipal gallery

„Waiblingen – Junge Stadt in alten Mauern", so wirbt das Stadtmarketing vollmundig auf der Homepage der 50 000 Einwohner-Gemeinde. Zumindest die alten Gemäuer, die stimmen: Das im nordöstlichen Teil des Stuttgarter Speckgürtels gelegene Städtchen besitzt eine Fachwerk-Altstadt samt historischem Rathaus und weitgehend intakter Stadtmauer, die charakteristische Stadtsilhouette zeichnet sich trotz der Planungen der 1960er- und 1970er-Jahre über der Auenlandschaft der Rems unverstellt ab. Wer dem vermeintlich ‚Jungen' in der Architektur auf die Spur kommen möchte, der muss sich an die Randzonen der historischen Substanz begeben: Auf einer vormals mit Lagerhallen bebauten Brache unmittelbar außerhalb, und doch in unmittelbarer Nachbarschaft zur Stadtmauer, zwischen historischer Gerbervorstadt und Flusslauf der Rems, liegt das Ensemble aus Kunstschule und städtischer Galerie; Letztere benannt nach dem Förderer des Baues, dem hiesigen Kettensägen-Produzenten Stihl und seinem Ableger, der Eva-Mayr-Stihl-Stiftung.

Zwei lang gestreckte Pavillonbauten – an den Ecken abgerundet und so gegeneinander versetzt, dass ein Durchgang zwischen ihnen entsteht – zeichnen sich mit ihren kühlen Industriebau-Fassaden aus transluzenten Glas-U-Profilen gegenüber der historischen Stadtkulisse aus Stein und Fachwerk deutlich ab. Trotz des gesuchten Kontrastes wurde das Ensemble so proportioniert und platziert, dass Sichtbezüge bewahrt und neue räumliche Zusammenhänge geschaffen werden konnten: Vis-à-vis zum alten Stadtmuseum entfaltet sich zwischen den Neubauten und einem neuen gläsernen Verwaltungsgebäude mit Museumscafé der neue ‚Museumsplatz', der jenseits der Engführung zwischen den beiden Volumen dynamisch in die neu angelegte „Remsterrasse" mündet.

"Waiblingen – A Young Town in Old Walls" – this is how the municipal marketing agency advertises this town with a population of 50,000. At least the "old walls" part is true: set in the northeastern part of Stuttgart's ring of outlying communities, Waiblingen has an Old Town full of preserved half-timbered buildings complete with a historic town hall and largely intact city walls. Despite 1960s and 1970s planning, a characteristic medieval skyline still rises over the banks of the Rems. Anyone trying to track down the supposedly "young" part of the architecture will have to move out to the fringes of the historic centre. There, on wasteland formerly occupied by warehouses right outside and yet directly adjacent to the city walls, between the historic tannery district and the river Rems, lies the ensemble of the art school, Kunstschule Waiblingen, and the municipal gallery, Galerie Stihl, the latter named for the building's patron, chainsaw manufacturer Stihl, and its foundation, the Eva-Mayr-Stihl-Stiftung.

Two longitudinal pavilions – rounded off at the corners and offset to create a passageway between them – stand out starkly with their cool industrial façades of translucent glass U-profiles from the

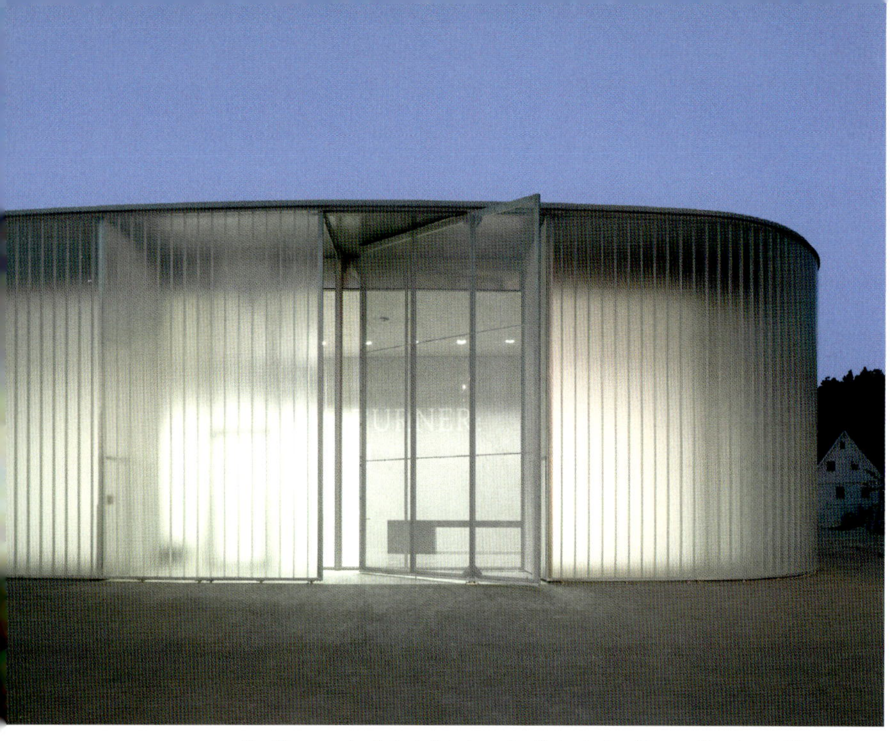

Der Eingang der Galerie ist ein sechs Meter hohes Tor aus Streckmetalllamellen.
The entrance to the gallery is a six-metre-high portal of expanded-metal blades.

Wie außen, so dominiert auch im Inneren der Bauten der Eindruck des unprätentiösen und doch zu höherer Askese veredelten Werkhallen-Charmes. Man betritt die Galerie durch ein sechs Meter hohes Tor aus Streckmetalllamellen: Dunkler Sichtbeton, grauer Magnesit-Estrich und die transluzenten, das einfallende Außenlicht weiß filternde Glaswände bestimmen den Eindruck rund um den langen Foyertisch aus lasiertem Fichtenholz. Jenseits des Foyers liegt der 600 Quadratmeter große, stützenlose Ausstellungsraum, der sich durch frei zu platzierende Stellwände flexibel bespielen lässt. Die Belichtung erfolgt allein durch die gläsernen Seitenwände, deren dreischalige Konstruktion nicht nur eine wärmedämmende, das Licht dämpfende Kapillarschicht, sondern auch Verdunklungsrollos aufnimmt, mit denen sich, manuell im 700 Millimeter breiten Zwischenraum der Fassadenschalung justierbar, der Raum weiter abdunkeln lässt. Indirektes Tageslicht von oben, wie im Entwurf der Architekten noch mit Sheddächern angedacht, ließ sich aus Kostengründen in dem mit 5,7 Millionen Euro vergleichsweise preiswerten Komplex nicht umsetzen. Leuchtschienen, die in die Decke eingelassen wurden, schaffen ein reduziertes Kunstlicht – für eine Galerie, die sich in erster Linie auf wechselnde Ausstellungen von Papierarbeiten verlegt hat, eine ausreichende, wenn auch wirkungsästhetisch nicht vollends überzeugende Lösung. Die konzentrierte, meditative Raumstimmung, die der Wechsel des natürlichen Tageslichts sanft belebt, wird unterstrichen durch präzise ausgeführte Details wie die imposanten, raumhohen Stahltüren, die zwischen Ausstellungshalle und den beiden Innenkernen mit Depotraum und WCs vermitteln.

historic backdrop of stone and half-timbered houses. Despite the deliberate contrast, the ensemble has been proportioned and placed in a way that makes visual reference to its setting and at the same time creates new spatial contexts. Across from the old municipal museum, a new 'Museum Square' is evolving between the new structures and a recently built glass building for the museum offices and café. Beyond the narrow passage between the art gallery and school, the vista opens up dynamically onto the newly constructed 'Rems Terrace'.

Just like their exteriors, the interiors of the two buildings have an unpretentious look with a typical factory-hall charm refined to a higher-level asceticism. One enters the gallery through a six-metre-high portal of expanded-metal blades to find a foyer of dark exposed concrete with a grey magnesite floor and translucent glass walls that filter the fall of light across the long counter of varnished spruce. Beyond the foyer is the 600-square-metre uninterrupted exhibition space, which can be divided as desired using partitions. Light comes from the glass side walls alone, the three-shell structure of which provides a heat-insulating, light-softening capillary layer as well as holding blinds that can be manually operated in the 700-millimetre intermediate space to darken the room. The shed roofs planned by the architects to provide indirect daylight from above were no longer possible within the 5.7-million-euro budget of this comparatively inexpensive complex. Light rails inserted in the ceiling provide a subdued artificial light instead – adequate for a gallery designed primarily for changing exhibitions of works on paper, although in terms of aesthetic effect not a completely satisfying solution. The concentrated, meditative ambience, gently enlivened by the changing natural daylight, is underscored by the carefully orchestrated details, such as the imposing, room-high steel doors between the exhibition hall and the two inner cores with storage and toilets.

The art school situated next to the gallery on the square – a proximity that encourages a close intermeshing of the event programmes of the two – is made of very similar materials, and yet the impression within is completely different. Here, closely packed workshops on two floors are grouped around a central foyer with light coming in from above. Room-high wooden sliding doors and glass partitions allow the studios on the ground floor to be connected to form a loft-like hall. When the ballet studio fuses with the foyer and the adjacent

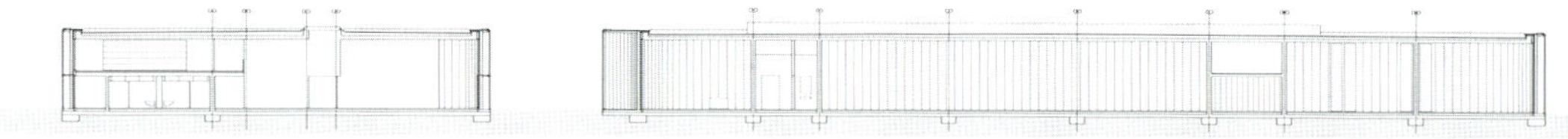

Schnitt | Section

Die vis-à-vis am Platz liegende Kunstschule – eine
Nachbarschaft, die zu enger Vernetzung des Veranstaltungspro-
gramms einlädt – ist von ganz ähnlicher Materialität, und doch
ist der Eindruck von Innen ein ganz anderer: In großer räum-
licher Dichte verteilen sich hier die Werkstatträume auf zwei
Etagen um ein zentrales, von oben belichtetes Foyer. Raumhohe Schiebetüren aus Holz und Zwischenwände aus Glas
erlauben es, die Ateliers im Erdgeschoss zu einer Loft-ähnlichen
Halle zu verbinden. Wenn das Ballettstudio mit dem Foyer und
der benachbarten Bildhauerwerkstatt zu einem großen Arbeits-
oder Veranstaltungsraum verschmelzen, erfüllen sich die
Räume mit Leben – auch die asketischen Sichtbetonwände
tragen die ersten Spuren davon.
Das Spiel der Ähnlichkeit der Volumina und der Verschieden-
heit der inneren Raumdispositionen verleiht dem Ensemble
eine besondere Spannung. Dass diese im Kontext einer historischen Altstadt so unprätentiös und ohne Adaption historisierender Elemente realisiert werden konnte, zeugt vom Mut der
Wettbewerbsjury und einer architektonisch tatsächlich ,jungen
Stadt'.

sculpture workshop to become a large space for
work or events, the rooms fill with life – even the
austere exposed concrete walls already bear the
first traces of activity.
The ensemble gains a unique tension from the
play between the similarity of the two volumes and
the utter difference in the disposition of rooms
within. That this could be realised in the context
of a historic town in such an unpretentious manner
and without including historicising elements
demonstrates the courage of the competition jury
and shows that Waiblingen is indeed, architecturally
speaking, a "young town".

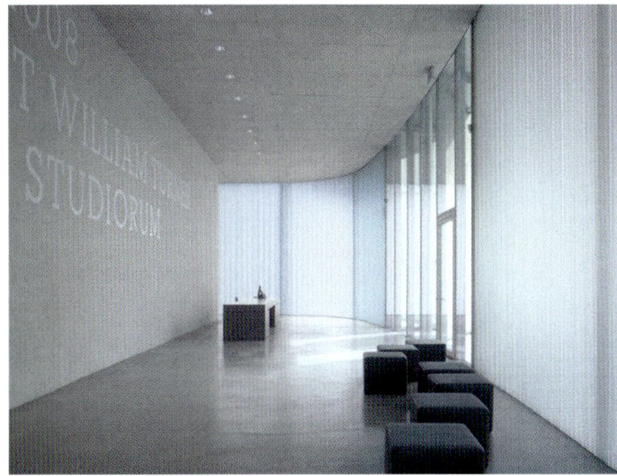

**Der Ausstellungsraum wird durch gläserne Seitenwände
belichtet. |** The exhibition space receives light through glazed
side walls.

Durchblick | View through the building

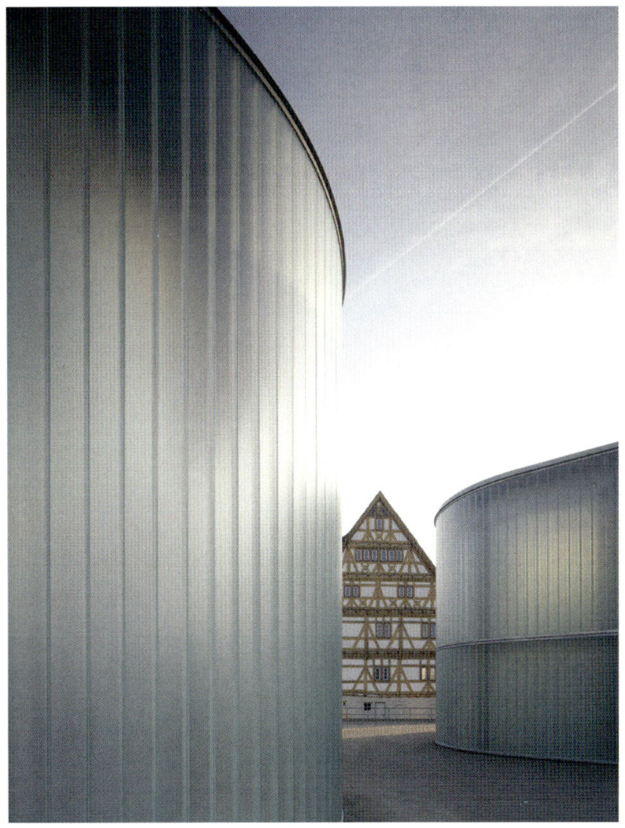

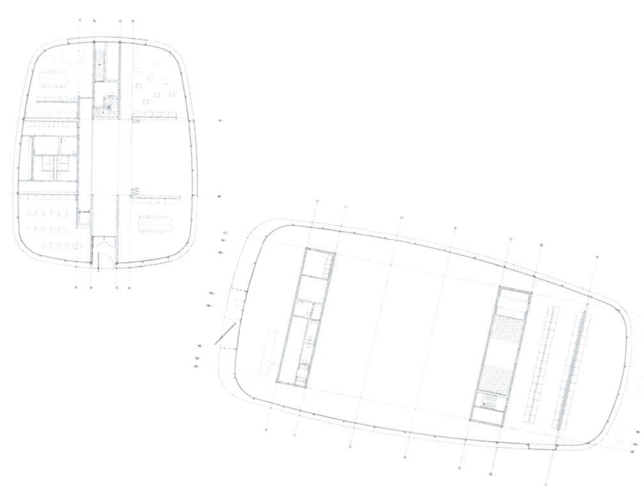

Grundriss Obergeschoss | Floor plan of upper level

Grundriss Erdgeschoss | Floor plan of ground floor

HIENDL_SCHINEIS

HAUS_L

TEXT SANDRA HOFMEISTER

14

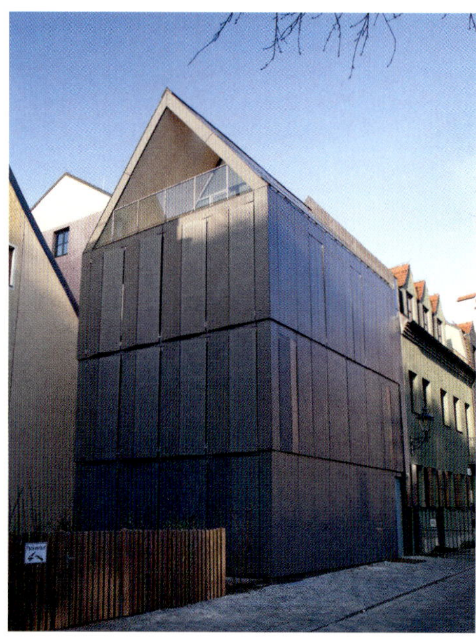

Die Außenhaut aus Faserzementplatten lässt sich komplett schließen und auffalten. | The outer skin of fibre cement panels can be closed completely and folded open again.

ARCHITEKTEN | ARCHITECTS

hiendl_schineis
Architektenpartnerschaft
Am Schanzl 10
94032 Passau

Mittlerer Lech 39
86150 Augsburg
www.hiendlschineis.com

MITARBEITER | TEAM

Andreas Selbertinger,
Christine Andrijanic

BAUHERR | CLIENT

Gabriele Lindermayr

TRAGWERK | STRUCTURE

Ingenieurgesellschaft
für das Bauwesen, Augsburg

FERTIGSTELLUNG | COMPLETION

Oktober 2007 | October 2007

STANDORT | LOCATION

Doktorgässchen 5
Domviertel
86152 Augsburg

FOTOS | PHOTOS

Eckhart Matthäus, hiendl_schineis

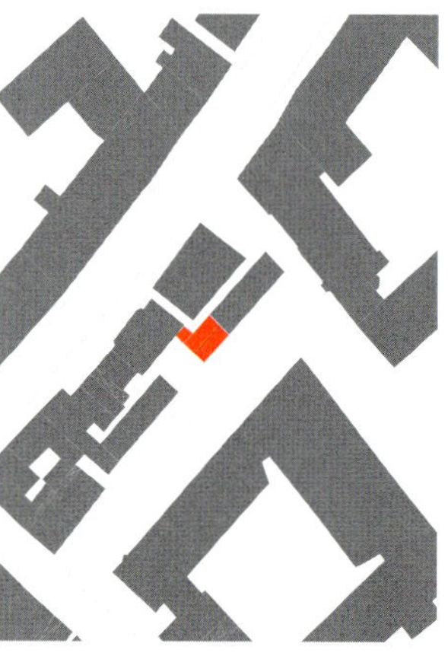

Lageplan | Site plan

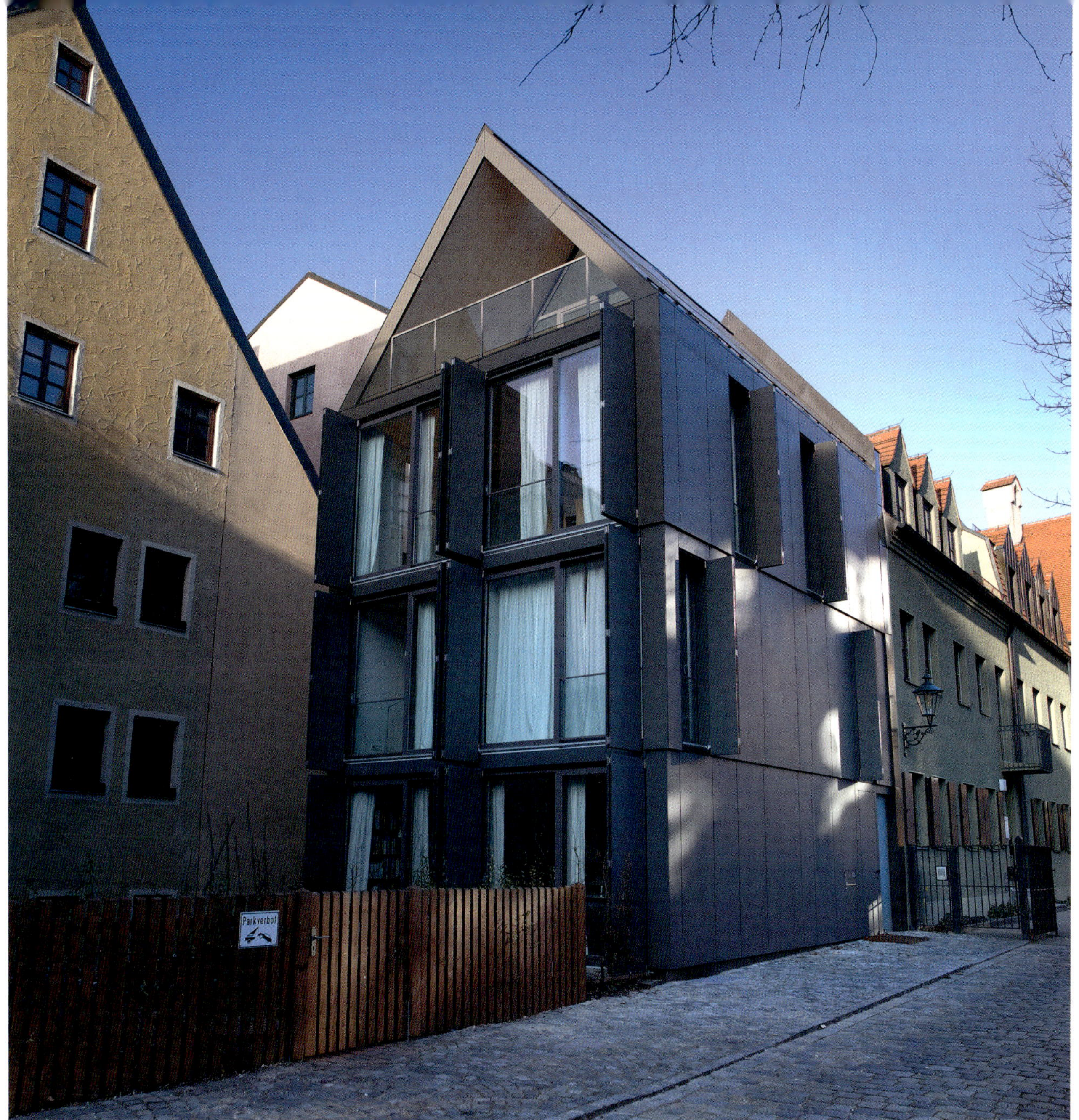

Referenz an historische Bürgerhäuser | Reference to historic townhouses

Das spitze Satteldach des Wohnhauses im Doktorgässchen reiht sich respektvoll in die ensemblegeschützte Häuserzeile am Rand der Augsburger Innenstadt ein – eine Referenz an historische Bürgerhäuser, deren Typologie die Architektin Regina Schineis in ihrem Entwurf interpretierend aufgriff. Augsburg ist eine barocke Stadt, die Fassaden des Neubaus hingegen verweisen auf ein unpathetisches modernes Architekturverständnis, das nicht auf Konfrontation, sondern auf die Ergänzung des historischen Bestandes aus ist. Geschosshohe durchgefärbte Faserzementplatten umhüllen die Holzständerkonstruktion auf allen Seiten, vom Erdgeschoss bis zum Dachfirst. Weder Dachrinnen noch -ziegel stören die makellose graubraune Oberfläche, deren Einheitlichkeit die klare Kubatur des dreigeschossigen Wohnhauses noch deutlicher hervortreten lässt. Vertikal wie Schuppen übereinandergelegt, strecken sich die Faserzementplatten entsprechend den zunehmenden Raumhöhen in den oberen Stockwerken. Dieser dezente Rhythmus wird durch ein verhaltenes Farbspiel unterstützt, das die Braun-

The steep gable roof of the residence on Doktorgässchen takes its place respectfully in the row of houses, protected buildings, on the outskirts of Augsburg city centre – making reference to the historic townhouses there, whose typology architect Regina Schineis has taken up and interpreted in a new way in her design. Augsburg is a Baroque city, but the façades of the new building reveal an undramatic, modern approach to architecture, one that is not bent on confrontation but rather aims to complement the historic buildings around it. Fibre cement panels the same height as the storeys enclose the wooden post-and-beam structure on all sides, from the ground floor to the roof ridge. Neither gutters nor roofing tiles disturb the immaculate grey-brown surface, whose uniformity highlights even further the clear cubic shape of the three-storey home. Vertically placed one above the

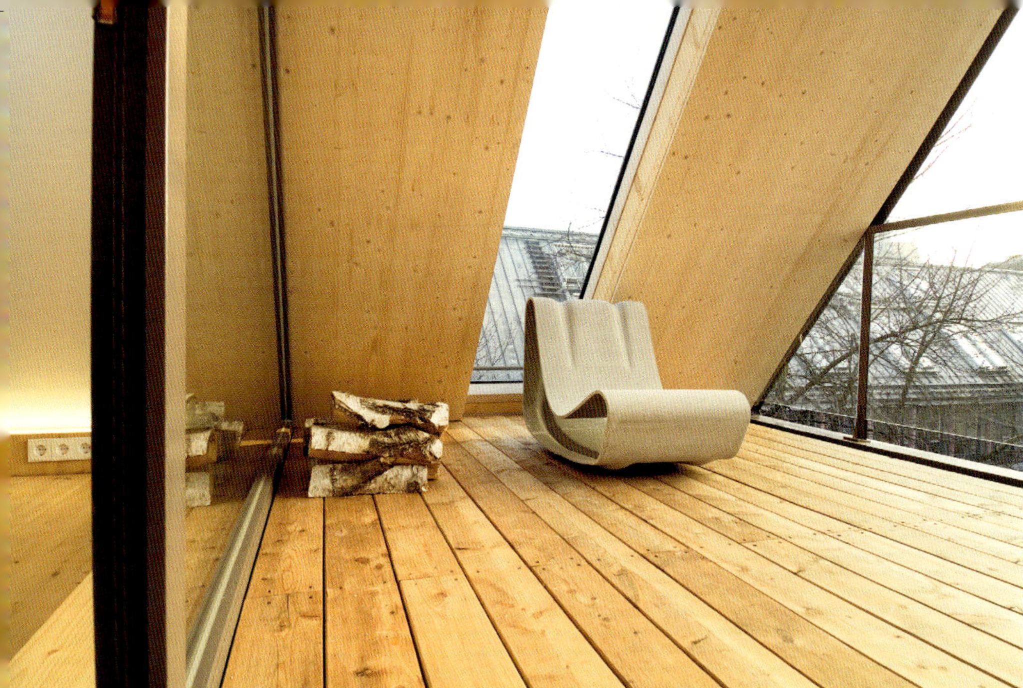

Terrasse im Dachgeschoss | Roof-level terrace

Weder Dachrinnen noch -ziegel unterbrechen die einheitliche Kubatur.
Neither gutters nor roofing tiles disturb the uniform cubic shape.

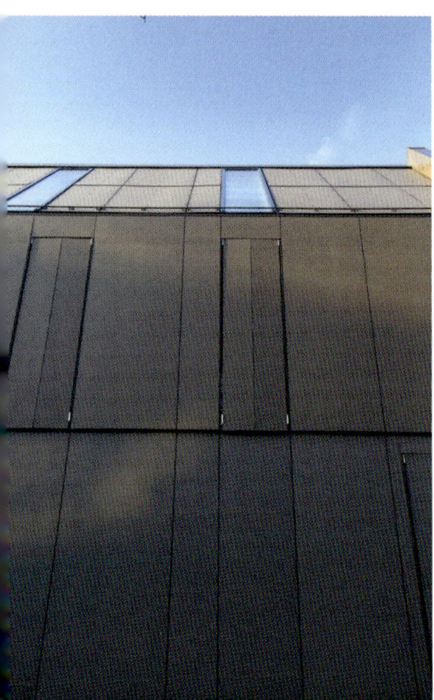

töne des durchgefärbten Materials nach oben heller werden lässt.
Diese gekonnte Differenzierung der Fassade macht die Raumaufteilung des Gebäudes sichtbar: Die zentralen Wohnbereiche
liegen in den oberen Geschossen, die mehr Licht erhalten.
Regina Schineis hat ein Wohnhaus entworfen, dessen kompakte
Architektur sich in Schichten und geschichteten Geschossen
präsentiert, die in die Höhe gestaffelt an Grundfläche dazu-
gewinnen. An einigen Stellen lässt sich die Außenhaut falten,
wegschieben und öffnen. Hinter den Faltschiebeläden – verschließbare Aluminiumrahmen, auf denen die Faserzementplatten angebracht wurden – verbergen sich raumhohe Fenster.
Der Nutzung entsprechend sind die Läden an einigen Stellen
geschlitzt. In geschlossenem Zustand bleiben sie beinahe
unsichtbar und ordnen sich dem einheitlichen Gesamtbild unter,
in offenem Zustand aber verändert sich die Außenwirkung des
Hauses: Zum Garten des Nachbargrundstücks öffnen sich dann
auf drei Stockwerken große Fensterflächen, die eine kompakte
Wohnraumstruktur erkennen lassen. Eine zurückgesetzte
Terrasse schließt das Dachgeschoss ab und reiht sich mit seiner
gläsernen Brüstung, die auch vor den Schiebefenstern in den
unteren Stockwerken zum Einsatz kommt, in die klaren Linien
des übersichtlichen Gebäudevolumens ein.
„Ich liebe dieses Ritual, die Läden im ganzen Haus abends zu
schließen und morgens zu öffnen", sagt die Hausherrin. Nach
Beratung mit der Architektin hat sie sich entschieden, den
maroden Vorgängerbau durch ein neues Haus mit ähnlicher
Kubatur zu ersetzen. Einzelne Teile des Rohbaus in Holzrahmenbauweise konnten kostengünstig vorproduziert und
zeitsparend auf der Baustelle montiert werden.
Im Inneren des Hauses breitet sich auf der überschaubaren
Grundfläche von 50 Quadratmetern eine kompakte Wohnland-
schaft aus. Eine schmale Holztreppe ohne Handlauf erschließt
die Stockwerke entlang der nordöstlichen Brandwand. Fensteröffnungen geben Blickachsen nach draußen frei und sorgen für

other like scales on a fish, the fibre cement panels
increase in height along with the rooms as the
storeys progress upward. Lending support to this
understated rhythm is a reserved colour scheme,
with the brown tones of the monochromatic material lighter on the upper floors. This skilful differen-
tiation of the façade makes the room divisions in
the building legible on the outside: the central living
areas are on the upper levels, which receive more
light.
Regina Schineis has designed a home whose
compact architecture presents itself in layers and
layered storeys, which become larger in area the
higher they are. In some places the outer skin of the
building is equipped with folding sliding shutters
that can be opened to let in light. Behind these
shutters – consisting of closable aluminium frames
onto which the fibre cement panels are affixed – are
floor-length windows. In some places the shutters
have slits to let in light. When closed they remain
nearly invisible and subordinate themselves to the
uniform overall surface of the building, but when
open they change the exterior effect of the house.
Large expanses of window facing the garden of the
neighbouring plot then open up on three storeys,
revealing a compactly structured living space. A
set-back terrace completes the roof storey, with a
glass balustrade – a feature also found in front of
the sliding windows in the lower storeys – that
harmonises well with the clean lines of the built
volume.
"I love this ritual of closing the shutters all over the
house at night and opening them in the morning",
says the lady of the house. After consulting with
the architect, she decided to replace the run-down
previous building with a new house similar in
silhouette. Wooden frame construction was chosen,
which made it possible to prefabricate some parts
of the shell inexpensively and then assemble them
on site, saving time.
Inside the house, a compact domestic landscape
spreads out over the modest 50-square-metre
footprint. A narrow wooden stairway without a
hand-rail provides access to the various levels along
the northeastern firewall. Window openings provide
views outside and illuminate the landings. The
pared-down but homely atmosphere is characte-

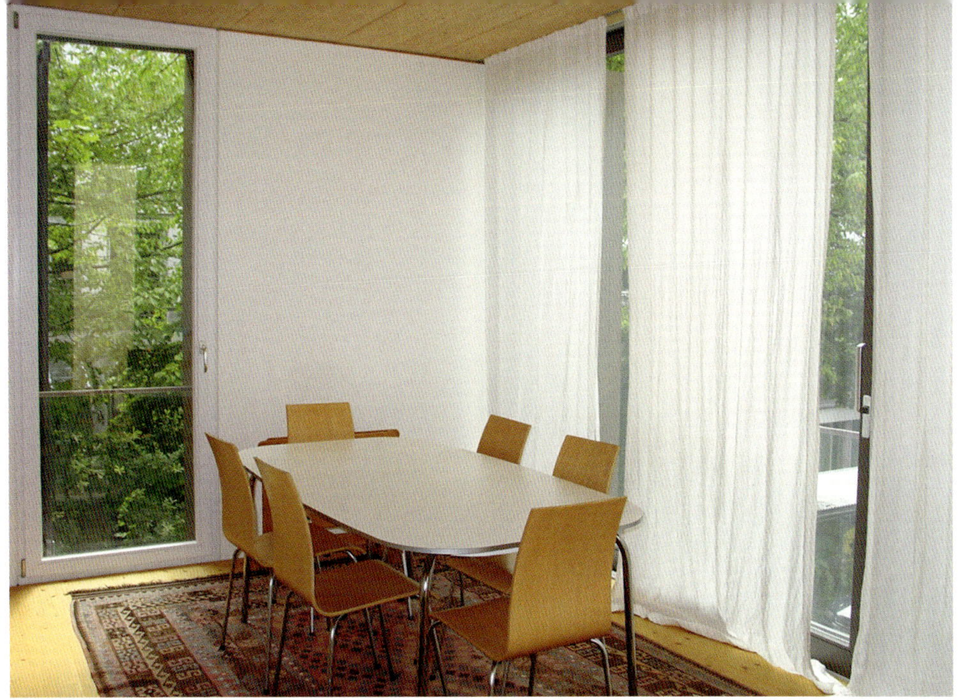

Essbereich | Dining area

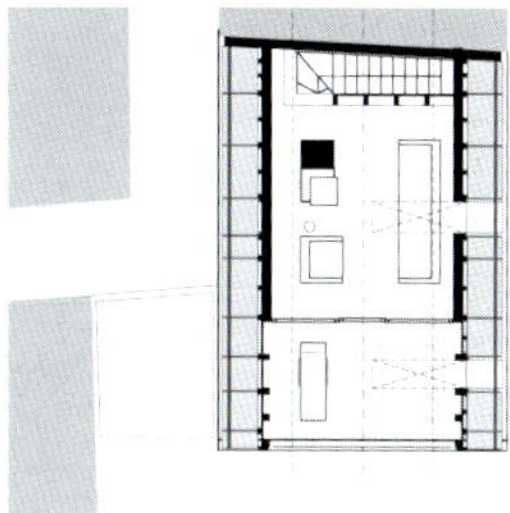

Grundriss Dachgeschoss
Floor plan of attic storey

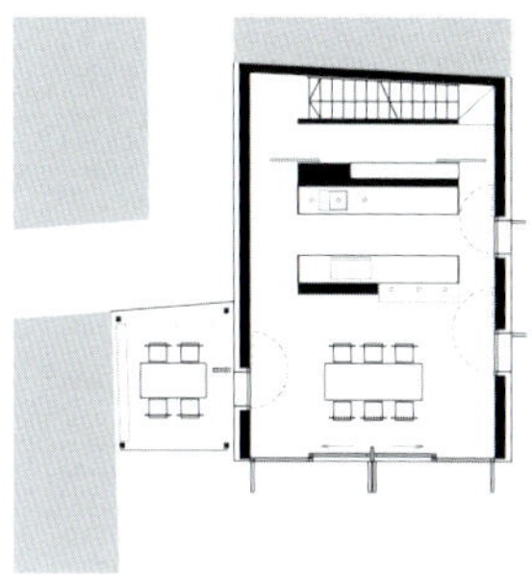

Grundriss 2. Obergeschoss
Floor plan of 2nd floor

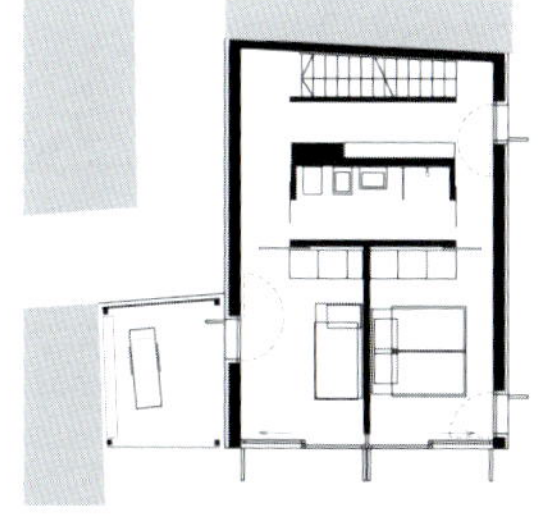

Grundriss 1. Obergeschoss
Floor plan of 1st floor

helle Treppenabsätze. Das schlichte, wohnliche Ambiente zeichnet sich durch die geschickte Raumorganisation und ein behagliches Raumklima aus. Unbehandelte Böden aus Weißtanne und weiß gehaltene Wände charakterisieren die Atmosphäre. Das Haus ist mit Holzfasern gedämmt und kommt dank des zentralen Versorgungsblocks in allen Geschossen ohne abgehängte Decken aus. Über dem Arbeitszimmer im Erdgeschoss gruppieren sich im ersten Stock zwei Schlafräume um ein mittiges Bad. Sämtliche Türen sind als Schiebeelemente ausgeführt und verschwinden unauffällig in den dafür vorgesehenen Wandschlitzen. Der Wohnbereich im zweiten Stock öffnet sich zum Garten – ein lichtdurchfluteter Raum mit geschosshohen Fenstern. Die zentrale Küche fügt sich mit weißen Schrank- und Arbeitsflächen in die zurückhaltende Raumsprache. Ein kleiner Balkon erweitert den Wohnbereich – die Stahlkonstruktion trennt das Wohnhaus von seinem nordwestlichen Nachbarn.

Ganz oben, unter dem spitzen Dach des Hauses, breitet sich ein helles Zimmer mit Kamin, verglastem Giebel und vorgelagerter überdachter Terrasse aus. Lange Lichtbänder werfen abends indirektes Licht an die steilen Dachschrägen. Durch die schmalen Fensterschlitze im Dach fällt der Blick über die Augsburger Innenstadt, und im Hintergrund ragt der barocke Zwiebelturm der Heilig-Kreuz-Kirche in den Himmel.

rised by deft spatial organisation and a comfortable room climate. Untreated floors of white pine and white walls give the interior its feel. The house has woodfibre insulation and makes do without suspended ceilings thanks to a central supply block on all floors. Above the office on the ground floor are two bedrooms grouped around a bathroom on the first floor. All doors slide into slots in the wall, disappearing when open. The living area on the second floor opens onto the garden – a light-flooded space with floor-to-ceiling windows. The central kitchen with its white cabinets and work surfaces fits the low-key character of the spaces. A small balcony extends the living space, its steel structure separating the house from its north-western neighbour.

At the very top, underneath the pointed roof, is a brightly lit room with a fireplace, glazed gable and roofed terrace. At night, long bands of light indirectly illuminate its steeply pitched walls. Glimpses can be caught of the Augsburg city centre through narrow window slits in the roof, and in the background the Baroque onion-dome church tower of the Heilig-Kreuz-Kirche rises into the sky.

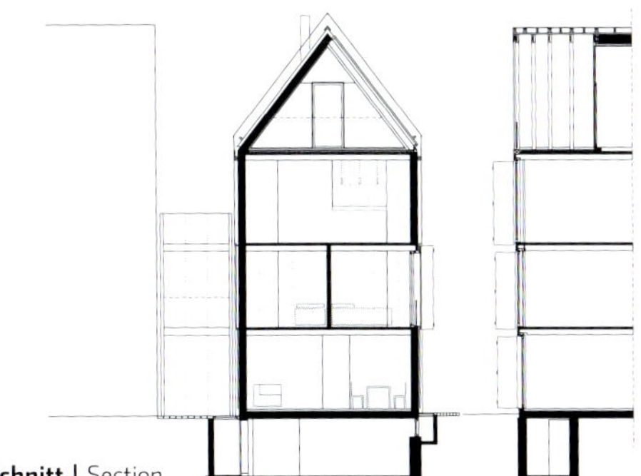

Schnitt | Section

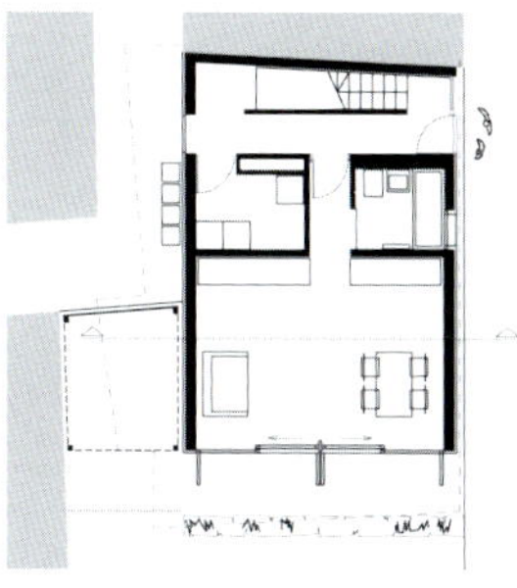

Grundriss Erdgeschoss
Floor plan of ground floor

J. MAYER H.

DUPLI. CASA

TEXT DOROTHEA DESCHERMEIER

15

ARCHITEKTEN | ARCHITECTS
J. MAYER H. Architekten
Bleibtreustrasse 54
10623 Berlin
www.jmayerh.de

MITARBEITER | TEAM
Jürgen Mayer H., Georg
Schmidthals, Thorsten Blatter,
Simon Takasaki, Andre Santer,
Sebastian Finckh

LOKALER KONTAKTARCHITEKT
ARCHITECT ON SITE
AB Wiesler, Stuttgart

BAUHERR | CLIENT
Privat | private

TRAGWERK | STRUCTURE
Dieter Kubasch

HAUSTECHNIK
M&E ENGINEERS
Ingenieurbüro Hans Wagner,
Filderstadt

BAUPHYSIK | BUILDING PHYSICS
Ingenieurbüro
Dr. Schaecke + Bayer,
Waiblingen-Hegnach

FERTIGSTELLUNG | COMPLETION
2008

STANDORT | LOCATION
bei | near **Ludwigsburg**

FOTOS | PHOTOS
David Franck

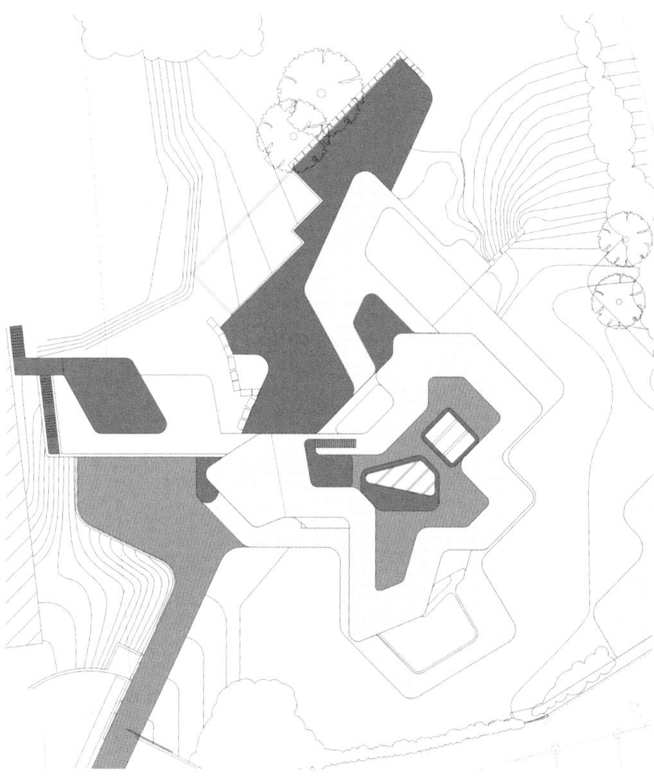

Lageplan | Site plan

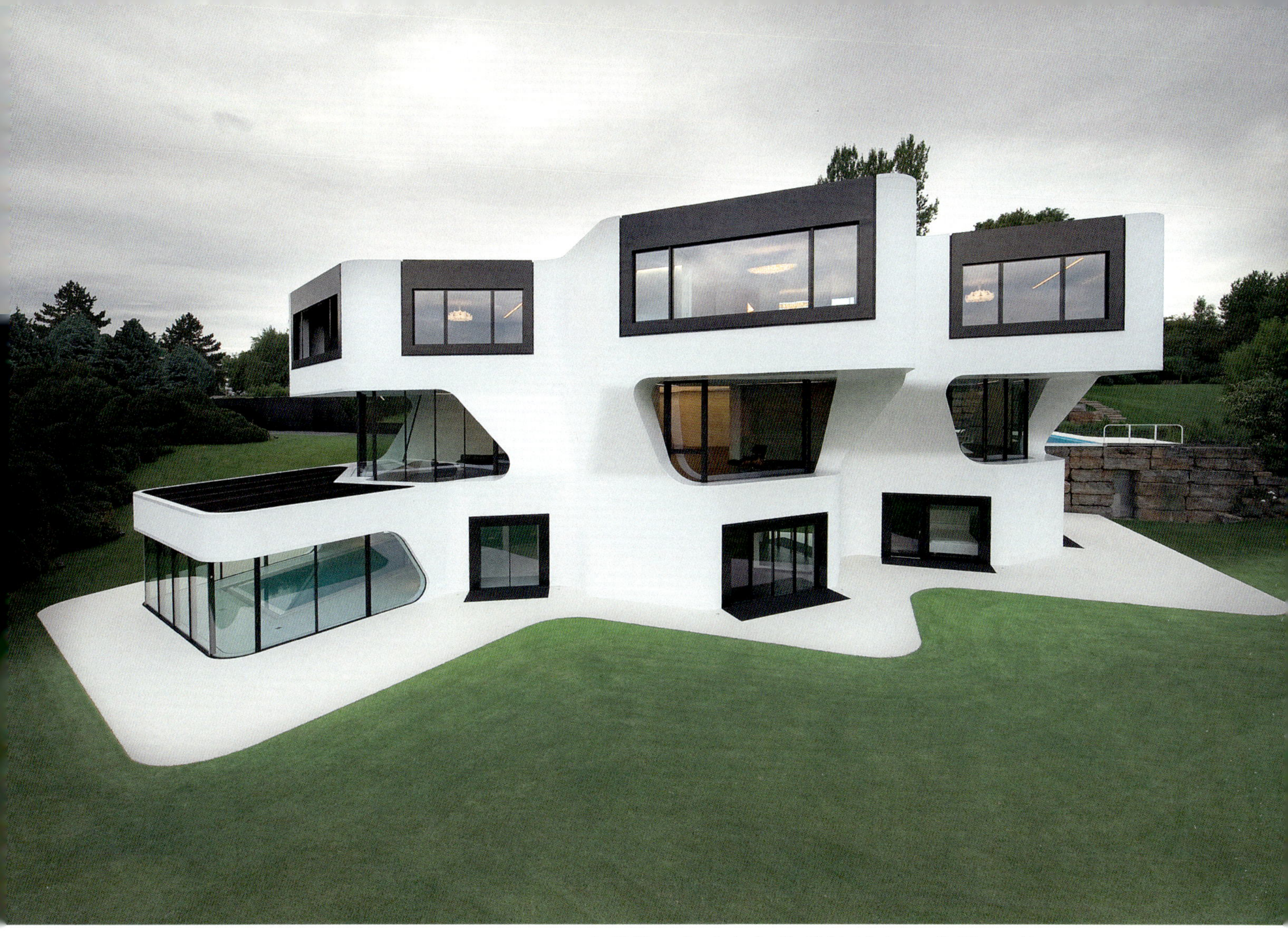

Wie hingegossen schmiegt sich die Dupli.Casa an den Hang des Neckarufers und hebt sich leuchtend weiß vom Grün der Natur ab, was den artifiziellen Habitus des Gebäudes noch unterstreicht. Die Grundidee der Dupli.Casa basiert auf dem komplexen ‚footprint' des Vorgängerbaus von 1984, der aus zahlreichen Um- und Anbauten resultiert. Die Bauherrenfamilie, bereits Auftraggeber des Bestandbaus, wollte ein neues Haus, aber kein neues Wohngefühl. Ihr Anliegen war es, die emotionale Verankerung auch im Neubau zu spüren, ‚Familienarchäologie', nennt Mayer H. das. Die Umrisslinie der alten Villa bleibt also als Kennung erhalten, wird über ein eingeschobenes gläsernes Erdgeschoss hinaus extrudiert und als dupliziertes Oberge- schoss zum ursprünglichen Gartengeschoss verdreht. Wie um diese Bewegung sichtbar zu machen, wird die Außenhaut zwischen den beiden Geschossen schräg verzogen und plastisch durchgebildet. Was wie dehnbares Material anmutet und den Eindruck von Weichheit hervorruft, sind in Wirklichkeit Kuben aus Porenbeton, einem Material, das den Vorteil hat, leicht und wärmedämmend zu sein. Einmal an der Stahlbetonkonstruktion angebracht, werden sie unter Zuhilfenahme von Schablonen so lange zurechtgeschliffen, bis sie die richtigen Rundungen annehmen. Die Illusion, und mit ihr einhergehend auch die Irri-

Dupli.Casa clings to a slope overlooking the river Neckar as if poured on, standing out in glowing white from the green of the natural landscape surrounding it, which has the effect of further underscoring the artificial air of the building. The basic idea behind Dupli.Casa was to retrace the complex footprint of the house before it, which was built in 1984 but since then had undergone a series of extensions and modifications. The clients, who had also built the previous house, wanted a new building, but not a whole new layout. They wanted to feel emotionally rooted in their new house, to maintain their 'family archaeology' as Mayer H. calls it. The floor plan of the old villa was thus preserved for identification, but was extruded out over an inserted glazed ground floor, with a duplicated upper floor set above the original garden storey and then twisted. As if to make this rotation visible, the outer skin between the two levels warps into a fluid sculptural relief. What looks a like pliable, malleable substance is however actually composed of cubes of aerated concrete – a material that has the

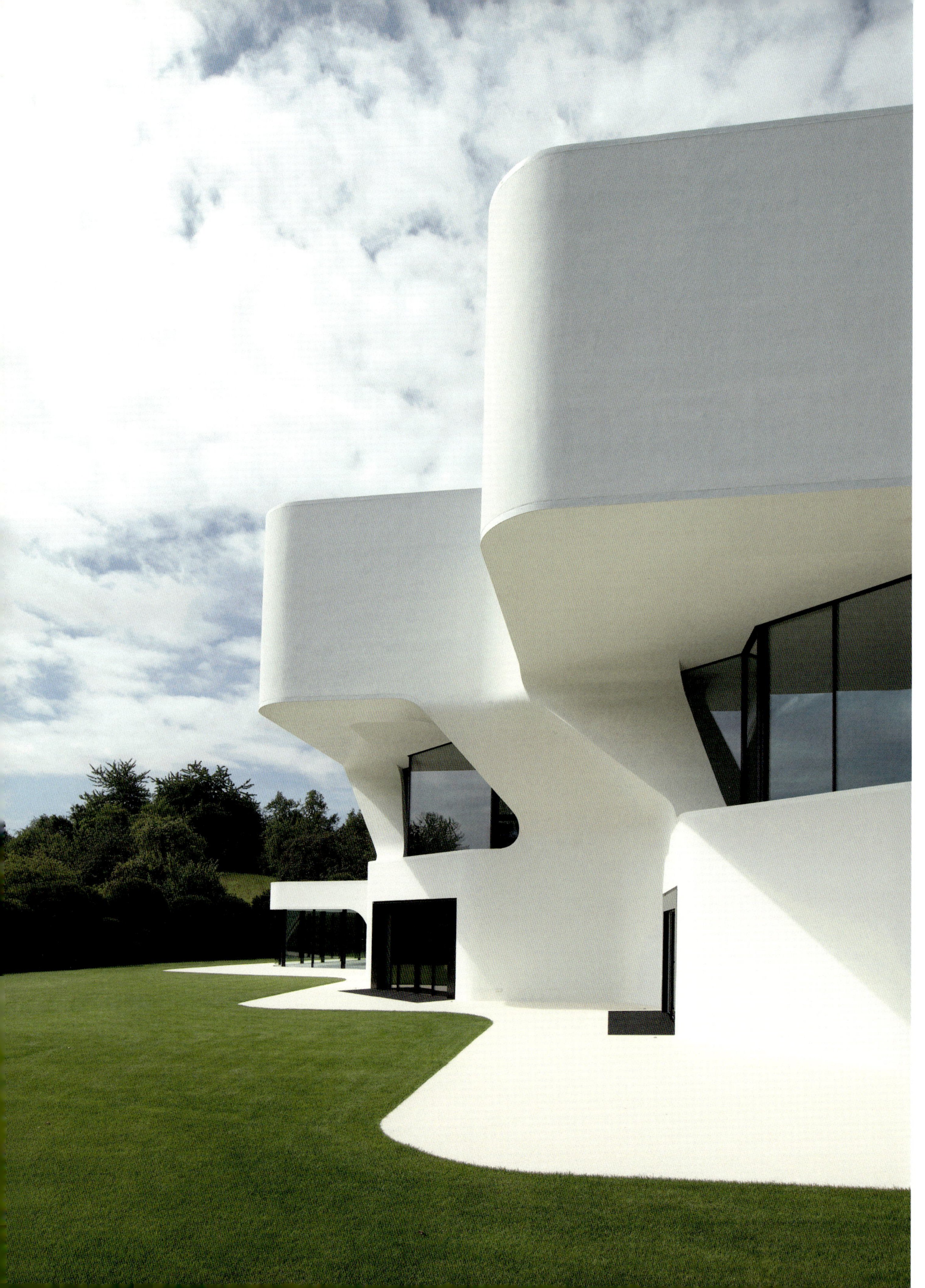

tation, die beim Betrachter ausgelöst werden, sind Konstanten im Werk von Mayer H. Bei der Mensa in Karlsruhe und dem Pavillon in Sevilla gaukelt einem eine drei Millimeter dicke, aufgespritzten Polyurethanschicht Elastizität vor, während sich unter ihr eine Holzkonstruktion verbirgt. Da Mayer H. sich der Architektur über den Kunstbegriff nähert, insbesondere über die Skulptur, erlaubt er es sich, einigen Kardinaltugenden, durch die sich die deutsche Architektur international auszeichnet, aus dem Weg zu gehen, wie zum Beispiel den Fragen nach Ehrlichkeit in Material und Konstruktion. Diese Begriffe scheren Meyer H. wenig, er spielt nach anderen Regeln, was bei den Kollegen und Fachleuten nicht selten Befremdung hervorruft. Mayer H. formt Architektur wie ein Künstler seine Plastik. Der Entwurfsprozess wird dabei weniger von der Überhöhung technischer Details oder der Funktionsgebundenheit als vielmehr von der Idee einer Gesamtatmosphäre beherrscht.

Die Oberflächenbearbeitung ist ihm wichtig, die plastische Durchbildung und eine eklatante Form. Die Perfektion in der Ausführung bleibt da manchmal auf der Strecke. Auch die Dupli.Casa weist den einen oder anderen Makel auf. So ist die Außenhaut zum Beispiel nicht so homogen, wie man es sich wünschen würde, Skulpturen haben schließlich selten Abtropfkanten. Wer aber wie Mayer H. neue Formen und Materialien konjugiert und von der Form hin zur Ausführung denkt und nicht umgekehrt, der muss wohl ab und an auch mit einer technischer Unausgegorenheit rechnen, wie sie dem Architekten oftmals vorgehalten wird.

Auf der glatten Oberfläche der Villa setzen die schwarzen Fensterprofile mit Schattenfugen grafische Akzente und ziehen sich im Obergeschoss bis zur Dachkante hoch, die mit Polyurethan verblendet ist. Das Material wird auch auf den Abschwemmflächen verwendet, wo das wartungsintensive Weiß besonders schmutzgefährdet ist. Dach, Mauern und Geschosse verschmelzen in der Dupli.Casa zu einer Gesamtform, die in weißen Tartanringen, die als Terrassen dienen, in den Rasen ausläuft.

In den großzügigen Wellnessbereich im Gartengeschoss der Villa sind Teile des Bestandpools integriert. Ein mit Ranken verziertes „1984", das in seinen Boden eingelassen ist, schimmert durch das Wasser. Wie ein Grundstein oder ein in der Tiefe des Wassers ruhender Schatz verweist das Datum auf die Bau- und damit Familiengeschichte, auf der der Neubau gründet.

Das Obergeschoss beherbergt die privaten Räume, während das

advantage of being lightweight and heat insulating. Once affixed to the ferroconcrete structure, these concrete blocks were filed away using templates until the desired curvature was attained. The illusion, and with it the puzzlement provoked in the viewer, are constants in the work of Mayer H. In a university dining hall in Karlsruhe and a pavilion in Seville that he designed, a three-millimetre-thick sprayed-on polyurethane layer masquerades as an elastic structure, while underneath the building is actually made of wood. Because Mayer H. approaches architecture from the perspective of art, especially of sculpture, he ventures to circumvent some of the cardinal virtues attributed internationally to German architecture, such as questions of honesty in materials and construction. These concepts mean little to Mayer H. – he plays according to a different set of rules, which not infrequently has the effect of alienating colleagues and critics. Mayer H. shapes architecture as an artist forms a sculpture. His design process is dominated not so much by the exaggeration of technical details or a dedication to function as by the idea of an overall feeling to be achieved.

Surface finishing is important to him, along with plastic shape and a spectacular form. In the process, perfection of execution sometimes falls by the wayside. Dupli.Casa, too, exhibits one or two flaws. For example, the outer skin is not as homogeneous as one would wish – after all, sculptures rarely need

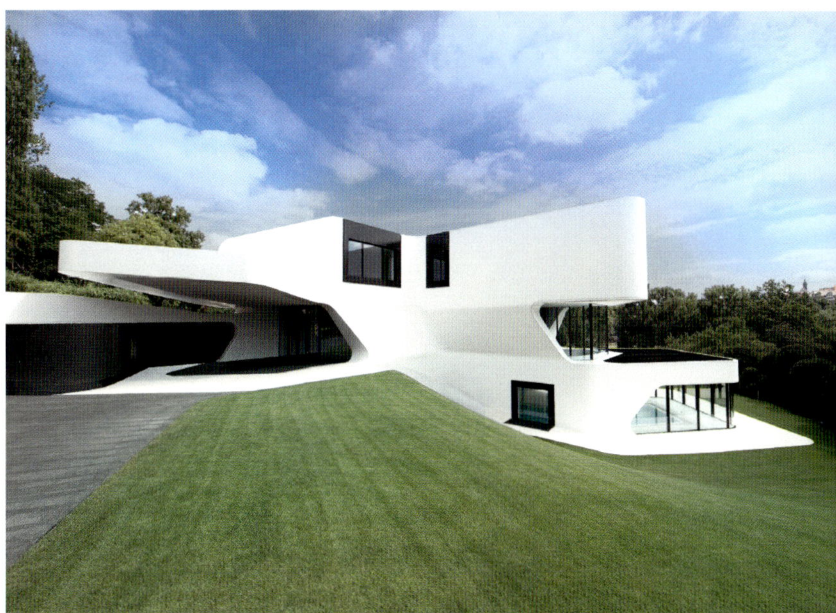

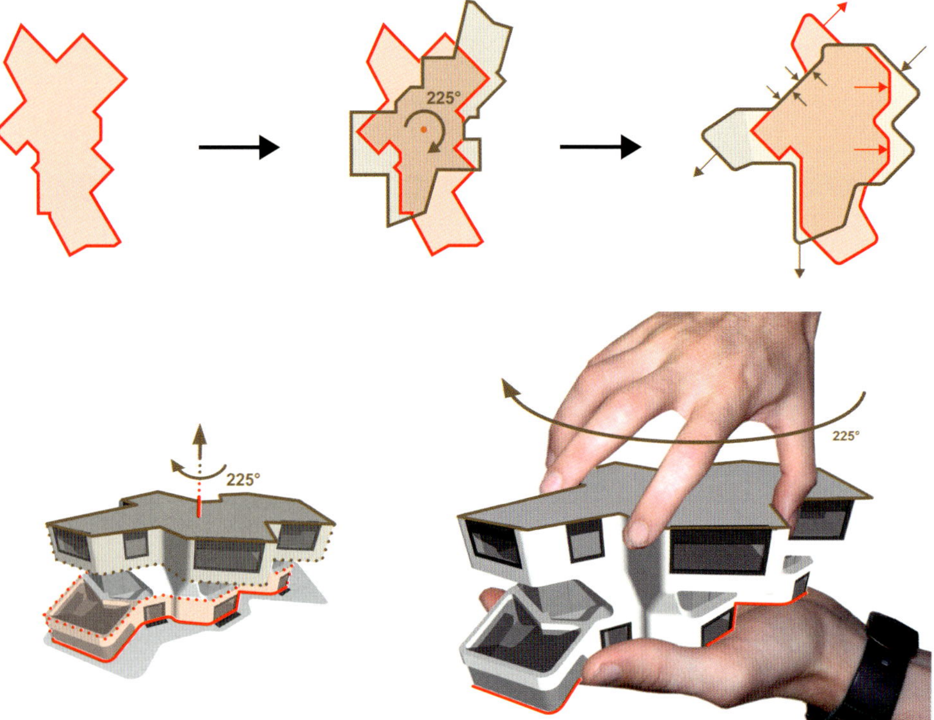

Konzept | Concept

mittlere als öffentlicher Bereich fungiert: Über ein geschoss-übergreifendes, lichtes Atrium betritt man das Haus. Von hier aus öffnen sich Wohnzimmer, Esszimmer und Studio der Hausherrin. Obwohl sie alle in einem Kontinuum mit Durch- und Ausblicken zusammenfließen, behalten die einzelnen Bereiche ihre Intimität, da sie fast tropfenförmig an die Lobby anschließen und jeweils eine eigene Räumlichkeit ausbilden. Die bodentiefen Öffnungen der soft-edge Panormafenster sind in die durch den vorgeblendeten Porenbeton stellenweise bis über zwei Meter tiefen Außenwände eingeschnitten. Das verdrehte Obergeschoss kragt schützend über sie hinaus, so dass sich die Assoziation einer sicheren weißen Höhle einstellt. Von hier aus lässt sich der weite Ausblick zum Deutschen Literaturarchiv auf der gegenüberliegenden Neckarseite erst recht genießen.

drip edges. Anyone who, like Mayer H., conjugates new forms and materials, thinking up the form first and then the execution, rather than the other way round, must presumably reckon with a certain lack of technical sophistication now and then, a criticism often directed at his work.

Set against the villa's fluid white surfaces, the black window profiles with their shadow seams provide a graphic note, on the upper storey continuing all the way up to the roof edge, which is concealed behind polyurethane. This material is also used on areas exposed to water run-off, where the high-maintenance white surface is particularly likely to become soiled. The roof and outer walls of Dupli.Casa melt into an overall form that oozes out onto the lawn in white tartan rings that serve as terraces.

In the spacious spa area on the garden level, part of the existing swimming pool has been integrated into the new structure. A "1984" adorned with tendrils and set into the bottom of the pool shimmers through the water. Like a foundation stone or a treasure resting deep beneath the sea, this date refers to the history of the house and family, the basis for the new building.

The upper level contains the private rooms, while the middle storey functions as a more public zone, the entrance leading in through a light-filled atrium that connects all the floors. The atrium gives onto the living room, dining room and the studio of the lady of the house. Although they all flow together in a continuum of lines of sight and views outside, each area nonetheless retains its intimacy and its own spatial unity. Connected to the lobby almost like droplets, each constitutes an independent space. The floor-length soft-edged panoramic windows are carved into the outer walls, which are up to two metres thick in places due to the cladding of aerated concrete. The twisted upper floor juts out protectively over them, evoking associations with a safe white cave. This is the perfect place to enjoy the sweeping view over the Neckar to the Deutsches Literaturarchiv on the opposite bank.

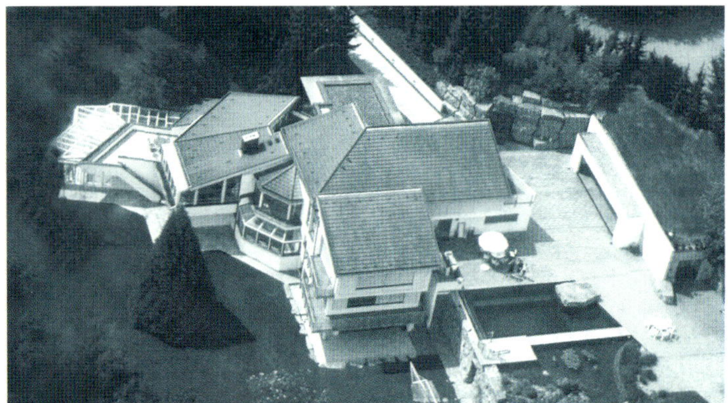

Der Vorgängerbau von 1984 | The previous building from 1984

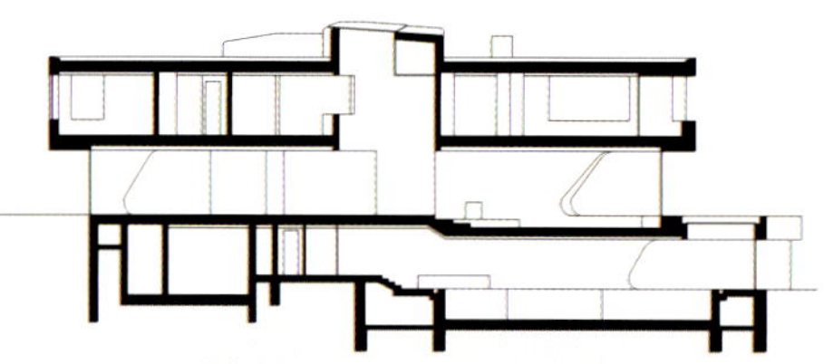

Schnitt | Section

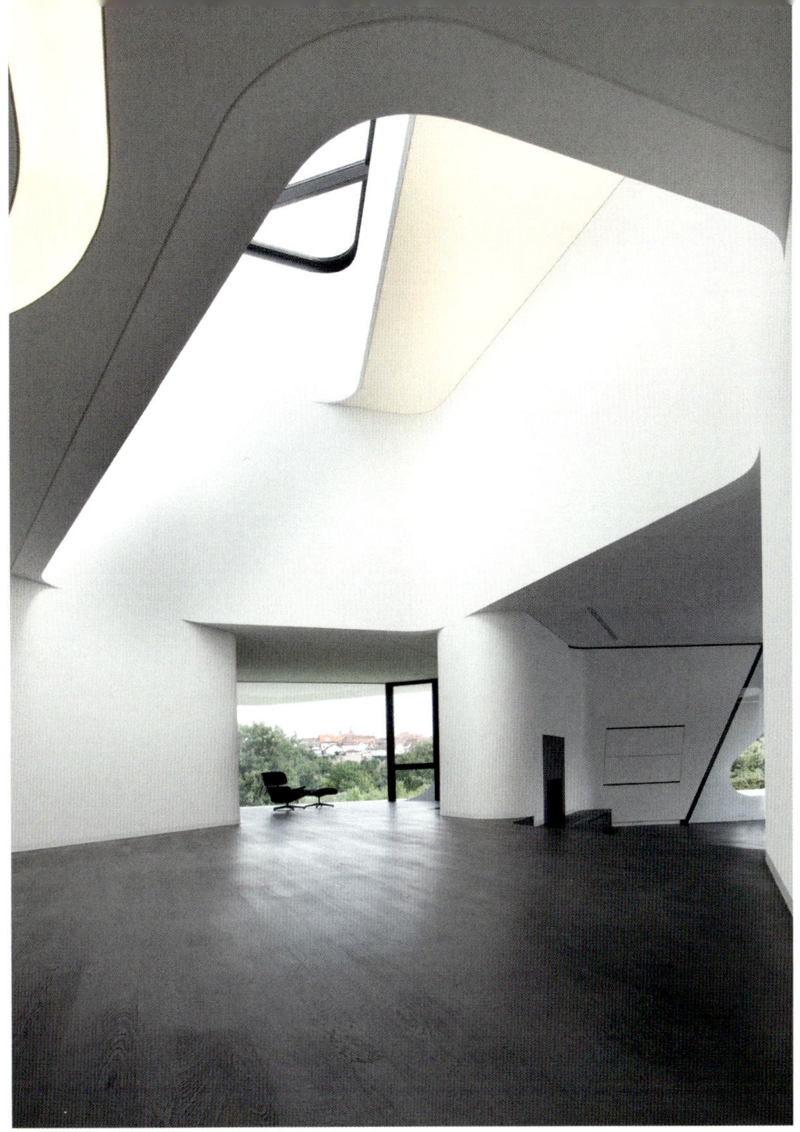

Atrium | Atrium

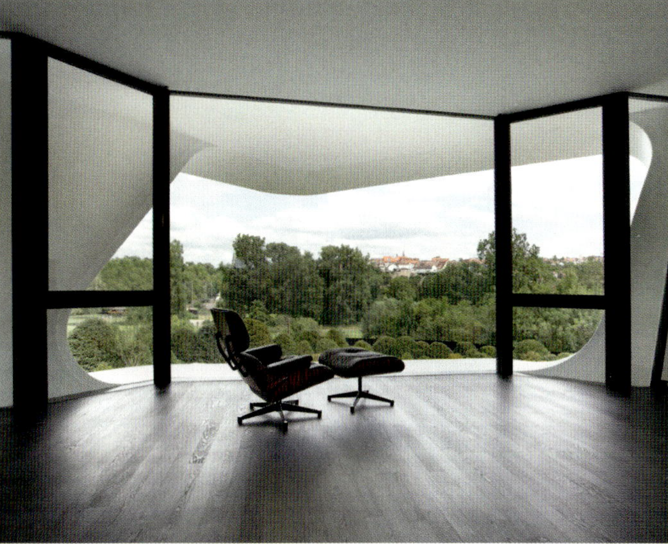

Ausblick | View outside

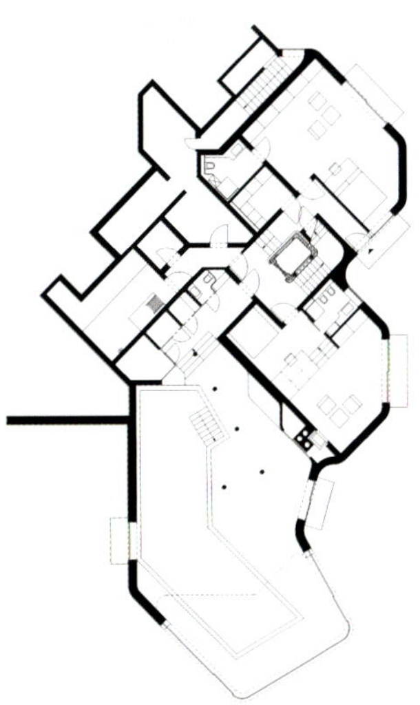

Grundriss Gartengeschoss | Floor plan of garden level

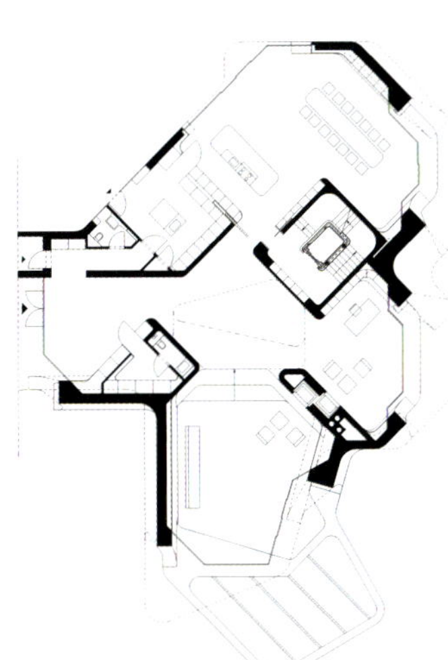

Grundriss Erdgeschoss | Floor plan of ground floor

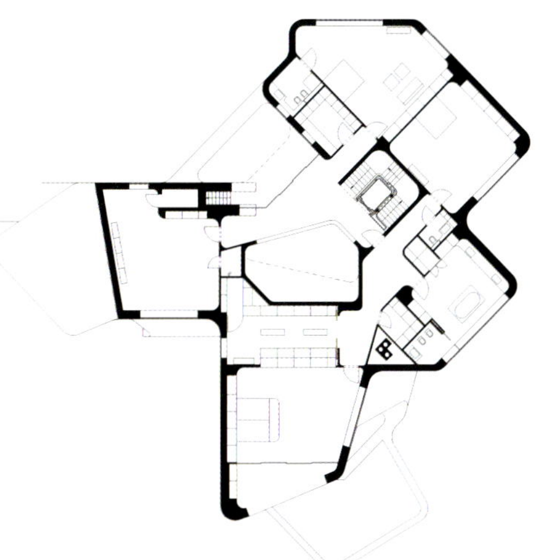

Grunriss Obergeschoss | Floor plan of upper level

RAINER MARIA KRESING – ANDREAS DEILMANN

HANSE CARRÉ

TEXT KAREN JUNG

16

ARCHITEKTEN | ARCHITECTS

Arbeitsgemeinschaft
Rainer Maria Kresing –
Andreas Deilmann
Lingener Str. 12
48155 Münster
www.kresing.de

MITARBEITER | TEAM

T. Vöge (Projektleitung
| project management),
B. Jung, M. Piehl, S. Weidig,
S. Sikorsky, B. Hafkenscheid,
M. Wefelshüten, A. Höing

BAUHERR | CLIENT

Projektentwicklung
Hanse Carré GmbH & Co. KG,
Münster

TRAGWERK | STRUCTURE

Gantert & Wiemeler, Münster

FERTIGSTELLUNG | COMPLETION

2009

STANDORT | LOCATION

Hanse Carré
Stubengasse 32–34
Beginengasse 10
48143 Münster

FOTOS | PHOTOS

Christian Richters

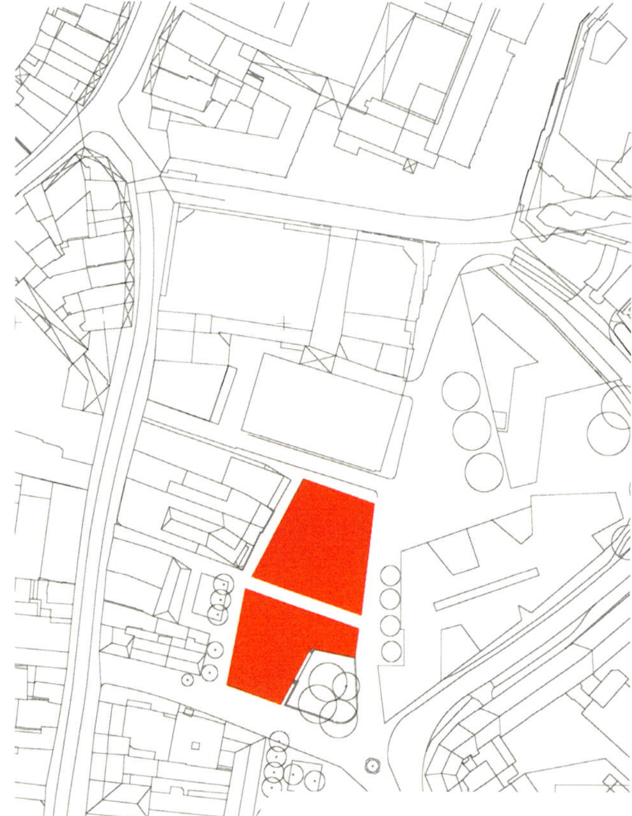

Lageplan | Site plan

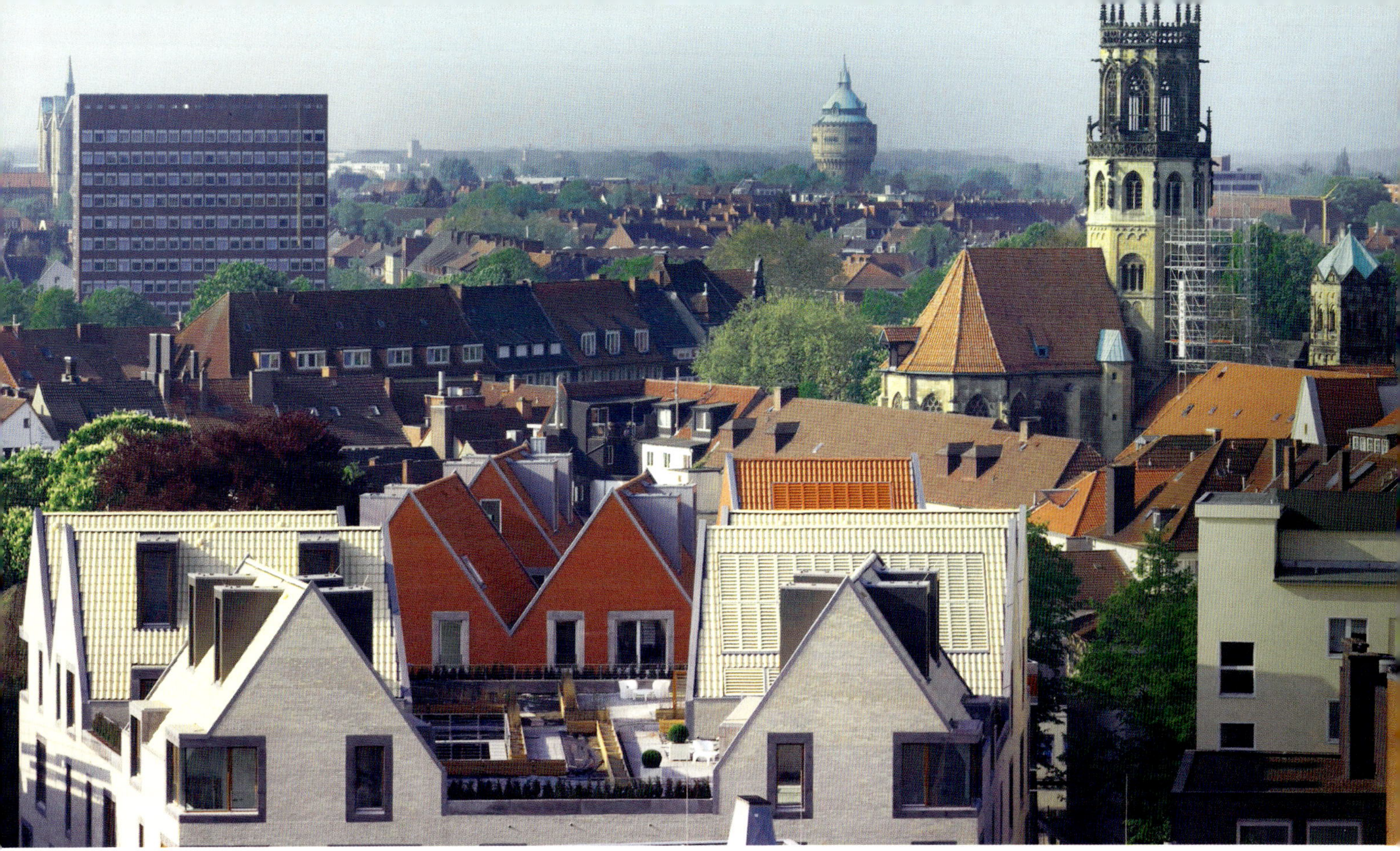

Zeitgenössische Variante ortstypischer Giebelhausstrukturen
Contemporary variation on the gabled houses typical of the area

Der französische Architekt Bernhard Huet hatte Ende der 1980er-Jahre in einem Aufsatz den Gegensatz von ‚Architektur' als freier Kunst und ‚Stadt' als Ort der Konvention betont. Die Stadt sei Sache der Gesellschaft, sagte er, die Architektur hingegen sei Sache des Einzelnen. Eine Arbeit in der Hansestadt Münster zeigt jedoch, dass es gelingen kann, diesen Widerspruch zum Wohle der Stadt und der Architektur zu lösen.

In unmittelbarer Nähe zu Münsters guter Stube, dem Prinzipalmarkt, stellt der Architekt Rainer Maria Kresing mit dem Hanse Carré eine sehr überzeugende Neuinterpretation des giebelständigen Kaufmannshauses vor. Möglich wurde dieses neue Gebäudeensemble durch den Abriss des sogenannten Overberg-Hauses aus den 1950er-Jahren, welches zuletzt die Bezirksregierung beherbergt hatte. Umnutzungskonzepte scheiterten und so entschloss sich der Architekt, zusammen mit dem Projektentwickler Andreas Deilmann das Grundstück zwischen der Ludgeristraße und der Stubengasse zu erwerben und hier ein Stück Stadt zum Wohnen und Arbeiten zu schaffen.

Anstelle des einstigen Solitärs entstand ein wie gewachsen aussehendes Ensemble aus zwei Stadthäusern und einem gläsernen Pavillon, das den Maßstab der innerstädtischen Bebauung aufnimmt und den Stadtgrundriss überzeugend weiterführt. So werden die zur belebten Ludgeristraße führenden Gassen in leicht gebrochener Geometrie und damit ganz natürlich an die Stubengasse angebunden; sogar ein zuvor unattraktiver

In an essay written in the late 1980s, French architect Bernard Huet emphasised the difference between 'architecture' as free art and 'city' as a locus of convention. The city belongs to society, he said, while architecture belongs to the individual. A current project in the Hanse City of Münster shows that this contradiction is capable of being resolved to the benefit of both the city and architecture.

In close proximity to Münster's 'best address', the Prinzipalmarkt, architect Rainer Maria Kresing presents a very satisfying reinterpretation of the traditional gabled merchant's house. This new building ensemble was made possible by the demolition of the so-called Overberg Haus from the 1950s, formerly the seat of the district government. Various proposed conversion schemes failed, and thus the architect, together with project developer Andreas Deilmann, decided to purchase the plot between Ludgeristrasse and Stubengasse and to create here a new place for city residents to work and live.

Instead of a single building, an organic-seeming ensemble of two townhouses and a glass pavilion takes up the dimensions of the other city-centre

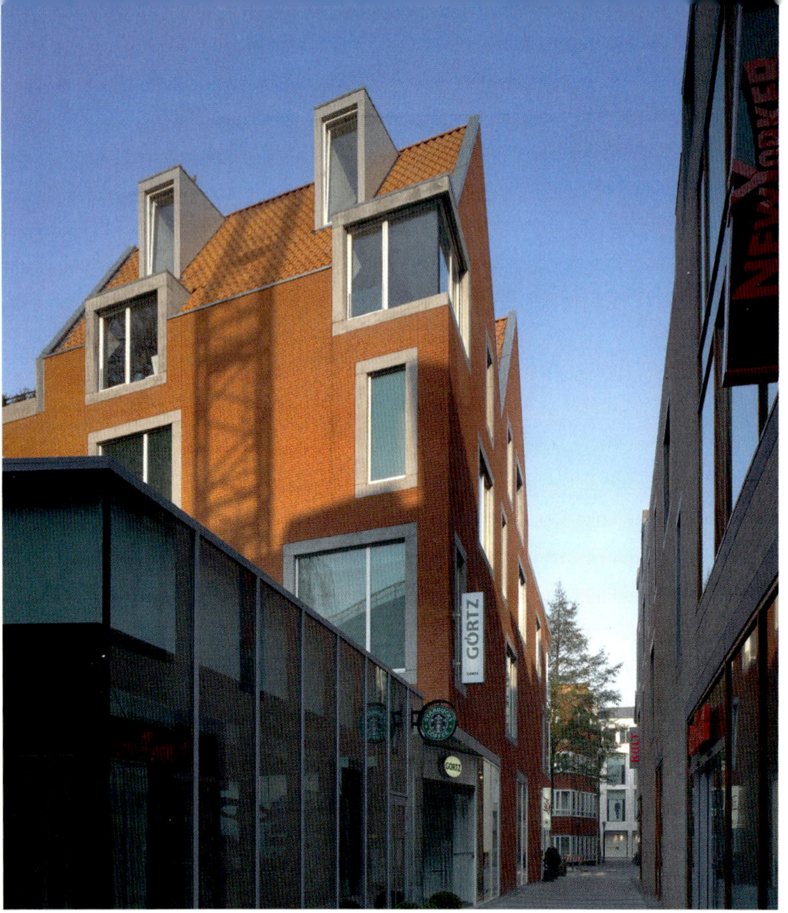

Stadtbausteine in Ziegelrot und Sandsteinfarbe
City building blocks in brick red and sandstone colour

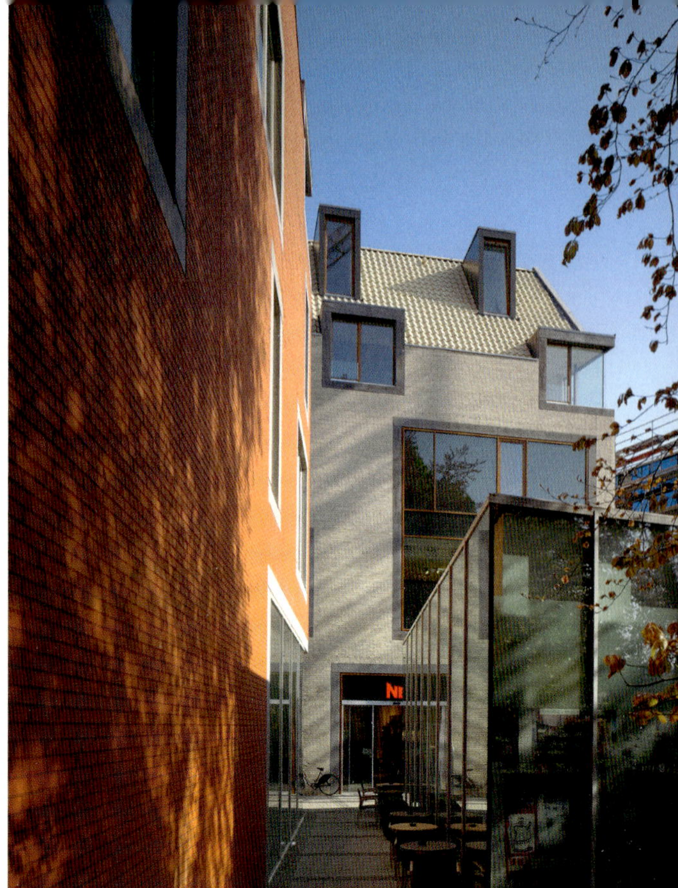

Ensemble aus zwei Stadthäusern und einem gläsernen
Pavillon | Ensemble of two townhouses and a glass pavilion

Wirtschaftshof wird zum intimen Quartiersplatz ausgebildet – ein Zugewinn an stadträumlicher Qualität, die es bisher an diesem Ort nicht gab.

Typologisch sind die neu geschaffenen Stadthäuser des Hanse Carrés dem Münsteraner Giebelhaus, wie es den Prinzipalmarkt prägt, verwandt. Dem Ort verpflichtet, nimmt die Architektur sowohl dessen Formensprache als auch dessen Nutzung als Kaufmannshaus auf. Auch dort liegen die Wohnräume zumeist unter dem Dach, während alle anderen Geschosse im Laufe der Zeit dem Verkauf von Waren dienlich gemacht wurden.

Wie die Kaufmannshäuser sind auch die Häuser des Hanse Carrés in ihrer Ästhetik zurückhaltend, beherrschen aber durch ihre formale und ästhetische Präsenz den Ort. Doch so klar sie als einfache giebelständige Häuser den Raum fassen, so sehr überraschen sie in ihrer typologischen Varianz. Die Drehung der Giebel um jeweils 90° lässt bereits ein Mehr an Komplexität erkennen, es entsteht ein Stadtraum mit allseitig öffentlichem Charakter – anders als bei einer Blockrandbebauung oder den historischen Giebelhäusern, die eine Vorder- und eine Rückseite haben.

Bei genauerem Hinsehen entpuppen sich die Gebäude als drei-geschossige Geschäftshäuser mit aufgesetzten kleinen Giebel-häusern. Diese bilden zum einen die Giebel der Stadthäuser und sind zugleich frei stehende Wohnhäuser, die über eine Dach-terrasse zugänglich sind. Sie sind stadträumlich umso bemer-kenswerter, als sie mit ihren Sockeln zu einem städtischen Haus verschmelzen.

Die zweigeschossigen Dachhäuser sind bei einer Größe von ca. 120 Quadratmetern geschickt aufgeteilt und überraschen mit enormen Raumhöhen und wunderbaren Ausblicken über die Dächer die Stadt. Die von Eibenhecken umgrenzten

buildings while convincingly fitting in with the surrounding layout. The narrow alleyways leading to busy Ludgeristrasse, though slightly altered in geometry, are thus given a natural connection to Stubengasse; and what used to be an unappealing commercial courtyard has now become an intimate city square – a boon to a setting that previously lacked quality of urban life.

In terms of typology, the new Hanse Carré town-houses are related to the traditional Münster gabled houses that dominate the skyline on Prinzipalmarkt. In fact, the architecture shows its commitment to this setting by adopting both the formal vocabulary used and the commercial function of the houses. In the old-time merchants' houses, the living spaces were usually located under the roof, with all the other floors being devoted over time to the sale of goods.

The houses of the Hanse Carré also share the reserved aesthetic of the merchants' houses, although they exude a formal and visual presence that dominates the scene. Yet as much as they relate to their surroundings as simple gabled houses, they exhibit a surprisingly individual typology. The twisting of the gable by 90° in each case already signifies greater complexity, leading to a city space that is open on all sides – unlike perimeter block development or historic gabled houses that have a defined back and front.

Upon closer scrutiny, we realise that these buildings are in reality three-storey business premises topped

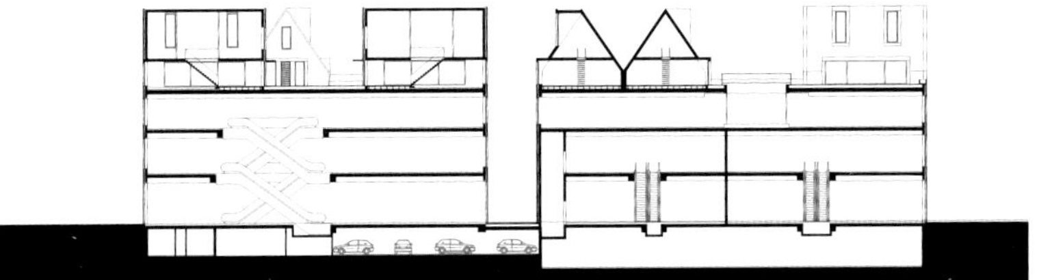

Schnitt | Section

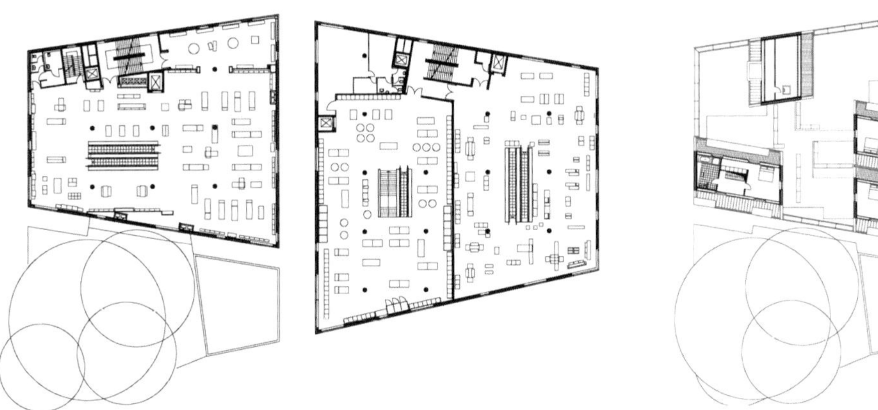

Grundriss 1. Obergeschoss | Floor plan of 1st floor

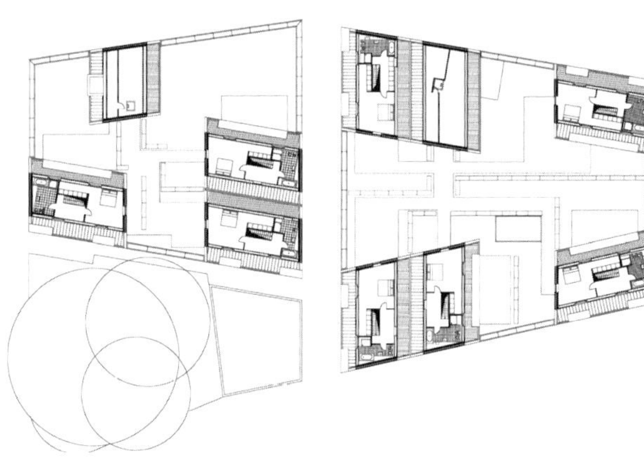

Grundriss 4. Obergeschoss | Floor plan of 4th floor

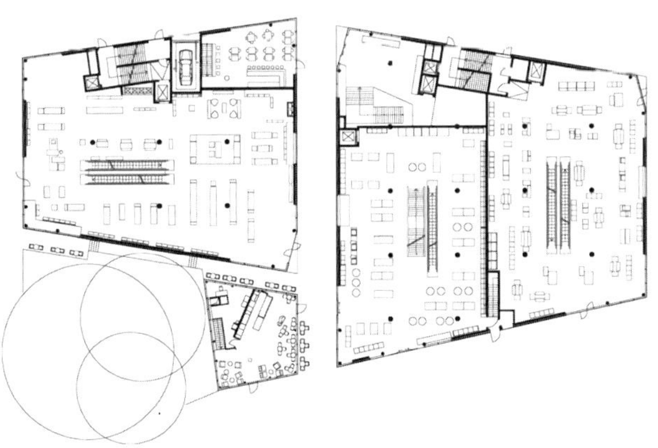

Grundriss Erdgeschoss | Floor plan of ground floor

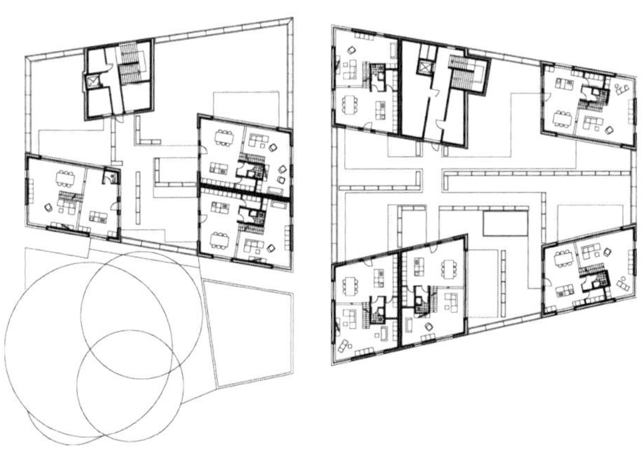

Grundriss 3. Obergeschoss | Floor plan of 3rd floor

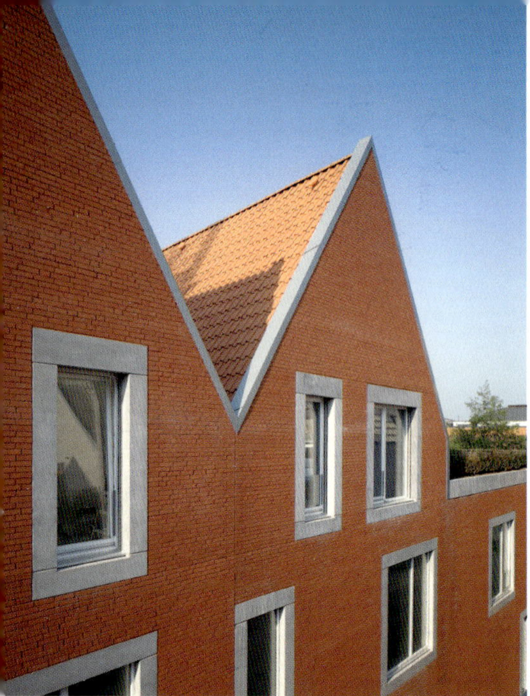

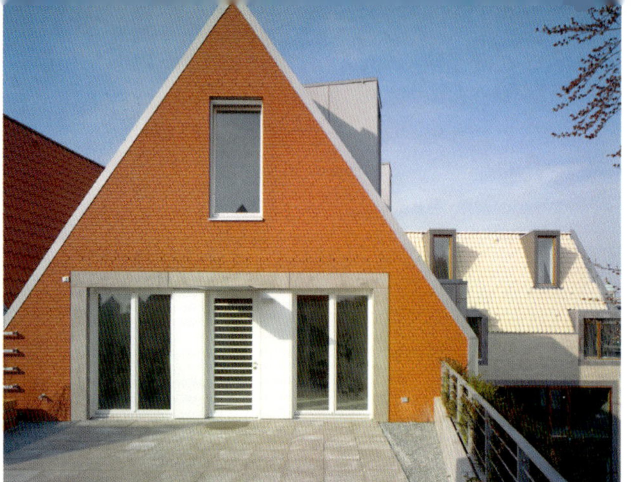

Die Dachhäuser verbinden sich mit ihrem Sockel zu einem städtischen Haus.
The rooftop apartments fuse with their base to form a city building.

großzügigen Dachgärten sind jeweils einer Wohnung zugeordnet und stellen eine luxuriöse Alternative zum Balkon dar. Als Fassadenmaterial wählte der Architekt dem Ort entsprechend einen Klinker. Um das Spiel beider Häuser zu betonen und die Bausteine der Stadt als eben solche auch ablesbar zu machen, entschied man sich für unterschiedliche Ausführungen – mal sandsteinfarben, mal rot. Die Fenstereinfassungen sind kontrastierend in eingefärbtem Sichtbeton ausgeführt, als Reminiszenz an die traditionellen Sandsteineinfassungen. Die Verfugungen der Klinkervorsatzschale sind jeweils dem Farbton angepasst und erzeugen so eine homogene, leicht strukturierte Wandfläche, in der das einzig bestimmende Element das Fenster ist, das so zum Ornament wird.

Auch für die technischen Anforderungen wurden fantasievolle Lösungen gefunden. Die Kombination von Wohn- und Verkaufsräumen, von Tiefgaragennutzung und aufwendiger Haustechnik ist heutzutage unter gestalterischen Gesichtspunkten eine besondere Herausforderung. Kresing Architekten lösten das Problem, indem sie die Zu- und Abluftöffnungen für die Klimaanlagen in die Giebelflächen integrierten und sie regelrecht unter Lamellen in den Dachflächen verschwinden ließen. So konnten die Dachterrassen wirklich Terrassen und die Dächer wirkliche Dächer werden, ohne dass diese Flächen in erster Linie zur Aufnahme der Gebäudetechnik genutzt wurden.

Haus und Stadt sind an diesem Ort eine Symbiose eingegangen. Das Quartier wurde bereichert, ohne verfälscht zu werden. Kunst und Konvention wurden versöhnt.

by small gabled houses. These residences both form the gables of the townhouses and are free-standing houses accessible via a rooftop terrace. They are all the more remarkable in this urban context as, thanks to their bases, they meld together into a single city building.

With approx. 120 square metres of floor space, the two-storey rooftop houses have cleverly conceived layouts and feature astonishingly high ceilings and lovely views over the rooftops of the city. Each house has its own spacious rooftop garden bordered by yew hedges, a luxurious alternative to a balcony. For the façades the architect chose a type of brick that fits the location. In order to underscore the interplay between the two houses and to make the building blocks of the city identifiable, two different treatments were chosen – one sandstone-coloured, the other red. The window casings are done in exposed concrete dyed in contrasting colours as a reminiscence of the traditional sandstone casings. The joints between the facing bricks are adapted to these tones, creating a homogeneous, slightly textured wall surface in which the windows are the only articulating element and thus become ornamental.

Imaginative solutions were also found for the technical requirements. The combination of residential and commercial use, of a public underground garage and elaborate technical facilities, is a special challenge these days in terms of design. Kresing Architekten solved this problem by integrating the air intake and exhaust openings for the air conditioning systems in the gable surfaces, making them veritably disappear under blades in the roof. The rooftop terraces can thus be true terraces, and the roofs real roofs, without the surfaces being used primarily as a place to stow all the building services.

House and city have entered into a symbiosis on this site. The quarter has been enriched without being defaced. Art and convention are reconciled.

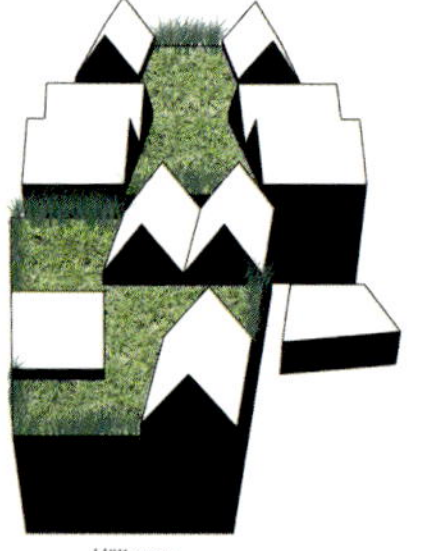

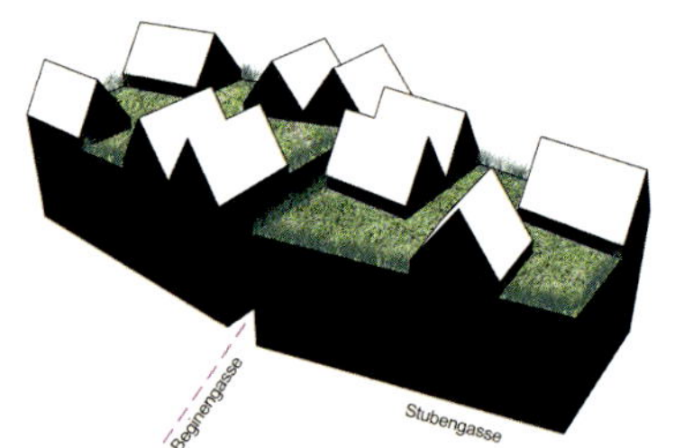

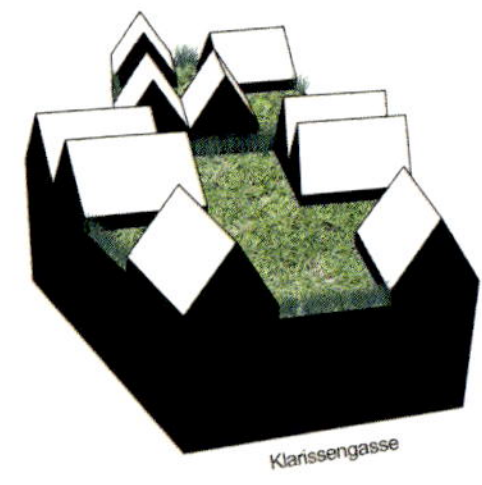

Baukörper | Building structure

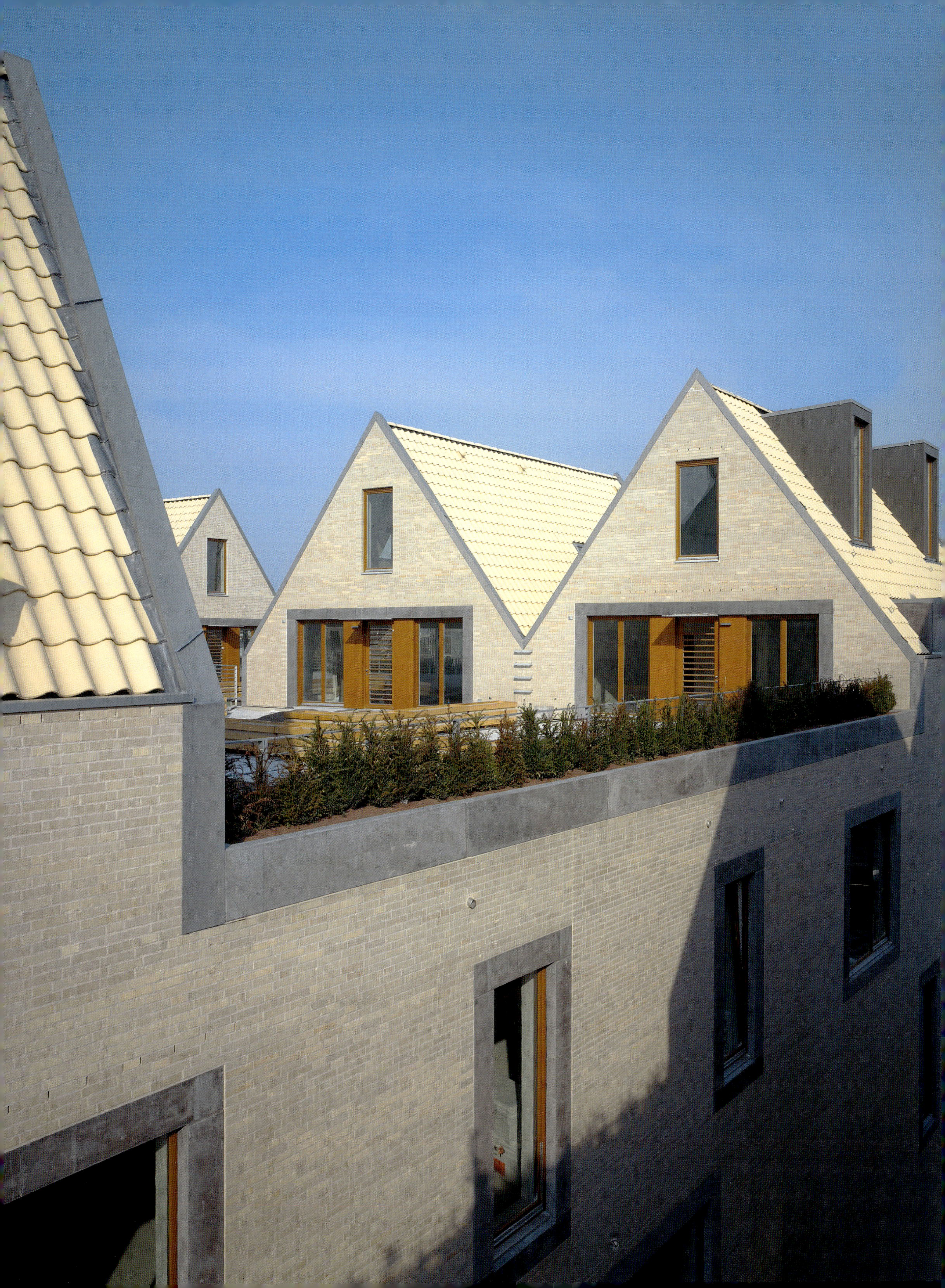

ARCHITEKT | ARCHITECT

MASSIMILANO FUKSAS

GEBÄUDE | BUILDING

MYZEIL – EINKAUFSZENTRUM

TEXT OLIVER ELSER

17

ARCHITEKTEN | ARCHITECTS

Massimiliano e Doriana Fuksas
Architetto
Piazza del Monte di Pietà, 30
00186 Rom | Rome
Italien | Italy

Schleusenstraße 17
60327 Frankfurt
www.fuksas.it

MITARBEITER | TEAM

Christian Knoll
(**Projektleiter** | project manager),
Tim-Philipp Brendel
(**Projektleiter** | project manager
von | from **2003 bis** | to **2005**),
Jens Vorbröker,
Kai Binnewies, Julia Gensicke,
Doriana O. Mandrelli (Design),
Gianluca Brancaleone
(**Modellbauleiter**
director of model building),
Nicola Giabati,
Frauke Stenz (Modellbau Team
model building team)

STÄDTEBAULICHER RAHMEN-
PLAN, BAUANTRAG GESAMT-
ENSEMBLE | URBAN MASTER PLAN,
BUILDING APPLICATION FOR
COMPLETE ENSEMBLE

KSP Engel und
Zimmermann Architekten,
Frankfurt am Main

BAUHERR | CLIENT

PalaisQuartier GmbH & Co. KG
über die MAB Development GmbH

TRAGWERK | STRUCTURE

Krebs und Kiefer, Darmstadt;
Weischede Herrmann und
Partner GmbH, Stuttgart
(**Tragwerksplanung Rohbau**
structural design of skeleton)
Knippers Helbig
advanced engineering, Stuttgart
(**Sonderkonstruktion**
Dach und Fassade | special
construction of roof and façade)

LANDSCHAFTSARCHITEKTEN
LANDSCAPE ARCHITECTS

BWP Endreß,
Frankfurt am Main

FERTIGSTELLUNG | COMPLETION

2009

STANDORT | LOCATION

MyZeil, Zeil 106,
60313 Frankfurt am Main
www.myzeil.de
www.palaisquartier.de

FOTOS | PHOTOS

Karsten Monnerjahn

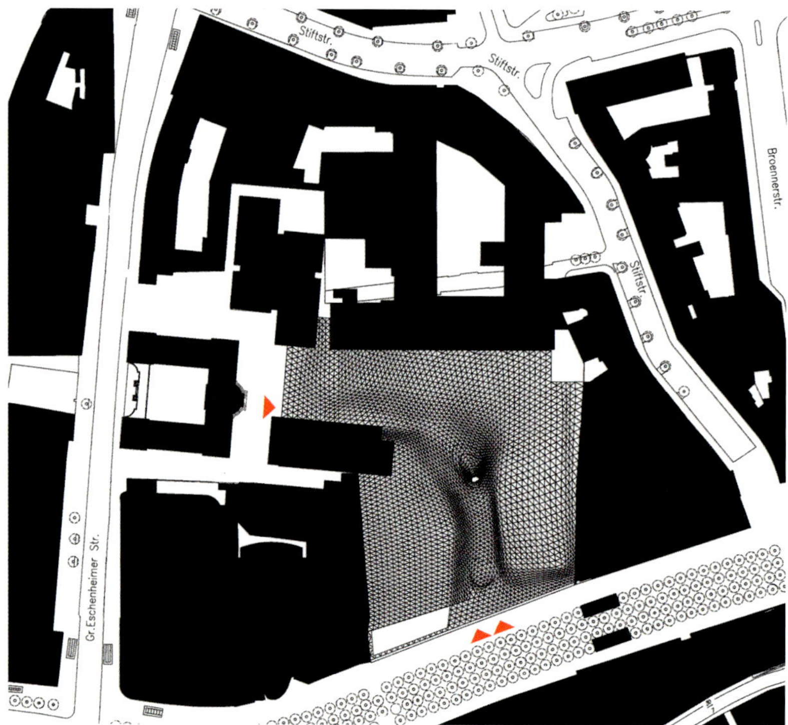

Lageplan | Site plan

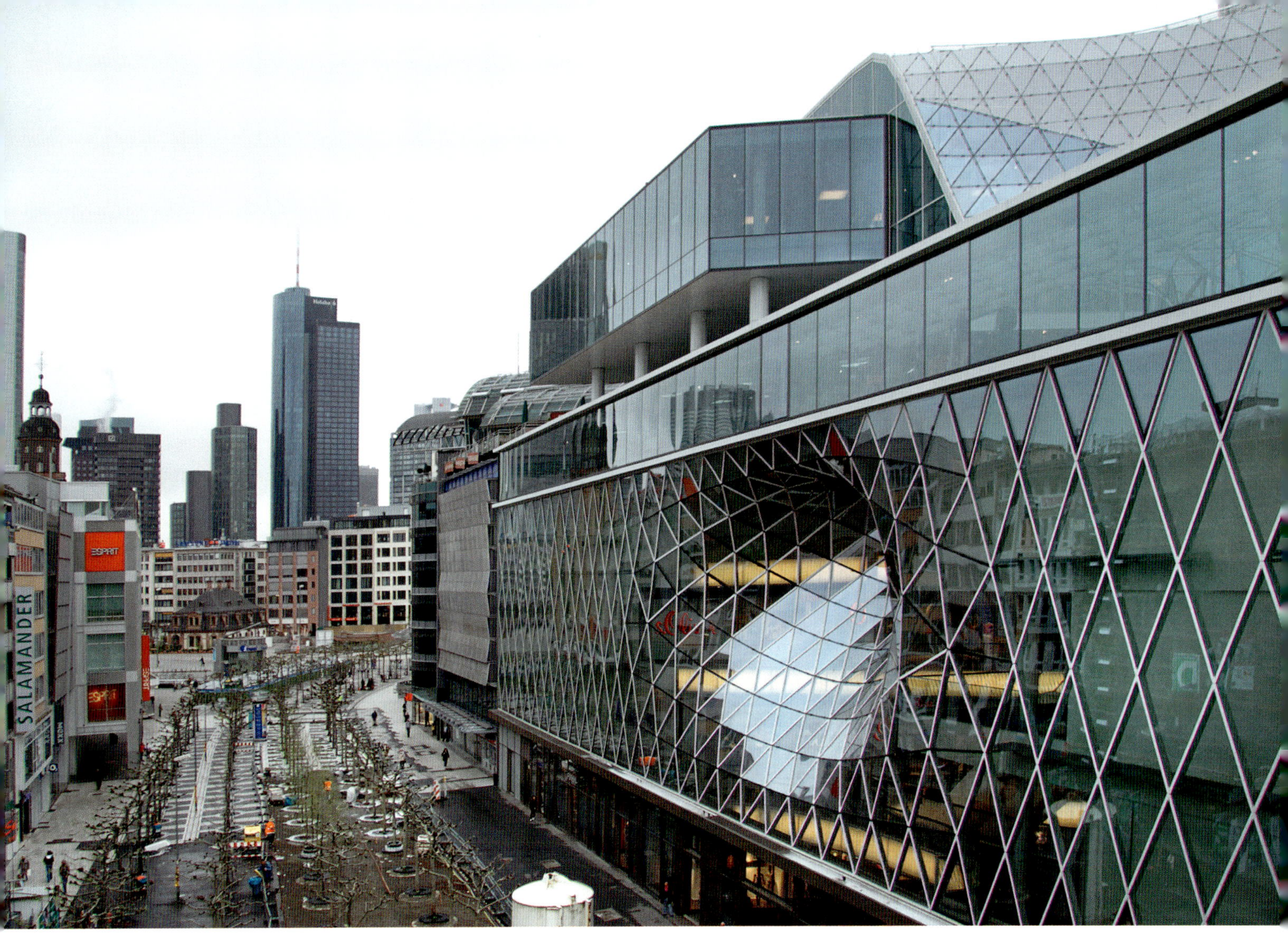

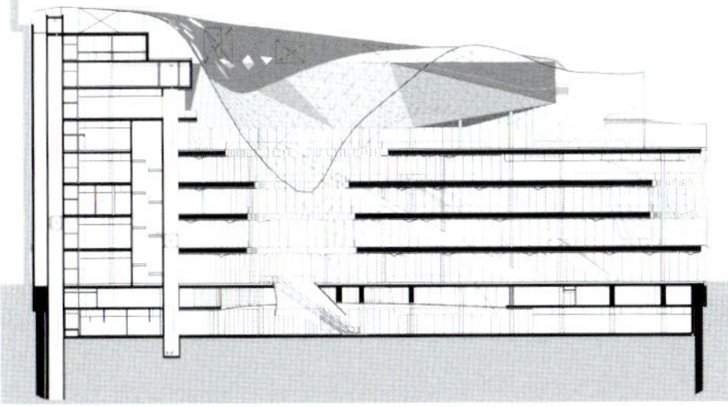

Es sieht fast so aus, als wäre ein Meteorit in die Glasfassade gedonnert.
It looks almost as if a meteorite had crashed into the glass façade.

Schräg von der Seite betrachtet, sieht es aus, als sei ein Meteorit in die Glasfassade gedonnert. Die Zeil, Frankfurts ‚Einkaufszone', hat eine gewaltige, von Weitem sichtbare Delle bekommen. Von Nahem betrachtet, und das tun derzeit viele und recken ihre Handykameras in die Höhe, ist die Delle ein Krater, hat der glühende Himmelsbrocken ganze Arbeit geleistet. Die neue Shoppingmall wurde glatt durchschlagen, die staunenden Passanten blinzeln, starren, knipsen in ein Loch hinein und sehen am Ende des Durchstoßkanals nichts als den puren Himmel. Ein Schauspiel mit beinahe metaphysischem Beigeschmack. Dass die Architekturgeschichte kaum mehr als eine Handvoll Gebäude aufbietet, die ein zum Himmel hin offenes Loch haben –, das Pantheon oder die Neue Wache Tessenows beispielsweise – wird hier, auf der Zeil, wohl die

Seen obliquely from the side, it looks like a meteorite has crashed into the glass façade of the building. An enormous dent, visible from a distance, has been made in the Zeil, Frankfurt's downtown shopping district. Viewed from up close, as many are now doing, stretching their cellphone cameras aloft, this dent is actually a crater – and the red-hot rock from outer space did a pretty thorough job of it. The hole pierces right through the new shopping mall; astounded passers-by blink, stare and take snapshots into the hole, peering through and seeing nothing but sky at the other end. This is a spectacle that smacks almost of the metaphysical. The fact that architectural history offers hardly more than a handful of buildings with a hole open to the sky – the Pantheon or Tessenow's Neue Wache in Berlin come to mind – is probably not of great interest to most people here on the Zeil, and this comparison isn't entirely apt anyway. But the fact that MyZeil behaves in an extremely strange manner is plain to see from the looks on all the faces.

Put in banal terms, this gesture is the most brutal of symbols of what the new shopping centre is

Schnitt | Section

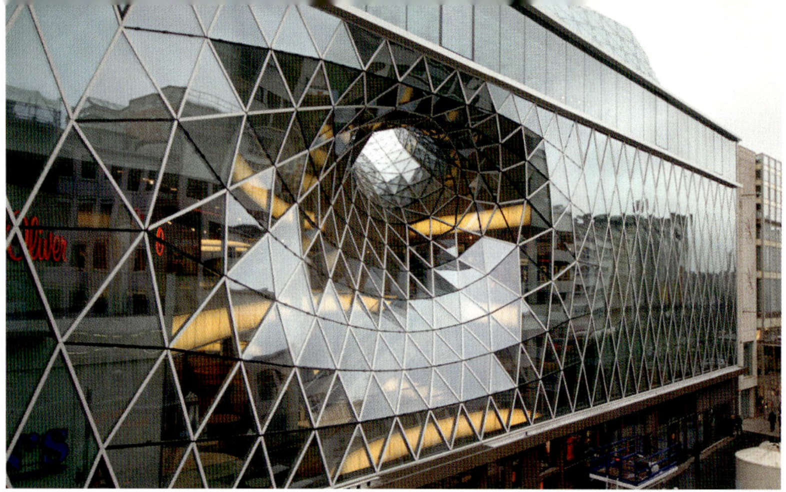

Durchblick zum Himmel | Looking through the building to the sky beyond

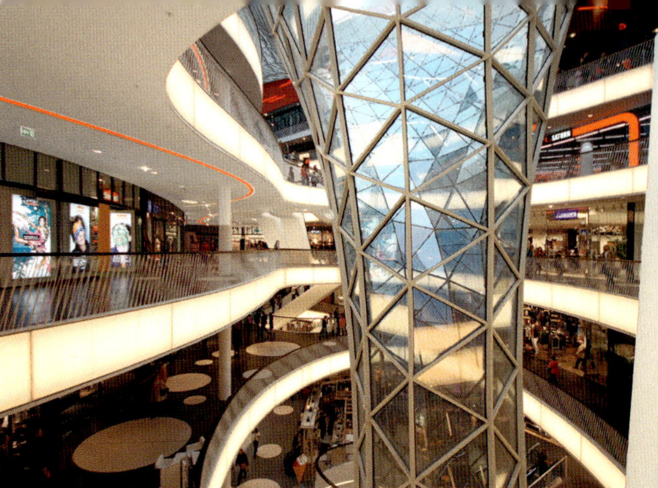

Neonlichtschlangen | Snake-like neon lights

wenigsten berühren, und auch wenn der Vergleich ohnehin nicht ganz stimmig ist, so ist die Tatsache, dass sich „MyZeil" extrem seltsam gebärdet, doch in allen Gesichtern abzulesen. Banal gesprochen, ist die Geste das brutalstmögliche Zeichen dafür, was durch das neue Einkaufszentrum erreicht werden soll: Die Kundenströme aus der west-ost-orientierten Zeil nach Norden umzuleiten, die Massen hineinströmen lassen. Das 1,7 Hektar große Gelände im Zentrum der Innenstadt war bis vor wenigen Jahren ein abgeriegelter Bezirk, belegt mit Funktionsgebäuden von Post und Telekom und damit in der Stadtwahrnehmung ausgeklammert. Das niederländische Unternehmen MAB Bouwfonds errichtete auf dieser Fläche nicht nur „MyZeil", sondern auch ein noch nicht ganz fertiggestelltes Hochhauscluster (Architektur: KSP Engel und Zimmermann), die zurechtgeschrumpfte Reproduktion eines Thurn-und-Taxis'schen Barockpalais' und eine Blockrandbebauung an der Stelle, wo vor Kurzem noch das Verlagsgebäude der „Frankfurter Rundschau" stand, ein Schmuckstück der stromlinienförmigen 1950er-Jahre.

Wie aktuell gerade der Schwung der Nachkriegsmoderne heute wieder sein kann, zeigt sich im Inneren von „MyZeil": Die Einkaufsebenen werden von nierenförmigen Luftöffnungen durchstoßen, um die sich Geländer winden, deren spaghetti-dünne Streben vor 50 Jahren schon einmal in Mode waren. Über den Köpfen winden sich Neonlichtschlangen. Es sind Details und Motive, die einerseits den Schwung der filigranen Netzhülle aufnehmen, gleichzeitig aber jeden Gedanken an die austausch- und abwaschbare Glitzerinnenwelt der Malls der vergangenen Jahre vertreiben. Angefangen beim dunkelgrauen, mit weißen Kreisflächen gesprenkelten rauen Terrazzoboden über die breiten hölzernen Handläufe bis hin zur Wegeführung, die hier mal nicht so eng an den Geschäften vorbeiführt, als solle einem das Geld ganz von selbst herausgepresst werden. Dies alles ist so stimmig, so großzügig, im Grunde so sympathisch, und vielleicht sogar wirklich ‚mai Zeil', wie der Hesse sagen würde, weil die Zeil ja nicht nobel ist, sondern ein Shoppinggelände für nahezu alle. So gesehen, erschöpft sich die spektakuläre Außengeste tatsächlich nicht in einem banalen „ihr Käuferlein kommet", sondern der Blick durchs Gebäude hindurch in den Himmel kündigt einen Mehrwert gegenüber vergleichbaren Projekten an, der tatsächlich eingelöst wird,

intended to do: redirect toward the north the customers streaming down the west-to-east-oriented Zeil and let the masses pour in. Until a few years ago the 1.7-hectare site in the inner city was a blocked-off area occupied by functional buildings for Deutsche Post and Deutsche Telekom, and thus a disregarded part of the cityscape. Then the Dutch company MAB Bouwfonds came along and developed here not only MyZeil, but also a cluster of high rises that is not quite finished yet (architecture: KSP Engel und Zimmermann), along with a reproduction of a Baroque Thurn and Taxis palace, shrunk to fit the plot, and a perimeter block development on the spot where just a short time ago the "Frankfurter Rundschau" newspaper building still stood, a jewel of 1950s streamlining.

Just how up-to-date the jaunty curves of post-war Modernism can look today can be seen in the interior of MyZeil. The shopping levels are pierced by kidney-shaped openings embraced by railings whose spaghetti-thin bars were once in style 50 years ago. Over shoppers' heads neon lights writhe like snakes. These details and motifs take up the sweep of the filigree net that forms the building's outer skin while banishing any trace of the hygienic, interchangeable glitter-world of the malls of past years. This starts with the rough dark grey terrazzo floor sprinkled with white circles and continues with wide wooden handrails and a walkway layout that doesn't press visitors so close to the stores that it seems as if the money is to be squeezed out of their pockets involuntarily. The interior is so coherent, so generously conceived, and so downright likeable that perhaps people will indeed view it as 'mai Zeil', as the Hessian locals would say, because the Zeil is not an elitist enclave, but really a shopping centre for nearly everyone. Seen in this light, the building's spectacular outward gesture is more than simply a blatant open invitation, a vortex drawing shoppers irresistibly inward. Instead, the view through the structure to the sky beyond announces added value

Weitläufiger Innenraum | Vast interior

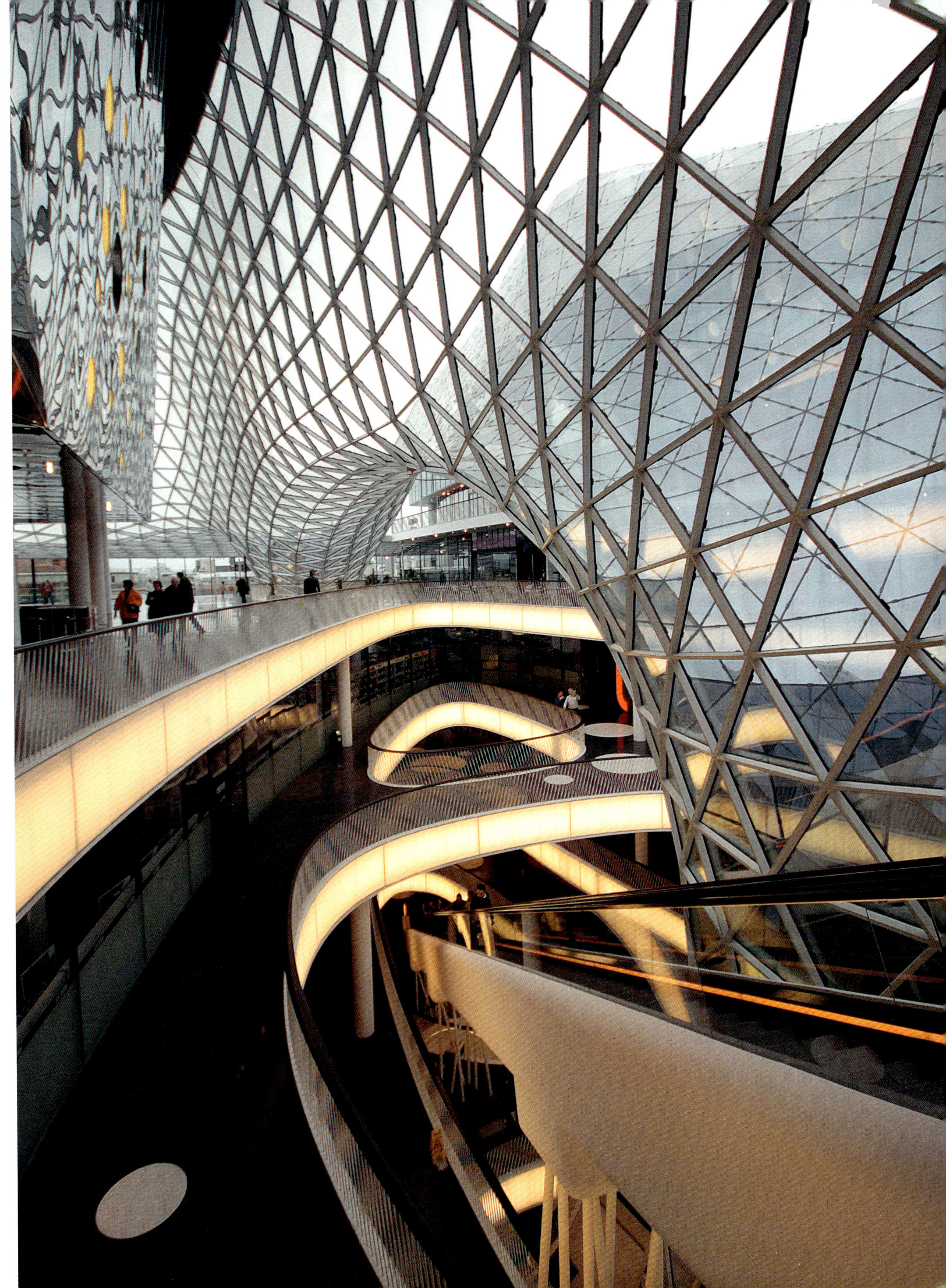

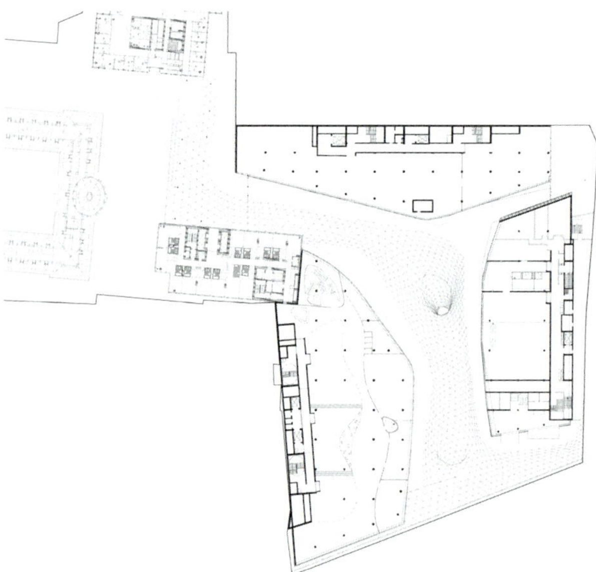

Grundriss 6. Obergeschoss | Floor plan of 6th floor

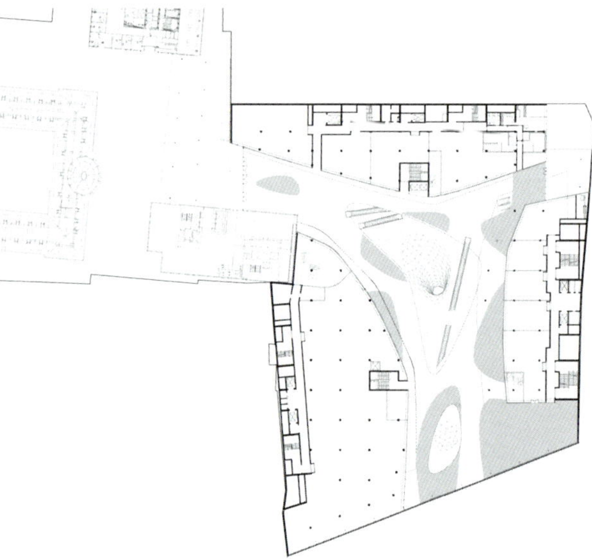

Grundriss 4. Obergeschoss | Floor plan of 4th floor

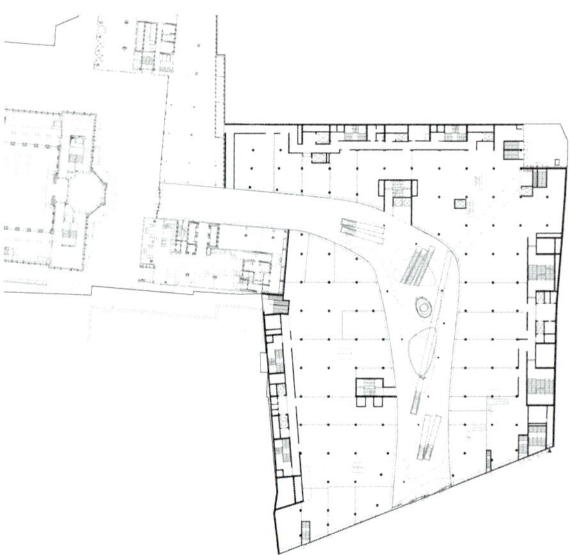

Grundriss Erdgeschoss | Floor plan of ground floor

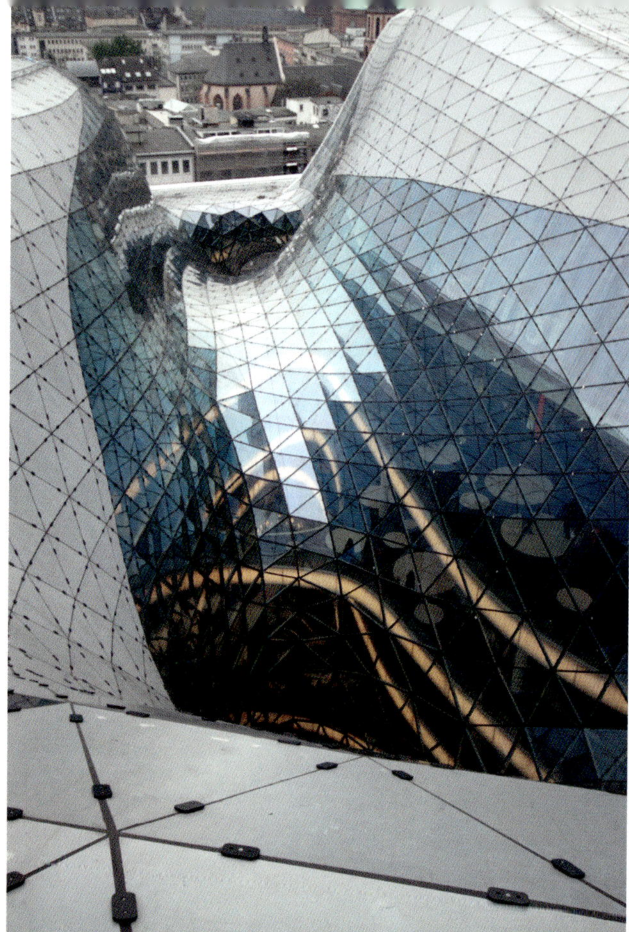

Dachlandschaft | Roof landscape

und entwickelt eine Verführungskraft, die in der Eigenwerbung von „MyZeil" mit einem von fast nichts verhüllten Fotomodell trefflich umgesetzt wird. Die vielbestaunten Phalli der Frankfurter Hochhaus-Silhouette haben endlich ihr weibliches Pendant bekommen.

Wären da nicht der Dreck und die im Detail oft schlampige Ausführung. Dass ein so raffiniertes Dach schwer zu reinigen ist, war vorauszusehen. Aber warum sind die Rolltreppen mit weißen Gipsverkleidungen eingepackt, auf denen die Besucher gleich vom ersten Tag an ihre Spuren hinterlassen konnten? Warum ist der Innenausbau bisweilen so schäbig, die Decke mit den herausgestülpten Lampen so lieblos ausgeführt?

Doch das wäre noch zu beheben. Auch die Leichtbauwände hinter der Zeilfassade könnten verschwinden, die vor allem bei Nacht demonstrieren, dass der Bau weniger transparent ist, als er zunächst scheint. Schwerer wiegt, dass nun eine Art südhessischer Bilbao-Effekt zu befürchten ist: Nur einen Häuserblock entfernt soll die den Goetheplatz säumende Bebauung der 1950er-Jahre teilweise verschwinden. Der Investor hat internationale ‚Star-Architekten' um Ideen gebeten, darunter auch Fuksas. Es wird ignoriert, was in Frankfurt ohnehin selten ist: Solide, unaufgeregte und damit in bestem Sinne städtische Architektur. Deren Wert zu erkennen, würde den Phantomschmerz der zerstörten Altstadt erst gar nicht entstehen lassen.

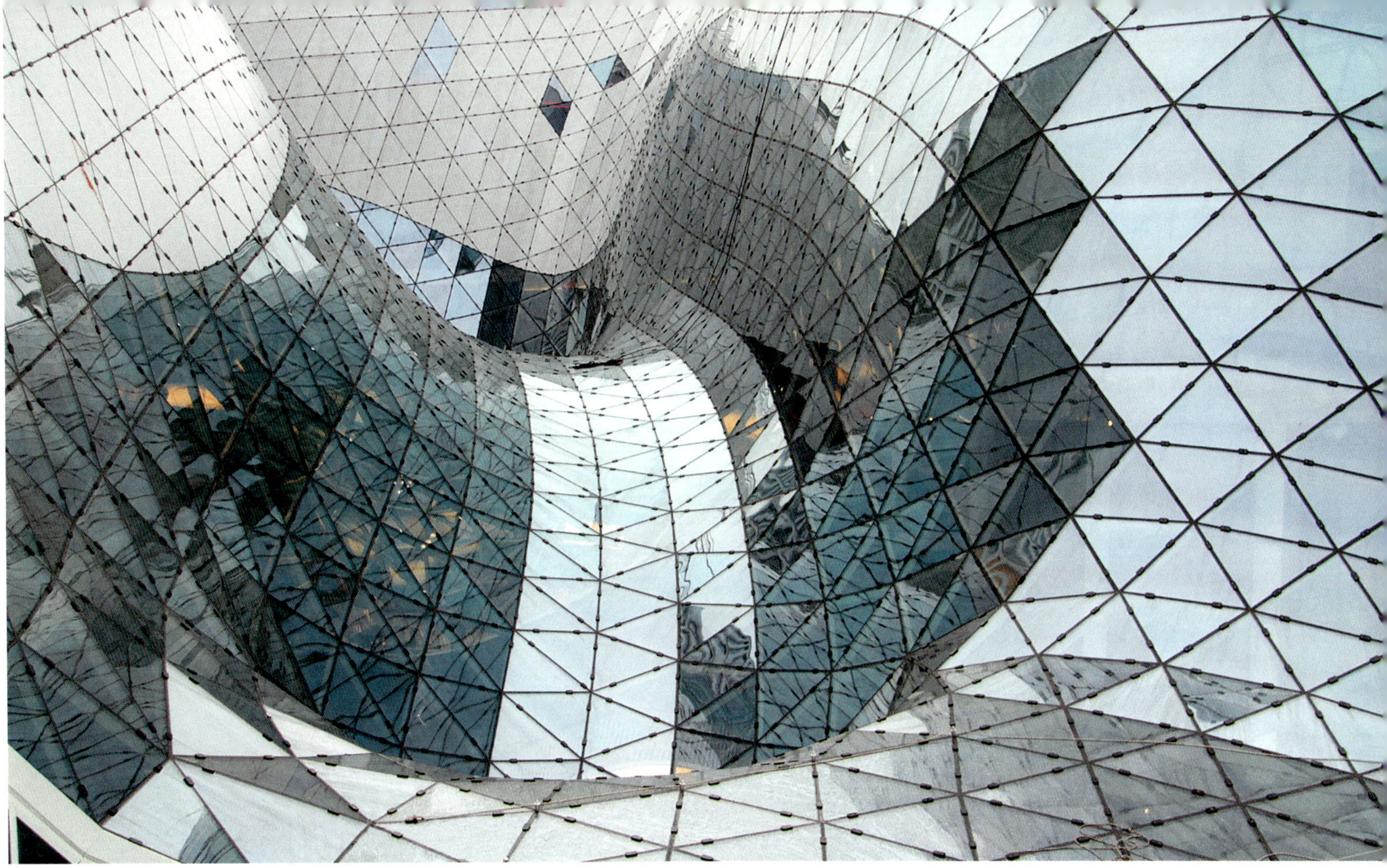

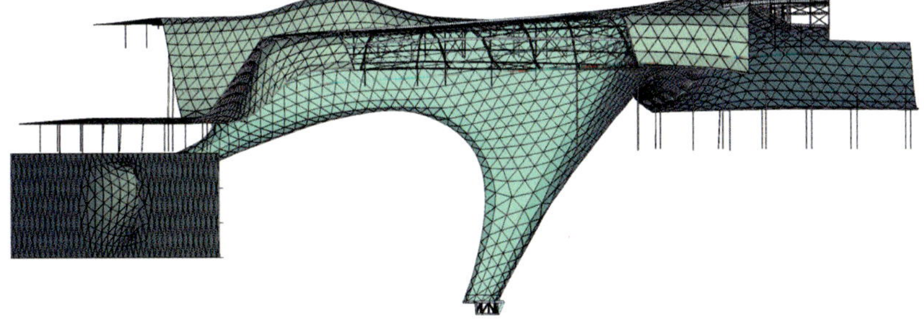

in relation to other, comparable projects. This added value is palpable within, developing a seductive force aptly symbolised in the MyZeil advertisements by a model whose charms are barely concealed by a flimsy windswept piece of fabric. The much-marvelled-at phalli of Frankfurt's skyline have finally been given a female counterpart.

If only it weren't for the dirt and the sometimes clumsily realised details. It was easy to foresee that such a sophisticated roof would be hard to clean. But why are the escalators clad in white plaster on which visitors left unsightly traces on the very first day? Why is the interior finishing so shabby in some places, the ceiling so lacklustre with its protruding lamps?

But these things could be fixed. And the lightweight walls set up behind the Zeil façade could also be made to vanish, demonstrating as they do, especially at night, that the building is far less transparent than it may at first appear. More serious is the danger that a kind of south Hessian Bilbao effect could come to pass here. Just one block away, some of the 1950s buildings lining Goetheplatz await the wrecking ball. The investor has asked international 'star architects' to propose ideas, among them Fuksas. Something is being ignored here that is already rare enough in Frankfurt: solid, unspectacular, and hence in the best sense urban, architecture. Recognising its value would prevent the phantom pain of the destroyed Old Town from being felt at all.

Dachkonstruktion | Roof structure

MECK ARCHITEKTEN

GEBÄUDE | BUILDING

DOMINIKUSZENTRUM

TEXT CHRISTIAN SCHITTICH

18

ARCHITEKTEN | ARCHITECTS

meck architekten
Kellerstraße 39
81667 München | Munich
www.meck-architekten.de

MITARBEITER | TEAM

Wolfgang Amann, Peter
Fretschner (Projektleitung
project management),
Susanne Frank, Johannes
Dörle, Alexander Sälzle,
Werner Schad (Ausschreibung
supplier tenders),
Wolfgang Kusterer
(Bauleitung | site management)

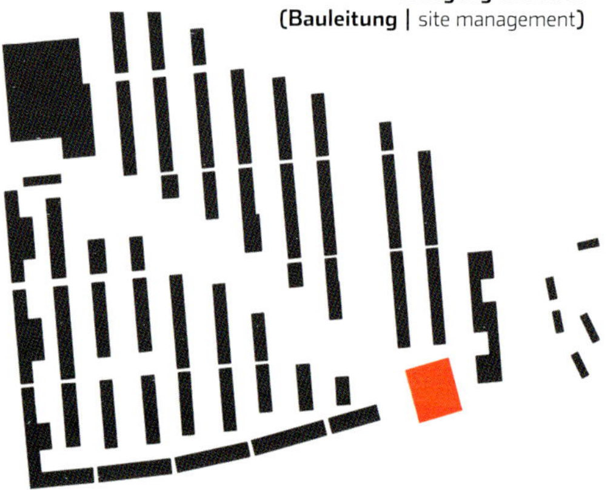

Lageplan | Site plan

BAUHERR | CLIENT

Katholische Kirchenstiftung
St. Gertrud,
Caritaszentrum München Nord,
Erzbischöfliches Jugendamt,
Erzbischöfliches
Ordiniariat München,
Baureferat (Maßnahmeträger)

TRAGWERK | STRUCTURE

Statoplan, Wolf Eglinger,
München | Munich

LANDSCHAFTSARCHITEKTEN
LANDSCAPE ARCHITECTS

Burger Landschaftsarchitekten,
München | Munich

KUNST AM BAU | ART

„Raumikone 2"
(blaue Raumfassung
| blue room setting)
und „Lichtikone"
(Mariendarstellung | Madonna):
Anna Leonie,
München | Munich
nach der Konzeption von | based
on a concept by meck architekten

„Credo" (Oberlicht | skylight):
Andreas Horlitz,
München | Munich
nach der Konzeption von | based
on a concept by meck architekten

Kreuz Andachtsraum | crucifix
in the chapel: Rudolf Bott, Neuburg

Schriftziegel | character tiles:
Stephanie Krieger (Typographie,
Grafik | typography, graphics),
Barbara Butz-Glas, Bad Tölz
(Ausführung | execution)

4 Wandbilder | 4 murals:
Friedhelm Falke, Köln | Cologne

Erdbilder | floor pictures:
Ekkeland Götze, München | Munich

Türgriffe Gruppenräume | door
handles in group rooms: Herman
Biegelmayr, München | Munich

Liturgisches Tuch | liturgical cloth:
Maja Vogl

Typografie | typography:
ks_visuell, Stephanie Krieger,
München | Munich

FERTIGSTELLUNG | COMPLETION

2008

STANDORT | LOCATION

Hildegard-von-Bingen-Anger 1–3
80937 München | Munich

FOTOS | PHOTOS

Michael Heinrich

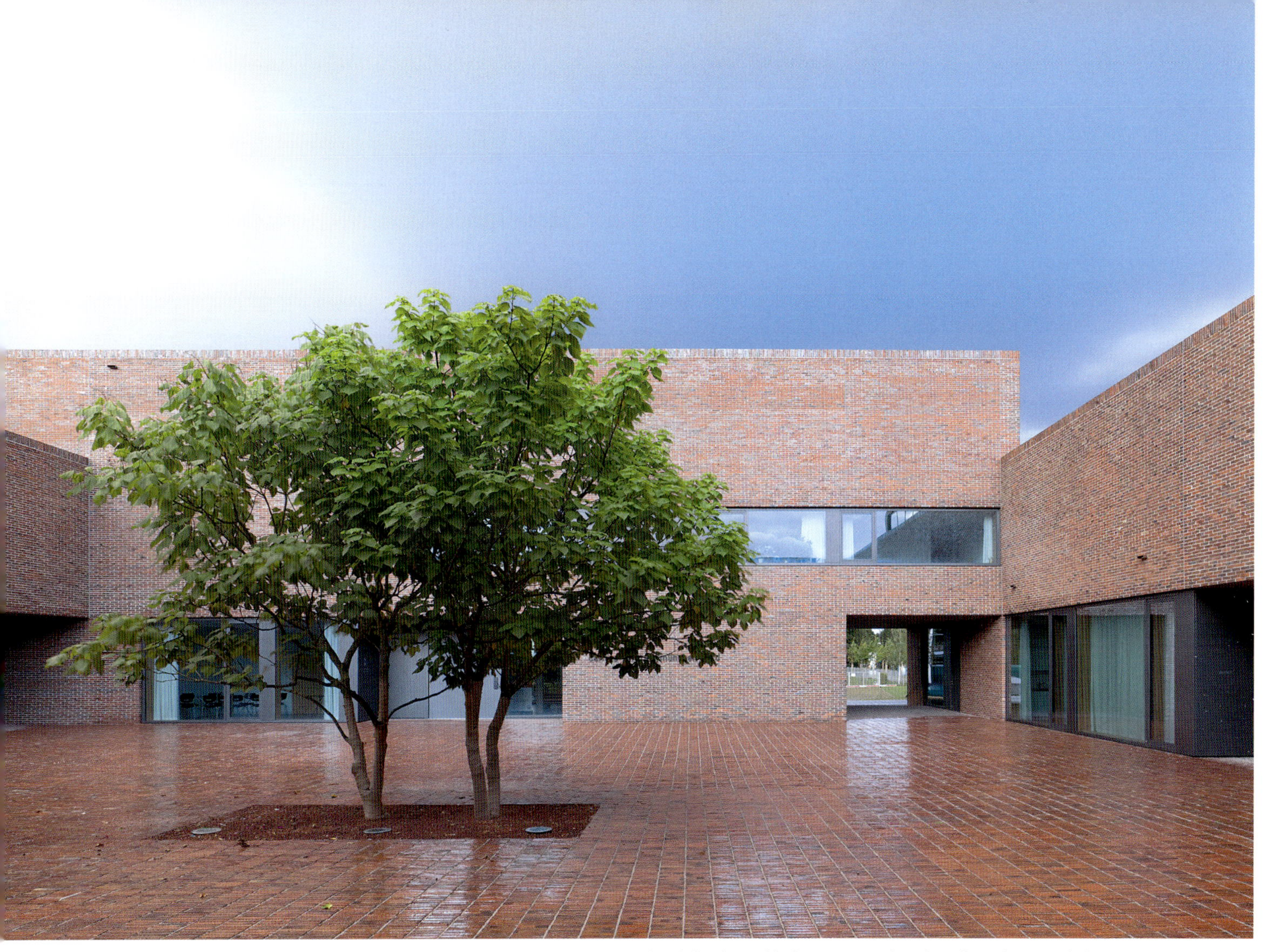

Das neue Quartier Nordheide im Norden von München ist kein Ort, an dem man ein architektonisches Kleinod erwartet: In kurzer Zeit auf dem Areal eines ehemaligen Truppenübungsplatzes aus dem Boden gestampft, zeigen die meisten Bauten eher mittelmäßige Qualität. Hier leben zahlreiche Menschen in schwierigen Verhältnissen: Arbeitslose, Geringverdiener, Alleinerziehende; der Ausländeranteil ist mit beinahe 23 Prozent besonders hoch. An der südöstlichen Ecke der Siedlung sieht sich der Besucher indes unvermittelt mit einem besonderen Bauwerk konfrontiert, das durch seine raue ziegelrote Hülle und seine klare Formensprache auffällt. Und das mit seinem markanten ruhigen Baukörper einen städtebaulichen Identifikationspunkt bildet.

Das im Sommer 2008 geweihte Dominikuszentrum von Meck Architekten geht auf den Gewinn eines beschränkten Realisierungswettbewerbs zurück und vereinigt verschiedene kirchliche Einrichtungen: Einen Andachtsraum als Außenstelle einer benachbarten Mutterpfarrei, ein Pfarrheim sowie Kindergarten

The new Nordheide Quarter in northern Munich is not the kind of place where one expects to stumble upon an architectural gem. Most of the buildings here, which sprouted up practically overnight on a former military training ground, are of merely mediocre quality. A large number of people live here in difficult circumstances: some unemployed, others low-income earners or single parents. At almost 23 percent, the ratio of foreigners is particularly high. Now, at the southwest corner of this district, the visitor suddenly comes upon a special edifice that stands out from the rest with its rough brick-red shell and clear formal vocabulary – and whose markedly serene aspect forms an identifying hallmark on the urban landscape.

Consecrated in summer 2008, the Dominikuszentrum by Meck Architekten is the result of an invitation-only competition to combine various

und Caritas-Zentrum. Diese Einrichtungen verteilen sich auf vier Gebäudeflügel, die einen annähernd quadratischen Innenhof umschließen. Ein Trompetenbaum bildet das Zentrum des für alle offenen Hofes.

Allein der Andachtsraum überragt die übrigen Gebäudeteile. Das ist – mit den 300 in seine Fassaden eingemauerten kleinen Bronzekreuzen, die der Betrachter nur bei genauem Hinschauen erkennt – der einzige dezente Hinweis auf die religiöse Zweckbestimmung der Einrichtung. Es gibt aus Rücksicht auf die Menschen der verschiedenen Völker, Religionen, Sprachen und Kulturen, denen man die Tore offen halten, die man integrieren will, keinen Glockenturm und kein überdimensionales Kreuzzeichen.

Charakteristisch für das neue Dominikuszentrum ist das vorgeblendete rot schimmernde Mauerwerk aus einem hochwertigen, in alter Handwerkstechnik gefertigten Torfbrandklinker – ein natürliches Material, das den Urbaustoff Erde symbolisieren und mit seiner Größe und haptischen Qualität für den menschlichen Maßstab und eine zeitüberdauernde Baukultur stehen soll. Der souveräne Umgang mit diesem, aber auch den anderen Materialien, ist eine der wesentlichen Qualitäten des Projekts. Alle Außenflächen sind mit dem Klinker verkleidet: Fassaden und Bodenbeläge, die Deckenuntersichten, ebenso die Treppenstufen und Rampen, so dass der gesamte Baukörper wie aus

church institutions under one roof: a chapel as branch of a neighbouring mother parish, a parish hall, a kindergarten and a centre for Caritas, the welfare organisation of the Catholic Church in Germany. These facilities are distributed among four building wings that enclose a nearly square-shaped inner courtyard. A trumpet tree forms the focal point for the courtyard, which is open to all. The chapel alone towers in height over the remaining parts of the building. This is the sole, subtle indicator – along with 300 small bronze crosses set into its façade, visible only upon close scrutiny – that this building has a religious function. Out of respect for the various peoples, religions, languages and cultures to whom the gates are to be kept open here, and who are to be integrated within its embrace, the building has no bell tower and no oversized crucifix.

The signature feature of the new Dominikuszentrum is its shimmering red walls of high-grade bricks fired in peat according to an age-old method – a natural material meant to symbolise earth as the archetypal building material and, with its size and tactile qualities, designed to stand for the human dimension and for a timeless architectural culture. The masterful treatment of this and the other materials employed here is one of the prime qualities of the project. All outside surfaces are clad in these bricks: façades and ground coverings, slab undersides, steps and ramps, so that the entire structure seems to have been cut out of a single enormous brick block. This impression is further enhanced by an assiduous attention to detail that makes sure to omit anything superfluous. No metal coverings, projections or cornices disrupt the clean lines. The architects dovetail the individual surfaces with great precision, but break up their

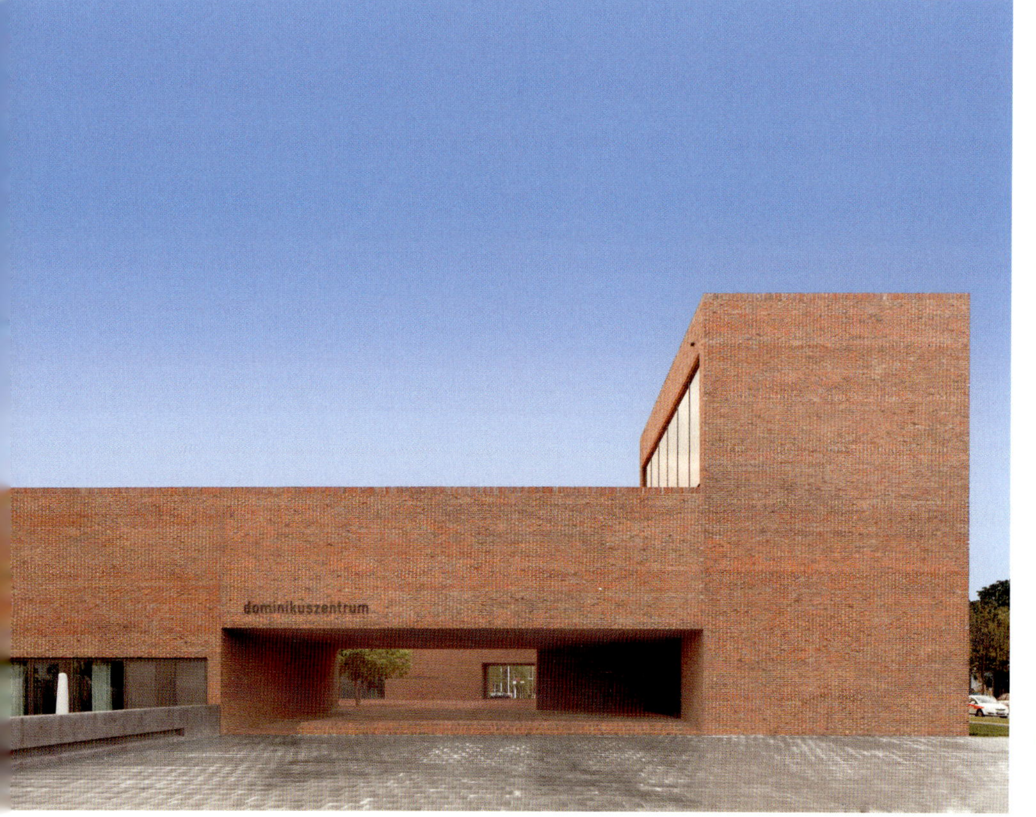

Charakteristisch für das Dominikuszentrum ist das vorgeblendete rote Mauerwerk aus Torfbrandklinker.
A distinguishing feature of the Dominikuszentrum is its red masonry of peat-fired brick.

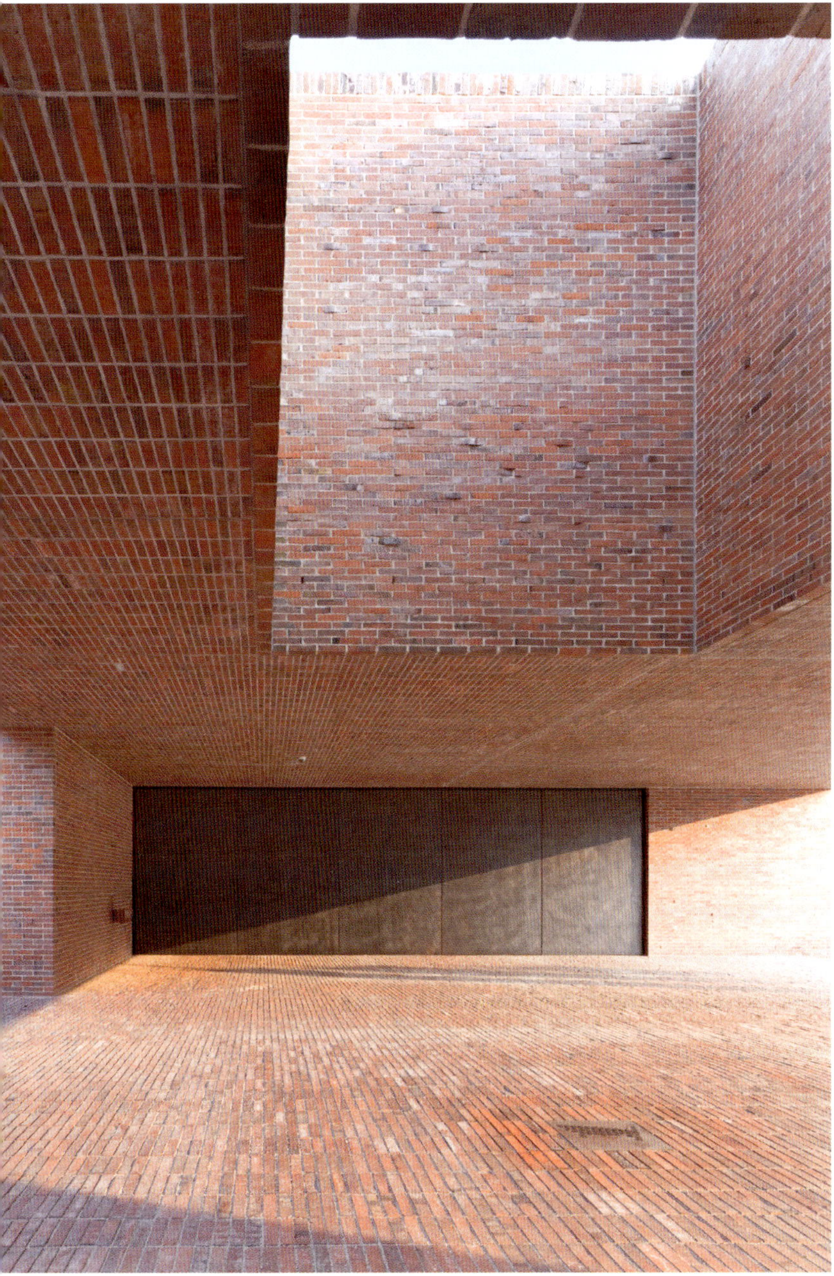

Alle Außenflächen sind einheitlich mit Klinker verkleidet.
All exterior walls are clad in a uniform brick surface.

einem einzigen mächtigen Ziegelblock geschnitten erscheint. Verstärkt wird dieser Eindruck durch eine sorgfältige Detailausbildung, die auf alles Überflüssige verzichtet. Keine Blechabdeckungen, Vorsprünge oder Gesimse stören die klaren Linien. Präzise fügen die Architekten die einzelnen Flächen aneinander, lockern sie aber durch unregelmäßige Steine auf, die den Fassaden Lebendigkeit und Plastizität verleihen. Auch die Innenwände und der Boden der Kapelle sind mit dem Torfbrandklinker bekleidet, der in diesem hervorgehobenen Raum eine besondere Behandlung erfährt: Nach dem Konzept von Andreas Meck leuchtet das Mauerwerk hier in tiefem Blau. Von Hand trug die Künstlerin Anna Leonie bis zu 27 pigmentierte Lasurschichten auf, durch die das Trägermaterial Ziegel hindurchschimmert und die Farbe Blau in unterschiedlichen Nuancen zur Geltung bringt. Verstärkt wird dieser Effekt durch das gedämpfte Tageslicht, das schräg von oben über ein erhöht angeordnetes Fenster in den Raum fällt. Auch mit diesem 4,70 x 13 Meter großen Oberlicht wurde einfühlsam Kunst in das Architekturkonzept integriert. Nach dem Entwurf von Andreas Horlitz überlagern sich auf insgesamt sechs Glas- und Schriftebenen die Worte des Glaubensbekenntnisses mit Auszügen einer mittelalterlichen Handschrift. Neben seinem semantischen Gehalt führt das auch zu einer wirkungsvollen Filterung des Lichts.

Die Möblierung der Kapelle aus hellem Eichenholz strahlt eine ähnlich robuste Sinnlichkeit aus wie die rauen Ziegelwände. Die gesamte Inneneinrichtung bis hin zu dem Gestell für die Opferkerzen, aber auch die Ausstattung aller anderen Bereiche wurde von den Architekten gleichermaßen akkurat gestaltet wie das Gebäude selbst. Genau darin liegt seine wesentliche Qualität. Allen Entwurfsebenen, von der städtebaulichen Einbindung über die Grundrissorganisation bis zum kleinsten Detail ist dieselbe Sorgfalt gewidmet worden, bei gleichzeitigem Verzicht auf jegliche laute Gesten oder kurzlebige Effekte. Das Ergebnis ist eine eindrucksvolle Architektur, wie sie heute selten geworden ist. Eine Architektur, die zu ihrer Entstehung neben einem sensiblen Architekten auch einen Bauherrn wie die Katholische Kirche braucht, der nicht an kurzfristige Rendite, sondern in langen Zeitdimensionen denkt.

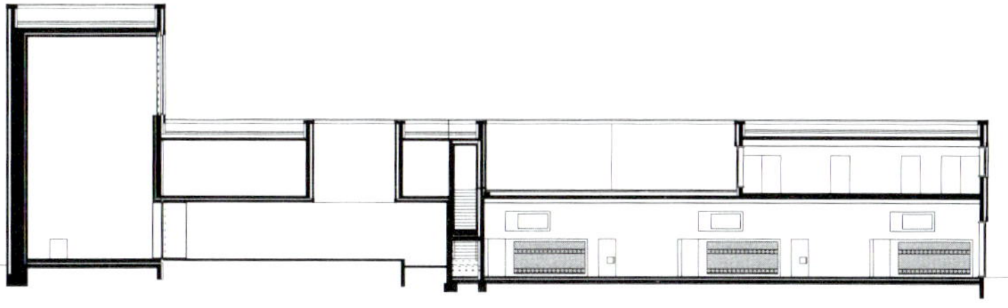

Schnitt Durchwegung Kirchenzentrum | Section of passage through the church community centre

Schnitt Kapelle-Kindergarten | Section of the chapel kindergarten

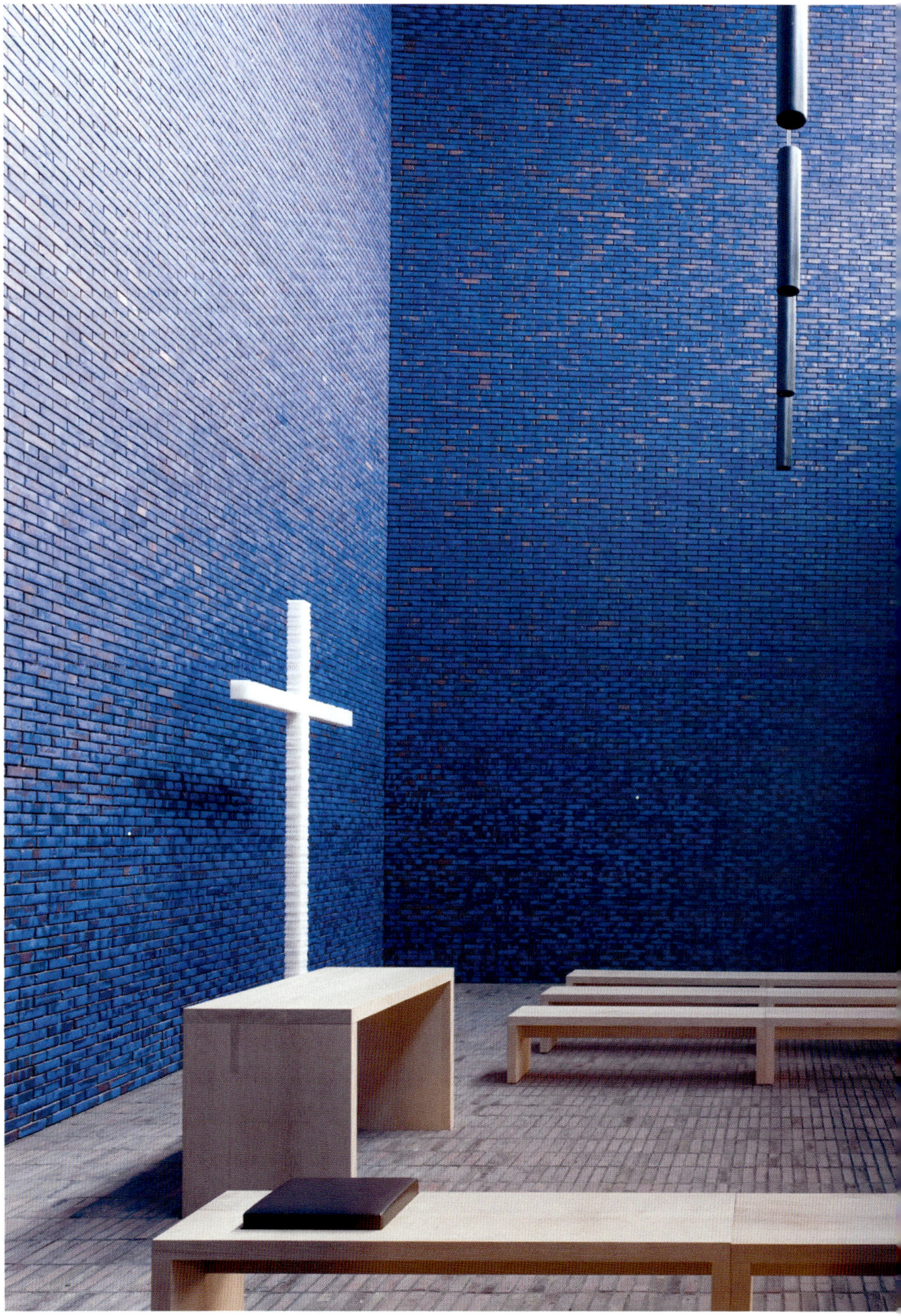

monotony by incorporating irregular stones, lending
the façades liveliness and plasticity. The interior
walls and floor of the chapel are likewise covered
in the peat-fired brick, but here it was treated to a
very special handling. Following a concept devised
by Andreas Meck, the walls of the chapel glow in
blue rather than red. Artist Anna Leonie applied
up to 27 layers of blue glaze by hand to achieve
this effect, allowing the original colour of the brick
to filter through in places while the blue tone
takes on a variety of subtly modulated nuances.
Muted daylight shines down at a slant from a high
clerestory window, further enhancing the effect.
This skylight, sized 4.70 x 13 metres, provided a
further opportunity to sensitively integrate art into
the architectural concept. In a design by Andreas
Horlitz, the words of the Apostles' Creed overlap
with lettering from a medieval manuscript across
six layers of glass and text. In addition to conveying
semantic content, this artwork also effectively
filters the light.

The light-hued oak furnishings in the chapel exude
a robust sensuality similar to that of the red brick
walls. The architect designed all the interior décor,
up to and including the stand for the votive candles
as well as the fittings for all other areas, with the
same degree of care he devoted to the building
itself. And therein lies its essential quality. Meticulous attention has been lavished on all levels of the
building's design, from its integration into the urban
surroundings, to the organisation of the ground
plan, down to the smallest detail, while however
foregoing any loud gestures or short-lived special
effects. The result is a stirring brand of architecture
that has grown rare these days. An architecture
calling for both a sensitive architect and a client like
the Catholic Church that is not out for quick profit
but rather thinks in terms of lasting value.

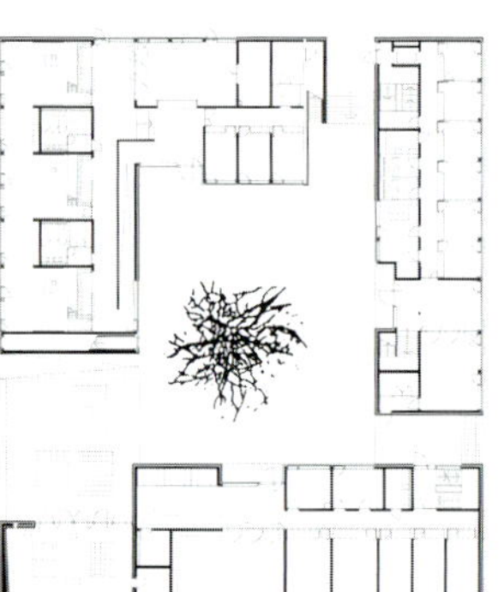

Grundriss Ebene 0 | Floor plan of Level 0

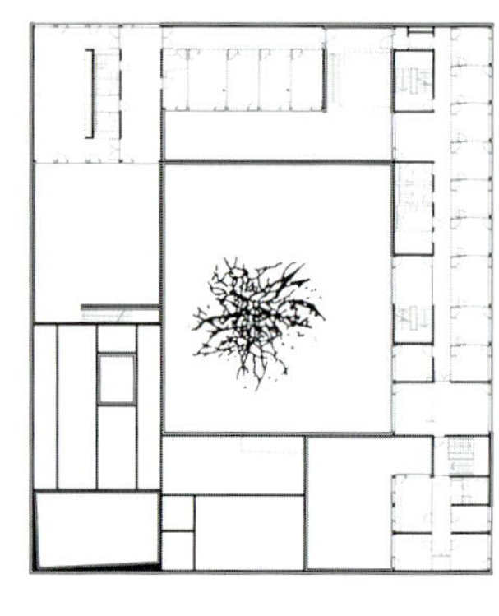

Grundriss Ebene 1 | Floor plan of Level 1

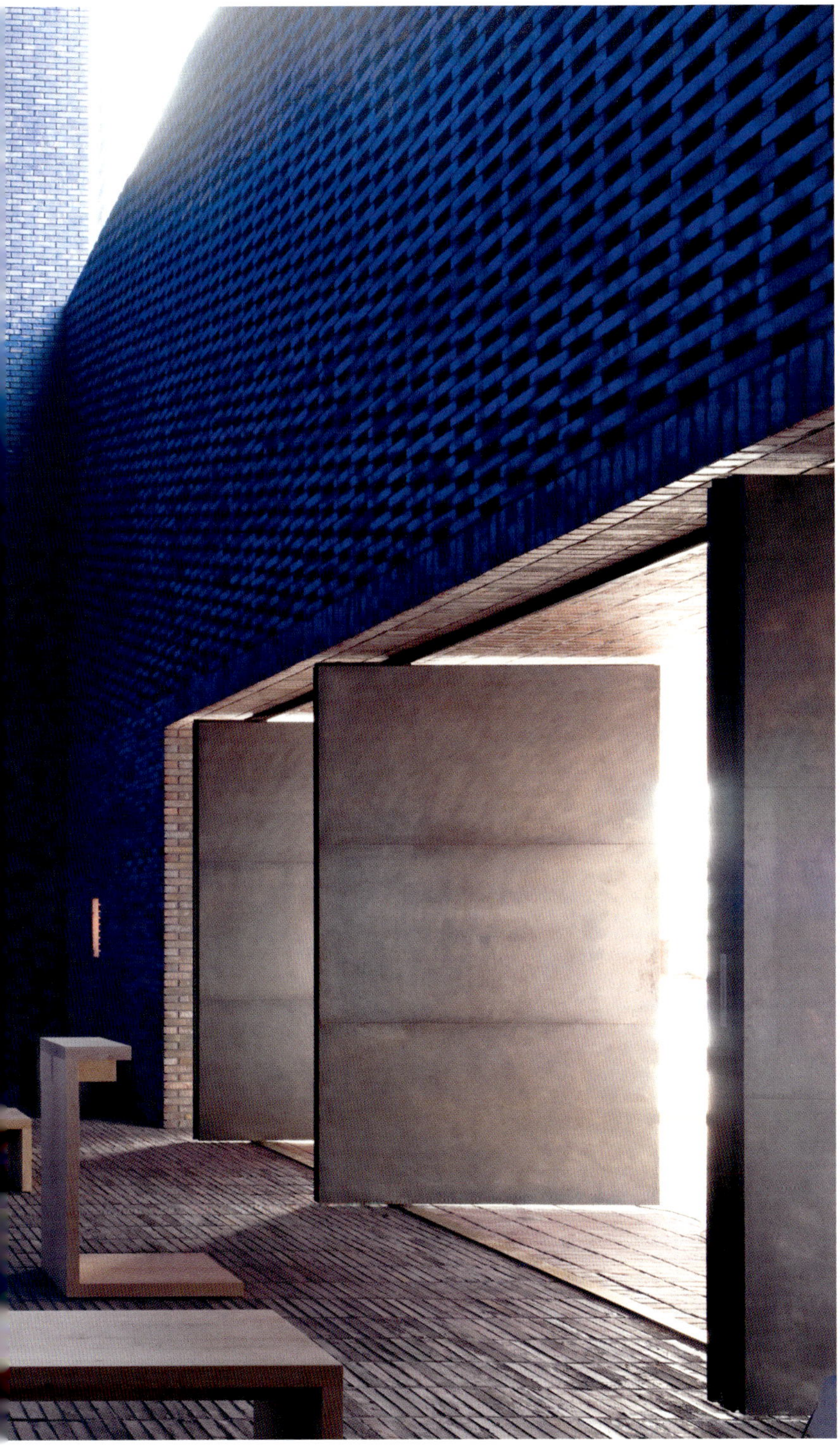

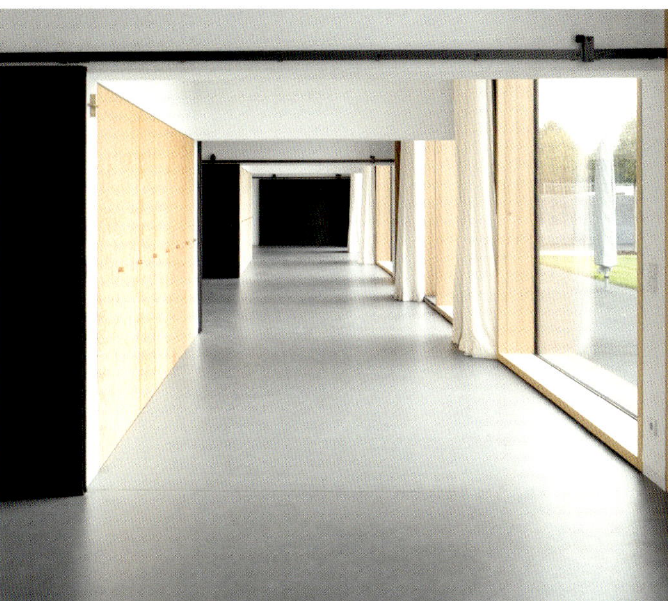

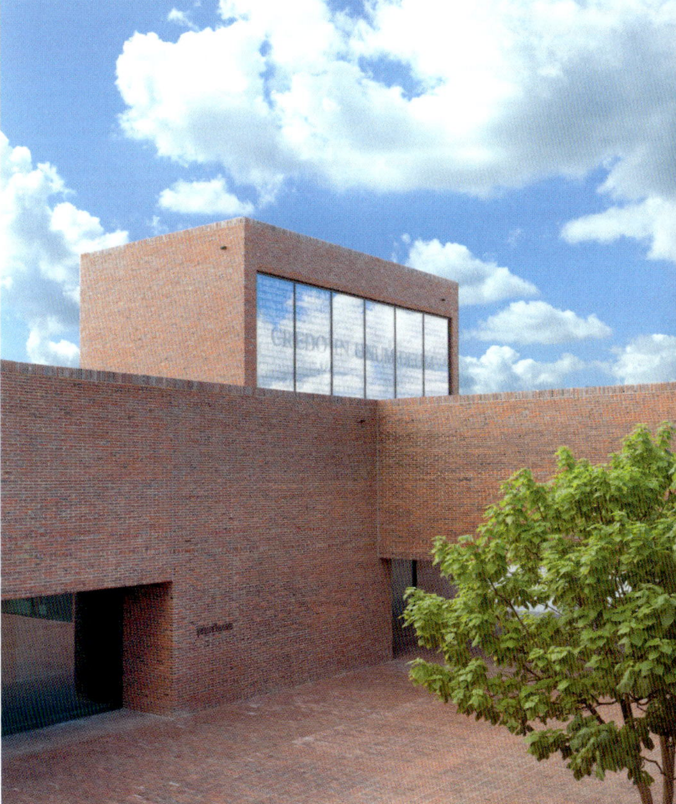

Die großen Fenster öffnen das Gebäude zum Hof. | The large window opens up the building to the courtyard.

Der Andachtsraum überragt die anderen Gebäudeteile. | The chapel towers over the rest of the building.

NIETO SOBEJANO

ERWEITERUNG KUNSTMUSEUM MORITZBURG

TEXT LAYLA DAWSON

19

ARCHITEKTEN | ARCHITECTS

Nieto Sobejano
Arquitectos, S.L.P.
Fuensanta Nieto –
Enrique Sobejano
Talavera 4 L-5
28016 Madrid
Spanien | Spain
www.nietosobejano.com

MITARBEITER | TEAM

Sebastian Sasse
(Projektarchitekt | project architect);
Vanesa Manrique, Nina Nolting,
Olaf Syrbe, Miguel Ubarrechena
(Wettbewerbsteam | compe-
tition collaborators);
Udo Brunner, Nina Nolting,
Dirk Landt, Susann Euen,
Siverin Arndt (Projektteam
project collaborators); ,
Nieto Sobejano Arquitectos S.L.P.
Fuensanta Nieto – Enrique Sobe-
jano, Sebastian Sasse, Johannes
Stumpf, Karl Heinz Bosse
(Bauleitung | site management)

HAUSTECHNIK | M&E ENGINEERS

Rentschler und Riedesser,
Jürgen Trautwein

DACHKONSTRUKTION | ROOF CONSTRUCTION

Dornhöfer GmbH

BAUHERR | CLIENT

Stiftung Moritzburg
Land Sachsen-Anhalt

TRAGWERK | STRUCTURE

GSE, Jorg Enseleit

FERTIGSTELLUNG | COMPLETION

2008

STANDORT | LOCATION

Friedemann-Bach-Platz 5
06108 Halle
www.stiftung-moritzburg.de

FOTOS | PHOTOS

Roland Halbe

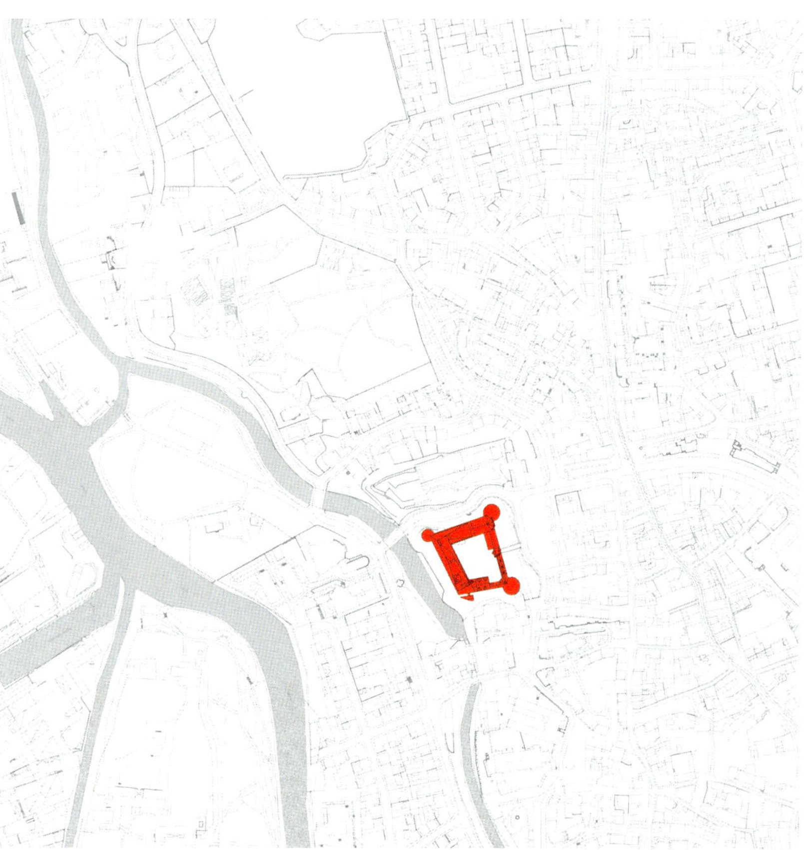

Lageplan | Site plan

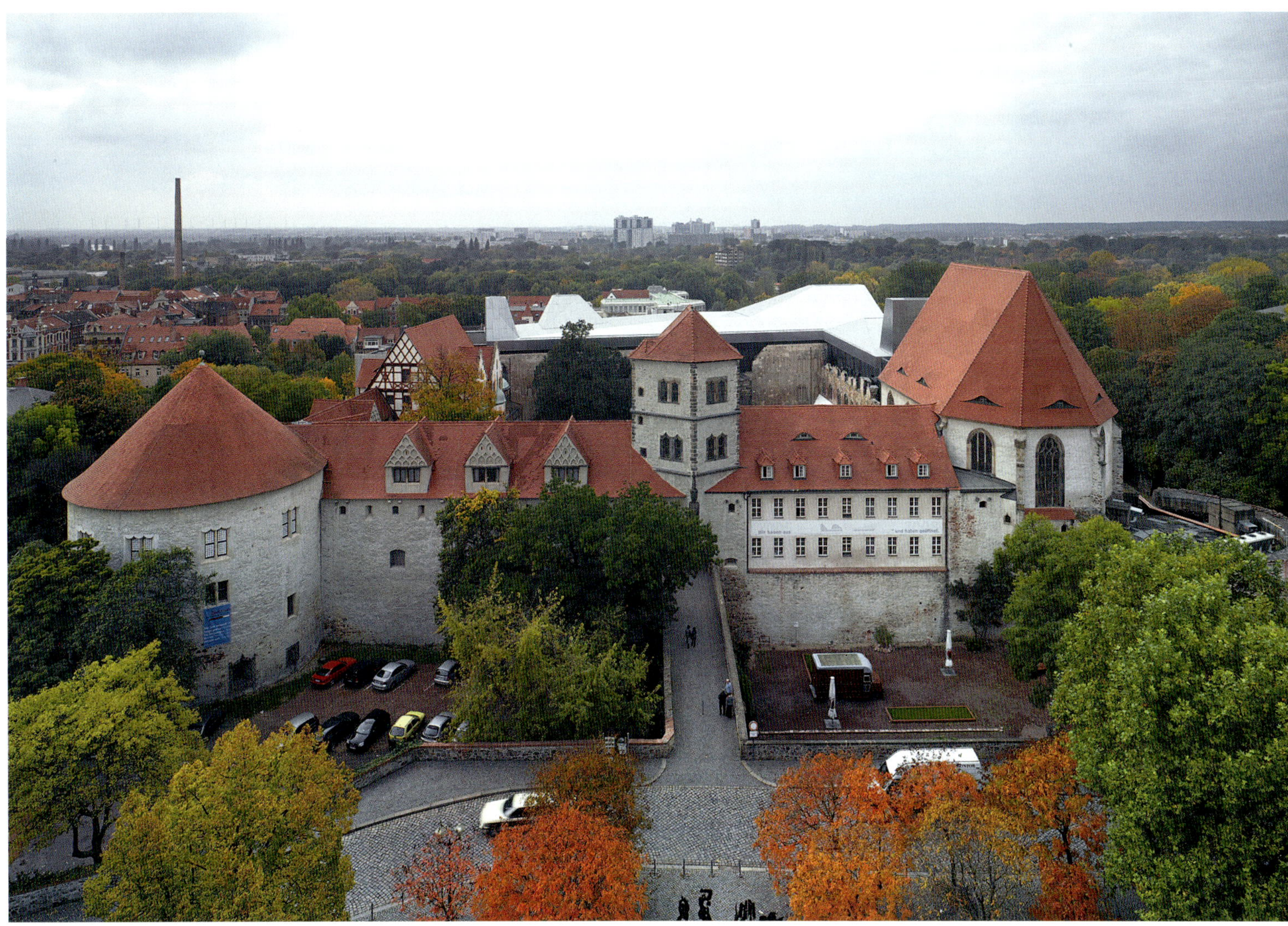

Die Erweiterung des Museums Moritzburg ist in der Vogelperspektive erkenntlich an dem asymmetrisch gefalteten Aluminiumdach. | The extension of the Moritzburg Museum can be recognised from the sky by its asymmetrically folded aluminium roof.

Ist es ein Vogel? Ist es ein Flugzeug? Das asymmetrisch gefaltete Aluminiumdach des Museums Moritzburg, dessen Linienführung an einen Stealth-Bomber erinnert, schwebt über alten Festungsmauern, die seit dem Spätmittelalter Kriege überdauert haben. Dieser Fremdkörper aus Glas und Metall, der auf zwei Etagen neue Ausstellungsflächen schafft, ist in die Mauerruinen des Nord- und Westflügels eingepasst. Wie Chirurgen bei einer Herzoperation haben die Architekten Nieto Sobejano Räume des 21. Jahrhunderts in eine historische Hülle eingepflanzt und einer Ruine neues Leben eingehaucht.
Die 500 Jahre alte Moritzburg ist ein Sammelsurium historischer Rekonstruktionen. Innerhalb der Burgmauern befinden sich Reste der Residenz der Magdeburger Erzbischöfe, deren Schutzpatron Mauritius der Anlage ihren Namen gab; ein ehemaliges Lazarettgebäude; ein Torhaus, in dem Lyonel Feininger wohnte, als er seine Halle-Serie malte; eine Neorenaissance-Replik des Talamts, das ursprünglich in der Innenstadt stand und als Sitz der Salzgrafen und Zunfthaus der Salzsieder diente; und eine Kapelle, für deren dringend erforderliche Restaurierung bisher die Mittel fehlten. Die Bruchsteinmauern, die einen trapezförmigen Innenhof umschließen, ragen wie Klippen über den Mühlgraben, einen Nebenarm der Saale, auf.

Is it a bird? Is it a plane? The asymmetrically folded aluminium roof of the Moritzburg Foundation, with lines similar to a Stealth bomber, hovers over ancient ramparts, themselves survivors of wars stretching back to the late Middle Ages. This alien body of glass and metal, incorporating two new levels of galleries, has been inserted between the ruined, shard-like, walls of the north and west wings. Architects Nieto Sobejano, like surgeons performing heart surgery, have fitted 21st-century spaces into a historic container, and given new life to a ruined body.
The Moritzburg fortress is a 500-year-old ragbag of historical reconstructions. Within the keep there are the remains of a Magdeburg archbishop's residence, dedicated to Saint Mauritius, a former military hospital, a gatehouse tower in which Lyonel Feininger lived while painting his Halle series, a copy of a neo-Renaissance villa, the Talamt, that originally stood in the city as association headquarters for the salt mining and production owners, and a church in need of restoration, for which there is,

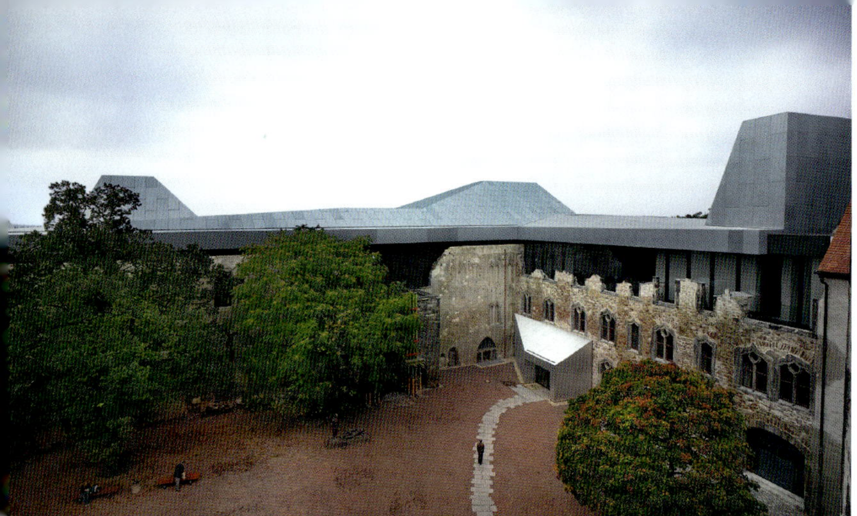
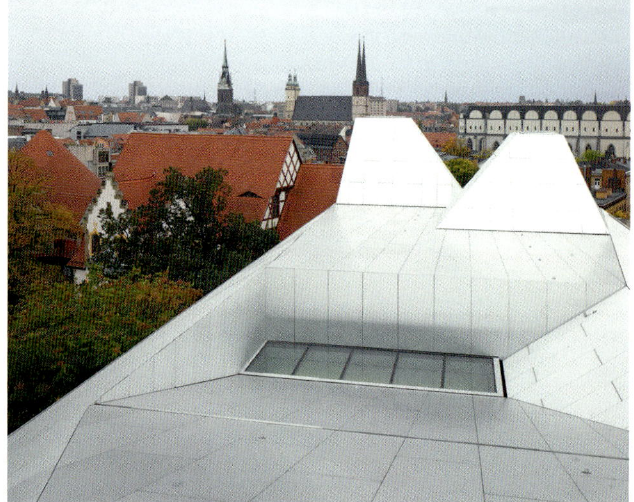

Durch ‚Kamine' im Dach fällt von oben Tageslicht in die Räume. | 'Chimneys' in the roof let in daylight from above.

Von den ursprünglich zwei Toren blieb im Laufe der Jahrhunderte nur noch eines übrig. Heute gelangen Besucher über eine gepflasterte Fußgängerbrücke in die Burg. Der Wassergraben, der die Burganlage einst schützte, ist mittlerweile verlandet, mit Gras bewachsen und dient als Parkplatz.

Als Nieto Sobejano 2004 den Wettbewerb der Stiftung Moritzburg für die Erweiterung der Ausstellungsflächen gewannen, die Platz für eine Dauerausstellung der „Brücke"-Sammlung Hermann Gerlingers sowie für Sonderausstellungen bieten sollte, stellte der Auftraggeber hohe Anforderungen. Der Entwurf für eine Erweiterung des Museums um 2000 Quadratmeter Ausstellungsfläche im Nord- und Westflügel, verbunden mit einem neuen Erschließungstrakt, Foyer, Museumsshop, Café und Servicebereichen, musste die Ansprüche zahlreicher Sponsoren befriedigen: den EU-Fond für Regionalentwicklung, Bund und Land, die Zeit-Stiftung und elf weitere Förderer, die von der Lotto-Toto-Gesellschaft bis zu Kulturstiftungen von Industrieunternehmen und Banken reichten. Das Budget war dagegen für einen solch anspruchsvollen Bau viel zu niedrig angesetzt. Das Entwurfskonzept ging von verschachtelten Boxen aus, die von der neuen Dachkonstruktion abgehängt werden sollten. Die bröckelnden Außenmauern wurden mit Betoninjektionen stabilisiert und mit einem Ringbalken versehen. Ein Dach aus Aluminiumguss, wie die Architekten es zunächst geplant hatten, erwies sich als zu schwer und zu kostspielig. Nun trägt eine Stahlkonstruktion mit einer Dachhaut aus Aluminium die abgehängten Boxen, die über den größeren Sälen im Erdgeschoss schweben und Ausstellungsflächen im Obergeschoss schaffen. Um die Dachlast weiter zu verringern, bestehen auch diese hängenden Säle aus einer Stahlkonstruktion, die mit Gips-

as yet, no money. The enclosing limestone walls, protecting a trapezoid inner courtyard, rise like cliffs over the Mühlgraben, an arm of the river Saale. Over the centuries two gateways into the keep have been reduced to one. Nowadays visitors enter over a cobbled footbridge. The moat below, where water once formed a defensive barrier, is now a grassed car park.

When Nieto Sobejano won the 2004 Halle competition to provide new exhibition halls for a permanent collection, the Hermann Gerlinger "Brücke" collection, and temporary shows, client expectations were high. The design for a 2,000-square-metre extension, built into the north and west wings, and linked by a new circulation core, entrance foyer, shop, café, and utilities, had to satisfy a wide range of sponsors: from the EU Fund for Regional Development, federal and regional governments, the Zeit Bucerius Foundation, and eleven other bodies, from Lotto Toto to industrial and banking cultural foundations. In contrast, the budget, for a building of such quality, was set far too low.

The design concept is of boxes within boxes, all hung from the new roof. The crumbling outer stone walls were strengthened with injected concrete and crowned with a ring beam. The architect's first choice, a cast aluminium roof, proved too heavy and expensive. Instead, a steel skeleton, clad in aluminium sheet, carries the box-like second-floor halls, which are suspended over the larger halls at first-floor level. In order to further reduce the roof load, these hanging halls are also steel frames, clad in gypsum board. Old and new have become one, but at no point do old and new actually touch. A design strategy of gaps and recessed joints gives

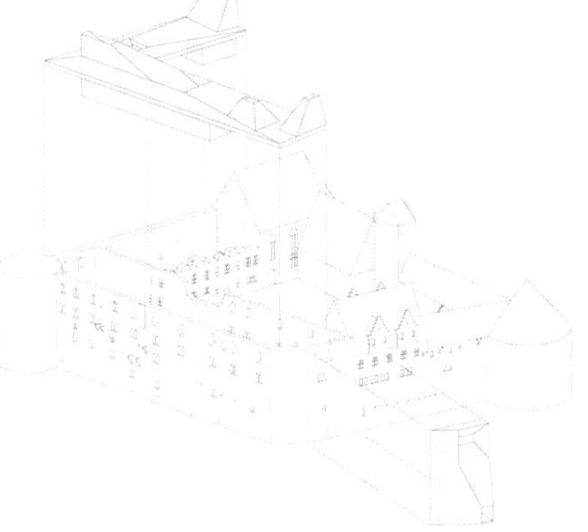

Axonometrie mit neuem Dach und Eingang für die Erweiterung des Museums Moritzburg
Axonometric view of new roof and entrance to the extension of the Moritzburg Museum

Fassade zum Innenhof: Die Stahlkonstruktion des Daches trägt abgehängte Ausstellungsboxen, die über den Sälen im Erdgeschoss schweben. | Façade looking onto inner courtyard: the steel roof structure supports suspended exhibition boxes that float over the ground-floor galleries.

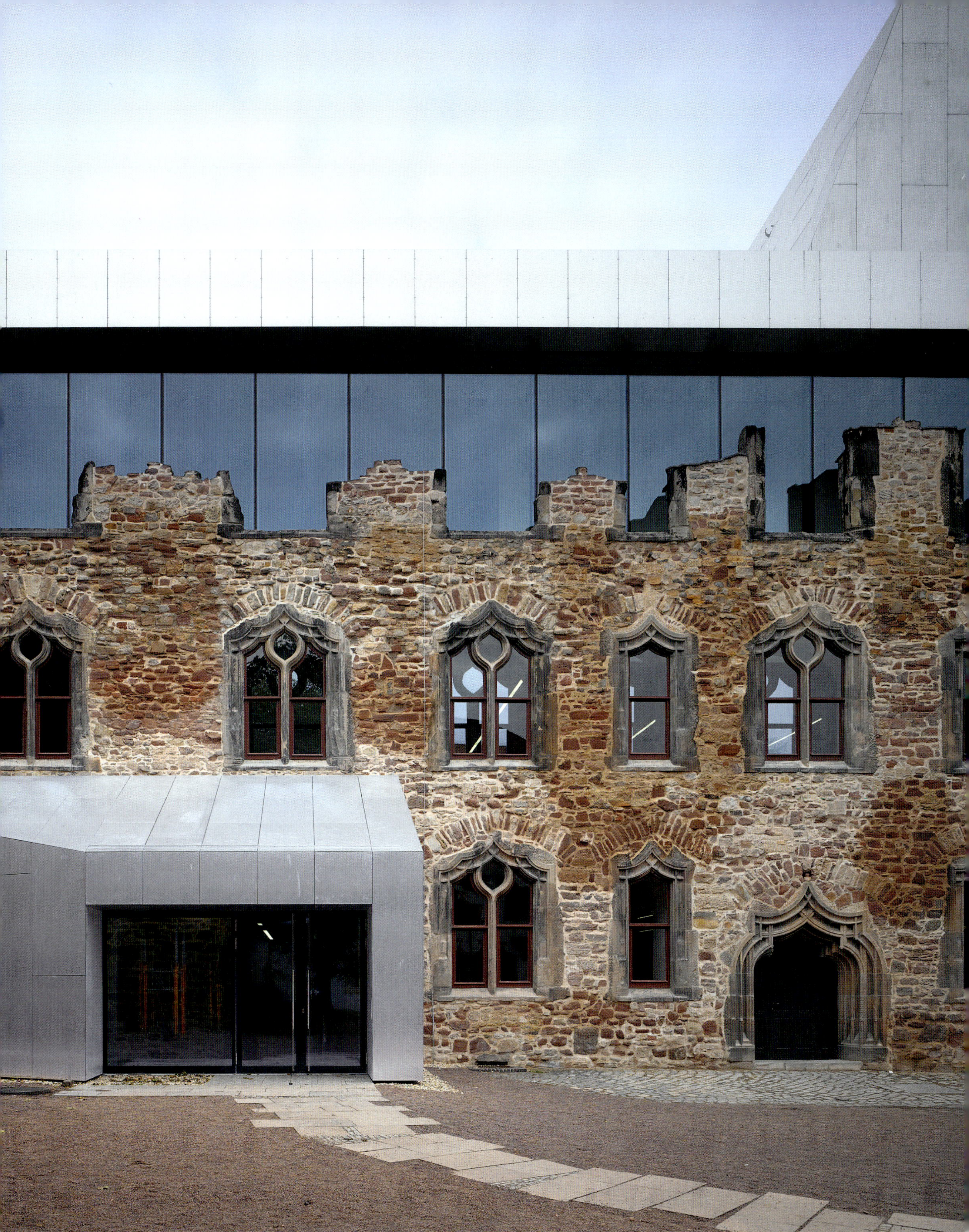

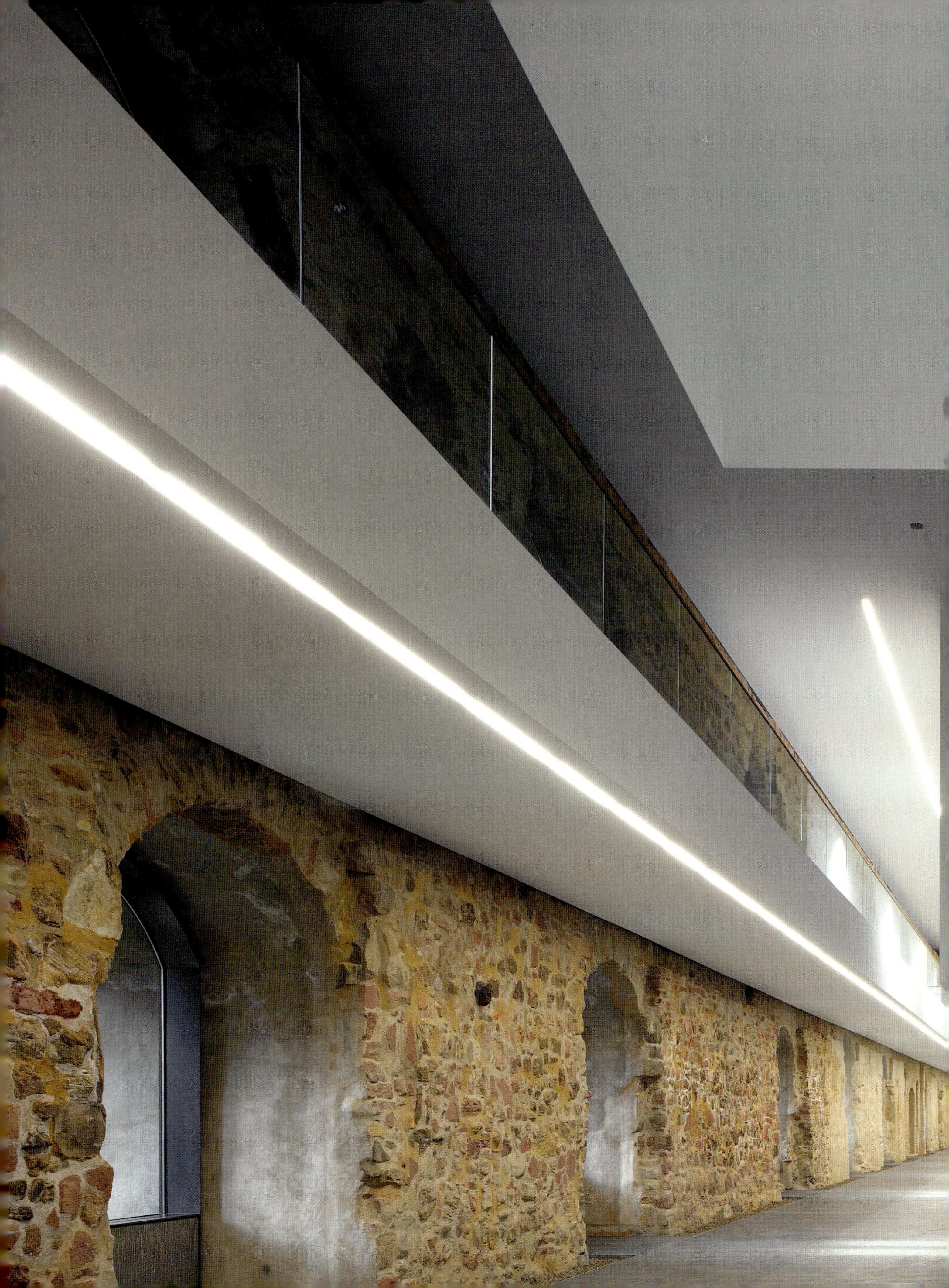

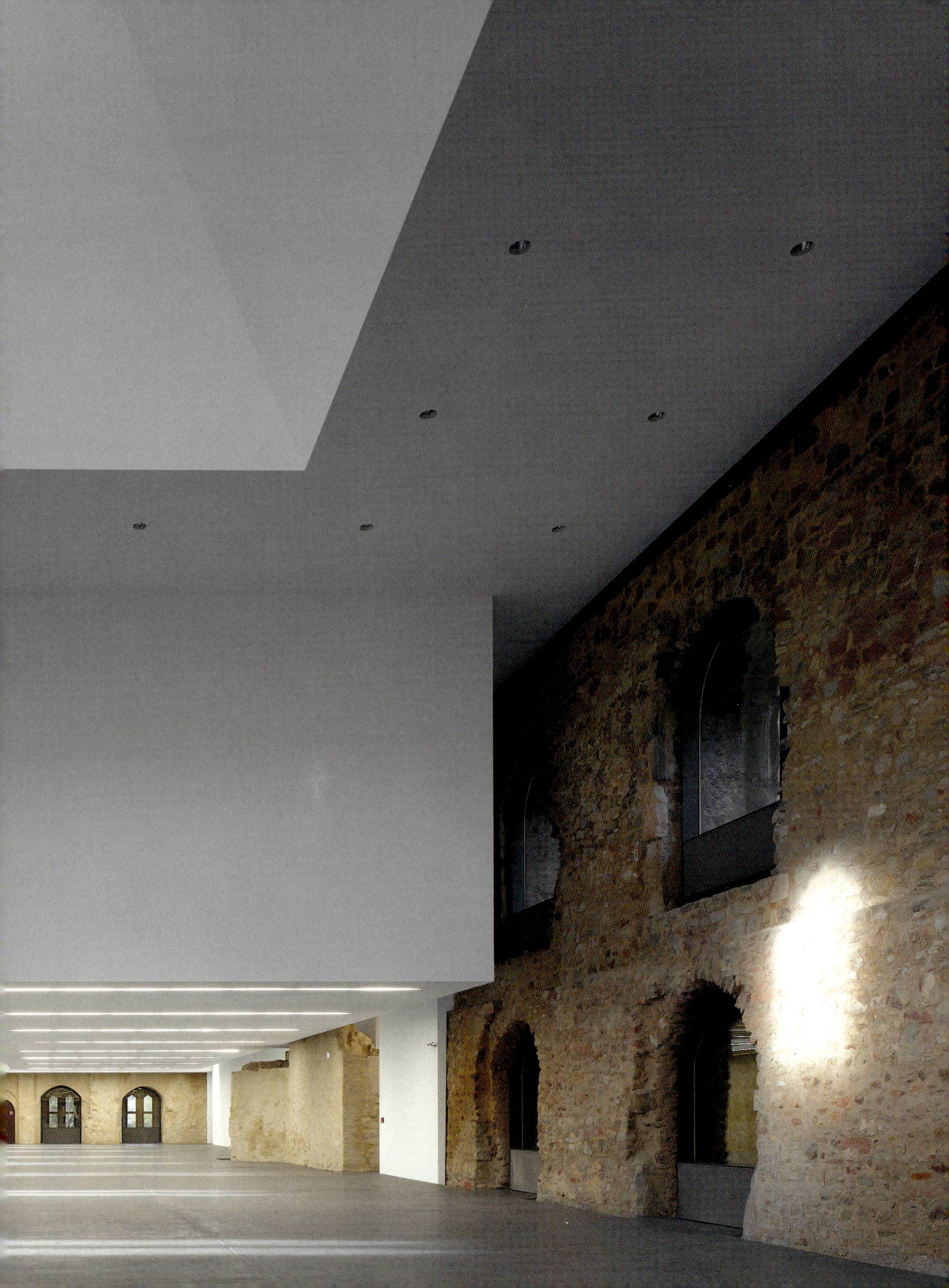

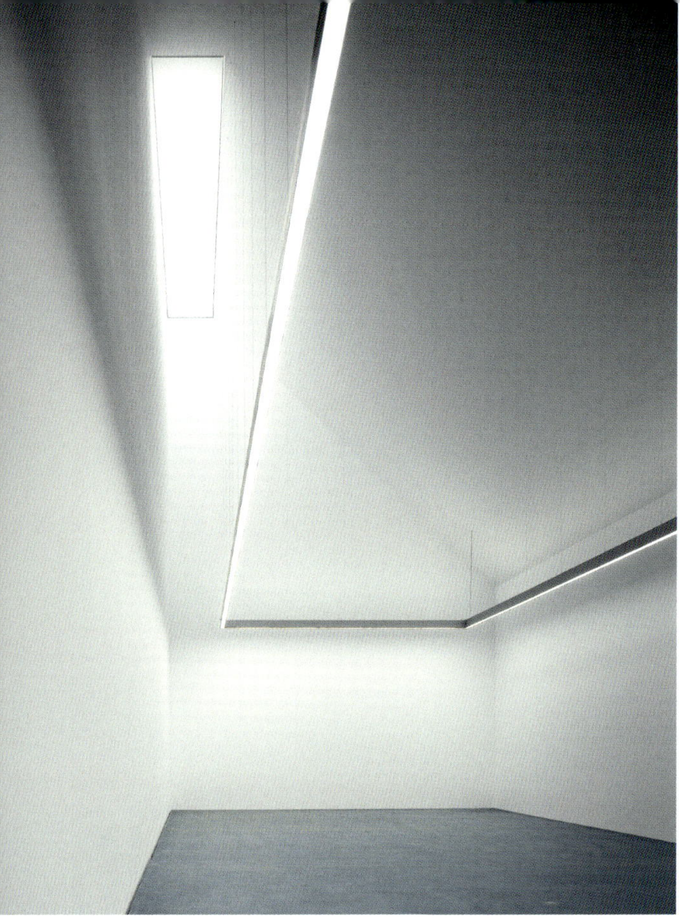

2. Obergeschoss, Ausstellung West: Ausstellungsbox
2nd floor, west: exhibition box

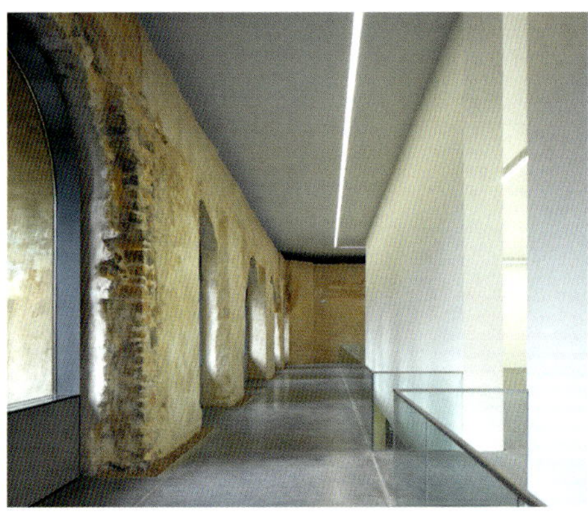

2. Obergeschoss, Galerie: Das Gestaltungskonzept
arbeitet mit Lücken und Fugen zwischen Alt und Neu.
2nd floor, gallery: The design concept works with gaps and
joints between old and new.

kartonplatten verkleidet ist. Alt und Neu sind eins geworden, obwohl sie sich an keiner Stelle berühren. Das Gestaltungskonzept, das mit Lücken und Fugen arbeitet, vermittelt die Illusion, dass weiße Behälter schwerelos in einer erdverbundenen Gebäudehülle aus rohem Stein hängen. Hohlräume zwischen neuen und alten Wänden dienen der Isolation und verbergen technische Einrichtungen. Polierte Betonböden und Treppen schweben zwischen den Geschossen, sind aber von den Wänden durch Kiesstreifen getrennt. Von außen springt die Verbindung von Mauern und Dach in einer Schattenfuge zurück, die den Eindruck schwerelosen Schwebens verstärkt. Die Lichteffekte lassen Lyonel Feiningers Einfluss erkennen. Durch ‚Kamine' im Dach dringen von oben Lichtkegel in die Räume. Ganz ähnlich ‚schleust' ein neuer Eingang aus Aluminium Besucher in das Gebäude. Die durchdachte Architektur, die nach den ursprünglichen Vorgaben entwickelt wurde, respektiert die vielfältige Vorgeschichte des Gebäudes und vereint erfolgreich seine unterschiedlichen Funktionen. Dank eines motivierten Politikers und kompromissloser Architekten hat Halle einen Weltklassebau erhalten. Die minimalistische Palette der Architekten und die gelungene Bändigung der Haustechnik, deren Kabel, Rohre und Lüftungen sich als bloße Schlitze in der Wandverkleidung präsentieren, schaffen eine ruhige Umgebung, die die klassische moderne Kunst vorteilhaft zur Geltung bringt. Leider wirkt die Anordnung der Raumteiler in der Dauerausstellung mit Werken der „Brücke" bedrückend und unsensibel für die Architektur, aber das ist nun mal das Vorrecht eines Bauherrn.

Halle ist zwar eine schrumpfende Stadt, aber Dank des Föderalismus verteilt sich Kultur auf die verschiedenen Regionen und gilt als öffentliches Gut, das noch nicht vollends privatisiert oder zentralisiert ist. Analog zum ‚slow food' sind Museen ‚slow culture', die letzten Bastionen der Kontemplation angesichts des Turbokonsums. Das Museum Moritzburg hat mit einem einzigartigen Bauwerk nicht nur den Standard der Region gehoben, sondern sich auch eine nützliche Waffe im wirtschaftlichen Wettbewerb urbaner Zentren zugelegt.

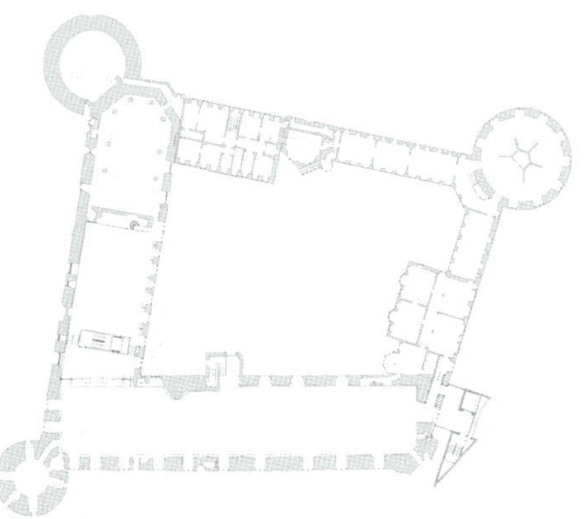

Grundriss Ebene 0 | Floor plan of Level 0

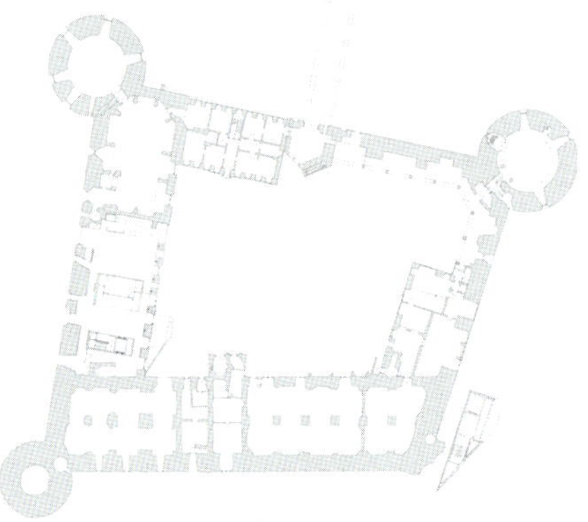

Grundriss Ebene 1 | Floor plan of Level 1

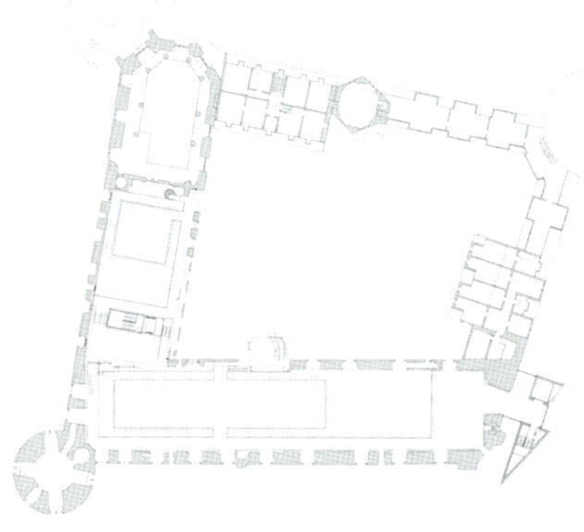

Grundriss Ebene 2 | Floor plan of Level 2

the illusion of white pods hanging, weightlessly, within an earth-bound rough stone shell. Air spaces between new and historic walls help insulation, and hide technical services. Polished concrete floors and stairs flow through the levels but are separated from the walls by gravel-filled borders. Externally, the joint between roof and walls is recessed and hidden in shadow, adding to the illusion of weightless suspension. Lyonel Feininger's influence is seen in the lighting effects. Shafts of light pierce the halls from above, through 'chimneys' in the roof. Similarly visitors are 'funneled' through a new aluminium entrance.

This meticulous architecture, developed from the original brief, respects the many pre-histories, while successfully connecting disparate functions. Thanks to a motivated politician and uncompromising architects, Halle has gained some world-class accommodation. The architect's minimalist palette, and successful disciplining of the service engineers' wires, vents and pipes to mere slits in the skin, has created a calm environment, against which classical modern art stands out to advantage. Unfortunately, in the Brücke gallery, the curator's layout of partitions is oppressive and insensitive to the architecture, but that is a client's prerogative. Halle is a shrinking city but, thanks to federalism, culture is dispersed among the regions, and still seen as public property, not yet fully privatised or centralised. Museums, like 'slow food', are 'slow culture', the last bastions of contemplation in the face of turbo consumption. Not only has Moritzburg raised regional standards with a unique piece of architecture, it has also armed itself with a useful weapon in the economic war between urban centres.

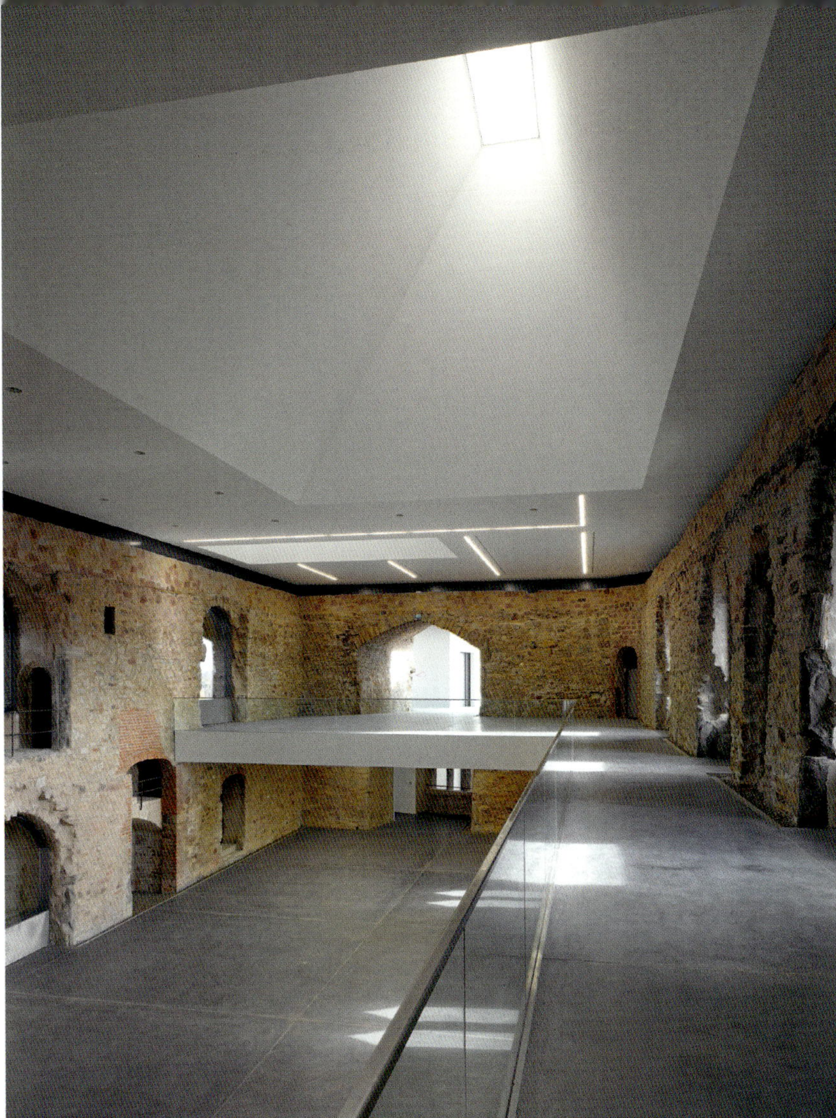

2. Obergeschoss, Galerie: Die Lichteffekte lassen Lyonel Feiningers Einfluss erkennen. | 2nd floor, gallery: the light effects betray Lyonel Feininger's influence.

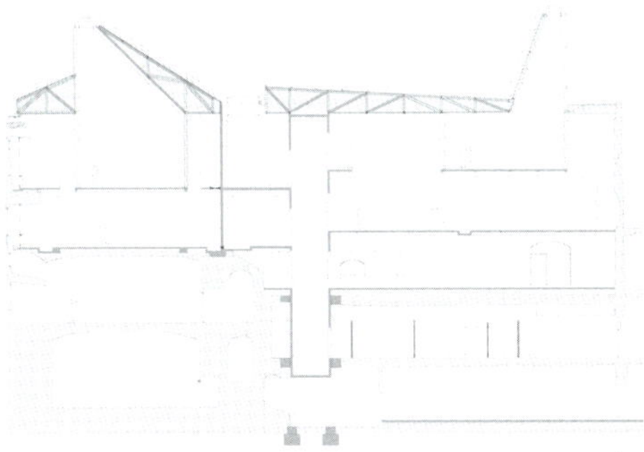

PETER HAIMERL

„BIRG MICH, CILLI!"

TEXT DIETER BARTETZKO

20

ARCHITEKTEN | ARCHITECTS

HAI MERLIN,
Studio für Architektur
Peter Haimerl
Lothringer Straße 13
81667 München | Munich
www.zoom-town.eu

MITARBEITER | ASSOCIATE

Jutta Görlich

BAUHERR | CLIENT

Jutta Görlich,
Peter Haimerl

TRAGWERK | STRUCTURE

a.k.a. ingenieure
München | Munich

FERTIGSTELLUNG | COMPLETION

2008

STANDORT | LOCATION

Eben 4
94234 Viechtach

FOTOS | PHOTOS

Edward Beierle,
Gero Wortmann,
Jutta Görlich

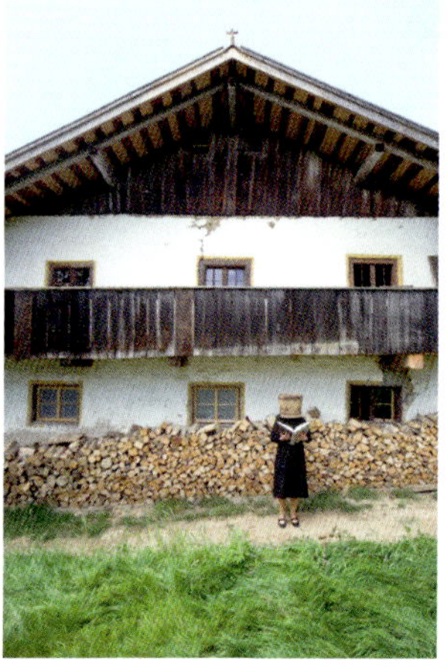

Die Auferstehung eines Bauernhauses
The resurrection of a farmhouse

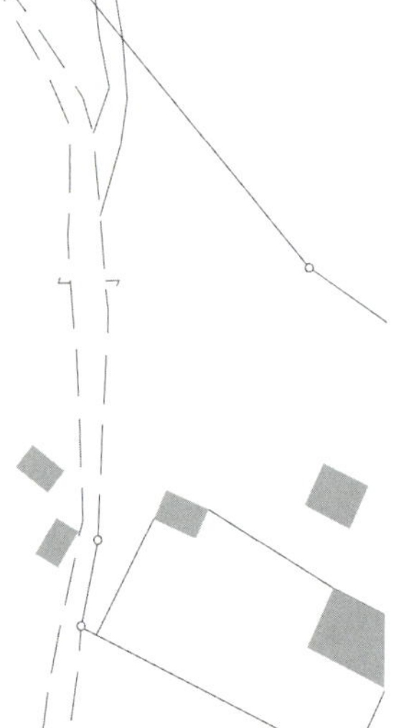

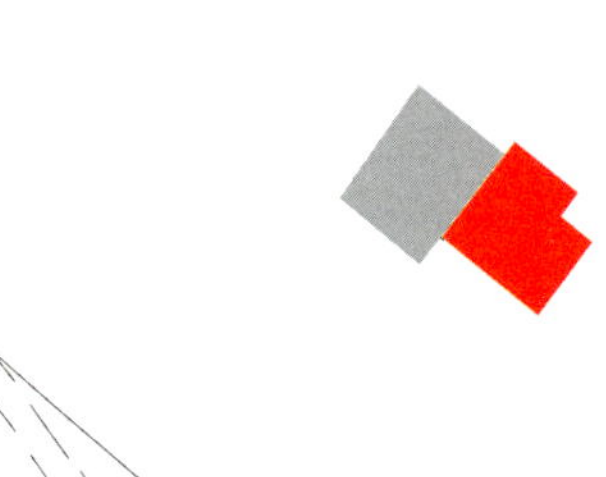

Lageplan | Site plan

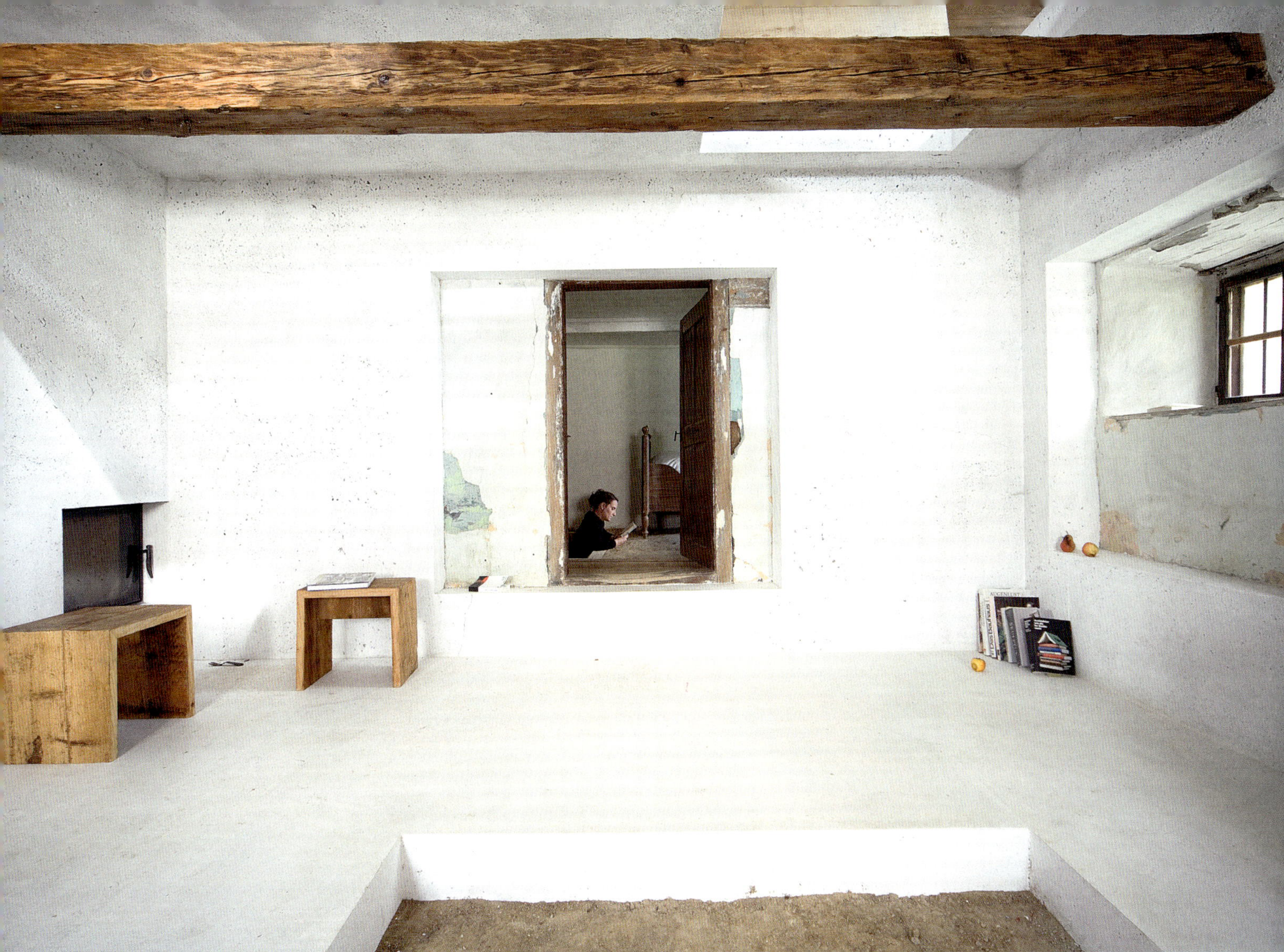

Die Fotografie strahlt etwas leise Beunruhigendes aus: Eine junge Frau in einem formlosen schwarzen Kleid steht vor einem verfallenen geduckten Haus. Ringsum eine abschüssige Wiese, uralte Obstbäume, aus deren Kronen abgestorbene Äste ragen, dahinter dichter ansteigender Wald. Die Frau hat ein hölzernes Behältnis über den Kopf gestülpt, einen Scheffel, das alte bäuerliche Messgerät für Korn. Es macht sie blick- und hilflos, gespenstisch und komisch, gefährdet und doch grenzenlos selbstbewusst.

Jutta Görlich heißt die Frau, ist Künstlerin und hat diese Aufnahme samt einer Serie weiterer verfremdeter Fotografien inszeniert, deren Schauplatz das erwähnte Bauernhaus im Bayerischen Wald nahe der tschechischen Grenze ist. Das wiederum hat ihr Mann, der Architekt Peter Haimerl, bearbeitet. Bearbeitet, denn von einer Sanierung oder einem Umbau im landläufigen Sinne kann man hier nicht sprechen.

Was Haimerl vorfand, war ein um 1840 erbauter Kleinbauernhof weitab vom Dorf. Das Haus, in dem traditionsgemäß Mensch und Vieh Wand an Wand und mitsamt ihren Vorräten lebten, war gegen 1890 aufgestockt worden. Den Dachstuhl hatte man angehoben und das Giebeldreieck als Ziegelmauer vorgeblendet; ein scharfer Kontrast zum wunderbaren, nach jahrhundertealten Traditionen gemauerten Bruchsteingefüge des Erdgeschosses. Verputz tarnte die schroffen Unterschiede und Baunähte.

Bis 1974 war der Hof bewohnt, dann stand er leer. Mit der Folge, dass der Architekt ein marodes Anwesen vorfand: eingesunkene Balken, rissige Wände, bröckelnder Putz innen wie außen. Eine Seitenwand hatte dem Druck des Hangs nachgegeben, in den sie eingetieft stand und einzustürzen drohte.

The photograph exudes a vague feeling of unease: a young woman in a shapeless black dress stands before a low-slung, tumbledown house. All around is a sloping meadow, ancient fruit trees from whose crowns dead boughs rise, behind them a dense forest spreading up a hillside. The woman has a wooden vessel stuck over her head, a bushel that farmers once used to measure out grain. It renders her blind and helpless, spectral and comical, endangered and yet endlessly self-assured.

Jutta Görlich is the woman's name; she is an artist and staged this scene herself, along with a series of other strange photographs, all of them set at the aforementioned farmhouse in the Bayrischer Wald (Bavarian Forest) near the Czech border. The house in turn was reworked by her husband, architect Peter Haimerl. 'Reworked' because one can hardly speak here of a renovation or remodelling in the conventional sense.

What Haimerl found was a small farm built in 1840 far away from the village. In keeping with tradition, the residents and their livestock lived in close quarters in the farmhouse, together with their food stores, and an additional storey was added in 1890. The roof was raised and the gable triangle superimposed as a brick wall – a stark contrast to the wonderful quarry stone of the ground floor, laid in accordance with centuries-old traditions. Plaster camouflaged the abrupt disparities and building seams.

The farm was inhabited until 1974, and afterward stood empty. The architect came upon a dilapidated property: sunken beams, cracked walls, crumbling plaster, inside and out. One of the side walls had

133

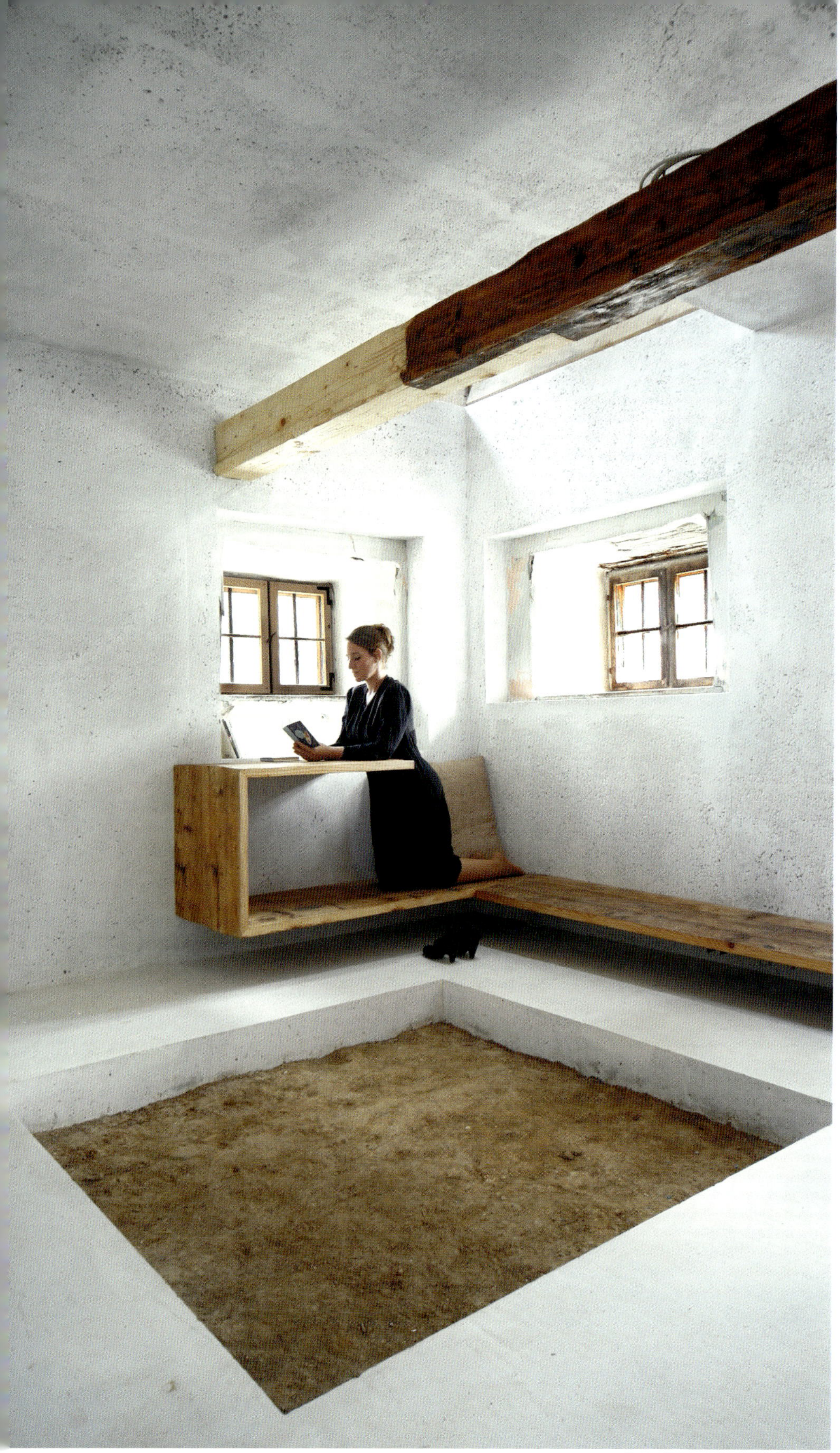

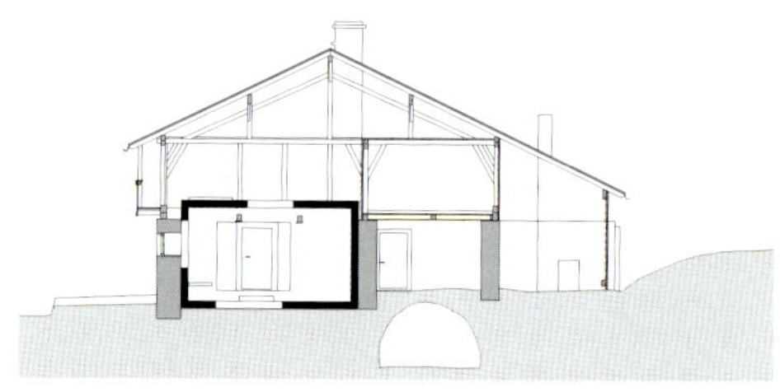

Schnitt | Section

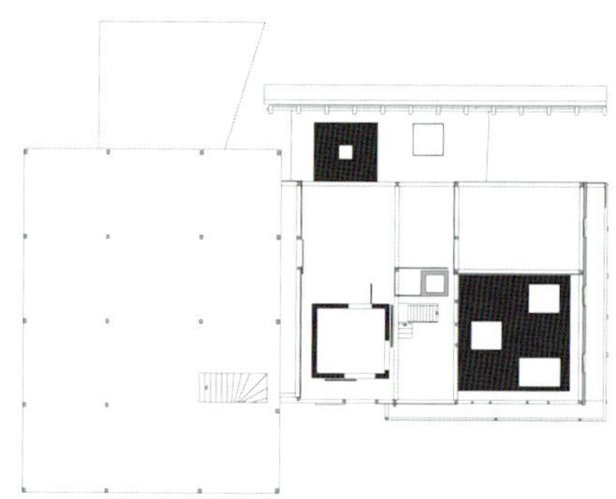

Grundriss Obergeschoss | Floor plan of upper floor

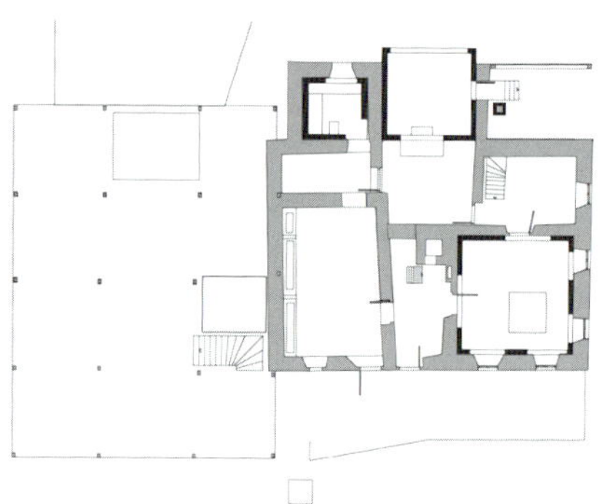

Grundriss Erdgeschoss | Floor plan of ground floor

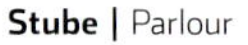

Stube | Parlour

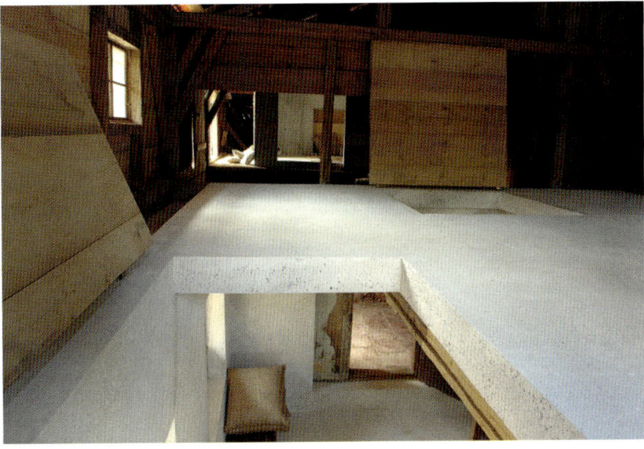

Freideck | Open celling

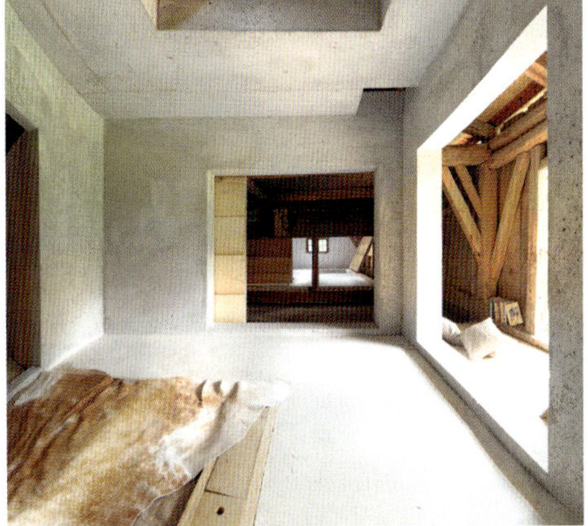

Schlafzimmer | Bedroom

Die Pläne einer schonenden Sanierung zur Wiederherstellung im ursprünglichen Stil rückten Peter Haimerl immer ferner, je länger er sich mit dem Bau beschäftigte. Wo immer er nämlich hinsah, traten die Spuren gelebten Lebens und vergangener Handwerke zum Vorschein, was immer er anpackte, drohte unter seinen erneuernden Händen endgültig zu verschwinden oder bis zur Unkenntlichkeit umgearbeitet zu werden. Nach etwa 150 Entwürfen zwischen Dekonstruktivismus und Neohistorismus entschloss sich der Architekt zu absoluter Zurückhaltung.

Cilli Sigl hieß die letzte Bewohnerin, eine Bäuerin, die Peter Haimerl als Kind noch erlebt hatte, herb, selbstständig, gemeinsam mit ihrer stillen Schwester das Anwesen bewirtschaftend. Überall trat sie dem Architekten und seiner Frau entgegen, in Gestalt bizarrer Kleidungsstücke, alter Möbel, des Herds oder ausgeblichener Kalender und Heiligenbilder, die noch an den durchfeuchteten Wänden hingen. Geradezu gebannt von diesem Widerschein einer versunkenen Welt, griffen Peter Haimerl und Jutta Görlich zur zugleich sensibelsten und radikalsten Maßnahme: die Künstlerin sammelte und ordnete alle Hinterlassenschaften der Bewohner, der Architekt ließ das Haus weitgehend unangetastet – und stellte unter dem Motto: „Birg mich, Cilli", vier Betonkisten hinein.

Stellte? Nein, Peter Haimerl schuf Implantate, die er behutsam wie ein Chirurg in den alten Baukörper pflanzte. Konkret: Er verfiel auf den Schweizer Misapor-Beton, eine Spezialmischung aus Quarz und Zement, dampfdiffusionsdicht, ein idealer, wie natürlich wirkender Wärme- und Kältedämmer, nicht seidig glatt, aber doch den Eindruck haptischer Geschmeidigkeit ausstrahlend. Der hohe Quarzanteil des Betons baute zudem eine symbolische Brücke zum Bayerischen Wald, denn der wird vom ‚Pfahl' durchzogen, einer Art Rückgrat, geformt aus reinem Quarz.

Nachdem er anfangs die Holzdecke der alten ‚Stube' herausgerissen hatte, sollte nichts mehr vom historischen Bestand verrückt oder beseitigt werden. Also erstellte Peter Haimerl die Schalung und die Versteifungen in einem komplizierten labyrinthischen Gefüge und gewährleistete damit das behutsame Mit- und Nebeneinander von bruchsteinernen und hölzernen Wänden und denen aus Misapor. Am 30. Juni 2007 – eine Schüttung aus Schaumglasschotter war am Boden ausgebracht – wurden die neuen Kuben direkt durch das marode Dach ausgegossen.

Es sind Zellen der „Zweiten Moderne" geworden, freundlich trotz Purismus, die zu etwa einem Drittel das Innere bestimmen. Den Auftakt bildet die ehemalige ‚Stube', geräumig, mit Fenstern, deren Maße die alten wiederholen, und einem glasgeschlossenen Kamin dort, wo sich die alte Heizstelle befand. Zwei mächtige Balken unterhalb der Betondecke, die nun nichts mehr tragen, hat Haimerl als Wächter der Geschichte integriert. Den Boden bestimmt eine annähernd quadratische Öffnung, die den Blick auf die Tonerde freigibt, auf der sich das Haus

buckled under the pressure of the incline in which it was embedded and threatened to collapse.

The more he occupied himself with the structure, the further Haimerl departed from his plans to restore the house to its original style. Wherever he looked, he found traces of the life lived within the walls and of the previous workmanship; whatever he touched threatened to crumble for good under his reviving hands or required reworking beyond recognition. After coming up with some 150 designs, running the gamut from Deconstructivism to neo-Historicism, the architect chose a course of absolute restraint.

Cilli Sigl was the name of the house's last resident. Haimerl remembered the farm woman from his childhood: dry, independent, running the farm with her quiet sister. The architect and his wife encountered her everywhere they looked – in the form of bizarre garments, old furniture, the stove or faded calendars and pictures of saints that still hung on walls permeated with damp. Enthralled by these reflections of a lost world, Peter Haimerl and Jutta Görlich seized upon what was at once the most sensitive and most radical measure of all: the artist collected and organised all of the former inhabitants' effects and the architect left the house largely untouched – and installed within it four concrete boxes, under the motto: "Birg mich, Cilli" ("Harbour. me, Cilli").

Installed? No, the boxes are more like implants, which Haimerl inserted in the old structure as carefully as a surgeon. He came up with the idea of using Swiss Misapor concrete, a special mixture of quartz and cement that is damp-proof and an ideal natural heat and cold insulator, not silky smooth but exuding the impression of haptic softness. The high ratio of quartz in the concrete at the same time builds a symbolic bridge to the Bayrischer Wald, which is traversed by the 'Pfahl', a kind of spine of pure quartz.

After starting off by tearing out the wooden ceiling of the old parlour, nothing more of the historic building fabric was to be shifted or eliminated. Haimerl instead executed the framework and the bracing in a complex labyrinthine arrangement, thus ensuring the gentle coexistence and intermeshing of quarry stone and wood walls with the new ones made of Misapor. On 30 June 2007 – after a packed bed of foamed glass granulate had been laid on the floor – the cubes were poured directly through the rotting roof.

These became cells of 'Second Modernism', congenial despite their purist pedigree, which now determine the look of about one-third of the interior. The prelude is the former parlour – spacious, with

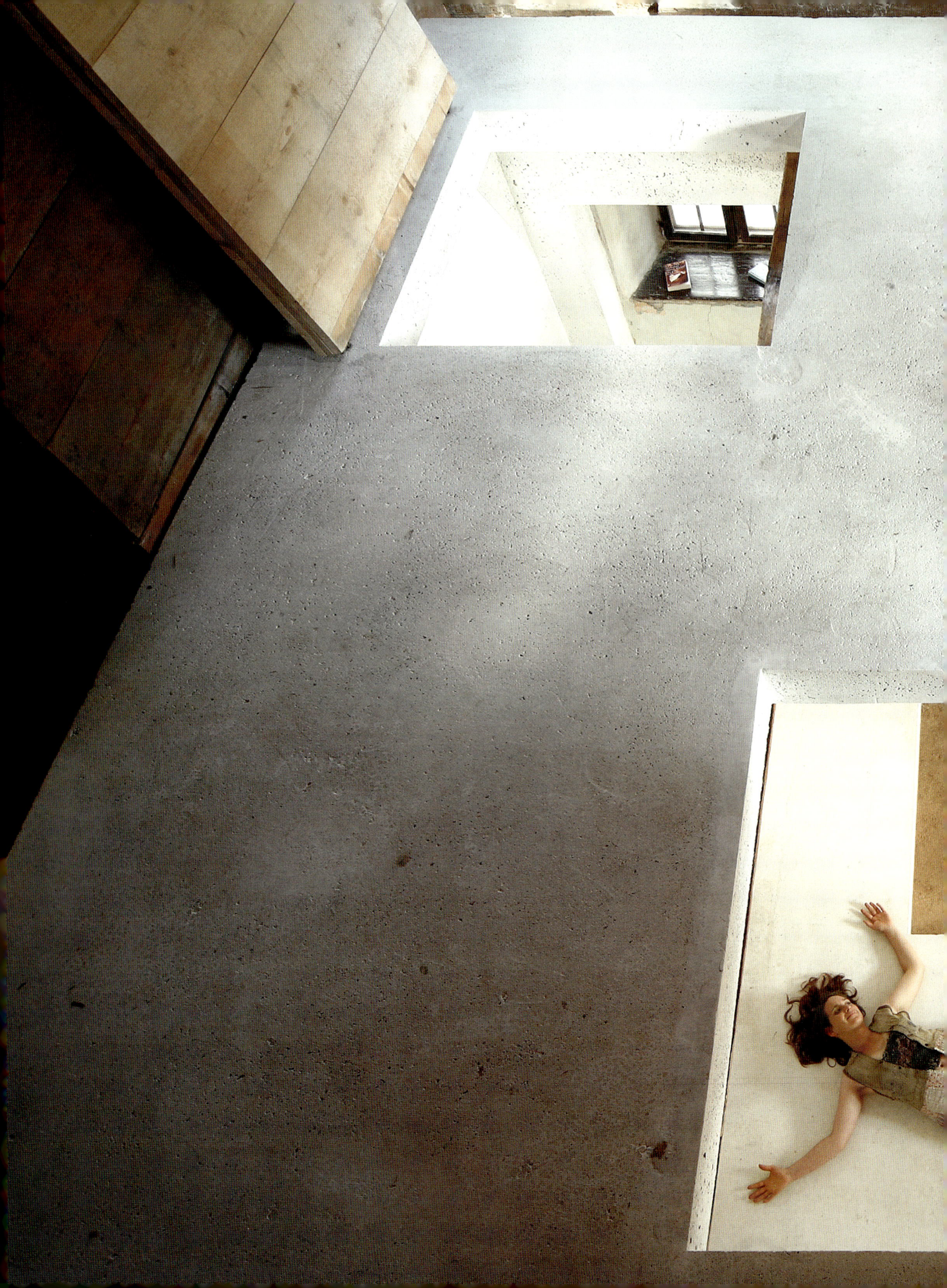

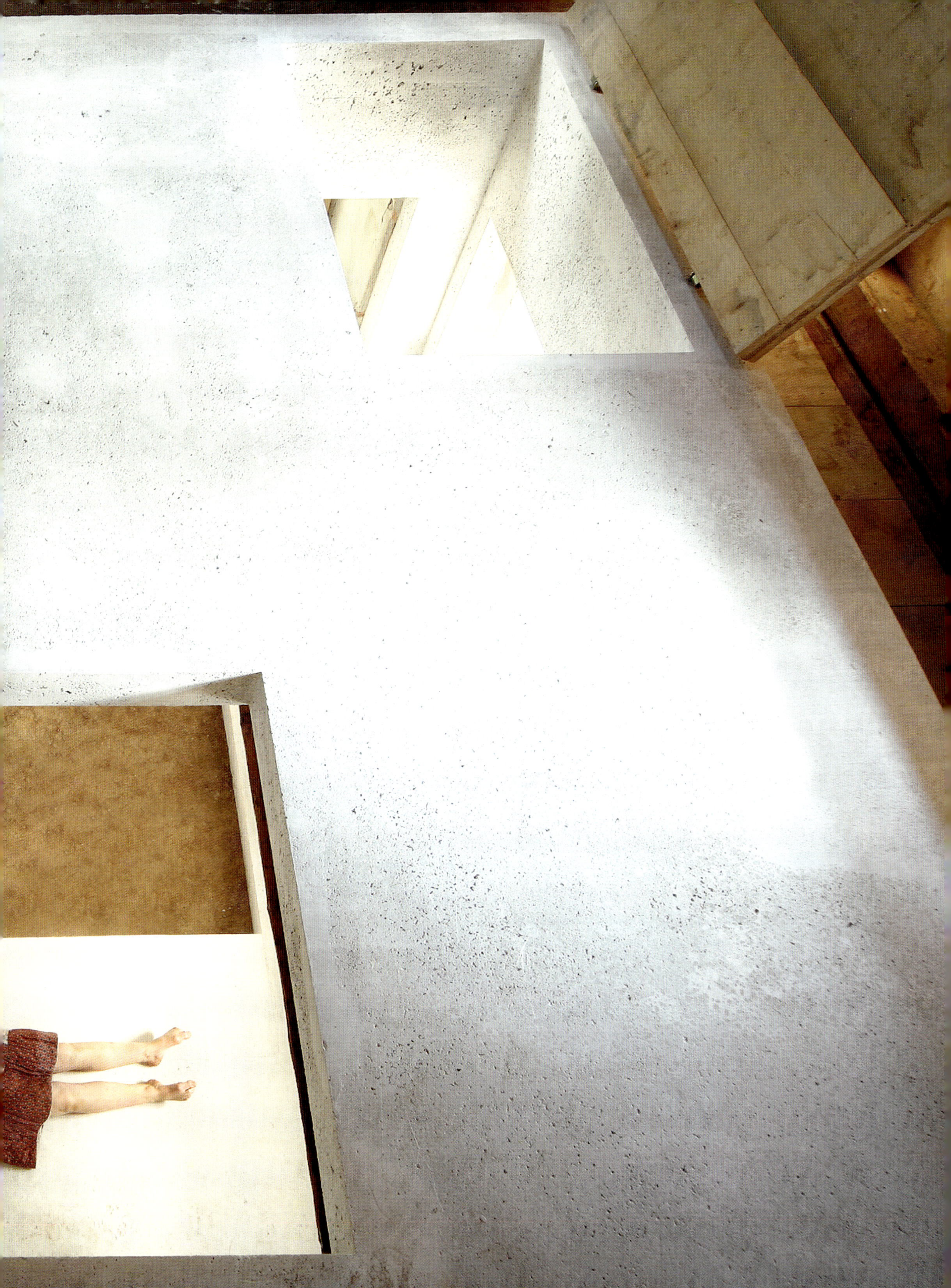

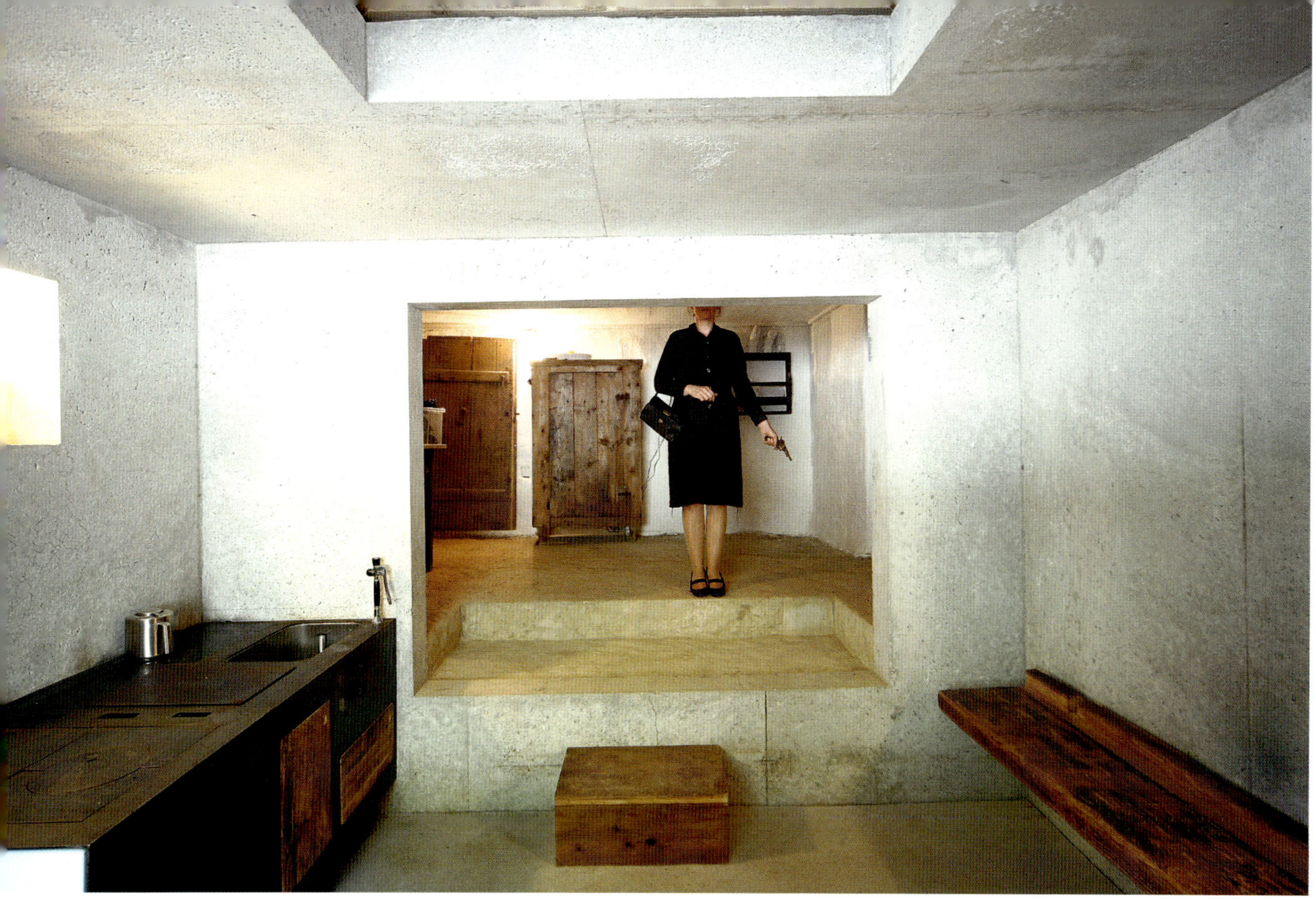

Küche | Kitchen

erhebt. Das ergibt einen fast mythischen Akzent und erinnert
an die Herdstelle im Zentrum des griechischen Megaron, des
Urhauses der abendländischen Kultur.
Die Betondecke zeigt zwei quadratische, bei Bedarf mit hölzernen Luken verschließbare große Öffnungen. Durch sie schaut
man in den Dachstuhl, den einstigen Kornspeicher mit seinen
wunderlich gebogenen Hölzern.
Wie in der ‚Stube' die Bänke (schlicht und elegant geformt,
wie dem Bauhaus entsprungen), aus dem honiggelben alten
Holz eines in der Nähe abgebrochenen historischen ‚Getreide-
kastens', kontrastieren auch in der Küche, dem zweiten Beton-
kubus, Alt und Neu. Haimerl hat den alten Herd technisch
aufgerüstet und mit einem Wasserbecken kombiniert; trotzdem
wird er so beheizt wie zu Zeiten Cilli Sigls. Der „Herrgotts-
winkel" aus Beton öffnet sich hin zur alten Bruchsteinwand,

windows whose dimensions echo those of the old
ones, and a glass-fronted fireplace where the old
hearth once stood. Haimerl has integrated two
massive beams beneath the concrete ceiling; they
no longer support anything, but instead stand
as guardians of the building's history. The floor
i s dominated by an almost square opening that
reveals a glimpse of the clay on which the house
was built. This lends an almost mythical accent,
reminiscent of the hearth at the centre of the Greek
megaron, the original house of Western civilisation.
In the concrete ceiling there are two large square-
shaped openings that can be closed if needed with
wooden hatches. They provide a view of the attic,
where grain was once stored, with its whimsically
bent wood beams.
While in the parlour the benches (simple and
elegant in shape, as if originating from the
Bauhaus), made of honey-yellow wood salvaged
from one of the historic 'grain boxes' dismantled
nearby, form a contrast to the concrete walls, old
and new meet again in the kitchen, the second
concrete cube. Haimerl has upgraded the old stove
with new technology and combined it with a sink,
but it is still heated the same way as in the days of
Cilli Sigl. The concrete dining corner opens to the
old stone wall, while the new panorama window
provides a view of the restabilised slope beyond.
Behind the kitchen is the bathroom, with a tub and
wash basin of poured Misapor concrete that have
a contemporary, clean-lined rationality and yet still
recall age-old troughs.

Küche | Kitchen

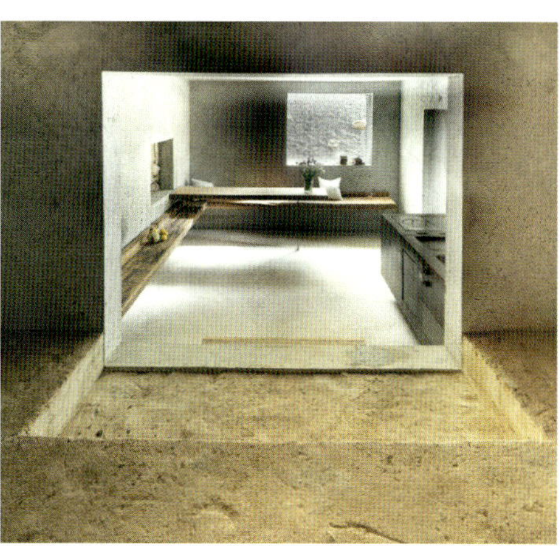

das neue Panoramafenster gibt den Blick auf den wieder gefes-
tigten Hang frei. Dahinter das Bad: Wanne und Waschbecken
aus Misapor gegossen, dennoch nicht schroff, und trotz zeitgemäßer Sachlichkeit an die alten Tränken und Tröge erinnernd.
Im Obergeschoss das Schlafzimmer als weitere Betonzelle,
direkt daneben die alte hölzerne Austragswohnung: Ausblicke
in die wunderbare Waldlandschaft, die nicht durch gewalt-
same neue Einbrüche, sondern nach dem Muster der alten
Fenster entstanden sind. Mit einem Schritt von Zimmer zu
Zimmer wechselt man immer wieder vom 19. ins 21. Jahrhundert. Vor den Betonwänden stehen (zuweilen ramponiert) die
angestammten alten Möbel, an Bretterwänden wie am Misapor
hängen Heiligenbildchen. Und doch ist nirgendwo „Jodelhüt-
tenrenovierung", wie Haimerl es formuliert, zu sehen, sondern
überall ein respektvolles Nebeneinander von Gestern und Heute,
von bäuerlichem Pragmatismus und zeitgenössischer Radika-
lität, bis am Ende doch (selbst den Außenputz ließ Haimerl
nicht nachbessern) der Respekt vor dem Überkommenen über-
wiegt.

Bauen im Bestand heißt derzeit – und fast schon bis zum Über-
druss – allerorten die Losung zeitgenössischen Bauens. Ernst
nehmen sie die wenigsten Betroffenen. So müsste denn die
Denkmalpflege Peter Haimerl geradezu anbeten. Welcher
Sanierer vor ihm wäre derart pietätvoll mit einem historischen
Ensemble umgegangen, hätte dermaßen sensibel zeitgenös-
sisches und historisches Bauen zusammengebracht? Doch auch
die deutsche Architektenszene sollte Haimerl feiern. Schließlich
hat er ihr gezeigt, wie man ohne jeden faulen Kompromiss Altes
bewahrt, indem man bedingungslos Neues zur Anwendung
bringt. Ein Betonbauer, der sanft wie ein Mediziner dem hinfäl-
ligen und im konkreten Fall obendrein unscheinbaren baulichen
Erbe wieder auf die Füße hilft, ein asketischer Romantiker im
Zeichen strikter „(Zweiter) Moderne" – so etwas hat es bei uns
noch nie gegeben.

On the upper floor the bedroom is enclosed by a
further concrete cell, and directly adjacent is the
old wooden 'Austragswohnung', where the retired
farmer lived once his heirs had taken over the
farm. Views over the lovely forest landscape have
been created not through violent new openings in
the walls, but by following the pattern of the old
windows. Walking from room to room, one continu-
ally moves back and forth between the 19th and 21st
centuries. The old (and sometimes battered) furniture stands before the concrete walls; pictures of
saints hang from both wood-panelled and Misapor
walls. And yet nowhere do we find "yodel-cottage
renovation", as Haimerl puts it. Instead, there is a
respectful side-by-side of yesterday and today, of
farmerly pragmatism and contemporary radical-
ism, until in the end (Haimerl didn't even touch up
the external plaster) it is an appreciation for what
remains that stands out most.

"Building within the existing fabric" is the catch-
word everywhere today – we almost can't bear to
hear it anymore. Very few actually take it seriously,
so the preservationists must practically worship
Peter Haimerl. Which other restorer would have
treated a historic ensemble with the same degree
of reverence, and would have brought together
contemporary and historic architecture with so
much sensitivity? The German architecture scene,
too, should give Haimerl the acclaim he deserves.
After all, he has demonstrated how it is possible
without any lacklustre compromises to preserve the
old by unconditionally applying the new. A builder in
concrete who, gentle as a doctor, helps the frail, and
in this case unprepossessing, architectural legacy
back onto its feet, an ascetic romantic committed
to a strict 'Second Modernism' – the like has never
been seen before in this country.

Ein Betonbauer, der einem unscheinbaren baulichen Erbe wieder auf die Füße hilft, ein asketischer Romantiker im Zeichen strikter (Zweiter) Moderne. | A builder in concrete who helps an unprepossessing piece of architectural heritage back onto its feet, an ascetic romantic committed to a strict (Second) Modernism.

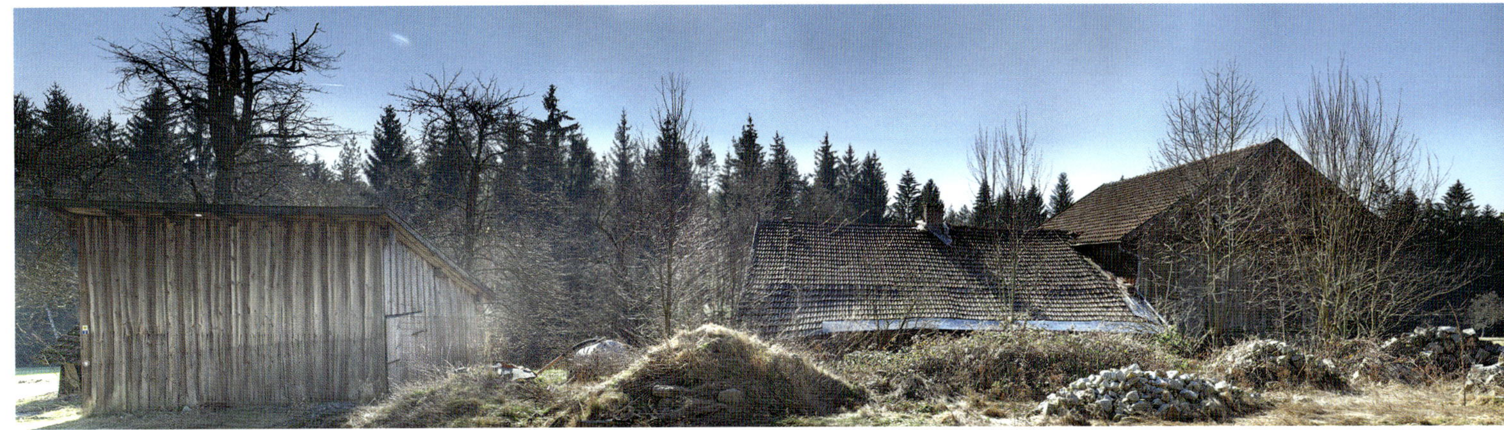

SAUERBRUCH HUTTON

GEBÄUDE | BUILDING

MUSEUM BRANDHORST

TEXT ELISABETH PLESSEN

21

ARCHITEKTEN | ARCHITECTS

Sauerbruch Hutton
Lehrter Str. 57
10557 Berlin
www.sauerbruchhutton.com

MITARBEITER | TEAM

Prof. Matthias Sauerbruch,
Louisa Hutton, Juan Lucas Young,
David Wegener, Peter Apel,
Rasmus Jörgensen, Mareike
Lamm, Jürgen Bartenschlag,
Philip Engelbrecht,
Andrea Frensch, Michaela Kunze

BAUHERR | CLIENT

Freistaat Bayern
Bayerisches Staatsministerium
für Wissenschaft, Forschung
und Kunst
Staatliches Bauamt München 1
(Projektleitung | project
management)

TRAGWERK | STRUCTURE

Ingenieurbüro Fink, Berlin

LANDSCHAFTSARCHITEKTEN
LANDSCAPE ARCHITECTS

Adelheid Gräfin Schönborn,
München | Munich

FERTIGSTELLUNG | COMPLETION

2008

MUSEUMSERÖFFNUNG
MUSEUM OPENING

Mai | May 2009

STANDORT | LOCATION

Theresienstraße 35A
80333 München
www.museum-brandhorst.de

FOTOS | PHOTOS

Andreas Lechtape,
Haydar Koyupinar, Noshe

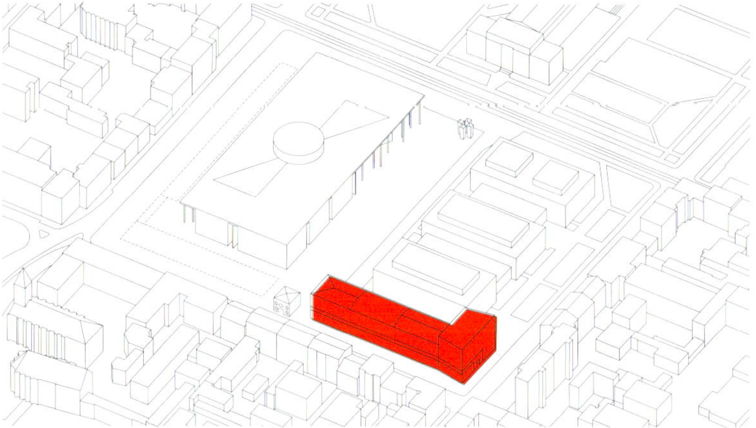

Isometrie | Isometric drawing

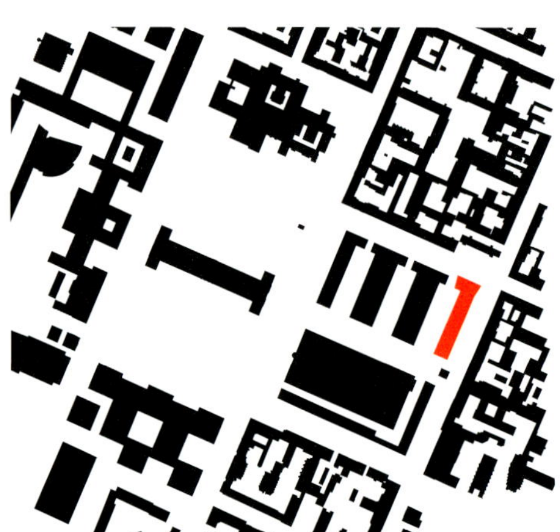

Lageplan | Site plan

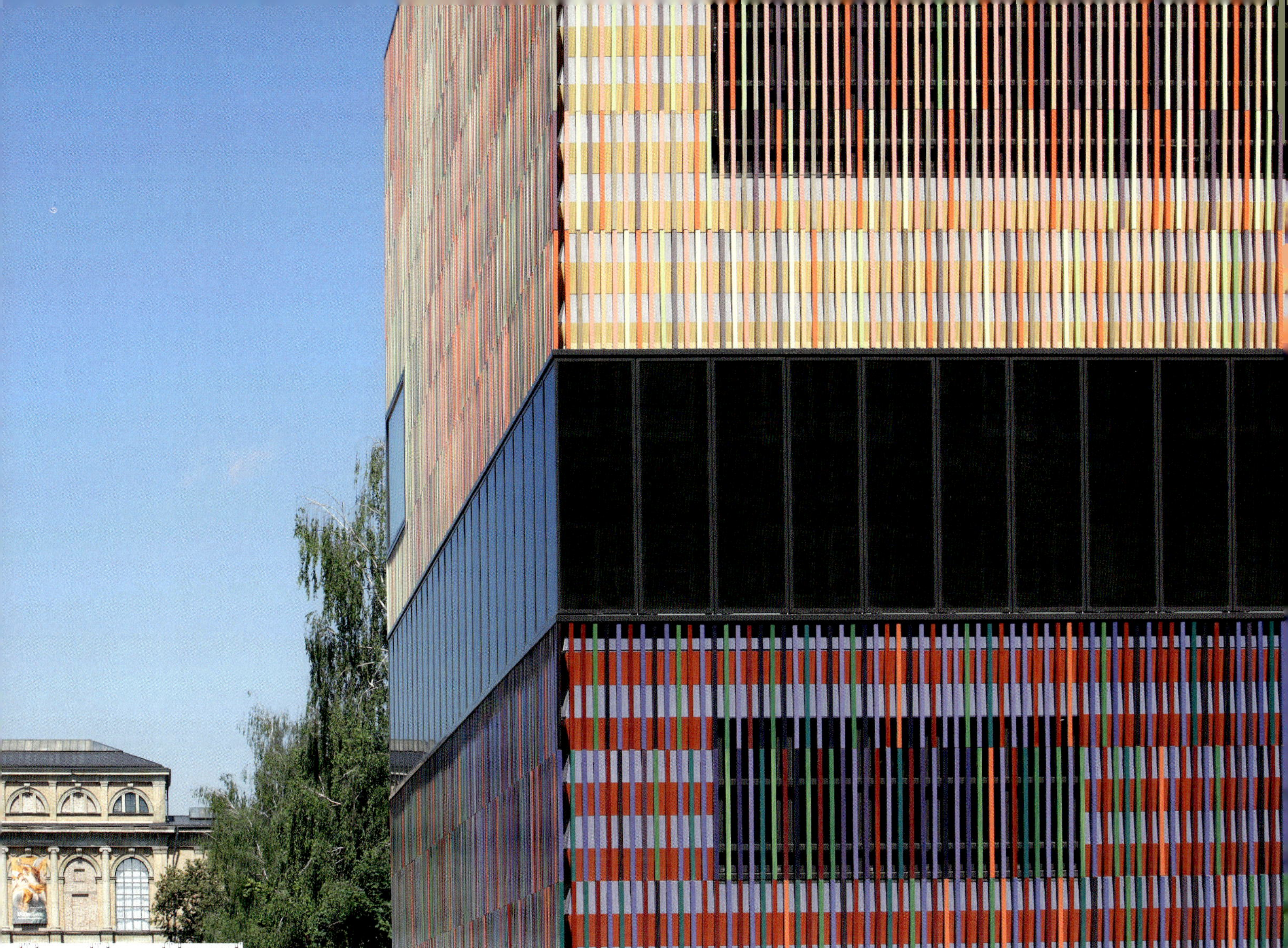

Museumsareal München: Museum Brandhorst mit der Alten Pinakothek im Hintergrund
Munichh's Museum Quarter: Museum Brandhorst with the Alte Pinakothek in the background

Museumsareal, der Name hat sich mittlerweile für das Gebiet der Münchner Maxvorstadt eingebürgert, wo sich Klenze / Döllgasts Alte Pinakothek, von Brancas Neue Pinakothek und Braunfels 2002 eröffnete Pinakothek der Moderne befinden. Die drei Bauten bilden einen konzentrierten Raum des Kunsterlebens, der bislang nicht ‚gefasst' im städtischen Kontext liegt. Mit der Sammlung Brandhorst ist nun ein weiterer Schritt getan, das Areal städtebaulich zu rahmen.

Als 2002 das Sammlerehepaar Brandhorst der Stadt seine Sammlung Moderner Kunst unter der Prämisse anbot, ein angemessenes Gebäude zu erhalten, schrieb diese einen Wettbewerb aus, den Sauerbruch Hutton gewannen. Das Grundstück, ursprünglich als dritter Bauabschnitt der Pinakothek der Moderne vorgesehen – was zu heftigsten Auseinandersetzungen mit Braunfels führte – schließt das ‚Areal' zur Türken- / Theresienstraße ab. Keine einfache Aufgabe, auf engstem Raum, neben (noch) bestehenden Institutsbauten der Universität, einen eigenständigen Baukörper zu platzieren. Direkter Nachbar auf der gegenüberliegenden Straßenecke ist zudem ein Wohngebäude von Sep Ruf, dem die Sammlung bedauerlicherweise ein wenig zu nahe rücken musste.

'Museumsareal' (Museum Quarter) – this description is now commonly used to refer to the Maxvorstadt area of Munich, where Klenze / Döllgast's Alte Pinakothek, von Branca's Neue Pinakothek and Braunfels' Pinakothek der Moderne, opened in 2002, can be found. The three buildings comprise a concentrated space for experiencing art – one that until now has not really been 'accommodated' within the urban context. But with the Brandhorst Collection a further step has now been taken toward giving the district a proper urban planning framework.

When in 2002 Udo and Anette Brandhorst offered to give their collection of modern art to the city on condition that a suitable building be provided to house it, Munich held a competition to find an architect, choosing Sauerbruch Hutton as winner. The site, which was originally set aside for the third building phase of the Pinakothek der Moderne – giving rise to vehement disputes with Braunfels – bounds the 'museum quarter' on the Türken- / Theresienstrasse side. It was no easy task to squeeze an independent

141

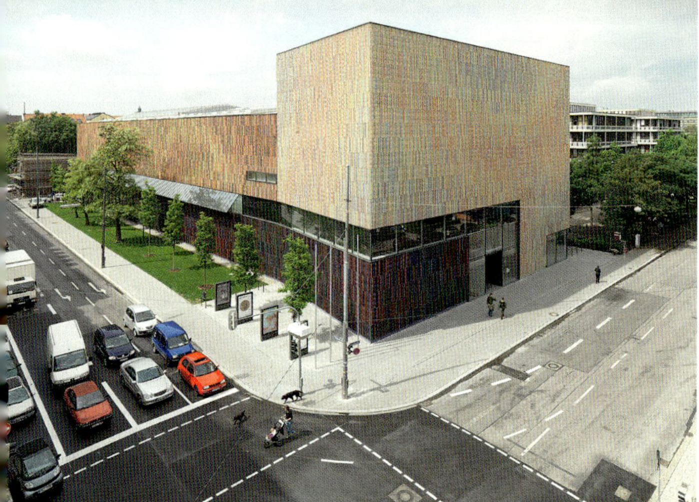

Die Sammlung Brandhorst rahmt das Museumsareal zur Türken- und Theresienstraße hin. The Brandhorst collection frames the Museum Quarter on the Türken- and Theresienstrasse side.

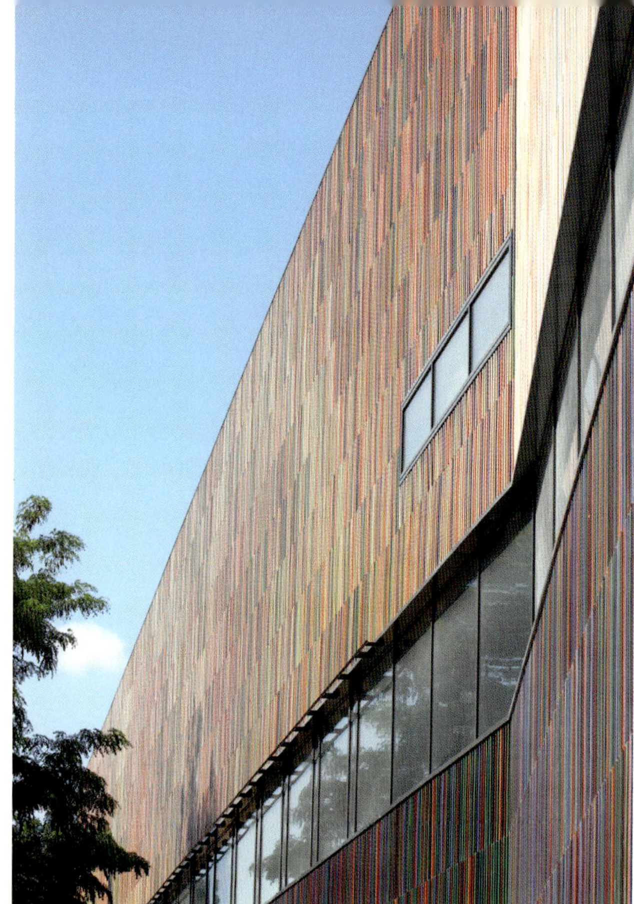

(Lärmschutz-)Fassade mit einem Farbspiel aus vertikalen Keramikstäben | (Sound-insulating) façade with play of colour formed by vertical ceramic rods

Sauerbruch Huttons Antwort ist ein lang gestreckter Riegel entlang der Türkenstraße, der zur Ecksituation hin von einem höheren, turmartigen Körper mit leicht ausgestellten Seiten abgeschlossen wird. Eine aufwendige (Lärmschutz-)Fassade, ein Farbspiel aus vertikal angeordneten Keramikstäben, hinter denen horizontal angeordnet perforierte farbige Blechbänder liegen, vermittelt den Eindruck, als sehe man ein in der Hitze leicht flirrend verzerrtes Gebilde. Es sind ‚nur‘ 23 Farben, die, zu Farbfamilien angeordnet, das Volumen des Längskörpers in ein dunkleres, von klaren Rot-, Blau- und Grüntönen dominiertes Erdgeschoss und ein helleres, orangerotes Obergeschoss teilen. Dem markanten Turm sind pastellige Töne zugeordnet. So soll die Sammlung im Straßenraum wie ein abstraktes modernes Gemälde wirken. Ein wenig respektlos könnte man meinen, das Gebäude habe sich die Gewänder eines bekannten hochpreisigen italienischen Modelabels übergestreift, die ihm eine eigenwillige Zeitlosigkeit verleihen.

Ein offensichtlicher Kritikpunkt ist die Lage des Eingangs, der sich von den Pinakotheken weg und zur Theresienstraße hinwendet. Eine gläserne Drehtür markiert eher beiläufig das Entree, dessen Ausstattung fast wie eine Reminiszenz an die 1950er-Jahre und damit an den Sep-Ruf-Bau erscheint. Die Wände, im unteren Bereich fast umlaufend mit hölzernen Einbauten gefasst, darüber in einem intensiven dunklen Rot und Lichtgrau, beleuchtet durch gläserne Lichtschalensegmente in den gevouteten Öffnungen der hohen Decke, lassen eine fast sakrale Stimmung entstehen. Schon hier zeigt sich, wie durchgängig im ganzen Museum, die sorgfältige Detaillierung und präzise handwerkliche Ausführung.

Aus dem Foyer zieht die hölzerne Verkleidung den Besucher fast sogartig in die großräumige offene Treppenhausskulptur mit ihren nach oben hin sich verjüngenden hölzernen Brüstungen. Ab hier ist der gesamte Ausstellungs- und Erschließungsbereich durchgehend mit einem Bodenbelag aus

structure into such a narrow space, next to (still) existing university buildings. An apartment building by Sep Ruf, on the corner directly across the street, is a bit too close for comfort.

Sauerbruch Hutton's answer is a longitudinal building along Türkenstrasse, terminating at the corner in a higher, tower-like element with slightly outward-flaring sides. An elaborate (sound-insulated) façade – a play of colour created by vertical ceramic rods over a horizontally striped perforated sheet-metal skin – evokes the impression of a distorted image slightly shimmering in the heat. There are 'only' 23 colours here, arranged into colour families, dividing the volume of the longitudinal structure into a darker ground floor, dominated by clear red, blue and green tones, and a lighter-coloured, orange-red upper storey. The striking tower has been cast in pastel hues. The collection is thus meant to look like an abstract modern painting adorning the streetscape. One might even say a bit disrespectfully that the building has garbed itself in a gown created by a well-known upscale Italian fashion label, lending it an idiosyncratic, timeless appeal.

An obvious point of criticism is the location of the entrance, which turns away from the Pinakothek buildings toward Theresienstrasse. A glass revolving door marks the entrance lobby, almost as an afterthought, where the furnishings almost seem like a throwback to the 1950s and thus seem to pay

Im Bereich des Erdgeschosses dominieren klare Rot-, Blau- und Grüntöne; das Obergeschoss flirrt in hellerem Orangerot und dem Turm sind Pastellfarben zugeordnet. | On the ground floor, clear red, blue and green tones dominate, while the upper level shimmers in lighter orange-red and the tower is rendered in pastels.

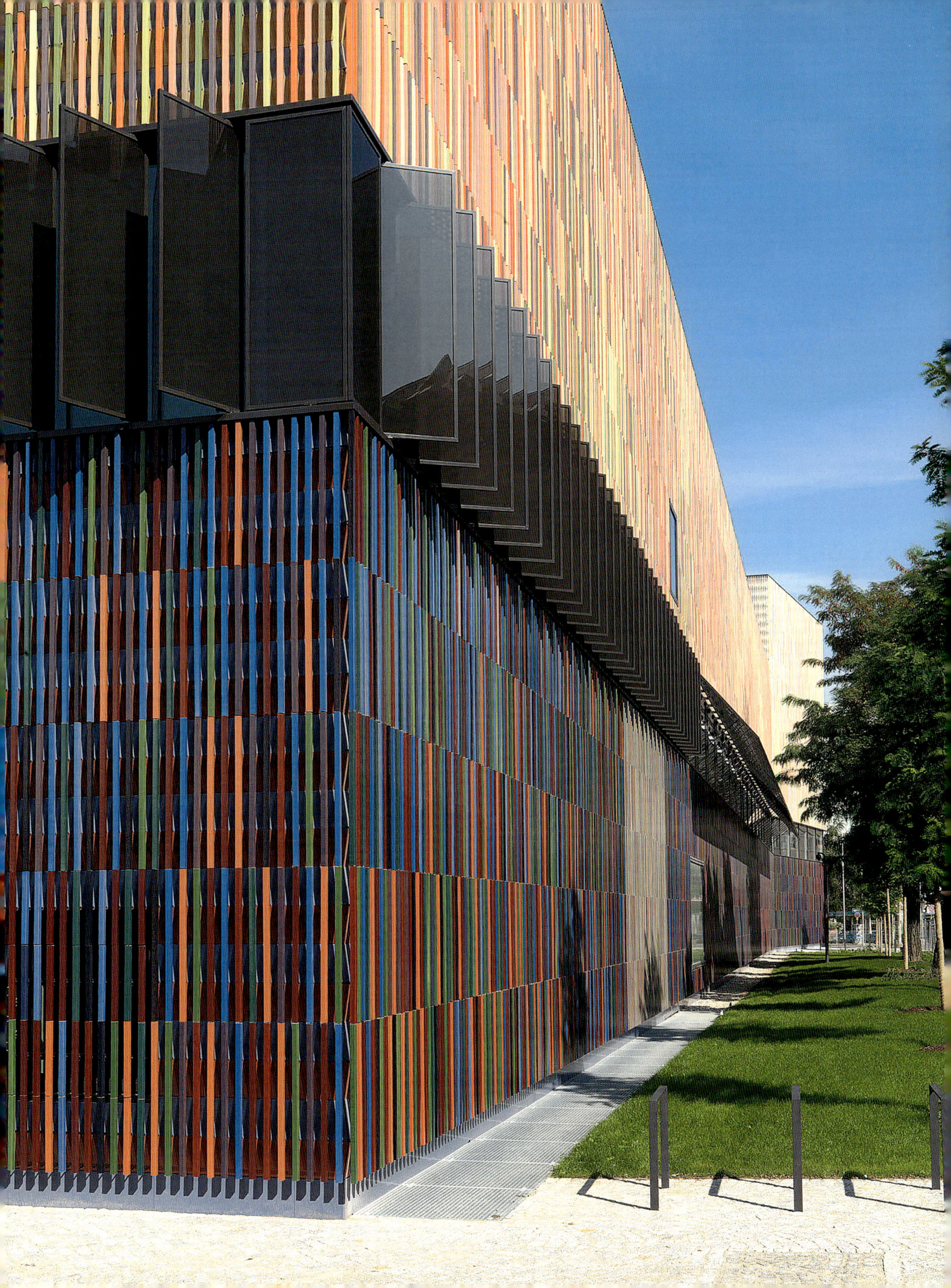

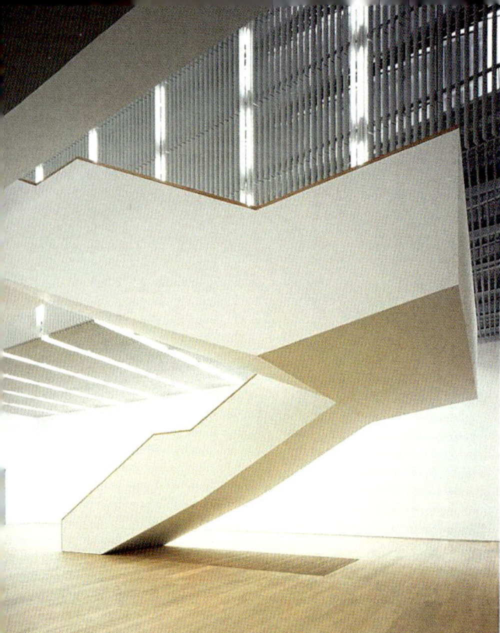

Treppenskulptur im Foyer | Stairway as sculpture in the foyer

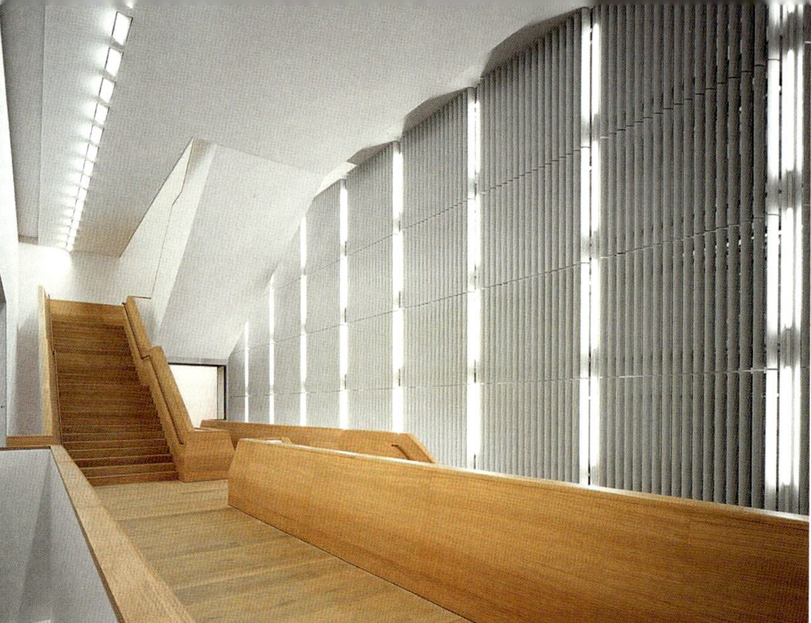

Treppenlandschaft | Stairway landscape

dänischer Eiche versehen. Ein wenig erinnert die Treppenlandschaft an eine Orgelempore, ein Eindruck, der durch die an der Fassade vertikal angeordneten Metalllamellen zur Lichtlenkung und Verschattung verstärkt wird.

Im Erdgeschoss finden sich die kleineren Kabinette, im Obergeschoss die großen, hohen Ausstellungsräume und im Untergeschoss ein offener Ausstellungsbereich, an den sich ebenfalls kleinere Kabinette anschließen. Die hohen Säle ebenso wie die Kabinette sind zurückhaltend gestaltet, die Wände in gebrochenem Weiß, mit satiniertem Glas belegte Türen und Stürze säumen die Raumenfiladen. Großflächige Tageslichtdecken in den Sälen und kleine Lichtfelder in den Kabinetten tauchen die Räume in ein klares, weiches Licht. Bis ins Untergeschoss hin dringt durch raffinierte Lichtlenkungssysteme Tageslicht, dem nach Bedarf Kunstlicht zugeschaltet werden kann.

Eigenwillig stimmig auf allen Ebenen, so lässt sich der Museumsbau der Sammlung Brandhorst beschreiben. Mag man sich mit der Fassade anfreunden können oder nicht, sie ist ebenso konsequent, sowohl unter gestalterischen als auch gebäudetechnischen Gesichtspunkten, konzipiert wie das gesamte Innere: nie laut, immer ein wenig anders als erwartet – dabei nicht effekthaschend. Das Museum gibt den Kunstwerken die Ruhe, die sie verdienen, nimmt sich dabei zurück, ohne allerdings ganz in den Hintergrund zu treten, denn die Noblesse seiner Materialien und Ausführung und deren bildhafte Evokationen bleiben präsent.

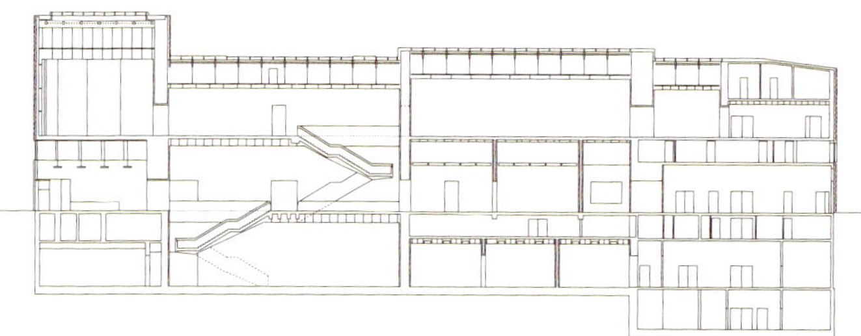

Längsschnitt | Longitudinal section

tribute to the Sep Ruf building opposite. The walls,
in the lower area featuring wooden installations
along almost their entire length, with a colour
scheme of intense dark red and light grey above,
are illuminated by segmented windows in the
haunched openings of the high ceiling, creating an
almost church-like mood. Here we can already feel
the careful detailing and precise craftsmanship that
characterise the entire museum.

From the foyer the wooden panelling almost sweeps
the visitor into the generously proportioned open
sculptural staircase with its upward tapering wooden
railings. From this point the entire exhibition area
and corridors have Danish oak floors. The stairway
looks something like an organ loft – an impression
that is further enhanced by the metal blades
arranged vertically across the façade for regulating
the fall of light and shade.

On the ground floor are smaller galleries and on
the upper floor large, high-ceilinged exhibition
spaces, while the underground level is an open exhibition area with more smaller rooms adjoining.
The high galleries as well as the smaller spaces
provide a restrained backdrop for the artworks, with
walls in off-white and doors of frosted glass border-
ing the suites of rooms. Vast daylight ceilings in
the galleries and smaller fields of light in the lesser
spaces immerse the rooms in a clear, soft light.
Through a clever system of reflectors, daylight
penetrates down to the underground level, with
artificial light available as needed.

Individualistically coherent on all levels – this is one
way to describe the museum that has been built
for the Brandhorst Collection. Whether or not one
can become accustomed to the façade, in terms
of both aesthetics and building engineering it is
conceived just as logically as the entire interior:
never loud, always slightly different than expected
– but never stagy. The museum gives the artworks
the tranquillity they deserve, withdrawing but never
completely receding into the background, because
the refinement of its materials and execution and
their vivid evocations maintain a presence.

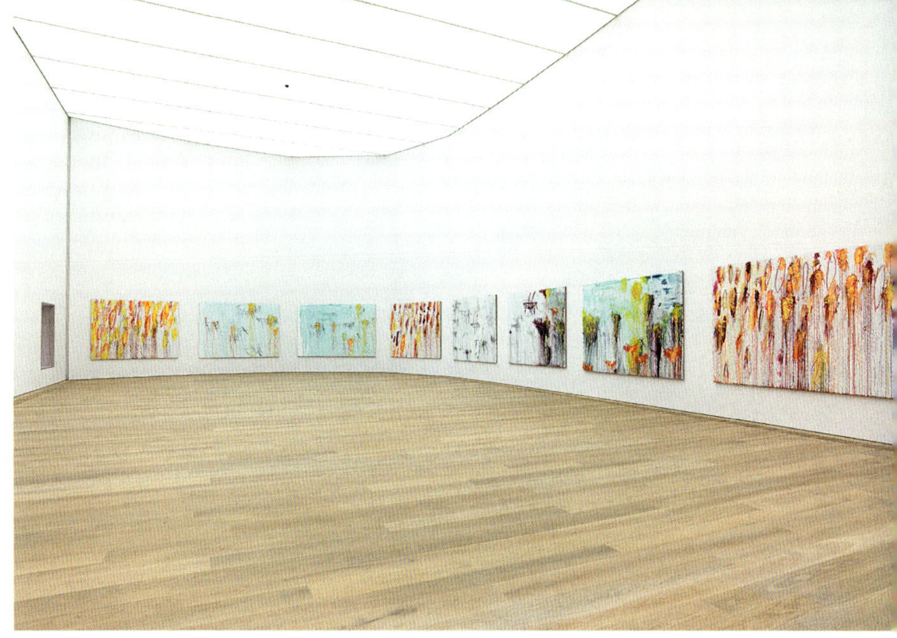

Innenansicht mit dem Werk Lepanto von Cy Twombly | Interior with "Lepanto" by Cy Twombly

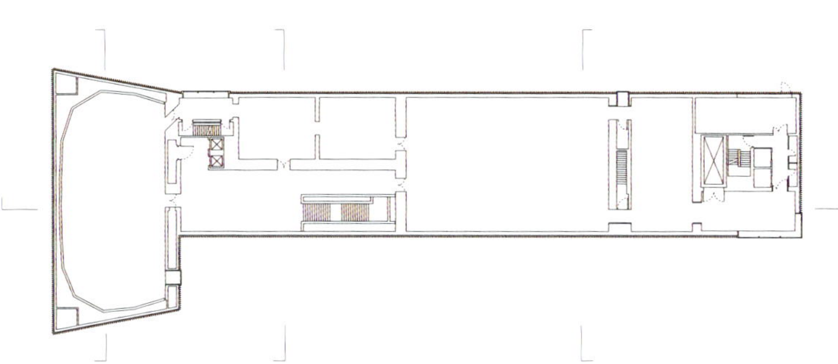

Grundriss Obergeschoss |Floor plan of upper level

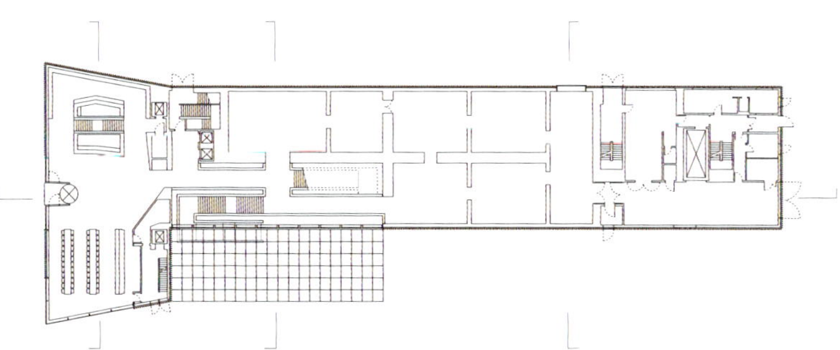

Grundriss Erdgeschoss | Floor plan of ground floor

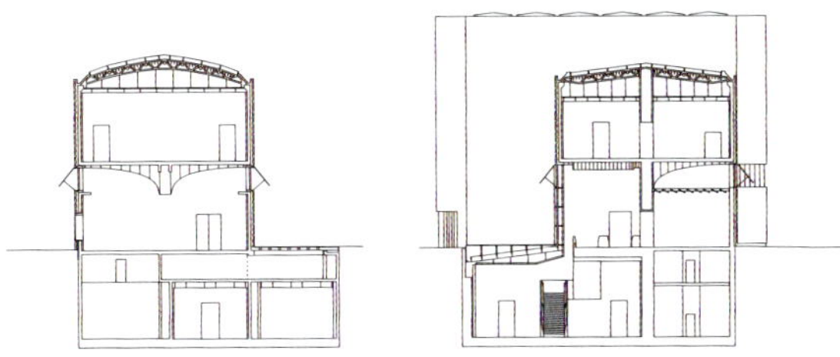

Querschnitte | Cross-sections

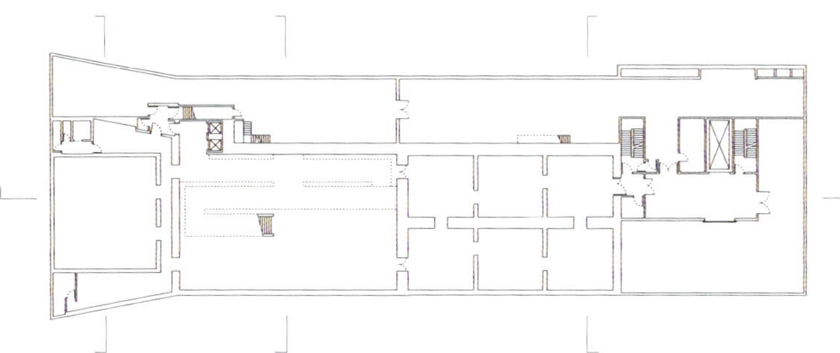

Grundriss Untergeschoss | Floor plan of basement

STEFAN GIERS UND SUSANNE GABRIEL

GEBÄUDE | BUILDING

LANDMARKE LAUSITZER SEENLAND

TEXT CHRISTINA GRÄWE

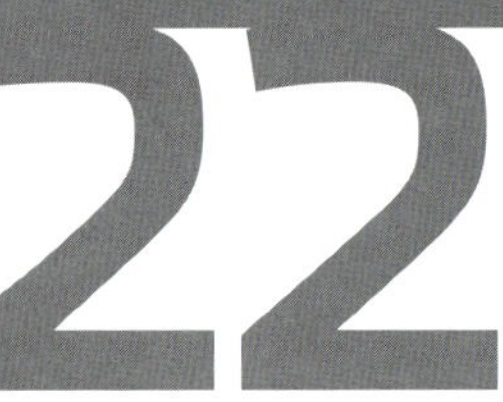

ARCHITEKTEN | ARCHITECTS

Architektur & Landschaft
Stefan Giers, Architekt;
Susanne Gabriel,
Landschaftsarchitektin
Preysingplatz 2
81667 München | Munich
www.architekturundlandschaft.de

BAUHERR | CLIENT

Stadt Senftenberg

TRAGWERK | STRUCTURE

Seeberger, Friedl und Partner,
Pfarrkirchen

BAULEITUNG
SITE MANAGEMENT

Fischer Projektmanagement
GmbH, Leipzig

LANDSCHAFTSARCHITEKTEN
LANDSCAPE ARCHITECTS

Architektur & Landschaft

FERTIGSTELLUNG | COMPLETION

2008

STANDORT | LOCATION

Mündung des Sornoer Kanals
in den Sedlitzer See bei
01968 Senftenberg-Kleinkoschen
Mouth of the Sorno Canal,
on Lake Sedlitz near
01968 Senftenberg-Kleinkoschen

FOTOS | PHOTOS

Thomas Spier

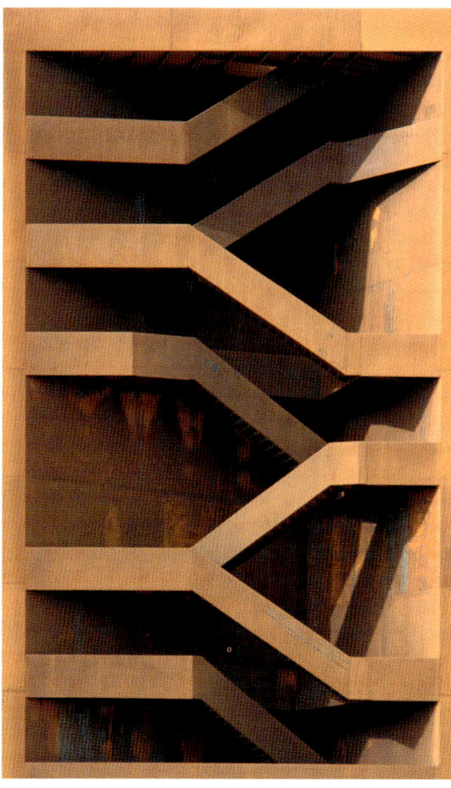

Treppenläufe
Flights of stairs

Lageplan | Site plan

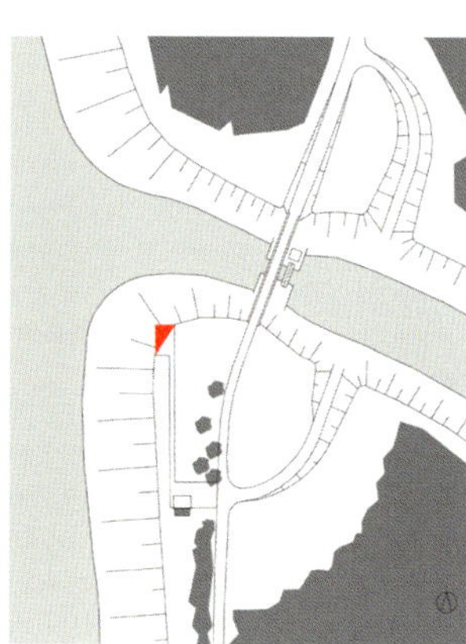

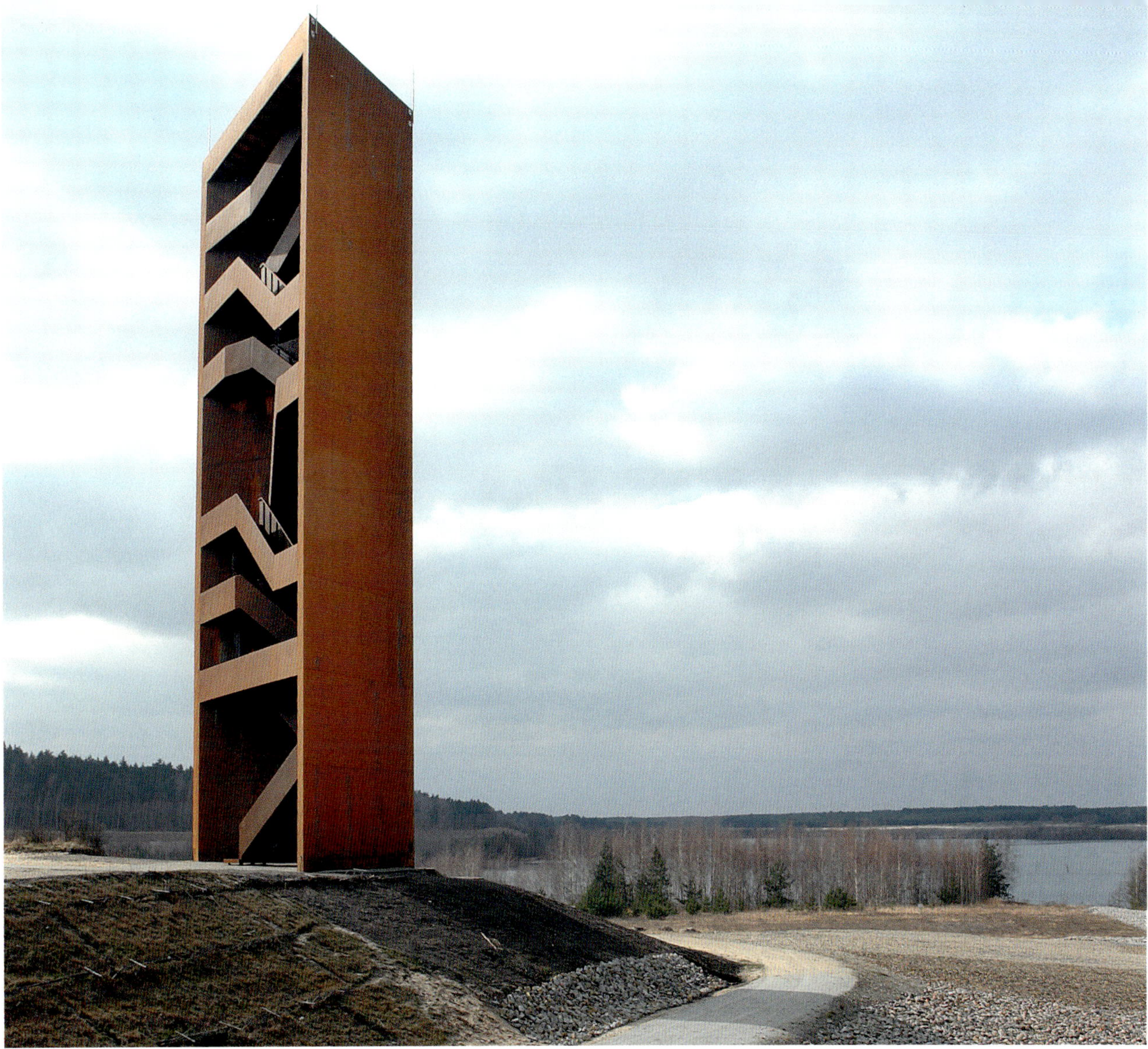

Die Landmarke mit Blick über vier Seen | The landmark with view over four lakes

Anders als in den berühmten Treppenbildern des holländischen Künstlers M. C. Escher haben diese Treppenläufe ein klares Ziel: die Aussichtsterrasse der 30 Meter hohen Landmarke Lausitzer Seenland. Doch zunächst erscheint der Aufstieg als verwirrendes Stufen-Zickzack, wenn man sich dem rostigen Turm auf seiner geöffneten Seite nähert. Der Blick nach oben lässt mit jedem Schritt eine neue Perspektive entstehen. Je nachdem in welchem Winkel die Sonne einfällt, verstärkt sich dieser Eindruck durch das zusätzliche Spiel aus Licht und Schatten.

Jedes ,Stockwerk' bildet einen anderen Raum. Mal führen schmale Gänge entlang der schluchtartig aufsteigenden Außenwände der Skulptur auf dreieckigem Grundriss, mal öffnet sich ein breiter Absatz balkonartig zur Landschaft. Oben angekommen versteht der Besucher einmal mehr, warum der Turm eine Doppelfunktion besitzt: Neben der eines Orientierungspunktes in der weiten Landschaft der ehemaligen Tagebaugruben bietet sich ein 360°-Panorama über nicht weniger als vier Seen. Aus der Brüstung ausgestanzte Buchstaben anstelle hilflos angeklebter Schildchen geben an, was der Betrachter erspäht oder auch die Entfernung der Nachbarländer Tschechien und Polen per Luftlinie. Erst auf den zweiten

Unlike the famous stairway pictures by Dutch artist M. C. Escher, these stairs actually lead somewhere: to the viewing platform atop the 30-metre-high Landmarke Lausitzer Seenland. At first, though, when one approaches the rusty tower from its open side, the ascent looks like a confusing zigzag of stairs. Looking upward as one climbs, every step opens up a new perspective. Depending on the angle of the sun, this impression is further enhanced by the play of light and shadow.

Every 'storey' forms another space. Sometimes narrow passageways lead along the canyon-like outer walls of the sculpture with its triangular floor plan, and sometimes a wide landing opens up onto the landscape like a balcony. Having arrived at the top, the visitor understands even better why the tower has a double function: besides serving as an orientation point in the vast landscape of this former strip-mining region, it also provides a 360-degree panorama across no less than four lakes. Letters punched out of the parapet take the place of clumsily stuck-on signs to indicate what the

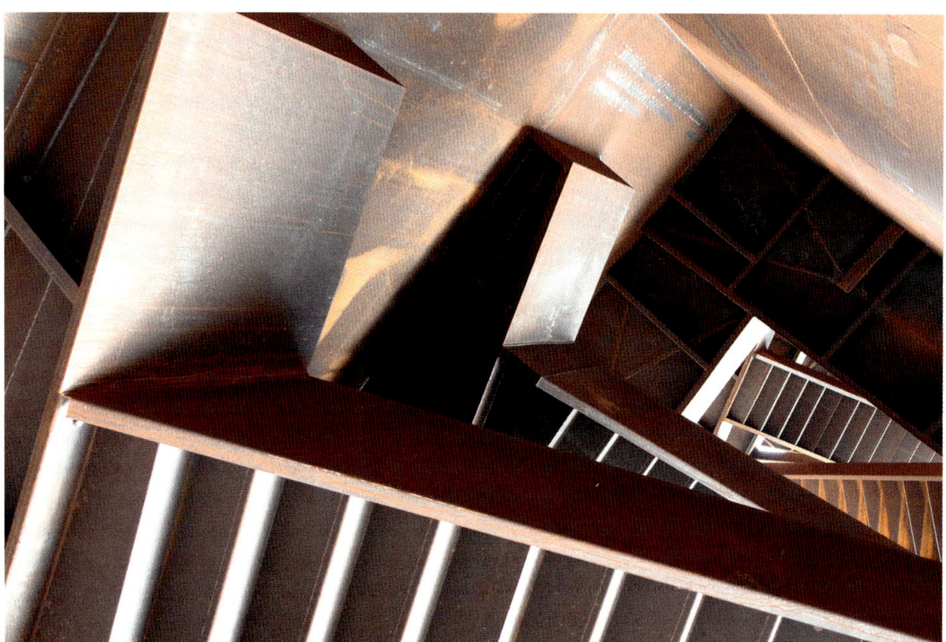

Der Blick nach oben lässt mit jedem Schritt neue Perspektiven entstehen. | The view upward opens up new perspectives with every step.

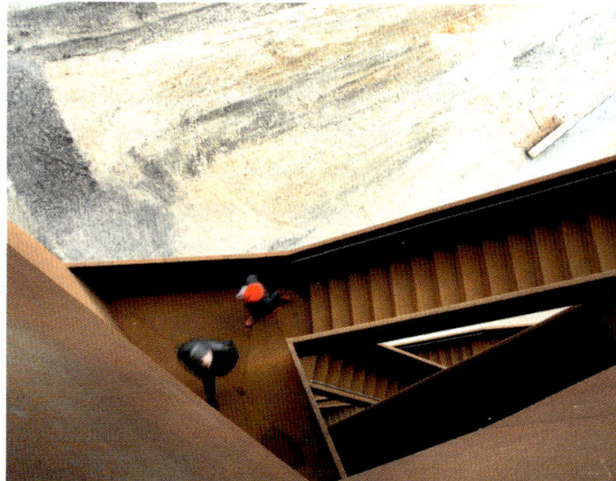

Aufstieg | Ascent

Blick entdeckt man ein eckiges Rohr mit Schlitz und aufgeschweißtem Euro-Zeichen, eine originelle Spendenbox: Jede eingeworfene Münze kullert lautstark durch den Kanal, der über die gesamte Höhe des Turms zurück bis zum ersten Treppenabsatz reicht. Dort können die Spenden hinter einer verschließbaren Klappe hervorgeholt werden.

Der ‚Rostturm' entstand im Rahmen der auf zehn Jahre angelegten Internationalen Bauausstellung (IBA) Fürst-Pückler-Land. Deren Ziel ist die Verwandlung der von Braunkohle-Kratern geprägten Landschaft in eine Abfolge von Seen durch die allmähliche Flutung der Gruben und die Erschließung der Landschaft für Touristen.

Die Stadt Senftenberg lobte 2005 einen internationalen Wettbewerb für den Entwurf einer Landmarke aus. Stefan Giers und Susanne Gabriel gewannen ihn mit dem Vorschlag, an die Geschichte der rauen Landschaft mit einem ruppigen Aussichtsturm aus rostendem Cortenstahl zu erinnern. Aber nicht abschreckend sollte der Bau wirken: Die Öffnung des Dreiecks zum Wegenetz (und einem Kiosk aus demselben Material) verstehen die Architekten als „einladende Geste". Zur Böschung sind die beiden anderen Seiten geschlossen und ragen wie ein Pfeil Richtung Sedlitzer See.

Die Konstruktion besteht aus rechteckigen geschweißten Hohlkörpern aus sechs und zehn Millimeter starkem Flachstahl, auf

viewer is looking at, along with the distance to the neighbouring countries, the Czech Republic and Poland. Only at second glance does one notice an angular pipe with a slit and a welded-on euro sign – an original donation box. Every coin tossed in rolls loudly through a channel that runs down the entire height of the tower to the first landing. There, the donations can be retrieved through a locked door. The 'rusty tower' was built as part of the ten-year Internationale Bauaustellung (IBA – International Building Exhibition) Fürst-Pückler-Land. The goal is to transform the crater-pocked former lignite-mining region into a sequence of lakes by gradually flooding the mines and developing the landscape for tourists.

In 2005 the Senftenberg municipal authority announced an international competition for the design of a landmark. Stefan Giers and Susanne Gabriel won with their proposal to recall the history of this industrial landscape with a rough-hewn viewing tower made of rusting Corten steel. The structure is not meant to put visitors off, however: the opening of the triangle to the network of roads and paths leading up to it (and to a kiosk made of the same material) is intended to function as an 'inviting gesture'. The other two sides, bordered by an embankment, are closed and project like an arrow toward Lake Sedlitz.

The structure is composed of hollow rectangular welded elements made of flat steel, six to ten millimetres thick, on which serial numbers can still be seen and whose colour will change over the years with its exposure to the elements. Borrowed from shipbuilding, these prefabricated hollow pieces, stacked one on top of another, clang and echo with

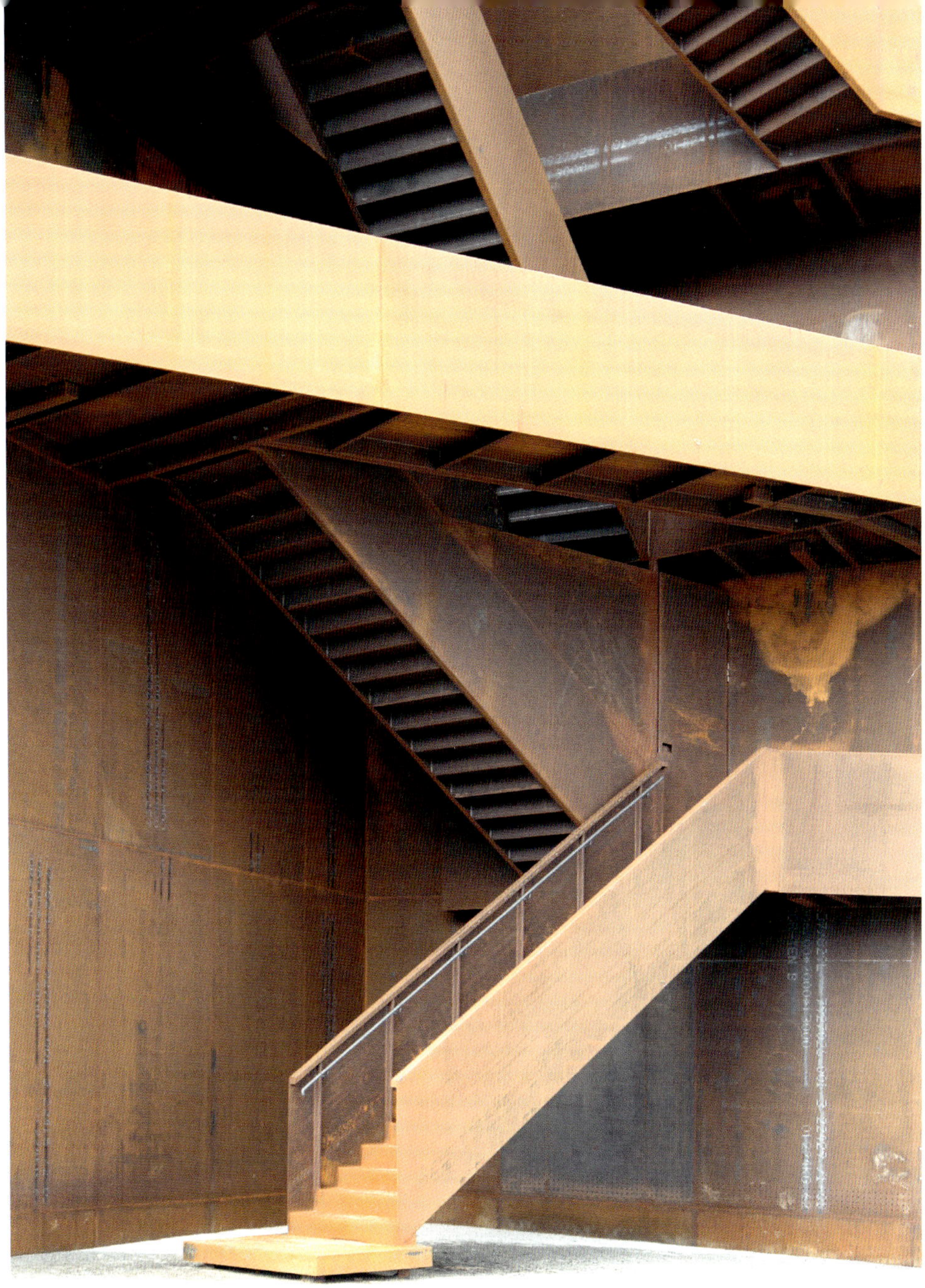

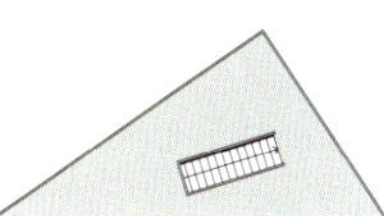

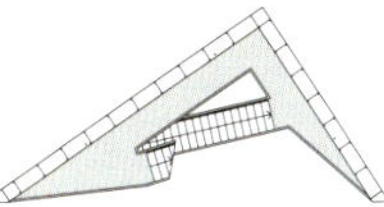

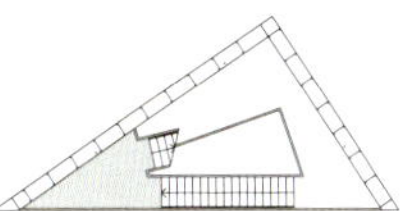

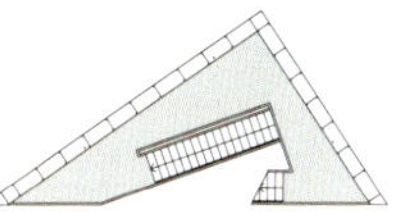

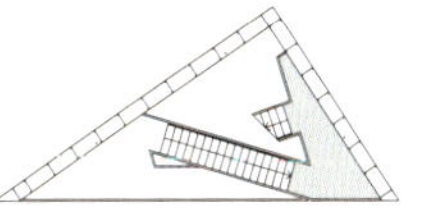

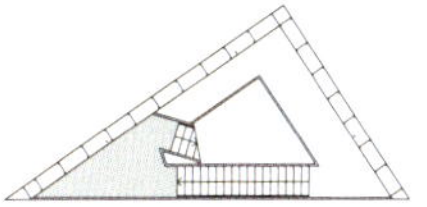

Treppe | Stairway

denen die Seriennummern sichtbar geblieben sind und deren
Farbe sich durch die Witterung im Lauf der Jahre ändern wird.
Die dem Schiffsbau entlehnten vorgefertigten Hohlkörper sind
übereinander gestellt und verursachen bei jedem Schritt
Klänge. Der Besucher erlebt Auf- und Abstieg auch akustisch.
Die Realisierung der Landmarke mit einer Bausumme von 1
Million Euro war phasenweise unsicher. Die Lausitzer und
Mitteldeutsche Bergbau- Verwaltungsgesellschaft kam der
Bauherrin Stadt Senftenberg zur Hilfe: Am 23. Oktober 2008
wurde der Turm feierlich eröffnet. Zum Auftakt der Saison
2009 wurde bereits Anfang März gedrängt, die Aussichtsplatt-
form, die im Winter wegen Glatteisgefahr geschlossen ist,
wieder zugänglich zu machen.

every step. Visitors thus experience the ascent and
descent acoustically, too.
It was uncertain at times whether the landmark with
its construction budget of 1 million euros would
be realised. The Lausitzer und Mitteldeutsche
Bergbau- Verwaltungsgesellschaft (Lausitz and
Central German Mining Administration Company)
then came to the aid of the Senftenberg local authority, and the tower was opened with a ceremony on
23 October 2008. To kick off the 2009 season, at
the beginning of March visitors were already putting
pressure on the city to open the tower, which is
closed in winter due to the danger of slippery ice.

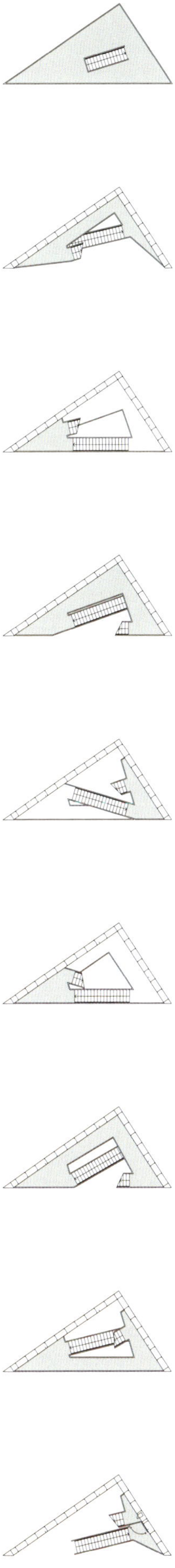

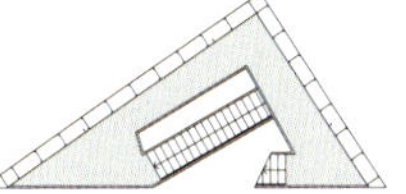

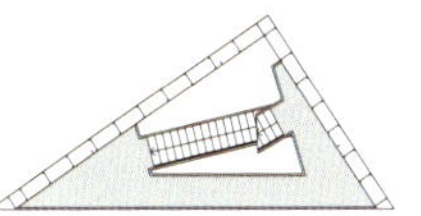

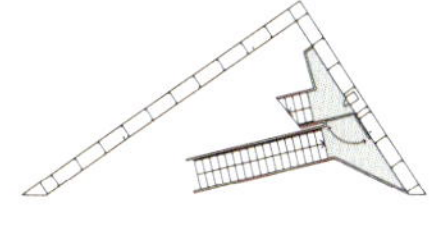

Grundrisse | Floor plans

WEBERWÜRSCHINGER

GEBÄUDE | BUILDING

3 ZWEIFAMILIENHÄUSER

TEXT ENRICO SANTIFALLER

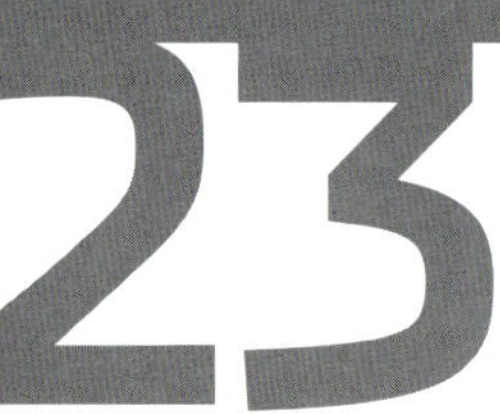

ARCHITEKTEN | ARCHITECTS

WEBERWÜRSCHINGER GmbH
Michael Weber,
Klaus Würschinger
und Haye Bakker
Urbanstraße 116
10967 Berlin
www.weberwuerschinger.com

MITARBEITER | TEAM

Joana Mendo, Rui Alves,
Katharina Bonhag,
Lea Niewöhner, Ralf Klabunde

BAUHERR | CLIENT

Wilhelm Weber

TRAGWERK | STUCTURE

Bräutigam Consult,
Ernst Bräutigam

LANDSCHAFTSARCHITEKTEN
LANDSCAPE ARCHITECTS

WEBERWÜRSCHINGER GmbH

FERTIGSTELLUNG | COMPLETION

Oktober 2007 | October 2007

STANDORT | LOCATION

Mooslohstraße 54
92637 Weiden

FOTOS | PHOTOS

Mirco Taliercio

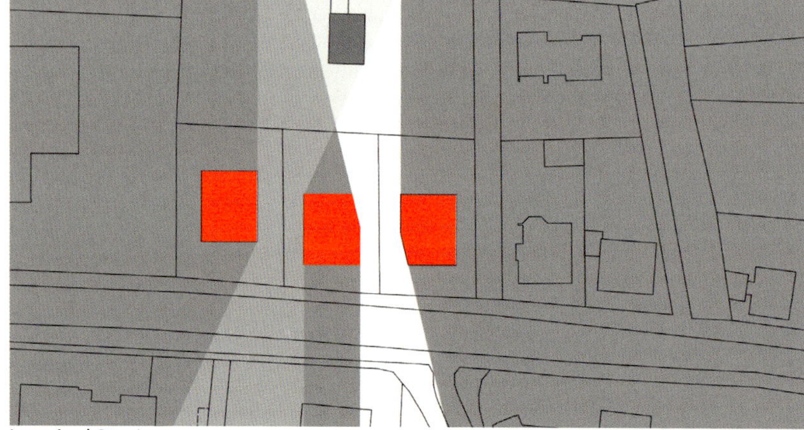

Lageplan | Site plan

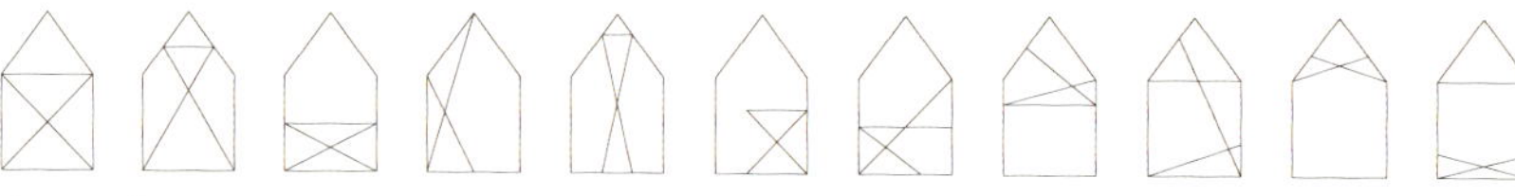

Konzept | Concept

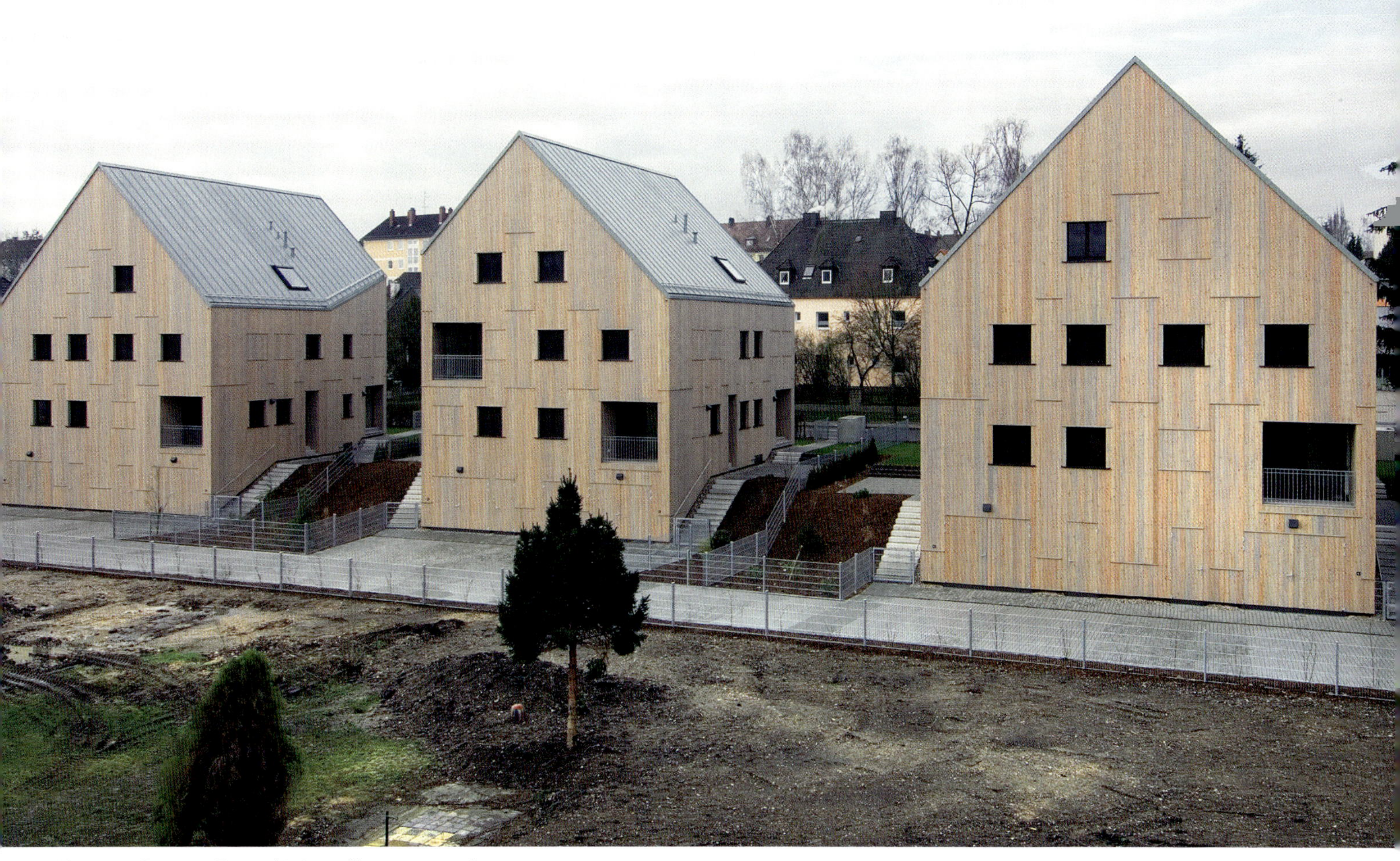

Urhütten im Supersize-Format | Archetypal huts in supersize format

Seit die Bush-Administration 2005 beschlossen hatte, den Truppenübungsplatz Grafenwöhr weiter auszubauen, sind in der mittleren Oberpfalz ganze Dörfer aus dem Nichts entstanden. Geplant wird nach einem von der Bundesanstalt für Immobilienaufgaben herausgegebenen „Informationsgeheft", das auf 26 Seiten ebenso penibel wie rigide von Raumgrößen über die Dimensionen für den Kühlschrank bis zu Vorhangleisten alles festgelegt, um für alle US-Soldaten gleiche Wohnverhältnisse zu gewährleisten. Obwohl die Miete mit 5,50 Euro pro Quadratmeter für großstädtische Verhältnisse eher niedrig ist, lohnt es sich für Investoren, bereits bei geringem Eigenkapital zu bauen. Ein zwischenstaatliches Abkommen sichert Mehrwertsteuer-Freiheit zu; die Bundesanstalt gibt eine zehnjährige Mietgarantie mit einer Option auf zweimal fünf weitere Jahre. Weil sich mit dem Geheft rund 80 Prozent der Ausschreibung erledigen lassen, beschränkt sich die Kreativität der Bauträger meist auf die Namensfindung: ob „Haus Georgia", „Haus California" oder „Haus Arizona", meist entbehrt diese Einheitsware jeglichen architektonischen Anspruchs. Mitten in dieser Bauunkultur des rasch Dahingezimmerten schufen Michael Weber und Klaus Würschinger ein seltenes Juwel. Sechs Doppelhaushälften konnten nach Entwürfen der aus Weiden stammenden Architekten an ihrem Heimatort realisiert werden – sechsmal ein Beleg, der zeigt, dass trotz aller Standardisierung Ortsbezogenheit, trotz aller Reglementierung Individualität, trotz Rendite Nachhaltigkeit möglich ist.

Das Stadtviertel Moosloh und die gleichnamige Ausfallstraße sind kein städtebauliches Glanzstück: ein paar ungeschlachte Zehngeschosser, sozialer Wohnungsbau aus den 1970ern, Mehrfamilienhäuser mit gewerblicher Nutzung im Erd-

Ever since the Bush administration decided in 2005 to expand the Grafenwöhr military training area, whole villages have been sprouting out of the ground in the central Oberpfalz region. According to a 26-page 'Information Booklet' published by the Bundesanstalt für Immobilienaufgaben (Federal Real Estate Office), which painstakingly details a set of rigid specifications, from room sizes to the dimensions of the refrigerator and curtain rods, the same living conditions are to be provided for all US soldiers. Although at 5.50 euros per square metre the rent is quite low by the standards of city living, it is worthwhile even for investors with modest capital to build here. An agreement between the US and Germany ensures exemption from sales tax, and the Bundesanstalt provides a ten-year rent guarantee, with an option for two further five-year periods. As some 80 percent of the tender is covered in the booklet, the creativity of the building developers is usually limited to coming up with cute names for the houses. But whether they're called "Haus Georgia", "Haus California" or "Haus Arizona" – these cookie-cutter homes are usually bereft of any higher architectural aspirations. Right in the midst of this non-architecture of rapidly thrown-together housing, Michael Weber and Klaus Würschinger have now managed to set down a rare gem. Six semi-detached houses have been erected according to the plans of the two Weiden-based architects in their hometown – proving sixfold that despite standardisation it is still possible to relate a home to its location, that despite regimentation it is still possible to create individu-

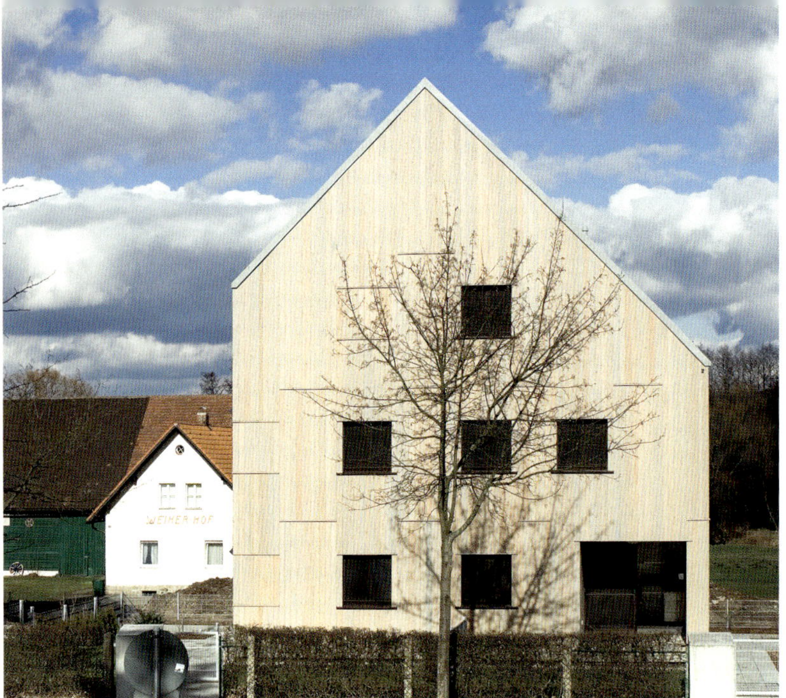

Blickbeziehung zur Umgebung | Views out onto the surroundings

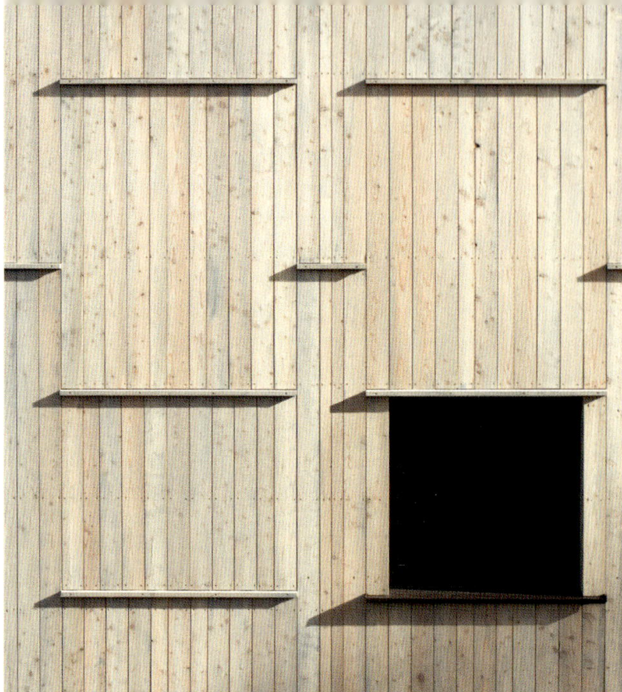

**Die Sturzhölzer deuten mögliche zukünftige Fassaden-
öffnungen an.** | The horizontal lintels hint at possible future
façade openings.

geschoss und Einfamilienhäuser mit Satteldächern und
Vorgärten, brav giebelständig aufgereiht. Höhepunkt ist der
zurückgesetzte Weiherhof, der letzte, bis in die 1990er-Jahre
noch bewirtschaftete Ackerbürger-Bauernhof in Weiden,
sowie ein Landschaftsschutzgebiet entlang eines kleinen
Baches. Wesentlicher Bestandteil des Entwurfs war, die
Blickbeziehungen zu diesem Ort des kollektiven Gedächt-
nisses zu erhalten. Aus diesem Grund sind die Volumina der
Gebäude, die als punktförmige Hausarchetypen ohne Dach-
überstand ausgebildet wurden, abgeschnitten. Die Urhütten
haben allerdings Supersize-Format: Jedes der Häuser bietet
derzeit 280 Quadratmeter Wohnfläche. Wenn die amerika-
nischen Mieter dereinst ausziehen, kann die Wohnfläche mit
dem Ausbau der Dachgeschosse, Loggien und Garagen auf
jeweils 450 Quadratmeter erweitert werden. Derzeit beherbergt jedes Haus eine 5- und eine 4-Zimmer-Wohnung, aber
im ausgebauten Zustand können dort gewerbliche Nutzungen,
Wohnungen verschiedenster Größe vom Appartement über
Maisonnetten bis hin zu Mehr-Generationen-Wohnungen untergebracht werden. Die Architekten entwickelten elf verschiedene Varianten, wobei das Sockelgeschoss, heute dient es
als Garage für Pick-ups, barrierefrei zugänglich ist. Auf diese
Weise können die Hauseigner nach Ablauf der Mietgarantie
flexibel auf geänderte Anforderungen des Immobilienmarktes
reagieren. Neben den Flächenreserven ist auch die Variabilität
im Grundriss konstruktiv vorgeplant: Zwischen den Außen-
wänden aus Betonmauersteinen ist eine Stahlbetondecke
gespannt, bis auf die Umfassungswände der innen liegenden
Treppenhäuser können alle Raumbegrenzungen entfernt oder
an anderer Stelle errichtet werden. Die derzeit getrennte
Erschließungszone, der alle Neben- und Funktionsräume zugeordnet sind, kann problemlos in eine gemeinsame umgewan-
delt werden, ebenso die Loggien in Zimmer.
Die Fassade wurde mit gehobeltem, vorvergrautem Lärchenholz
verschalt – ein heimisches Material, das auch an dem hinter den
Häusern hervorlugenden Stall des Weiherhofes zu finden ist.

ality, and that despite the drive for profit it is still
possible to ensure lasting value.
The district of Moosloh and the arterial road of the
same name are not exactly urban planning highlights. There are a few cloddish ten-storey buildings,
council housing from the 1970s, apartment houses
with commercial tenants on the ground floor, and
single-family homes with pitched roofs and front
gardens, arranged obediently gable on gable. The
highlights are the Weiherhof set back somewhat
from the road, the last of Weiden's farms, which
was still operating during the 1990s, and a
landscape conservation area on the banks of a small
stream. A major aim of the design was to preserve
a vista onto this scenery of collective memory.
For this reason, the buildings' volumes, which are
realised as archetypical pitch-roofed houses without
projecting eaves, were truncated in places so as
not to obstruct the view. However, these primeval
huts have been inflated to a supersize format: each
house contains 280 square metres of living space.
When the American tenants one day move out, the
floor area can be expanded to 450 square metres
by converting the attic storeys, loggias and garages.
At the moment each house contains a 5-room and
a 4-room apartment. Once extended, they could
house commercial tenants and apartments in a
wide variety of sizes, from studio or maisonette all
the way to multi-generation homes. The architects
developed eleven different versions, with the ground
floor, which today serves as a garage for pick-ups,
always barrier-free. In this way the house owners
can react flexibly to the requirements of the real
estate market once the rent guarantee has expired.
In addition to spatial reserves, variability of the floor
plan is also built into the design: a ferroconcrete

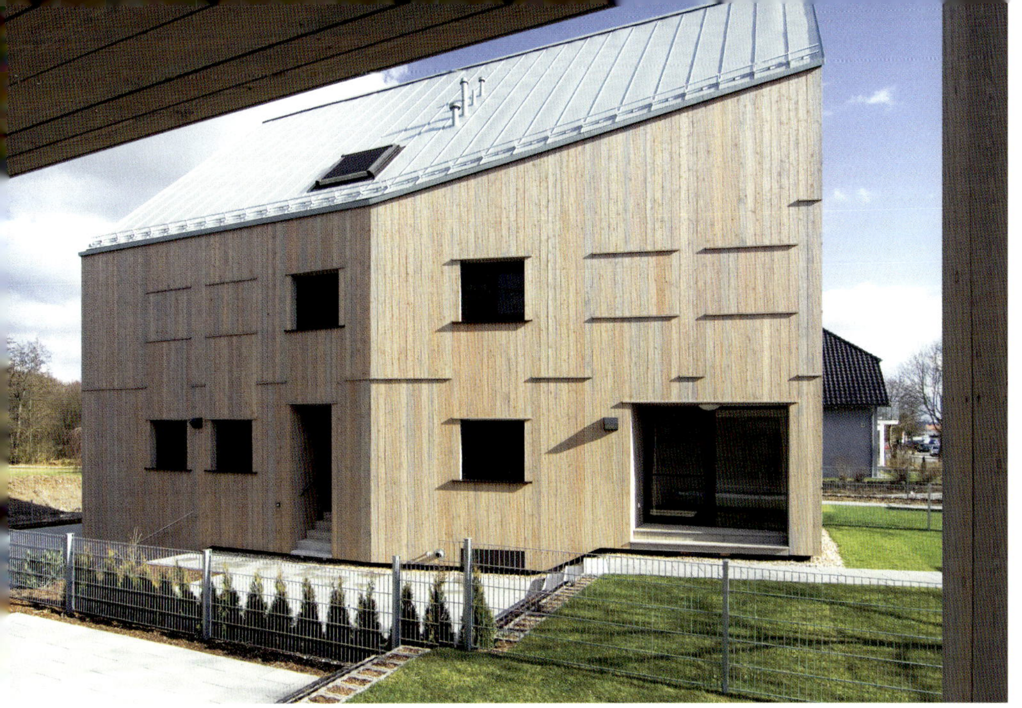

Fassadenschalung aus heimischem vorvergrauten Lärchenholz – wie beim Stall des benachbarten Weiherhofes | Façade clad in native pre-weathered larchwood – like the stall of the neighbouring Weiherhof farm

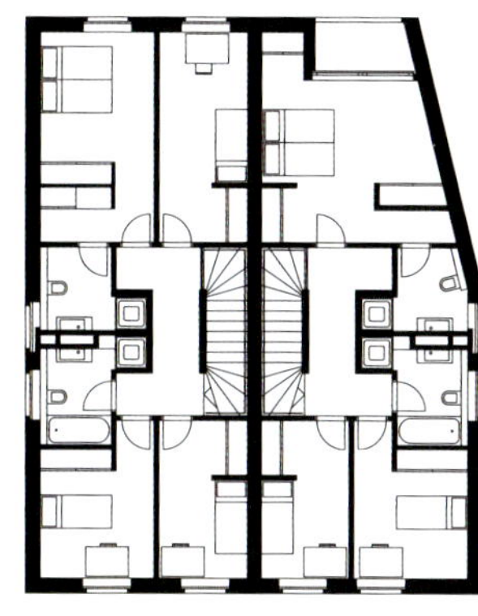

Grundriss 1. Obergeschoss
Floor plan of 1st floor

Um Kosten zu reduzieren, griff man auf Lagerware in gängigen Größen zurück. Die bauphysikalisch notwendigen horizontalen Sturzhölzer setzten die Architekten ein, um mögliche zukünftige Fassadenöffnungen anzudeuten. Fassade und Volumetrie, scheinbare Reduzierung auf die Urform des Hauses bei gleichzeitiger Vergrößerung, traditioneller Werkstoff und in dieser Gegend eher ungewöhnliche, internationale Bewohner: Die Architekten spielen ein herrlich dialektisches Spiel mit der Wahrnehmung. Sie erzählen von einem Zwei-Phasen-Konzept, von dem Vorher-Nachher-Prinzip, das den Bauten zugrunde liegt. Die drei Häuser sind gute Gebrauchsarchitektur und dennoch poetisches Erlebnis. Der lange vergessenen Oberpfalz, in jüngster Zeit durch einige bemerkenswerte Architekturen aufgefallen, konnten Weber und Würschinger einen weiteren bemerkenswerten Baustein hinzufügen.

ceiling is hung between the concrete brick external walls, meaning that, except for the walls enclosing the interior staircases, all internal dividing walls can be removed or shifted as needed. The entry zone, which is currently separate for each apartment and contains all ancillary and utility rooms, can easily be converted into a common area, just as the loggias can be made into rooms.

The façade was clad in planed, pre-weathered larchwood – a native material that also covers the stall of the Weiherhof, which can be glimpsed behind the houses. To reduce costs, stock materials in commonly available sizes were chosen. The architects used the horizontal lintels that were required for the physical integrity of the structures to hint at possible future openings in the façades. Façade and volumetry, apparent reduction to the most basic house shape but in an oversized version, traditional materials and international residents that are not the rule in this region: the architects play a wonderfully dialectic game with our perception. They tell of a two-phase concept, of the before-and-after principle on which the buildings are predicated. The three houses are sound utilitarian architecture and yet provide a poetic experience. The long-forgotten Oberpfalz, which has suddenly attracted attention of late with some notable architectural projects, has now been given a further distinguished feature by Weber and Würschinger.

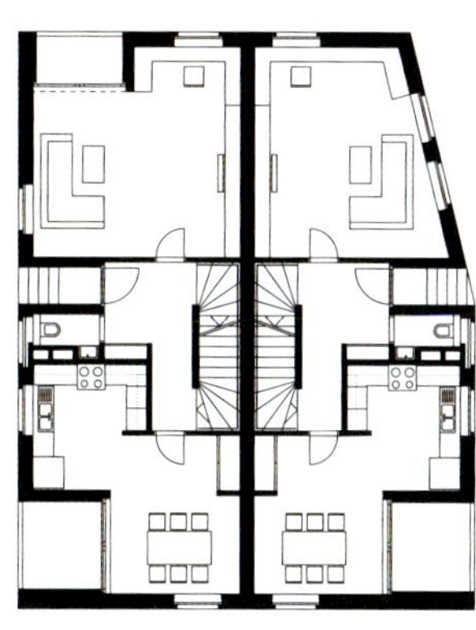

Grundriss Erdgeschoss
Floor plan of ground floor

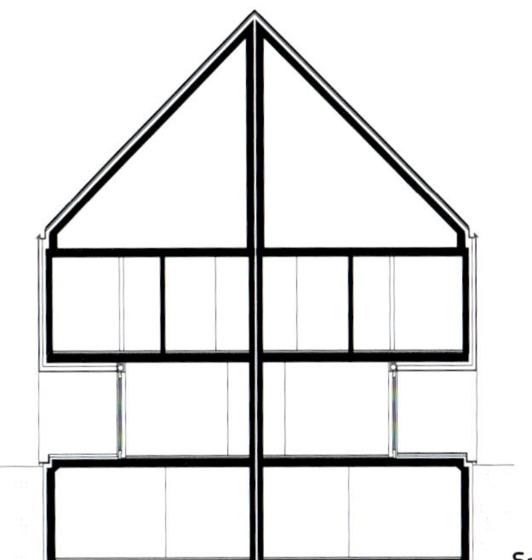

Schnitt | Section

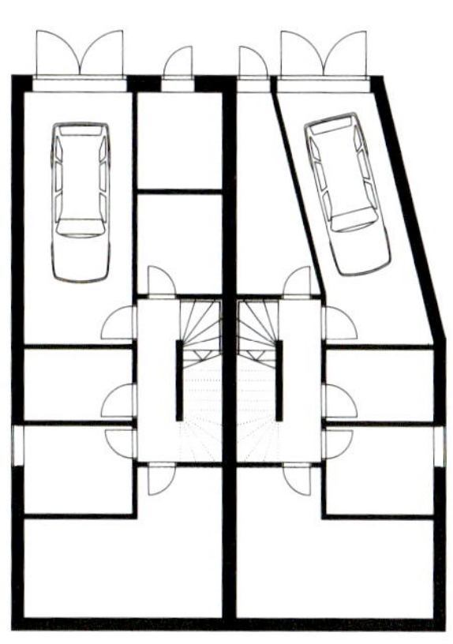

Grundriss Kellergeschoss
Floor plan of basement

WEINMILLER ARCHITEKTEN

GEBÄUDE | BUILDING

L-BANK

TEXT HANS IBELINGS

24

ARCHITEKTEN | ARCHITECTS

Weinmiller Architekten
Gesine Weinmiller,
Michael Großmann
Kurfürstendamm 178/179
10707 Berlin
www.weinmiller.de

MITARBEITER | TEAM

Nils Stelter, Nadja Häupl,
Michael Zeichardt,
Thekla Pohl, Therese Strohe,
André Lücke, Jörn Kriedemann

BAUHERR | CLIENT

L-Bank
Schlossplatz
76113 Karlsruhe

TRAGWERK | STRUCTURE

Leonhardt, Andrä & Partner
Beratende Ingenieure VBI, GmbH
Stuttgart

LANDSCHAFTSARCHITEKTEN
LANDSCAPE ARCHITECTS

Agence Ter
Karlsruhe

FERTIGSTELLUNG | COMPLETION

2008

FOTOS | PHOTOS

Maximilian Meisse

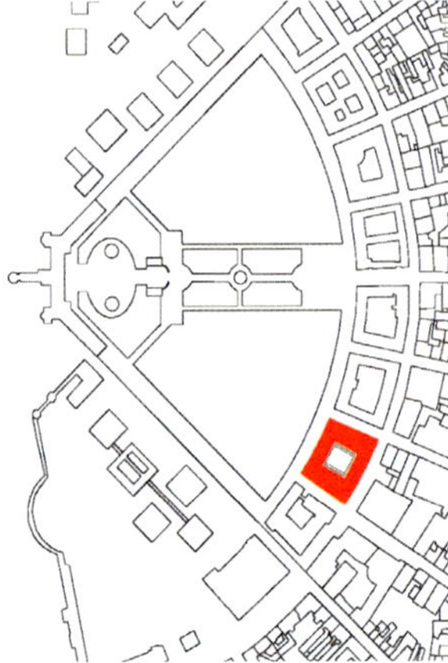

Lageplan | Site plan

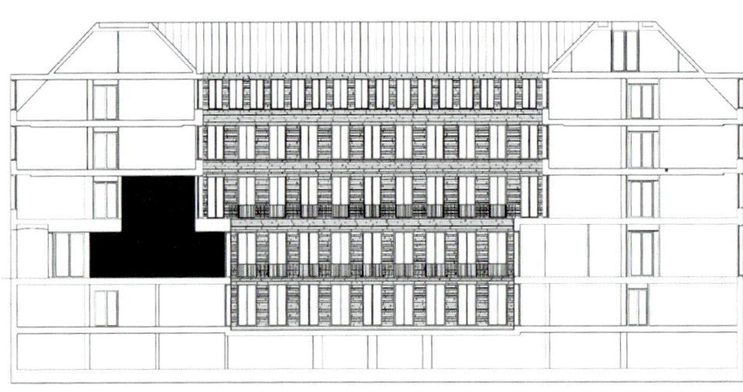

Schnitt | Section

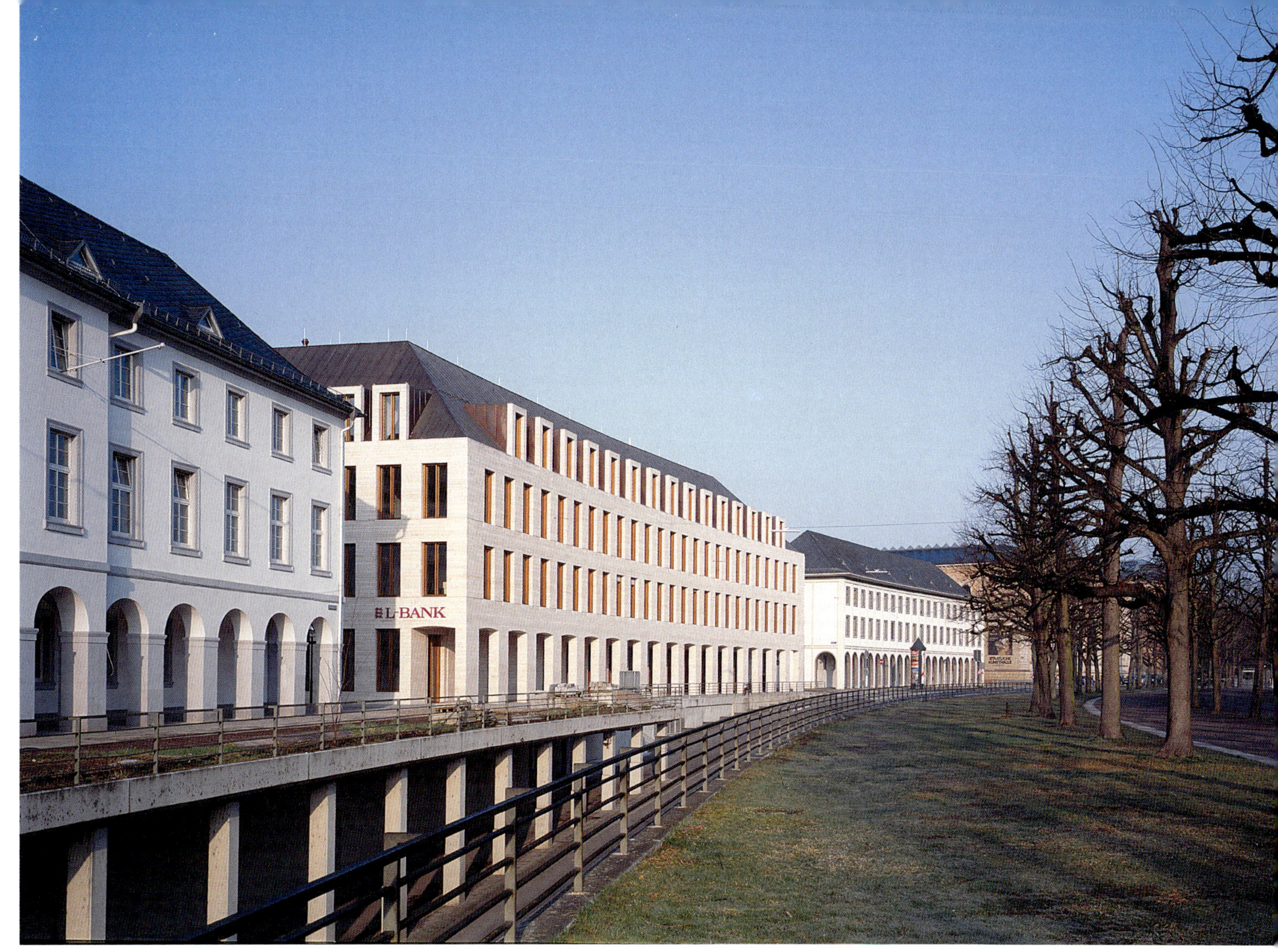

Die neue Architektur passt in die barocke Idealplanung Karlsruhes mit ihrer neoklassizistischen Ergänzung aus der zweiten Hälfte des 18. Jahrhunderts. | The new architecture fits in with the Baroque plan of Karlsruhe as an ideal city with its neo-classical additions from the latter half of the 18th century.

Mit Fassaden aus französischem Kalkstein, bronzefarbenen Fensterrahmen, geschosshohen Türen aus Nussholz und einer zwei Stockwerke hohen, mit Olivenholz und Fußböden aus Kirchheimer Muschelkalk ausgestalteten Halle ist dies eine Architektur, die in Bezug auf Gediegenheit und Luxus keinen Zweifel lässt. Kennzeichnend für die von Weinmiller Architekten aus Berlin entworfene L-Bank in Karlsruhe ist, dass die Fassaden nicht aus den üblichen, dem Gebäude vorgehängten dünnen Natursteinplatten bestehen, sondern tatsächlich aus Stein hochgezogen sind. Dieses Mauerwerk unterstreicht den tektonischen Charakter des Bauwerks.

Die Architektur von Gesine Weinmiller und Michael Großmann passt in die barocke, auf die erste Hälfte des 18. Jahrhunderts zurückgehende Idealplanung Karlsruhes und ihrer neoklassizistischen Ergänzung aus der zweiten Hälfte des 18. Jahrhunderts. An diesem Ort ist dies ein Kontext, den es selbstverständlich und unvermeidlich zu respektieren gilt: Auch bei der Wiederinstandsetzung nach den schweren Zerstörungen im Zweiten Weltkrieg wurde diesem Umstand durchaus Rechnung getragen. Diese Behutsamkeit hat zu einer außergewöhnlichen Wiederaufbaumoderne mit historisierender Tendenz geführt. Auch alles, was später am Schlossplatz, Zirkel und Marktplatz gebaut wurde, fügt sich mehr oder weniger und besser oder schlechter der Dominanz der Gesamtum-

With French limestone façades, bronze window frames, floor-to-ceiling walnut doors, a two-storey lobby with olivewood trim and floors of Kirchheim muschelkalk, or shell limestone, this is architecture that leaves no doubt as to its solidity and sumptuousness. Characteristically, the façades of the L-Bank building in Karlsruhe, rather than consisting of curtain walls of thin slabs of natural stone, are actually built of stone. This stonework underscores the structure's tectonic character.

Designed by Berlin-based Weinmiller Architekten – Gesine Weinmiller and Michael Großmann – the building's architecture fits into the early 18th-century Baroque ideal planning of Karlsruhe and its late 18th-century neo-Classical completion, which provide the location with a context that is naturally and inevitably to be respected. During reconstruction after the severe damage suffered in World War II this context was, in fact, heeded, leading to an exceptional reconstruction Modernism with Historicist overtones. Everything that was subsequently built at Schlossplatz, Zirkel and Markt also more or less and for better or worse accepts this dominance of context, even if invariably displaying some period specificity. The same holds true

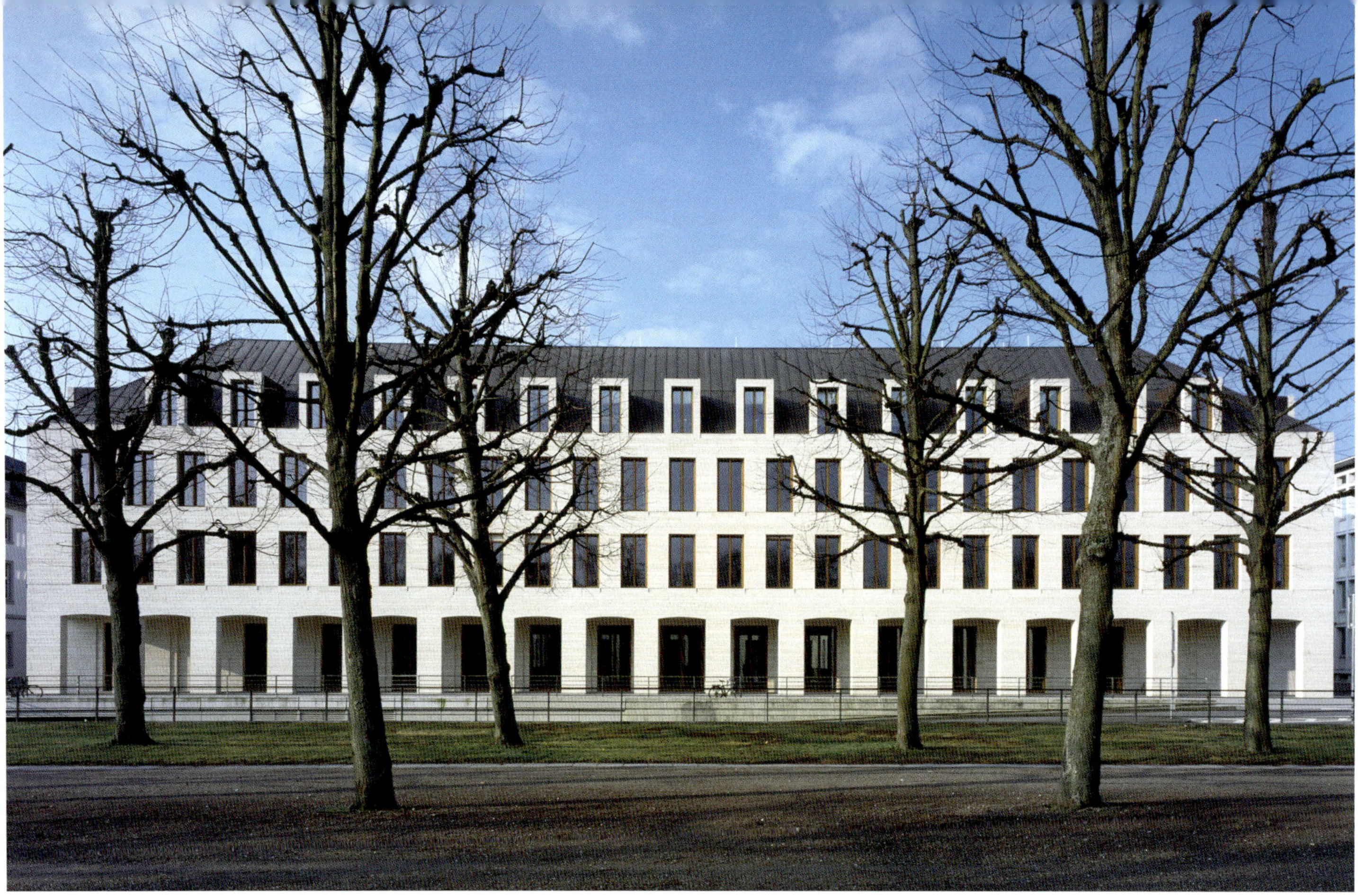

Die Abstraktion ihrer monolithischen Außenflächen und ebenso der Innenräume weist die L-Bank als Gebäude des 21. Jahrhunderts aus. | The abstraction of its monolithic exterior surfaces and its interiors identifies the L-Bank as a building of the 21st century.

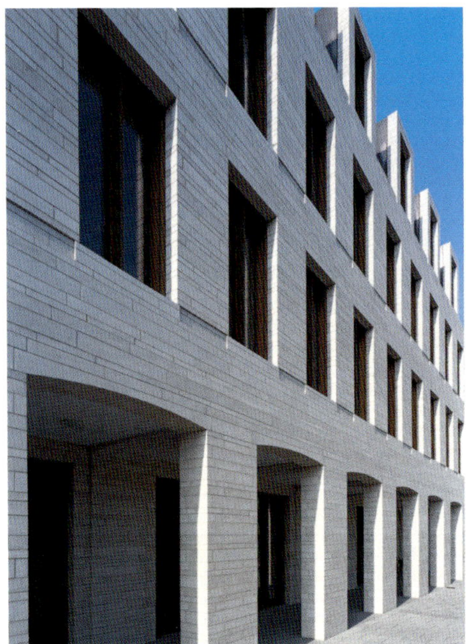

Fassaden aus massivem französischem Kalkstein
Façades of solid French limestone

gebung, auch wenn die Entstehungszeit zwangsläufig immer durchschlägt. Dies gilt ebenso für den Neubau des Büros Weinmiller Architekten, das nach einem begrenzt offenen Wettbewerb mit vorgeschaltetem Bewerbungsverfahren den Auftrag für den Neubau der mit mehreren Adressen am Schlossplatz vertretenen L-Bank erhielt. Der Neubau schließt die letzte Lücke, die der Krieg ins historische Zentrum geschlagen hatte. Die Architektur des Büros Weinmiller passt sich sichtlich der Umgebung an, die Konformismus verlangt. Gleichzeitig ist aber die neue L-Bank, in der bis zu 400 Menschen arbeiten können, unübersehbar ein Gebäude des 21. Jahrhunderts. Und sei es nur aufgrund der Abstraktion, die zu der Vereinfachung passt, welche in der Gegenwartsarchitektur aller Art – vom Neomodernismus David Chipperfields bis zur Solidität Adolfo Natalinis oder der ephemeren Leichtigkeit von SANAA – wiederzufinden ist. Diese Abstraktion zeigt sich nicht nur in den monolithischen steinernen Außenflächen, sondern auch im Inneren, so etwa in den aus einem Stück gefertigten Möbeln aus Corian in der Cafeteria und im Fitnessraum im Untergeschoss.

Dass sich das Gebäude einfügt, war von den Architekten ausdrücklich so gewollt: Sie wollten keinen Solisten hervorbringen, sondern einen Chorsänger, der im Chor mitsingt, ohne sich im Ton zu vergreifen. Das ist ihnen perfekt gelungen: Die L-Bank kommt ohne jeden aus dem Rahmen fallenden Innovationsdrang oder Formwillen aus. Veränderungen können hier nur behutsam durchgeführt werden, und das wurde in diesem Fall fachmännisch realisiert. Das Dachgeschoss beispielsweise wurde so weit erhöht, dass dort funktionale Büroräume untergebracht werden konnten, ohne das Karlsruher Modell der zwei Geschosse plus geneigtem Dach zu durchbrechen. Dass das Gebäude aus diesem Grund eine Spur größer ist, fällt kaum auf, zumal da auf äußerst subtile Weise auch das Dach des in das

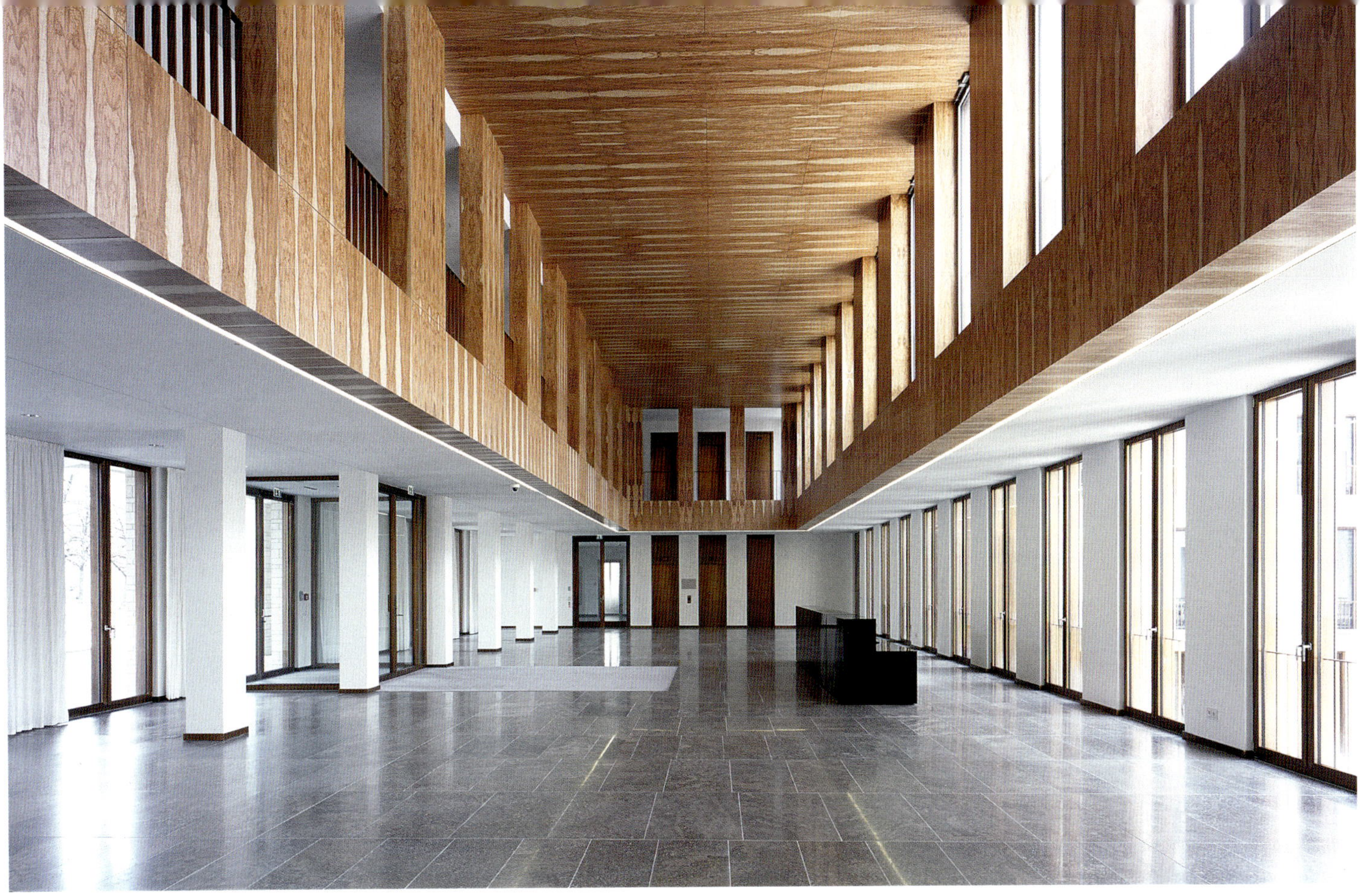

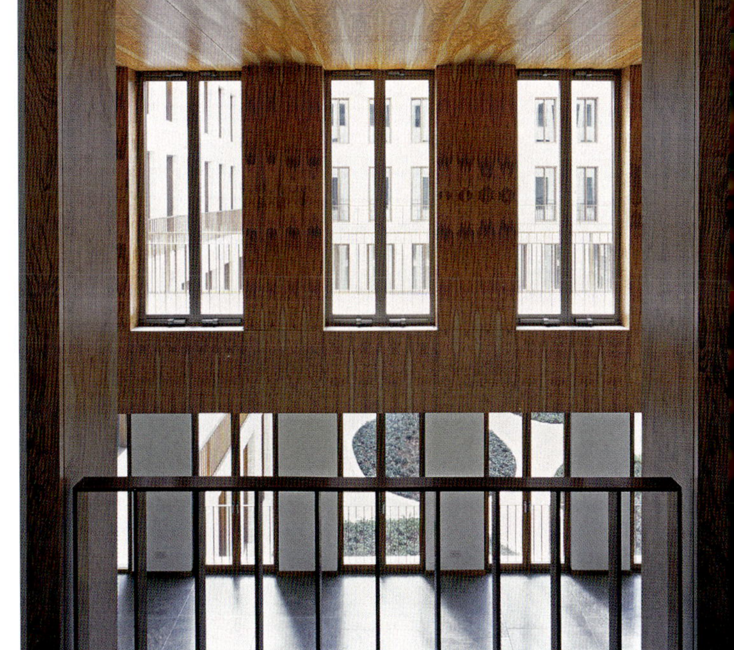

Zweigeschossige Halle, ausgestattet mit Olivenholz und Fußböden aus Kirchheimer Muschelkalk. | Two-storey hall with olivewood fittings and floors of Kirchheim shell limestone.

for the new building of L-Bank, which has several addresses at Schlossplatz. Following a limited competition with a preset application procedure, Weinmiller Architekten were commissioned to design the bank's new building, which was to close the last hole the war had ripped in the historic city centre.

Weinmiller's architecture in obvious ways adapts to this environment, which calls for conformism. At the same time, however, the new L-Bank building, where up to 400 people can work, is unmistakably a structure of the 21st century. Even if only on account of its abstraction, which goes with the simplification found in so much contemporary architecture, from the neo-Modernism of David Chipperfield to the solidity of Adolfo Natalini or the ephemeral lightness of SANAA. This abstraction is evident not only in the monolithic stone exterior, but also in the interior, as for instance in the solid Corian furniture in the cafeteria and the fitness room in the basement. The architects explicitly intended the building to fit in: they did not want to create a soloist, but rather a choir boy who would sing along in the choir without hitting a wrong note. And they were successful in this: the L-Bank building is devoid of any misplaced innovative urge or formal impulse. Changes can be implemented only cautiously here, and in this case it was done expertly. The attic storey, for instance, was raised to allow the creation of useful office spaces, without deviating from the Karlsruhe standard of two storeys plus slanted roof. That the building is slightly taller because of this is hardly

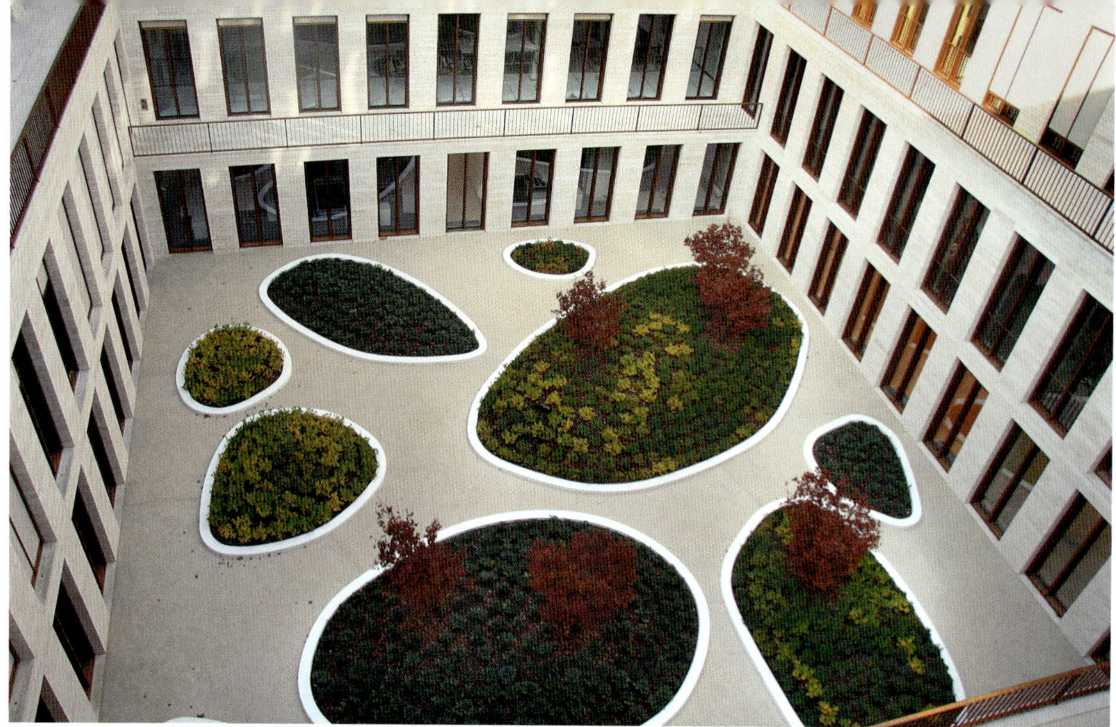

Das Gebäude umschliesst einen von Agence Ter gestalteten Innenhof. | The building encloses an inner courtyard designed by Agence Ter.

Bankgebäude integrierten neoklassizistischen Denkmals am Zirkel erhöht wurde. Dieses Denkmal, bis vor Kurzem die einzige Bebauung auf dem als Parkplatz genutzten Grundstück, wurde eher renoviert als restauriert, jedenfalls ohne einem unnötigen Hang zu historischer Reinheit nachzugeben. Das Motiv des Lichthofs des Denkmals wiederholt sich in den Lichthöfen der drei Treppenhäuser des Neubaus.

Das strenge Regelmaß der L-Bank – ein Wesensmerkmal des Klassischen – wird durch die leichte Krümmung der beiden Längsseiten und die nicht parallel zueinander verlaufenden Seitenfassaden durchbrochen, eine Folge der städtebaulichen Anlage Karlsruhes. Dies nimmt der Architektur eine etwaige Trockenheit, so wie der menschliche Maßstab Karlsruhes einer etwaigen erdrückenden Monumentalität vorbeugt. Das Gleiche gilt für den von Agence Ter gestalteten Hofgarten, der mit seinen elliptischen Formen für ein Gegengewicht zur überwiegenden Rechteckigkeit der Architektur sorgt.

In einem Gebäude, dessen Form in spezifischer Weise reduziert ist, in dem sich Details auf ein Minimum beschränken und wo sich die Farbe innerhalb einer begrenzten Palette aus vorwiegend Braun-, Bronze- und Beigetönen bewegt, sind es am Ende wesentliche architektonische Eigenschaften wie Proportionen, Raum und Licht, die die Qualität bestimmen.

noticeable, especially since the roof of the Classical monument on Zirkel that was integrated into the bank building was also raised in a very subtle way. Until recently the only structure on a site that served as a parking lot, this monument was not so much restored as renovated, that is, without a misplaced penchant for historical purity. The atrium inside the monument is echoed by the atriums in the three stairwells of the new building.

The L-Bank building's strict regularity – a quintessentially Classical quality – is disrupted both by the slight curvature of the two long fronts and by the fact that the façades on the sides of the building do not run parallel, a consequence of the way the city of Karlsruhe was laid out. This keeps the architecture from being dry or dull, just as the human scale of Karlsruhe prevents a monumentality that could have been overwhelming. The same holds true for the courtyard garden designed by Agence Ter, which with its elliptical shapes counterbalances the architecture's predominant orthogonality.

In a building formally reduced in this way, with detailing kept to a minimum and colour falling within a limited palette of mainly brown, bronze and beige, quality is ultimately determined by essential architectural properties such as proportions, space and light.

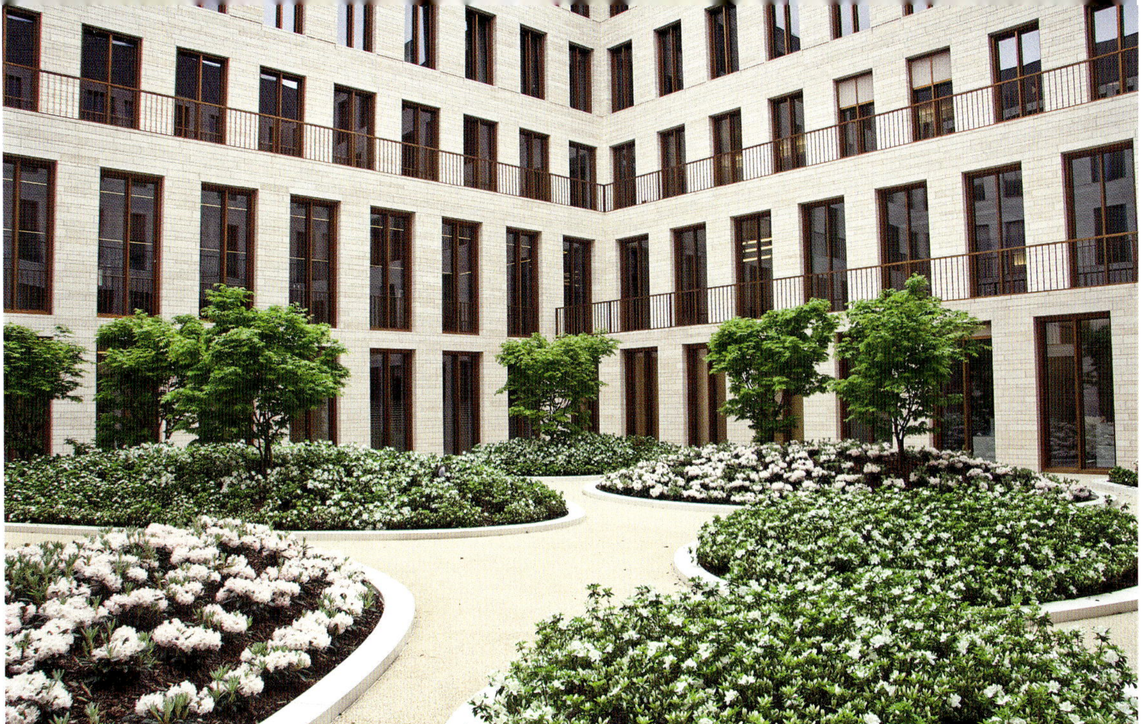

Innenhof im Frühling mit Rhododendron-Inseln | Inner courtyard in the spring with rhododendron islands

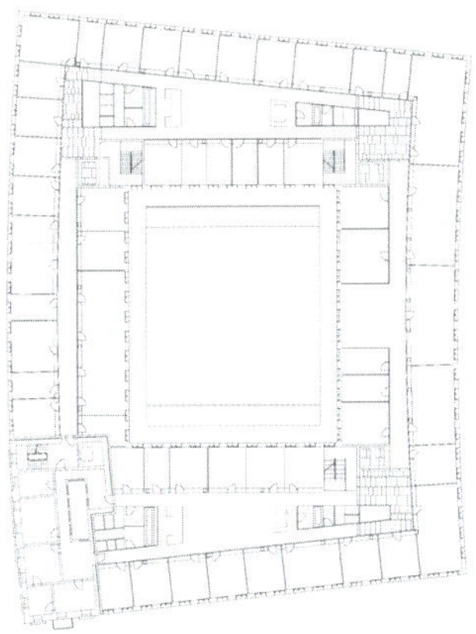

Grundriss 2. Obergeschoss | Floor plan of 2nd floor

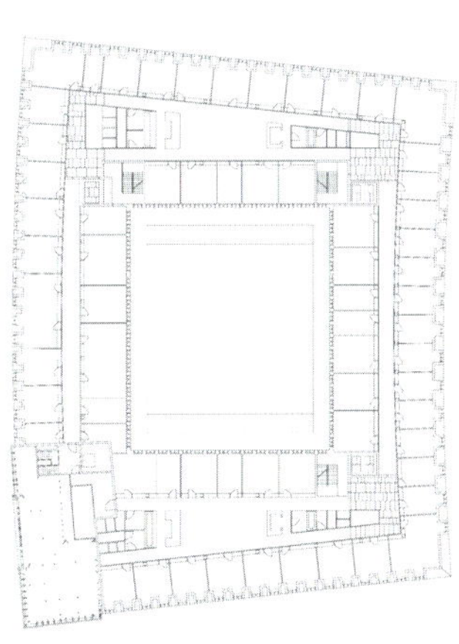

Grundriss 3. Obergeschoss | Floor plan of 3rd floor

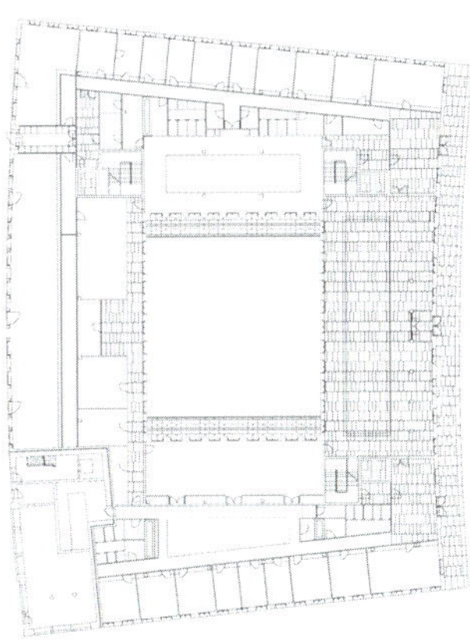

Grundriss Erdgeschoss | Floor plan of ground floor

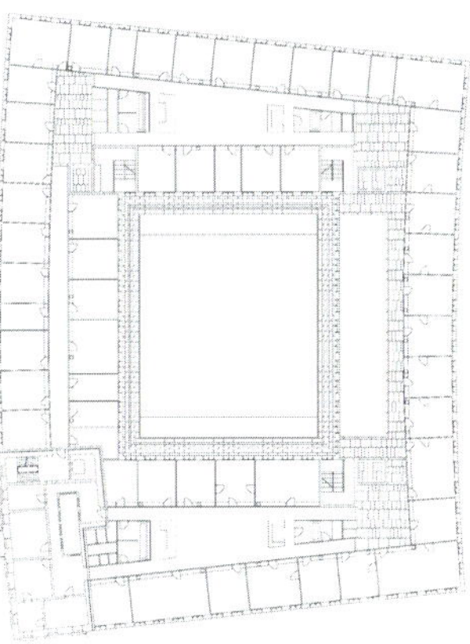

Grundriss 1. Obergeschoss | Floor plan of 1st floor

EINE BESTANDSAUFNAHME: MODERNE, MOBILITÄT, MARKE
TAKING STOCK: MODERNITY, MOBILITY, BRANDING
GENERATION AUDI

MICHAELA BUSENKELL

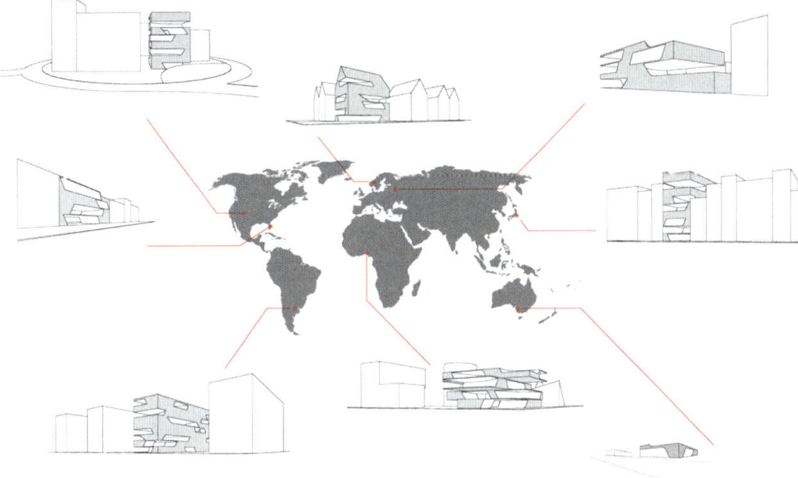

Globale Adaption: Position im Kontext | Global adaptation: position in context

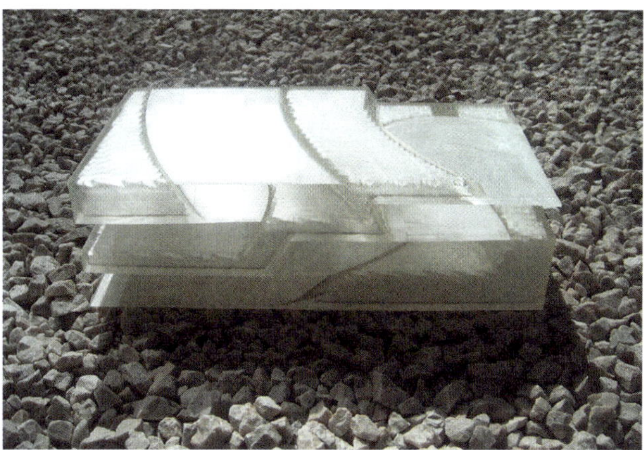

Modell | Model

„Modern society is a society on the move. Central to the idea of modernity is that of movement, that modern societies have brought about some striking changes in the nature and experience of motion or travel."
Scott Lash, John Urry, Economies of Signs and Space, London 1994, S. 225.

L'ESPRIT NOUVEAU

Le Corbusier proklamierte in den 1920er-Jahren den Geist der neuen Zeit: Er entwickelte eine dynamische Architektur für den dynamischen Menschen und führte Autos, Schiffe und ‚Zirkulation' in den Bereich der Baukunst ein. In seiner Schrift „Vers une Architecture" von 1923 platzierte er Bilder neuer Automobile neben einer Ansicht des Parthenon um zu verdeutlichen, dass das Ziel der Arbeit von Ingenieuren und Architekten das gleiche sei: Ökonomie, Gebrauchsfähigkeit, Standardisierung und Emanzipation durch Technik und Wissenschaft.[1]
Bereits im Jahr 1909 hatte das Futuristische Manifest das Fanal zum Aufbruch in die Zukunft gegeben und den neuen Götzen Geschwindigkeit inthronisiert: In der berühmten Passage über das aufheulende Automobil, „schöner als die Nike von Samothrake", verkündete Filippo Tommaso Marinetti die Schönheit der mechanischen Geschwindigkeit. Doch erst in der Nachkriegszeit brach mit der Massenmotorisierung die mobile Zukunft für Jedermann an und der immens anwachsende Verkehr wurde zum Indikator dafür, in welchem Ausmaß sich die Gesellschaft räumlich und sozial in Bewegung setzte. Gleichzeitig erwuchsen dem Traum von der Mobilität die Leuchttürme der neuen Lebenskultur: Tankstellen, Parkhäuser, Bushaltestellen, Fußgängerzonen und -unterführungen, Raststätten oder Drive-in-Schalter. Von der Autobahn über die autogerechte Stadt, die das Kraftfahrzeug zum Maß der Stadtplanung machte, bis hin zur Suburbanisierung durch die neue Wohnmobilität ist die Geschichte der Moderne auch eine Geschichte der modernen Mobilität.
Le Corbusier benannte das Maison Citrohan (1920), erst in der Stuttgarter Weißenhofsiedlung realisiert, nach seiner bevorzugten Automarke Citroën, er legte das Erdgeschoss der Villa Savoye (1930) auf den Wendekreis eines Voison C14 von 1929 aus. Gerne ließ er auch seine Immobilien im Geleit eleganter Limousinen fotografieren, als Kontext für das gute Leben, das mit seinen Bauten assoziiert werden sollte. Das ‚Langfenster' (fenêtre en longueur) des Ozeandampfers übernahm er als Motiv der Bewegung in sein Fünf-Punkte-Manifest einer neuen Architektur[2] und implementierte es im Einfamilienhaus, was in Frankreich um 1930 ebenso heftige architektonische Kontroversen auslöste wie das flache Dach zeitgleich in Deutschland.

CARCHITECTURE

Heute wird die Liaison von Architektur und Automobil von den Automobilherstellern selbst in Szene gesetzt – in Form von Markenarchitektur, die infolge des Bilbao Effekts zur Blüte gelangte[3]. Nachdem zu Beginn der Jahrtausendwende Volkswagen mit der Autostadt Wolfsburg und der gläsernen Manufaktur

"Modern society is a society on the move. Central to the idea of modernity is that of movement, that modern societies have brought about some striking changes in the nature and experience of motion or travel."
Scott Lash, John Urry, Economies of Signs and Space, London 1994, p. 225.

L'ESPRIT NOUVEAU

In the 1920s Le Corbusier proclaimed the spirit of a new age. He developed a dynamic architecture for the modern man on the move and introduced automobiles, ships and "circulation" into the architectural field. In his manuscript "Vers une Architecture" from 1923 he placed pictures of new automobiles next to a view of the Parthenon in order to underscore that engineers and architects shared the same aims: economy, usability, standardisation and emancipation through technology and science.[1]
As early as 1909 the "Futurist Manifesto" had sounded the fanfare for striding off into the future, enthroning Speed as its new idol. In a famous passage on the roaring motorcar, "more beautiful than the Victory of Samothrace", Filippo Tommaso Marinetti embraced the beauty of mechanical momentum. But it was only with the mass motorisation of the post-war period that the mobile future dawned for Everyman, the huge growth in traffic attesting to the degree to which society was picking up speed both spatially and socially. The dream of mobility gave birth to the beacons of the modern lifestyle: gas stations, car parks, bus stops, pedestrian zones and tunnels, motorway rest areas and drive-ins. From the motorway to the car-friendly city that made the automobile the measure of urban planning, and all the way to suburbanisation through the new flexibility in commuting, the history of Modernism is also a history of modern mobility.
Le Corbusier named his Maison Citrohan (1920), first realised in Stuttgart's Weissenhof development, after his favourite make of car, Citroën; he laid out the ground floor of the Villa Savoye (1930) to correspond to the turning radius of a 1929 Voison C14; and he liked to have his projects photographed with elegant sedans parked out front to signify the good life that was to be associated with his buildings. He adopted the 'long window' (fenêtre en longueur) of an ocean liner as a motif of movement in his five-point manifesto for a new architecture[2] and used it in a single-family home, setting off architectural debates in France in the 1930s that were just as vehement as those coursing through Germany regarding the new flat roof.

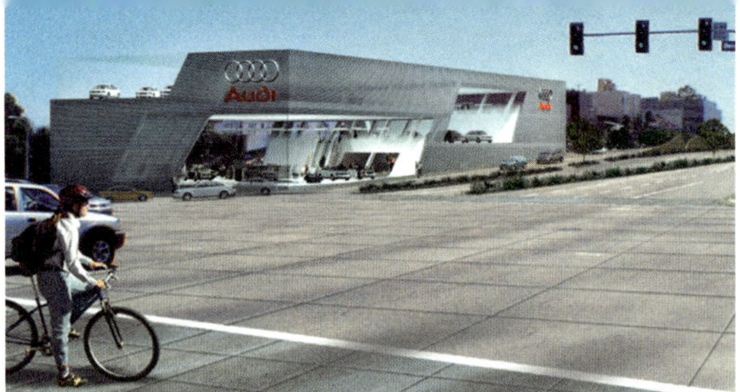

Konzeptstudie für US-amerikanische Standorte | Concept study for US locations

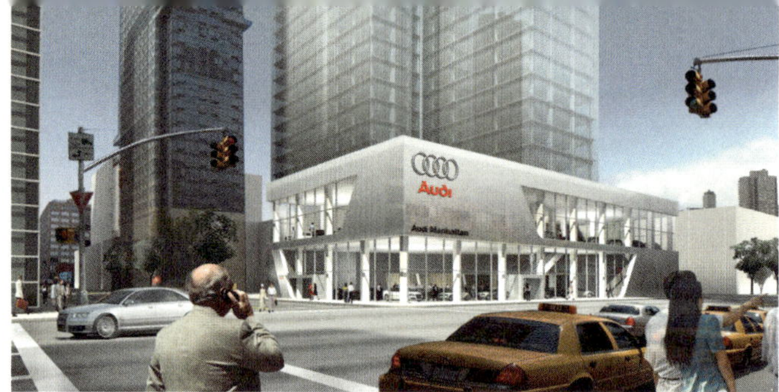

Orlando (in Planung) | Orlando (in planning)

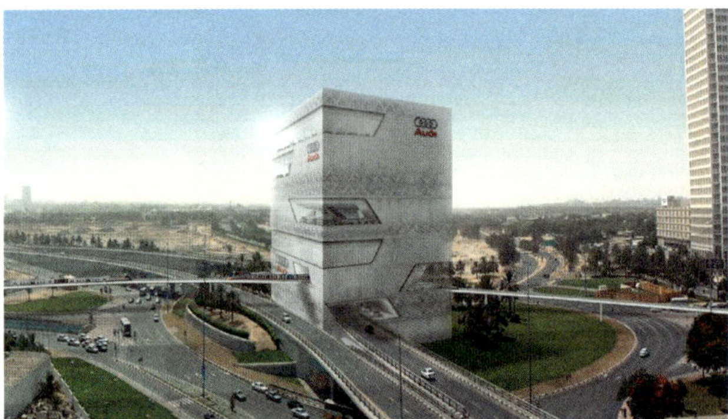

Konzeptstudie für Standorte in den Arabischen Emiraten | Concept study for locations in the Arab Emirates

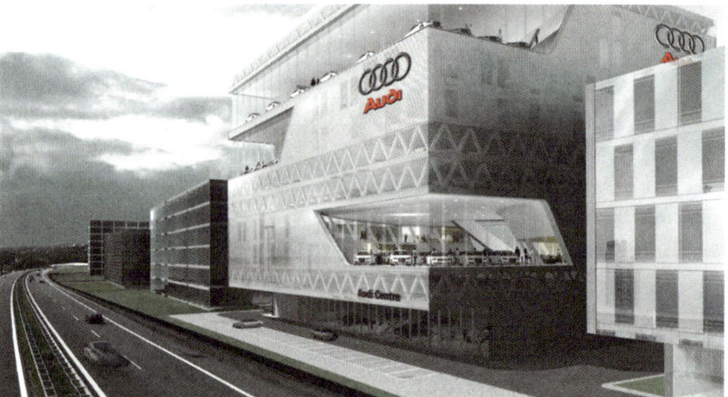

Konzeptstudie für europäische Standorte | Concept study for European locations

Dresden sowie Audi mit seinem Forum mit Museum in Ingolstadt (alle Bauten von Henn Architekten) eine neue Form des automobilen Themenparks inszenierten, folgten als bekannteste Beispiele das Mercedes-Benz Museum in Stuttgart-Untertürkheim (UN Studio, 2006, siehe DAM Jahrbuch 2006), das BMW-Werk in Leipzig (Zaha Hadid, 2005, siehe DAM Jahrbuch 2005) und die BMW-Welt in München (Coop Himmelb(l)au, 2007, siehe Deutsches Architektur Jahrbuch 2008/09) oder, die vorerst letzte spektakuläre Geste, das Porsche Museum in Stuttgart-Zuffenhausen (siehe S. 62ff.).

Die kulturell codierten Superzeichen sollen gemeinhin ein Bild von Dynamik und Geschwindigkeit evozieren, das die Gesetze der Schwerkraft vergessen macht. Auch wenn sich längst die Frage stellt, ob wir immer noch größere und schnellere Autos benötigen – und nicht vielmehr nachhaltigere und intelligentere Mobilitätskonzepte mit weniger Schadstoffemissionen – „… wird uns versprochen, dass der Showroom, so wie die Autos selbst, uns mehr und mehr bieten wird. Der neue, waghalsigere, größere Showroom gräbt das Automobil tiefer in das Bewusstsein des Konsumenten und erweitert die Marke in die Psychogeografie unserer Städte, Räume die unser ständig wachsendes Bedürfnis nach Konsumenten-Identität bedienen". schreibt Clare Dowdy in „Carchitecture" (Birkhäuser, 2001).[4] Doch sind heute Hierarchien und Statusbegriffe anhand von Maximaldefinitionen noch relevant? Professor Peter Kruse, Psychologe und Organisationsberater, erläutert im Zusammenhang seiner Studie „Wertewelt Mobilität", dass die Ursachen des aktuellen Einbruchs der Autoverkäufe nicht nur in Klimadebatte, Ölpreis und Finanzkrise liegen, sondern auch in einer Produktpolitik, die vorwiegend auf Motorenstärke und Technologie setzt. Sofern Status für die Befragten überhaupt noch eine Rolle spiele, so Kruse, dann nicht mehr im Zusammenhang exklusiver Qualität, sondern ökologischer Unbedenklichkeit, sozialer Gerechtigkeit und funktionaler Zweckmäßigkeit. Auch die Erlebniskategorie Fahrspaß sei heute zunehmend mit veränderten Assoziationen belegt. Brachten die Konsumenten Fahrspaß bisher in Verbindung mit Dynamik, Geschwindigkeit, Freiheit, Sicherheit und Komfort, so nennen sie heute: Vernunft, Sparsamkeit, soziale Verantwortung, menschliche Nähe und Schönheit.[5]

CARCHITECTURE

Today, auto makers themselves are setting the stage for the liaison of architecture and automobile – in the form of the brand architecture that has flourished as a consequence of the 'Bilbao effect'.[3] After Volkswagen ushered in the new millennium by creating a new form of automotive theme park with its Autostadt Wolfsburg and Gläserne Manufaktur (Transparent Factory) in Dresden, joined by Audi with its Forum and Museum in Ingolstadt (all designed by Henn Architekten), others quickly followed suit, the best known being the Mercedes-Benz Museum in Stuttgart-Untertürkheim (UN Studio, 2006, see DAM Architecture Annual 2006), the BMW plant in Leipzig (Zaha Hadid, 2005, see DAM Architecture Annual 2005) and BMW Welt in Munich (Coop Himmelb(l)au, 2007, see DAM Architecture Annual 2008/09) or, the most recent spectacular gesture, the Porsche Museum in Stuttgart-Zuffenhausen (see p. 62ff.).

The culturally encoded super-icons are in general meant to evoke an image of dynamism and speed that seems to suspend the laws of gravity. Even if we may long since be asking ourselves whether we really need cars that keep getting bigger and faster – and not instead more sustainable and intelligent mobility concepts with fewer emissions – "… we are promised that the showroom – like cars themselves – will offer us more and more. The new, bolder, bigger showroom edges the automobile deeper into the consumer's consciousness, extending the brand into the psychogeography of our cities, spaces that serve our ever-increasing desire for consumer identity", writes Clare Dowdy in Carchitecture (Birkhäuser, 2001).[4] But are hierarchies and notions of status based on maximum definitions still really relevant today? Professor Peter Kruse, psychologist and management consultant, explains in his study "Wertewelt Mobilität" (The World of Mobility Values) that the causes behind the current drop in automotive sales can be found not only in the climate debate, oil prices and financial crisis, but rather in product policies geared primarily toward engine power and technology. If status still plays a role at all for the people he surveyed, says Kruse, then it is no longer in connection with exclusive quality but more with environmental

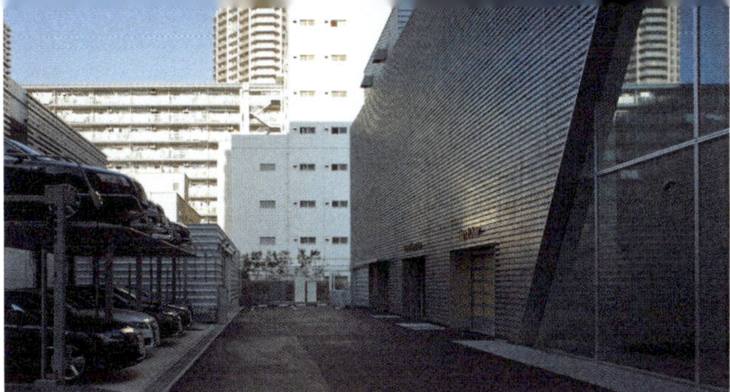

Audi Terminal Tokio (2008) | Audi terminal Tokyo (2008)

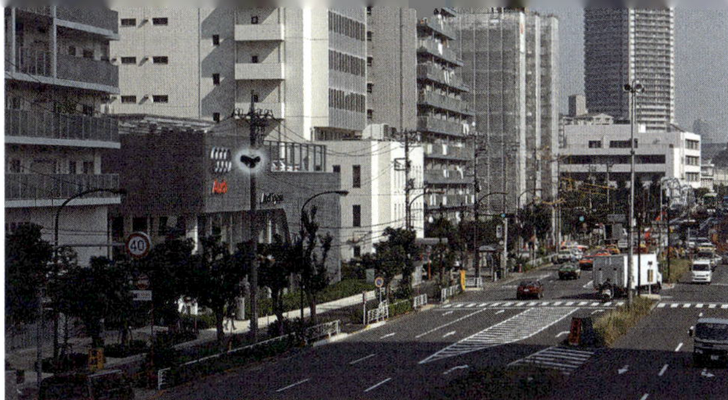

Audi Terminal Tokio (2008) | Audi terminal Tokyo (2008)

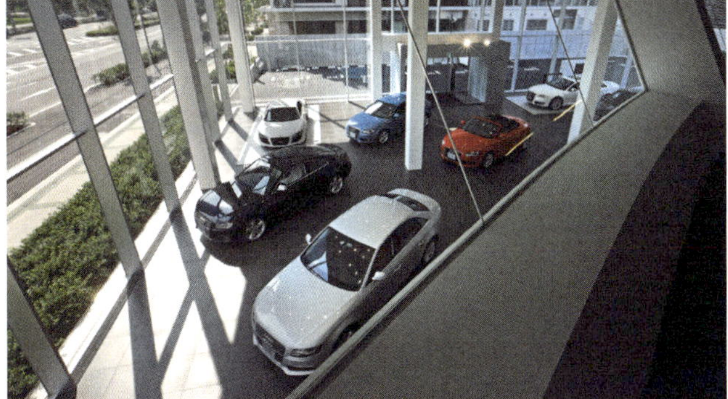

Audi Terminal Tokio (2008) | Audi terminal Tokyo (2008)

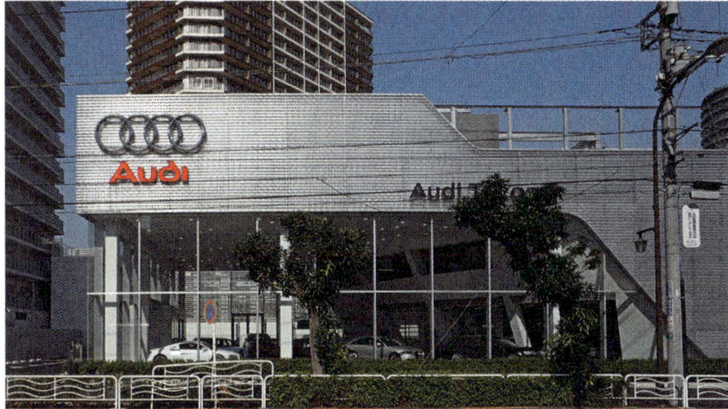

Audi Terminal Tokio (2008) | Audi terminal Tokyo (2008)

SERIE

Auch das neue Audi-Autohaus soll seine Marke kommunizieren. Doch hier wird keine kulturelle Typologie bemüht, um das Markenimage zu transzendieren. Auch die bauliche Rhetorik ist bar jeder halsbrecherischen Architekturakrobatik des ‚Außergewöhnlichen'. Bei Audi geht es um die Reprogrammierung des profanen Autohauses, in serieller Ausführung und mit globaler Identität. Weltweit soll es gebaut werden, die Marke überall wiedererkennbar sein, aber das Gebäude dennoch mit einer kontextbezogenen Konfiguration an den jeweiligen Standort adaptiert werden können. Damit wird ein Thema wieder aufgegriffen und aktualisiert, mit dem bereits die Architekten der frühen Moderne auf das Automobil Bezug nahmen: Standardisierung und Serie, heute erweitert um den Faktor der lokalen Variation. Aktuell sind weltweit über 175 Projekte in Ausführung, darunter in Las Vegas, Taipeh, Buenos Aires und Prag (alle 2009) und Washington, Schanghai und Johannesburg (alle 2010). Bis 2012 sollen mehr als 350 neue Audi Autohäuser fertiggestellt werden.

Die Typologie des Autohauses gab es bereits, bevor der automobile Themenpark und das Automuseum en vogue kamen. Zumeist beheimatet an der Peripherie oder im Gewerbegebiet, kennt man sie als simple Kisten, deren robuste Farben und Details die Aura der street credibility entfalten. Eines der Autohäuser, das sich in den 1980er-Jahren in dieser Vorstadtszenerie mit einer eigenständigen Architektursprache absetzte, war der ‚Audi Hangar' (von Henn Architekten), dessen Charakteristika ein rundes asymmetrisches Dach und visuell dominante konstruktive Elemente waren. Seitdem haben sich nicht nur die Modellpalette und die Marke Audi verändert. In Zeiten der Renaissance der Städte sollte sich auch der Schauraum dorthin bewegen, wo die Menschen sind, und nicht umgekehrt – und zudem die Präsenz der Marke in den internationalen Metropolen verkörpern. Das Konzept des neuen ‚Audi Terminal' musste kraftvoll und tragfähig genug sein, um die Markenidentität und die qualitätvolle Umsetzung an einer Vielzahl von Standorten zu gewährleisten.

Aus einem Architektenwettbewerb ging der Entwurf von Allmann Sattler Wappner Architekten aus München mit dem Basiskonzept eines Schauraums hervor, der global reproduzierbar ist und an heterogenen Standorten eine durchgängige Identität und Prägnanz aufweist. Die Leitthemen Dynamik, Asymmetrie und Transparenz als wesentliche Merkmale dieser Corporate Architecture wurden in eine flexible konstruktive und räumliche Struktur umgesetzt, deren

soundness, social justice and functional practicality. The connotations of the 'driving pleasure' category of experience are likewise changing. While consumers previously associated driving pleasure with dynamism, speed, freedom, safety and comfort, today they cite rationality, frugality, social responsibility, human closeness and beauty.[5]

SERIES

Like the flagships listed above, the new Audi dealership is also designed to communicate its brand. But here, no cultural typology is brought into play in an effort to transcend the brand image. Nor does the architectural rhetoric perform any daring acrobatics meant to produce something 'out of the ordinary'. At Audi it's all about reprogramming the mundane car dealership, as a series model and with a global identity. This dealership model is to be built worldwide, making the brand instantly recognisable everywhere but with the building configuration adaptable to the context of the location. The theme being revisited and updated here is one with which the architects of early Modernism already made reference to the automobile: standardisation and series, today with the additional factor of local variation. Over 175 projects are currently underway worldwide, including dealerships in Las Vegas, Taipei, Buenos Aires and Prague (all in 2009) and in Washington, Shanghai and Johannesburg (all in 2010). By 2012 more than 350 new Audi dealerships are expected to be completed. The typology of the car dealership already existed before the automotive theme park and the car museum came into fashion. Usually located on the outskirts of a city or on an industrial estate, they are familiar to us as simple boxes whose robust colours and details radiate an aura of street credibility. One of the dealerships that stood out against the characteristic suburban scenery of the 1980s with its own independent architectural vocabulary was the 'Audi Hangar' (Henn Architekten), whose signature touches were a round, asymmetrical roof and visually dominant constructional elements. It's not only the model range and the Audi brand that have changed since then. In a period when cities were experiencing a renaissance, the showroom also had to edge closer to

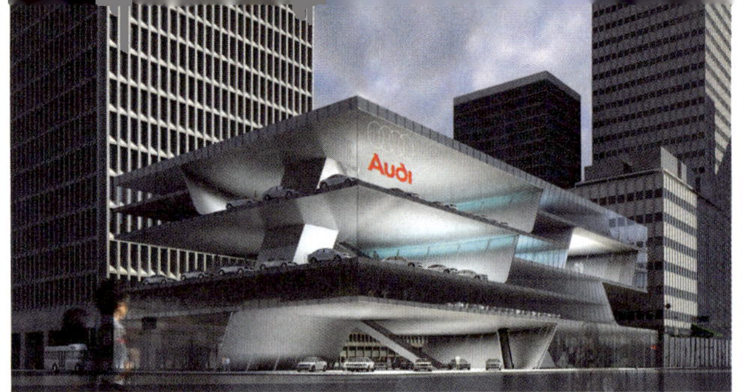
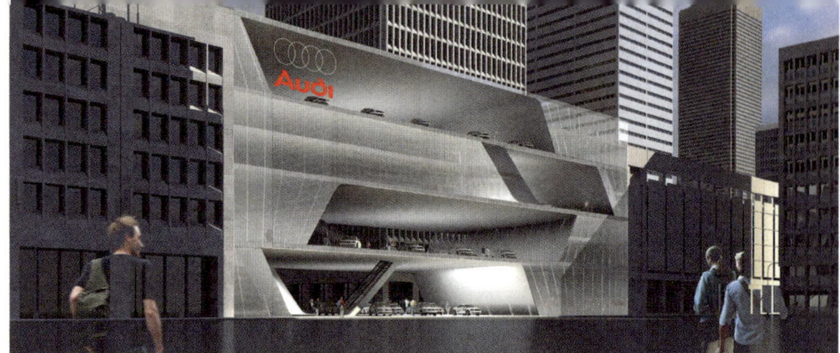

Standort: **Ecksituation** | Corner

Standort: **Blockrandsituation** | Mid-block

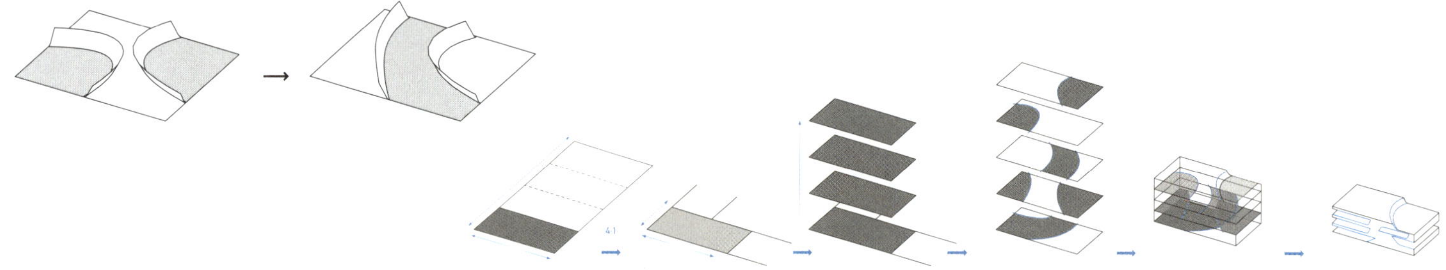

Die Kurve zur Verstärkung der räumlichen Dynamik
Curvature to reinforce the spatial dynamics

Räumliche Stapelung | Spatial stacking

Systematik modular aufgebaut und leicht skalierbar ist, um das Gebäude an die jeweilige Situation anpassen zu können. Durch die Modularität und Flexibilität der Basiskonfiguration kann der Terminal sowohl eingeschossig als auch zwei- oder mehrgeschossig errichtet werden. Mit übereinander angeordneten Ausstellungsräumen lassen sich zahlreiche Fahrzeuge auf einer vergleichsweise geringen innerstädtischen Grundstücksfläche präsentieren. Der Terminal kann in innerstädtischer Lage sowohl in eine Blockbebauung integriert werden, eine Eckrandsituation ausprägen als auch frei stehen. Bestehende Gebäude lassen sich ebenfalls in einen Schauraum mit den typischen Charakteristika umwandeln.

DYNAMIK

Der Baukörper ist funktional und entstammt konzeptionell der Familie der Container. Der Terminal ist eine zeitgemäße Aktualisierung dieser hermetischen Transitkiste und abstrahiert das industrielle Image ins Technoide: Ohne überflüssige Details, umgeben von einer perforierten Aluminiumhaut erscheint das neue Autohaus leicht, durchlässig und beinahe virtuell, da sich die aufgekantete gitterähnliche Alustruktur wie ein Weichzeichner um die Konturen legt. Das Spezifische der Fassade, das überall ablesbar sein soll, besteht im Wechselspiel von geschlossenen Aluminium-Abschnitten und schräg geschnittenen Schauraumfenstern, die mit der orthogonalen Geometrie des Baukörpers kontrastieren. Auch die beiden bestimmenden Materialien – Aluminium und Glas – finden sich überall wieder. Die Fensteröffnungen des Autohauses bilden die Schnittstelle zur Umgebung. Die expressiven Glasflächen ermöglichen zum einen den direkten Einblick in die innere Ausstellungsinszenierung der ‚Kurve'. Gleichzeitig wird die jeweilige Umgebung in den Innenraum einbezogen und sorgt für die lokale Verortung, so wie es auf den Renderings der Machbarkeitsstudien für verschiedene Städte zu sehen ist.

Das asymmetrische Kurvensegment des Ausstellungsraums, auf dem die Fahrzeuge präsentiert werden, simuliert eine reale Straßensituation und prägt das Leitbild der Dynamik. Dieses Element zieht sich durch das ganze Gebäude und wird noch verstärkt durch geneigte Umfassungswände, welche die Kurve im Inneren nachfahren und sich außen an den Schrägen der horizontalen Flächen der Glasschaufenster abbilden.

where the people are, not vice-versa, and also to embody the presence of the brand in international metropolises. The concept for the new 'Audi Terminal' would have to be powerful and workable enough to ensure a clear brand identity and high-quality realisation in a number of different places.

The competition to find an architect was decided in favour of Allmann Sattler Wappner Architekten from Munich, who came up with a basic concept for a showroom that can be globally reproduced, bringing the same identity and striking presence to heterogeneous locations. The guiding themes of dynamism, asymmetry and transparency as the key features of this corporate architecture were translated into a structure with a flexible design and spatial configuration, based on a system made up of modules that can easily be scaled to fit the situation. Thanks to the modularity and flexibility of the basic configuration, the Terminal can be constructed as a one-storey, two-storey, or multi-storey building. With showrooms arranged atop one another, numerous vehicles can be displayed on a relatively small inner-city floor plan. The Terminal can be integrated into an inner-city site or city block, form the corner closing off a block, or be freestanding. Alternatively, existing buildings can be converted into a showroom featuring the typical characteristics.

DYNAMISM

The body of the building is functional and stems conceptually from the container family. The Terminal represents a contemporary update of this hermetic transit box, abstracting the industrial image into a technoid style. Without any superfluous details and surrounded by a perforated aluminium skin, the new car dealership has a light and airy, almost virtual look, the mesh-like aluminium outer structure set on its edge softening the contours like a diffuser scrim. The distinguishing feature of the façade, one that is meant to be legible everywhere the building is constructed, is the interplay between closed aluminium sections and showroom windows cut out on a slant, contrasting with the orthogonal geometry of the main body of the building. We also

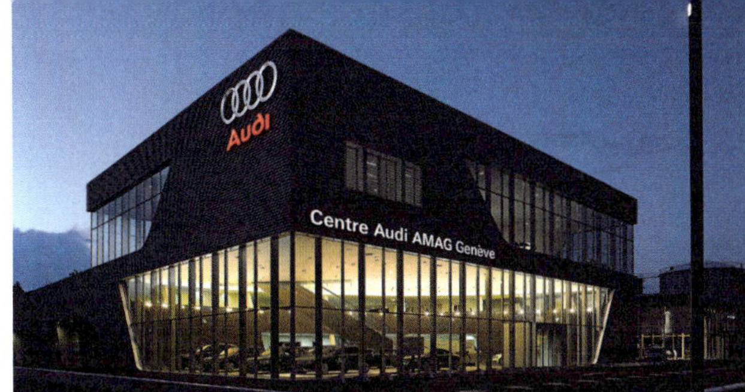

Genf (2008) | Geneva (2008)

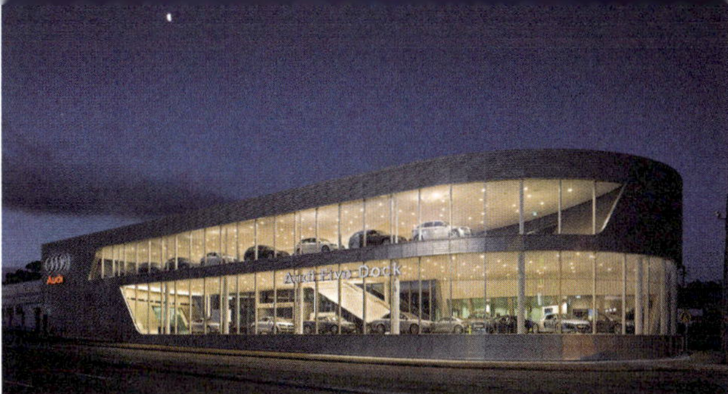

Sydney (2008) | Sydney (2008)

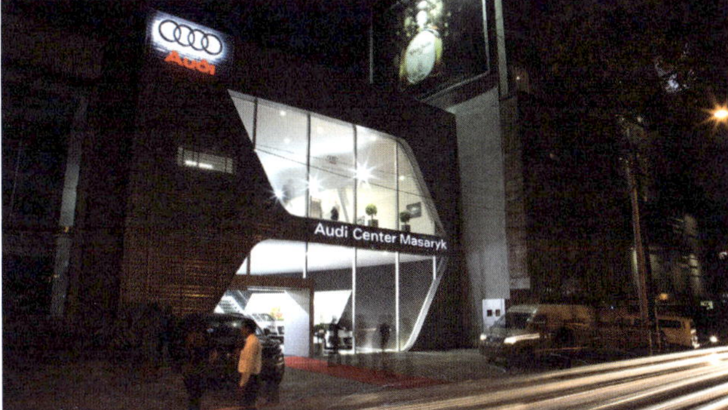

Mexico City (2008) | Mexico City (2008)

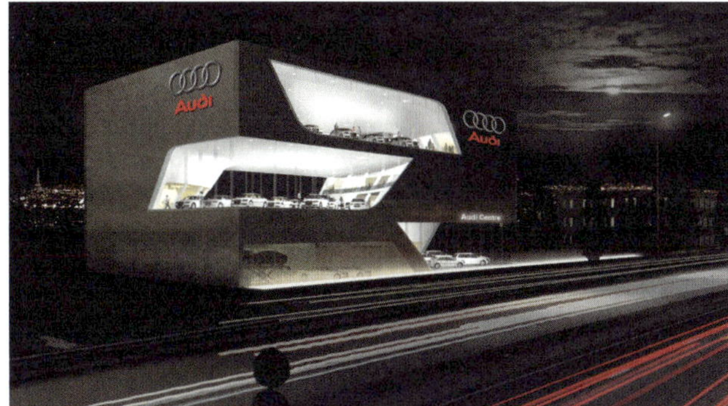

Paris (2011) | Paris (2011)

MANUAL UND PLANUNG

Die Aufgabe der Architekten war es, die maßgeblichen Richtlinien für die Gestaltung unterschiedlicher Gebäude in Form eines Handbuches festzulegen. In einem rund 250-seitigen Manual werden die Basis-Standards für Regeltypen, Varianten und Leitdetails der Baukörper im Kontext und für Fassade, Gebäudestruktur, Ausstellungsraum und Kundenzone vorgegeben. Die Angaben beschränken sich auf Optionen (z. B. für Materialien) oder Richtwerte. So werden beispielsweise keine spezifischen Angaben zur Neigung der Ausstellungswände oder zum Durchmesser einer Ausstellungskurve angegeben, sondern generelle Spielräume. Die endgültige Entscheidung trifft der jeweilige lokale Architekt, der für das Projekt verantwortlich ist. Die vom Münchner Büro Phase 1 entwickelte Möblierung ist ebenfalls standardisiert und kann aufgrund ihrer modularen Struktur an jeden individuellen Baukörper angepasst werden. Ursprünglich sollte auch ein Energiekonzept entwickelt werden, das Anpassungen an die verschiedenen Klimabedingungen zulässt. Doch bekanntlich ist es in der Umwelt- und Klimapolitik bisher nicht gelungen, global gültige Standards festzulegen – was eine einheitliche Planung problematisch macht. Daher soll nun jeweils im Einzelfall gemeinsam mit dem Bauherrn entschieden werden, wie die Architektur so energiesparend wie möglich geplant werden kann, um Heizungs- und Kühlungsanforderungen zu reduzieren.

Der Bau eines Terminals wird von einem lokalen Architekten und dem jeweiligen Händlerbetrieb als Bauherr in Abstimmung mit dem Audi-Importeur des entsprechenden Landes und dem Vertrieb der Audi AG in Ingolstadt durchgeführt. Von Anfang an ist auch der für die jeweilige Region oder das Land zuständige Terminal-Bauberater der Audi AG eingebunden. Nach der gemeinsamen Besichtigung des Grundstücks lädt die Audi AG den ausführenden lokalen Architekten zunächst zu einer mehrtägigen Schulung nach Ingolstadt ein. Das von Allmann Sattler Wappner entwickelte Manual und eine entsprechende Datenbank bilden die Grundlage für die Planung des Terminals in Abstimmung zwischen dem ausführenden lokalen Architekten und dem zuständigen Bauberater der Audi AG. Die Endabnahme des fertiggestellten Gebäudes erfolgt gemeinsam durch den Bauherrn, den ausführenden Architekten und den Bauberater der Audi AG. Neben baulich-technischen Fragen wird hier auch die Umsetzung von CI-Standards überprüft.

find the two dominant materials – aluminium and glass – everywhere we look. The window openings of the dealership form its interface with its surroundings, expressive expanses of glass that allow for a direct view into the interior exhibition setting in the 'curve'. At the same time, the outdoor setting is brought inside, anchoring the showroom in its local environment, as can be seen in the renderings executed for the feasibility studies for the various cities.

The asymmetrically curving segment of the showroom, on which the cars are presented, simulates the real situation on the road and conveys the desired dynamic image. This element recurs throughout the building, reinforced even further by sloping surrounding walls that follow the shape of the inside of the curve and are reflected on the outside by the slanted horizontal surfaces of the showroom windows.

MANUAL AND PLANNING

The architects were asked to set down the applicable guidelines for designing the different showrooms in a manual. On some 250 pages the basic standards for rule types, variations and key details are specified for the main body of the building in its particular context and for the façade, building structure, showroom and customer zone. The specifications merely suggest various options (e.g. for materials) or reference values. The angle of slant for the exhibition walls and the diameter of the exhibition curve are not defined precisely, for example, but are only general guidelines with scope for individualisation. The final decision is up to the local architect responsible for the project. The furnishings developed by Phase 1 in Munich are likewise standardised, but have a modular structure that can be adapted to the particulars of each building. Originally, an energy concept was to have been developed that would allow for adjustment to various climatic conditions. As we know, however, policymakers have not yet been able to establish globally applicable environmental and climate standards – which makes uniform planning problematic. Therefore, it is now up to the architect and client in each case to plan energy-saving architecture that reduces heating and cooling requirements.

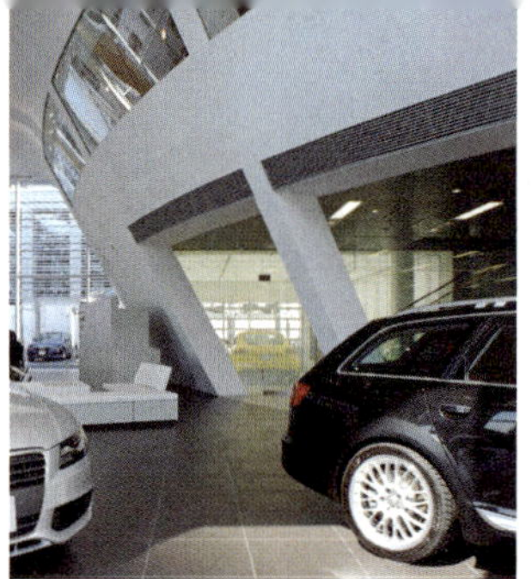
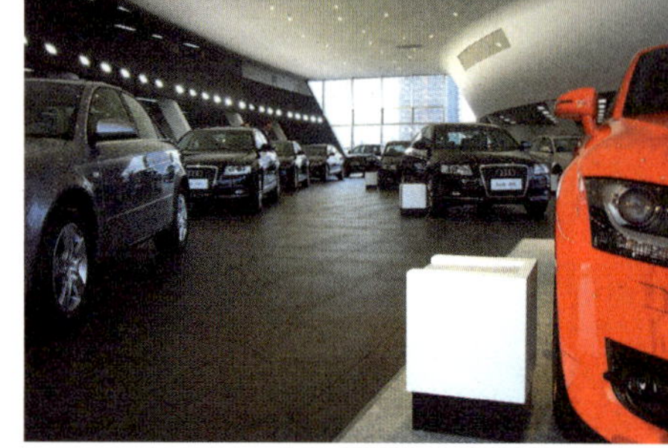

Tokio | Tokyo

Shaoxing (2008) | Shaoxing (2008)

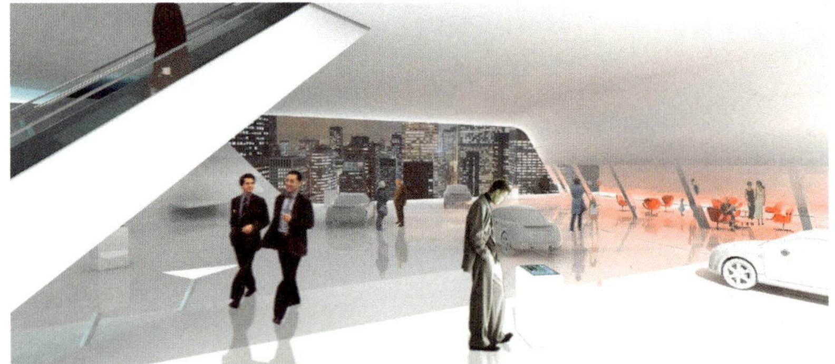
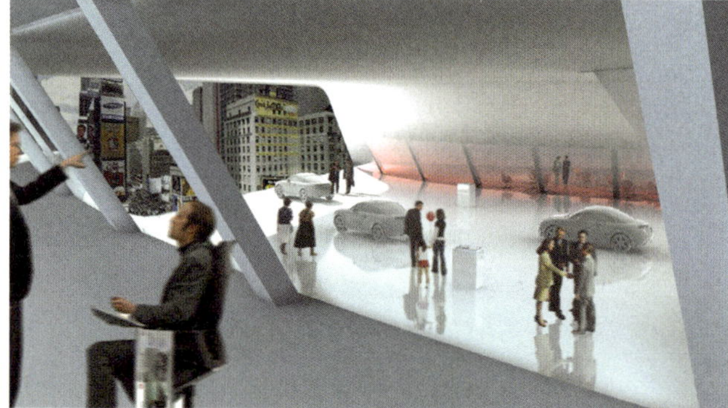

Innenraum Terminal mit schrägen Wänden und Blick auf den urbanen Kontext | Terminal interior with slanted walls and view out onto the urban context

IDENTITÄT

Auch wenn alle Gebäude auf denselben Vorgaben basieren, können die finalen Interpretationen unterschiedlich ausfallen. Ursprünglich überlegten Allmann Sattler Wappner Architekten, die Fassaden je nach Region unterschiedlich auszuführen – in den Rocky Mountains beispielsweise als Holzverschalung, die im Laufe der Jahre silbrig wird. Doch Audi zog es vor, die Markenidentität durch ein einheitliches Bild – Aluminium – auszudrücken. Wichtiger als der Standort ist die Audi-Identität, die bei allen Freiheiten der Umsetzung zur Geltung kommen muss. Le Corbusier plante Architektur als „Zirkulation" und „eine Stadt, die für Schnelligkeit gemacht ist" (Plan Voisin, 1925); der Chicagoer Fertighaushersteller General Houses – in Anlehnung an General Motors – übernahm in den 1930er-Jahren standardisierte Fertigungsmethoden der Automobilindustrie, um, wie sein Werbeslogan verkündete, „Häuser wie Fords" herzustellen.[6] Yona Friedman wiederum zielte in seinem Manifest der mobilen Architektur von 1958[7] darauf ab, dass jede Art von Gebrauch und Aneignung eines Gebäudes durch die Bewohner ermöglicht werden sollte; und die mobilen Räume und Städte der 1960er-Jahre, die Archigram entwarf, waren technologie-optimistische Utopien mit Anleihen an Comics, Science Fiction und der damaligen Raumfahrt. Das Programm der zeichenhaften Advertisement-Architektur verlagerte sich auf eine Dynamik des ‚Außergewöhnlichen', das diese Bauten versinnbildlichen und auf die Produkte übertragen sollen. Das Unschärfemoment, das dieser Forderung unterliegt, liefert bereits die Folie der formalen Allbereitschaft für Gebäude mit einem singulären ‚Wow-Faktor', der eine ganze Generation deutscher Markenarchitekturen prägt.

Angesichts dieser Bauten wirkt der Audi Terminal wie eine subversive Verweigerung der allzu strategischen Selbstzurichtung. Die kulturelle Halbwertzeit von Bildern kann recht kurz sein. Der Terminal kommuniziert nicht ‚retinale' – sprich: formal effektheischende –, sondern adäquate und intelligente konzeptuelle Architektur; kein optisches Wahrnehmungsmarketing, sondern eine nachhaltige architektonische Unternehmenskultur. Er verbindet Straßentauglichkeit mit Branding ohne waghalsige Klimmzüge, kommt verbindlich und unaufgeregt daher, gibt nicht vor, etwas anderes zu sein, als er ist. Das ist seine Stärke. Als smarter Hybrid aus Architektur und Automobil fügt der Audi Terminal sich in die Stadt ein, beinahe wie einer jener infrastrukturellen Knotenpunkte, welche die Identität der globalen Gesellschaft manifestieren.

Each Terminal is designed by a local architect with the respective dealership as client, and in association with the Audi importer in that country as well as Audi AG Sales in Ingolstadt. The Terminal consultant from Audi AG responsible for the region or country concerned is involved in the building project from the outset. After a joint inspection of the building site, Audi AG invites the local architect hired for the project to Ingolstadt for several days of training. The manual put together by Allmann Sattler Wappner and a corresponding database form the basis for the architect and the Audi AG adviser to jointly plan the Terminal. The final inspection of the finished building is made by the client, architect and Audi AG consultant. They examine not only construction and engineering issues but also the implementation of the corporate identity standards.

IDENTITY

Even though all buildings are based on the same set of specifications, the final interpretations can vary considerably. Initially, Allmann Sattler Wappner Architekten considered specifying a few different façades, depending on the region – for example, wood cladding in the Rocky Mountains that weathers to a silver patina over the years. But Audi preferred to express its brand identity by means of a uniform material – aluminium. More important than the location is the Audi identity, which, despite all creative scope, must shine through clearly.

Le Corbusier planned architecture as "circulation" and "a city made for speed" ("Plan Voisin", 1925); the Chicago maker of prefabricated houses General Houses – named after General Motors – adopted the standardised production methods of the automotive industry in the 1930s in order to make "houses like Fords", as its advertising slogan proclaimed.[6] Yona Friedman in turn proposed in his manifesto "Mobile Architecture" (1958)[7] that a building should allow its owners to adapt it to any kind of usage, while the mobile rooms and cities Archigram designed in the 1960s were technologically optimistic utopias with borrowings from comic books, science fiction and space travel.

The popular programme of symbolic advertising architecture shifted

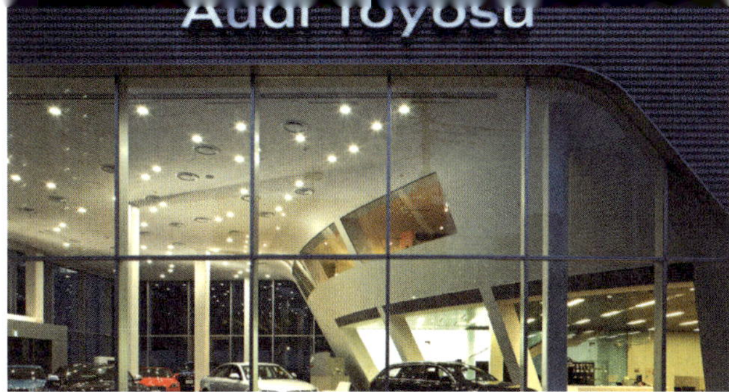

Tokio | Tokyo

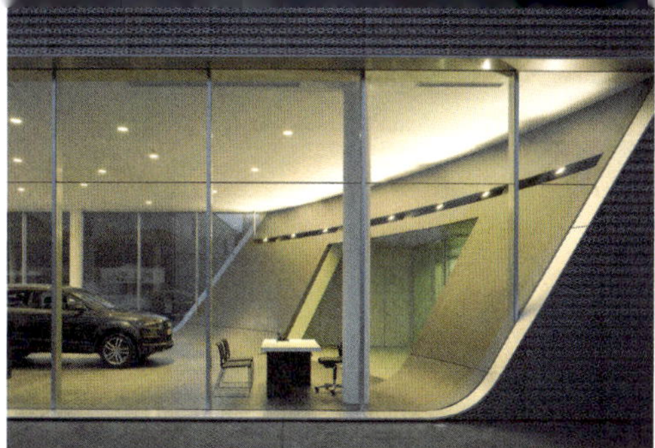

Sydney | Sydney

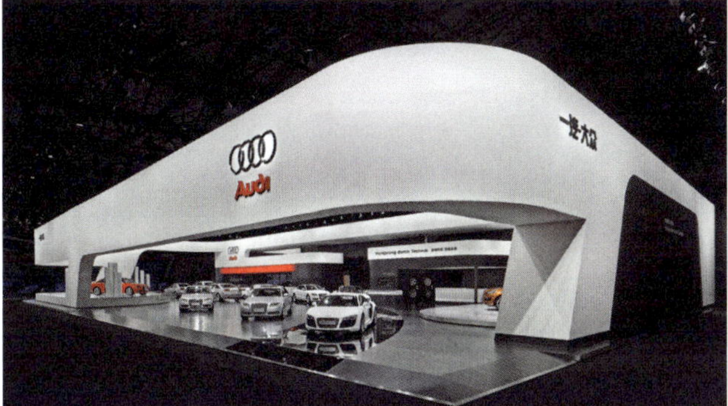

Messestand, Auto Schanghai, 2009 | Trade fair stand, Auto Shanghai, 2009

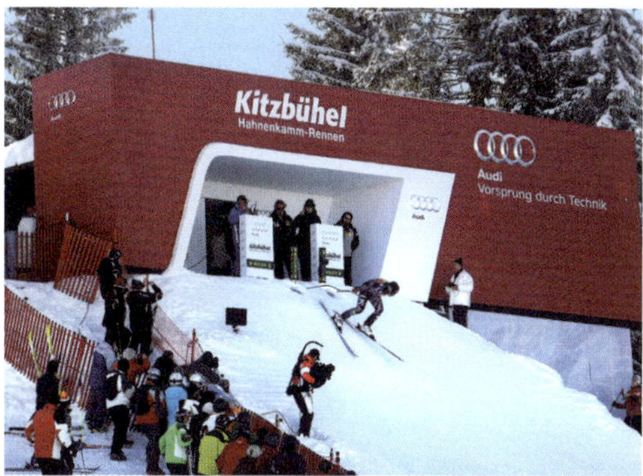

Starthaus des Hahnenkamm-Rennens, Kitzbühel, 2009
Start building for the Hahnenkamm Race, Kitzbühel, 2009

Und er ist mehr, als was er auf den ersten Blick erscheint. Die Komplexität des Konzeptes – in Form des zugrunde liegenden Manuals – erschließt sich erst im Hinblick auf die Serie. Das Konzept verbindet Serie, Marke und Globalität mit Architektur, überschreitet die Realisierung des singulären Gebäudes und schafft die fünfte Dimension, die diesem Markengebäude zugrunde liegt und seine Relevanz ausmacht.

[1] **Le Corbusier, „Ausblick auf eine Architektur", ,Bauwelt Fundamente'.**

[2] **Le Corbusier, „Les 5 Points d'une architecture nouvelle", 1926.**

[3] **Aufwertung von Orten bzw. Marken durch spektakuläre Architektur, die von Star-Architekten geplant wird.**

[4] **„ ... we are promised, that the showroom – like cars themselves - will offer us more and more. The new, bolder, bigger showroom edges the automobile deeper into the consumer's conasciousness, extending the brand into the psychogeography of our cities, spaces that serve our ever-increasing desire for consumer identy.", ,Carchitecture', Birkhäuser, S. 105.**

[5] **GDI Impuls 1. 2009, Wertewandel, S. 12ff.**

[6] **„Houses like Fords" by Douglas Putnam Haskell, in: ,Harper's Magazine', Februar 1934, http://www.harpers.org/archive/1934/02/0018679.**

[7] **„L'Architecture Mobile", 1958; das Manifest gilt zugleich als Gründungsdokument der „Groupe d'études d'architecture mobile (GEAM)".**

toward a dynamic of the 'extraordinary', meant to lend these buildings an emblematic stature that would then be associated with the products. The blurriness of this concept sets a pattern for the universal desire to create buildings with a singular 'wow factor' – an ambition that has shaped a whole generation of German brand architecture. Compared with such buildings, the Audi Terminal seems to represent a subversive denial of an all-too-strategic self-fashioning. The cultural half-life of pictures can be quite short. The Terminal does not communicate 'retinally' – in other words, with formal flamboyance – but rather through appropriate and intelligent conceptual architecture; not through optical awareness marketing, but through a sustainable corporate architectural culture. It combines street credibility with branding without having to turn cartwheels to do so, radiates calmness and authority, and doesn't try to be anything it is not. That is its strength. As a smart hybrid of architecture and automobile, the Audi Terminal blends into the cityscape, almost like one of those infrastructural hubs that manifest the identity of the global society.
And it is more than what it appears to be at first glance. The complexity of the concept - in the form of the manual on which it is based – only reveals itself when one studies the series as a whole. That concept combines series, brand and globality with architecture, exceeding the realisation of a singular building and creating the fifth dimension that makes this brand architecture so relevant.

[1] Le Corbusier, "Ausblick auf eine Architektur", 'Bauwelt Fundamente'.

[2] Le Corbusier, "Les 5 Points d'une architecture nouvelle", 1926.

[3] The upgrading of locations or brands through spectacular architecture designed by star architects.

[4] 'Carchitecture', Birkhäuser, p. 105.

[5] GDI Impuls 1. 2009, Wertewandel, p. 12ff.

[6] "Houses like Fords", by Douglas Putnam Haskell, 'Harper's Magazine', February 1934, http://www.harpers.org/archive/1934/02/0018679.

[7] "L'Architecture Mobile", 1958; the manifesto is also regarded as the founding document of the "Groupe d'études d'architecture mobile (GEAM)".

DEUTSCHER ARCHITEKTUR EXPORT
GERMAN ARCHITECTURE EXPORT

25 – 26

INTERNATIONAL
INTERNATIONAL

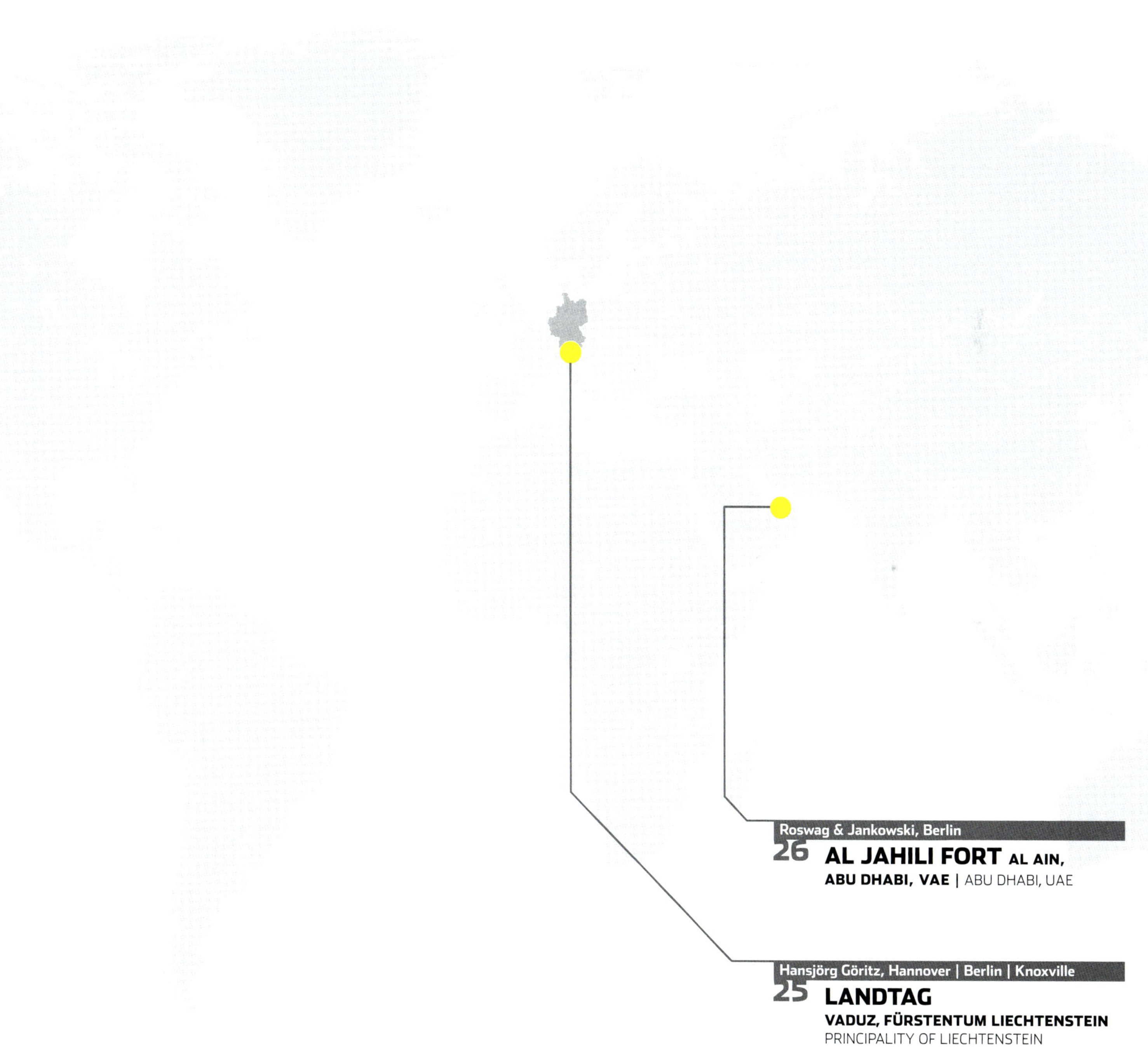

HANSJÖRG GÖRITZ

GEBÄUDE | BUILDING

LANDTAG

TEXT HUBERTUS ADAM

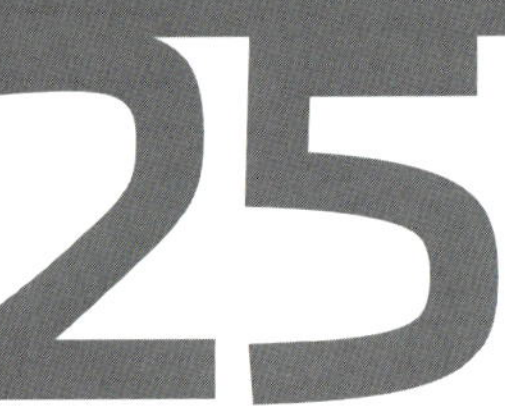

25

ARCHITEKTEN | ARCHITECTS

HansjörgGöritzArchitekturstudio
Professor Hansjörg Göritz
Architekt BDA DWB +
Werkgefährten
Hannover / Berlin / Knoxville
www.hansjoerggoeritz.com

Ausführung in örtlicher
Zusammenarbeit mit | Implemen-
tation in local collaboration with
FrickArchitekten AG
Im Krüz 52
9494 Schaan
www.frick-arch.li

MITARBEITER | TEAM

Anne-Claire von Braunmühl
(Projektleitung Gesamtplanung
project manager, overall planning),
Stefan Höpfinger (Projekt-
leitung Detailplanung | project
manager, detailed planning),
Mario Bearth, Marc Berliat
(Projektleitung Ausführung
project manager, execution),
Fritz Eggenberger (Bauleitung
site manager)

BAUHERR | CLIENT

Land Liechtenstein
vertreten durch das
Hochbauamt Vaduz
represented by the
Building Department Vaduz

TRAGWERK | STRUCTURE

Vogt Ingenieurbüro AG, Vaduz,
Hoch & Gassner AG, Triesen,
Conzett, Bronzini,
Gartmann AG, Chur

KUNST AM BAU | ART

Sabine Laidig
(Plenarsaal | plenary chamber),
Martin Frommelt (Lounge)

FERTIGSTELLUNG | COMPLETION

2008

STANDORT | LOCATION

Städtle 47
9490 Vaduz
Fürstentum Liechtenstein

FOTOS | PHOTOS

Jürg Zürcher

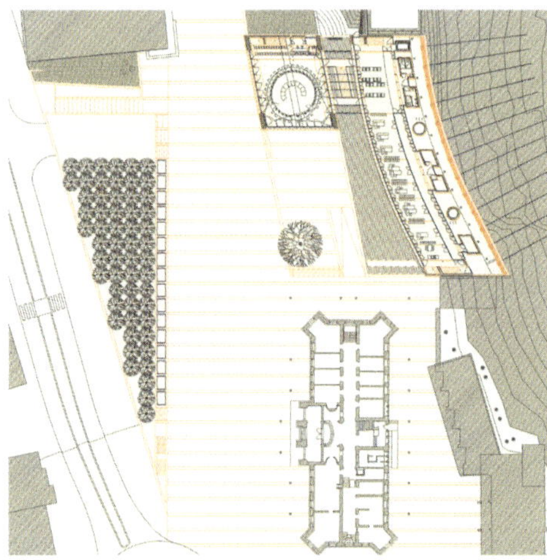

Grundriss 1. Obergeschoss | Floor plan of 1st floor

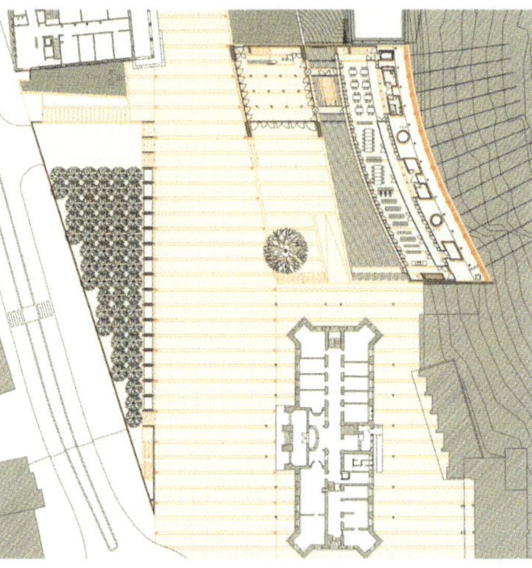

Grundriss Erdgeschoss | Floor plan of ground floor

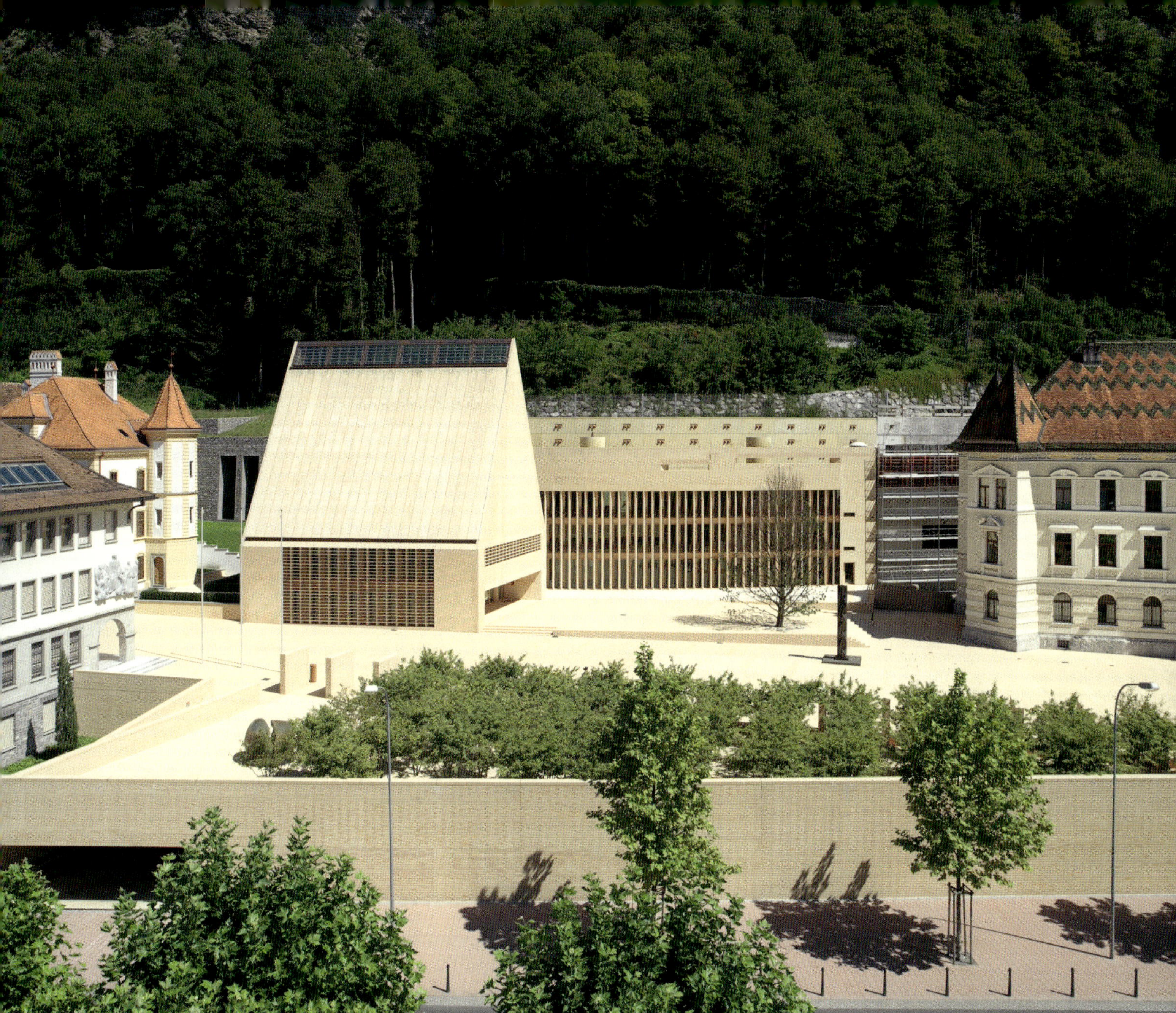

Das Ensemble des Landesparlaments aus geometrischen Baukörpern.
The National Parliament complex is made up of geometric elements.

Seit Mitte Februar des Jahres 2008 steht ein elementares Gebäude im Zentrum von Vaduz, dem Hauptort des Staates Liechtenstein: ganz aus hellem Klinker, mit seinem steil aufragenden Dach steinernes Zelt und Urhütte zugleich. Als Gegenpol zum Schloss hoch oben am steil aufragenden Hang markiert das neue Landtagsgebäude die Macht des Volkssouveräns.

Der Wettbewerb des Jahres 2000, aus dem der Hannoveraner Architekt Hansjörg Göritz als Sieger hervorgegangen war, stellte den zweiten Anlauf dar, ein adäquates Parlamentsgebäude des Kleinstaats zu schaffen und damit das Regierungsviertel in Vaduz zu erweitern. Schon 1987 hatte Luigi Snozzi einen Plan vorgelegt, dem Bereich zwischen Verweserhaus – dem früheren Sitz des fürstlichen Statthalters – und Pfarrkirche zu Zentrumsqualitäten zu verhelfen. Eine Volksabstimmung setzte 1993 Snozzis Konzept einer Hangfußbebauung mit davor stehenden Solitären ein Ende. Immerhin flossen die Ideen in einen Masterplan für das Regierungsviertel ein, dessen Realisierung nun begann. Göritz' Landtagsgebäude bildet das wichtigste Teilstück des Gesamtkonzepts. Mit einem geschwungenen Gebäude, das südlich unmittelbar an die als Stützmauer in Erscheinung tretende Erweiterung des Landesmuseums anschließt, greift er Snozzis Idee der Hangfußbebauung auf. Davor steht, an die nördliche

Since mid-February 2008, an elementary building has been added to the cityscape at the centre of Vaduz, capital of the Principality of Liechtenstein. Made completely of light-coloured clinker brink and with a deeply pitched roof, the structure resembles a stone tent or archetypical hut. As a counterpart to the castle looming above it on its cliff-top perch, the new parliament building proclaims the power of the citizenry below.

The competition held in 2000, won by Hanover architect Hansjörg Göritz, was the second attempt to create an adequate parliament building for the small nation and thus extend the Government Quarter in Vaduz. For the 1987 competition, Luigi Snozzi submitted a plan to help make the area between the Administrator's House (Verweserhaus) – former seat of the princely administrator – and St Florin's parish church feel more like a true city centre. A referendum in 1993 put an end to Snozzi's plans to build a structure at the foot of the cliff with a solitary building standing before it. But his ideas did become part of the master plan for the Government Quarter that then began to take shape.

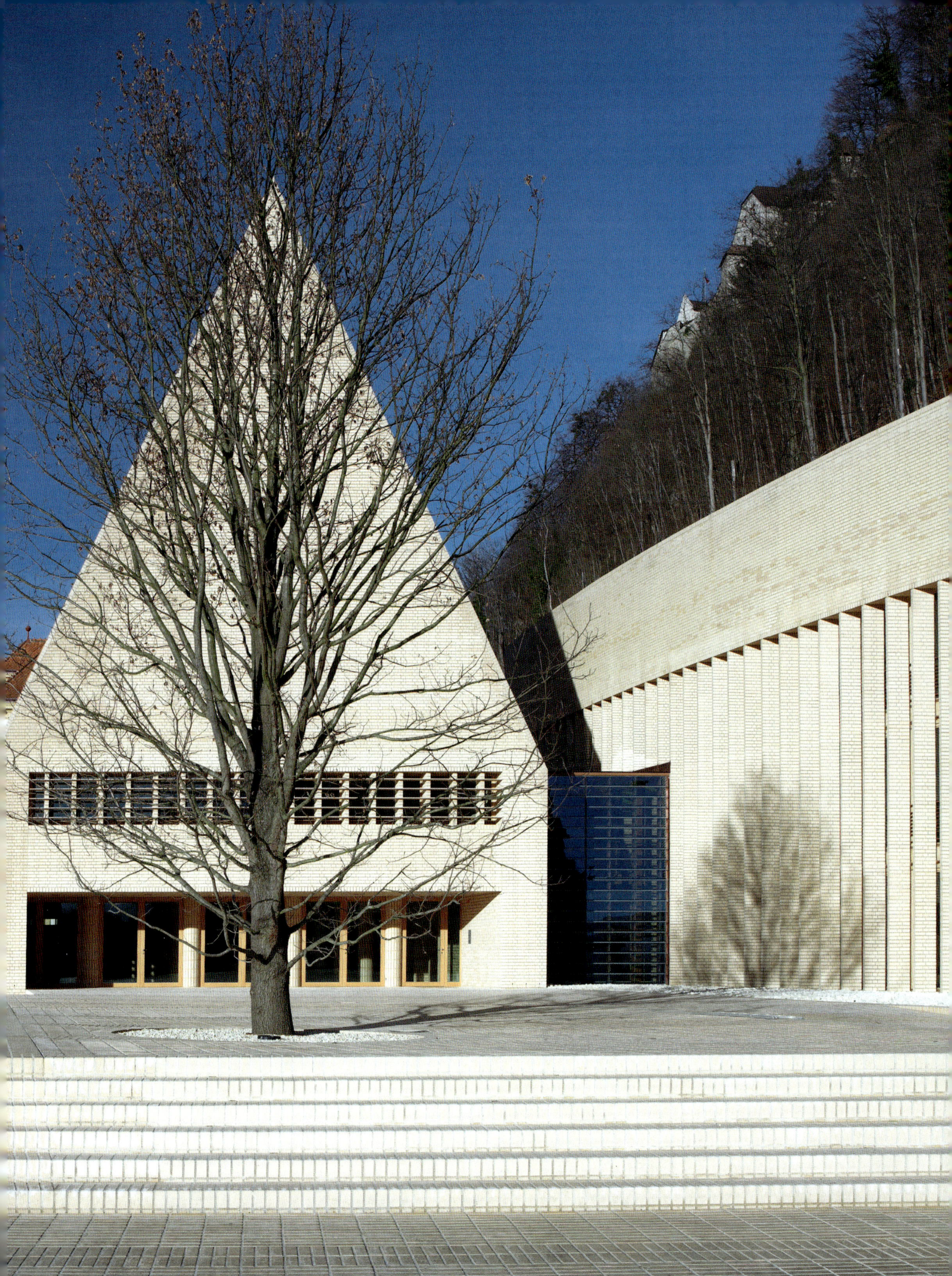

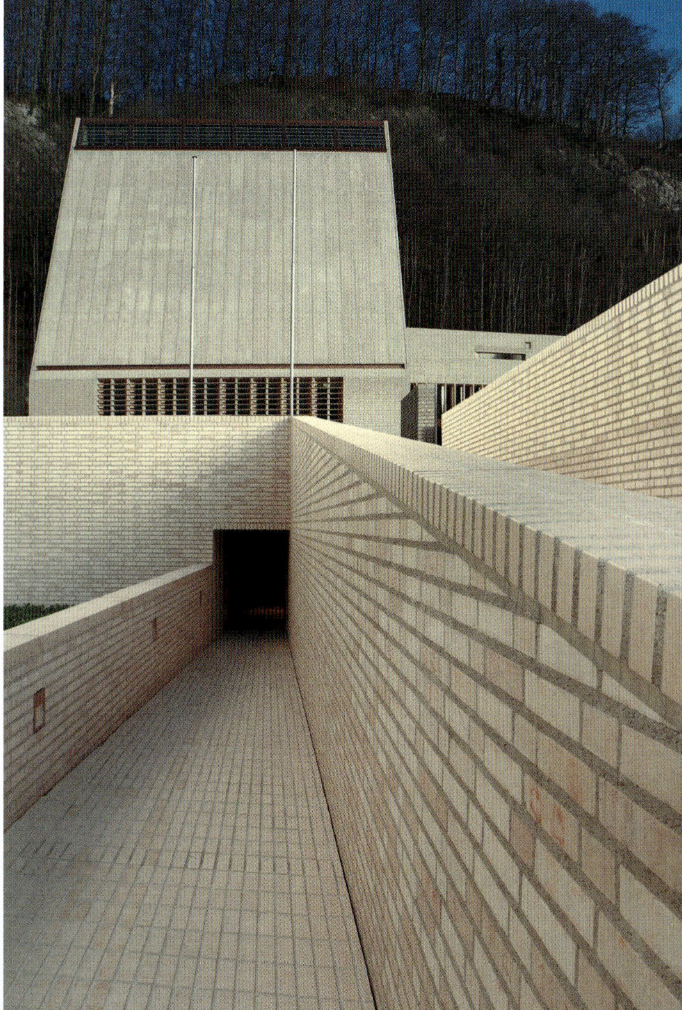

Rampe | Ramp

Grundstücksgrenze gerückt, das neue Parlamentsgebäude – nicht als reiner
Solitär, sondern in die Flucht der Städtlestrasse integriert. Mit seinem
markanten steilen Dach ist es zum neuen Wahrzeichen von Vaduz geworden.
„Hohes Haus" hat Göritz dieses Gebäude von Anbeginn genannt – und intuitiv
jenen Begriff verwendet, mit dem in Vaduz das Parlament bezeichnet wird, im
Gegensatz zum „Grossen Haus" der Regierung. Anders als bei Snozzis Entwurf
stehen „Grosses Haus" und „Hohes Haus" nicht direkt nebeneinander, sondern
– hinterfangen vom „Langen Haus" mit den Büros und Besprechungsräumen
des Landtags – einander gegenüber, so dass sich zwischen ihnen ein großer
Platz aufspannen kann. Dieser übergreift die inzwischen zur Fußgängerzone
umgewandelte Städtlestrasse und findet seinen Abschluss in dem rhythmisch
gegliederten Kabinettsgarten zwischen Äule- und Städtlestrasse. Bepflanzt mit
einem Hain aus weiß blühenden Kupferfelsbirnen, wirkt dieser Bereich wie
ein Hortus conclusus – und erfüllt mit der Mauer zur viel befahrenen Äulestrasse
ganz prosaisch die Funktion einer Lärmschutzwand für das neu entstandene
Forum.
Göritz' Entwurf besticht durch die Verbindung von Pathosformeln und einer
pragmatischen Selbstverständlichkeit. Besonders deutlich offenbart sich das im
„Hohen Haus". Im Parlamentssaal, der sich über der Rundpfeilerhalle des Foyers
im ersten Obergeschoss befindet, ordnete der Architekt die Plätze der Abgeord-
neten wie bei einer Tafelrunde in Kreisform an – und wählte den baulichen
Archetypus eines steilen (hier falschen) Gewölbes aus Ziegelstein. Man mag an
Kornhallen denken, an Kathedralen oder an geschichtete Steinhäuser des
südlichen Europas: Göritz schafft Luft über dem Parlament – gleichsam einen
spirituellen Raum, der sich über dem durch die Ziegelsteinpfeiler und die brise-
soleils aus Tonplatten belichteten Arbeitsraum öffnet. Repräsentative Geste und
alltägliche Arbeitswelt finden so zusammen. Dazu trägt die subtile Kunstinstal-
lation der Berliner Künstlerin Sabine Laidig ebenso bei wie die Tatsache, dass
Göritz in die Fugen zwischen den Ziegeln des Gewölbes Wollfilz integrieren ließ,
um einen kathedralartigen Hall zu vermeiden.
Sämtliche Besprechungssäle, Büros und sonstigen Nebenräume ordnete Göritz
im dreigeschossigen, mit einer Dachterrasse bekrönten Langhaus an, das, vom
Berghang abgerückt, von zwei Seiten belichtet wird.
Eine klare modulare Geometrie verbindet Kabinettsgarten, Platz und Bauten, deren
Oberflächen aus einem einzigen Material bestehen: schmalen, gelblichockerfar-
benen und somit warm wirkenden Ziegelsteinen eines Herstellers aus dem
Schweizer Jura. Kompliziert wurde die Geometrie dadurch, dass die Langseite

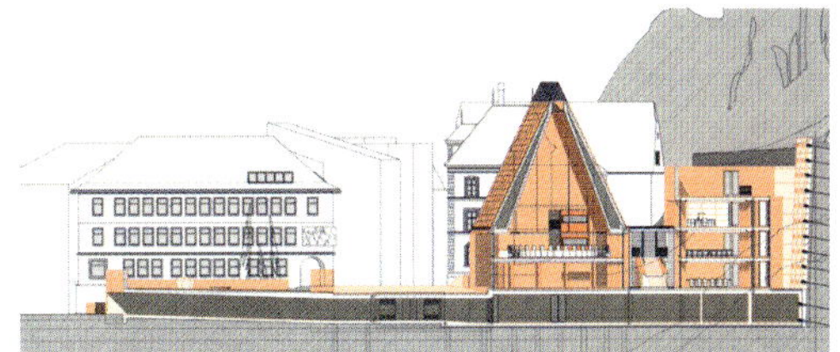

Schnitt | Section

Göritz's parliament building is the key component of this total concept.
With a curving building directly adjacent at the south to the State
Museum extension, which forms a retaining wall set against the slope,
Göritz's plan takes up Snozzi's idea of a structure hugging the side of
the hill. Before it stands the new parliament building, pushed to the
northern edge of the site – not as a purely solitary structure, but rather
falling into line with the buildings along Städtlestrasse. With its
strikingly pitched roof, the parliament has given Vaduz a new
landmark. Göritz referred to this building from the very start as the
"High House" – intuitively employing the same term used in Vaduz to
refer to the parliament, in contrast with the "Big House" of the
government administration. Unlike in Snozzi's design, the "Big House"
and the "High House" do not stand directly adjacent to each other,
but rather – set against the "Long House", holding parliamentary
offices and conference rooms – across from one another, with a large
square spreading out between them. The square overlaps
Städtlestrasse, which has now been converted into a pedestrian zone,
and ends in a rhythmically organised walled garden between
Äulestrasse and Städtlestrasse. Planted with a grove of white-blos-
somed juneberry trees, this area has the feeling of a hortus conclusus,
and – together with the wall – fulfils the very prosaic function of
protecting the newly created forum from the noise and bustle of
Äulestrasse.

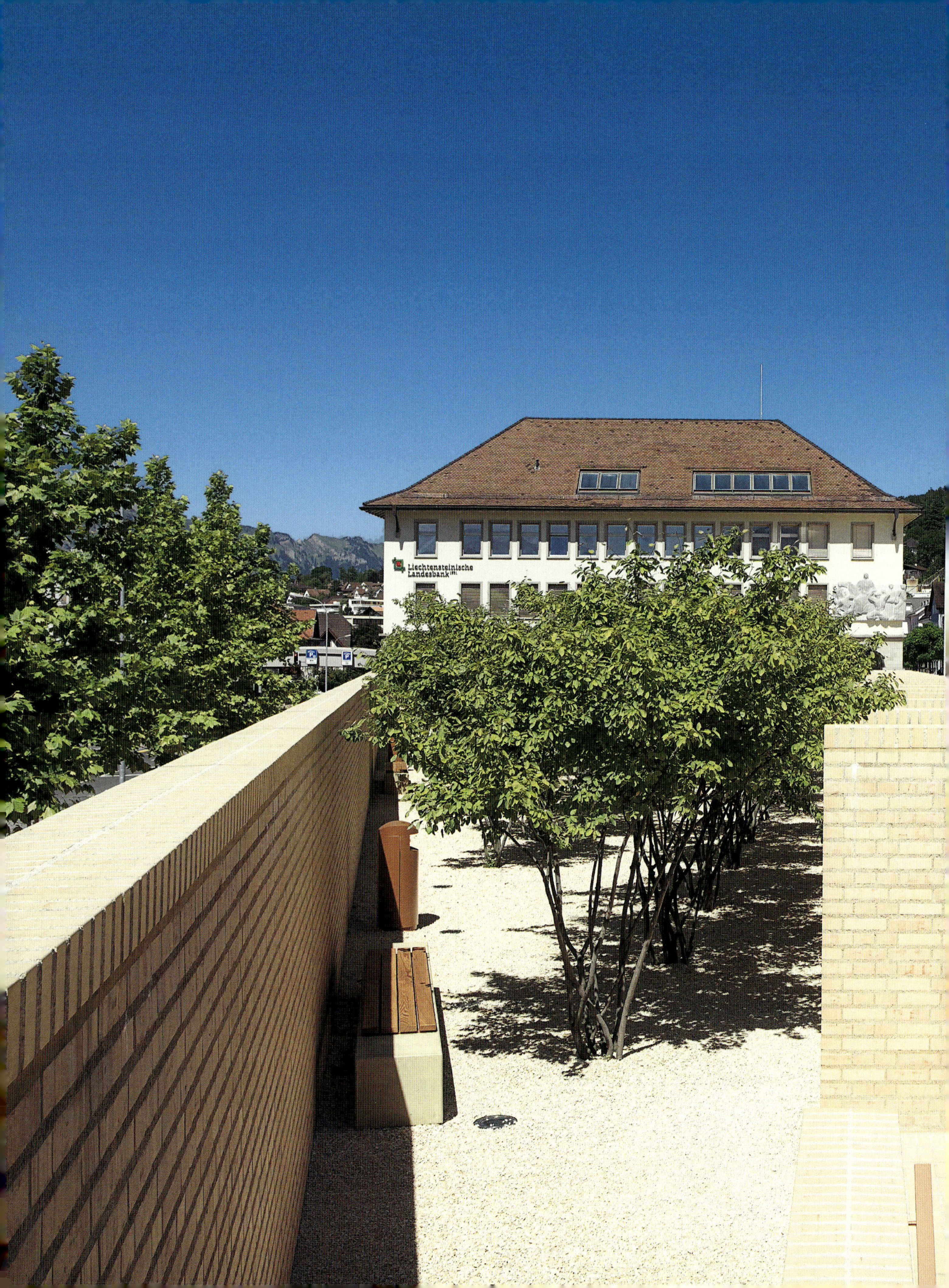

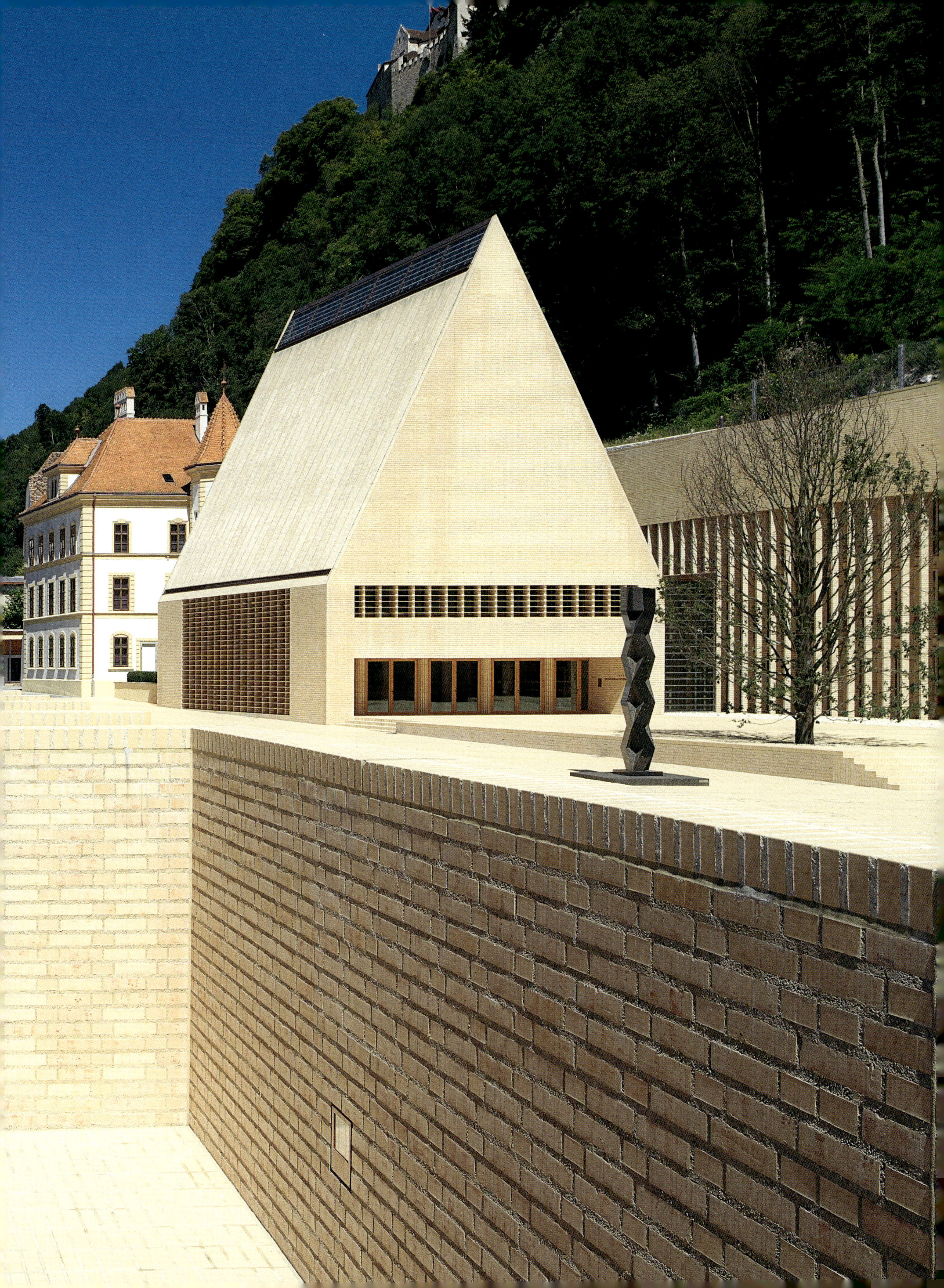

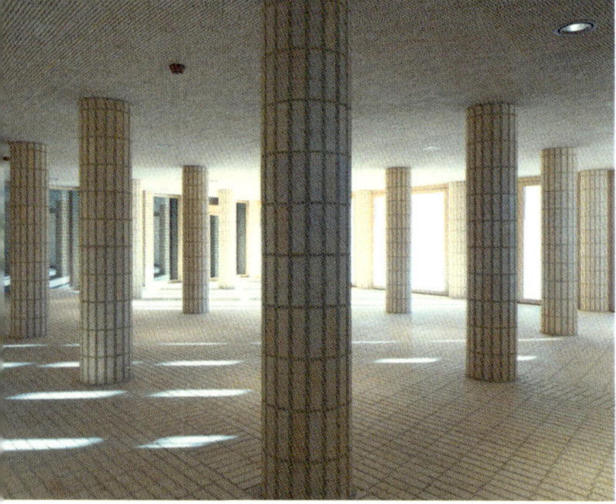

Eine Rundpfeilerhalle als Foyer für das „Hohe Haus"
A round-pillared hall as foyer of the "High House"

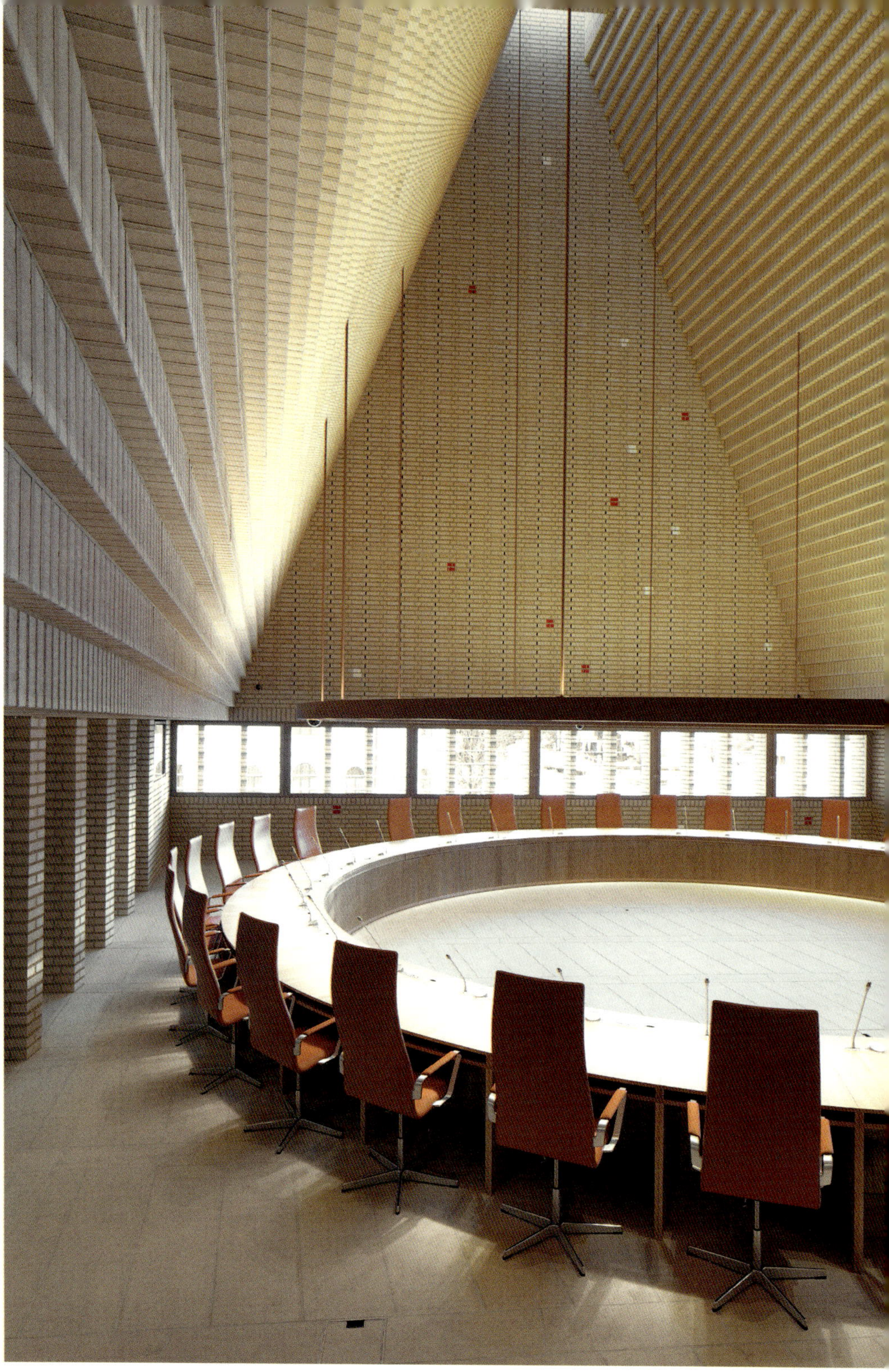

Der Parlamentssaal | Plenary Chamber

des „Hohen Hauses" durch eine imaginäre Linie zwischen Regierungsgebäude und Verweserhaus definiert ist, so dass der Grundriss ein Parallelogramm darstellt. Das Langhaus hingegen folgt der konvexen Kurve des Hangs.

Mit einer Präzision, wie sie anderenorts kaum möglich wäre, ist es dem Architekten und den ausführenden Handwerkern gelungen, die Herausforderung zu bewältigen. Entstanden ist ein durch Konsistenz, Präzision und urbane Setzung überzeugendes Ensemble.

Göritz's design appealingly combines emotion-evoking formulas and a pragmatic matter-of-factness. This is particularly notable in the "High House". In the Plenary chamber, located on the upper floor above a round-columned foyer, the architect arranged the representatives' seats at a round table, with all the allusions that invokes. Overhead, he chose the architectural archetype of a brick vault (in this case a fake one), whose aspect summons up images of granaries, of cathedrals, or of the layered stone houses of southern Europe. With it Göritz creates air space above the parliament – and at the same time a spiritual space that opens up above the workspace with its brick pillars and brise-soleils made of earthenware slabs. Ceremonial gesture and the workaday world are thus brought together. Contributing to this cohesion is the subtle art installation by Sabine Laidig from Berlin as well as the wool felt that Göritz integrated into the joints between the bricks of the vault in order to avoid cathedral-like echoes.

All conference rooms, offices and other ancillary rooms are arranged in the "Long House", crowned by a rooftop terrace and set far enough away from the slope to receive light on two sides.

A clear modular geometry unites the enclosed garden, square and buildings, all of which have surfaces of a single material: narrow bricks in a warm ochre-yellow tone from a manufacturer in the Swiss Jura region. The geometry is complicated by the fact that the longitudinal side of the "High House" is defined by an imaginary line drawn between the government building and the Administrator's House, giving the ground plan a parallelogram shape. The "Long House" by contrast follows the convex curve of the cliffside.

The architect and the craftsmen working on the project have managed to master the challenge presented by this project with a precision that would hardly have been possible in any other location. The result is an ensemble with a singularly satisfying consistency and precision – one that has created an attractive new urban setting.

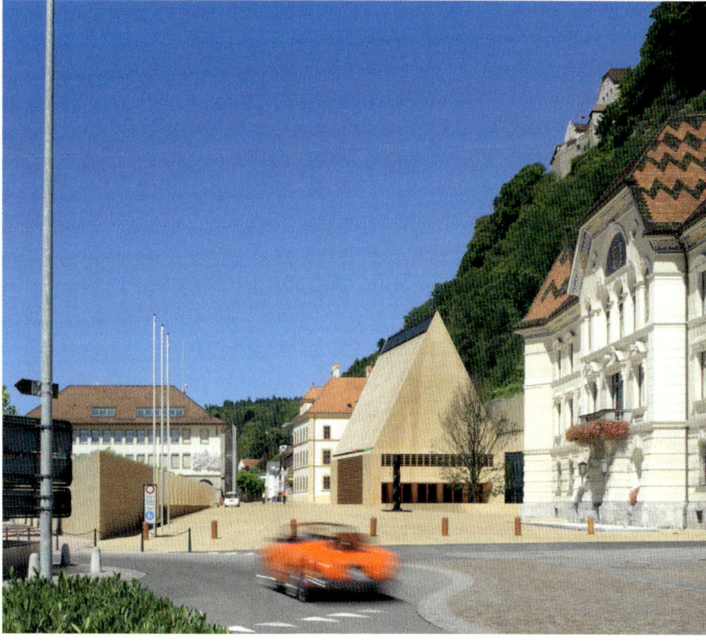

Das Forum des Landesparlaments | The Forum of the National Parliament

ROSWAG & JANKOWSKI

GEBÄUDE | BUILDING

AL JAHILI FORT

TEXT FRIEDERIKE MEYER

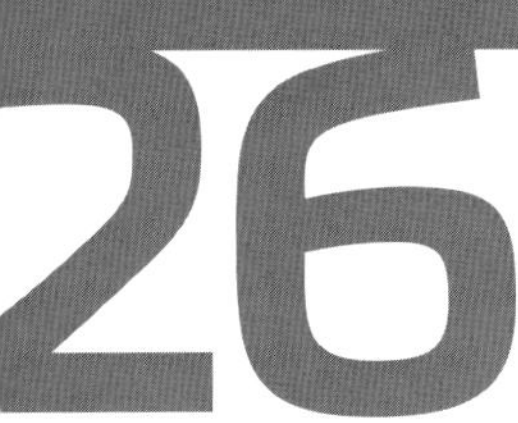

26

ARCHITEKTEN | ARCHITECTS

Roswag & Jankowski Architekten
Lehrter Straße 57, Haus 4
10557 Berlin
www.werk-a.de

MITARBEITER | TEAM

Eike Roswag, Guntram Jankowski,
Marine Miroux, Jan Schreiber,
Axel Huhn, Felix Affeld

BAUHERR | CLIENT

Abu Dhabi Authority for
Culture and Heritage (ADACH)
www.cultural.org.ae

TRAGWERK | STRUCTURE

ZRS Architekten Ingenieure
Christof Ziegert, Uwe Seiler

LANDSCHAFTSARCHITEKTEN
LANDSCAPE ARCHITECTS

Freianlage.de
Landschaftsarchitektur
Marko Höhn

**AUSSTELLUNGSGESTALTUNG,
GRAFIKDESIGN | EXHIBITION
DESIGN, GRAPHIC DESIGN**

Roswag & Jankowski Architekten
Designstudio Christiane Liebert
www.ch-liebert.de

FERTIGSTELLUNG | COMPLETION

Dezember 2008 | December 2008

STANDORT | LOCATION

Al Jahili Fort
Al Ain
Abu Dhabi, VAE
www.cultural.org.ae

FOTOS | PHOTOS

Torsten Seidel

Schnitt | Section

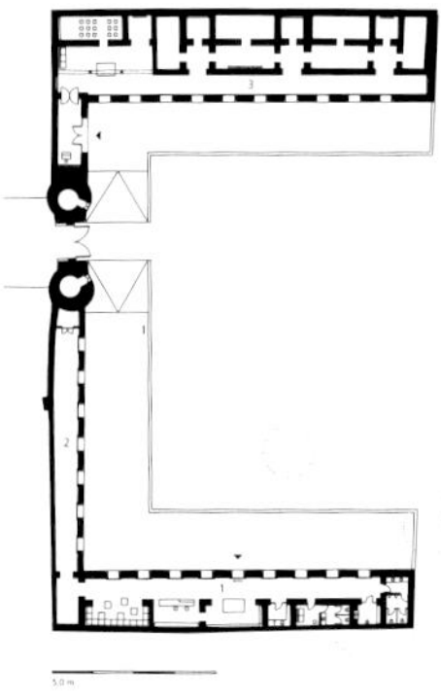

Grundriss | Floor plan

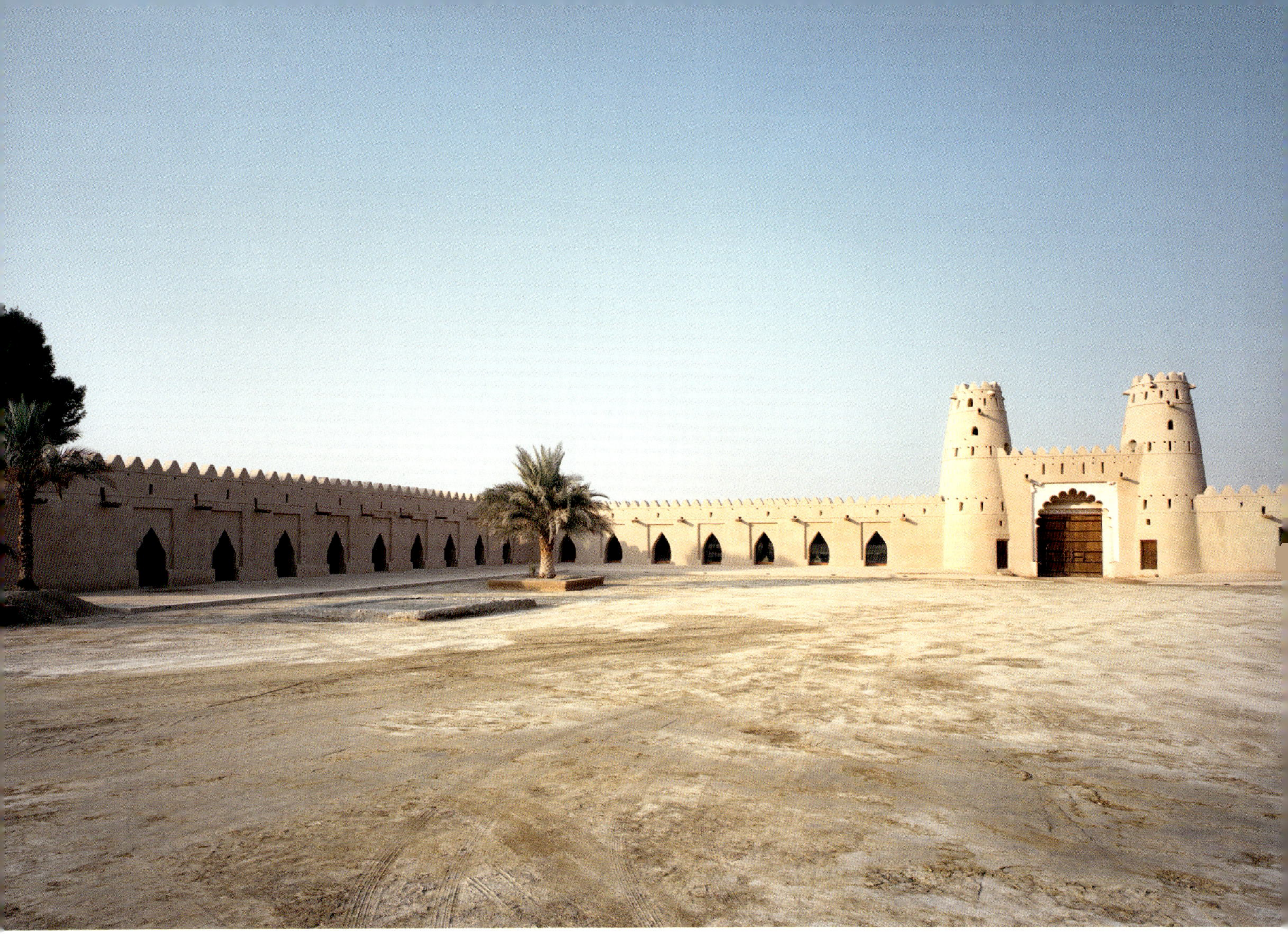

Hofansicht | Courtyard view

Luxushotels, Hochhäuser und Shoppingmalls. Mit diesen Klischees sind die Vereinigten Arabischen Emirate schnell erklärt. Doch 140 Autobahnkilometer abseits vom Bauboom an der Küste sucht die Oasenstadt Al Ain eine andere Identität. Als es um die Sanierung des Jahili Forts ging, waren die Berliner Eike Roswag und Christoph Ziegert gefragt: Sie haben Erfahrung mit Lehmbauten. Das Jahili Fort ist die berühmteste Festungsanlage der Vereinigten Arabischen Emirate. Sein runder Wachturm dient als Logo eines Trinkwasserherstellers, als Bild auf der 50 Dirham Note, und er hat dem UAE-Pavillon auf der Expo in Hannover Modell gestanden. Das Fort, Ende des 19. Jahrhunderts zur Verteidigung der Wasserquellen gebaut, steht für die Bautradition der Wüste: dicke Lehmwände und Dachbalken aus geviertelten Palmenstämmen.
Um diese Tradition kümmert sich die Abu Dhabi Authority for Culture and Heritage (ADACH) gemeinsam mit iranischen Geologen, britischen Archäologen und Handwerkern aus Deutschland. Seit ihrer Gründung vor drei Jahren

Luxury hotels, high rises and shopping malls: these are the clichés commonly used to describe the United Arab Emirates. 140 kilometres by motorway from the building boom on the coast, however, the oasis of Al Ain is searching for a different kind of identity. When plans were made to restore Jahili Fort, the developers called on Berlin architects Eike Roswag and Christoph Ziegert with their expertise in earth construction.
Jahili Fort is the most famous fortification in the United Arab Emirates. Its round watchtower serves as the logo for a drinking water supplier, as a picture on the 50-dirham note, and was used as model for the UAE pavilion at the World Expo in Hanover. Used to defend freshwater springs in the late 19th century, the fort stands for desert building traditions: thick earthen walls and roof beams of quartered palm trunks. This tradition is being preserved by the Abu Dhabi Authority for Culture and Heritage (ADACH), with the help of Iranian geologists, British archaeologists and craftsmen from Germany. Founded three years ago, the authority is in charge of managing Abu Dhabi's architectural heritage. This includes the 60 or so historic earthen structures in Al Ain, a city that grew up out of what were once seven separate oases and today has a population of half a million. Visitor centres are

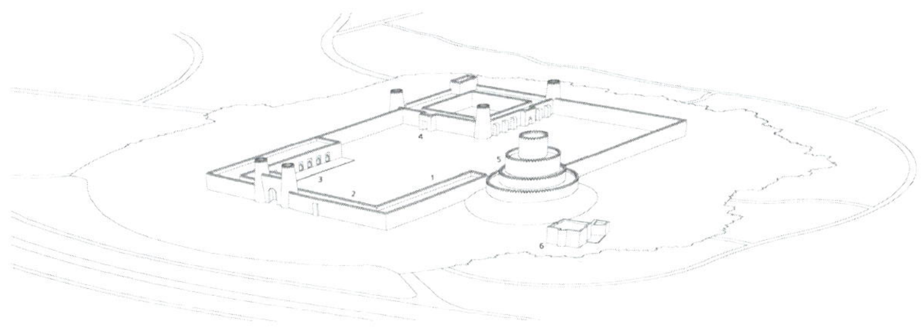

Axonometrie | Axonometry

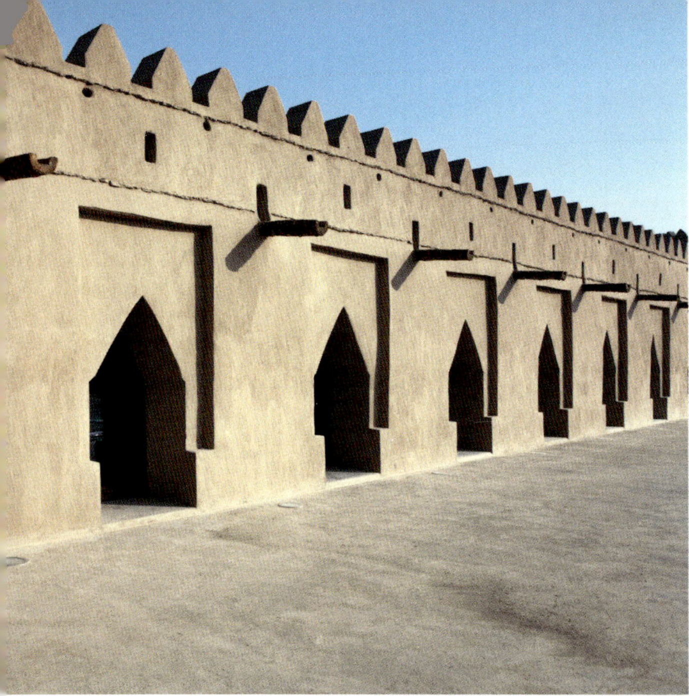

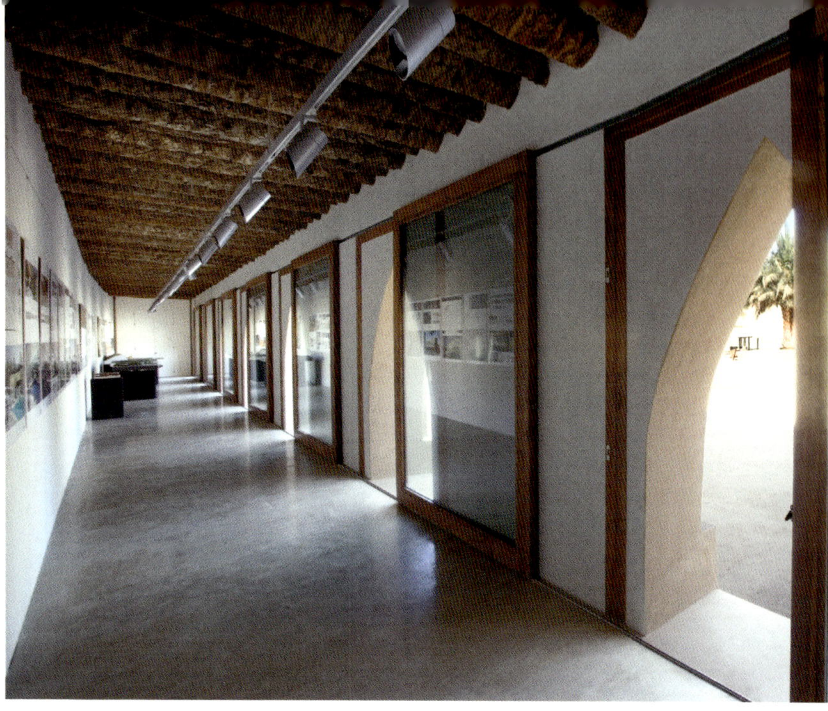

Fassadendetail | Façade detail

Die Öffnungen der Außenwände wurden mit Sonnenschutzglas geschlossen.
The openings in the outer walls are fitted with sun protection glass.

verwaltet die Behörde das baukulturelle Erbe des Emirats Abu Dhabi. Dazu gehören die rund 60 historischen Lehmbauten in Al Ain, einer Stadt, die aus einst sieben Oasen zusammengewachsen ist und heute eine halbe Million Einwohner zählt. Bei den Oasen sind Besucherzentren geplant, ein Hotel und ein neuer Markt. Wenn die Touristen genug haben von den klimatisierten Fantasiewelten in Dubai, so die Hoffnung, kommen sie nach Al Ain, um die Geschichte des Landes zu erkunden. Dr. Sami Al Masri, Leiter der Planungsabteilung, spricht von der Suche nach Identität und von kulturellem Dialog. Beim Umbau des Forts will er mit dem Berliner Büro Roswag & Jankowski Architekten ein Paradebeispiel für die Potenziale des Lehmbaus schaffen. Aufgabe der Architekten war es, die ungenutzte Anlage als Besucherzentrum mit Buchladen und Café und für eine Dauerausstellung über den britischen Reiseschriftsteller und Fotografen Wilfred Thesiger herzurichten.

Bereits während der Entwurfsphase wurde den Architekten bewusst, dass der Umbau mit Denkmalpflege nach deutscher Auffassung nicht viel zu tun haben würde. Sie konnten weder auf Untersuchungen der Bausubstanz, noch auf ausreichend Informationen über vorherige Nutzungen zurückgreifen. So mussten sie interpretieren oder einfach Annahmen treffen. Ihre Strategie: Das Charakteristische stärken und durch Notwendiges für die neue Nutzung ergänzen. Das Ziel: Die lokalen Baustoffe (wieder)verwenden – Lehm für Wände und Böden, Palmstämme und -blätter für das Dach.

Drei Flügel der Festungsanlage zum Museum umnutzen, hieß, ein konstantes Innenraumklima zu gewährleisten, vor allem während der bis zu 50 Grad heißen Sommertage. Roswag & Jankowski Architekten verschlossen die Öffnungen der 90 Zentimeter dicken Außenwände zwar mit Sonnenschutzglas und dämmten das Dach, eine Klimatisierung war trotzdem nötig. In den Wänden integrierten sie ein Kaltwassersystem, das durch Strahlungskühle angenehme Temperaturen garantiert. Zum Einbau haben sie den alten Lehmputz heruntergenommen, eingesumpft, durchgetreten und nach Installation der Leitungen wieder aufgebracht. Er wurde nicht wie früher üblich mit den

planned for the oases, along with a hotel and a new market. And when tourists have had their fill of the air-conditioned fantasy world of Dubai, hopes are that they will come to Al Ain to explore the history of this land. Dr. Sami Al Masri, director of the planning department, speaks of the search for identity and of cross-cultural dialogue. He hopes that the reconstruction of the fort with the help of Roswag & Jankowski Architekten from Berlin will become a showcase example of the potential offered by earth construction. The architects' brief was to transform the unused complex into a visitor centre with bookstore and café including a permanent exhibition on British travel writer and photographer Wilfred Thesiger.

Already during the planning phase the architects realised that this reconstruction project would not have much to do with historic preservation in the German sense. They were unable to draw on examinations of the building fabric or adequate information on previous uses and therefore had to come up with their own interpretations, or simply venture assumptions. The strategy they chose was to emphasise what was characteristic about the structure and add what was necessary for new uses. And their goal was to use or re-use local building materials – earth for walls and floors, palm trunks and leaves for the roof.

Converting three wings of the fortress into a museum meant creating a constant interior climate, especially on summer days when temperatures soar up to 50 degrees. Roswag & Jankowski Architekten fitted the openings in the 90-centimetre-thick outside walls with sun protection glass and insulated the roof, but they still had to install air conditioning. They built a cold-water system into the walls that guarantees pleasant temperatures through radiation coolness. To install the system, they took down the old loam

Händen verschmiert, sondern mit Richtscheiten glatt gezogen.
Die Kombination von traditioneller Bauweise und handwerk-
licher Präzision ist die augenscheinlichtste Qualität des
Projekts. „Je länger wir im Ausland arbeiten", resümiert Eike
Roswag den einjährigen Bauprozess, „desto besser lernen wir
die Regeln schätzen, die daheim immer als Hindernis
erscheinen." Deshalb haben Handwerker aus Deutschland die
indischen Arbeiter vor Ort ausgebildet – ein Aspekt des nach-
haltigen Bauens, der bei Roswag & Jankowski Architekten
ebenso dazugehört wie ein aufgeräumtes Design.
Mit den Möbeln und Leuchtobjekten aus weißem Corian, in die
dezente Ornamente gefräst sind, lassen sie westlichen Lifestyle auf östliche Tradition treffen. Kein technischer Schalter,
kein Ventil stört den Raumeindruck. Zurückhaltung lautet die
Botschaft, und - Lehm muss nicht immer nur braun sein. Die
Wände in den Kabinetten sind mit grauem Clayfix-Lehmfeinputz
veredelt, damit die Ästhetik der Wilfred-Thesiger-Fotografien in
den grafitfarbenen Rahmen besser zur Geltung kommt.
In den 1940er-Jahren hatte Thesiger als erster Europäer mit den
Beduinen das „Leere Viertel" der arabischen Wüste durchquert.
Seine Bilder erzählen vom Leben vor dem Ölboom, als es auf
dem Gebiet der heutigen Vereinigten Arabischen Emirate nur
Zelte, Lehmhäuser und Palmengärten, nur Beduinen und Kamele
gab – eine Zeit, deren wenige verbliebene Spuren erhalten und
mithilfe aus Deutschland wieder nutzbar gemacht werden
sollen.

plaster, soaked it, stamped it to an even consistency
and, after installing the supply lines, put it back on
the walls again. It was not smeared on by hand as
in the old days, but instead smoothed on with a
straightedge. The combination of traditional building methods and precise workmanship is the most
striking quality of the project. "The longer we work
abroad," says Eike Roswag, summing up the one-
year construction process, "the more we learn to
appreciate the rules that always seem such a
hindrance at home." This is why craftsmen from
Germany trained the Indian workers on site – an
aspect of sustainable building that is just as essential for Roswag & Jankowski Architekten as clear
design.
Thanks to furniture and lighting objects of white
Corian with restrained milled ornament, western
lifestyle meets eastern tradition. No technical switch-
es, valves or outlets disrupt the harmonious look of
these spaces. Understatement is the message here,
along with the news that earth doesn't always have
to be brown. The walls in the exhibition rooms are
finished with fine grey Clayfix plaster to better
bring out the aesthetic of Wilfred Thesiger's photographs with their graphite-coloured frames.
In the 1940s Thesiger was the first European to
cross the 'Empty Quarter' of the Arabian Desert.
His pictures tell of life before the oil boom, when on
the territory of today's United Arab Emirates there
was nothing but tents, earthen houses and palm
gardens, only Bedouins and camels. The few traces
that have survived from this period are now to be
preserved and, with help from Germany, put to good
use again.

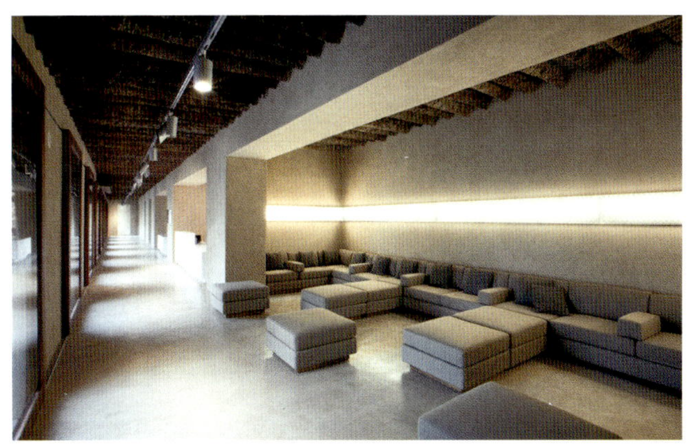

Lokale Baustoffe: Lehm für Wände und Böden, Palmstämme
und -blätter für das Dach | Local materials: earth for walls and
floors, palm trunks and leaves for the roof

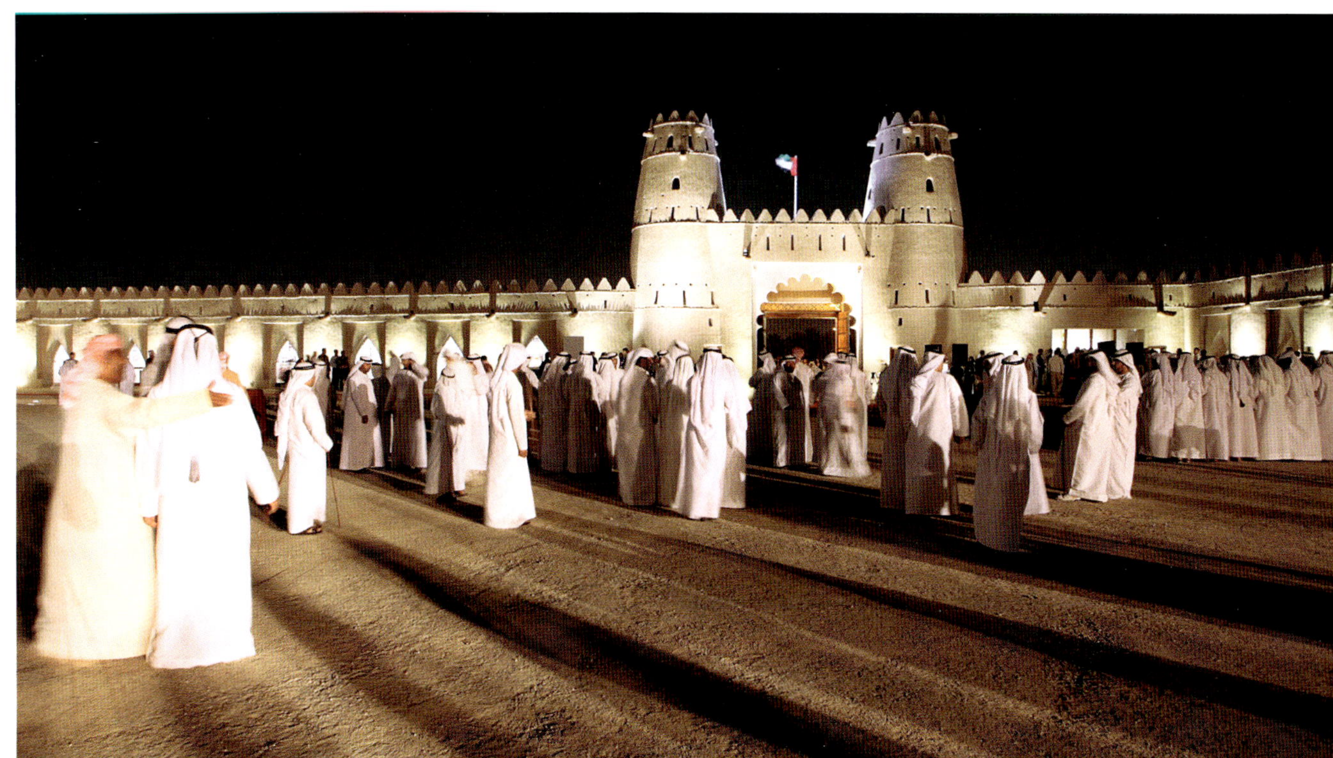

Eröffnung des
Forts | Opening
of the fort

DAM JAHRESBERICHT 2009
DAM ANNUAL REPORT 2009

Das Deutsche Architekturmuseum zeigte 2009 folgende Ausstellungen:

In 2009 the Deutsches Architekturmuseum hosted the following exhibitions:

Internationaler Hochhaus Preis 2008
International Highrise Award 2008
16. 11. 2008 – 04. 01. 2009

Maintor
Diplomarbeiten
TU Kaiserslautern
Diploma Theses
TU Kaiserslautern
13. 12. 2008 – 18. 01. 2009

New Urbanity
Die Europäische Stadt im 21. Jahrhundert
The European City in the 21st Century
06. 12. 2008 – 22. 02. 2009

Updating Germany
Projekte für eine bessere Zukunft – Deutscher Beitrag zur 11. Architekturbiennale Venedig 2008
Projects for a Better Future – German Contribution to the 11th International Architecture Biennial in Venice 2008
06. 12. 2008 – 22. 02. 2009

DAM Preis für Architektur in Deutschland 2008
DAM Award for Architecture in Germany 2008
Die 24 besten Bauwerke in / aus Deutschland
The 24 Best Buildings in / from Germany
17. 01. 2009 – 15. 03. 2009

Auszeichnung vorbildlicher Bauten im Land Hessen 2008
Architektenkammer Hessen
03. 03. 2009 – 22. 03. 2009

Bauhaus zwanzig-21
Bauhaus twenty-21
Fotografien von Gordon Watkinson
Photographs by Gordon Watkinson
07. 03. 2009 – 26. 04. 2009

Hawaii Moderne
Hawaiian Modern
Die Architektur von Vladimir Ossipoff
The Architecture of Vladimir Ossipoff
14. 03. 2009 – 14. 06. 2009

Zum Beispiel Schelling
For Example Schelling
Nachkriegsmoderne zwischen Erhalt und Abriss
Post-war Modernism between Preservation and Demolition
14. 02. 2009 – 12. 04. 2009

Las Vegas Studio
Bilder aus dem Archiv von Robert Venturi und Denise Scott Brown
Images from the Archives of Robert Venturi and Denise Scott Brown
28. 03. 2009 –16. 08. 2009

Europäischer Architekturfotografie-Preis 2009
European Prize of Architectural Photography 2009
Neue Heimat
New Homeland
25. 04. 2009 – 30. 06. 2009

Tezuka Architects
Erinnerte Zukunft
Nostalgic Future
09. 05. 2009 – 28. 06. 2009

Der Pavillon
The Pavilion
Lust und Polemik in der Architektur
Pleasure and Polemics in Architecture
11. 07. 2009 – 20. 09. 2009

Die weiße Stadt. Tel Avivs Moderne
The White City. Tel Aviv's Modern Movement
26. 06. 2009 – 13. 09. 2009

Bilden durch Bauen
Capacity Building Through Constructing
13 neue Universitäten in Äthiopien
13 New Universities in Ethiopia
18. 07. 2009 – 06. 09. 2009

M8 in China
Zeitgenössische chinesische Architekten
Contemporary Chinese Architects
29. 08. 2009 – 01. 11. 2009

Martin Elsaesser und das Neue Frankfurt
Martin Elsaesser and the New Frankfurt
10. 10. 2009 – 14. 03. 2010

Fernsehtürme | TV Towers
8.559 Meter Politik und Architektur
8,559 Meters of Politics and Architecture
03. 10. 2009 – 14.03. 2010

Ben Willikens – Abendmahl
31. 10. 2009 – 13. 12. 2009

DAM Preis für Architektur in Deutschland 2009
DAM Award for Architecture in Germany 2009
Die 25 besten Bauwerke in / aus Deutschland
The 25 Best Buildings in / from Germany
14. 11. 2009 – 17. 01. 2010

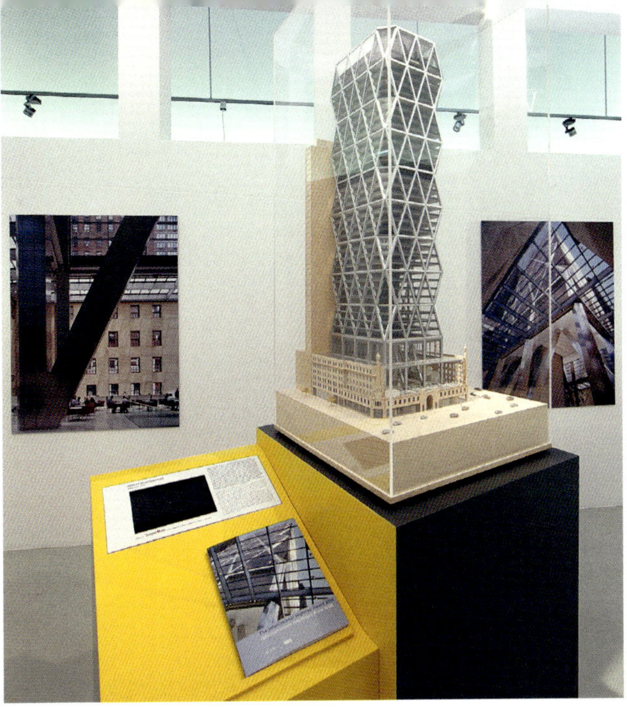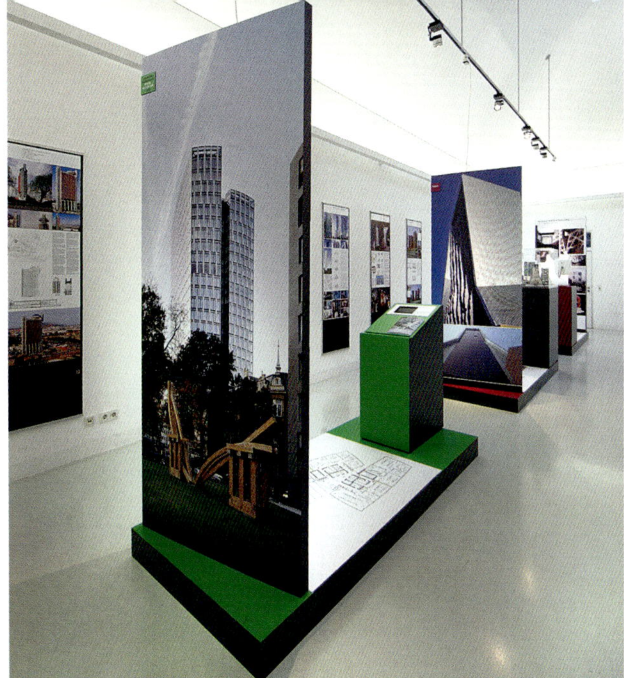

Ausstellung „Internationaler Hochhaus Preis 2008" | "International High-Rise Award 2008" exhibition

Dauerausstellung im DAM

Permanent exhibition at the DAM

Von der Urhütte zum Wolkenkratzer
From Primordial Hut to Skyscraper

DAM Ausstellungen auf Tour 2009

DAM touring exhibitions in 2009

Felsen aus Beton und Glas
Rocks of Concrete and Glass

Die Architektur von Gottfried Böhm
The Architecture of Gottfried Böhm
Köln, Museum für Angewandte Kunst
19. 01. 2009 – 26. 04. 2009
Burgau, RoMa Forum
23. 07. 2009 – 30. 09. 2009

Internationaler Hochhaus Preis 2008
International Highrise Award 2008
Frankfurt, Trianon, DekaBank Deutsche Girozentrale
29. 01. 2009 – 26. 03. 2009

Jean Prouvé

Die Poetik des technischen Objekts
The Poetry of the Technical Object
Wien, Hofmobiliendepot
10. 03. 2009 – 21. 06. 2009
Seoul, Daelim Museum
17. 09. 2009 - 29. 11. 2009

Megacity Network
Zeitgenössische Architektur in Korea
Contemporary Korean Architecture
Talinn, Eesti Arhitektuurimuuseum
20. 03. 2009 – 26. 04. 2009
Barcelona, Col.legi de Arquitectes de Catalunya (COAC)
30. 07. 2009 – 05. 09. 2009
Seoul, Korea, National Museum of Contemporary Art
12/2009 – 02/2010

Becoming Istanbul
Bahrain, Al Riwaq Gallery
05. 05. 2009 – 21. 06. 2009
Berlin, DAZ
15. 05. 2009 – 30. 06. 2009

A Lifetime of Architecture
Der Fotograf Julius Shulman
The Photographer Julius Shulman
Saarbrücken, Rathaus St. Johann
01. 10. 2009 – 31. 10. 2009

Vortragsreihen und Veranstaltungen

Lecture Series and Events

Architektur und Gesellschaft
Bauhaus – Architektur wird demokratisch
Arne Winkelmann, Yorck Förster
01. 04. 2009

Pecha Kucha Nights
PKN010: 12. 03. 2009, Palmengarten, Frankfurt am Main
PKN011: 04. 06. 2009, Weißfrauen Diakoniekirche, Frankfurt am Main
www.pechakuchanight.de

Nacht der Museen
Museum Night
Klänge und Architektur Hawaiis
Sounds and Architecture of Hawaii
25. 04. 2009

Werkschau Baustelle
Ordnungsamt, Meixner Schlüter Wendt
25. 05. 2009
Messehalle 11, Hascher + Jehle
23. 07. 2009
KfW Westarkaden, Sauerbruch + Hutton
27. 08. 2009

Städelschule Architecture Class
End-of-Year Reviews
Frank Barkow, Achim Menges, Klaus Bollinger + Manfred Grohmann, Beatriz Colomina, Nikolaus Hirsch
09. 07. 2009 + 10. 07. 2009

Symposien
Symposia

BAUKULTUR_IM_DIALOG – Baukultur im Klimawandel
Building Culture in Dialogue – Building Culture And Climate Change
Wolfgang Voigt, Mojib Latif, Boris Palmer, Werner Sobek, Stefan Forster, Beate Reinart, Michael Braum, Friedrich von Borries
DAM + Bundesstiftung Baukultur
30. 01. 2009

Nachhaltiges Bauen in der Zukunft. Solar Decathlon 2009
Sustainable Building In The Future. Solar Decathlon 2009
Peter Cachola Schmal, Isabell Schäfer, Manfred Hegger, Dr. Bernhard Bürklin, Hans-Dieter Hegner
DAM + TU Darmstadt
04. 02. 2009

Gefährdete Nachkriegsmoderne
Postwar Modernism At Risk
Dieter Bartetzko, Oliver Elser,
Arno Lederer, Ulrich
Maximilian Schumann,
Gerd Weiss
18. 02. 2009

Fragen an den Städtebau
Questions to Urbanism
Harald Bodenschatz,
Annette Becker, Michael
Hebbert, Vittorio Magnago
Lampugnani, Markus Neppl,
Ulrich Maximilan Schumann,
Wolfgang Sonne
20. 02. 2009

Raumschau | Schauraum.
Perspektiven der
Architekturausstellung –
6. AMM Symposium
Perspectives of Architectural
Exhibitions – 6.AMM Symposium
Jan R. Krause, Tassilo Eich-
berger, Peter Cachola Schmal,
Ursula Kleefisch-Jobst,
Ulrich Müller, Astrid Bornheim,
Ludwig Heimbach,
Adolf Krischanitz
DAM + AMM Hochschule
Bochum
20. 03. 2009

Architektur bringt Gäste
Architecture Attracts Visitors
Edwin Schwarz, Felizitas
Romeiß-Stracke, Max Dudler,
Matthias Alexander,
Peter Cachola Schmal
21. 04. 2009

Architektur und Mode.
Die zweite und dritte Haut
Architecture And Fashion.
The Second And Third Skin
Barbara Ettinger-Brinckmann,
Ralf Müll, Wolfgang Pehnt,
Lars Krückeberg,
Ruth Hanisch, Ingrid Loschek,
Sibylle Klose, Mark Wigley,
Christoph Mäckler
DAM + Akademie der
Architektenkammer- und
Stadtplanerkammer Hessen
24. 05. 2009

6. Werkstattgespräch –
Orte, die bewegen: Kunst am
Bau und Verkehrsarchitektur
Places That Move:
Art In The Architectural Context
And The Architecture Of Mobility
Asta von Buch, Eva Schweitzer,
Eva Maria Joeressen,
Aoife Rosenmeyer, Andreas
Sander-Carqueville, Carsten
Thiemann, Marie Neumüllers
DAM + BMVBS
11. 05. 2009

m8 in China – 8 zeitgenössische
chinesische Architekten
m8 in China – 8 Contemporary
Chinese Architects
ZHANG Bin, ZHOU Wei
(Atelier Z+), TONG Ming
(TM Studio), ZHANG Ke,
ZHANG Hong (standarchitec-
ture), WANG Shu (Amateur
Architects), XU Tiantian (DnA
Design and Architecture), ZHI
Wenjun, YIN Qian, Eduard
Kögel, Peter Cachola Schmal
28. 08. 2009

100 Jahre Tel Aviv
100 years Tel Aviv
Von der Sanddüne zum Weltkulturerbe
From sand dunes to world
cultural heritage
Peter Cachola Schmal, Wolfgang Voigt, Peter Loewy, Ines
Sonder, Ita Greenberg, Ron
Fuchs, Micha Gross
03. 09. 2009

Vorträge | Lectures

Peter Zumthor 16. 01. 2009

Dean Sakamoto, Bob Lijle-
strand, 13. 03. 2009

Takaharu + Yui Tezuka
08. 05. 2009

Brett Steele
SAC Dean's Honorary Lecture
10. 07. 2009

Frank Barkow + Regine
Leibinger
13. 11. 2009

Programm für Kinder und
Jugendliche
Program for children und
young people

LegoBaustelle
Lego Construction Site
26. 12. 2008 – 11. 01. 2009
14. 07. 2009 – 23. 08. 2009

Workshops 2009
Rosa Räume für Rapunzel –
Revisited
21. 02. 2009

Von Häusern und Menschen –
Fotografiewettbewerb
09. 03. 2009 – 12. 03. 2009
Wie wir wohnen
06. 04. 2009 + 07. 04. 2009

Architektur in Balance – Statik
(auch) am eigenen Leib
08. 04. 2009 + 09. 04. 2009

Das Bauhaus tanzt
16. 04. 2009 + 17. 04. 2009

Tag der Architektur:
Was macht ein Sonnenhaus
anders?
DAM + TU Darmstadt
27. 06. 2009 + 28. 06. 2009

Architektur mobil: auf den
Spuren von Yona Friedman
28. 06. 2009

Satourday 2008
Irrtümer und
Missverständnisse
08. 02. 2009

Formentanz
28. 03. 2009

Bionik – der Natur abgeschaut
30. 05. 2009

Lehrerfortbildung
Teacher Training

Was ist eigentlich dekonstruk-
tivistische Architektur?
14. 02. 2009 + 20. 06. 2009
+ 07. 11. 2009

Bauhaus – Architektur wird
demokratisch
01. 04. 2009 + 22. 04. 2009

Was ist eigentlich post-
moderne Architektur?
21. 03. 2009

Architektur im Unterricht.
Wie praktisch!
09. 05. 2009

Was ist eigentlich historische
Architektur?
23. 05. 2009 + 30. 05. 2009

Architektur + Gesellschaft,
das Neue Frankfurt
11. 11. 2009

Wohnen a Palladio
05. 12. 2009

Folgende Kataloge und
Veröffentlichungen sind
erschienen
The following catalogues and
books have been published

Bauhaus Zwanzig-21
Bauhaus twenty-21
Ideen für ein neues
Jahrhundert
Hrsg. | ed. Gordon Watkinson,
Birkhäuser Verlag
Deutsch
mit Beiträgen von | with
contributions from **Falk Jaeger,
Peter Cachola Schmal**

Takaharu + Yui Tezuka
Erinnerte Zukunft
Nostalgic Future
Hrsg. | ed. **Paul Andreas,
Peter Cachola Schmal**
Jovis Verlag
Deutsch / Englisch
mit Beiträgen von | with contri-
butions from **Taro Igarashi,
Joseph Grima, Paul Andreas**

Der Pavillon
The Pavilion
Lust und Polemik in der
Architektur
Pleasure and Polemics in
Architecture
Hrsg. | ed. **Peter Cachola
Schmal**
Verlag Hatje Cantz
Deutsch / Englisch
mit Beiträgen von | with
contributions from **Frank
Barkow + Regine Leibinger,
Barry Bergdoll, Ben van**

Berkel, Christian Brensing,
Kerstin Bußmann, Beatriz
Colomina, Nikolaus Hirsch,
Peter Cachola Schmal,
Werner Sobek

M8 in China
**Zeitgenössische chinesische
Architekten**
Contemporary Chinese Architects
Hrsg. | ed. **Peter Cachola
Schmal, ZHI Wenjun**
Liaoning Publishers / Jovis Verlag
Deutsch / Englisch
mit Beiträgen von | with contri-
butions from **Peter Cachola
Schmal, ZHI Wenjun,
Robert Ivy, Eduard Kögel**

Fernsehtürme
TV Towers
**8.559 Meter Politik und
Architektur**
8,559 Meters of Politics and
Architecture
Hrsg. | ed. **Friedrich von
Borries, Matthias Böttger,
Florian Heilmeyer
Liaoning Publishers | Jovis
Verlag
Deutsch / Englisch**
mit Beiträgen von | with con-
tributions from **Peter Cachola
Schmal, Rudolf Pospischil**

Martin Elsaesser
und das Neue Frankfurt
Martin Elsaesser
and the New Frankfurt
Hrsg. | eds.
**Peter Cachola Schmal,
Christina Gräwe, Thomas
Elsaesser, Jörg Schilling
Wasmuth Verlag,
Deutsch/Englisch**
mit Beiträgen von | with
contributions from **Thomas
Elsaesser, Christina Gräwe,
Christoph Mohr, Jörg Schil-
ling, Horst Peseke, Oliver M.
Piecha, Peter Cachola Schmal,
Wolfgang Voigt**

**Zu den wichtigsten Neuerwer-
bungen des DAM zählen**
The DAM's most important new
acquisitions include

Dokumente
Models, Drawings and Documents
Barkow Leibinger, Berlin

**Helge Bofinger, Wiesbaden
Delugan Meissl Associated
Architects, Wien**

**Eisele Staniek+ architekten
ingenieure, Darmstadt**

FAR Frohn & Rojas, Köln

Finsterwalder, Stephanskirchen

**Jörg Hempel Photodesign,
Aachen**

**INDEX Architekten BDA,
Frankfurt am Main**

**Jourdan & Müller Projekt-
gruppe Architektur und
Städtebau, Frankfurt am Main**

Mansilla+Tuñón, Madrid

**Richard Meier & Partners
Architects LLP, New York, NY**

**Meixner Schlüter Wendt Archi-
tekten, Frankfurt am Main**

**Muck Petzet Architekten,
München**

**querkraft architekten
ZT GmbH, Wien**

Dauerleihgabe | Permanent Loan:
**Gesellschaft der Freunde des
DAM**

4a Architekten GmbH, Stuttgart
Modell | Model,
**Wellnesspark ELSE-Club,
Moscow
Schenkung Architekten |**
Donation by architects

bayer | uhrig Architekten BDA,
Kaiserslautern
Modell | Model,
**Häuser für amerikanisches
Wohnen, Rodenbach
Schenkung Architekten |**
Donation by architects

Günter Bock (1918–2002)
Pläne und Fotografien |
Plans and photographs,
**Wohnhaus P., Bingen
Schenkung Bauherren |**
Donation by client

Gerber Architekten, Dortmund
Modell | Model,
**King Fahad National Library,
Riad, Saudi Arabia
Schenkung Architekten |**
Donation by architects

knerer und lang
Architekten GmbH, Dresden
Modell | Model,
**Sanierung Wohnzeile Prager
Straße, Dresden
Schenkung Architekten |**
Donation by architects

Rob Krier, Berlin
Zeichnungen und Modell |
Drawings and model,
**Berliner Schloss, Spreebogen
Dauerleihgabe Architekt |**
Permanent loan by architect

KSV Krüger Schuberth Vandreike
Planung und Kommunikation
GmbH, Berlin
Modell | Model,
**Museion, Museum for
Contemporary Art, Bozen
Schenkung Architekten |**
Donation by architects

Mass Studies, Seoul, Korea
Modell | Model,
**Matrix Building, Seoul,
Schenkung Architekten |**
Donation by architects

J. MAYER H., Berlin
Modell | Model,
**Metropol Parasol, Sevilla
Schenkung Architekt |**
Donation by architect

scopulus, Christian Werner,
Braunschweig
Modell | Model,
**Stadt Relief Berlin,
Edition Museumsinsel
Schenkung |** Donation by
Scopulus GBR

Staab Architekten GvAmbH,
Berlin
Modell | Model,
**German International
School, Sydney
Schenkung |** Donation by

German International School
terrain: loenhart&mayr
BDA landscape urbanism,
München
Modell / Model,
**Neue Olympia-
Skisprungschanze,
Garmisch-Partenkirchen
Schenkung Architekten /** Dona-
tion by architects

Ben Willikens, Stuttgart
**Raum 237, O. M. Ungers,
DAM, Frankfurt, Gemälde,
Acryl auf Leinwand |** Painting,
acrylic on canvas, **1999
Ankauf mit Unterstützung
durch |** Acquisition with
support by
**HPP Architekten + Kulturamt
der Stadt Frankfurt**

**Raum 236, O. M. Ungers
DAM, Frankfurt, Gemälde,
Acryl auf Leinwand |** Painting,
acrylic on canvas, **1999
Dauerleihgabe Künstler |**
permanent loan by artist

Karl Wimmenauer (1914–1997)
**Pläne und Zeichnungen
aus dem Nachlass
(verschiedene Projekte)**
Plans and drawings from
the estate (various projects)
Schenkung | Donation by
Christina Wimmenauer

Peter Zumthor
Modell | Model,
**Kolumba Museum, Köln, 2001
Dauerleihgabe |** Permanent loan
by **Erzbistum Köln**

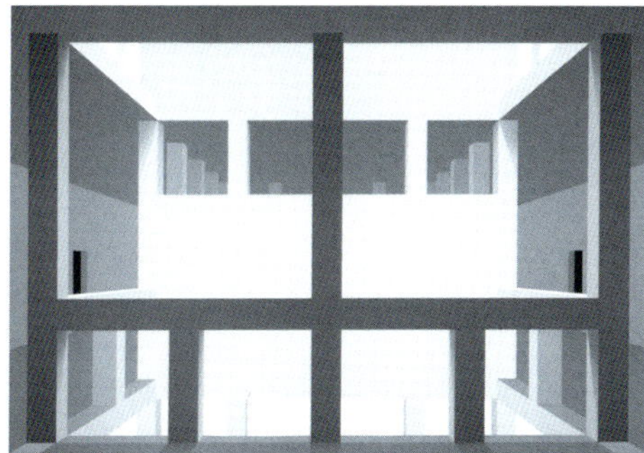

Ben Willikens, „Raum 237, O. M. Ungers Deutsches Architekturmuseum (Das Innenhaus)", 1999, 200 x 275 cm,
Acryl auf Leinwand/Ankauf 2008 | Ben Willikens, "Raum 237,
O.M. Ungers Deutsches Architekturmuseum (Das Innenhaus)",
1999, 200 x 275 cm, acrylic on canvas/purchased in 2008

Das DAM ist an der Auslobung wichtiger Architekturpreise beteiligt:
Seit 2007 zeichnet das DAM eines der im Deutschen Architektur Jahrbuch präsentierten Projekte mit dem DAM Preis für Architektur in Deutschland aus. Die Auszeichnung für das beste Projekt 2007 wurde Wandel Hofer Lorch + Hirsch für das Dokumentationszentrum Hinzert verliehen, Peter Zumthor 2008 für das Diözesanmuseum St. Kolumba in Köln und Barkow Leibinger 2009 für das Betriebsrestaurant TRUMPF in Ditzingen.
Der Internationale Hochhaus Preis (IHP) wird seit 2004 alle zwei Jahre von der Stadt Frankfurt am Main vergeben. Initiiert und organisiert wird er in partnerschaftlicher Kooperation vom DAM und der DekaBank, die außerdem den IHP finanziert. 2004 gewannen den Preis KPF Europe mit De Hooftoren in Den Haag, 2006 Jean Nouvel mit dem Torre Agbar in Barcelona und 2008 Foster + Partners mit dem Hearst Tower in New York. Der Preis besteht aus einer Statue des Künstlers Thomas Demand und einem Geldpreis von 50 000 Euro.
Der Europäische Architekturfotografie-Preis, alle zwei Jahre ausgelobt, wird bereits zum achten Mal vergeben. Zum ersten Mal fand die Preisverleihung und die Ausstellung der besten Wettbewerbsbeiträge im DAM statt, denn seit 2008 kooperieren der Auslober, die architekturbild e. V. und das DAM. Alle Fotos der bisherigen Preisträger der vergangenen 16 Jahre gehen in die Sammlung des DAM über. Der Preisträger der Edition 2009 unter dem Motto „Neue Heimat – New Homeland" ist Stephan Sahm aus München.
Als Mitglied des wissenschaftlichen Beirats für den Global Award For Sustainable Architecture der Cité d'architecture et du patrimoine in Paris beteiligt sich das DAM an diesem, seit 2007 erstmals verliehenen Preis, jeweils gekoppelt an einen Direktauftrag. Hermann Kaufmann aus Dornbirn gewann den ersten Preis, 2008 gewann Carin Smuts aus Sea Point, Südafrika, und 2009 wird der Preisträger einer der fünf Finalisten sein: Thomas Herzog aus München, Sami Rintala (Rinatala Eggertsson) aus Oslo, Diébédo Francis Kéré aus Berlin, Bijoy Jain (Studio Mumbai) aus dem indischen Mumbai und Patrick Bouchain et Loïc Julienne (Construire) aus Paris.
Das DAM ist außerdem Mitglied des Steering Committees für den alle zwei Jahre verliehenen EU Mies van der Rohe Preis für zeitgenössische Architektur in Europa. Die Preisträger 2009 sind die Architekten des norwegischen Architekturbüros Snøhetta, der Preis wurde ihnen für ihre Nationaloper in Oslo verliehen.

The DAM (German Architecture Museum) is involved in awarding some important architecture prizes.
Since 2007 the DAM has selected one of the projects presented in the German Architecture Annual to receive the DAM Award for Architecture in Germany. The award for best project in 2007 went to Wandel Hofer Lorch + Hirsch for their Dokumentationszentrum Hinzert, in 2008 to Peter Zumthor for Kolumba, the art museum of the archdiocese of Cologne, and in 2009 to Barkow Leibinger for their Betriebsrestaurant (company restaurant) for TRUMPF in Ditzingen.
The City of Frankfurt am Main has bestowed its International Highrise Award (IHP) every second year since 2004. The award is initiated and organised in partnership with the DAM and DekaBank, which also funds the IHP. In 2004 the winner was KPF Europe with De Hooftoren in The Hague, in 2006 Jean Nouvel with the Torre Agbar in Barcelona and in 2008 Foster + Partners with the Hearst Tower in New York. The prize consists of a statue by the artist Thomas Demand and a cash award of 50,000 euros.
The European Architectural Photography Prize, awarded every two years, is being presented in 2009 for the eighth time. As the award's sponsor, architekturbild e.V., has cooperated with the DAM since 2008, the award ceremony and the exhibition of the best competition entries took place at the DAM in 2008. All prize-winning photos from the past 16 years will become part of the DAM collection. The winner of the 2009 edition, the motto of which was 'Neue Heimat – New Homeland', is Stephan Sahm from Munich.
As a member of the research council of the Global Award For Sustainable Architecture of the Cité d'architecture et du patrimoine in Paris, which debuted in 2007 and is always coupled with a direct commission, the DAM also participates in this award. Hermann Kaufmann from Dornbirn was the first winner, and in 2008 Carin Smuts from Sea Point, South Africa received the award. In 2009 the five finalists are: Thomas Herzog from Munich, Sami Rintala (Rinatala Eggertsson) from Oslo, Diébédo Francis Kéré from Berlin, Bijoy Jain (Studio Mumbai) from Mumbai, and Patrick Bouchain et Loïc Julienne (Construire) from Paris.
The DAM is in addition a member of the steering committee for the biennial EU Mies van der Rohe Award for Contemporary Architecture in Europe. The award-winner in 2009 is the Norwegian architecture office Snøhetta, recognised for its National Opera in Oslo.

MÄZENE UND SPONSOREN
PATRONS AND SPONSORS

UND FOLGENDE UNTERSTÜTZER
AND THE FOLLOWING SUPPORTERS

Alle unsere Aktivitäten im vergangenen Jahr wären ohne die großzügige Unterstützung zahlreicher Sponsoren nicht möglich gewesen. Zu den Sponsoren, die das DAM unterstützt haben, zählen:
The museum's activities in the course of the last year would not have been possible without the generous support of our many sponsors, including:

DekaBank Deutsche Girozentrale, Frankfurt am Main; **Gemeinnützige Kulturfonds Frankfurt RheinMain GmbH,** Bad Homburg; **Bundesministerium für Verkehr, Bau und Stadtentwicklung (BMVBS),** Berlin; **Gesellschaft der Freunde des Deutschen Architekturmuseums e. V.,** Frankfurt am Main; **DFMG Deutsche Funkturm GmbH,** Münster; **Europäische Zentralbank,** Frankfurt am Main; **Architekten- und Stadtplanerkammer Hessen,** Wiesbaden; **eXperimente EINE KULTUR-INITIATIVE DER AVENTIS FOUNDATION,** Frankfurt am Main; **HPP Hentrich-Petschnigg & Partner – Architekten,** Düsseldorf; **Liaoning Science and Technology Publishing House (LSTPH), Shenyang,** China; **Copyright Department of China National Publications Import and Export Corporation (CNPIEC),** Beijing, China; **Josef Buchmann Immobilienverwaltung,** Frankfurt am Main; **Ströer Out of Home Media AG,** Köln; **Stiftung Polytechnische Gesellschaft,** Frankfurt am Main; **Universitätsbibliothek Johann Christian Senckenberg,** Frankfurt am Main; **OKALUX GmbH,** Marktheidenfeld; **s.boehme & co. KGaA,** Frankfurt am Main; **Hessischer Museumsverband,** Kassel; **Eternit Akademie,** Berlin; **Stiftung Städelschule für Baukunst,** Frankfurt am Main; **Kooperationspool der Stadt Frankfurt,** Frankfurt am Main; **Wüstenrot Stiftung Gemeinschaft der Freunde Deutscher Eigenheimverein e. V.,** Ludwigsburg; **Frankfurter Rundschau,** Frankfurt am Main; **world-architects.com,** Zürich; **Fr. Friedrich GmbH Darmstädter Speditions- und Möbeltransportgesellschaft mbH,** Darmstadt; **SKY-FRAME R&G Metallbau AG,** Ellikon a. d. Thur, Schweiz; **Bundesstiftung Baukultur,** Potsdam; **artur Architekturbilder Agentur GmbH,** Essen

AlienSkin Software, Raleigh NC; **architekturbild e. V.,** Stuttgart; **Autohaus G.V.O. GmbH,** Frankfurt; **Canson Infinity,** Herouville Saint Clair; **DESERVE GbR Raum und Medien Design,** Wiesbaden; **DICK GmbH,** Metten; **gainestranslations,** Frankfurt; **Hans Hundegger Maschinenbau GmbH,** Hawangen; **inditec Display & Messegestaltung GmbH,** Bad Camberg; **KNOLL International,** London; **PICTO,** Paris; **Schweizer Generalkonsulat,** Frankfurt; **TECNOLUMEN GmbH & Co. KG,** Bremen; **Thonet GmbH,** Frankenberg Eder; **Züco Dauphin Human Design AG,** Basel

GESELLSCHAFT DER FREUNDE DES DAM
THE SOCIETY OF FRIENDS OF THE DAM

Die Gesellschaft der Freunde des Deutschen Architektur Museums wurde im Jahr 1985 als eingetragener Verein ins Leben gerufen.

Das Hauptanliegen dieser Gesellschaft ist es, das Deutsche Architekturmuseum, Frankfurt am Main (DAM), in der Verwirklichung seiner öffentlichen Aufgaben ideell und materiell zu unterstützen und zu fördern.

Zu den Aufgaben und Zielen des Vereins gehören:
— Vermittlung, Ankauf und Überlassung von Plänen, Zeichnungen und Modellen deutscher und internationaler Architektur-Projekte und Architekten-Nachlässe bzw. -Vorlässe mit dem Ziel der wissenschaftlichen Bearbeitung und öffentlichkeitswirksamen Vermittlung der Arbeitsergebnisse durch das DAM. Vorhaltung eines großen Kontingents von Dauerleihgaben an das Archiv des DAM.
— Unterstützung bei der Planung, Vorbereitung und Durchführung von Ausstellungen, Auktionen, Veranstaltungen und anderen anstehenden Aufgaben. Einer der Schwerpunkte ist u. a. die Jugendarbeit bzw. Museumspädagogik.
— Herstellung von Kontakten zu Personen, Institutionen und Wirtschaftsunternehmen, die für die partnerschaftliche Unterstützung von Aktivitäten des DAM infrage kommen.
— Unterstützung des DAM bei verschiedenen Maßnahmen im Rahmen der Öffentlichkeitsarbeit.
— Vorhaltung und Überlassung einer Wohnung für Praktikanten. Erwerb eines Liefertransporters für das DAM 2009.

Mitglieder in diesem Verein sind Personen, Institutionen und Firmen, deren Anliegen es ist, einen Beitrag zur Förderung der Qualität der gebauten Umwelt zu leisten.

Der Vorstand wird jeweils über einen Zeitraum von fünf Jahren von der Mitgliederversammlung gewählt. Er setzt sich aus Persönlichkeiten aus den Bereichen Wirtschaft, Politik, Bildung, Bankwesen und Kultur zusammen. Dadurch ist gewährleistet, dass Informationen und Kontakte aus den unterschiedlichsten Bereichen zugunsten der Ziele der Gesellschaft der Freunde des DAM genutzt werden können.

Um einen intensiven Kontakt zu den Mitgliedern sicherzustellen, wird jährlich mindestens eine Versammlung durchgeführt, anschließend findet eine Sonderführung durch die laufende Ausstellung statt.

Wie Sie sich vorstellen können, erfordern die Aktivitäten der Gesellschaft in hohem Maße Geld, Ideen, ehrenamtliches Engagement und Idealismus. Unterstützen Sie uns bei unserem Vorhaben! Als Mitglied erhalten Sie das Jahrbuch des DAM bei Abholung unentgeltlich; auf alle anderen Publikationen des DAM erhalten Sie mit Ihrem Ausweis 20% Rabatt. Nur als Mitglied können Sie an speziellen Previews und Sonderführungen teilnehmen. Die Jahresgaben der Gesellschaft 1998 bis 2005 erhalten Sie zu einem Vorzugspreis. Es werden Architekturreisen für die Mitglieder angeboten, z. B. Reisen zu Architekturbiennalen (2006 Venedig, 2007 São Paulo, 2008 Venedig). Bitte informieren Sie sich auch speziell unter unserer Website: http//www.dam-online.de/Gesellschaft der Freunde.

Der Jahresmitgliedsbeitrag beträgt 95,00 EUR für Einzelmitglieder, für Studenten 50,00 EUR und für juristische Personen und Personenvereinigungen 920,00 EUR.

Vorstand: Marietta Andreas (Vorsitz), Prof. Johann Eisele (Stellvertretender Vorsitz), Prof. Helge Bofinger (Schatzmeister), Michael Bahrenberg, Barbara Ettinger-Brinckmann, Prof. Dr. Salomon Korn, Florian Schlüter, Francois Valentiny, Prof. Dr. Martin Wentz

The Society of Friends of the Deutsches Architekturmuseum was founded in 1985 as a registered non-profit organisation.

The society's main objective is to support and promote the Deutsches Architekturmuseum, Frankfurt/Main (DAM) both intellectually and materially in the execution of its public duties.

The organisation's duties and aims include:
— The mediation, purchase, and sale of plans, drawings and models of German and international architecture projects and architects' estates and bequeathals for the purpose of scientific handling as well as the effective public dissemination of the results of DAM's work. A large contingent of permanent loans is housed in the DAM archive.
— Support in the planning, preparation and realisation of exhibitions, auctions, events and other ongoing tasks. Focuses here include youth outreach and museum education.
— Establishing contact with persons, institutions and companies that come into question as potential partners for the support of DAM's activities.
— Supporting DAM with various PR-related measures.
— Maintaining an apartment for use by interns. Purchase of a delivery vehicle for DAM in 2009.

The organisation's members include persons, institutions and firms that are committed to making a contribution to improving the quality of our constructed environment.

The Board of Directors is elected for a period of five years by the General Meeting of the members. It is made up of representatives from the worlds of business, politics, education, banking and culture. This ensures that information from and contacts with a wide range of fields can be put to maximum use in furthering the objectives of the Society of Friends of DAM.

In order to keep in close contact with members, at least one General Meeting is held every year. It is followed by a special guided tour of the exhibition on show at the time.

As you can imagine, the Society's activities require a large amount of money, ideas, voluntary work and idealism. Why not support us in our objectives! As a member you will receive the DAM Annual free of charge when you pick it up yourself, as well as a 20% discount on all other DAM publications on presentation of your membership card. Only society members are entitled to attend special previews and take part in special tours. You can also obtain the society's annual gifts from 1998 until 2005 at a reduced rate. Architecture-related trips, for example to architecture biennials (2006 Venice, 2007 São Paulo, 2008 Venice) are organised for members. To find out more about these and other benefits of membership, please see our website: http//www.dam-online.de/Gesellschaft der Freunde.

Annual membership costs 95 EUR for private members, 50 EUR for students and 920 EUR for corporate bodies and associations.

The Board: Marietta Andreas (Chairperson), Prof. Johann Eisele (Deputy Chairperson), Prof. Helge Bofinger (Treasurer), Michael Bahrenberg, Barbara Ettinger-Brinckmann, Prof. Salomon Korn, Florian Schlüter, Francois Valentiny, Prof. Martin Wentz

Die Gesellschaft dankt folgenden Personen und Institutionen, die sich in besonderem Maße engagiert haben:
We would like to thank our special sponsors:

Architekten- und Stadtplanerkammer Hessen, Wiesbaden
Artemide GmbH, Fröndenberg
Auktionshaus Döbritz, Frankfurt am Main
aurelis Real Estate GmbH, Eschborn/Taunus
Bauverlag BV GmbH, Gütersloh
Beton Marketing Süd GmbH, Ostfildern
S. Boehme & Co. KGaA, Frankfurt am Main
Bund Deutscher Architekten im Lande Hessen e. V., Frankfurt am Main
Bund Deutscher Baumeister, Architekten und Ingenieure e. V., Berlin-Steglitz
Bund Deutscher Baumeister, Landesverband Hessen, Kassel
Bund Deutscher Baumeister, Bezirksgruppe Frankfurt, Frankfurt am Main
Deutsche Werkstätten Hellerau GmbH, Dresden
F. Dornbracht GmbH & Co. KG, Iserlohn
Frankfurter Allgemeine Zeitung, Frankfurt am Main
Gainestranslations, Frankfurt am Main
HOCHTIEF Projektentwicklung GmbH, Niederlassung Rhein-Main, Frankfurt am Main
Jo.Franzke Architekten, Frankfurt am Main
netzwerkarchitekten, Darmstadt
Treuhandverwaltung IGEMET GmbH, Frankfurt am Main
SSS Siedle + Söhne, Furtwangen
Xella International GmbH, Duisburg-Ruhrort

Kontakt | Contact

Gesellschaft der Freunde des Deutschen Architektur Museums e. V.
Geschäftsstelle: Deutsches Architekturmuseum
Schaumainkai 43
60596 Frankfurt am Main
Deutschland | Germany
Telefon | Tel.**: +49(0)69-97203366**
Mobil | Mobile**: +49(0)178-4475363**
Telefax | Fax**: +49(0)69-97203366**
E-Mail: freundeskreis.dam@stadt-frankfurt.de
http//www.dam-online.de/Gesellschaft der Freunde

Bankverbindung | Bank account:

Dresdner Bank AG
Frankfurt am Main
KONTO-NR. | Account number: **019 804 1500**
BLZ | Sorting code: **500 800 00**

HUBERTUS ADAM

***1965 in Hannover.
Studium der Kunstgeschichte, Archäologie und Philosophie in Heidelberg. 1996–98 Redakteur der Zeitschrift „Bauwelt" in Berlin. Seit 1998 Redakteur der Zeitschrift „archithese" in Zürich. Freier Architekturkritiker für die „Neue Zürcher Zeitung". Zahlreiche Zeitschriften- und Buchbeiträge sowie Bücher zur Architekturgeschichte des 20. Jahrhunderts und zur Architektur der Gegenwart.**

Born 1965 in Hanover. Studied art history, archaeology and philosophy in Heidelberg. 1996–98 editor of the magazine "Bauwelt" in Berlin. Since 1998 editor of the magazine "archithese" in Zurich. Freelance architecture critic for the "Neu Zürcher Zeitung" newspaper. Numerous magazine and book contributions as well as books on 20th-century architectural history and contemporary architecture.

PAUL ANDREAS

***1973 in Wolfsburg.
Studium der Kultur- und Kunstwissenschaft in Berlin und Paris; 2000 M. A. 2001 Japanisch-Studium in Tübingen und Kyoto.**

2003 freier Kurator am DAM. Kuratiert die Oscar-Niemeyer-Ausstellung im DAM. 2003–2005 wissenschaftlicher Mitarbeiter für Designgeschichte an der BU Wuppertal. Lebt als freier Journalist und Kurator in Düsseldorf. Seit 2007 Presse- und Öffentlichkeitsarbeit am DAM.

Born 1973 in Wolfsburg. Culture and art studies in Berlin and Paris; M. A. in 2000. Studied Japanese in Tübingen and Kyoto in 2001. Freelance Curator for the DAM. Curated the Oscar Niemeyer exhibition at the DAM in 2003. 2003–05 research assistant for design history at the University of Wuppertal. Lives and works as freelance journalist and curator in Düsseldorf. Public relations for the DAM since 2007.

WOLFGANG BACHMANN

***1951 in Ludwigshafen/Rhein. Studium der Agrarwissenschaften und Architektur. Diplom 1976 an der RWTH Aachen. Dissertation über die Architektur der Anthroposophen. Drei Jahre Berufspraxis in verschiedenen Architektur- und Ingenieurbüros, begleitend journalistische Tätigkeit. 1982 Redakteur der Zeitschrift „Bauwelt" in Berlin. Seit 1991 Chefredakteur der Zeitschrift**

„Baumeister" in München; außerdem schreibt er Kritiken, Glossen und Kurzgeschichten über Architektur und darüber hinaus. 2008 „Fachjournalist des Jahres" (2. Preis).

Born 1951 in Ludwigshafen/Rhein. Studied agriculture and architecture; degree from RWTH Aachen University in 1976. Dissertation on anthroposophically inspired architecture. Three years of professional practice in various architecture and engineering offices while also working as a journalist. From 1982 editor of the magazine "Bauwelt" in Berlin. Since 1991 editor-in-chief of the magazine "Baumeister" in Munich; also writes reviews, glosses and short histories of architecture and other themes. 2008 "Specialist Journalist of the Year" (2nd prize).

DIETER BARTETZKO

***1949 in Rodalben.
Studium der Kunstgeschichte, Soziologie und Germanistik in Marburg und Berlin; 1984 Promotion über die Theatralik der NS-Architektur. Seit 1994 Redakteur im Feuilleton der „Frankfurter Allgemeinen Zeitung", Ressort Architektur, Denkmalpflege und Archäologie.**

Born 1949 in Rodalben. Studied art history, sociology and German language and literature at Marburg and Berlin; 1984 doctoral thesis on the theatrical aspect of National Socialist architecture. Since 1994 editor of the architecture, conservation and archaeology section of the review pages of "Frankfurter Allgemeine Zeitung".

CHRISTIAN BRENSING

***1960 in Bad Ems.
1982–89 Studium der englischen Literatur und Kunstgeschichte in England; Abschluss M. A. Royal College of Art (RCA), London. 1989–90 wissenschaftlicher Assistent am Royal College of Art, London. 1990–92 Zaha Hadid Architects. London. 1993–2004 OveArup & Partners Consulting Engineers, London und Berlin. 2004–05 CBP Consulting Engineers, München. Seit 2006 freischaffender Berater, Autor und Kurator. Lebt in Berlin.**

Born 1960 in Bad Ems, West Germany. 1982–89 studied English literature and history of art in England, final degree M.A. Royal College of Art (RCA), London. 1989–90 assistant lecturer, Royal College of Art, London; 1990–92 Zaha Hadid Architects, London; 1993–2004 Ove Arup &

Partners Consulting Engineers, London and Berlin; 2004–05 CBP Consulting Engineers, Munich. Since 2006 freelance consultant, author and curator. Lives in Berlin.

MICHAELA BUSENKELL

***1962 in Schleswig. Aufenthalt in Brüssel, Heidelberg, Barcelona, 1992 Diplom Architektur TU München, Döllgastpreis. Bis 1996 Mitarbeit in Architekturbüros; 1996–99 Volontärin/ Redakteurin der Fachzeitschrift „AIT", Stuttgart; 1999–2005 Chefredakteurin von „a-matter, architecture and related". Kuratorische Beraterin Deutscher Pavillon, Architektur Biennale Venedig 2004. Seit 2005 freie Journalisten- und Kritikertätigkeit, seit 2007 freie wissenschaftliche Mitarbeiterin am DAM.**

Born 1962 in Schleswig. Lived in Brussels, Heidelberg, Barcelona; degree in architecture from the Technical University of Munich in 1992, Döllgast Award. Worked in architecture offices until 1996; 1996–99 volunteer/ editor of the trade journal "AIT", Stuttgart; 1999–2005 editor-in-chief of "a-matter, architecture and related". Member of the advisory board for the German Pavilion at the Venice Architecture Biennale in 2004. Since 2005 freelance journalist and reviewer; since 2007 freelance scientific collaborator at the DAM.

LAYLA DAWSON

***1949 in London. Architektin in England, im Nahen Osten und in Hong Kong. Lebt seit 1989 in Hamburg. Schreibt für „The Architectural Review", London, und andere internationale Fachpublikationen. Zahlreiche literarische Rezensionen. 2005 erschien das bisher letzte Buch zum Thema Architektur unter dem Titel „China's New Dawn" im Prestel Verlag. 2006 erschien „Brit and Brown" von Layla Shah 2006 im Arche Lite-**

ratur-Verlag und 2008 im Berliner Taschenbuch Verlag.

Born 1949 in London. Architect in England, the Middle East and Hong Kong. Since 1989 living in Hamburg and writing for "The Architectural Review" and other international architecture publications. For some years she has also published literary criticism. Her last book about architecture was "China's New Dawn", published 2005 by Prestel, and a novel "Brit and Brown" by Layla Shah, published 2006 by Arche-Literatur-Verlag, and 2008 by Berliner Taschenbuch Verlag in paperback.

DOROTHEA DESCHERMEIER

***1976 in Wasserburg am Inn. Studium der Kunstgeschichte und der Kirchengeschichte in München, Berlin und Bologna. 2007 Promotion an der Universität Bologna über die Firmenarchitektur des Energiekonzerns Eni. 2003–2008 Mitarbeit in der Galerie „Studio G7" für zeitgenössische Kunst, Bologna. Verschiedene Veröffentlichungen. Seit 2008 wissenschaftliche Volontärin am DAM.**

Born 1976 in Wasserburg am Inn. Studied art history and ecclesiastical history in Munich, Berlin and Bologna. Doctorate in 2007 from the University of Bologna with a dissertation on the corporate architecture of the Eni energy company. 2003–08 worked at Studio G7 gallery for contemporary art, Bologna. Various publications. Since 2008 research volunteer at the DAM.

OLIVER ELSER

***1972 in Rüsselsheim. Architekturstudium in Berlin. Zahlreiche Architekturkritiken für Zeitungen und Zeitschriften („Frankfurter Allgemeine Zeitung", „Süddeutsche Zeitung", „Texte zur Kunst", „Frankfurter Rundschau", „Bauwelt" etc.) sowie in Katalogen und Büchern. 2006–07 Lehrtätigkeit in Graz und Wien. Seit 2007 Kurator am DAM.**

Born 1972 in Rüsselsheim. Studied architecture in Berlin. Has written numerous architectural reviews for newspapers and magazines ("Frankfurter Allgemeine Zeitung", "Süddeutsche Zeitung", "Texte zur Kunst", "Frankfurter Rundschau", "Bauwelt" etc.) as well as catalogues and books. Taught in Graz and Vienna 2006–07. Since 2007 curator at the DAM.

YORCK FÖRSTER

***1964 in Hannover. Studium der Philosophie, Soziologie und Kunstpädagogik an der Universität Frankfurt am Main. Als freier Kurator für das DAM tätig.**

Born 1964 in Hanover. Studied philosophy, sociology and art education at the University of Frankfurt/Main. Works as freelance curator for the DAM.

CHRISTINA GRÄWE

***1965 in Idar-Oberstein. Ausbildung zur Krankenschwester. Studium von Spanisch und Kunstgeschichte an der FU Berlin sowie Architektur an der TU Berlin. Mitarbeit in verschiedenen Architekturbüros. 2003–05 Volontariat am DAM. Freie Kuratorin und Autorin.**

Born 1965 in Idar-Oberstein; trained as a nurse. Studied Spanish and art history at the Free University of Berlin and architecture at the Technical University of Berlin. Employed in various architectural practices; 2003–05 research volunteer at the DAM. Freelance curator and author.

SANDRA HOFMEISTER

***1970 in München. Studium der Kunstgeschichte und Romanistik in Berlin. 2004 Promotion in Italienischer Philologie. Publizistin und freie Journalistin für deutsch- und englischsprachige Zeitschriften mit Schwerpunkt Architektur, Kunst und Design.**

Born 1970 in Munich. Studied art history and romance languages in

Berlin. Doctorate in 2004 with dissertation on Italian philology. Publicist and freelance journalist for German- and English-language magazines, focusing on architecture, art and design.

CHRISTIAN HOLL

Zunächst Kunststudium in Stuttgart und Münster/Westfalen, dann Architekturstudium an der RWTH Aachen, in Florenz und an der Universität Stuttgart. 1997–2004 Redakteur der „db deutsche bauzeitung". 2004 Gründung von „frei04 publizistik" mit Ursula Baus und Klaus Siegele. Buchveröffentlichungen, freie Redakteurs-, Journalisten- und Kritikertätigkeit sowie Lehraufträge. Seit 2005 akademischer Mitarbeiter am Städtebau-Institut der Uni Stuttgart. Mitglied im Ausstellungsausschuss der „architekturgalerie am weißenhof", Stuttgart.

Studied art in Stuttgart and Münster/Westphalia, then architecture at RWTH Aachen University, in Florence and at the University of Stuttgart. 1997–2004 editor at "db deutsche bauzeitung". Founded "frei04 publizistik" in 2004 with Ursula Baus and Klaus Siegele. Has published books, worked as freelance editor, journalist and reviewer and held posts as lecturer. Since 2005 academic assistant at the Institute of Urban Planning at the University of Stuttgart. Member of the exhibition committee of "architekturgalerie am weissenhof", Stuttgart.

ULRICH HÖHNS

***1954 in Bothel. Architekturhistoriker und -kritiker, wissenschaftlicher Leiter des Schleswig-Holsteinischen Archivs für Architektur und Ingenieurbaukunst.**

Born 1954 in Bothel. Architectural historian and critic, research director of the Schleswig-Holstein Archive for Architecture and Engineering.

HANS IBELINGS
***1963 in Rotterdam.
Architekturhistoriker sowie
Herausgeber und Verleger der
zweimonatlich erscheinenden
Zeitschrift „A10 new
European architecture", die
er gemeinsam mit dem Grafik-
designer Arjan Groot im Jahr
2004 begründete. Ibelings war
zudem Kurator am
Netherlands Architecture
Institute in Rotterdam. Er ist
Autor und/oder Herausgeber
zahlreicher Publikationen,
darunter „Supermodernism:
Architecture in the Age of
Globalisation" (1998),
„The Artificial Landscape:
Contemporary Architecture,
Urban Design and Landscape
Architecture in the
Netherlands" (2000) und
„Unmodern Architecture:
Contemporary Traditionalism
in the Netherlands" (2004).**
Born 1963 in Rotterdam.
Architectural historian and
editor/publisher of "A10 new
European architecture", a
bimonthly magazine which he
founded together with graphic
designer Arjan Groot in 2004.
Ibelings has been a curator at
the Netherlands Architecture
Institute in Rotterdam. He is the
author and/or editor of several
publications, including "Super-
modernism: Architecture in the
Age of Globalisation" (1998),
"The Artificial Landscape:
Contemporary Architecture,
Urban Design and Landscape
Architecture in the Netherlands"
(2000) and "Unmodern Architecture: Contemporary Traditionalism
in the Netherlands" (2004).

FALK JAEGER
***1950 in Ottweiler/Saar.
Studium der Architektur
und Kunstgeschichte in
Braunschweig, Stuttgart
und Tübingen. Promotion
an der TU Hannover. Apl.
Professor für Architektur-
theorie und -kritik an der
TU Dresden. Freier Publizist,
Kurator und Architekturkritiker bei Tages- und
Fachpresse, Hörfunk und
Fernsehen. Lebt in Berlin.**
Born 1950 in Ottweiler/Saar.
Studied architecture and art
history at Brunswick, Stuttgart
und Tübingen. Doctorate from
Technical University of Hanover.
Professorship in architectural
theory and criticism at Technical
University of Dresden. Freelance
writer, curator, architecture
critic for newspapers and specialist
periodicals, radio and TV. Lives
in Berlin.

KAREN JUNG, *SCHMEINK
***1974 in Münster.
Studium der Architektur
an der Universität Karlsruhe
und ETH Zürich. Mitarbeit
in verschiedenen Architekturbüros. 1999–2002 Mitarbeiterin am Institut für Grund-
lagen der Architektur der
Universität Karlsruhe.
2005 Promotion an der
ETH Zürich bei Prof. Dr.
V. M. Lampugnani und Prof.
Dr. Á. Moravánszky zum
„Porösen Baublock".
2006–08 Volontärin und
seit 2008 freie Kuratorin
am DAM. Seit 2009 freie
Kuratorin am M:AI Museum
für Architektur und Ingenieurkunst NRW.**
Born 1974 in Münster.
Architecture studies at the
University of Karlsruhe and
Technical Universtiy (ETH)
Zurich. Worked in various architecture offices. 1999–2002
employee of the Institute for
the Fundamentals of Architecture at the University of Karlsruhe. Doctorate from ETH Zurich
under Prof. Dr. V. M. Lampugnani
and Prof. Dr. Á. Moravánszky in
2005 on the 'Porous Block'.
2006–08 research volunteer
and since 2008 freelance
curator at the DAM. Since 2008
freelance curator at the M:AI
Museum of Architecture and the
Art of Engineering NRW.

URSULA KLEEFISCH-JOBST
***1956 in Stuttgart.
Studium der Kunstgeschichte,
Archäologie und Germanistik
in Bonn, München und Rom:
Promotion. 1985–88
Forschungsprojekt an der
Biblioteca Hertziana in Rom.**
1989–90 Mitarbeiterin am
Landesdenkmalamt in Berlin.
2001–08 freie Kuratorin am
DAM. Seit 2008 leitende
Kuratorin am Museum für
Architektur und Ingenieur-
kunst NRW.
Born 1956 in Stuttgart. Studied
art history, archaeology and
German language & literature
in Bonn, Munich and Rome,
culminating in doctorate.
1985–88 research project at the
Biblioteca Hertziana in Rome.
1989–90 employee at the Berlin
Monument Authority. 2001–08
freelance curator at the DAM.
Since 2008 head curator at
the Museum of Architecture and
the Art of Engineering NRW.

STEFANIE LAMPE
***1984 in Heilbronn. Seit 2004
Studium der Kunstgeschichte
und Angewandten Kultur-
wissenschaften an der Universität Karlsruhe. Seit 2009
freie Mitarbeiterin im Bereich
Presse- und Öffentlichkeitsarbeit des DAM.**
Born 1984 in Heilbronn. Art
history and applied art studies at
the University of Karlsruhe since
2004. Since 2009 freelance
employee in the press and public
relations department of the DAM.

FRIEDERIKE MEYER
***1972 in Dresden.
Architekturstudium in Aachen
und Seattle, Design Build
Studio in Cuernavaca, Mexiko,
Kunstgeschichte in Dresden,
Öffentlichkeitsarbeit und Aus-
stellungen am Festspielhaus
Hellerau, Journalistenschule
in Berlin. Seit 2000 Redak-
teurin der „Bauwelt".**
Born 1972 in Dresden.
Architecture studies in Aachen
and Seattle, Design Build Studio
in Cuernavaca, Mexico, history
of art in Dresden, public relations
and curator at Festspielhaus
Hellerau, journalism studies in
Berlin. Since 2000 editor at
"Bauwelt" magazine.

ELISABETH PLESSEN
***1965 in Mönchengladbach.
1984–87 Studium der Kunst-
geschichte, Germanistik und**
Philosophie in Köln. 1987–93
Studium der Architektur an
der TU Stuttgart (Diplom).
1993–95 Masterstudiengang
Architektur (SCI-Arc), Los
Angeles. 1996–2000
Chefredakteurin der Zeitschrift
„beton", 2004–04 Geschäfts-
führende Redakteurin der
Zeitschrift „Baumeister".
Seit 2005 Lehraufträge für
Architekturkritik an der
HTWG Konstanz. Bis 2009
Chefredakteurin der „db
deutsche bauzeitung".
Born 1965 in Mönchengladbach.
Studied art history, German
language & literature and
philosophy in Cologne 1984–87.
Architecture studies 1987–93
at the Technical University of
Stuttgart (Diplom degree).
Master's in architecture (SCI-Arc)
in Los Angeles 1993–95.
1996–2000 editor-in-chief of
"beton" magazine, 2004–04
managing editor of "Baumeister"
magazine. Since 2005 lecturer
in architectural criticism at the
University of Applied Sciences
in Constance. Editor-in-chief of
"db deutsche bauzeitung"
until 2009.

HESTER ROBINSON
***1955 in London.
1974–81 Architekturstudium
an der Universität Cambridge,
England. Als Architektin in
London, Zürich, Heidelberg
und Frankfurt am Main tätig.
Architekturführungen in
London, Paris und Frankfurt.
Seit 2003 freie Mitarbeiterin
am DAM im Bereich Architek-
turvermittlung und Päda-
gogik.**
Born 1955 in London.
Studied architecture at Cambridge
University. Worked as an architect
in London, Zurich, Heidelberg
and Frankfurt/Main. Organises
and leads architectural tours in
London, Paris and Frankfurt/
Main. Since 2003 freelance work
at the DAM in the museum's
education programme.

ENRICO SANTIFALLER
***1960 in München.
Studium der Geschichte und
Soziologie; Redakteur der**

IN MEMORIOAM

TEXTE VON | TEXTS BY

IRENE MEISSNER & CAROLA WIESE,
WOLFGANG VOIGT

WALTER BELZ

(31. 1. 1927–6. 3. 2009)

Eine ganze Generation angehender Architekten wurde von Walter Belz, der von 1972 bis 1992 das Fachgebiet Entwerfen + Hochbaukonstruktion II an der heutigen TU Darmstadt leitete, unterrichtet. Die Maximen seiner Lehre waren Wahrhaftigkeit, Logik, Vernunft, Angemessenheit sowie die sinnvolle konstruktive Fügung der Bauteile. Entscheidend trug er zu der uns prägenden „Darmstädter Schule" bei. Die Sammlung seiner Vorlesungen „Zusammenhänge – Bemerkungen zur Baukonstruktion und dergleichen" wurde schnell zu einem zeitlos gültigen Lehrbuch. Unvergessen sind die Gespräche, Exkursionen und die kritische Ausstellung gegen die vertanen Chancen beim Wiederaufbau „Heimat Deine Häuser", die er 1963 mit Max Bächer und Hans Kammerer initiierte und auch in Darmstadt zeigte. Am Lehrstuhl befanden sich die Dias der ausgeführten Bauten separiert in einem Schrank in seinem Zimmer. Dort lernten wir zuerst seine Arbeit als Architekt kennen: Walter Belz, 1927 in Stuttgart geboren und aufgewachsen, studierte an der dortigen TH.

1955 begannen Rolf Gutbier und Hans Kammerer (1922–2000) mit ihm als freiem Mitarbeiter die gemeinsame Arbeit am Hochhausprojekt der Daimler Benz Hauptverwaltung. Nach dem Ausscheiden von Gutbier entstand 1963 die Partnerschaft Kammerer + Belz. Mit zahlreichen Wettbewerbsgewinnen avancierten sie zu einem der größten und federführenden deutschen Architekturbüros. Die Bauten spiegeln die Grundsätze seiner Lehre wider, einige waren ihm besonders wichtig: die eigene Hausgruppe in Stetten, die Calwer Passage und der mit dem Deutschen Architekturpreis ausgezeichnete Erweiterungsbau der Commerzbank in Stuttgart, das Wilhelm-Kempf-Haus in Wiesbaden-Naurod, die Deutsche Botschaft in Peking, das von ihm angeregte Provisorium der Freitreppe am Kleinen Schlossplatz oder der Stuttgarter Rathausumbau. Alle sind Beispiele für eine aus Ort und Material entwickelte und für die Bedürfnisse des Menschen geformte Architektur, die nun in seinem Sinne von KBK Architekten fortgeführt wird. Immer wieder nahm er Stellung zu aktuellen Fragen der Architektur, verfasste

‚Kritische Texte' und wirkte im Redaktionsbeirat der Zeitschrift „Der Architekt". Er engagierte sich als Landesvorsitzender und war Mitglied des Präsidiums des BDA Baden-Württemberg. Das Büro lenkte Walter Belz mit Weitblick und unternehmerischem Geschick, die Sicherung der Arbeitsplätze war ihm dabei immer ein soziales Anliegen. Die Praxis in Stuttgart und die Lehre in Darmstadt ergänzten sich. Der Abschied von der Hochschule fiel ihm schwer, den Kontakt zu den Mitarbeitern, die seine Ideale weitergeben, hielt er aufrecht. Walter Belz starb am 6. 3. 2009. Mit ihm ist ein großer Hochschullehrer, Architekt und Städtebauer und ein liebenswerter Mensch von uns gegangen.

A whole generation of up-and-coming architects were taught by Walter Belz, who from 1972 to 1992 directed the Department of Building Design + Construction II at what is today the Technical University of Darmstadt. The maxims guiding his teaching were truthfulness, logic, reason, appropriateness and the meaningful integration of parts into overall structure. He made a vital contribution to the "Darmstadt School", which has been so influential in shaping us. His collected lectures,

"Zusammenhänge – Bemerkungen zur Baukonstruktion und dergleichen" ("Contexts – Remarks on Building Design and Similar Themes"), soon became a timelessly pertinent textbook. The conversations and excursions with him remain unforgotten, as does his critical exhibition on the opportunities that were wasted in Germany's postwar reconstruction, "Heimat Deine Häuser", which he initiated in 1963 with Max Bächer and Hans Kammerer and also showed in Darmstadt. Slides of the buildings he completed were found in a cabinet in his department office at the university. This is where we first became acquainted with his work as an architect. Walter Belz, born in 1927 in Stuttgart, grew up in that city and studied at the Technical University there. In 1955 he began working as a freelancer on Rolf Gutbier and Hans Kammerer's (1922–2000) project to build a highrise as headquarters for Daimler Benz. After Gutbier resigned, Kammerer + Belz founded their own partnership in 1963. Winning numerous competitions, they advanced to become one of the largest German architecture firms and a leader in the field. The buildings reflected Belz's doctrines. Some of them were particularly important to him: his own group of houses in Stetten, the Calwer Passage and the

addition to the Commerzbank in Stuttgart, awarded the German Architecture Prize, the Wilhelm Kempf House in Wiesbaden-Naurod, the German Embassy in Beijing, the temporary steps erected on Kleiner Schlossplatz at his suggestion, or the conversion of Stuttgart's Rathaus. All are exemplary of an architecture based on site and materials, and shaped to fulfil human needs – the kind of architecture that is now being carried on as Belz would have wished by KBK Architekten. Belz frequently commented on topical architectural issues, wrote critical texts and was part of the editorial advisory board of the magazine "Der Architekt". He was state chairman of the Baden-Württemberg chapter of the Federation of German Architects (BDA) as well as a member of the executive committee. Walter Belz managed his architecture office with farsightedness and entrepreneurial skill, demonstrating a social conscience with his efforts to provide and safeguard jobs with the firm. His architecture practice in Stuttgart and teaching in Darmstadt proved mutually complementary. He took leave of the university with a heavy heart, but stayed in touch with his colleagues, who passed on his ideals to others.

Walter Belz passed away on 6 March 2009. We mourn the loss of a great university teacher, architect and urban planner and an endearing human being.

Irene Meissner, Carola Wiese

HANS SCHILLING
(4. 4. 1921–19. 2. 2009)

Der 1921 in Köln geborene Hans Schilling gehörte mit Rudolf Schwarz, Karl Band, Fritz Schaller, Gottfried Böhm und einigen anderen zur Pioniergeneration des Kölner Wiederaufbaus nach dem Zweiten Weltkrieg. Die starke Ausstrahlung der Domstadt wurde vor allem von dem radikal neu aufgefassten katholischen Kirchenbau im Kölner Erzbistum genährt, für den die genannten Architekten unter der intellektuellen Führung von Schwarz die Maßstäbe setzten. Der Autodidakt Schilling begann als Bauzeichner seines Lehrmeisters Karl Band, dessen Mitarbeiter er bis Anfang der 50er-Jahre blieb. Die Serie seiner eigenen Kirchen begann 1952 mit der Friedenskirche zu den Heiligen Engeln im total zerstörten Wesel, deren Grundriss er über den Mauern eines zerstörten Forts entwickelte. Ganz von selbst ergab sich ein parabelförmiger Chor, der der von Schwarz vorgeschlagenen liturgischen Form des ‚heiligen Wurfes' entsprach. Zu internationaler Bekanntheit brachte es Schilling mit der Kirche Neu St. Alban (1957–59), die er als monumental aufsteigende Backsteinskulptur in den Kölner Stadtgarten setzte. St. Alban entstand aus braunen Trümmerziegeln, die zu Schillings ureigenem Material wurden. Auch in St. Alban gibt es den parabelförmigen Chor, an dem man auch viele andere Kirchen Schillings erkennt. Der Schillingsche Chor und ein polygonaler Grundriss mit fächerförmig zum Altar angeordneten Sitzreihen bildeten einen Kirchentypus mit Wiedererkennungswert, den er viele Male erfolgreich variierte. Aber auch bei den profanen Aufgaben setzte er unverwechselbare Bauten in das Kölner Stadtbild, die noch heute beeindrucken, wie das Ringhof-Haus mit kühn auskragendem Flugdach (1960) oder das schmale „Em Hahnen", das jedem auffällt, der den Alten Markt durchwandert, weil es glaubwürdig demonstriert, wie der Maßstab des Alten mit neuer Form zu füllen war. Um 1980 folgten einige Jahre fruchtbarer Zusammenarbeit mit dem deutlich jüngeren Peter Kulka, mit dem er das Maternushaus als Tagungszentrum des Kölner Bistums (1978–83) in das Domviertel baute: als bergendes Halbrund mit abgeschlossener Rückseite zur verkehrstosenden Stadtautobahn. Kurz vor seinem Tod hatte Hans Schilling seine Zeichnungen in die sicher geglaubte Obhut des Historischen Archivs der Stadt Köln gegeben. Als man ihn zwei Wochen später in seiner Heimatstadt beerdigte, ahnte niemand die bevorstehende Katastrophe. Für Schilling gab es an diesem Tag ein zweifaches Begräbnis. Denn nur Stunden nach seiner Beisetzung versank sein Nachlass mitsamt dem Archivgebäude und allen anderen darin gelagerten Schätzen im Kölner Untergrund. Aber noch stehen Schillings Kirchen und viele seiner Bauten und erzählen von der Gestaltungskraft dieses urkölnischen Modernisten.

Born in 1921 in Cologne, Hans Schilling was one of the pioneering generation of architects who rebuilt Cologne after the Second World War – among them Rudolf Schwarz, Karl Band, Fritz Schaller, Gottfried Böhm and a few others. The strong post-war aura of the cathedral city was nourished above all by the radical new approach taken to the design of Catholic churches in the Cologne archdiocese, for which the above-named architects, under the intellectual leadership of Schwarz, set the tone. An autodidact, Schilling started his career as an architectural draughtsman working for Karl Band, a job he maintained until the early 1950s. He began designing his own churches in 1952 with the Friedenskirche zu den heiligen Engeln in the razed town of Wesel, echoing in his floor plan the walls of a demolished fort. The parabola-shaped choir thus arose quite naturally, at the same time corresponding to the liturgical 'sacred cast' form propagated by Schwarz, meant to focus the congregation's attention forward on the altar. Schilling rose to international fame with his Neu St. Alban church (1957–59), which he set in Cologne's Stadtgarten park as a monumentally soaring brick sculpture. St. Alban was made of bricks salvaged from the ruins of the war, which would become Schilling's signature material. St. Alban again exhibits the parabolic choir that is a distinct feature of many of Schilling's churches. The Schilling choir and a polygonal floor plan with rows of pews fanning out from the altar became a recognisable church type that Schilling repeated in several successful variations. But he also left his inimitable mark on Cologne's secular architecture with buildings that still impress us today, such as the Ringhof-Haus with its daringly cantilevered flying roof (1960) or the narrow Em Hahnen building that everyone notices who walks across the Alter Markt, because it so convincingly demonstrates how the old canon could be filled with new forms. There followed around 1980 several years of fruitful collaboration with Schilling's much younger colleague Peter Kulka, with whom he designed the Maternushaus, a conference centre for the Cologne archdiocese located in the cathedral quarter (1978–83). This structure is conceived as a sheltering semi-circle with a rear wall closed to the heavy traffic on the city through-road. Shortly before his death, Hans Schilling entrusted his drawings to what he thought was safekeeping in the historical archives of the city of Cologne. When he was buried two weeks later in his hometown, no one could have known that catastrophe was imminent. For Schilling, the day was like a double burial. Only hours after his funeral, his bequest sank into the ground beneath Cologne along with the entire archive building and all the other treasures harboured there. Fortunately, Schilling's churches and many of his other edifices still bear silent witness to the creative talents of this true native of Cologne and Modernist.

Wolfgang Voigt

Sämtliche hier nicht aufgeführte Abbildungen wurden uns freundlicherweise von den Architekten für die Publikation ihrer Projekte in diesem Buch zur Verfügung gestellt. Sollten unabsichtlich Referenzen nicht erfolgt sein, bitten wir um Entschuldigung und eine entsprechende Mitteilung an das DAM.

All photographs not listed here were either kindly made available to us by the architects for the publication of their projects in this book. Any omissions are entirely unintentional. We apologise to anyone not acknowledged and would request that details be addressed to DAM.

Umschlag und Umschlaginnenseite | Cover and Inside Front Cover
Stephan Sahm

1–11 Stephan Sahm
23 Uwe Dettmar
25 links | left © Stiftung Preußischer Kulturbesitz / David Chipperfield Architects; Foto | Photo: Joerg von Bruchhausen
25 rechts | right © Stiftung Preußischer Kulturbesitz / David Chipperfield Architects, Foto | Photo: Ute Zscharnt
26 links | left schneider+schumacher Architekturgesellschaft mbH, Frankfurt am Main

26 rechts | right schneider+schumacher Architekturgesellschaft mbH, Frankfurt am Main; Foto | Photo: Frank Hellwig
27 Architekt Daniel Libeskind AG
28 links |left DBM, Deutsches Bergbaumuseum Bochum
28 rechts | right NMFE GmbH / Imaging Atelier, 2009
29 links | left Kuehn Malvezzi
29 oben rechts, unten | top right, below Franco Stella
30 links | left Historisches Museum Frankfurt am Main; Foto | Photo: Uwe Dettmar
30 rechts | right Zooey Braun Fotografie
31 Hans-Christian Schink
34–39 Tomas Riehle / arturimages
41–43 Lukas Roth, Köln
44 Ralf Lehm
45 Roland Halbe Fotografie
46 oben links | top left Roland Halbe Fotografie
46 oben rechts | top right Johannes-Maria Schlorke
47–48 Roland Halbe Fotografie
49 Johannes-Maria Schlorke
50–51 Frank Ockert
52–54 Quirin Leppert
57–59 Rainer Mader
61–63 ORCH Chemollo
64–65 Hertha Hurnaus
66–68 Roland Halbe Fotografie
69 oben | top Roland Halbe Fotografie

69 unten | below Hertha Hurnaus
71–73 Roger Frei, Zürich
75–77 Barbara Staubach, Frankfurt am Main
78–79 Frank Heinen
80–81 Barbara Staubach, Frankfurt am Main
82–87 Michael Heinrich
88 Florian Holzherr
89 Florian Nagler
90–91 Florian Holzherr
93–95 Christian Richters
96–98 Eckhart Matthäus
99 Regina Schineis
101–103 David Franck, www.davidfranck.de
105 David Franck, www.davidfranck.de
107–111 Christian Richters
113–117 Karsten Monnerjahn
119–123 Michael Heinrich
125–131 Roland Halbe Fotografie
132–134 Edward Beierle
135 Gero Wortmann
136–138 oben | top Edward Beierle
138 unten | below Jutta Görlich
139 Gero Wortmann
141 Foto | Photo: Andreas Lechtape, 2008 / © Museum Brandhorst, München
142 links | left Foto | Photo: Haydar Koyupinar, 2008 / © Museum Brandhorst, München
142 rechts | right Foto | Photo: Andreas Lechtape, 2008 / © Museum Brandhorst, München

143 Foto | Photo: Haydar Koyupinar, 2008 / © Museum Brandhorst, München
144 Foto | Photo: Noshe, 2008 / © Museum Brandhorst, München
145 Foto | Photo: Haydar Koyupinar, 2008 / © Bayerische Staatgemäldesammlungen / Museum Brandhorst, München
146–149 Thomas Spier
151–153 Mirco Taliercio, www.mirco.net
155–159 Maximilian Meisse
161 links | left Audi / Allmann Sattler Wappner
161 rechts | right Audi / Allmann Sattler Wappner
162 Audi / Allmann Sattler Wappner
163 Audi
164 Audi/Allmann Sattler Wappner
165 oben, unten links | above, below left Audi
165 unten rechts | below right Audi / Allmann Sattler Wappner
166 oben | top Audi
166 unten | below Audi / Allmann Sattler Wappner
167 Audi
171–177 Jürg Zürcher Fotografie
179–181 Torsten Seidel
183 Uwe Dettmar
185 © DAM, Frankfurt am Main

CAPITAL INTEGRITY CHAIR

Design Zhu Xiaojie

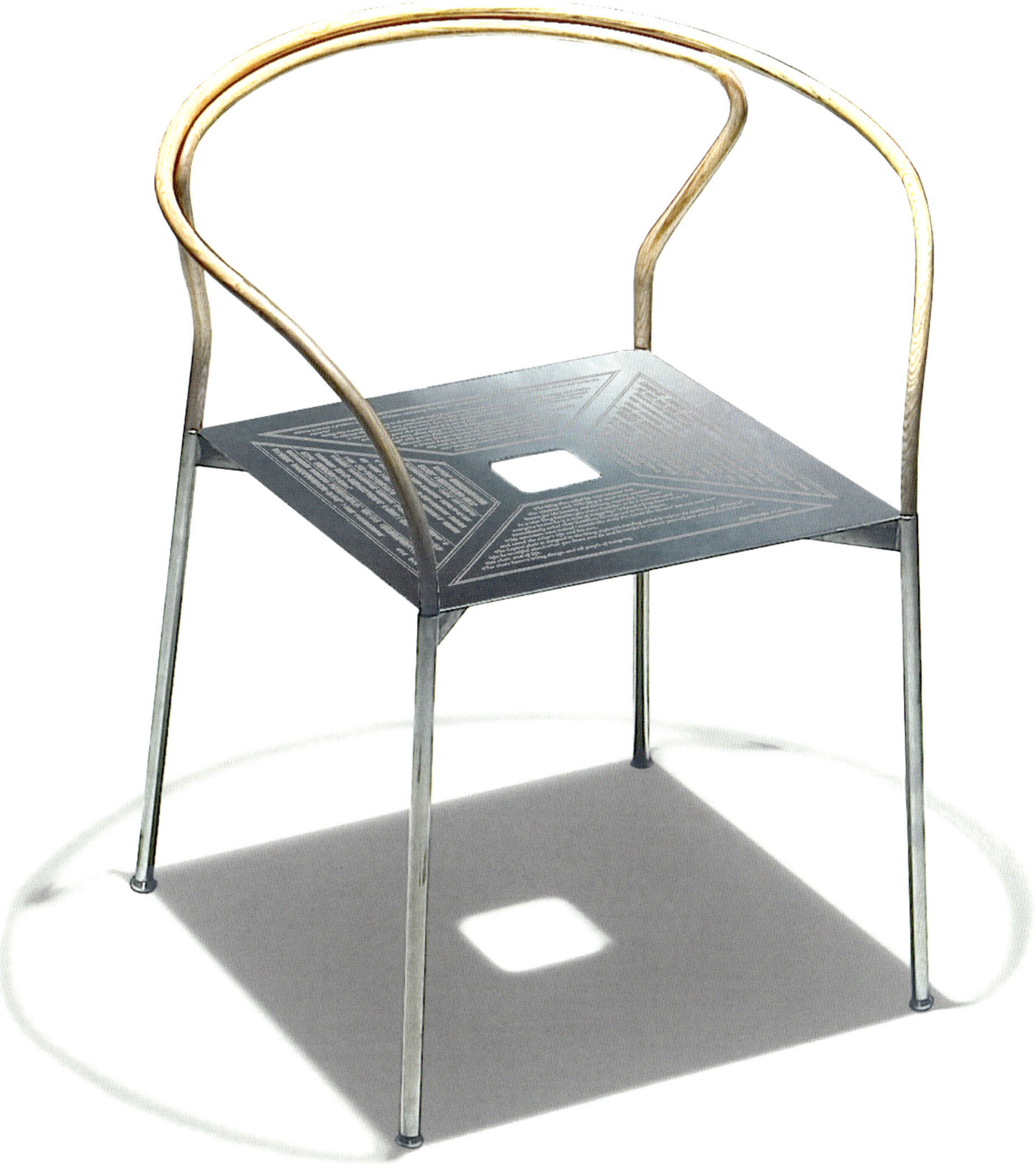

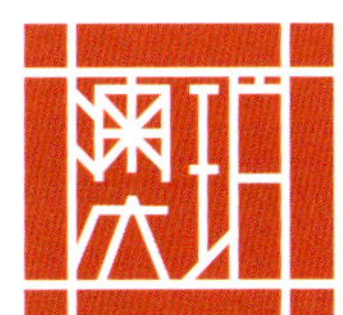

OPAL FURNITURE CO. LTD, No. 1 Yucangdong road, Economic Development Zone, Wenzhou
Tel: +86 (0)577 8655 1234, Fax: +86 (0)577 8655 2345, E-mail: opal-zhu@vip.163.com, **www.opal-furniture.com**

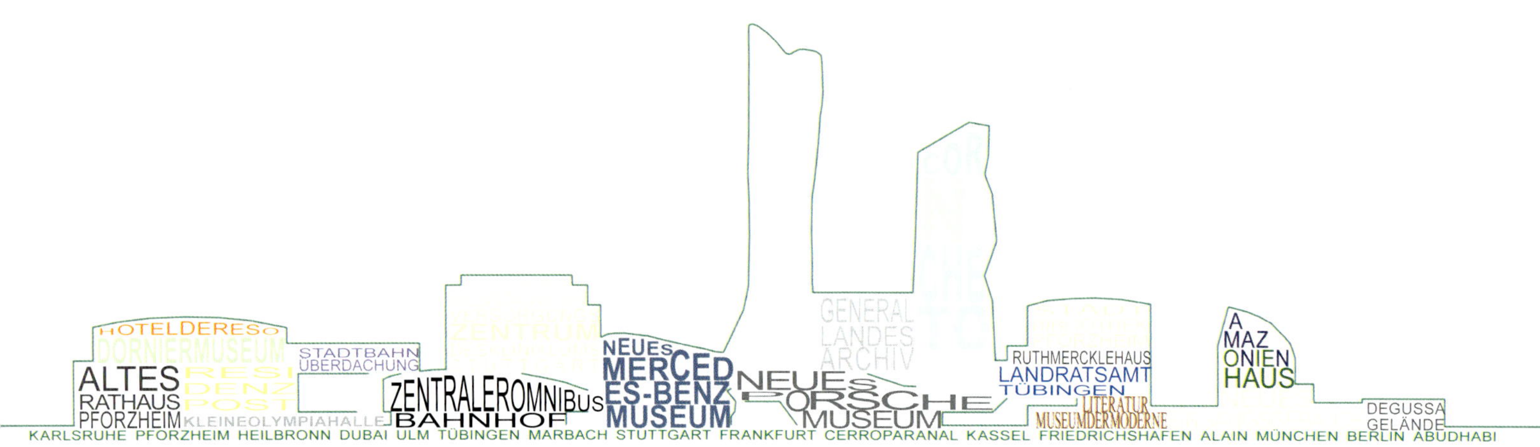

WENZEL + WENZEL

FREIE ARCHITEKTEN | DIPL.-ING. | PARTNERSCHAFT

Komplizen für Visionäre

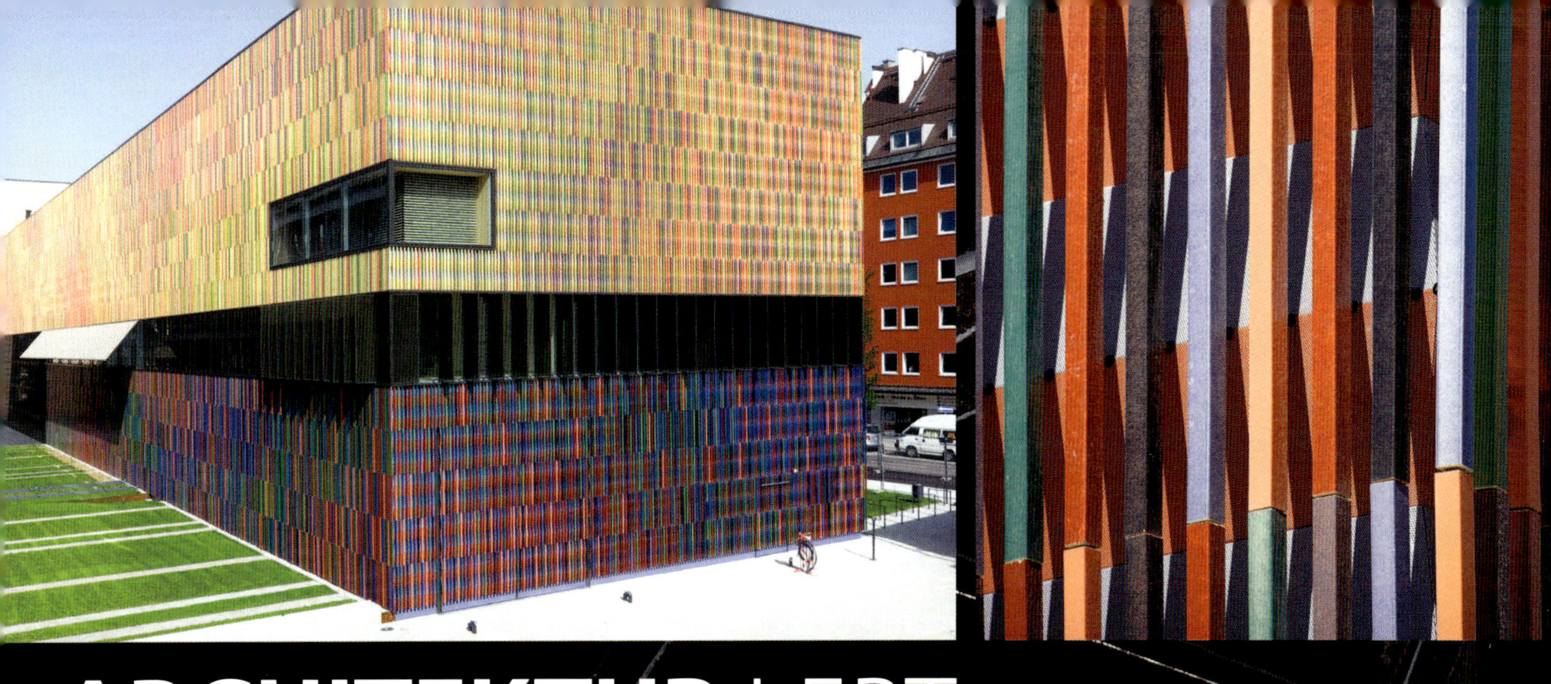

ARCHITEKTUR LEBT VON IDEEN

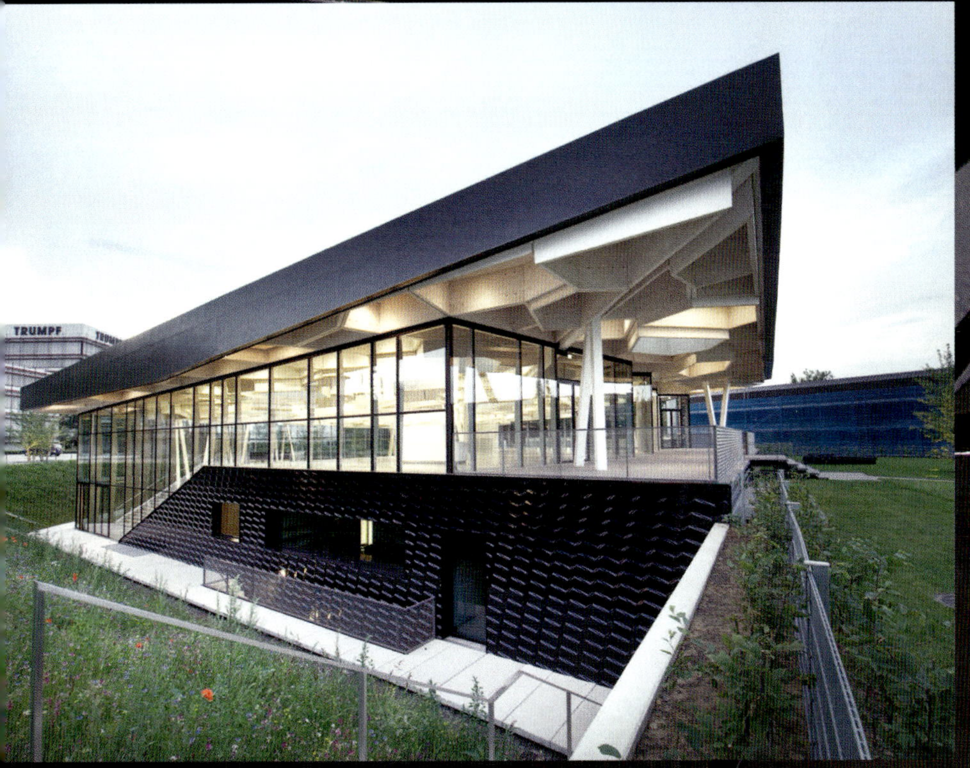

Ideenreiche Architektur unter Verwendung des
TERR**A**RT®-Fassadensystems:

Museum Sammlung Brandhorst in München,
Architekt: Sauerbruch & Hutton, Berlin

TRUMPF Betriebsrestaurant Ditzingen,
Architekt: Barkow Leibinger

NBK | Ceramic
ARCHITECTURAL TERRACOTTA

NBK Keramik GmbH & Co.
Reeser Strasse 235
D - 46446 Emmerich
FON: +49 (0) 28 22/81 11- 0
FAX: +49 (0) 28 22/81 11- 20
email: info@nbk.de

www.nbk.de

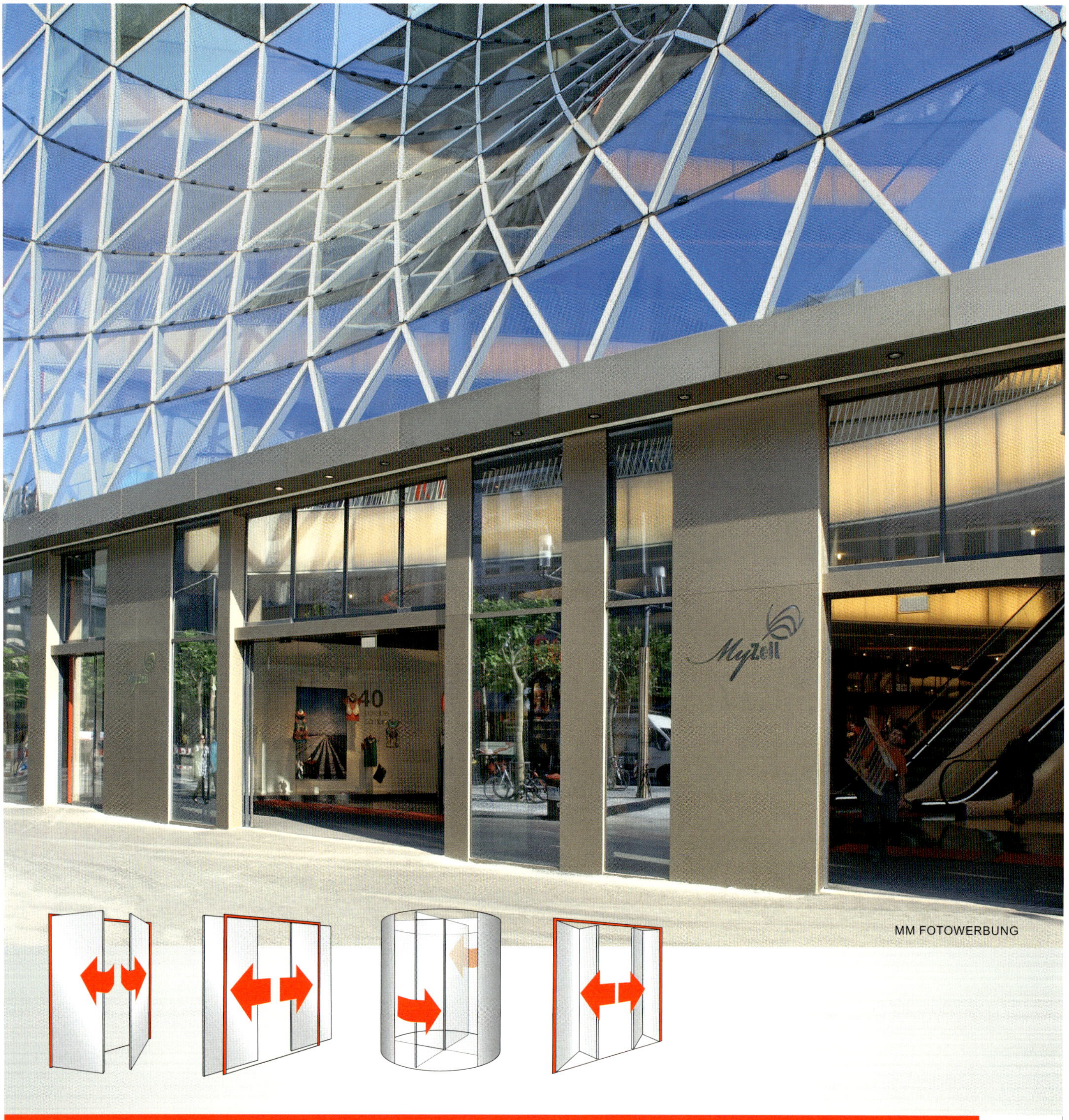

Die neue Generation
automatischer Türsysteme:
www.imotion.net

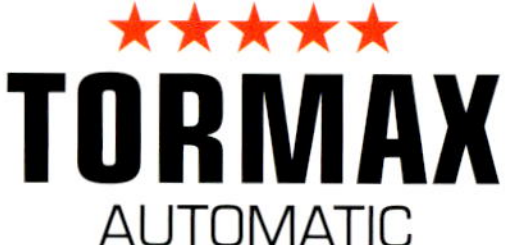

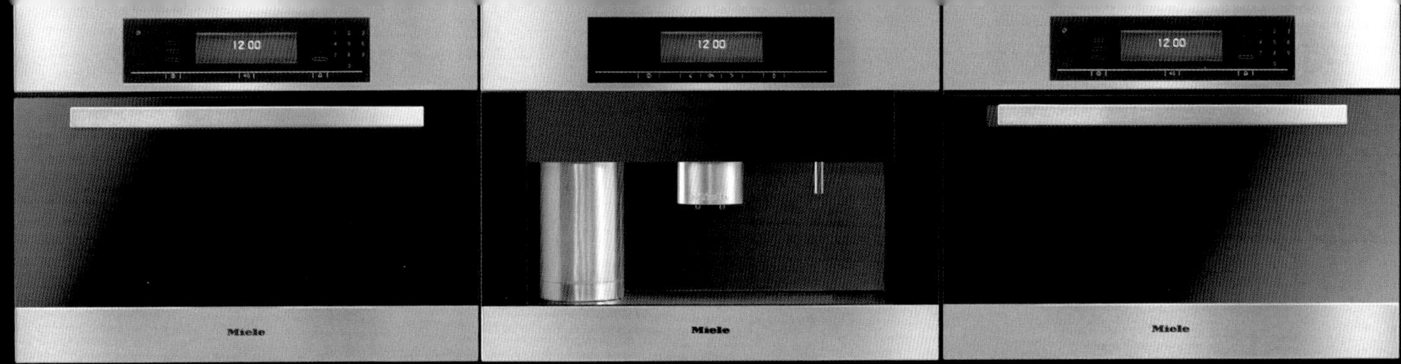

20 Jahre Lebensdauer – für ein Gebäude Voraussetzung, für ein Küchengerät ein Qualitätsmerkmal. Miele prüft alle seine Geräte im Non-Stop-Dauertest auf 20 Jahre Lebensdauer. Für die Architektur bedeutet das ein Zugewinn an Qualität, denn wer bei der Planung auf Miele setzt, entscheidet sich für nachhaltige Ausstattung und steigert damit den Wert eines Gebäudes.

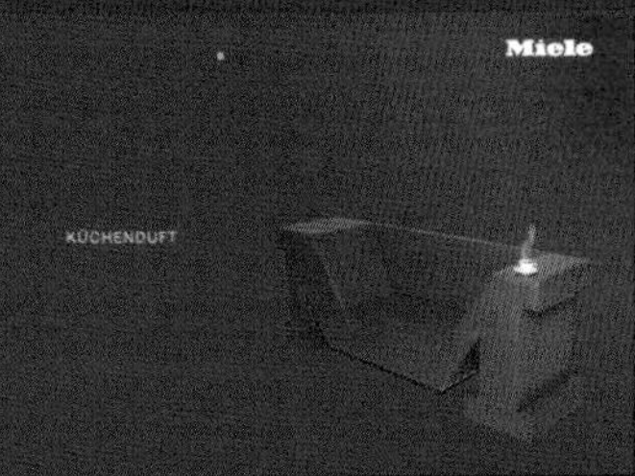

Das Miele Buch „Küchenduft"
können Projektentwickler,
Architekten, Innenarchitekten
und Planer kostenlos anfordern:
architekten@miele.de
www.miele.de

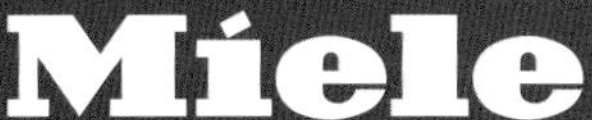

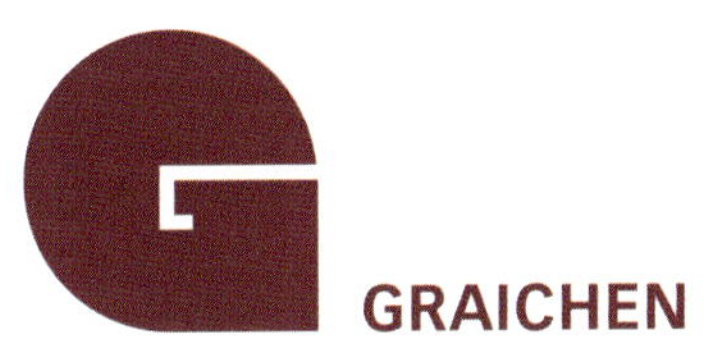

GRAICHEN

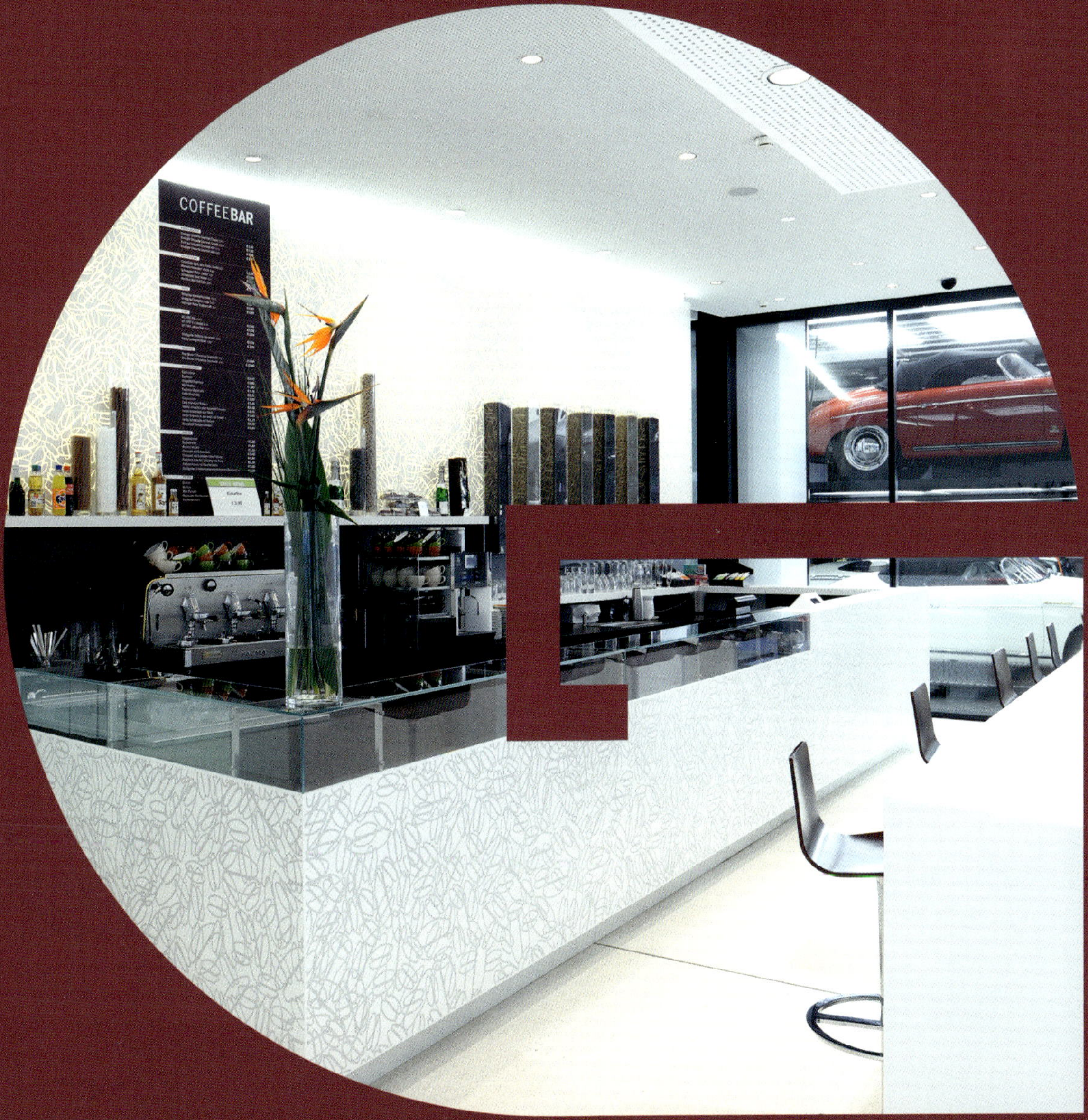

Meisterhafte Aussichten

GRAICHEN Bau- und Möbelwerkstätten GmbH
Gewerbegebiet Süd
Ringstraße 9, 04654 Frohburg

T +49.34348.691-0
F +49.34348.691-20
graichen@graichen-gmbh.de
www.graichen-gmbh.de

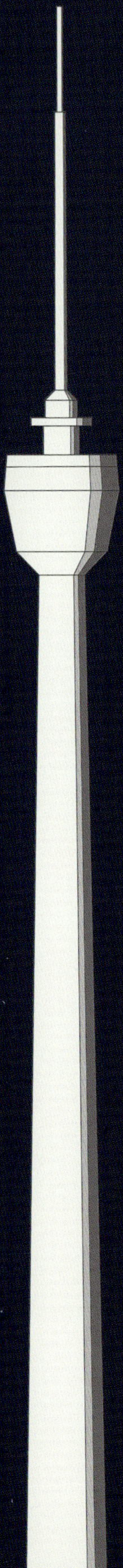

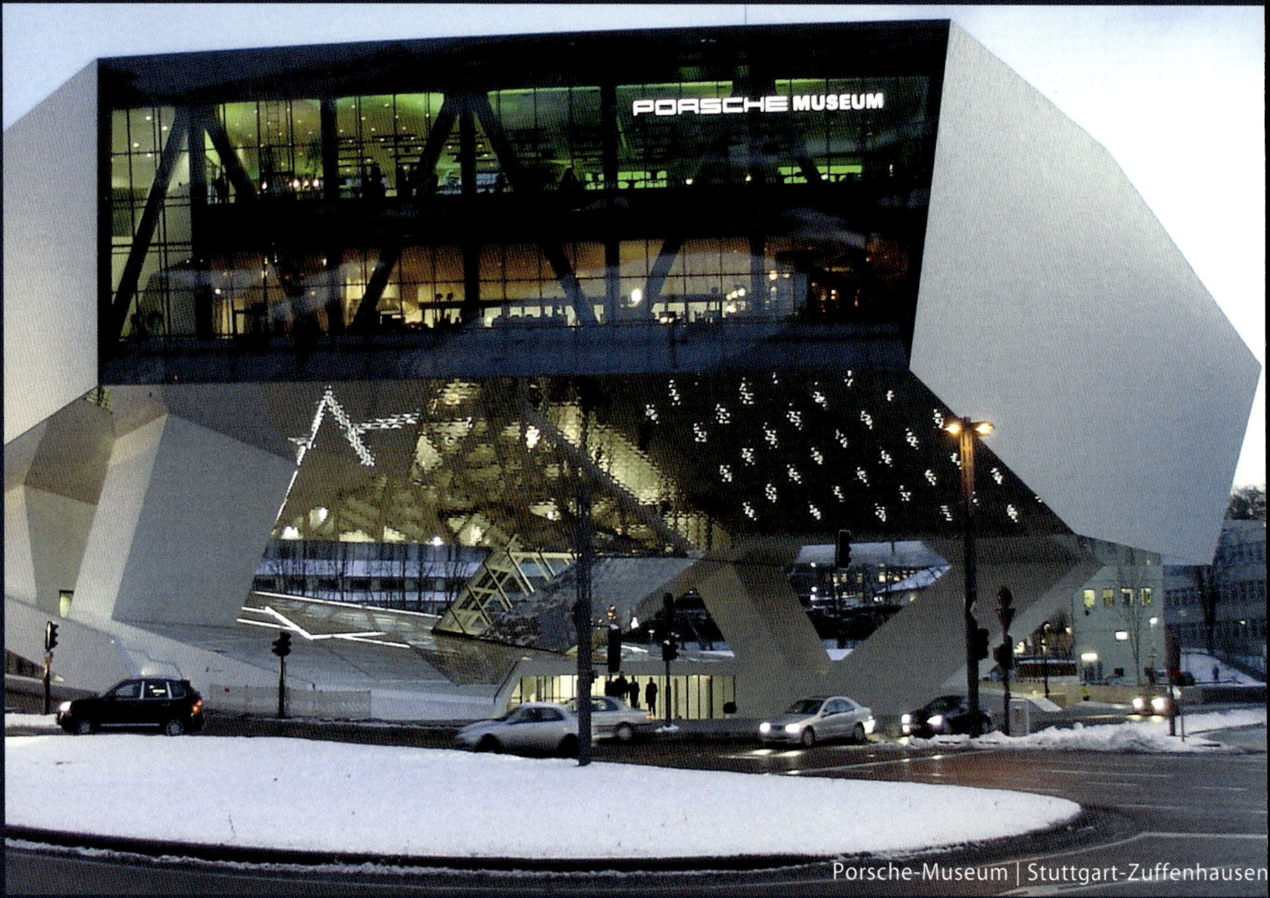

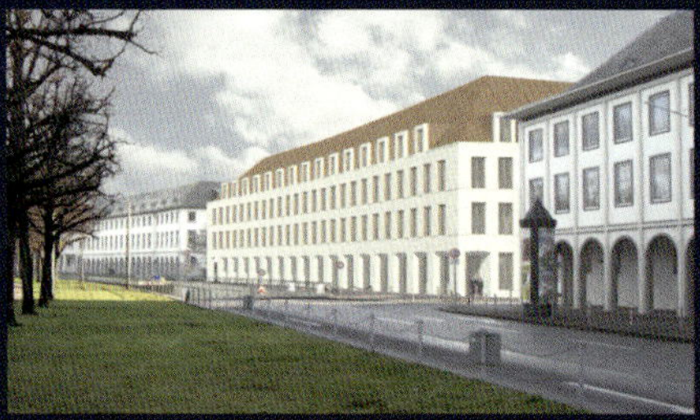

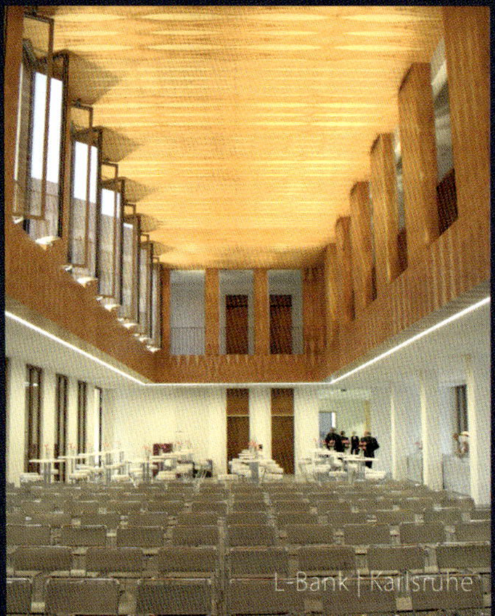

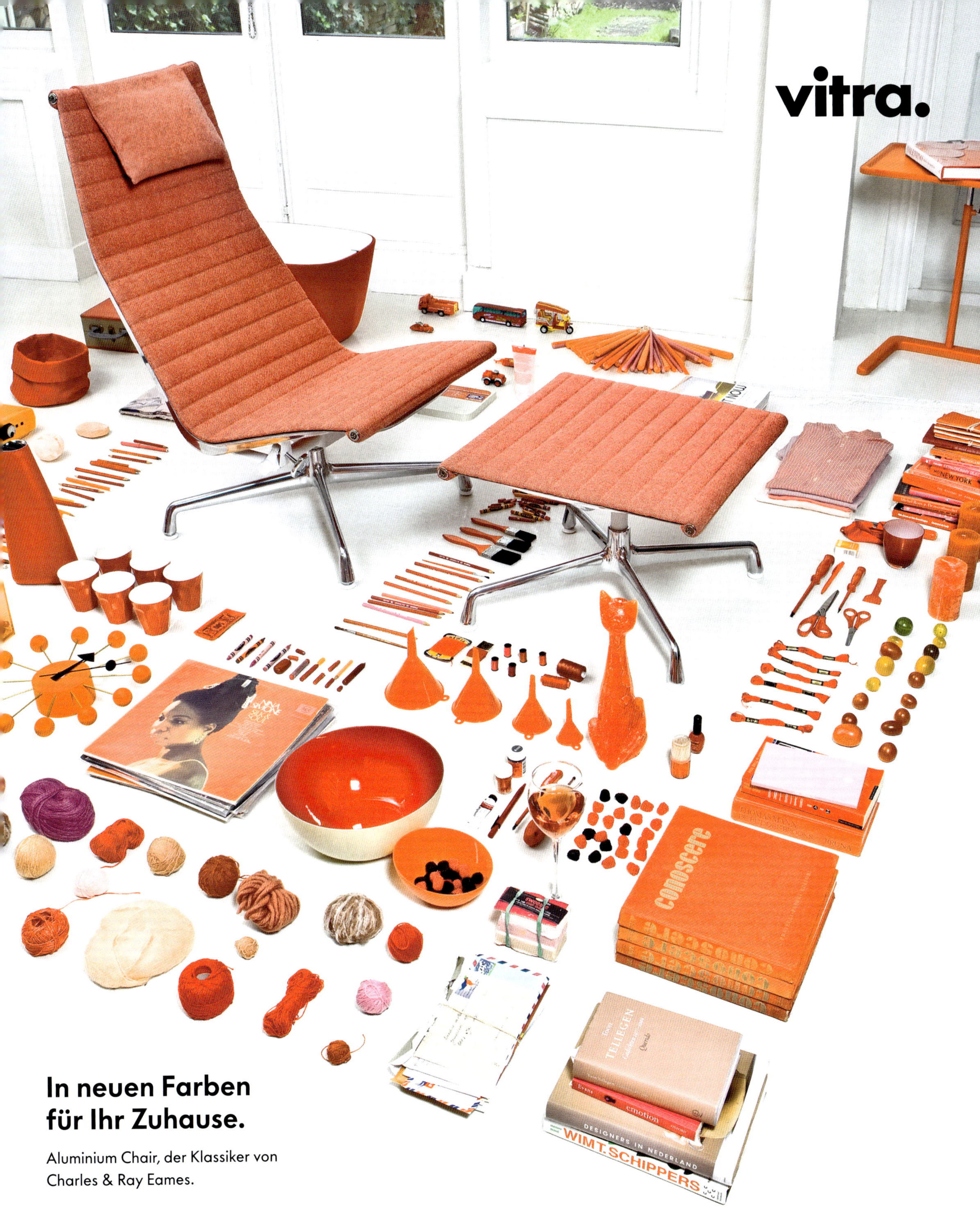

vitra.

In neuen Farben
für Ihr Zuhause.

Aluminium Chair, der Klassiker von
Charles & Ray Eames.

Vitra ist der einzige legitimierte Hersteller der Möbel von Charles & Ray Eames für Europa und den Mittleren Osten. © Vitra ® Der Vitra Aluminium Chair zählt zu den bedeutendsten Entwürfen des Möbeldesigns
im 20. Jahrhundert. Es gibt ihn in einer Vielfalt zeitgemäßer Farben. In welcher davon der Klassiker am besten in Ihr Zuhause passt, entdecken Sie bei Ihrem Vitra Händler. Tel. 00 80022 55 84 87, www.vitra.com

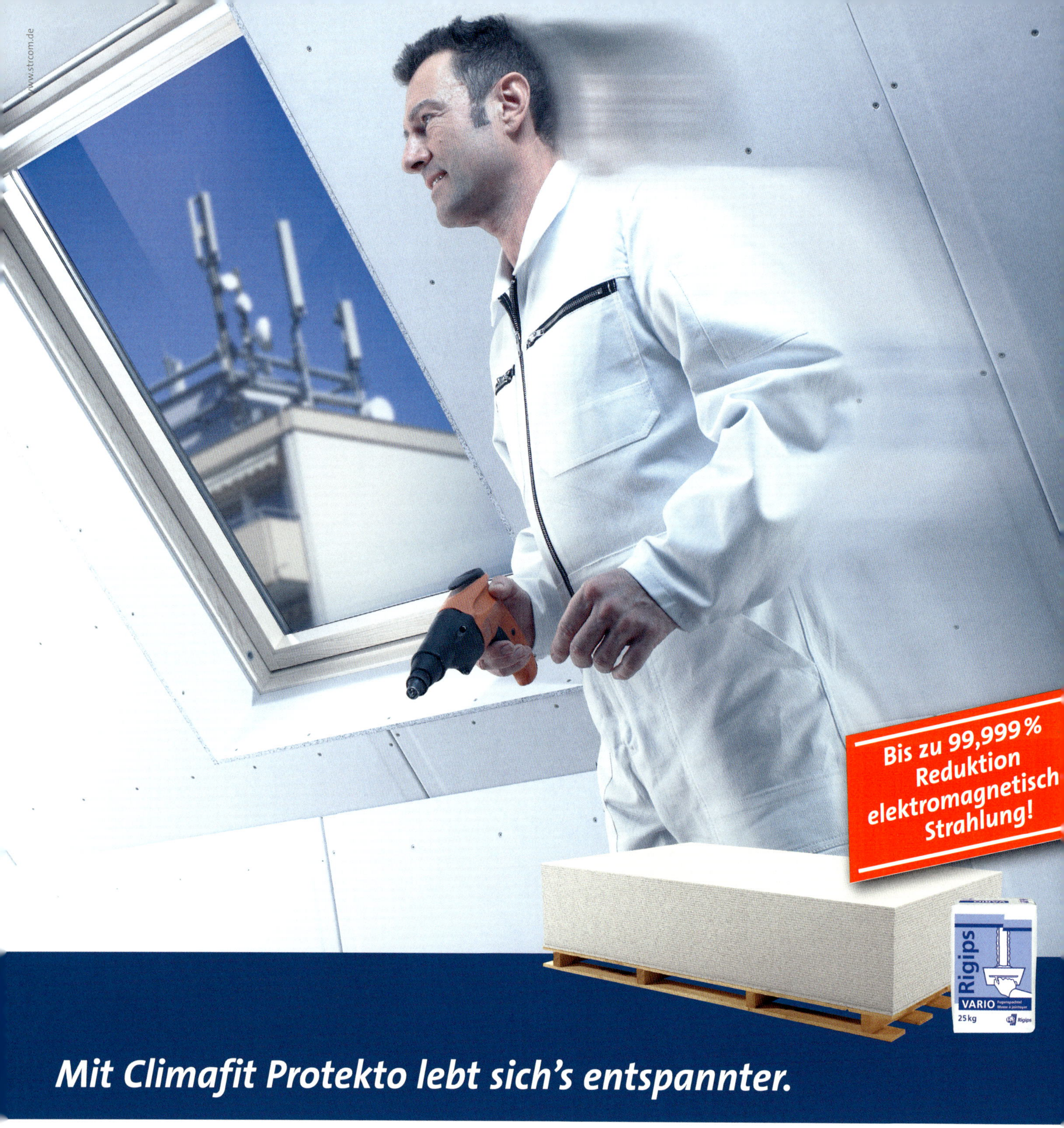

Mit Climafit Protekto lebt sich's entspannter.

Künstlich erzeugte Strahlung ist schon heute allgegenwärtig und wird noch weiter zunehmen. Rigips bietet hier wirksamen Schutz durch die effektive Reduzierung elektromagnetischer Strahlung. Die neue und einzigartige **Climafit Protekto-Lösung** überzeugt dabei durch eine Reihe entscheidender Vorteile:

- **Sowohl hoch- als auch niederfrequente elektromagnetische Felder werden um bis zu 99,999 % reduziert**
- **Elektromagnetische Strahlung wird weitestgehend absorbiert, nicht bloß reflektiert**

Trockenbau, Putze und Dämmstoffe. Aufeinander abgestimmte Systeme aus einer Hand.
Mehr erfahren Sie unter **www.rigips.de**.

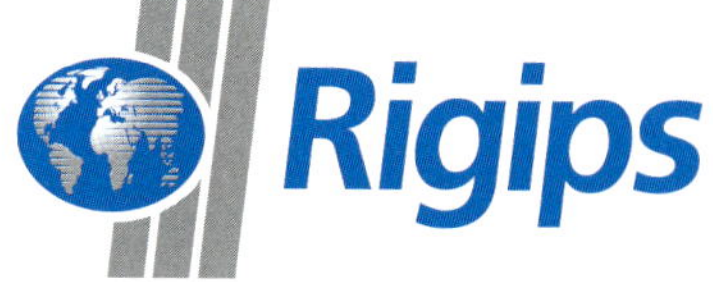

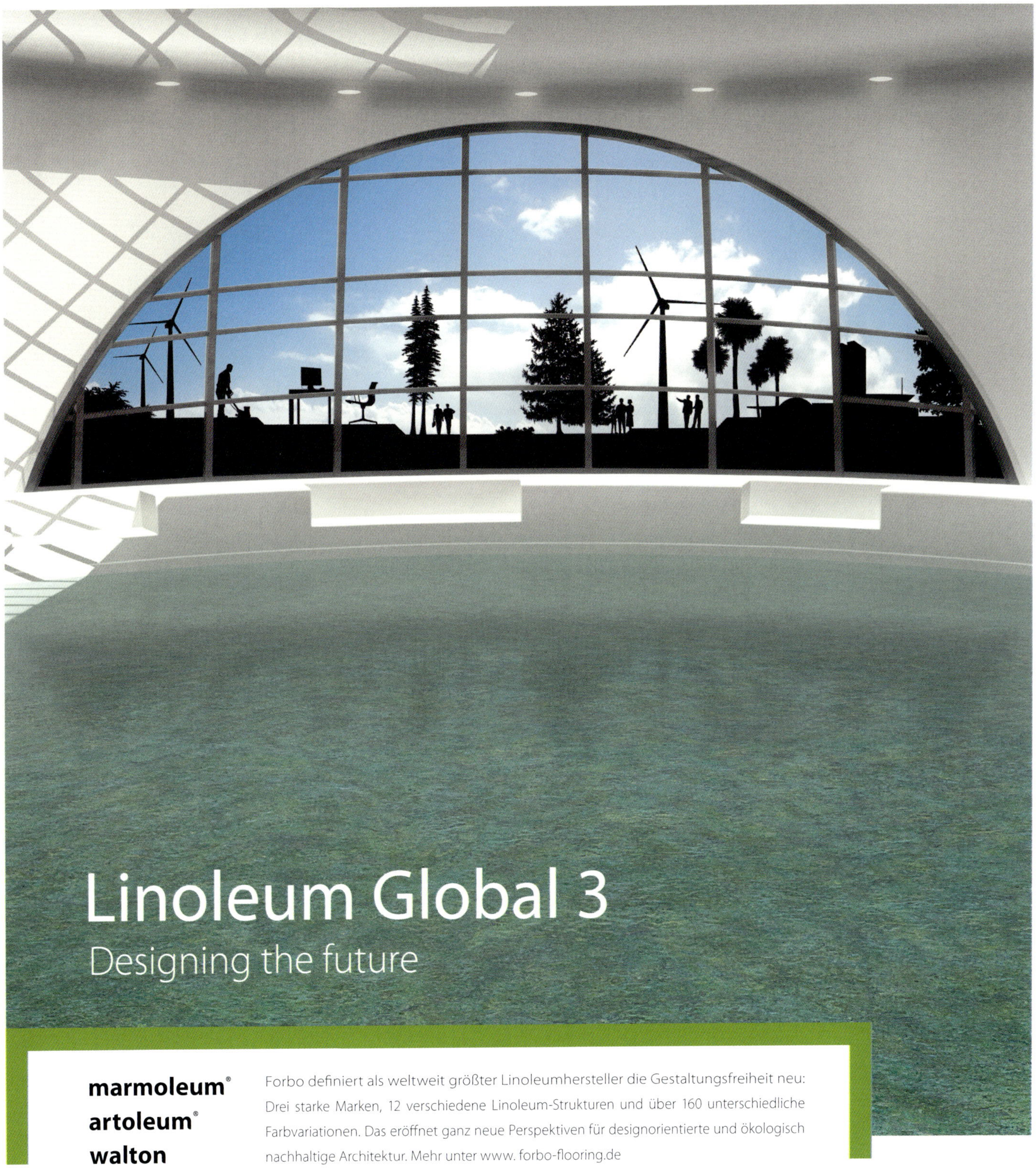

Linoleum Global 3

Designing the future

marmoleum®
artoleum®
walton

Forbo definiert als weltweit größter Linoleumhersteller die Gestaltungsfreiheit neu: Drei starke Marken, 12 verschiedene Linoleum-Strukturen und über 160 unterschiedliche Farbvariationen. Das eröffnet ganz neue Perspektiven für designorientierte und ökologisch nachhaltige Architektur. Mehr unter www.forbo-flooring.de

creating better environments

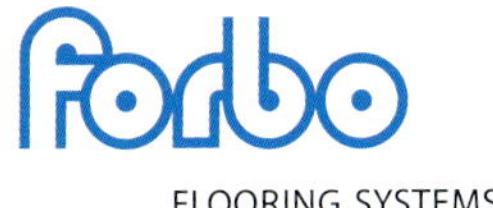

24 Stunden Sonnenwärme.

Der Traum vom solaren Heizen ist Wirklichkeit. Die neue patentierte Solarheizung von Consolar liefert erstmals die komplette Wärme fürs Haus mit nur einem System – und das rund um die Uhr. Circa 85 % der Energie gewinnt die Solarheizung SOLAERA direkt aus der Sonne – das ist mehr als doppelt so viel wie bislang möglich war.

Solar heizen. Auch bei Nacht.

Selbst bei Dunkelheit fangen die Hybridkollektoren die Sonnenwärme ein – ohne Erdsonden. So sparen Sie 50 bis 70 % der CO_2-Emission im Vergleich zu Öl, Gas und anderen Wärmepumpen.

Lassen Sie die Sonne ins Haus.

Unser Portfolio umfasst neben den Komplettanlagen auch Solaranlagen zur Warmwasserbereitung und Heizungsunterstützung, Hochleistungs-Kollektoren und Zimmeröfen mit Holz oder Pellets.

Gestalten Sie die Zukunft.
Mit Solartechnologie der neuesten Generation.

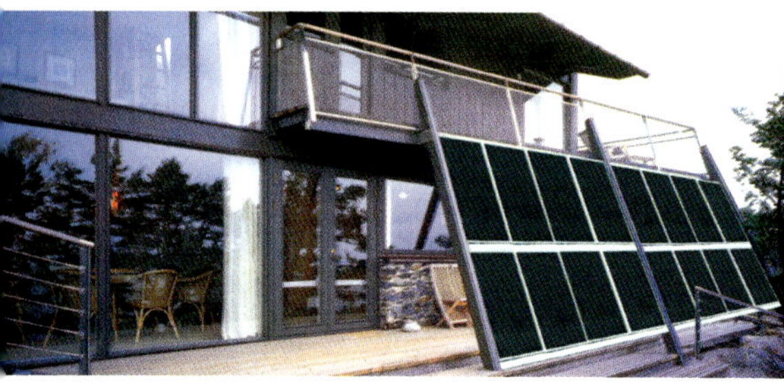
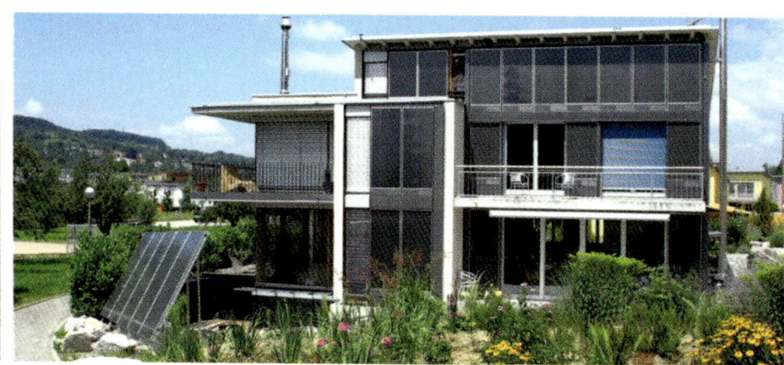
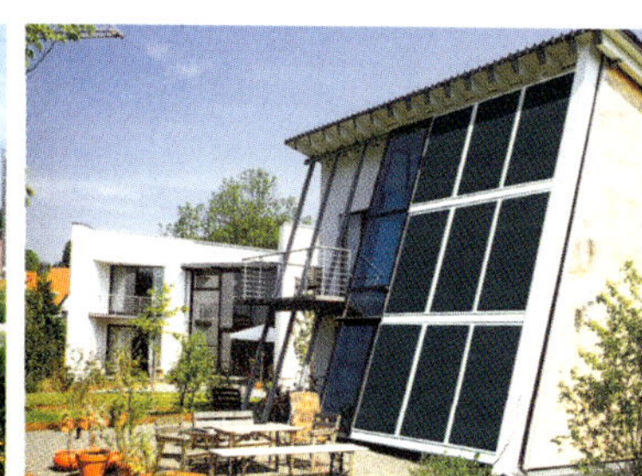

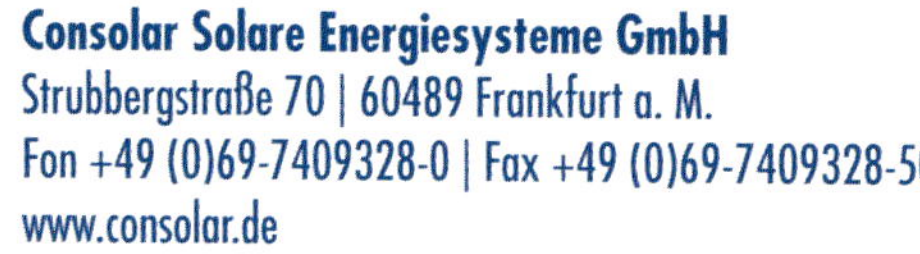

Consolar Solare Energiesysteme GmbH
Strubbergstraße 70 | 60489 Frankfurt a. M.
Fon +49 (0)69-7409328-0 | Fax +49 (0)69-7409328-50
www.consolar.de

Hocheffiziente Solaranlagen

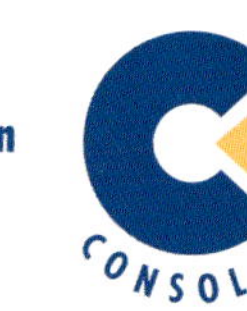

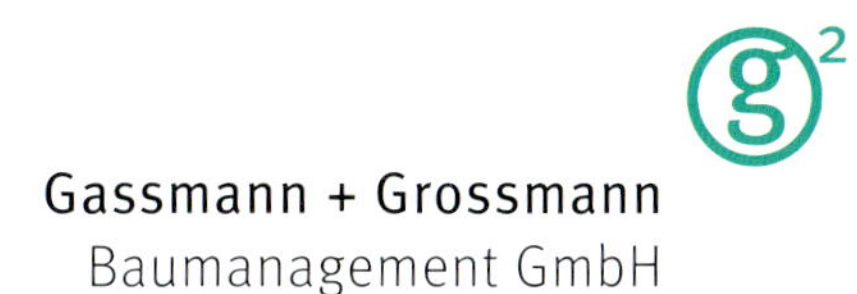

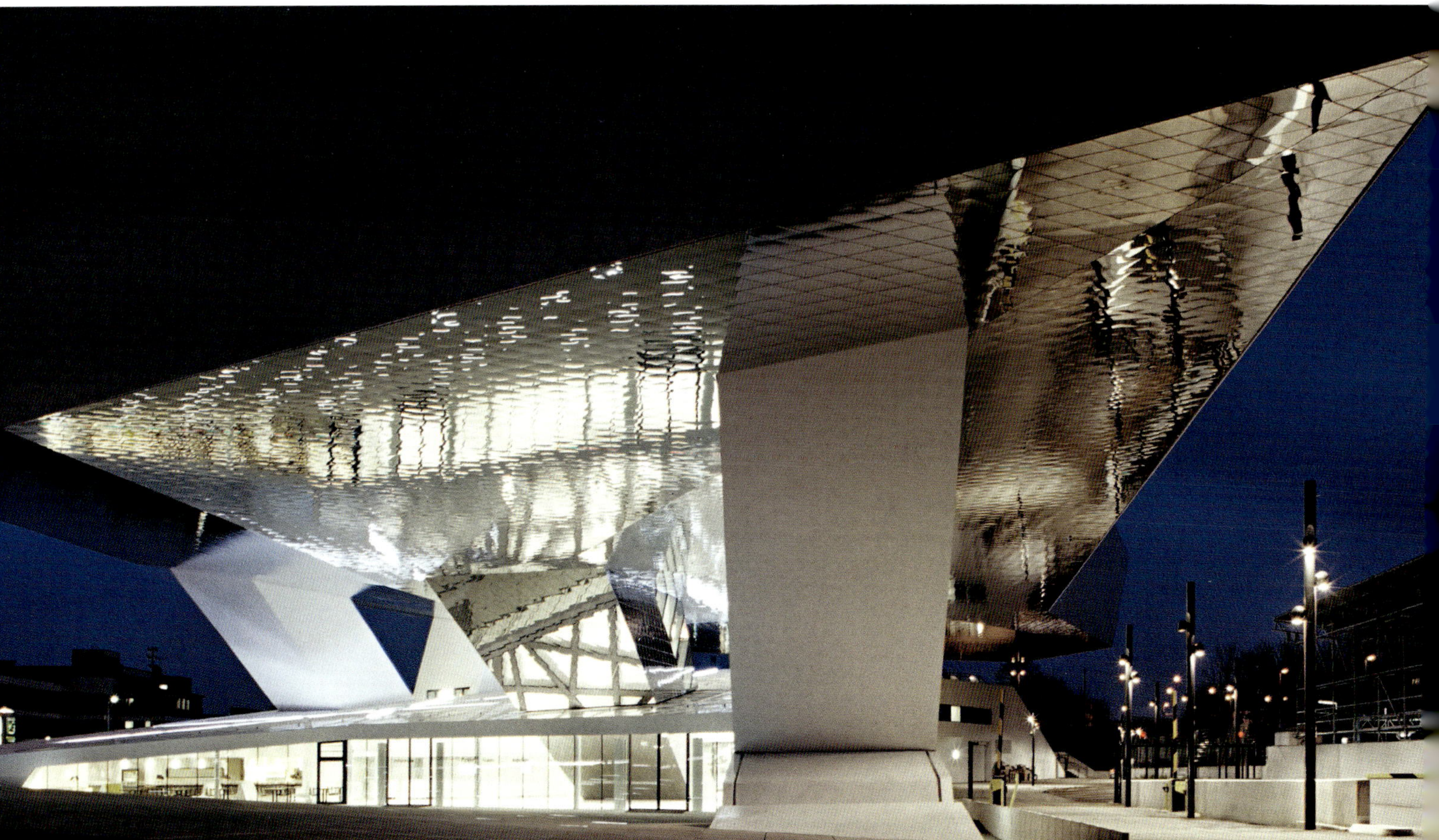

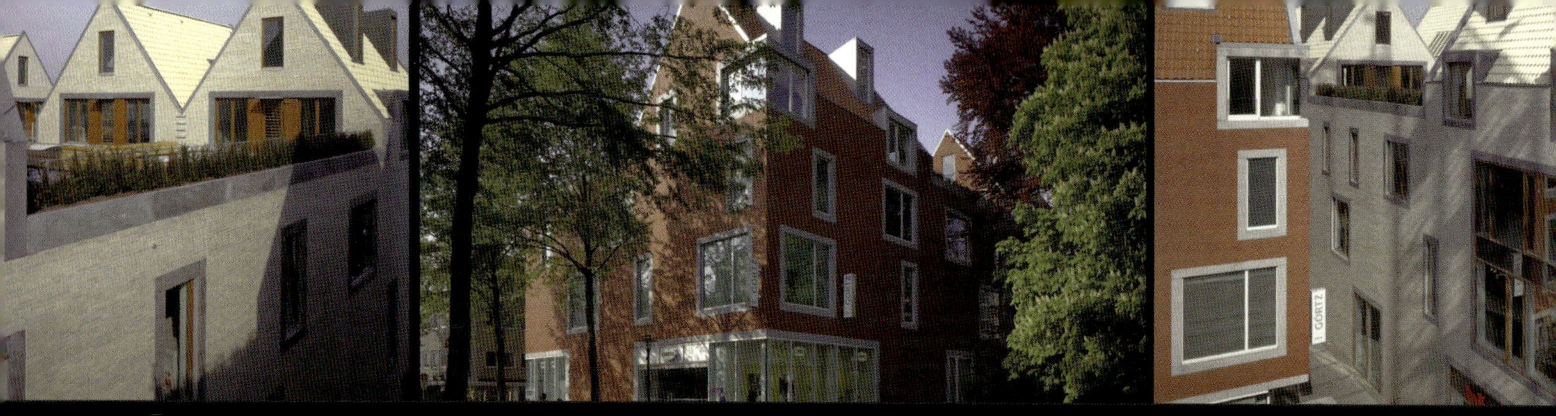

DER MÜNSTERZIEGEL®

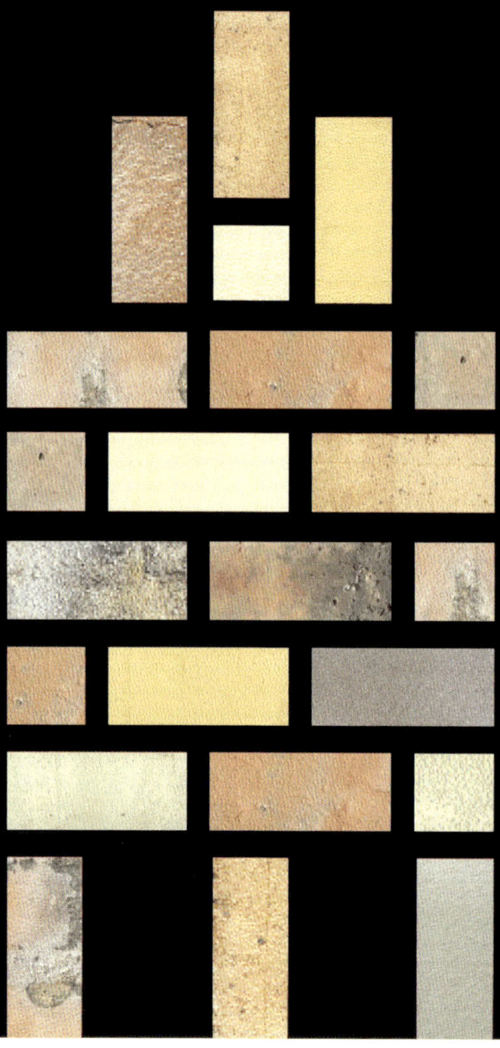

Der Münsterziegel prägt da[s]
Bild der neuen Architektur a[m]
Hanse-Carrée.

Erste Wahl für eine gut[e]
Adresse.

Architekt:
Rainer Kresing, Münster

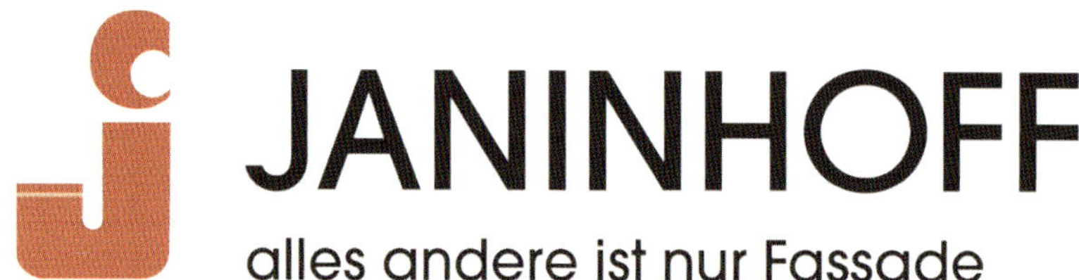

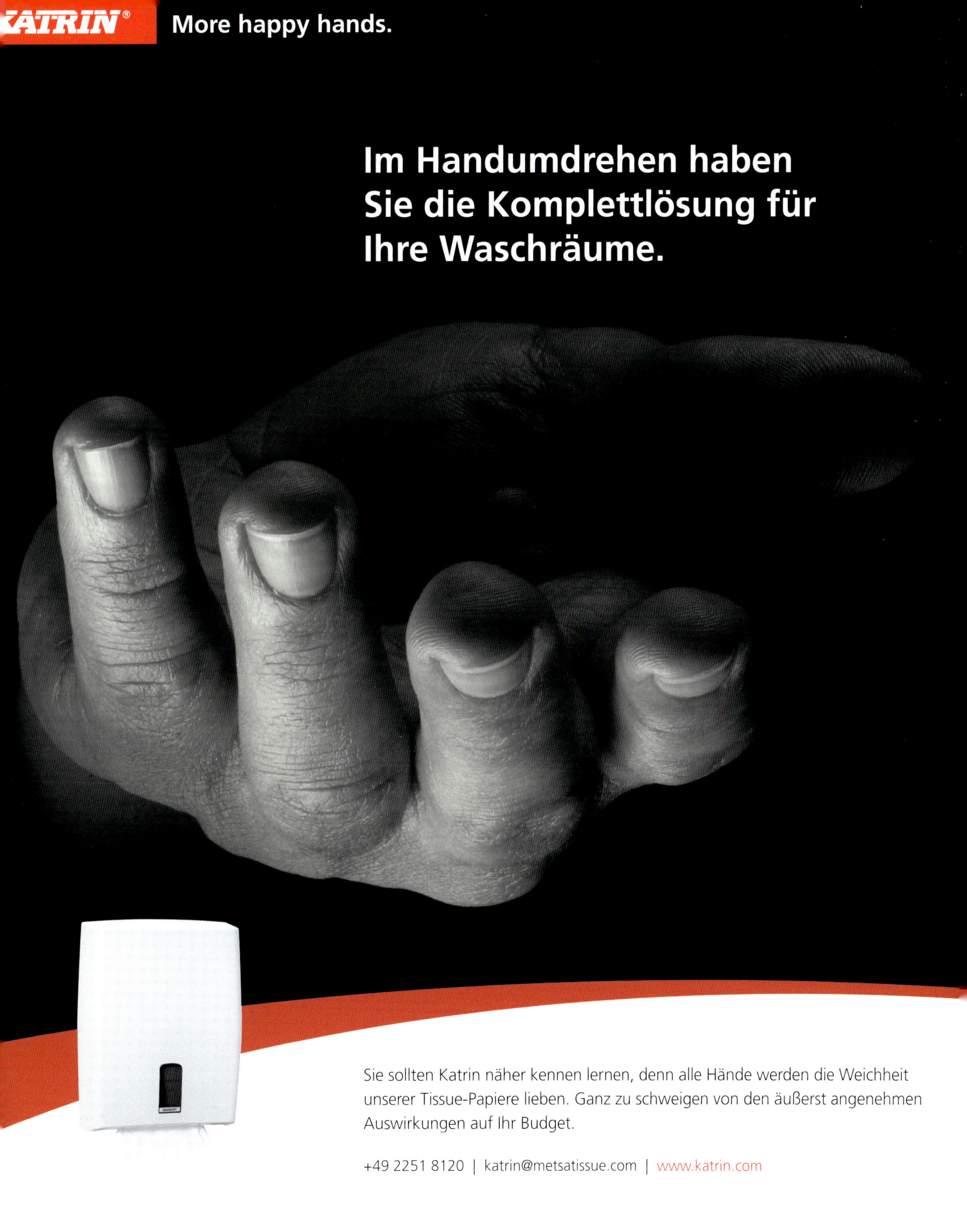

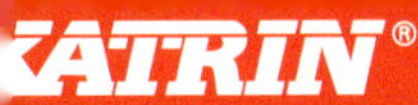

KATRIN®

More happy hands.

Im Handumdrehen haben
Sie die Komplettlösung für
Ihre Waschräume.

Sie sollten Katrin näher kennen lernen, denn alle Hände werden die Weichheit
unserer Tissue-Papiere lieben. Ganz zu schweigen von den äußerst angenehmen
Auswirkungen auf Ihr Budget.

+49 2251 8120 | katrin@metsatissue.com | www.katrin.com

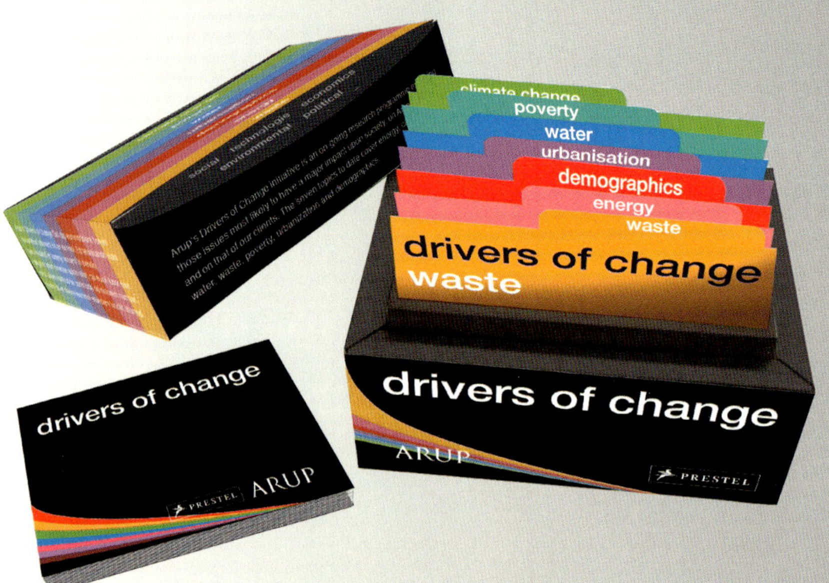

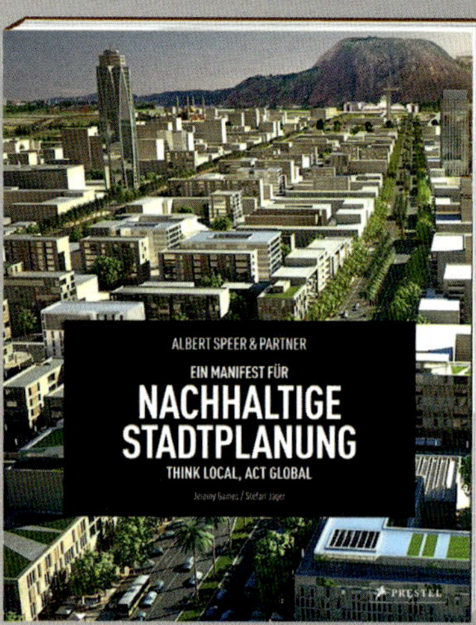

"... we shape a better world."

DRIVERS OF CHANGE
Chris Luebkeman
englisch, 175 Karten in einer Box mit Buch
ISBN 978-3-7913-4224-5
€ 49,95 (D) / CHF 84,00

Think local, act global.

**ALBERT SPEER UND PARTNER:
EIN MANIFEST FÜR
NACHHALTIGE STADTPLANUNG**
Jeremy Gaines, Stefan Jäger
deutsch, Flexo-Einband
ISBN 978-3-7913-4206-1
(engl. ISBN 978-3-7913-4207-8)
€ 29,95 (D) / CHF 49,90

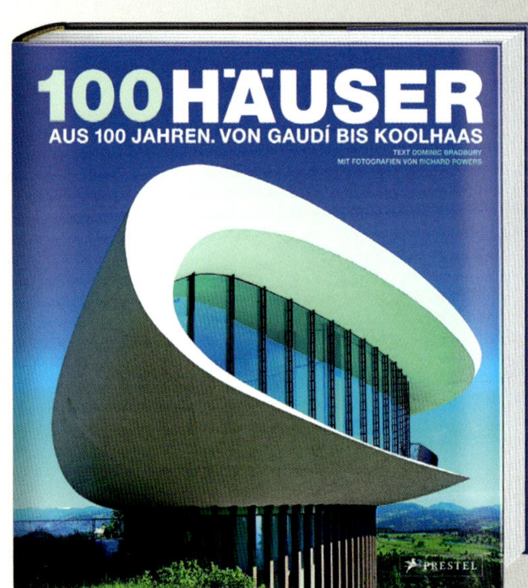

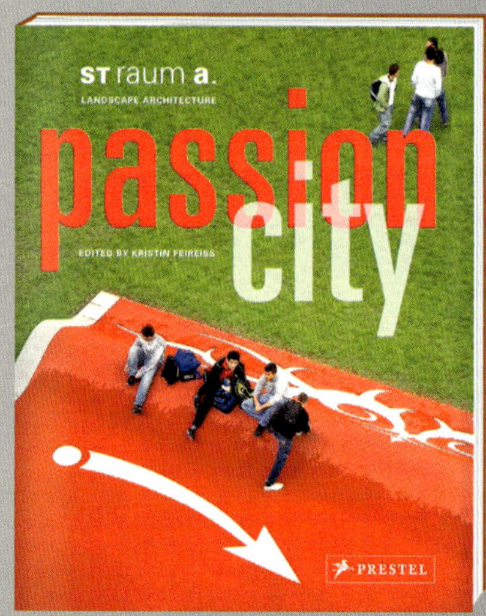

Ikonen der Wohnhaus-Architektur

**100 HÄUSER AUS 100 JAHREN.
VON GAUDÍ BIS KOOLHAAS**
Dominic Bradbury, Fotos: Richard Powers
deutsch, gebunden mit Schutzumschlag
ISBN 978-3-7913-4322-8
€ 59,00 (D) / CHF 99,90

Stadtraum – für Menschen

**PASSION CITY
ST RAUM A. LANDSCHAFTSARCHITEKTUR**
Kristin Feireiss
deutsch/englisch, Flexo-Einband
ISBN 978-3-7913-4305-1
€ 39,95 (D) / CHF 68,00

ARCHITEKTUR

Sitz in Deutschland. Weltweit aktiv.
Investitionsfokus: Premium-Objekte!

Sie haben interessante Bestandsobjekte in hochwertigen Lagen anzubieten? Dann sprechen Sie mit einem der führenden deutschen Investoren! Mit einem verwalteten Immobilien-Vermögen von rund 18,1 Mrd. Euro und einem Bestand von über 400 Immobilien in 23 Ländern auf vier Kontinenten ist Deka Immobilien der richtige Ansprechpartner für Sie!

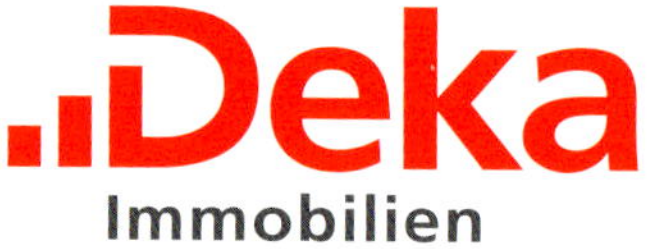

Deka Immobilien GmbH

Nehmen Sie Kontakt auf! www.deka-immobilien.de

Finanzgruppe

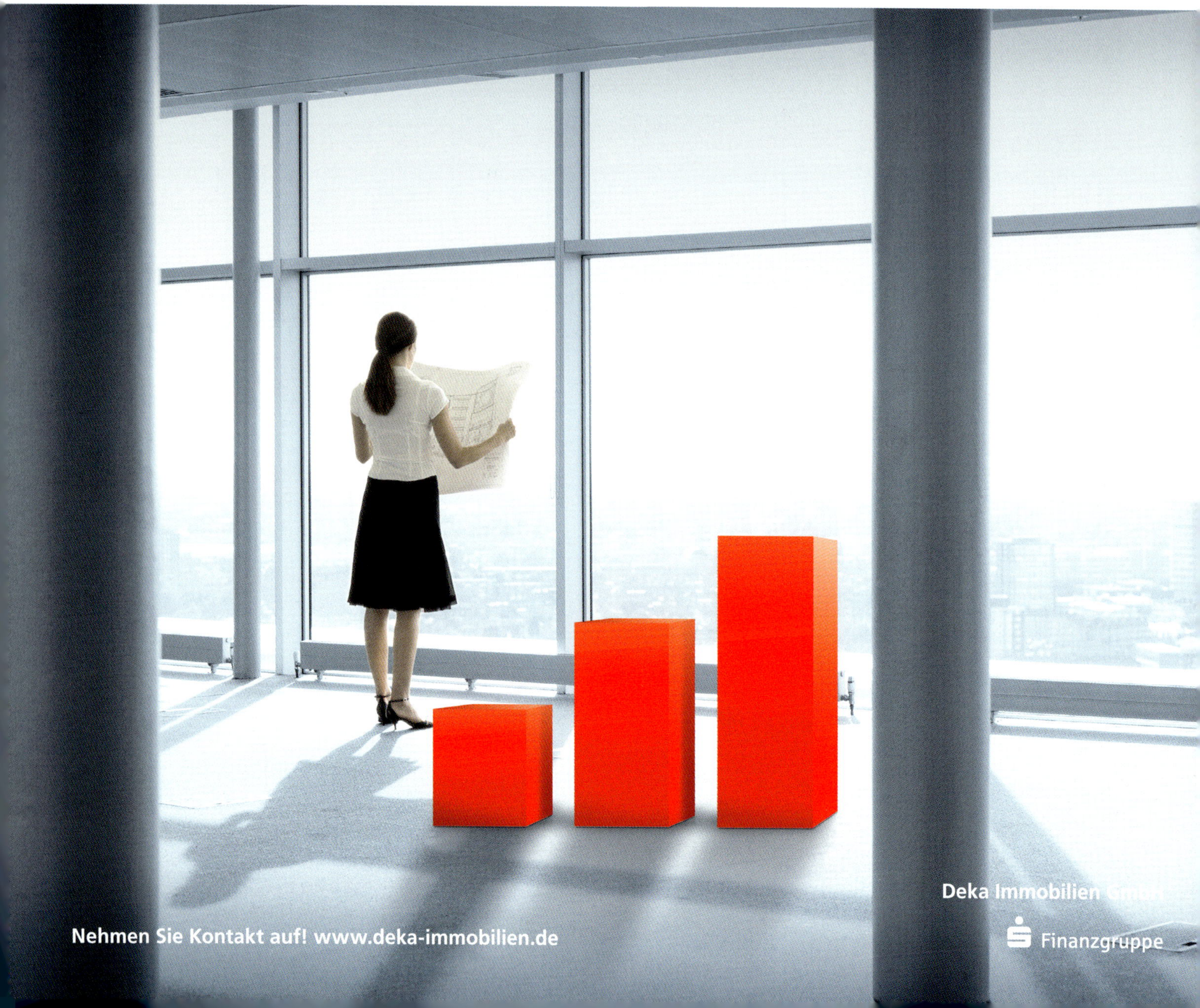

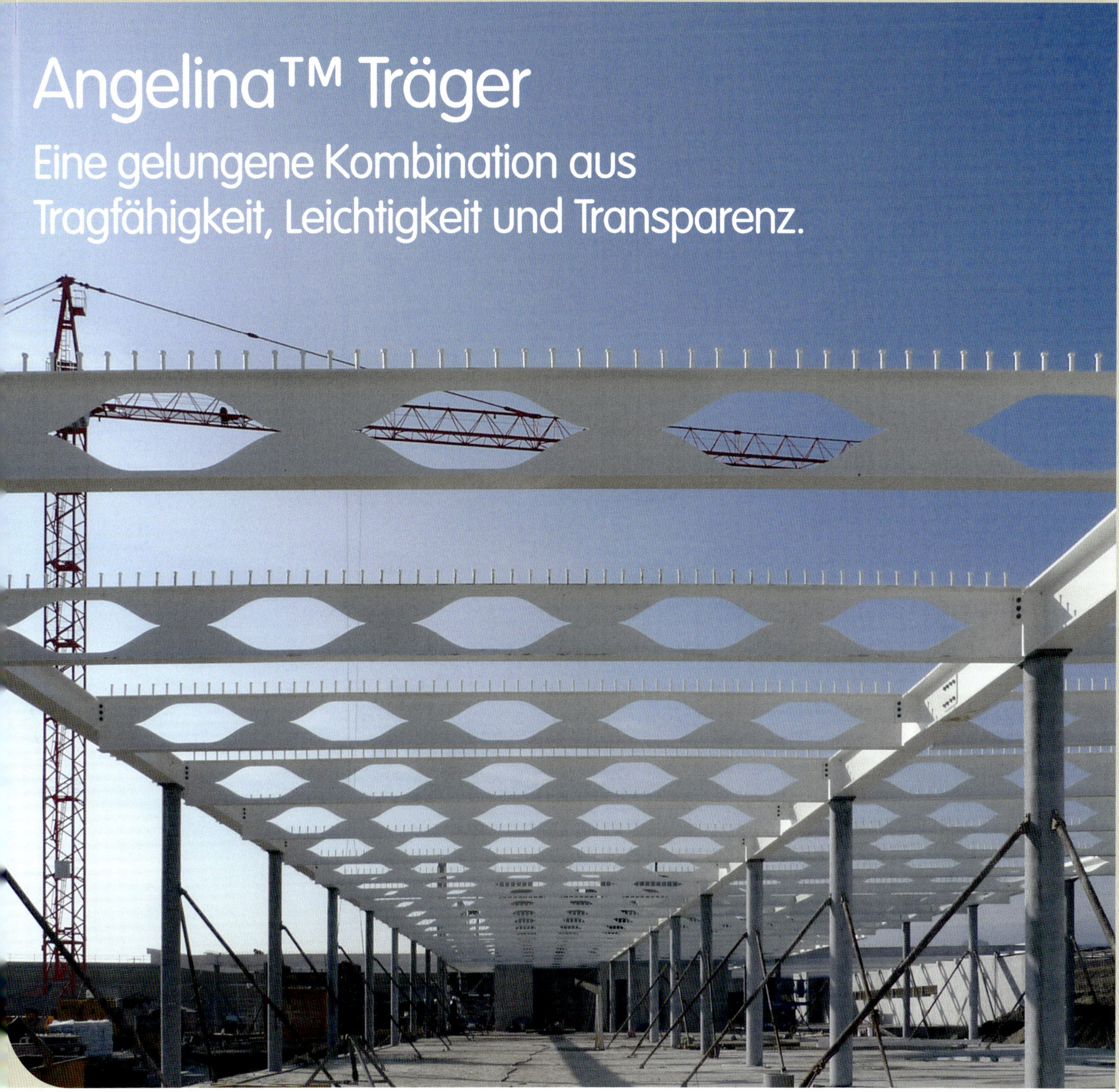

Angelina™ Träger

Eine gelungene Kombination aus Tragfähigkeit, Leichtigkeit und Transparenz.

transforming
tomorrow

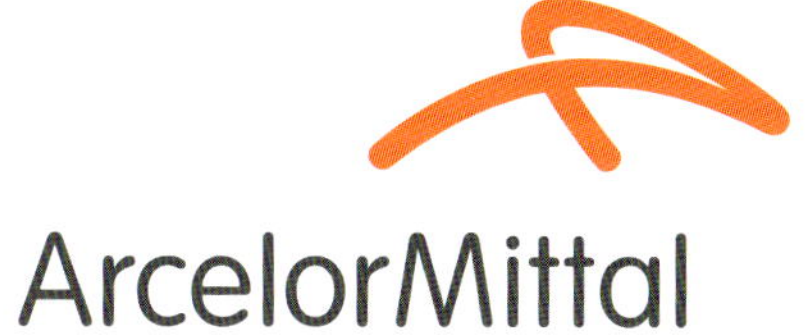

ArcelorMittal Commercial Long Deutschland GmbH
Subbelrather Straße 13 · D-50672 Köln · Tel. +49-221-572 90 · Fax +49-221-572 92 65
Herzogstraße 6A · D-70176 Stuttgart · Tel. +49-711-667 40 · Fax +49-711-667 42 40 · www.arcelormittal.com/sections

IMPRESSUM | IMPRINT

Herausgegeben von | Edited by **Peter Cachola Schmal und I** and **Michaela Busenkell**
im Auftrag des | on behalf of **Dezernats für Kultur und Wissenschaft, Kulturamt der Stadt Frankfurt am Main**

© **Prestel Verlag München, Berlin, London, New York, 2009**
© **Deutsches Architekturmuseum, Frankfurt am Main, 2009**
© **für die abgebildeten Werke bei den Architekten und Künstlern, ihren Erben oder Rechtsnachfolgern;
Abbildungsnachweis siehe Seite 194** | For the artworks with the architects and artists, their heirs or assigns;
picture credits see page 194

Umschlag-Rückseite | Back cover: **Ozeaneum Stralsund**

**Urhebernennungen stammen von den beteiligten Architekten selbst. Für die Richtigkeit dieser Angaben
übernehmen das Deutsche Architekturmuseum und der Prestel Verlag keine Gewähr.**
Names of copyright holders of the material used have been supplied by the architects themselves. Neither the Deutsches
Architekturmuseum nor Prestel Verlag shall be held responsible for any omissions or inaccuracies.

**Die Deutsche Nationalbibliothek verzeichnet diese Publikation in der deutschen Nationalbibliografie;
detaillierte bibliografische Daten sind im Internet über http://dnb.ddb.de abrufbar.**
The Deutsche Nationalbibliothek holds a record of this publication in the Deutsche Nationalbibliografie;
detailed bibliographical data can be found under: http://dnb.ddb.de

Library of Congress Control Number is available.
British Library Cataloguing-in-Publication-Data: a catalogue record for this book is available from the British Library.

Prestel Verlag
Königinstraße 9
80539 München
Tel. +49 (0)89 24 29 08-300
Fax +49 (0)89 24 29 08-335

www.prestel.de

Prestel Publishing Ltd.
4 Bloomsbury Place
London WC1A 2QA
Tel. +44 (0)20 7323-5004
Fax. +44 (0)20 7636-8004

www.prestel.com

Prestel Publishing
900 Broadway, Suite 603
New York, N.Y. 10003
Tel. +1 (212) 995-2720
Fax +1 (212) 995-2733

**Prestel books are available worldwide. Please contact your nearest bookseller or one of the above addresses
for information concerning your local distributor.**

Deutsches Architekturmuseum
Schaumainkai 43
60596 Frankfurt am Main
Tel. +49 (69) 212-38 844
Fax +49 (69) 212-36 31-86
E-Mail: info.DAM@stadt-frankfurt.de

www.dam-online.de

Redaktion und Koordination DAM I Editorial direction and coordination DAM: **Michaela Busenkell**
Assistenz DAM | Assistant DAM: **Dorothea Deschermeier**
Projektleitung Prestel | Project management Prestel: **Gabriele Ebbecke**
Übersetzung aus dem Deutschen | Translation from the German: **Jennifer Taylor**
Übersetzung aus dem Englischen | Translation from the English: **Ulrike Bischoff**
Übersetzung aus dem Niederländischen | Translation from the Dutch: **Bram Opstelten**
Lektorat | Copyediting: **Dr. Willfried Baatz (deutsch** | German**), John Sykes
(englisch** | English**) für** | for **alpha & bet VERLAGSSERVICE, München**
Gestaltung | Design: **LIQUID I Agentur für Gestaltung, Augsburg**
Herstellung | Production: **Simone Zeeb**
Satz | Typesetting: **LIQUID | Agentur für Gestaltung, Augsburg**
Lithografie | Lithography: **Repro Ludwig, Zell am See**
Druck und Bindung | Printing and binding: **Druckerei Uhl, Radolfzell**

Anzeigenverkauf | Advertising sales:
medienpunkt.e.K., Raimund T. Arntzen
Am Aichberg 3
86573 Obergriesbach
Tel. +49 (0)8251-8880852
E-mail: zentrale@medienpuntonline.de

Gedruckt in Deutschland auf chlorfrei gebleichtem Papier
Printed in Germany on acid-free paper

ISSN 1865-3545
ISBN 978-3-7913-4367-9 (Buchhandelsausgabe | Trade edition**)**
ISBN 978-3-7913-6245-8 (Museumsausgabe | Museum edition**)**